# HENRI BERGSON: A BIBLIOGRAPHY

# HENRI BERGSON: A BIBLIOGRAPHY

The first in the series of **BIBLIOGRAPHIES OF FAMOUS PHILOSOPHERS** edited by Richard H. Lineback and published by the Philosophy Documentation Center.

# HENRI BERGSON

# A BIBLIOGRAPHY

By

**P. A. Y. GUNTER**

Published By

**PHILOSOPHY DOCUMENTATION CENTER**
**BOWLING GREEN UNIVERSITY**
**BOWLING GREEN, OHIO 43403**
**U. S. A.**

Library of Congress Card Number:  74–78456

ISBN  0-912632-31-3

# CONTENTS

# PART I

# INTRODUCTION

Henri Louis Bergson (1859-1941) is the most distinguished French philosopher of the last hundred years.  The literature, psychology, and religious thought of our time have all felt the transforming impact of his conceptions, while few aspects of contemporary philosophy remain entirely unaffected by his critiques of scientific materialism and mathematical time or by his concepts of creative evolution, intuition, and psychological duration.  But though the philosophy of Bergson has provoked an immense, often highly interesting literature, no general reference work detailing this literature now exists.  The present bibliography is an effort to fill this gap.

To do so has not been in every respect a simple or an easy task.  The "Bergson Literature" is a highly varied body of writing, spanning over eighty years of philosophical reflection and analysis. Standard bibliographic sources, whether philosophical or other, scarcely give a full account of its contents.  To achieve, or rather to approach, a full account, it is necessary to search widely, often in sources which would seem to have little to do with philosophy per se.

In part the highly diverse character of this literature is due to the popular vogue of Bergson's thought.  To an unusual extent for an academician, Bergson reached beyond the confines of academic philosophy.  Political leaders, journalists, writers, and literary critics--to name a few--felt called upon to write about his "new philosophy."  Their articles, in newspapers, books, or even popular magazines, were often enthusiastic but sometimes less than precise, and they lent a "literary" and "high fashion" aura to Bergson's philosophy which scarcely represented its true content.  However uneven in tenor and however scattered its products, no complete catalogue of the Bergson literature can neglect "Popular Bergsonism."

Professional philosophers, though from a different viewpoint and usually with greater caution, also responded to the challenge of Bergson's thought.  During the decades 1900-1920, the period of his most decisive influence, philosophical journals bristled with articles on Bergson's philosophy, and books detailing or discounting his ideas issued regularly from the press.  On the occasion of Bergson's visit to Columbia University in 1912, John Dewey concluded:

"No philosophic problem will ever exhibit just the same face and aspect that it presented before Professor Bergson invited us to look at it in its connexions with duration as a real and vital fact."[1]

Dewey's insight is attested by the presence in this bibliography
not only of items by the majority of the most eminent philosophers
of our time, but by the abundance of items on Bergson by philosophers of all ranks, nationalities, and viewpoints.

There is a danger, however, in becoming a symbol of <u>Zeitgeist</u>,
either at a scholarly or a popular level.  Philosophical fashions
and popular moods are notoriously changeable, and their ebb is lia-
ble to be as devoid of balanced reflection as their flood.  World
War I was decisively to end the Bergson vogue.  In the aftermath
of that disastrous struggle prewar verities, especially those with
an optimistic bent, had a hollow sound indeed.  It would not be
fair to say that in the new context interest in Bergson's philosophy simply vanished.  Rather, that interest gradually but percep-
tibly waned, even where the diffuse but still recognizable influence of his thought persisted.

Meanwhile Bergson's health declined, sapped by a crippling
arthritis which reduced him to the status of a near invalid.  He
was to continue to read, meditate, and write.  In parallel fashion,
commentary on his philosophy both <u>pro</u> and <u>con</u> was to continue
throughout his life, though with decreased intensity and in dimin-
ished volume.  Indeed, it continues up to the present time, and
shows no signs of ceasing.  Much of this later commentary attains
a profounder balance and a more just assessment of Bergson's value
and meaning than that produced during the heyday of his popularity.

In introducing such a bibliography it is necessary to explain
the way in which it is organized, the extent to which it has been
annotated, and a number of other factors.  Before entering into
such an explanation, however, it will be helpful to give a general
account of the development of Bergson's thought.  Such an account
should help to "situate" his philosophy and its significance.  It
should also make for easier access to many of the specific topics
with which he dealt.


I.


What did Bergson say that so won the interest of his contemporaries?  In part, his influence stemmed from the subjects with
which he dealt.  Biological evolution, the unconscious mind, psychological time, laughter, the nature of dreams, the revolt against
mechanism--all were "in the air" around the turn of the century.
In part also Bergson's impact stemmed from the contrasts which he
drew between different kinds of knowledge and the different sorts
of reality to which he believed these kinds of knowledge apply.

That is, Bergson held that true knowledge can be gained only by "intuition." And he contrasted intuition with other, for him more artificial, modes of thought.

According to Bergson, intuition penetrates into the flux of things, adopting their ever-changing, dynamic character. By contrast, the intellect deals in so-called clear and distinct ideas, and by means of them constructs static and mechanical pictures of reality. To intuition the universe appears as a continuous process within which novel and hence unpredictable events emerge. To intellect, by contrast, the world appears predictable, repetitious, machine-like. The goal of philosophy on Bergson's terms is to get as close to the "stream of reality" as possible, overcoming the static and fragmentary concepts imposed by the intellect. Philosophy thus attempts to "live" or "experience" reality, not merely to represent it or enclose it in a fixed system. In philosophical intuition we get past all such symbols of reality to reality itself. "Metaphysics," Bergson teaches, "is the science which claims to dispense with symbols."[2]

The term "intuition" and the consequent contrast between "intuition" and "intellect" were first employed by Bergson in An Introduction to Metaphysics (1903). But his earlier books, Time and Free Will (1889) and Matter and Memory (1896), had already suggested this distinction, or some distinction like it, by sharply contrasting the all-important experience of "duration" with the various ways in which our ordinary mathematical and spatial concepts can misrepresent it. In Time and Free Will the experience of duration is approached and analyzed from a purely psychological standpoint. Psychological or "inner" time, Bergson shows, is qualitative, heterogeneous, and dynamic. No two of its moments are identical and none of its components are spatially isolable and distinct. When we try to represent the becoming of our mental life by means of spatial symbolism we inevitably disfigure it, transforming wholeness into fragmentation, novelty into repetition, and freedom into mechanical determinism. Yet, Bergson concludes, we are free, at least when we cast aside our "spatialized" and "superficial" self and express the profound self which we otherwise habitually submerge and neglect. The decisions which significantly express our freedom, Bergson claims, are the result of a long personal history of reflection, hesitation, and effort. They are, hence, relatively rare. But they are decisive and, since they express something novel, unpredictable.

This dynamic and indeterministic concept of personal freedom is retained in Matter and Memory. But it is reshaped there in the effort to show that the "inner" self can exist as an integral yet controlling factor in the human body. Almost since the time of

Descartes scientific study of the brain and nervous system has been taken as proving that the body is closed to any influence from the mind. More recently the facts of neurology have been used to support the thesis that mind-states are so many "reflections" of the brain apparatus. If this latter theory is true, then it makes no sense to say that the self can originate novel, unpredictable acts, while if the former is true, then any such act can scarcely be expressed through the body.

Bergson's solution of this difficulty shows a characteristic blend of commonsense intelligence and speculative daring. Beginning with a complete re-evaluation of the brain's function, he proceeds to challenge orthodox concepts of perception and, on the strength of this challenge, to propose a new concept of the brain's relations to thought. Underlying all modern formulations of the mind-body problem, Bergson holds, is the unquestioned assumption that the brain has a purely speculative, disinterested function. This assumption may seem plausible enough. Yet even a cursory examination shows the obvious fact that the brain and perceptual organs are structured adaptively. That is, they are formed in such a way as to allow us to relate effectively to the most easily manipulable aspects of things. Like all tools, Bergson insists, the neural system has a highly selective, and to that extent limited, function. And this function prevents it, by its very nature, from picturing, mirroring, or otherwise replicating external reality in any comprehensive sense.

It does not follow from this, Bergson is quick to point out, that we are somehow cut off from our natural environment. Far from it. In "pure perception," he holds, we participate fully in the processes of the world around us. (We thus have, if you like, an intuition or direct perception of matter.) What needs to be explained, therefore, is not that we perceive, but that we perceive so little, not that we are directly aware of the world but that our sense organs select and represent to us so little of it; and, it must be added, represent this little in a very schematic, essentially static way. Bergson's concepts of perception and of matter lead him to some prophetic insights into the basic theories of physics. They also lead him to a strikingly novel and suggestive concept of the limitations and potential scope of neurophysiology.

The pragmatic function of the brain forbids any thoroughgoing one-to-one correspondence between brain state and external physical reality. But it must equally forbid any such one-to-one correspondence between state of mind and the state of the brain. The brain is viewed by Bergson as an instrument of the active, conscious self, but an instrument in a very special sense. The brain does not, Bergson observes, give rise to consciousness. It does not, as one

materialist insisted, "secrete thought in the way that the liver
secretes bile." To the contrary, the brain limits consciousness.
forcing us to attend to the very particular, very pressing demands
of ordinary life. The kind of nervous system we have channels our
awareness towards particular objects, permits us to recall only the
elements of our past experience that help us to deal with these objects. Without such limitations we might be more disinterested, we
might gain a fuller intuition of the richness of the inter-related-
ness of the world, Bergson speculates. But we would live in rever-
ie: diffuse, undirected, devoid of focus. Bergson thus terms the
brain the organ of "attention to life."[3] By being forced to attend
to life, we are coerced into consciousness. The free inner self of
Time and Free Will, it thus turns out, could only exist over and
against a brain and nervous system which are at the same time both
its opposite and its instrument.

If this concept of mind-body relationships is correct, one
would be ill-advised to look for the mind's higher functions within the adaptive mechanisms of the nervous system. We should instead, to use more recent terminology, merely look for the complex
of "cybernetic" systems through which practical adaptation is made
possible.

"He who could penetrate into the interior of a brain and see
what happens there, would probably obtain full details of
these sketched-out, or prepared movements; there is no proof
he would learn anything else."[4]

At the time when Matter and Memory was written, the most thoroughly
investigated brain-function was memory, along with the maladies of
memory, the aphasias. Prolonged and intensive study of the literature of aphasiology convinced Bergson that memories are not stored
in the brain. Rather than containing the immense wealth of memory
(Bergson, like Freud, believes that the entire mass of memories is
preserved in the unconscious mind.) the brain is selective; it prevents us from being inundated with random recollections by focusing
on our present context only those memories which are relevant to it.
What the neural physiologist studies is "rote" or "habit" memory,
i.e., the capacity to repeat previously learned performances, as
when we repeat a poem or a telephone number we have memorized.
Such performances are always present; they have no intrinsic reference to a past. But when it comes to memories of the past per se,
Bergson teaches, the brain limits what we can recall, but does not
create recollection itself.

The focus of Bergson's earlier writings explains to a large degree the number of items in this bibliography concerned with neurology, psychopathology, and general psychology. It also explains the

presence there of items devoted to literary topics.  Bergson's psychological theories including especially those of <u>Laughter</u>, 1901,
have had a profound effect on many poets, novelists, and dramatists
of our time.  Bergson belongs thus to the psychologists and <u>litté-
rateurs</u> as well as to the philosophers.

    But he belongs to the biologists as well.  <u>Creative Evolution</u>
(1907) contains both Bergson's critique of mechanistic biology and
a metaphysical vision on a grand scale.  It was to make him inter-
nationally famous--and fashionable--almost overnight.  The biological theory of evolution has been used to substantiate a materialistic conception of life, according to which life is "nothing but"
its material constituents, while evolution consists simply in a
string of fortunate coincidences preserved by natural selection.
Bergson, needless to say, was thoroughly critical of this explanation.  Like all mechanistic theories, he saw, it relies on a spatialized concept of time.  In the world of Darwinian evolution nothing exists but empty space, internally changeless particles, and
random motion, with motion itself conceived, strictly, as a series
of instantaneous positions and as, in any case, strictly reversible.
What is left of time in such a universe, except a word occasionally
uttered by theorists?  But those who use the word, unconsciously
(and, Bergson insists, inconsistently) fall back on actual, expe-
rienceable duration in order to give that word any real meaning.
The basic goal of <u>Creative Evolution</u>, therefore, is to replace the
abstract, homogeneous, verbal time of Darwinism with an ongoing,
organically interrelated, creative process.

    In carrying out this program Bergson was led to propose a con-
troversial contrast between life and non-living matter, a contrast
not unlike that drawn between mind and body in <u>Matter and Memory</u>.
While biological evolution proceeds in the direction of increased
diversity, activity, and efficiency, non-living matter drifts in
the opposite direction, towards homogeneity, passivity, repetition.
In other words, life proceeds in an opposite direction to that of
entropy.  <u>Creative Evolution</u> describes biological evolution as the
development of a "life force" or "<u>élan vital</u>" in radically new and
unforeseeable directions.  This force or tendency must contend with
the resistance of matter, which presents itself as an obstacle to
organization.  Not every direction attempted by life has succeeded;
witness the number of species which have degenerated, stagnated,
or become extinct.  Those main directions which life has taken, however, exhibit successes which would only have been possible thanks
to the obstacle presented by matter.  For Bergson life depends on
matter, even while working against it.

    Animal life shows two main directions, the vertebrates, culmi-
nating in the higher primates and man, and the arthropods, culmina-

ting in the social insects.  While the emergence of man as an in-
telligent, reflective creature is treated by Bergson as a major
triumph of vitality over entropy and of organization over random-
ness, he contends that human consciousness is of a special kind,
and embodies special limitations.  Insect societies depend upon
"instinct", an unlearned knowledge which, Bergson holds, is primarily turned towards life.  But the intelligence of vertebrates is
turned towards matter, i.e., towards dealing not with basic life
functions but with whatever can be treated, potentially, as a tool.
A wasp like the sphex "knows" how to sting a caterpillar on its
nerve centers so as to paralyze it without killing it.  But man has
succeeded primarily through his capacity to harness natural forces
and put them at the service of his machines.

It is no wonder, then, that human intelligence, which has
spent its history adapting itself more accurately and successfully
to non-living matter, should begin to understand evolution materi-
alistically and mechanically.  But all such viewpoints fail to do
justice to the dynamic of the evolutionary advance.  To fully understand evolution we must employ our entire conceptual capacity.
That is, we must employ intuition, which is

" . . . instinct that has become disinterested, self-conscious,
capable of reflecting on its object and of enlarging it indefinitely."[5]

Though Bertrand Russell retorted angrily to such assertions that
intuition must therefore be at its best in "bats, bees, and Bergson," it is clear that Bergson preached no return to primitive instinct.  As he insisted over and over again intuition is intellec-
tually sophisticated reflection; only, it is a reflection uniquely
capable of following the dynamic of nature without spatializing or
otherwise "freezing" it.

The quarter of a century between Creative Evolution and The
Two Sources of Morality and Religion (1932) was a time of relative
silence for Bergson.  His health confined him physically and limited his writing time, in his own words, to "hours, even minutes"
per day.[6]  Mind-Energy (1919) and The Creative Mind (1933) are for
the most part reissues of previously published essays.  (An exception is the two prefaces to The Creative Mind.)  Duration and Simultaneity (1922), his criticism of Einstein's theory of relativity,
evidences his long-standing interest in the problems and concepts
of modern physics and is intimately bound up with his basic concepts of time and space.  Yet it is a program piece, designed to
meet specific objections urged at a specific time, and is not a central part of the overall development of his thought.  The culmina-
tion of Bergsonism is to be found in the expansive religious vision

of The Two Sources of Morality and Religion.

Classical Christian theology has traditionally emphasized the "timeless," i.e., eternal and unchanging aspects of God.  The theology of Bergson, by contrast, emphasizes those respects in which God can be said to be active and dynamic.  Christian theology has also relied on highly rationalistic proofs of the existence and nature of God.  For Bergson, however, any proposed "proof" of God must depend on the confirmation provided by mystical experience.  For it is the mystic who achieves an immediate awareness (in the broadest sense, an intuition) of God.  Bergson is quick to point out that this mystical intuition leads to action and expresses a creative love of one's fellow man.  He also insists that the mystical intuition, like all intuition, is "supra" and not "infra"-rational, i.e., that it is not an unthinking or blindly irrational experience.

If the mystic's message is what Bergson says it is, then there is certainly a resistance to it on the part of human societies. The mystic would draw men into the "open society."  But he must overcome the "closed society."

"Never shall we pass from the closed society to the open society, from the city to humanity, by any mere broadening out. The two things are not of the same essence."[7]

The mystic must grapple with and overcome the moral entropy of society.  The difficulties involved in doing so must necessarily be enormous, but The Two Sources of Morality and Religion embodies Bergson's belief that human social evolution exhibits the gradual triumph of the open over the closed society.  It is clear from Bergson's discussion that this triumph is only possible because of both the negation and the possibilities afforded by the closed society. Of the major world religions Christianity has most fully embodied the impetus towards the open society and offered a creative ethics to mankind, Bergson concludes.  In the teachings of the Christian mystics we find God's love most profoundly fulfilled.

This brief survey of the development of Bergson's thought scarcely does justice to the variety of subjects with which he dealt or the originality of his approach.  In particular, a more extended account should be given of the dialectical relations which Bergson establishes between intuition and intellect, an account which would clarify the nature of his critique of scientific mechanism.  Such a synoptic view of his philosophy, however, helps to make clear the basic topics to be covered in a Bergson bibliography. It also, along with the description given above of the "Bergson vogue" of the early decades of this century, helps to suggest some of the problems encountered in collecting and organizing the

Bergson literature.

## II.

This bibliography almost certainly contains the bulk of the Bergson literature, or at least that part of it published in French, English, German, Spanish, Italian, Portuguese, and possibly the Scandinavian languages as well. Optimism on this point is supported by a number of factors. For one, it has been possible to examine previously published Bergson bibliographies in detail. The degree of overlap among these provides considerable insurance that at least the most important entries have been noted, while each bibliography contains items not noted elsewhere. Moreover, several years of reading in this literature have made it possible also to track down numerous references not included in any of the Bergson bibliographies or in any of the standard bibliographic works devoted as a whole or in part to philosophy. Finally, it has been possible to spend time doing research in several libraries with extensive holdings in late nineteenth and twentieth century philosophy. Among these are the Bibliothèque nationale in Paris, the Library of Congress in Washington, D.C., and the Latin-American collection of the University of Texas at Austin. The Rice University and Johns Hopkins University libraries have also proved extremely helpful.

It is probable, of course, that in spite of repeated surveys of the literature, important entries have been overlooked. But it is unlikely that one, painstakingly applying several mutually compatible bibliographic methods across the bulk of the available literature, will miss much that is essential. This author does not wish, in any case, to claim exhaustive completeness; and he welcomes any further bibliographic information on Bergson which may be added to that which he has catalogued so far.

Several points of detail concerning the nature of this bibliography should be pointed out here. For one, no attempt has been made to edit out items which are of doubtful value, or of extreme brevity, or which are only concerned in part with Bergson, his critics, and his followers. Any one of these might prove useful to a scholar interested in some aspect of Bergson's influence, personal life, or times. For the same reason articles or even quotes have been included by various authors simply because they provide either an interesting perspective on Bergson's thought or a valuable insight into the general impression which philosophers or others have had of him. (Some quotes have been included simply because the author does not think that a sense of humor should be excluded even from bibliographic research.)

But while all relevant materials encountered in the course of
compiling this reference work have been included, there has been no
attempt to give a complete catalogue of certain classes of entries.
No effort has been made, for example, to locate either all the news-
paper articles concerning Bergson or all the reviews of books and
articles which concern themselves, in part or as a whole, with his
philosophy.  Unpublished materials on Bergson which have been
brought to the author's attention have not been included unless
cited in other bibliographic sources.  Nor has there been an attempt to give a complete list of letters from various authors and
philosophers to Bergson.  Many such letters remain to be published
elsewhere.  Finally, no attempt has been made to include all translations of works on or by Bergson.  The translations cited provide
a representative, but by no means complete, selection.  An attempt
has been made, however, to include all available letters or other
materials written by Bergson himself, however brief or however minimally related to basic philosophical issues.  It has been possible
to add five or six items by Bergson to the already very full collection of this material published recently in France.  (Cf. below,
Mélanges.)

In comprehensiveness this bibliography outdistances others
which have appeared so far.  The Bergson bibliography published in
1913 by Columbia University contains 496 items, 86 by Bergson.  The
Bergson bibliography of 1941, edited by Alfredo Coviello and published in Argentina, contains 1056 items, of which Bergson is the
author of 198.  Since 1941 numerous Bergson bibliographies have
been published (Cf. Index: Sources Used in Compiling This Bibliography).  All of these, though immensely useful, are small in comparison with the above two volumes.  For example, the bibliography
published by the Revue Internationale de Philosophie in 1950 contains 215 items; the bibliographies published in Volume 4 of Les
Etudes Bergsoniennes include 205 items.  The bibliography published
in Rose-Marie Mossé-Bastide, Bergson éducateur (1955), contains
1796 items, 288 of which are by Bergson.  Georges Mourélos, Bergson et les niveaux de la réalité (1964), contains a bibliography
with 245 entries.  By contrast this present bibliography contains
4381 items, 472 of which are by Bergson.  In addition, while many
entries included here are incomplete, it has been possible to add
bibliographic information to, and sometimes to complete, many par-
tial or fragmentary entries found elsewhere.  It has also been possible to correct numerous mistakes found in other bibliographies.
No doubt errors remain to be corrected, including some which the
author himself has introduced or allowed to go on uncorrected.
For both sorts of error apologies are offered.

It would be desirable, given world enough and time, to include
a thorough annotation for every item included in the bibliography.

This has not been possible for several reasons.  For one, it has
not been possible to obtain access to a large number of items.  For
another, the author does not have a linguistic background in several of the languages represented.  Equally determining is the time
factor.  The author is unwilling to forestall publication for two
or more years while the task of annotation is completed.  He has
been engaged in compiling this bibliography for six years and is
satisfied to publish it in its present form.  Annotations of second-
ary sources are intended to give very general information concerning content and, occasionally, to suggest an evaluation.

There is no difficulty in gaining access to items written by
Bergson.  This is due to the existence of both the centenary edition of Bergson's works (cited in the text as Edition du Centenaire)
and the more recently published Mélanges (1972), which includes not
only the text of Durée et simultanéité and André Robinet's translation of Bergson's Latin thesis, but a remarkably complete collection of letters, book reviews, talks, and articles by Bergson.
Thanks to this latter source it has been possible to annotate almost all of the entries by Bergson.  As in the case of entries concerning Bergson, the annotations of items by Bergson are intended
to be brief.  They give a general description of the content of an
item, with little or no explanation of details.  This is true of
the annotations both of Bergson's books and of his letters and articles.

Of the various Bergson bibliographies only one (the Columbia
University bibliography, 1913) contains annotations of certain of
Bergson's writings.  Only one bibliography of which I am aware contains annotations of works concerning Bergson.  This is the bibliographic material published in the Giornale di metafisica in 1959
and subsequently republished in the proceedings of the Congrès Bergson.  Except for the present volume, then, no bibliography current-
ly exists in which the annotation of works on and by Bergson is
attempted.

In matters of punctuation, capitalization, and form The MLA
Style Sheet, Second Edition, has been followed.  This has provided
consistency, but has necessitated making changes in numerous entries.  For example, colons have been substituted for commas,
dashes, semicolons, and other punctuations which separate titles
and subtitles.  This is true even in the "borderline cases" in
which is is questionable whether the latter part of a title is a
subtitle or not, e.g., in cases where a title is followed not by a
subtitle in the ordinary sense, but by dates.  In languages other
than French, English, German, Italian, Spanish, or Portuguese, however, entries have been left in the form in which they have been
found.  This includes Swedish, Danish, Dutch, Russian, Czech, Pol-

ish, Rumanian, Finnish, Japanese, Latvian, Arabic, Hebrew, and
Turkish language entries.  Other deviations from MLA conventions
are the result of efforts to achieve visual clarity.  (That is, ab-
breviations like "p." and "pp." are sometimes included in order to
clearly distinguish page numbers from year or volume numbers.)  All
entries in the section concerning Bergson are catalogued in alpha-
betical order.  Articles (e.g., "a," "the," "an") are disregarded
in establishing this order.  Unsigned reviews of books and articles
are alphabetized by means of the book or article title.  Thus "Review of Creative Evolution by Henri Bergson" is catalogued under
'C', while "Review of Matter and Memory by Henri Bergson" is catalogued under 'M', etc.  All entries in the section by Bergson are
arranged, insofar as possible, in chronological order by year and
alphabetically within a given year.  Throughout the bibliography,
titles beginning with Bergson's name (e.g., M. Bergson, Henri Bergson, Enrico Bergson) are all alphabetized under 'B'.

It might be thought that bibliographic research is boring.
While the sheer clerical labor necessary to render a bibliography
as precise and as consistent as possible certainly lacks exhilara-
tion, the discovery and exploration of a significant literature on
a significant topic involves an excitement of its own.  The compila-
tion and study of the Bergson literature has provided many fascinat-
ing insights into the period in which Bergson wrote, the manner in
which contemporaries viewed his thought, and the many movements and
criticisms which he engendered and to which he reacted.  Equally interesting has been the discovery of unexpected analogies between
Bergson's thought and that of other philosophers, scientists, and
artists.  Finally, over and above the intellectual history of a period and the discovery of suggestive analogies, there is the matter
of philosophical "influence."  In Bergson's case this is not merely
an academic or a historical matter.  Bergson believed that the intuition of duration is potentially fruitful for all areas of human
discourse, science, philosophy, and the arts included.[8]  He offered
his philosophical method, no less than did Bacon, Descartes, or
Kant, as one which may lead to profitable explorations.  For this
reason, innumerable works have been included in this bibliography
which, though not expressly concerned with Bergson, nonetheless
bear the unmistakable imprint of his philosophy.  It may sound odd
to say, but though Bergson was a dialectical philosopher and in the
broadest sense an idealist, he was a verificationist and a positivist as well.  To the extent that his philosophy was able to suggest
fruitful directions of research, we can say that his contentions
have been verified.

I would like to thank North Texas State University for several
research grants, which have made it possible to employ a research
secretary and utilize interlibrary loans.  Without such support

this bibliography would have been much delayed and far less extensive.  Mrs. Camille Barnes and Miss Diana Haas are due a vote of
thanks for their work as research secretaries: work that was often
tedious, always painstaking, but extremely helpful.  Mrs. Brenda
Brown, Mrs. Patti Sikorsky, Mrs. Kathy Alcoze, and Mrs. Mary West,
successively (but, most unfortunately, not simultaneously) secretaries of the Department of Philosophy at North Texas State University, have earned undying gratitude by typing entries on seemingly
endless packets of 5" x 8" cards.  Professor Mary Christine
Markovsky of Our Lady of the Lake College is to be thanked for her
bibliographic suggestions.  For her help in typing and correcting
the galley proofs (particularly for her assistance with French language entries), Ms. Marcy St. John is due a debt of gratitude.
Finally, I wish to express my appreciation to Miss Nellie Whitmore
and Miss Johnnye Cope of the North Texas State University Library
for their good humor, generous help, and many useful suggestions.

P. A. Y. Gunter, Ph.D.
North Texas State University
Denton, Texas

## FOOTNOTES

1 John Dewey, "Preface," A Contribution to a Bibliography of Henri Bergson (New York: Columbia University Press, 1912), xii.

2 Henri Bergson, "An Introduction to Metaphysics," The Creative Mind (New York: Philosophical Library, 1946), 191.

3 Henri Bergson, "Introduction," Matter and Memory (London: Allen and Unwin, 1950), xviii.

4 Ibid.

5 Henri Bergson, Creative Evolution (New York: Modern Library, 1944), 793.

6 Floris Delattre, "Les Dernières Années de Bergson," Revue Philosophique de la France et de l'Etranger, 131, Nos. 2-3 (mars-août 1941), 125-138.

7 Henri Bergson, The Two Sources of Morality and Religion (Garden City, New York: Doubleday, 1954), 267.

8 See on this point the writings of Milič Čapek and Vittorio Mathieu. See also my "Introduction" to Bergson and the Evolution of Physics (Knoxville, Tennessee: University of Tennessee Press, 1969), 3-42.

# PART II

# WORKS BY BERGSON

### 1877

1    "Solution d'un problème mathématique."  Nouvelles Annales
     Mathématiques, 11, 17, 1878, 266-276; Ecrits et paroles,
     1, 3-9; Mélanges, 247-256.  This is Bergson's solution of
     a mathematical problem, for which he won first prize.

### 1878

2    "Sur Un Problème de Pascal."  Etude sur Pascal et les géo-
     mètres contemporaines, suivi de plusieurs notes scientifi-
     ques et littéraires.  Ed. Adolphe Desboves.  Paris:
     Delagrave, 1878, 129-130.  Also in Mélanges, 254-255.
     This is a solution by Bergson of a mathematical problem
     first posed by Pascal.

### 1882

3    "La Spécialité."  Angers: Lachèse et Dolbeau, 1882, 16.
     Also in Journal de Maine-et-Loire, No. 182, 4 août 1882,
     264; M. Antier.  Le Lycée David d'Angers depuis ses ori-
     gines jusqu'à nos jours.  Angers: Editions de l'Ouest,
     1947, 137-142; Ecrits et paroles, 1, 10-16; Mélanges,
     257-264.  In this talk, given at the distribution of prizes
     at Angers on 3 August 1882, Bergson discusses the limita-
     tions of specialization.

### 1883

4    Extraits de Lucrèce: Avec un commentaire des notes et une
     étude sur la poésie, la philosophie et la langue de
     Lucrèce.  Paris: Delagrave, 1883, 159 (Eighth edition,
     1912).  Also in Ecrits et paroles, 1, 17-56 (L'Avant-
     propos); Mélanges, 265-310.  This is Bergson's translation
     of Lucretius' philosophical poem De Rerum Natura, with
     commentary.

5    Lucrèce: Extraits de Lucrèce: Avec un commentaire, des notes
     et une étude sur la poésie, la philosophie, la physique,
     le texte et la langue de Lucrèce.  2e éd.  Paris: Dela-
     grave, 1955, 160.

TRANSLATIONS

6        "Lucrecio." Enciclopedia de educación. Trans. Emilio
         Oribe. Enero 1946, 3-93.

7        The Philosophy of Poetry. Ed., trans., and in part
         recast by Wade Baskin. New York: Wisdom Library, 1959,
         83. This work consists of Bergson's notes on Lucretius'
         poetry and on the nature of poetry in general. It does
         not contain any of Bergson's translation of Lucretius.

8        "Traduction de l'ouvrage de James Sully. Les Illusions
         des sens et de l'esprit." Paris: Ballière et Cie., 1883.
         There is in this edition no mention of Bergson's name as
         translator. For notes concerning Bergson's translation
         Cf. Mélanges, 311.


                              1884


9        "Le Rire: De qui rit-on? Pourquoi rit-on?" Moniteur du
         Puy-de-Dôme, 21 février 1884. Also in Mélanges, 313-315.
         This is a journalistic account of Bergson's talk which is
         signed P. M. Here Bergson discusses the nature and causes
         of laughter.


                              1885


10       "Cours à la Faculté de Clermont-Ferrand." Bulletin Mensuel
         de l'Académie de Clermont, No. 77, décembre 1885, 147.
         Also in Mélanges, 332. This is an outline of two courses
         taught by Bergson. The course on the history of philos-
         ophy included Aristotle, Malebranche, and Spinoza. The
         course on general philosophical topics included discus-
         sions of matter, mind, the principal proofs of God's
         existence, and basic systems of ethics, including util-
         itarianism.

11       "La Politesse." Palmarès du Lycée Clermont-Ferrand, distri-
         bution des prix du 30 juillet 1885. Ed. Colbert. 1885.
         Also in Moniteur du Puy-de-Dôme, 6 août 1885; Mélanges,
         317-332. For later version Cf. entry under 1882.

## 1886

12    "Cours à la Faculté de Clermont-Ferrand." Bulletin Mensuel
de l'Académie de Clermont, No. 86, septembre 1886, 40-41.
Also in Mélanges, 342. This is an outline of two courses
taught by Bergson. The course on general philosophical
topics included lectures on psychology, the attributes of
God, scepticism, and idealism. The course on the history
of philosophy included lectures on Aristotle's ethics and
politics, Stoicism and Epicureanism, modern British empiricism, and nineteenth-century French philosophy.

13    "Une Inspection générale." Dauphin Meunier. "Une Leçon de
M. Henri Bergson en 1886." Le Figaro, Supplément littéraire, 21 février 1914, p. 3, col. 3-4. Also in Mélanges,
341. This is a brief mention of a lecture by Bergson on
pessimism.

14    "De La Simulation inconscient dans l'état d'hypnotisme."
Revue Philosophique de la France et de l'Etranger, 22,
69-75; Mélanges, 333-341. This is a sceptical critique
of thought-reading experiments carried on by hypnotized
subjects.

## 1887

15    "Cours à la Faculté de Clermont-Ferrand." Bulletin Mensuel
de l'Académie de Clermont, No. 98, septembre 1887, 40.
Also in Mélanges, 343. This is an outline of two courses
taught by Bergson. The course on general philosophical
topics included lectures on psychophysics, habits, freewill and determinism, and philosophical method. The
course on the history of philosophy included lectures on
Bacon, Malebranche, and Leibniz.

## 1888

16    "Cours à la Faculté de Clermont-Ferrand." Bulletin Mensuel
de l'Académie de Clermont, No. 108, juillet 1888, 363.
Also in Mélanges, 345. These two lectures, one on philosophical psychology and the other on the history of philosophy, were never given.

1889

17    Essai sur les données immédiates de la conscience. Paris:
      Félix Alcan, 1889, 185. This book states the fundamental
      themes of Bergson's philosophy. Psychological duration,
      Bergson holds, cannot be "spatialized." Psychological
      duration is by nature dynamic and qualitative, and hence
      cannot be predicted. The individual is capable of acts
      which are in the fullest sense free and unpredictable.

18    Essai sur les données immédiates de la conscience. Genève:
      Skira, 1946, 190.

19    Essai sur les données immédiates de la conscience. Paris:
      Presses Universitaires de France, 1961, 184. A new
      edition.

      TRANSLATIONS

20    Ensayo sobre los datos inmediatos de la conciencia.
      Madrid: Francisco Beltrán, 1919, 184. 2e ed. 1925,
      192.

21    O bezpośrednich danych świadomości: z upoważniena autora
      przełożyla K. Bobrowska. Warzawa: Wende, 1913, 167.

22    Saggio sui dati immediati della coscienza. "Traduzione
      e Note Cura di Niso Ciusa." Torino: S.E.I., 1951, 85.

23    Saggio sui dati immediati della concienza: A cura di
      Vittorio Mathieu. Torino: Casa Paravia, 1952.

24    Saggio sui dati immediati della coscienza. Trans.
      Giuseppe Cavallaro. Roma: Signorelli, 1957, 99.

25    Saggio sui dati immediati della coscienza. Trans.
      G. Bartoli. Torino: Boringhieri, 1964, 231.

26    Time and Free Will: An Essay on the Immediate Data of
      Consciousness. Authorized trans. F. L. Pogson. London:
      Swan Sonnenschein and Co., Ltd.; New York: Macmillan,
      1910, xxiii, 252 (Library of Philosophy).

27    Time and Free Will: An Essay on the Immediate Data of
      Consciousness. Trans. F. L. Pogson. New York: Harper,
      1960, 262.

28    Vremiâ i svoboda voli: S prilozheniem traktata togo zhe
      avtora Vvedenie v metafiziku. Trans. S. Hessen and
      M. Grünwald. St. Petersburg, Russia, 1912, 238.

29    Zeit und Freiheit: Eine Abhandlung über die unmittel-
      baren Bewussteinstatsachen. Jena: Diederichs, 1911,
      189.

30    Zeit und Freiheit: Eine Abhandlung über die unmittel-
      baren Bewussteinstatsachen. Meisenheim am Glan: West-
      kultuverlag Hain, 1949, 200.

31    Quid Aristoteles de Loco Senserit. Thesim Facultati Lit-
         terarum Parisiensi, proponebat H. Bergson, Scholae Nor-
         malis olim Alumnus, Lutetiae Parisorum, Edebat F. Alcan,
         Bibliopola, MDCCCLXXXIX, 82. Also in Etudes Bergso-
         niennes, 2, 29-104; Mélanges, 2-56 (Trans. Robert
         Mossé-Bastide). English translation in Ancients and
         Moderns. Ed. John K. Ryan. Washington: Catholic Univer-
         sity of America Press, 1970, 368, 12-72. This is an expo-
         sition and criticism of Aristotle's doctrine of "place".
         Aristotle, Bergson holds, illicitly substitutes the con-
         cept of place for that of space. Aristotle thereby
         avoids, rather than resolves, problems which Bergson
         believes are connected with the idea of space.


                                1891


32    "Compte rendu de La Genèse de l'idée de temps de G. Guyau."
         Revue Philosophique de la France et de l'Etranger, 31,
         No. 1, janvier 1891, 185-190. Also in Ecrits et paroles,
         1, 75-82; Mélanges, 349-356. This is a thorough analysis
         and criticism of Guyau's thesis that the concept of time
         is derived from that of space.


33    "Lettre à L. Dauriac: 6 juillet 1891." Ecrits et paroles,
         3, 196 (résumé). Also in Mélanges, 356; Bibl. Victor-
         Cousin. This letter is concerned with Dauriac's Croyance
         et réalité and the concept of substance suggested by Dau-
         riac.

34    "Lettre à Félix Ravaisson: 2 novembre 1891." Revue de Méta-
         physique et de Morale, 45, No. 2, avril 1938, 195-196.
         Also in Mélanges, 357. Here Bergson thanks Ravaisson for a
         copy of an article on pedagogy and agrees with his con-
         clusions.

1892

35    "La Politesse." Palmarès du Lycée Henri-IV, distribution
      des prix du 30 juillet 1892, 17-27. Also in Ecrits et
      paroles, 1, 57-68; Mélanges, 317-332. In this talk Berg-
      son considers the true meaning of politeness.

1895

36    "Le Bon Sens et les études classiques: Discours prononcé
      lors de la distribution du Concours général, 30 juillet
      1895." Palmarès général, 5-17. Also: Concours général.
      Distribution des prix, année 1895. Paris: Delalain, 1895,
      5; Le Bon Sens et les études classiques. Clermont-Fer-
      rand: L'Epervier, 1947, 74. Suivi d'un propos par Blaise
      Romeyer; "Bon Sens et justice." La Nef, 4, No. 32,
      juillet 1947, 61-72; Mélanges, 359-372. "El buen sentido
      y los estudios clásicos." Trans. Armando D. Delucchi.
      Revista de Filosofia, (Argentina) 22, Nos. 12-13, 1963,
      83-92. In this essay Bergson considers what we ought to
      mean when we say that someone has "good sense."

37    "Lettre à O. Gréard: 15 avril 1895." Ecrits et Paroles,
      1, 83. Also in Mélanges, 359. The definition of "bon
      sens", i.e., good sense, is discussed in this letter.

1896

38    "Cours sur Descartes." Rose-Marie Mossé-Bastide. Bergson
      éducateur. Paris: Presses Universitaires de France, 1955,
      336-337. Also in Mélanges, 374. This is a general de-
      scription by Bergson of a course taught by him concerning
      the philosophy of René Descartes.

39    Matière et mémoire: Essai sur la relation du corps avec
      l'esprit. Genève: Skira, 1946, 262. In this work Berg-
      son broadens his psychology to include a theory of per-
      ception and a theory of mind-body relationships. Psy-
      chological duration, Bergson holds, is not located in the
      brain, which is an "organ of attention to life" and not a
      storehouse of memories or of thoughts. The increasing
      complexity of the brain gives broader scope to human free-
      dom.

40    Matière et mémoire: Essai sur la relation du corps avec
      l'esprit. Paris: Félix Alcan, 1896, iii, 279.

      TRANSLATIONS

41    Materie und Gedächtnis: Eine Abhandlung über die Bezieh-
      ung zwischen Körper und Geist. Trans. Julius Franken-
      berger. Jena: Diederichs, 1919, 264.

42    Materie une Gedächtnis: Essays zur Beziehung zwischen
      Körper und Geist. Trans. W. Windelband. Jena: Die-
      derichs, 1908, xvi, 264.

43    Materie und Gedächtnis und andere Schriften.   Frankfurt:
      Fischer, 1964, 489 (Fischer Paperbacks).

44    Materia y memoria: Ensayo sobre la reación del cuerpo
      con el espíritu. Trans. Martín Navarro. Madrid, 1900,
      336.

45    Materia y memoria. Trans. Martín Navarro. La Plata,
      Argentina: Ed. Calomino, 1943, 269.

46    Matter and Memory. Authorized Trans. Nancy Paul and
      W. Scott Palmer. London: Swan Sonnenschein and Co.;
      New York: Macmillan, 1911, xx, 359 (Library of Phil-
      osophy). Bergson wrote a special introduction to this
      translation of Matter and Memory.

47    "Mémoire et reconnaissance." Revue Philosophique de la
      France et de l'Etranger, 41, 1896, 225-248, 380-399.
      Cf. apparat critique, Edition du Centenaire, 1491-1496,
      1496-1501. This essay is republished in Matière et
      mémoire.

48    "Perception de matière." Revue de Métaphysique et de Mo-
      rale, 4, No. 2, mai 1896, 257-277. Cf. "Apparat critique,"
      Edition du Centenaire, 1501-1502. Appears in Matière et
      mémoire.


                              1897


49    "Compte rendu des Principes de métaphysique et psychologie
      de Paul Janet." Revue Philosophique de la France et de
      l'Etranger, 44, novembre 1897, 526-551. Also in Ecrits
      et paroles, I, 98-128; Mélanges, 375-410.

50       "Lettre à G. Lechalas."  G. Lechalas.  "Compte rendu de
         Matière et mémoire."  Annales de Philosophie Chrétienne,
         36, 1897, 154, 328, 333.  Also in Ecrits et paroles, I,
         95-97; Mélanges, 410-413.  Here Bergson states his candi-
         dacy for the Chair of Modern Philosophy at the Ecole Nor-
         male.


                                1900


51       "Bergson au Congrès international de philosophie: 2 août
         1900."  Revue de Métaphysique et de Morale, 8, 1900, 525,
         531, 532.  Also in Mélanges, 417-418.  This essay includes
         a discussion of Evellin's "antinomies."

52       "Bergson au Congrès international de philosophie: 3 août
         1900."  Revue de Métaphysique et de Morale, 8, 1900, 566,
         574, 575, 582.  Also in Mélanges, 418.  This essay
         includes a discussion of the nature of idealism, and of
         Edouard Le Roy's paper on science and liberty.

53       "Communication au VIe Congrès internationale de psycholo-
         gie."  Revue de Métaphysique et de Morale, 8, 1900, 803.
         Mélanges, 435.  This is a brief mention of Bergson's
         address on intellectual effort.  It occurs in an article
         by N. Vaschide.

54       "Lettre à L. Dauriac: 4 décembre 1900."  Etudes Bergsonien-
         nes, 3, 196.  Also in Mélanges, 436-437.  Bergson's con-
         cept of laughter is discussed in this letter.

55       "Note sur les origines psychologiques de notre croyance à
         la loi de causalité."  Bibliothèque du congrès interna-
         tional de philosophie, I.  Philosophie générale et méta-
         physique.  Paris: Armand Colin, 1900, 1-15.  Also in
         Ecrits et paroles, I, 129-137; Mélanges, 419-428.  Belief
         in the law of causality, Bergson holds, is based on the
         coordination of our tactile impressions with our visual
         impressions.  The continuation of visual impressions into
         tactile impressions generates motor habits which are ten-
         dencies to action.

56       "Note sur les origines psychologiques de notre croyance à
         la loi de causalité."  Revue de Métaphysique et de Morale,
         8, 1900, 655-664.  Mélanges, 428-435.  This is an abstract
         of Bergson's paper followed by a discussion.

57    "Le Rire."  Revue de Paris, 7, Nos. 23 et 24, 1900, 512-544,
      759-790; 8, No. 1, 1900, 146-179.  In this essay Bergson
      describes laughter as a reaction against mechanical and
      rigid forms of behavior.  Laughter is thus a weapon used
      by society against those who fail to adapt to their social
      or physical contexts.

58    Le Rire: Essai sur la signification du comique.  Paris:
      Félix Alcan, 1900, vii, 204; Genève: Skira, 1945, 134;
      Paris: Fequet et Baudier, 1947, 107; Edition du Centenaire,
      381-485.

      TRANSLATIONS

59    Hatzekhok.  Trans. Jacob Levy.  Jerusalem: Rubin Mass.,
      1947, 123.

60    Das Lachen.  Meisenheim am Glan: Westkulturverlag Hain
      1949, 112.

61    Laughter: An Essay on the Meaning of the Comic.  Author-
      ized Trans. Cloudesly Brereton and Fred Rothwell.
      New York: Macmillan, 1911, vii, 200.

62    La risa.  Trans. Amalia Haydée Raggio.  Buenos Aires:
      Ed. Losada, 1939, 154.

63    La risa: Ensayo sobre la significación de lo cómico.
      Valencia: Promoteo, 1914, 219.

64    La risa: Ensayo sobre la significación de lo cómico.
      Trans. P. Girosi.  Buenos Aires: Tor, 1939.

65    Il riso: Saggio sul significato del comico.  Trans.
      A. Cervesato and C. Galli.  Bari: Laterza e Figli, 1916.

66    Il riso: Saggio sul significato del comico.  Trans.
      F. Stella.  Milano: Rizzoli, 1961, 166.

67    Skrattet: En undersokning av Komikens vasen.  Trans.
      Algot Ruhe.  Stockholm, 1910, 172.

68    Smiech: Studyum o komicie.  "Wiedza i zycie; zagadniena
      z pradu wspolczesnego w dziedzinie wiedzy, sztuki i
      zycia spolecznego."  Ser. 2, vol. 2, 1902.

1901

69    "Collège de France: Cours de M. Bergson sur l'idée de
cause." Revue de Philosophie, 1, No. 3, avril 1901,
385-388. Mélanges, 439-441. This article is signed
"J. C.".

70    "Cours du Collège de France: 26 décembre 1901." Archives
du Collège de France, 1, 1901, 71-72. Also in Mélanges,
512. Brief mention is made of a course on the idea of
time and on Plotinus' sixth Ennead in this essay.

71    "Cours du Collège de France: Philosophie grecque et latine."
Archives du Collège de France, 1, 1901, 55-56. Also in
Ecrits et paroles, 1, 138; Mélanges, 438. Bergson discusses here the concept of causality held by both ancients
and moderns.

72    "Election à l'Académie des sciences morales et politiques:
14 décembre 1901." Séances et Travaux de l'Académie des
Sciences Morales et Politiques, 157, 1902, p. 289. Also
in Mélanges, 511.

73    "Réception à l'Académie des sciences morales et politiques: 21 décembre 1901." Séances et Travaux de l'Académie des Sciences Morales et Politiques, 157, 1902, p. 291.
Also in Mélanges, 511.

74    "Le Rêve." Bulletin de l'Institut Général Psychologique,
1re Année, No. 3, mai 1901, 97-122. Also in Revue Scientifique, 4e Sér. 15, No. 23, 8 juin 1901, 705-715. This
article appears with many emendations in L'Energie spirituelle, 1919, Edition du Centenaire, 878-897. Cf. Notes,
1566-1558; Etudes Bergsoniennes, 6, 61-86; Mélanges,
443-463. In this brief essay Bergson developes his theory
of the nature of dreams. According to Bergson the mechanism of dreams is like that of normal perception. As is
the case in ordinary sense perception, both sense impressions and memories are necessary to create the dream.
But the sleeper, unlike the waking man, is relaxed from
the attitude of control.

TRANSLATIONS

75    Dreams. Trans. with Intro. Edwin E. Slosson. New York:
Huebsch, 1914, 57.

76    <u>Dreams</u>.  Trans. with Intro. Edwin E. Slosson.  London:
      Unwin, 1914, 62.

77    "Such Stuff as Dreams are Made on: A Study of the Mecha-
      nism of Dreaming."  <u>Independent</u>, 76, Nos. 3396-3387,
      23 October and 30 October 1913, 160-163, 200-203.


                              1902


78    "Collège de France: Cours de M. Bergson."  <u>Revue de Philo-
      sophie</u>, 2, No. 6, octobre 1902, 828-832.  Also in <u>Mélan-
      ges</u>, 513-517.  Here an account is given of a course on the
      concept of time.

79    "Cours du Collège de France."  <u>Revue de Philosophie</u>, 4, No. 1,
      janvier 1904, 105-111.  Also in <u>Mélanges</u>, 573-578.  An
      article by Léonard Constant on Bergson's course (1902-1903)
      on the history of the concept of time.

80    "Cours du Collège de France: Philosophie grecque et latine."
      <u>Archives du Collège de France</u>, 3, 1903, p. 96.  Also in
      <u>Ecrits et paroles</u>, 1, p. 191; <u>Mélanges</u>, 572.  A brief ac-
      count is given of courses presented in 1902-1903 on book
      two of Aristotle's <u>Physics</u> and on the history of the idea
      of time.

81    "Discussion à la Société française de philosophie: La Place
      et le caractère de la philosophie dans l'enseignement
      secondaire par M. Belot."  <u>Bulletin de la Société Fran-
      çaise de Philosophie</u>, 3, 2 février 1903, 44-66.  Also in
      <u>Ecrits et paroles</u>, 1, 187-190; <u>Mélanges</u>, 568-571.  This
      discussion concerns the place of philosophy in secondary
      education and was given on 18 December 1902.

82    "Discussion à la Société française de philosophie: Le Voca-
      bulaire philosophique."  <u>Bulletin de la Société française
      de Philosophie</u>, 2, juillet 1902, pp. 157, 160, 161.  Also
      in <u>Ecrits et paroles</u>, 1, p. 174; <u>Mélanges</u>, 551-552.  This
      discussion is concerned with an analysis of the terms
      "evidence" and "absolute."

83    "L'Effort intellectuel."  <u>Revue Philosophique de la France
      et de l'Etranger</u>, 5, janvier 1902, 1-27.  Also, with
      many revisions, in <u>L'Energie spirituelle</u>, 1919; <u>Edition du
      Centenaire</u>, 930-959 (Notes, 1568-1569); <u>Etudes Bergso-
      niennes</u>, 6, 97-126; <u>Mélanges</u>, 519-550.  This is Bergson's

classic study of the characteristics of intellectual
effort. Intellectual creativity involves both a general
idea or schema and the concrete, detailed images through
which the schema must be embodied. The movement from
abstract idea to concrete images may meet with resistance
from idea or images, Bergson holds, and insofar as this
produces hesitation, there is the sense of obstacle and
effort characteristic of intellectual endeavor.

84    "De L'Intelligence." Palmarès du Lycée Voltaire, 6, No. 75,
1902, 1-9. Also in Bulletin de l'Union pour la Vérité, 21
No. 6, 15 avril 1914, 424-436; Ecrits et paroles, 1,
175-181; Mélanges, 553-560. In this talk Bergson defines
intelligence, in a broad sense, as the collaboration of
"intuition" and "intellect." Intelligence succeeds, Bergson holds, through an effort of concentration.

85    "Philosophie grecque et latine." Archives du Collège de
France, 2, 1902, 49-50. Also in Ecrits et paroles, 1,
p. 173; Mélanges, 512-513. A brief description of a
course on Plotinus' sixth Ennead and the concept of time
is made in this essay.

86    "Rapport sur la Fondation Carnot: 6 décembre 1902." Séances
et Travaux de l'Académie des Sciences Morales et Politiques, 159, 1903, 52-62. Also in Ecrits et paroles, 1,
182-186; Mélanges, 561-566. This report concerns the
problems and hopes of a charitable institution.

1903

87    "Cause et raison chez Cournot." Bulletin de la Société
Française de Philosophie, 1, No. 8, août 1903, 209. Also
in G. Tarde. La Philosophie sociale de Cournot, 229;
Ecrits et paroles, 1, p. 199; Mélanges, 589. This is a
brief discussion by Bergson of Cournot's distinction between cause (i.e., actual causal factors) and reason
(i.e., principle of explanation).

88    "Compte rendu de An Essay on Laughter de. J. Sully." Revue
Philosophique de la France et de l'Etranger, 56, octobre
1903, 402-410. Also in Ecrits et paroles, 1, 213-221;
Mélanges, 594-603. Bergson analyzes Sully's concept of
laughter and subjects it to a brief criticism. Sully,
Bergson holds, has two distinct concepts of laughter but
does not provide a clear transition between them.

89    "Cours du Collège de France: Histoire des théories de la mé-
      moire." Revue de Philosophie, 4, No. 12, décembre 1904,
      801-814. Also in Mélanges, 614-625. The brain as a memo-
      ry-bank, the association of ideas, the function of the
      brain, memory versus perception, different kinds of memo-
      ry, aphasias, epiphenomenalism, etc., are ideas discussed
      in this account of a course given by Bergson in 1903-1904.

90    "Cours du Collège de France: Philosophie grecque et latine."
      Archives du Collège de France, 4, 1904, p. 77. Also in
      Mélanges, 613; Ecrits et paroles, 1, p. 222. This is a
      brief account of courses on 'Book Lambda' of Aristotle's
      Physics and on the evolution of concepts of memory.

91    "Discussion au groupe d'études des phénomènes psychiques."
      Bulletin de l'Institut Général Psychologique, 4, No. 1,
      janvier 1904, 28-31. Also in Ecrits et paroles, 1,
      209-212; Mélanges, 606-609. This discussion concerns
      high frequency radiation emitted by the nervous system and
      light penumbras surrounding the human body purportedly
      seen by "sensitives."

92    "Introduction à la métaphysique." Revue de Métaphysique et
      de Morale, 29, janvier 1903, 1-36. Also in Edition du
      Centenaire, 1392-1432 and 1537-1539. In this essay Berg-
      son developes his theory of knowledge. Intuition, he
      states, is capable of grasping things from within and fol-
      lowing their fluid, ever-changing duration. Intellect,
      however, must be seen as viewing things from without by
      means of static concepts. Philosophy is primarily the
      effort to achieve intuitive insight.

      TRANSLATIONS

93    Einführung in die Metaphysik. Authorized Trans. M. Sus-
      mann. Jena: Diederichs, 1909, 58.

94    La filosofia dell'intuizione: Introduzione alla meta-
      física, ed. estratti altre opera, a cura di Giovanni
      Papini. Lanciano, Italy: Carabba, 1908, 126.

95    Introducción a la metafísica. Trans. Carlos Sabat
      Ercasty. Montivideo: García y Cía, 1944, 65.

96    Introduccíon a la metafísica. Trans. Rafael Moreno.
      México: Centro de estudios filosoficos, Universidad
      nacional autónoma de México, 1960, 50.

97        Introducción a la metafísica y la intuición filosófica.
         Buenos Aires: Siglo viente, 1966, 144.

98        Introduction à la métaphysique. Trans. B. Fogarasi.
         Budapest: Politzer, 1910, 41.

99        Introduction to Metaphysics. Authorized Trans. T. E.
         Hulme. New York: Putnam's Sons, 1912, 92.

100       Introduction to Metaphysics. Authorized Trans. T. E.
         Hulme. London: Macmillan, 1913, 79.

101       Introduction to Metaphysics. Trans. Mabelle L. Andison.
         New York: Philosophical Library, 1961, 84.

102       Introduction to a New Philosophy: Introduction à la
         Métaphysique. Trans. Sidney Littman. Boston: John W.
         Luce and Co., 1912, 108.

103       Introduzione alla metafisica. Ed. B. Brunello.
         Bologna: Zanichelli, 1949, 95.

104       Introduzione alla metafisica. Trans. Vittorio Mathieu.
         Bari: Laterza, 1957, 103.

105       Introduzione alla metafisica. Trans. Armando Vedaldi.
         Firenze: Sansoni, 1958, 125.

106       Intuition och intelligence: Inledning till metafysiken.
         Trans. Algot Ruhe. Stockholm: 1911. "Med ett forord ab
         professor Axel Herrlin."

107       Intuition og verdensankuelse. Trans. Knud Ferlov.
         Copenhagen: Gad, 1914.

108       Vremia svobodi voli: S. prilozheniem traktata togo zhe
         avtora Vvedenie v metaphysiku. Trans. S. Hessen and
         M. Grünwald. St. Petersburg: Russkaia mysl', 1912, 238.

109       Wstep do metafizyki. Trans. Kazimir Bteszyński. Kraków:
         Gebethner, 1910, 104.

110       "Lettre à M. L. Brunschvicg: 26 février 1903." Bulletin de
         la Société Française de Philosophie, 3, 1903, 101-103.
         Also in Ecrits et paroles, 1, 194-196; Mélanges, 585-587.
         The concept of "moral liberty" is discussed in this let-
         ter.

111     "Lettre à A. Dayot." Le Livre d'or de Renan. Paris:
        Joanin, 1903, p. 137. Also in Mélanges, 610. Bergson
        accepts a position on a committee to build a monument to
        Renan.

112     "Lettre à W. James: 6 janvier 1903." Revue des Deux Mondes,
        15 octobre 1933, 793-794. Also in Ecrits et paroles, 1,
        192-193; Mélanges, 579-581. In this letter Bergson's
        "durée" and William James' "stream of consciousness" are
        compared.

113     "Lettre à W. James: 25 mars 1903." Revue des Deux Mondes.
        15 octobre 1933, 797-798. Also in Ecrits et paroles, 2,
        197-198; Mélanges, 587-589. In this letter Matter and
        Memory is discussed.

114     "Lettre à Ch. Péguy: 22 février 1903." Etudes Bergsonien-
        nes, 8, p. 14. Also in Mélanges, 582-583. Bergson po-
        litely criticizes Péguy in this letter for publishing
        "An Introduction to Metaphysics" in Cahiers de la Quin-
        zaine. Metaphysics, Bergson holds, does not always mix
        well with political and social thought.

115     "Préface à l'Esquisse d'un système de psychologie ration-
        nelle d'E. Lubac." E. Lubac. Esquisse d'un système de
        psychologie rationnelle. Paris: Félix Alcan, 1903,, vii-x.
        Also in Ecrits et paroles, 1, 204-207; Mélanges, 610-612.
        This is a discussion of the intuitional method in psychol-
        ogy.

116     "Rapport sur le concours pour le prix Halphen, à décerner en
        1903." Séances et Travaux de l'Académie des Sciences
        Morales et Politiques, 160, 1903, 540-544. Also in Ecrits
        et paroles, 1, 200-203; Mélanges, 590-594. Bergson awards
        a prize to Boirac and Magendie for their Leçons de psycho-
        logie appliquée à l'éducation.

117     "Rapport sur l'Esquisse d'un système de psychologie ration-
        nelle d'E. Lubac." Séances et Travaux de l'Académie des
        Sciences Morales et Politiques, 161, 1904, p. 337. Also
        in Ecrits et paroles, 1, p. 208; Mélanges, 605-606. Berg-
        son treats Lubac's treatise as a series of suggestions,
        some highly penetrating, for the study of psychological
        phenomena.

1904

118    "Le Cerveau et la pensée." L'Energie spirituelle, Edition
       du Centenaire, 959-974 et 1530-1531. This paper was read
       at the International Congress of Philosophy at Geneva in
       1904 and published in the Revue de Métaphysique et de Mo-
       rale, 12, No. 6, novembre 1904, 859-908, under the title
       "Le Paralogisme psycho-physiologique." This essay is a
       criticism of the notion that there is an equivalence or
       parallelism between mind states and brain states. Whether
       viewed from the side of mind or the side of body, Bergson
       holds that the parallelist thesis engenders insoluble con-
       tradictions.

119    "Cours du Collège de France: Philosophie moderne." Archives
       du Collège de France, 5, 1905, p. 90. Also in Ecrits et
       paroles, 1, p. 234; Mélanges, 648-649. These are courses
       which were given in 1904-1905 on the evolution of the con-
       cept of liberty and on Spencer's First Principles, partic-
       ularly Spencer's concept of "force."

120    "Demande de transfert à la chaire de philosophie moderne."
       Mélanges, 637-638.

121    "Discussion au Groupe d'études des phénomènes psychiques:
       Les Courbes respiratoires pendant l'hypnose." Bulletin
       de l'Institut Général Psychologique, 5, No. 2, mars 1905,
       155-164. Also in Ecrits et paroles, 1, 225-228; Mélanges,
       639-642. A discussion of breathing rhythms during succes-
       sive stages of hypnosis.

122    "Discussion à la Société française de philosophie: Binet,
       Esprit et matière." Bulletin de la Société Française de
       Philosophie, 5, No. 3, mars 1905, 94-99. Also in Ecrits
       et paroles, 1, 229-233; Mélanges, 643-648. A discussion
       of agreements and disagreements of Bergson and Binet on
       the function of the nervous system in perception. Berg-
       son denies that his theory transforms sensory nerves into
       motor nerves.

123    "Lettre à Ch. Péguy: 19 juillet 1904." Etudes Bergsonien-
       nes, 8, 15-16. Also in Mélanges, 630-631. This letter is
       concerned with obtaining a scholarship for a young friend
       of Péguy.

124    "Lettre à Ch. Péguy: 23 novembre 1904." Etudes Bergsonien-
       nes, 8, p. 17. Also in Mélanges, 642-643. This letter is

concerned with Bergson's courses on the evolution of the
problem of liberty and on passages in Herbert Spencer's
First Principles.

125    "Rapport sur un ouvrage de Victor Mortet: Notes sur le texte
des 'Institutions' de Cassiodore." Séances et Travaux de
l'Académie des Sciences Morales et Politiques, 162, octobre 1904, p. 485. Also in Ecrits et paroles, 1, p. 223;
Mélanges, 628-629. This account is brief and expository.

126    "Rapport sur un ouvrage de J. Ruskin: La Bible d'Amiens:
Préface et traduction de Marcel Proust." Séances et Travaux de l'Académie des Sciences Morales et Politiques,
62, octobre 1904, 491-492. Also in Ecrits et paroles,
1, p. 224; Mélanges, 629-630. Bergson lauds Proust's interpretation of Ruskin's thought.

127    "Réplique à E. Faguet." Journal des Débats, Feuilleton, La
Semaine dramatique, 10 octobre 1904. Also in Mélanges,
631-637. This is a reply to Faguet's criticisms of Bergson's concept of laughter. According to Bergson, Faguet
oversimplifies his "definition" of laughter.

127a   "La Vie et l'oeuvre de Ravaisson." Séances et Travaux de
l'Académie des Sciences Morales et Politiques, 161, 1904,
673-708. Also in Mémoires de l'Académie des Sciences Morales et Politiques, 25, 1907, 1-43; Edition du Centenaire, 1450-1481 et 1539. In this essay Bergson follows
the development of Félix Ravaisson's philosophy while
chronicling the details of his life. Ravaisson's philosophy is in certain ways vague, Bergson holds, but that is
because its form "is the form of an inspiration."

1905

128    "Bergson et le médium Eusapia Palladino." Bulletin de
l'Institut Général Psychologique, 8, No. 5-6, 415-546.
Also in Mélanges, 673-674. Bergson was an observer in
telekinesis experiments.

129    "Lettre à W. James: 15 février 1905." Revue des Deux Mondes,
15 octobre 1933, 798-799. Also in Ecrits et paroles, 2,
235-236; Mélanges, 651-652. This letter concerns radical
empiricism and the significance of the unconscious.

130    "Lettre à W. James: 20 juillet 1905." Revue des Deux Mondes,
15 octobre 1933, 802-804. Also in Ecrits et paroles, 2,

241-242; Mélanges, 671-672.  Binet's theories of matter and perception are discussed in this letter.

131    "Lettre au directeur de la Revue Philosophique sur sa rela-tion à James Ward et à William James."  Revue Philosophi-que de la France et de l'Etranger, 60, août 1905, 229-231. Also in Ecrits et paroles, 2, 239-240; Mélanges, 656-658. Bergson denies any influence of James and Ward on the de-velopment of his concept of "durée réelle."

132    "Rapport sur L'Ame et le corps d'Alfred Binet."  Séances et Travaux de l'Académie des Sciences Morales et Politiques, 165, 1906, 166-167.  Also in Ecrits et paroles, 2, 251-252; Mélanges, 671-672.  Binet's theories of matter and perception are discussed in this essay.

133    "Rapport sur un ouvrage de M. Ossip-Lourié: Le Bonheur et l'intelligence."  Séances et Travaux de l'Académie des Sciences Morales et Politiques, 164, juillet 1905, 114 (Séance du ler avril 1905).  Also in Ecrits et paroles, 2, 237; Mélanges, 653-654.  This is a brief account of a book which attempts to define the nature of happiness.

134    "Rapport sur le Prix Bordin à décerner en 1905: Mémoires sur Maine de Biran."  Séances et Travaux de l'Académie des Sciences Morales et Politiques, 165, janvier 1906, 152-162 (Séance du 8 novembre 1905).  Also in Ecrits et paroles, 2, 243-250; Mélanges, 662-671.  Here Bergson examines two studies of the philosophy of Maine de Biran, assessing the strengths and weaknesses of each.  First prize is awarded to the study titled La Vie de l'esprit commence avec le premier effort voulu.

## 1906

135    "Cours au Collège de France sur les théories de la volonté." Revue de Philosophie, 7, No. 7, ler juillet 1907, 70-91. Also in Mélanges, 685-704.  These are notes by P. Fontana on Bergson's course given in 1906-1907.  In this essay on the theory of volition Bergson considers scientific mate-rialism and the positions of Schopenhauer and William James.  He deals in particular with the nature of volun-tary attention and muscular effort.

136    "Cours au Collège de France sur les théories de la volonté: Suite."  Revue de Philosophie, 7, No. 10, ler octobre

1907, 407-428.  Also in Mélanges, 704-722.  These are
notes by P. Fontana on Bergson's course which was given in
1906-1907.  In this essay on the nature of volition (a
continuation of a previous essay) Bergson considers the
effects of volition on the entire mental life, both in
the case of particular mental acts and in the case of
longer periods of time.  In the latter case, Bergson
holds that they have to do with character.

137    "Cours du Collège de France: Philosophie moderne." Archives
       du Collège de France, 7, 1907, p. 80.  Also in Ecrits et
       paroles, 2, p. .259; Mélanges, 684.  Bergson's courses,
       which were taught in 1906-1907, on the concept of volition
       and on Herbert Spencer's Principles of Psychology are
       discussed here.

138    "L'Idée de néant."  Revue Philosophique de la France et de
       l'Etranger, 31, No. 10, octobre 1906, 449-466.  This essay
       is republished in Ch. IV of L'Evolution créatrice.  Berg-
       son holds here that the idea of "nothing" is a pseudo-idea.

139    "Lettre à A. Bourgeois: 9 mai 1906."  Etudes Bergsoniennes,
       9, p. 21.  Also in Mélanges, 681.  This concerns Cahiers
       de la Quinzaine.

140    "Lettre à Ch. Péguy: 9 mai 1906."  Etudes Bergsoniennes, 8,
       p. 20.  Also in Mélanges, 680-681.  This concerns Cahiers
       de la Quinzaine.

141    "Rapport sur un ouvrage de M. Jacques Bardoux: Essai d'une
       psychologie de l'Angleterre contemporaine: Les Crises bel-
       liqueuses."  Séances et Travaux de l'Académie des Sciences
       Morales et Politiques, 165, mai 1906, 683-684 (Séance du
       10 février 1906).  Also in Ecrits et paroles, 2, 253-254;
       Mélanges, 676-678.  This is a rather brief examination of
       a study of industrial and political factors in Great Brit-
       ain during the late nineteenth and early twentieth centu-
       ries and of the British attitude towards war.

142    "Rapport sur un ouvrage de P. Gaultier: Le Sens de l'art.
       Préface d'Emile Boutroux."  Séances et Travaux de l'Acadé-
       mie des Sciences Morales et Politiques, 167, mars 1907,
       425-426 (Séance du 24 novembre 1906).  Also in Ecrits et
       paroles, 2, 257-258; Mélanges, 682- 684.  This concerns the
       place of emotion in aesthetics.

143    "Rapport sur un ouvrage de G.-H. Luquet: Idées générales de
       psychologie."  Séances et Travaux de l'Académie des Sci-

ences Morales et Politiques, 168, 1907, 425-426 (Séance
du 5 mai 1906). Also in Ecrits et paroles, 2, 255-256;
Mélanges, 679-680. This is a discussion of Luquet's Bergsonian psychology.

## 1907

144   "Enquête sur l'enseignement de la philosophie: Discussion
avec Binet sur l'influence de la philosophie de Bergson
sur les élèves des lycées." Bulletin de la Société Française de Philosophie, 8, janvier 1908, 12, 14, 21-22
(Séance du 28 novembre 1907). Also in Ecrits et paroles,
2, 277-278; Mélanges, 746-747. Here Bergson protests
strongly against anti-scientific interpretations of his
thought.

145   L'Evolution créatrice. Paris: Félix Alcan, 1907, 403.
This is Bergson's criticism of mechanistic biology. Bergson holds that evolution is the result of a creative force
in nature which must overcome the obstacle of inert matter
in order to produce new, unforseeable life forms. The
human intellect, which is the result of a particular direction taken by evolution, cannot fully understand the evolutionary advance. Such understanding must be achieved
through intuition, which is instinct made reflective and
flexible.

146   L'Evolution créatrice. Genève: Skira, 1946, 374.

TRANSLATIONS

147   Creative Evolution. Authorized Trans. Arthur Mitchell.
New York: Holt and Co., 1911, 407.

148   Creative Evolution. Authorized Trans. Arthur Mitchell.
London: The Macmillan Co., 1964, 425.

149   Evolución creadora. Trans. Carlos Malagarriga. Madrid:
Renacimiento, 1912.

150   Evolución creadora: Abreviatura de Fernando Vela.
Buenos Aires: Revista de Occidenta Argentina, 1947, 192.

151   L'evoluzione creatrice. Trans. U. Segre. Milano:
Corbaccio, 1936, 226. The first edition was published
in 1925.

152    L'evoluzione creatrice. "Introduzione e Commento a Cura
di Paolo Serini." Milano-Verona: Mondadori, 1935, 282.

153    L'evoluzione creatrice. Napoli: Libreria scientifica,
1947, 208.

154    L'evoluzione creatrice. Trans. Armando Vedaldi. Firenze: Sansoni, 1963, 224. The first edition of this translation was published in 1951.

155    L'evoluzione creatrice. Trans. G. Penati. Brescia,
Italy: La Scuola, 1961, 140.

156    L'evoluzione creatrice. Trans. Giancarlo Penati. 3e ed.
Brescia, Italy: La Scuola, 1968, 136.

157    L'evoluzione creatrice, a cura di Francesco Albergamo.
Mazara, Italy: Società Editrice Siciliana, 1952, 84.

158    L'evoluzione creatrice: Antologia a cura di Vittorio
Mathieu. Bari, Italy: Laterza, 1957, 210.

159    L'evoluzione creatrice: Estratti. Trans. L. Ferrarino.
Bari, Italy: Laterza, 1959, 242.

160    Ewolucja twórcza. Trans. Florian Znaniecki. Warsaw:
Ksiazka i Wiedza, 1957, 318. This is a new edition of
the 1912 translation, which is preceded by an essay by
Leszek Kotakowski entitled "Bergson, the Antinomy of
Practical Reason."

161    La Nociono di la tempo: Unesma pagini de la Kreante
evoluciono. Trans. Paulo Dienes. Budapest: Ido-
editerio, 1919, 20.

162    Schopferische Entwicklung. Trans. G. Kantorowicz. Jena:
Diederichs, 1912, 373.

163    Den skapende utveckling. Trans. Algot Ruhe. Stockholm:
1911, 345.

164    Den skabende udvikling. Authorized Trans. Knud Ferlov.
Copenhagen: Gad, 1914.

165    "Lettre à E.-J. Lotte: 26 août 1907." Bulletin Joseph
Lotte, 104, mars 1940, 281-282. Also in Quoniam. De La
Sainteté, 75-76; Etudes Bergsoniennes, 8, p. 22; Mélanges,
735. This is about Lotte's article on L'Evolution créatrice.

166    "Lettre à G. Papini." Nouvelles Littéraires, 15 décembre
       1928.  Also in Ecrits et paroles, 1, p. 204; Mélanges,
       736.  This letter, written in 1907, is about the cessa-
       tion of the publication of Leonardo.

167    "Lettre au directeur de la Revue du Mois après l'article de
       Le Dantec sur L'Evolution créatrice." Revue du Mois, 4,
       No. 9, 10 septembre 1907, 351-354.  Also in Ecrits et Pa-
       roles, 2, 264-267; Le Dantec.  Science et conscience, Ch.
       VI; Mélanges, 731-735.  This is a discussion of Le Dan-
       tec's misinterpretation of Bergson's theory of evolution:
       absolute and relative motion, epiphenomenalism, mathema-
       tism, and "élan vital."

168    "Rapport sur le concours pour le Prix Le-Dissez-de-Penanrun:
       Ouvrage de F. Evellin: La Raison pure et les antinomies et
       ouvrage de G. Belot: Etudes de morale positive." Séances
       et Travaux de l'Académie des Sciences Morales et Politi-
       ques, 169, janvier 1908, 91-102 (Séance du 26 octobre
       1907).  Also in Ecrits et paroles, 2, 268-276; Mélanges,
       736-746.  Kant's antinomies are discussed here along with
       Belot's utilitarianism.

169    "Rapport sur un ouvrage de J. Bardoux (suite): Essai d'une
       psychologie de l'Angleterre contemporaine: Les Crises poli-
       tiques: Protectionnisme et radicalisme." Séances et Tra-
       vaux de l'Académie des Sciences Morales et Politiques, 169,
       janvier 1908, 105-107 (Séance du 29 juin 1907).  Also in
       Ecrits et paroles, 2, 262-263; Mélanges, 728-730.  This is
       an account of a study of protectionism and free trade in
       Britain.

170    "Réponse à Frédéric Charpin sur la question religieuse."
       Mercure de France, 69, No. 241, 15 juillet 1907, 34.  Also
       in Frédéric Charpin.  La Question religieuse.  Paris: 1908,
       p. 272; Ecrits et paroles, 2, 308; Mélanges, 730-731.
       Bergson claims here that religious feeling is not destined
       to fade away.

171    "Résumé par Bergson de ses cours sur Formation et valeur des
       idées générales et sur Principes de la connaissance de
       Berkeley." Archives du Collège de France, 7, 1907, p. 89.
       Also in Ecrits et paroles, 2, 279; Mélanges, 748.  In this
       description of two courses given at the Collège de France,
       Bergson mentions problems concerning the relations between
       language and thought and concerning the different possible
       kinds of general ideas.  Bergson's course on Berkeley in-
       cluded an attempt to define idealism and an analysis of
       Berkeley's theory of general ideas.

1908

172    "A Propos de L'Evolution de l'intelligence géométrique:
       Réponse à un article d'E. Borel." Revue de Métaphysique
       et de Morale, 16, No. 1 janvier 1908, 28-33. Also in
       Ecrits et paroles, 2, 280-285; Mélanges, 753-758. In this
       essay Bergson denies Borel's claim that he conceives
       mathematics and geometry not to have changed since the
       Greeks.

173    "Discussion à propos du Vocabulaire philosophique: Interven-
       tions à propos des mots 'immédiat' et 'inconnaissable'."
       Bulletin de la Société Française de Philosophie, 8, août
       1908, 331-333, 340-341. Also in Ecrits et paroles, 2,
       300-303; Mélanges, 771-772. Here Bergson gives his defi-
       nitions of the words "immediate" and "unknowable."

174    "Lettre à Alfred Binet: 30 mars 1908." Année Psychologique,
       14, 1908, 230-231. Also in Ecrits et paroles, 2, 292-293;
       Mélanges, 726-727. This letter is about Bergson's method
       of writing and the difficulties of introspection.

175    "Lettre à H. Wildon Carr." Proceedings of the Aristotelian
       Society, N.S. 9, 1908-1909, 59-60. This is about Zeno,
       the nature of motion, the future of the sciences, and the
       limitations of "intelligence."

176    "Lettre à L. Dauriac: 2 décembre 1908." Etudes Bergsonien-
       nes, 3, p. 96 (in part). Also in Mélanges, 781 (complete).
       Bergson discusses agoraphobia, dreams, and abnormal psy-
       chology in this letter.

177    "Lettre à W. James: 9 mai 1908." Revue des Deux Mondes, 8,
       Sér. 17, No. 20, 15 octobre 1933, 810-811. Also in
       Ecrits et paroles, 2, 294-295; Mélanges, 765-766. This is
       about the early history of Bergson's thought.

178    "Lettre à W. James: 23 juillet 1908." Revue des Deux
       Mondes, 8, Sér. 17, No. 20, 15 octobre 1933, 813-814.
       Also in Ecrits et paroles, 2, 304-305; Mélanges, 775-777.
       In this letter Bergson comments favorably on the essay
       written about him by James.

179    "Lettre à G. Sorel: Avril 1908." Etudes Bergsoniennes, 3,
       p. 48n. Also in Mélanges, 764. This is a brief fragment
       concerning the difficulty of conceiving evolution through
       concepts.

180     "Lettre à J. de Tonquédec: 12 mai 1908." Etudes par des
        Pères de la Compagnie de Jésus, 130, No. 1, 1912, 516.
        Also in J. de Tonquédec. Sur La Philosophie bergsonienne,
        1936, 60-61; Ecrits et paroles, 2, p. 269; Mélanges,
        766-767. In this letter Bergson states that he is not a
        pantheist.

181     "Rapport sur un ouvrage d'A. Bazaillas: Musique et incon-
        science." Séances et Travaux de l'Académie des Sciences
        Morales et Politiques, 169, juin 1908, 719-720 (Séance du
        1er février 1908). Also in Ecrits et paroles, 2, 288-289;
        Mélanges, 759-760. This is an expository review of
        Bazaillas' study of music, Schopenhauer, and the uncon-
        scious.

182     "Rapport sur un ouvrage de Boirac: La Psychologie inconnue."
        Séances et Travaux de l'Académie des Sciences Morales et
        Politiques, 170, juillet 1908, 119-120 (Séance du 28 mars
        1908). Also in Ecrits et paroles, 2, 290-291; Mélanges,
        760-762. Hypnotism, telepathy, and causality in psychol-
        ogy are discussed in this article.

183     "Rapport sur un ouvrage de M. Georges Dwelshauvers: La Syn-
        thèse mentale." Séances et Travaux de l'Académie des
        Sciences Morales et Politiques, 170, novembre-décembre
        1908, 623-624 (Séance du 8 juin 1908). Also in Ecrits et
        paroles, 2, 298-299; Mélanges, 769-770. Brain and con-
        sciousness, the unconscious, and introspection are dis-
        cussed in this essay.

184     "Rapport sur un ouvrage de J. Merlant: Sénancour." Séances
        et Travaux de l'Académie des Sciences Morales et Politi-
        ques, 169, juin 1908, 720-721 (Séance du 18 janvier 1908).
        Also in Ecrits et paroles, 2, 286-287; Mélanges, 751-752.
        This is a brief description of a book on the poet and
        religious thinker Sénancour (1770-1846).

185     "Rapport sur un ouvrage de J.-P. Nayrac: La Fontaine."
        Séances et Travaux de l'Académie des Sciences Morales et
        Politiques, 170, septembre 1908, 484 (Séance du 23 mai
        1908). Also in Ecrits et paroles, 2, 297; Mélanges,
        768-769. Here Bergson discusses a psychological and
        literary study of the writer La Fontaine.

186     "Remarque sur l'organisation des congrès de philosophie
        après le compte rendu fait par H. Delacroix sur le Con-
        grès international de philosophie de Heidelberg." Bulle-
        tin de la Société Française de Philosophie, 19, janvier

1909, 11-12 (Séance du 28 octobre 1908).  Also in <u>Ecrits</u>
<u>et paroles</u>, 2, 306-307; <u>Mélanges</u>, 779-780.  Here Bergson
suggests that papers read at the next philosophical congress be confined by and large to general philosophical
topics instead of concentrating on problems in the philosophy of particular sciences.

187    "Résumé par Bergson de ses cours sur <u>Nature de l'esprit et</u>
<u>rapport de l'esprit à l'action cérébrale</u> et sur la <u>Siris</u>
de Berkeley." <u>Annuaire du Collège de France</u>, 9, 1909,
p. 76.  Also in <u>Ecrits et paroles</u>, 2, p. 209; <u>Mélanges</u>,
782.  Here Bergson gives a general account of two courses.
The first is concerned with the mind-body problem, the
second with Berkeley's later thought as expressed in his
book <u>Siris</u>.  These courses were given in 1908-1909.

188    "Le Souvenir du présent et la fausse reconnaissance." <u>Revue</u>
<u>Philosophique de la France et de l'Etranger</u>, 66, No. 4
décembre 1908, 561-593.  Also in <u>Edition du Centenaire</u>,
897-930, 1523-1528.  An explanation of the phenomenon of
"déjà vu" through the wandering of attention is given in
this essay, which is republished in <u>L'Energie spirituelle</u>.


                          1909


189    "Discours sur Gabriel Tarde: 12 septembre 1909." <u>Mélanges</u>,
799-801.  This is a speech delivered on the occasion of
the dedication of a monument to Tarde.

190    "Discussion à propos de l'ouvrage de Georges Dwelshauvers:
<u>L'Inconscient dans la vie mentale</u>." <u>Bulletin de la Socié-</u>
<u>té Française de Philosophie</u>, 10, No. 2, janvier 1910,
31-46 (Séance du 25 novembre 1909).  Also in <u>Ecrits et</u>
<u>paroles</u>, 2, 325-331; <u>Mélanges</u>, 803-810.  In this highly
interesting discussion, which includes an exchange between
Bergson and Dwelshauvers, the terms "conscious" and "unconscious" are clarified.

191    "Discussion à propos du <u>Vocabulaire philosophique</u>: Interven-
tion à propos du mot 'intuition'." <u>Bulletin de la Société</u>
<u>Française de Philosophie</u>, 9, 1909, p. 274 (Séance du 1er
juillet 1909).  Also in <u>Ecrits et paroles</u>, 2, p. 322;
<u>Mélanges</u>, 796-797.  This is a discussion of scientific
knowledge as a precondition of intuition.

192   "Lettre à A. Bourgeois: 6 juillet 1909." Etudes Bergsonien-
      nes, 8, p. 23.   Also in Mélanges, 797.   This brief note
      concerns Cahiers de la Quinzaine.

193   "Lettre à W. James: 21 janvier 1909." Revue des Deux Mondes,
      8, Sér. 17, No. 20, 15 octobre 1933, 816-817. Also in
      Ecrits et paroles, 2, p. 310; Mélanges, 785-786. This is
      about Fechner's Zend-Avesta and the hypothesis of a world-
      soul.

194   "Lettre à W. James: 9 avril 1909." Revue des Deux Mondes,
      8, Sér. 17, No. 20, 15 octobre 1933, p. 817. Also in
      Ecrits et paroles, 2, p. 315; Mélanges, 790. Bergson con-
      gratulates James for his article in the Hibbert Journal on
      the philosophy of Bergson.

195   "Lettre à W. James: 30 avril 1909." Revue des Deux Mondes,
      8, Sér. 17, No. 20, 15 octobre 1933, 817-818. Also in
      Ecrits et paroles, 2, 316-316; Mélanges, 791. In this
      letter Bergson discusses Fechner's Zend-Avesta and certain
      of James' ideas concerning the philosophy of religion.

196   "Lettre à W. James: 28 octobre 1909." Revue des Deux Mondes,
      8, Sér. 17, No. 20, 15 octobre 1944, 818-819. Also in
      Ecrits et paroles, 2, 323-324; Mélanges, 801-802. In this
      letter Bergson comments on James' The Meaning of Truth and
      upon the difficulties which James' philosophy will find in
      being understood.

197   "Lettre à Giuseppe Prezzolini: 12 juillet 1909." Il tempo
      della voce.   Ed. Giuseppe Prezzolini.   Milano e Firenze:
      Coedizione Longanese e Vallecchi, 1960, 239-242.

198   "Lettre à N. Söderblom: 27 juillet 1909." H. Sunden. La
      Théorie bergsonienne de la religion, 37. Also in Mélanges,
      797-798. In this letter Bergson declines an invitation to
      give lectures at Uppsala on the philosophy of religion.
      His views on the subject are not yet precise and formula-
      ble.

199   "Préface aux Pages choisies de Gabriel Tarde, par ses fils."
      Paris: Michaud, 1909, 223. Also in Ecrits et paroles, 2,
      332-334; Mélanges, 811-813. Bergson here presents the
      basic ideas of Tarde.

200   "Rapport sur un ouvrage de J. H. Boex-Borel (J. H. Rosny-
      aîné): Le Pluralisme: Etude sur la discontinuité et l'hété-
      rogénéité des phénomènes." Séances et Travaux de l'Acadé-

mie des Sciences Morales et Politiques, 172, 1909, 517-519
(Séance du 21 juin 1909).  Also in Ecrits et paroles, 2,
319-321; Mélanges, 794-796.

201     "Rapport sur un ouvrage de Georges Bohn: La Naissance de
        l'intelligence."  Séances et Travaux de l'Académie des
        Sciences Morales et Politiques, 172, 1909, 144-145 (Séance
        du 1er mai 1909).  Also in Ecrits et paroles, 2, 317-318;
        Mélanges, 792-793.  This is about comparative psychology,
        intelligence, and tropisms.

202     "Rapport sur un ouvrage de M. Henri Delacroix: Etudes
        d'histoire et de psychologie du mysticisme."  Séances et
        Travaux de l'Académie des Sciences Morales et Politiques,
        171, mai 1909, 670-671 (Séance du 20 janvier 1909).  Also
        in Ecrits et paroles, 2, 313-314; Mélanges, 788-790.  This
        is a brief, expository review of Delacroix's study of mys-
        ticism.

203     "Rapport sur un ouvrage de M. Emile Meyerson: Identité et
        réalité."  Séances et Travaux de l'Académie des Sciences
        Morales et Politiques, 171, mai 1909, 664-666 (Séance du
        23 janvier 1909).  Also in Ecrits et paroles, 2, 311-312;
        Mélanges, 786-788.  This is a résumé of Meyerson's posi-
        tion in Identity and Reality.


                              1910


204     "Cours au Collège de France: La Théorie de la personne
        d'après Bergson."  Etudes par des Pères de la Compagnie de
        Jésus, 129, No. 4, 1911, 449-485.  Also in Mélanges, 847-
        875.  These notes were taken by Jules Grivet in 1910-1911.
        This lecture provides significant insights into Bergson's
        psychology and his interpretation of the psychology of his
        era.

205     "Discussion pour le Vocabulaire philosophique sur le mot
        'liberté'."  Bulletin de la Société Française de Philoso-
        phie, 10, No. 7, 1910, 164-166 (Séance du 7 juillet 1910).
        Also in Ecrits et paroles, 2, p. 349; Mélanges, 833-834.
        In this essay liberty is discussed as involving both self-
        determination and indetermination; liberty is "situated"
        between these two terms.

206     "'Une Heure chez Henri Bergson' par Georges Aimel."  Paris-
        Journal, 11 décembre 1910.  Also in Ecrits et paroles, 2,

354-355; Mélanges, 843-844. Here Bergson discusses philosophy and art, literary creativity, symbolism, and Debussy.

207  "Lettre à I. Benrubi: 14 juin 1910." I. Benrubi. Essais et témoignages, 373. Also in Mélanges, 832. This letter is about Benrubi's articles concerning Bergson, Nietzsche, and Rousseau.

208  "Lettre à W. James: 21 mars 1910." Revue des Deux Mondes, 8, Sér. 17, No. 20, 15 octobre 1933, 819-820. Also in Ecrits et paroles, 2, 335-336; Mélanges, 816-817. This letter is about James' "The Moral Equivalent of War" and "A Suggestion about Mysticism." Bergson also discusses a dream he has experienced as a possible "uncovering."

209  "Lettre à E.-J. Lotte: 15 juillet 1910." Bulletin Joseph Lotte, 104, mars 1940, p. 282. Also in Quoniam. De La Sainteté, 76; Etudes Bergsoniennes, 8, p. 30. Also in Mélanges, 834. In this letter Bergson praises Lotte's articles concerning L'Evolution créatrice.

210  "Lettre à E.-J. Lotte: 20 septembre 1910." Etudes Bergsoniennes, 8, p. 30. Also in Mélanges, 835. In this letter Bergson regrets that he is unable to see M. Lotte at the present time.

211  "Lettre à Ch. Péguy: 14 janvier 1910." Etudes Bergsoniennes, 8, p. 24. Mélanges, 815-816. Bergson suggests a time at which he and Péguy might meet.

212  "Lettre à Ch. Péguy: 4 juin 1910." Feuillets de l'Amitié Charles Péguy, 30, p. 9. Also in Etudes Bergsoniennes, 8, p. 27; Mélanges, 828. In this letter Bergson arranges to spend time with Péguy.

213  "Lettre à Ch. Péguy: 20 juin 1910." Feuillets de l'Amitié Charles Péguy, 30, 9-10. Also in Etudes Bergsoniennes, 8, p. 29; Mélanges, 832-833. In this letter Bergson returns, with regrets, a manuscript by Berth.

214  "Lettre à Ch. Péguy." Etudes Bergsoniennes, 8, p. 31. Also in Mélanges, 842. Bergson discusses a recent issue of the Cahiers de la Quinzaine with Péguy.

215  "Rapport pour le concours Charles-Lévêque à décerner en 1910: L'Ouvrage d'Hannequin: Etudes d'histoire des sciences et d'histoire de la philosophie." Séances et Travaux de

l'Académie des Sciences Morales et Politiques, 174, 1910,
496-501 (Séance du 22 octobre 1910). Also in Ecrits et
paroles, 2, 350-353; Mélanges, 835-839. Here Bergson
awards a prize to a posthumously published study of modern philosophy.

216     "Rapport pour le concours de Coenobium." Coenobium, 6, No.
        1, janvier 1912, 176-192. Also in Ecrits et paroles, 2,
        362-363; Mélanges, 840-841. In these notes, written in
        1910, Bergson discusses the relative merits of several
        works, some valuable, some not.

217     "Rapport sur un ouvrage de Lionel Dauriac: Le Musicien poète
        R. Wagner; Etude de psychologie musicale." Séances et
        Travaux de l'Académie des Sciences Morales et Politiques,
        173, juin 1910, 803-805 (Séance du 16 avril 1910). Also
        in Ecrits et paroles, 2, 337-339; Mélanges, 818-820. This
        is an expository review of Dauriac's book on Richard Wag-
        ner.

218     "Rapport sur un ouvrage de M. André Joussain:  Le Fondement
        psychologique de la morale." Séances et Travaux de l'Aca-
        démie des Sciences Morales et Politiques, 173, juin 1910,
        816-817 (Séance du 14 mai 1910). Also in Ecrits et paro-
        les, 2, 340-341; Mélanges, 825-826. This is about an
        attempt to found morality on "sentiment."

219     "Rapport sur un ouvrage de Barret Wendell: La France d'au-
        jourd'hui. Trans. G. Grappe. 2e éd." Séances et Travaux
        de l'Académie des Sciences Morales et Politiques, 174,
        juillet 1910, 146-148 (Séance du 11 juin 1910). Also in
        Ecrits et paroles, 2, 346-348; Mélanges, 829-831. In this
        brief essay, Bergson discusses a book about the French
        national character and its basic "seriousness."

220     "Réponse à l'article de W. B. Pitkin, 'James and Bergson'."
        Journal of Philosophy, Psychology, and Scientific Meth-
        ods, 7, No. 14, 7 July 1910, 385-388. Also in Ecrits et
        paroles, 2, 342-345; Mélanges, 820-824. In this article
        Bergson defends himself against Pitkin's interpretation of
        his thought.

221     "Résumé par Bergson de ses cours sur La Personnalité et sur
        le Traité de la réforme de l'entendement." Archives du
        Collège de France, 11, 1910, 114. Also in Ecrits et paro-
        les, 2, 356-357; Mélanges, 845-846. This is a brief ac-
        count by Bergson of lectures on the problem of personality
        and on Spinoza.

## 1911

222   <u>Choix de textes</u>. Notice par René Gillouin. Paris: Louis
      Michaud, 1911, 222.

223   "Entretien avec E.-J. Lotte: 21 avril 1811." <u>Bulletin
      Joseph Lotte</u>, 104, mars 1940. 282-285. Also in <u>Etudes
      Bergsoniennes</u>, 8, 37-41; <u>Mélanges</u>, 879-882. This is
      about Bergson's proposed book on morality, mysticism, and
      the decadence of Europe.

224   "Interview par Jacques Morland: 19 août 1911." <u>L'Opinion</u>,
      4e Année, No. 33, 19 août 1911, 241-242. Also in <u>Mélanges</u>,
      939-944. Here Bergson discusses his divergent influence,
      his philosophical method, syndicalism, positivism, and the
      younger generation.

225   "L'Intuition philosophique." <u>Edition du Centenaire</u>, 1345-
      1365, 1534-1535. In this essay Bergson discusses the man-
      ner in which intuition functions in philosophy. He ap-
      plies his concept of philosophic intuition to Spinoza and
      to Berkeley. This essay is republished in <u>La Pensée et le
      mouvant</u>.

226   "Lettre à Madame W. James: Juin 1911." <u>Revue des Deux
      Mondes</u>, 15 octobre 1933, p. 821. Also in <u>Mélanges</u>, 939.
      This is about Bergson's introduction to James' <u>Pragmatism</u>.

227   "Lettre à E.-J. Lotte: 19 avril 1911." <u>Etudes Bergsoniennes</u>,
      8, p. 36. Also in <u>Mélanges</u>, 879. Bergson arranges a meet-
      ing with Lotte in this letter.

228   "Lettre à E.-J. Lotte: 20 septembre 1911." <u>Etudes Bergso-
      niennes</u>, 8, p. 45. Also in <u>Mélanges</u>, 944. Bergson here
      suggests that Lotte may be able to visit with him in Paris.

229   "Lettre à Ch. Péguy: 3 février 1911." <u>Etudes Bergsoniennes</u>,
      8, 33. Also in <u>Mélanges</u>, 878. This letter is about finan-
      cial backing for <u>Cahiers de la Quinzaine</u>.

230   "Lettre à Ch. Péguy: 3 mai 1911." <u>Etudes Bergsoniennes</u>, 8,
      43-44. Also in <u>Mélanges</u>, 883-884. This letter is about
      Péguy's <u>Pages choisies</u>.

231   "Lettre à F. Znianiecki: 3 décembre 1811." <u>Ecrits et pa-
      roles</u>, 3, p. 654. Also in <u>Mélanges</u>, 960. This is about
      the Polish translation of <u>L'Evolution créatrice</u> and Berg-

son's opinion of the difficulties involved in translating
this major work.

232    "Life and Consciousness." Hibbert Journal, 10, Part 1,
October 1911, 22-44. Also in L'Energie spirituelle, 1919,
Edition du Centenaire, 815-836; Etudes Bergsoniennes, 6,
5-36; Mélanges, 916-938. This is the Huxley Lecture, delivered at the University of Birmingham, 29 May 1911, with
some additions. Bergson deals in this essay with the
threefold problem of consciousness, of life, and of their
relations to each other. The mind-body problem, evolution,
and the limitations of science and philosophy are discussed.

233    "La Nature de l'âme." Etudes Bergsoniennes, 7, 9-16. Also
in Mélanges, 944-959. This article consists of four lectures given 21, 23, 28, and 30 October 1911, at Leeds University. Bergson, in these lectures, examines the nature
of mind and suggests how the action of the mind on the
body ought to be represented. He deals in turn with the
possible objections to his view based on science and on
philosophical assumptions.

234    La Perception du changement: Conférences faites à l'université d'Oxford les 26 et 27 mai 1911. Oxford: Clarendon
Press, 1911, 37. Also, with numerous corrections, in La
Pensée et le mouvant, Edition du Centenaire, 1365-1392
(A note on the text occurs on 1576); Etudes Bergsoniennes,
6, 133-168; Mélanges, 888-914. This consists of two lectures on the nature of change, the difficulties encountered in explaining change, and the manner in which we can
resolve certain philosophical problems by understanding
the nature of change.

TRANSLATIONS

235    Filosofen och livet. Trans. svenska av Algot Ruhe.
Stockholm: Fyra föredrag, 1911, 77.

236    Vospruatie izmienchivosti. St. Petersburg, 1912.

237    "Les Réalités que la science n'atteint pas." Foi et vie,
14, No. 14, 16 juillet 1911, 421-422. Also in Ecrits et
paroles, 2, 359-360; Mélanges, 885-887. In this essay
Bergson claims that, though limited, science possesses
certainty. Philosophy, however, has its own method and
object.

238    "Résumé de ses cours sur L'Idée d'évolution et sur Les Principes généraux de la philosophie de Spinoza." Archives du
Collège de France, 12, 1912, p. 38. Also in Ecrits et paroles, 2, p. 361; Mélanges, 961. This is a general description by Bergson of courses on the idea of evolution
and on Spinoza's philosophy, which were given in 1911-1912.

239    "'Vérité et réalité': Introduction." Le Pragmatisme, par
William James. Paris: Flammarion, 1911, 312, i-xvi. Also
in La Pensée et le mouvant, Edition du Centenaire, 1440-
1450 et 1539. This is a general account of the philosophy of William James.


1912


240    "Avant-propos à l'ouvrage de Rudolph Eucken: Le Sens et la
valeur de la vie." Paris: Félix Alcan, 1912, i-iv. Also
in Ecrits et paroles, 2, 371-372; Mélanges, 971-973. In
this foreword Bergson discusses, in very general terms,
the significance and character of Eucken's thought.

241    "Conférence à Foi et vie sur l'âme et le corps." L'Energie
spirituelle, Edition du Centenaire, 836-860, 1517-1520.
Also in Gustave Le Bon, Ed. Le Matérialisme actuel.
Paris: Flammarion, 1913, 7-48. This is an explanation of
Bergson's mind-body theory.

242    "Discours prononcé sur la tombe d'Henri Franck: 27 février
1912." Henri Franck, 2 décembre 1888-25 février 1912,
Paris, 1912. Also in Ecrits et paroles, 2, p. 367; Mélanges, 965-966. This a brief yet eloquent funeral ora-
tion.

243    "Letter of Recommendation for T. E. Hulme. 1912." T. E.
Hulme. Speculations. London: Routledge and Kegan Paul,
1949, 271, viii. Bergson asserts here that Hulme will
pursue a creative career in modern art.

244    "Lettre à L. Dauriac: 26 mai 1912." Etudes Bergsoniennes,
3, 196-197. Also in Mélanges, 968. This is a résumé of
a letter. It is about Bergson's attitude towards Kant.

245    "Lettre à L. Dauriac: 18 août 1912." Etudes Bergsoniennes,
3, p. 197. This is a résumé of a letter on Meyerbeer.

246    "'Lettre à Gilbert Maire." Cited in Gilbert Maire. "La Philosophie de G. Sorel." Cahiers du Cercle Proud'hon, 2,

mars–avril 1912, 65.  Also in Ecrits et paroles, 2, p.
370; Mélanges, 971.  Bergson's relation to Sorel is discussed here.

247    "Lettre à Ch. Péguy: 21 mai 1912."  Feuillets de l'Amitié
Charles Péguy, 30, p. 11.  Also in Etudes Bergsoniennes,
8, 45–46; Mélanges, 967.  This letter concerns the possible publication of "L'Ame et le corps" in Cahiers de la
Quinzaine.

248    "Lettre à M. Edouard Le Roy à la suite de deux articles pa-
rus dans la Revue des Deux Mondes sur la philosophie nouvelle, 1er et 15 février 1912."  Ecrits et paroles, 2,
364.  Also in the preface to E. Le Roy.  Une Philosophie
nouvelle.  Paris: Félix Alcan, 1912, iv–v.  In this fragment of a letter Bergson congratulates Le Roy for his interpretation of his (i.e., Bergson's) philosophy.

249    "Lettre à J. de Tonquédec: 20 février 1912."  Etudes par des
Pères de la Compagnie de Jésus, 130, 20 février 1912, 514–
516.  Also in Sur La Philosophie bergsonienne.  Paris:
Beauchesne, 1946, 59–60; Ecrits et paroles, 2, 365–366;
Mélanges, 963–964.  This is about Bergson's philosophical
method.

250    "Réponse à l'enquête de Jules Bertaut sur la jeunesse."  Le
Gaulois, 15 juin 1912.  Also in H. Massis.  Les Jeunes Gens
d'aujourd'hui.  Paris: Plon, 1913, 284–286; Ecrits et paroles, 2, 368–369; Mélanges, 968–970.  Here Bergson holds
that there is a profound change in the youth of France––a
sort of moral renaissance.


## 1913


251    "The Bergson Lectures."  Columbia Alumni News, 4, No. 26,
21 March 1913, 397–399.  Also in Mélanges, 978–981.  The
general notes on Bergson's lectures were taken by W. T.
Bush.  The lectures outline Bergson's epistemology and his
ideas on the mind-body dualism.

252    "Cours à Columbia University: Spirituality and Liberty."
The Chronicle, 13, 6 March 1913, 214–220.  Also in Mélanges, 981–989.  The following topics are discussed in
this lecture: the need of a new philosophy, free will
means moral health, the memory has no special home in the
brain, the relation of vital phenomena to science, life

mentally and morally an effort, and immortality unproved but man may live after death.

253   "Discours au Comité France-Amérique." France-Amérique, juin 1913, 341-350. Also in Revue Internationale de l'Enseignement, 33, No. 7, juillet 1913. 95-105; Ecrits et paroles, 2, 378-388; Mélanges, 990-1001. Here Bergson gives his impressions of New York, of Columbia University, and of Franco-American idealism.

254   "Fantômes de vivants et recherche psychique." Proceedings of the British Society for Psychical Research, 26, 1913, 462-479. Also in Annales des Sciences Psychiques, 23e Année, No. 11-12, 321-329 (free translation); L'Energie spirituelle, 1919, Edition du Centenaire, 870-878, 1566 (translation differs significantly from the above); Etudes Bergsoniennes, 6, 37-60; Mélanges, 1002-1019. This is the Presidential address given before the British Society for Psychical Research. In it Bergson applies his mind-body theory, particularly his theory of "attention to life," to the problems of parapsychology.

255   "Lettre à I. Benrubi: 14 juillet 1913." I. Benrubi. Souvenirs sur Henri Bergson, 86. Also in Henri Bergson. Essais et témoignages, page de garde; Mélanges, 1024. This letter is on creativity as the goal of human life.

256   "Lettre à L. Dauriac: 19 mars 1913." Etudes Bergsoniennes, 3, p. 197 résumé. Also in Mélanges, 990. This letter is about Bergson's trip to the United States.

257   "Lettre à Fr. Grandjean: 12 juin 1913." Fr. Grandjean. La Doctrine de M. Henri Bergson. Also in Mélanges, 1020. This letter concerns Grandjean's book on Bergson.

258   "Lettre à Fr. Grandjean: 22 août 1913." Henri Bergson. Essais et témoignages, 372-373. Also in Mélanges, 1024-1025. Bergson affirms his decision, in this letter, not to allow publication of opinions expressed in conversation.

259   "Lettre à Marie-Anne Léon: 12 mars 1913." Catalogue Henri Bergson de la Bibliothèque Nationale, cote 273. Also in Mélanges, 989. This is a brief segment of a letter. Bergson states that reality flows.

260   "Lettre à A. Mitchell." A. Mitchell. "Studies in Bergson's Philosophy." Bulletin of the University of Kansas, January 1914. Also in Mélanges, 1030-1031. This letter is a

discussion of intuition as the basis for the posing of
philosophical problems, the status of matter and of rest,
and the unity of action and knowledge.

261    "Lettre à Thureau-Dangin: 25 septembre 1913." Archives de
       l'Académie Française, Série A.  Also in Mélanges, 1025.
       In this letter Bergson proposes his candidacy for the
       French Academy.

262    "Lettre sur le jury de cour d'assises: 19 octobre 1913." Le
       Temps, 19 octobre 1913, p. 4, col. 2-3.  Also in Ecrits et
       paroles, 2, 389-392; Mélanges, 1026-1030.  Here Bergson
       discusses the "theatrical" weaknesses of Parisian juries
       and their overindulgence towards "crimes of passion."

263    "Mission à l'Université Columbia." Archives du Collège de
       France, 13, 1913, 87-88.  Also in Ecrits et paroles, 2,
       373-374; Mélanges, 976-977.  This is a discussion of a
       course for students entitled "Esquisse d'une théorie de la
       connaissance."  The public course was entitled "Spiritua-
       lité et liberté."

264    "La Philosophie de Claude Bernard." La Pensée et le mouvant,
       Edition du Centenaire, 1433-1440, 1539.  In this essay
       Bergson discusses the thought of the French physiologist
       Claude Bernard.  Bergson explores Bernard's biological
       concepts and his concept of the nature of scientific meth-
       od.  Bernard, Bergson insists, breaks with the idea that
       science can be a complete, perfected system.

265    "Rapport sur un ouvrage de J. M. Baldwin: Le Darwinisme dans
       les sciences morales."  Also in Séances et Travaux de
       l'Académie des Sciences Morales et Politiques, 180, 1913,
       329-331 (Séance du 14 juin 1913); Ecrits et paroles, 2,
       375-377; Mélanges, 1020-1023.  This is a discussion of
       Darwinism in psychology, Weissman's theory of "intra-se-
       lection," and the theory of "organic selection."

266    "Significado de la evolución." Trans. Malagarriga. Atlan-
       tida, 9, No. 27, marzo 1913, 348-379.  Cf. also note on
       475.


                              1914


267    "Discours de Bergson élu président de l'Académie des
       sciences morales et politiques." Séances et Travaux de
       l'Académie des Sciences Morales et Politiques, 181, 1914,

130-133 (Séance du 10 janvier 1914).  Also in Ecrits et
paroles, 2, 393-395; Mélanges, 1034-1037.  This essay is
on the importance of the moral and political sciences.

268     "Discours prononcé à l'Académie des sciences morales et po-
        litiques."  Séances et Travaux de l'Académie des Sciences
        Morales et Politiques, 192, 1914, p. 325.  Also in Le Fi-
        garo, 9 août 1914; Le Temps, 8 août 1914; Mélanges, 1102.
        Bergson here conveys the thanks and the admiration of the
        French people for the Belgians' brave struggle against
        the German invaders.

269     "Discours prononcé à l'occasion du décès de Ludovic Beau-
        chet."  Séances et Travaux de l'Académie des Sciences Mo-
        rales et Politiques, 181, 1914, 327-328 (Séance du 17 jan-
        vier 1914).  Also in Ecrits et paroles, 2, 396-397; Mélan-
        ges, 1044-1045.  This is a brief review of the life and
        writings of a French legal scholar.

270     "Discours prononcé à l'occasion du décès de Charles Wadding-
        ton."  Ecrits et paroles, 11, 398-400.  Also in Séances
        et Travaux de l'Académie des Sciences Morales et Politi-
        ques, 181, 1912, 441-445 (Séance du 21 mars 1914); Ecrits
        et paroles, 2, 398-400; Mélanges, 1046-1049.  This is an
        account of the life and writings of a French philosopher
        and historian of philosophy.

271     "Discours sur la signification de la guerre."  Séances et
        Travaux de l'Académie des Sciences Morales et Politiques,
        183, 1915, 139-168.  Also in (among many others) Revue
        Universitaire, 23, No. 10, 19 décembre 1914, 233-242;  La
        Signification de la guerre, 7-29; Hibbert Journal, 13, No.
        3, 1915, 465-475; Mélanges, 1107-1129.  This is Bergson's
        concluding speech as president of the Academy.  The open-
        ing and closing sections express Bergson's attitude to-
        wards the war.  The middle section includes necrologies,
        the award of prizes, etc.

        TRANSLATION

272     "Life and Matter at War."  The Meaning of War.  Trans.
        H. Wildon Carr.  London: Fisher Unwin, 1946, 47.

273     "La Force qui s'use et celle qui ne s'use pas."  Bulletin
        des Armées de la République, No. 42, 4 novembre 1914,
        p. 1.  Also in La Signification de la guerre, 40-42;
        Mélanges, 1105-1106.  This is a discussion of French
        "force morale" versus German "force matérielle."

TRANSLATION

274    "The Force Which Wastes and that Which Does not Waste."
The Meaning of War. Trans. H. Wildon Carr. London:
Fisher Unwin, 1916, 47.

275    "Hommage à A. Ribot." Séances et Travaux de l'Académie des
Sciences Morales et Politiques, 182, 1914, p. 468. Also
in Mélanges, 1104. In this essay Bergson works to prevent
expulsion of German members from the Academy.

276    "Hommage au roi Albert et au peuple belge." Daily Telegraph,
London. Also in La Signification de la guerre, 45-46;
Mélanges, 1129-1130. Here Bergson expresses his admira-
tion for the Belgian defense against Germany.

277    "Interview recueillie par Gremil: 16 février 1914." La Dé-
pêche de Toulouse, 16 février 1914. Also in Mélanges,
1038-1040. This interview includes a brief account of
Bergson's early life, a discussion of the place of system
in philosophy, of determinism in history, etc.

278    "Lettre à A. Bourgeois: 19 septembre 1914." Feuillets de
l'Amitie Charles Péguy, 1, p. 5. Also in Etudes Bergsoniennes, 8, p. 57; Mélanges, 1103. In this letter Bergson
asks M. Bourgeois for the address of Mme. Péguy.

279    "Lettre à A. Bourgeois: 21 septembre 1914." Feuillets de
l'Amitié Charles Péguy, 1, p. 5. Also in Etudes Bergsoniennes, 8, p. 57; Mélanges, 1104. In this letter Bergson
conveys the news of Péguy's death.

280    "Lettre à E.-J. Lotte: 12 février 1914." Archives Charles
Péguy. Also in Etudes Bergsoniennes, 8, p. 47; Mélanges,
1038. Bergson here thanks Lotte for some kind words.

281    "Lettre à Ch. Péguy: 27 février 1914." Feuillets de l'Amitié
Charles Péguy, 30, p. 12. Also in Esprit, 1953, 337;
Etudes Bergsoniennes, 8, p. 49; Mélanges, 1042. This letter concerns a personal misunderstanding between Bergson
and Péguy.

282    "Lettre à Ch. Péguy: 4 mars 1914." Etudes Bergsoniennes, 8,
p. 51. Also in Mélanges, 1043. This letter concerns the
arranging of a meeting between Bergson and Péguy.

283    "Lettre à Ch. Péguy: 10 mars 1914." Etudes Bergsoniennes,
8, p. 52. Also in Mélanges, 1044. Here Bergson sets a
time for a meeting with Péguy.

284    "Lettre à Ch. Péguy: 21 avril 1914." Etudes Bergsoniennes,
       8, 52-53. Also in Mélanges, 1086-1087. This concerns an
       issue of Cahiers de la Quinzaine to be dedicated to Berg-
       son.

285    "Lettre à Ch. Péguy: 4 mai 1914." Etudes Bergsoniennes, 8,
       53-54. Also in Mélanges, 1087. In this letter Bergson
       thanks Péguy for his "Note sur la philosophie bergso-
       nienne."

286    "Lettre à Ch. Péguy: 17 mai 1914." Etudes Bergsoniennes, 8,
       54-55. Also in Mélanges, 1088. This letter is about
       Péguy's "Note sur la philosophie bergsonienne."

287    "Lettre à Ch. Péguy: 9 juillet 1914." Etudes Bergsoniennes,
       9, p. 56. Also in Mélanges, 1094. This letter is about
       the Bergson edition of Cahiers de la Quinzaine.

288    "Lettre à F. Vandérem: 27 février 1914." Le Figaro, 29 fé-
       vrier 1914, p. 1, col. 6. Also in Mélanges, 1040-1041.
       This letter contains replies to criticisms, a discussion
       of Bergson's lectures, his philosophical method, and the
       character of his conclusions.

289    "The Problem of Personality." Etudes Bergsoniennes, 7,
       65-88. Also in Mélanges, 1051-1086. These are the Gif-
       ford Lectures for 1914. This edition includes both an Eng-
       lish version and a French translation by André Robinet.
       The following topics are discussed: personality and philo-
       sophical system; the history of the problem of personality:
       Plotinus, Kant; the problem of unity of personality; the
       unconscious; and disorders of personality.

290    "Rapport sur un ouvrage de Jacques Bardoux: Croquis d'outre-
       manche." Ecrits et paroles, 11, 401-402. Also in Séances
       et Travaux de l'Académie des Sciences Morales et Politi-
       ques, 182, 1914, 94-95 (Séance du 28 mars 1914); Ecrits et
       paroles, 2, 401-402; Mélanges, 1049-1051. This concerns a
       study of Great Britain.

291    "Rapport sur un ouvrage de Jacques de Coussange: La Scandina-
       vie: Le Nationalisme scandinave." Séances et Travaux de
       l'Académie des Sciences Morales et Politiques, 183, 1915,
       229-231 (Séance du 11 juillet 1914). Also in Ecrits et
       paroles, 2, 410-412; Mélanges, 1098-1101. This is a
       review of a book on the revival of nationalism in the
       Scandinavian nations.

292    "Rapport sur un ouvrage d'Edouard Dolléans: Le Chartisme."
       Ecrits et paroles, 11, 407-409.  Also in Séances et Tra-
       vaux de l'Académie des Sciences Morales et Politiques, 183,
       1915, 117-119 (Séance du 11 juillet 1914); Ecrits et paro-
       les, 2, 406-409; Mélanges, 1085-1098.  This is a discus-
       sion of English political and social movements of the
       early nineteenth century.

293    "Rapport sur un ouvrage de Jean Finot: Progrès et bonheur."
       Séances et Travaux de l'Académie des Sciences Morales et
       Politiques, 182, 1914, 448-451 (Séance du 27 juin 1914).
       Also in Ecrits et paroles, 2, 403-406; Mélanges, 1090-
       1095.  The conditions of happiness and the reality of
       progress are discussed in this review.


                                1915


294    "Discours à l'Académie des sciences morales et politiques:
       Renouvellement du bureau de l'Académie."  Séances et Tra-
       vaux de l'Académie des Sciences Morales et Politiques, 183,
       1915, 133-135.  Also in La Signification de la guerre, 33-
       35; Le Temps, 17 janvier 1915, in modified form; Mélanges,
       1131-1133.  This is a discussion of French "esprit" and
       German mechanism.

295    "Discours sur la guerre et la littérature de demain."  Revue
       Bleue, 8-15 mai 1915, 162-164.  Also in Mélanges, 1151-
       1156.  Here Bergson states that the future cannot be pre-
       dicted, that it depends on choices made in the present.
       He illustrates this thesis by examples taken from the
       First World War.

296    "Lettre à Jacques Chevalier: 14 mars 1915."  Chevalier.
       Bergson, 64.  Also in Mélanges, 1146.  This letter gives
       an account of Bergson's preoccupation with the war.

297    "Lettre à P. Grimanelli: 6 février 1915."  Revue Positiviste
       Internationale, No. 2, 15 février 1915, 94-95.  Also in
       Mélanges, 1144-1145.  This letter contains Bergson's opin-
       ion of Auguste Comte.

298    "Lettre à A. Hébrard: 19 janvier 1915."  Le Temps, 24 jan-
       vier 1915, p. 1.  Also in Mélanges, 1136-1141.  This is a
       correction of the account in Le Temps of Bergson's speech
       before the Académie des sciences morales et politiques.
       It includes a reply to Bergson by the editors of Le Temps.

299    "Lettre à Harald Höffding: 15 mars 1915." Höffding. La
       Philosophie de Bergson, 157-165. Also in Ecrits et paro-
       les, 3, 455-458; Mélanges, 1146-1150. The version in the
       latter of two sources is corrected by Bergson. Here Berg-
       son claims that the concept of duration is more signifi-
       cant than that of intuition. This is a much-quoted letter.

300    "Lettre à H. M. Kallen: 28 octobre 1915." Journal of Phi-
       losophy, Psychology, and Scientific Methods, 12, No. 22,
       October 1915, 615-616. Also in Riley. "Le Bergsonisme en
       Amérique." Revue Philosophique de la France et de l'Etran-
       ger, 1921, 92-93; Descoqs. Praelectiones Theologiae nat-
       uralis, 1, p. 397; Ecrits et paroles, 3, p. 433 in short-
       ened form; Mélanges, 1191-1194. Here Bergson refutes Kal-
       len's attempt to liken his views to those of traditional
       metaphysics. He also affirms that his views are not un-
       like those of William James.

301    "Lettre à Giuseppe Prezzolini: 3 juillet 1915." Il tempo
       della voce. Ed. Giuseppe Prezzolini. Milano e Firenze:
       Coedizione Longanese e Vallecchi, 1960, 689.

302    "La Philosophie française." Revue de Paris, 3, mai-juin
       1915, 236-256. Also in La Science française. Paris:
       Larousse, 1915, 1, 15-37; La Philosophie. Paris: Larousse,
       1915, 27; Reedited with E. Le Roy. La Science française.
       Paris: Larousse, 1933, 1-26 (many corrections); Ecrits et
       paroles, 2, 413-436; Mélanges, 1157-1189. Bergson claims
       in this essay that France has been the great initiator of
       new ideas in the evolution of modern philosophy.

303    "Progrès matériel et progrès moral." Le Temps, 19 janvier
       1915, p. 1. Also in Mélanges, 1134-1136. This is a re-
       port of Bergson's speech at the Académie des sciences mo-
       rales et politiques, 16 January 1915, by A. Hébrard.

304    "Rapport sur La Science française publié par le Ministère
       de l'instruction publique." Séances et Travaux de l'Aca-
       démie des Sciences Morales et Politiques, 185, 1916, 103-
       104. Also in Ecrits et paroles, 3, 453-454; Mélanges,
       1189-1191.

## 1916

305    "Au Périodique La Razón." La Razón (Madrid), No. 70, 14
       mayo 1916. Also in Mélanges, 1236. This essay is about
       France and Spain.

306    "Conférence de Madrid: La Personnalité." España (weekly),
       6 mayo 1916. Also in Etudes Bergsoniennes. 9, 57-118;
       Mélanges, 1215-1235. This is a general account of Berg-
       son's theory of personality: mind and brain, artistic
       creativity, unity of states of consciousness, personal
       effort, dissociation of personality, fatigue, and creation
       and life.

307    "Conférence de Madrid sur l'âme humaine." España (weekly),
       2 mayo 1916. Also in Etudes Bergsoniennes, 9, 11-56;
       Mélanges, 1200-1215. This is a general exposition of
       essential aspects of Bergson's philosophy: science and phi-
       losophy, creative evolution, conservation of energy, mind-
       body parallelism, the aphasias, etc.

308    "Discours prononcé à la Résidence des Etudiants à Madrid, le
       1er mai 1916." Manuel G. Morente. La Filosofía de Henri
       Bergson. Madrid: Residencia de Estudiantes, 1917, 15-23.
       Also in Ecrits et paroles, 111, 445-448; Mélanges, 1195-
       1200. This essay is about philosophical method and about
       the relations between France and Spain.

309    "Rapport sur un ouvrage de Jacques Chevalier: La Notion du
       nécessaire chez Aristote et chez ses prédécesseurs."
       Séances et Travaux de l'Académie des Sciences Morales et
       Politiques, 185, 1916, 484-486 (Séance du 1er juillet
       1916). Also in Ecrits et paroles, 3, ·451-452; Mélanges,
       1238-1240. This is about necessity vs. contingency in
       Aristotle. Aristotle is unable to make these concepts
       consistent, Chevalier holds, because he lacks the idea of
       creation.

310    "Rapport sur un ouvrage de Paul Gaultier: La Mentalité alle-
       mande et la guerre." Séances et Travaux de l'Académie des
       Sciences Morales et Politiques, 195, 1916, 483-484 (Séance
       du 1er juillet 1916). Also in Ecrits et paroles, 3, 449-
       450; Mélanges, 1236-1238. The German mystique of force is
       discussed here.


                              1917


311    "L'Amitié franco-américaine." L'Amérique, Nos. 3-4, 17-24
       juin 1917, 15-17. Also in France-Amérique, 1967, 7-10;
       Mélanges, 1257-1268. This is a discussion of America,
       its idealism, and its entry into World War I.

312    "Article sur les Etats-Unis." Le Petit Parisien, 4 juillet
       1917. Also in Mélanges, 1269-1270. This is a discussion
       of the motivations which led the United States to enter
       World War I.

313    "Communication à l'Académie des sciences morales et politi-
       ques." Le Figaro, 10 juin 1917, 1, col. 1-2. Also in
       Mélanges, 1253-1256. This is a report by Gabriel Hanotaux
       of Bergson's speech before the Academy concerning his mis-
       sion in the United States.

314    "Compte rendu de la séance du 9 juin 1917 à l'Académie des
       sciences morales et politiques." Le Temps, 11 juin 1917,
       2, col. 6. Also in Mélanges, 1256-1257. This is an un-
       signed newspaper report of Bergson's speech. Bergson dis-
       cusses the American attitude towards the war.

315    "Discours au banquet de la Société France-Amérique, à New
       York." France-Amérique, 1917, 8-16. Also in Mélanges,
       1243-1248. This is a rousing speech on behalf of a "holy
       war."

316    "Lettre à Alfred Loisy: 20 juillet 1917." Cited in Loisy.
       Mémoires pour servir l'histoire religieuse de notre temps.
       Paris: Emile Nourry, 1931, 3, 348. Also in Ecrits et pa-
       roles, 3, p. 460; Mélanges, 1270. This letter is a dis-
       cusion of Bergson's philosophy of religion, which indi-
       cates the importance of mystical experience and religion.

317    "Lettre à Agenor Petit: 27 janvier 1917." A. Petit. Berg-
       son et le rationalisme. 1921. Also in Ecrits et paroles,
       3, p. 459; Mélanges, 1241-1242. The intelligence, Bergson
       holds, has a role to play both in philosophy and in meta-
       physics.

318    "Lettre: 16 août 1917." Labyrinthe, 2, No. 13, 1945, p. 7.
       Also in Mélanges, 1271-1272. This is about the possibil-
       ity of a League of Nations.

319    "La Mission française en Amérique." "Préface à Viviani."
       La Mission française en Amérique. Paris, 1917, 1-7. This
       article concerns Bergson's attempt to influence America to
       enter the First World War.

1918

320    "Allocution au Centre interallié pour le Mother's Day."
       Mélanges, 1306-1307. This was originally in an article
       by Georges Drouilly. Le Gaulois, 13 mai 1918. The topic
       discussed is the American intervention in the First World
       War.

321    "Discours de réception de Bergson à l'Académie française: 24
       janvier 1918." Institut de France, Académie française.
       Paris: F. Didot, 1918, 3-41; Librarie Académique, Paris:
       Perrin, 1918, 1-44. Also in Journal Officiel de la Répub-
       lique Française, 50, No. 25, 1918, 961-966; Ecrits et pa-
       roles, 3, 461-484; Mélanges, 1275-1302. This is about
       Emile Ollivier, his political career, and his philosophy.

322    "Lettre à Albert Adès: 20 avril 1918." Adès chez Bergson.
       Paris, 1949, 130-131. Also in Mélanges, 1304. Here Berg-
       son opposes the use of statements on philosophical sub-
       jects made in conversation.

323    "Lettre à Albert Adès: 26 avril 1918." Adès chez Bergson.
       Paris, 1949, 132-133. Also in Mélanges, 1305-1306. In
       this letter Bergson expresses his unwillingness to be
       quoted in interviews.

324    "Lettre à P. Imbart de la Tour: 2 décembre 1918." La Biblio-
       thèque de Louvain: Séance commemorative du quatrième anni-
       versaire de l'incendie. Paris: Perrin, 1919. Also in
       Mélanges, 1308-1310. This letter is about Belgian resis-
       tance to German aggression and the burning of the library
       of Louvain University.

325    "Notes pour Adès." Adès chez Bergson, 1949, 124-125. Also
       in Mélanges, 1302-1303. This is a point by point criti-
       cism of Adès' article "La Philosophie de Bergson dans la
       vie." Unity of the self, relations of past and present,
       self and society, concept of God, and anarchism are some
       of the ideas discussed.

1919

326    "L'Amitié indestructible: 2 mars 1919." Vie Universitaire,
       mai 1919, 3-5. Also in C. Bouglé and P. Gastinel.
       Qu'est-ce que l'esprit française? Paris: Garnier, 1920,

63-66 in shortened form; Ecrits et paroles, 3, 485-488;
Mélanges, 1312-1316. The topic discussed here is France,
the United States, and their common idealism.

327   "A Propos de la nature du comique: Notes et discussions."
Revue du Mois, 20, No. 119, 1919, 514-517. This is a
reply to criticisms by Delage in a prior number of the
same journal.

328   "Conférence à Strasbourg 'Sur l'âme humaine'." Journal
d'Alsace et de Lorraine, No. 122, 13 mai 1919. Also in
Mélanges, 1316-1319. This is an account by A. Birckel of
Bergson's talk. Bergson claims that the spiritual in man
must overcome the mechanical. Other topics discussed are
Germany, minds and bodies, psychic research, and the function of the intellect.

329   L'Energie spirituelle: Essais et conférences. Paris: Félix
Alcan, 1919, 227. The essays included in this book are:
"La Conscience et la vie," "L'Ame et le corps," "Fantômes
de vivants et recherche psychique," "Le Rêve," "Le Souvenir du présent et la fausse reconnaissance," "L'Effort intellectuel," and "Le Cerveau et la pensée."

330   L'Energie spirituelle: Essais et conférences. Genève: Skira,
1946, 202.

TRANSLATIONS

331   La energía espiritual: Ensayos y conferencias. Trans.
Eduardo Ovejero y Maury. Madrid: Daniel Jorro, 1928,
324.

332   Henkinen tarmo. Trans. J. A. Hollo. Porvoo-Helsinki:
Werner Söderström, 1958, 208.

333   Mind-Energy: Lectures and Essays. Trans. H. Wildon Carr.
New York: Henry Holt, 1920, 262.

334   Die seelische Energie. Jena: Diederichs, 1928, 190.

335   Sjalslig kraft: Studier och föredrag. Trans. Algot
Ruhe. Stockholm: Wahlstrom and Widstrand, 1921, 181.

336   "French Ideals in Education and the American Student." Living Age, 303, No. 3938, December 1919, 775-777. This is
the English translation of "L'Amitié indestructible."

1920

337   "Fragment d'une lettre à G. Sorel: 1920."  Etudes Bergsonien-
      nes, 3, p. 52.  Also in Mélanges, 1326.  Bergson finds
      Sorel's conclusions favorable towards religious emotion.

338   "Lettre à Jacques Chevalier: 28 avril 1920."  Chevalier.
      Bergson.  Paris: Plon, 1934, 296, 304.  Also in Ecrits et
      paroles, 3, 489; Mélanges, 1322.  In this letter Bergson
      explains the terms "intelligence," "intellectual," and
      "supra-intellectual."  The latter term defines intuition.

339   "Lettre à M. Proust: 30 septembre 1920."  J. Guitton.  Voca-
      tion de Bergson, 40-41.  Also in Mélanges, 1326.  This is
      about Proust's success and the acuity of his introspective
      method.

340   "Lettre à l'administrateur du Collège de France: 3 octobre
      1920."  Mélanges, 1327.  In this letter Bergson expresses
      his desire to retire from teaching.

341   "Le Possible et le réel."  Nordisk Tidskrift for vetensdag,
      november 1930, 441-456.  Swedish translation, Mgr. Söder-
      blöm.  Also in La Pensée et le mouvant, 1934, Edition du
      Centenaire, 1331-1345; Etudes Bergsoniennes, 7, 127-132;
      Mélanges, 1322-1326 résumé.  This lecture was delivered at
      Oxford in 1920 and never has been published as a whole.
      The thesis of this lecture is that possibility does not
      precede actuality; there is less in the "possible" than in
      the real and not more, as traditional philosophy has held.

1921

342   "Henri Bergson on Moral Values and Other Subjects."  Person-
      alist, 62, No. 2, 1961, 178-180.  This article contains
      replies by Bergson to various questions posed to him by
      R. F. Piper in 1921.

343   "Lettre à Le Figaro: 25 février 1921."  Le Figaro, 25 fé-
      vrier 1921.  Also in Mélanges, 1331-1332.  Here Bergson
      denies any participation in a committee to aid Russian ref-
      ugees.

344   "Préface."  Woodbridge Riley.  Le Génie américain: Penseurs
      et hommes d'action.  Paris: Félix Alcan, 1921, i-iv.  Also

in Ecrits et paroles, 3, 495-496; Mélanges, 1336-1338. This is a review of a book on important thinkers and early religious movements in the United States.

345    "Rapport sur un ouvrage de René Gillouin: Une Nouvelle Phi-losophie de l'histoire moderne et française." Séances et Travaux de l'Académie des Sciences Morales et Politiques, 196, 1921, 167-170 (Séance du 9 juillet 1921). Also in Ecrits et paroles, 3, 492-494; Mélanges, 1333-1336. This is a discussion of the mystique of imperialism.

346    "Rapport sur un ouvrage d'Ossip-Lourié: La Graphomanie: Essai de psychologie morbide." Séances et Travaux de l'Académie des Sciences Morales et Politiques, 196, 1921, 520-522 (Séance du 12 février 1921). Also in Ecrits et paroles, 3, 490-491; Mélanges, 1330-1331. Bergson claims that the study of the irresistible desire to write does not necessarily enlighten psychology.

1922

347    "Appel...en faveur des travailleurs intellectuels autri-chiens et de la vie intellectuelle en Autriche." Archives de l'Unesco, C. 731, M. 443, 1922, XII, 1-2. Also in Ecrits et paroles, 3, 520-522; Mélanges, 1363-1366. Vari-ous means of aiding Austria's intellectual community are suggested here.

348    "Avant-propos." J. Alexander Gunn. Modern French Philoso-phy, a Study of the Development since Comte. London: Fisher Unwin, 1922, 358, 8-9. Also in Ecrits et paroles, 2, 536-537; Mélanges, 1387-1388. Bergson gives a general account of the structure and subject matter of Gunn's book.

349    "Comment doivent écrire les philosophes?  Ce que pensent... M. Henri Bergson." Monde Nouveau, 4e Sér., 6, No. 25, 15 décembre 1922, 228-233. Also in Bourquin, Ed. Comment doivent écrire les philosophes? Paris: Editions du Monde Nouveau, 1923, 166.

350    "Commission internationale de coopération intellectuelle: Questions relatives à la propriété scientifique, artis-tique et littéraire." Archives de l'Unesco, A. 61, 1922, XII et C. 559, 1922, XII, p. 33. Also in Mélanges, 1348. This concerns the need for international copyright laws.

351    "Commission international de coopération intellectuelle:
       Rapport de la Commission approuvé par le Conseil de la
       S.D.N. le 13 septembre 1922." <u>Archives de l'Unesco</u>
       A. 61, 1933, XII et C. 559, 1922, XII, 1-6. Also in
       <u>Ecrits et paroles</u>, 3, 504-515; <u>Mélanges</u>, 1352-1363. In
       this essay there is a general enquiry into the state of
       intellectual life, a discussion of help to nations in
       which intellectual life is menaced, of an international
       organization for scientific documentation, and of inter-
       national cooperation in scientific research, etc.

352    "Commission internationale de coopération intellectuelle:
       Rapport sur la première session tenue à Genève du ler au
       6 août 1922." <u>Société des Nations</u>, 1922, 2-6. Also in
       <u>Ecrits et paroles</u>, 3, 504-515. Bergson intervenes at
       several points during this discussion.

353    "Commission internationale de coopération intellectuelle:
       Résolution du Président concernant les recherches archéo-
       logiques." <u>Archives de l'Unesco</u>, A. 61, 1922, XII et
       C. 559, 1922, XII, p. 28. Also in <u>Mélanges</u>, 1347-1348.
       Here Bergson calls for international cooperation to pre-
       serve archeological treasures.

354    "Commission internationale de coopération intellectuelle:
       Sous-Commission de bibliographie: Première séance à Paris
       20 décembre 1922." <u>Archives de l'Unesco</u>, C.I.C.I./B./
       P.V.1. Also in <u>Mélanges</u>, 1379-1383. Here Bergson dis-
       cusses the problem of world libraries and international
       bibliographic libraries.

355    "Commission internationale de coopération intellectuelle:
       Sous-Commission de bibliographie: 21 décembre 1922."
       <u>Archives de l'Unesco</u>, C.I.C.I./B./P.V.1 Also in <u>Mélanges</u>,
       1383-1386. Here Bergson discusses, with Mme. Curie and
       others, the problems of creating an international biblio-
       graphic index.

356    "Discours de clôture du président de la Commission interna-
       tionale de coopération intellectuelle: Genève, 5 août
       1922." <u>Première session de la Commission internationale
       de coopération intellectuelle</u>. Genève, 1922, 36-37. Also
       in <u>Ecrits et paroles</u>, 3, 516-519; <u>Mélanges</u>, 1349-1352.
       This is a general discussion of the goals and the accom-
       plishments of the Commission.

357    <u>Durée et simultanéité</u>. Paris: Félix Alcan, 1922, 245.

358    Durée et simultanéité. 2e édition augmentée. Paris: Félix
       Alcan, 1923, 289. This edition, like all subsequent edi-
       tions, contains three appendices: "Le Voyage en boulet,"
       "Réciprocité de l'accélération," and "Le 'Temps propre'
       et la 'Ligne d'Univers'."

359    "Durée et simultanéité." Mélanges. Paris: Presses Univer-
       sitaires de France, 1972, 1692, 57-244.

360    Durée et simultanéité: A Propos de la théorie d'Einstein.
       3e éd. Paris: Félix Alcan, 1926, 289.

361    Durée et simultanéité: A Propos de la théorie d'Einstein.
       7e éd. Paris: Presses Universitaires de France, 1968,
       216 (Bibliothèque de Philosophie Contemporaine). This is
       the first posthumous reprinting.

       TRANSLATION

362    Duration and Simultaneity. Trans. Leon Jacobson.
       Indianapolis, Indiana: Bobbs-Merrill, 1965, 190. The
       introduction is by Herbert Dingle.

363    "Les Etudes gréco-latines et la réforme de l'enseignement
       secondaire." Séances et Travaux de l'Académie des
       Sciences Morales et Politiques, 199, 1923, 60-71. Also in
       Revue de Paris, 30, No. 9, 1er mai 1923, 5-18; Ecrits et
       paroles, 3, 523-534; Mélanges, 1366-1379. This is a dis-
       cussion of the vital role of classical studies in French
       education.

364    "Lettre à Karen Stephen: 1922." Karen Stephen. The Misuse
       of Mind. London: Kegan Paul, 1922, 107. Also in Ecrits
       et paroles, 3, p. 535; Mélanges, 1386-1387. This is a
       preface to Karen Stephen's Misuse of Mind. In it, Bergson
       praises Stephen's logical rigor.

365    "Préface à La Fierté de vivre de Pierre-Jean Ménard." Mélan-
       ges, 1389-1391. This is an introduction to the notes of a
       physician-philosopher killed in World War I. It discusses
       the place of heroism in human affairs.

366    "Remarques sur la théorie de la relativité." Bulletin de la
       Société Française de Philosophie, 22, No. 3, juillet 1922,
       102-113 (Séance du 6 avril 1922). Also in Ecrits et pa-
       roles, 3, 497-503; Mélanges, 1340-1347. This article has
       been translated, with an introduction, in Bergson and the
       Evolution of Physics. Ed. P. A. Y. Gunter, 123-135.

1923

367    "Commission internationale de coopération intellectuelle:
       L'Enseignement de l'Esperanto: 31 juillet 1923." Archives
       de l'Unesco, C. 570, M. 224, 1923, XII, p. 40. Also in
       Mélanges, 1414-1416. Here Bergson discusses both the ad-
       vantages and the drawbacks of an artificial international
       language.

368    "Commission internationale de coopération intellectuelle:
       Rapport sur la deuxième session tenue à Genève du 26 juil-
       let au 2 août 1923. 15 août 1923." Société des Nations,
       A. 31, 1923, 12, 3-10. Also in Ecrits et paroles, 3, 542-
       559; Mélanges, 1398-1414. This is a detailed account of
       the work to be accomplished by the Commission and the
       problems it will encounter.

369    "Discours d'ouverture du président de la Commission interna-
       tionale de coopération intellectuelle: 26 juillet 1923."
       Deuxième session de la Commission internationale de coopé-
       ration intellectuelle, 1923, Procès-verbaux, 7. Also in
       Ecrits et paroles, 3, 540-541; Mélanges, 1397-1398. Here
       Bergson welcomes back the members of the Commission and
       urges them to seek practical goals.

370    "Discours prononcé au banquet offert à Xavier Léon pour le
       trentième anniversaire de la Revue de Métaphysique et de
       Morale." Trentenaire de la Revue de Métaphysique et de
       Morale. Hommage à M. Xavier Léon. Paris: Presses Univer-
       sitaires de France, 1924. Also in Ecrits et paroles, 3,
       566-569; Mélanges, 1425-1428. This talk was given 27 De-
       cember 1923. Bergson congratulates Xavier Léon in this
       talk for his great contribution to French philosophy.

371    "Lettre à Floris Delattre: 9 mai 1923." Revue Philosophique
       de la France et de l'Etranger, 1941, p. 134. Also in
       Mélanges, 1394. In this fragment Bergson discusses his
       ill health, particularly his insomnia.

372    "Lettre à Floris Delattre: 23 ou 24 août 1923." Revue An-
       glo-américaine, 13, No. 5, juin 1936, 392-393. Also in
       Ecrits et paroles, 3, 560-561; Mélanges, 1417-1418. Here
       Bergson describes his "durée" as being more continuous
       than William James' "stream of thought."

373    "Lettre à R. de Flers: 27 avril 1923." Le Figaro, 28 avril
       1923, 1, col. 3. Also in Mélanges, 1394. In this letter
       Bergson denies any knowledge of or influence by Laggrond.

374    "Lettre à A. Suarès: 1923." M. Dietschy. Le Cas André
       Suarès, p. 292. Also in Mélanges, 1429. In this frag-
       ment of a letter Bergson thanks Suarès for one of his
       books.

375    "Proposition de crédit supplémentaire pour la Commission de
       coopération intellectuelle." Journal Officiel de la Socié-
       té des Nations, 1923. Suppléments Spéciaux, No. 17, 78-80.
       "Rapport de M. Bergson devant la Commission financière de
       l'Assemblée de la Société des Nations, Genève, le 26 sep-
       tembre 1923." Also in Ecrits et paroles, 3, 562-566; Mé-
       langes, 1419-1424. This is about the financial affairs
       of the Commission.

376    "Rapport sur un ouvrage d'Alfred Tarde: Le Maroc: Ecole
       d'énergie." Séances et Travaux de l'Académie des Sciences
       Morales et Politiques, 201, 1924, 435-436 (Séance du 30
       juin 1923). Also in Ecrits et paroles, 3, 538-539; Mélan-
       ges, 1395-1396. This is about the "first chapter" of a phi-
       losophy of colonization.

377    "Réunion du conseil supérieur de l'éducation nationale: 3
       juillet 1923." Mossé-Bastide. Bergson éducateur, p. 171.
       Also in Mélanges, 1395. This article is about the impor-
       tance of a classical education.

## 1924

378    "Appel en faveur de la vie intellectuelle en Hongrie: 5 no-
       vembre 1924." Journal Officiel de la Société des Nations,
       2, 1924, 1811. Also in Ecrits et paroles, 3, 581-582;
       Mélanges, 1459-1461. Here Bergson makes a plea for jour-
       nals, books, and research funds for Hungary.

379    "Commission internationale de coopération intellectuelle:
       Ouverture de la session: 25 juillet 1924." Archives de
       l'Unesco, A. 20, 1924, XII, p. 9. Also in Mélanges, 1454-
       1455. Bergson welcomes Albert Einstein to the Commission
       and congratulates him on his success as a scientist.

380    "Commission internationale de coopération intellectuelle:
       Sous-Commission de bibliographie." Archives de l'Unesco,
       C.I.C.I./6e session/P.V.3. Also in Mélanges, 1452-1454.
       This article is a discussion of an international bibliog-
       raphy for the social sciences.

381    "Lettre à Fl. Delattre: 3 décembre 1924." Revue Philosophi-
       que de la France et de l'Etranger, mars 1941, 134. Also
       in Mélanges, 1462. This is a discussion of Bergson's ill-
       ness.

382    "Lettre à E. Peillaube: Juillet 1924." Revue de Philosophie,
       24, No. 4, juillet 1924. Translated in P. A. Y. Gunter.
       Bergson and the Evolution of Physics, 189-190. Also in
       Mélanges, 1450-1451. Bergson claims that Metz fails to
       understand his replies to criticisms of Duration and Sim-
       ultaneity. He states that there is nothing more to say
       on this subject.

383    "Lettre du président de la Commission au secrétaire de la
       Confédération internationale des travailleurs intellectu-
       els: 26 juillet 1924." Procès-verbal de la quatrième ses-
       sion de la Commission internationale de coopération intel-
       lectuelle, Annexe 1, 50. Also in Ecrits et paroles, 3,
       579; Mélanges, 1456-1457. In this letter Bergson dis-
       cusses the fact that the Confédération internationale des
       travailleurs intellectuels has been denied permission to
       send a voting member to the C.I.C.I. meetings. A non-vot-
       ing member, however, is to be allowed to attend.

384    "Lettre du président de la Commission de coopération intel-
       lectuelle à l'Association internationale des journalistes:
       28 juillet 1924." Procès-verbal de la quatrième session
       de la Commission internationale de coopération intellec-
       tuelle. Annexe 7. Also in Ecrits et paroles, 3, 580;
       Mélanges, 1457-1458. This is a discussion of the fact
       that journalists were not allowed to attend meetings of
       C.I.C.I. However, a public session of the Commission was
       planned.

385    "Mémoire sur l'échange international des publications."
       Journal de la Société des Nations, janvier-juin 1924.,
       Annexe 607a, 576-580. Also in Ecrits et paroles, 3, 570-
       578; Mélanges, 1463-1470. In this document, the findings
       of the International Commission for Intellectual Coopera-
       tion on the possibility of the free international exchange
       of publications are summarized.

386    "Préface." Floris Delattre. Extraits de correspondance de
       W. James. Paris: Payot, 1924, 7-12. Also in Ecrits et
       paroles, 3, 583-586; Mélanges, 1470-1474. In this brief
       essay, Bergson discussed the vision and personality of
       William James.

387    "Rapport sur La Révolution physique et la science de J.
       Sageret." Séances et Travaux de l'Académie des Sciences
       Morales et Politiques, 205, 1926, 300-301. Also in Mélan-
       ges, 1461-1462. Here Bergson points out parallels in the
       scientific thinking of Le Dantec, Einstein, and J. H.
       Rosny-aîné. In all these cases, he shows that becoming
       triumphs over being.

388    "Les Temps fictifs et le temps réel." Revue de Philosophie,
       24, mai 1924, 241-260. Translated, with an introduction,
       in Bergson and the Evolution of Physics. Ed. P. A. Y.
       Gunter, 165-186. Also in Mélanges, 1432-1339. This is
       a reply to criticisms of Duration and Simultaneity by
       André Metz. Bergson claims that Metz fails to understand
       the reciprocity of reference systems in the special theory
       of relativity and the reciprocity of acceleration in the
       general theory. The experiments which Metz appeals to,
       further, are incapable of proving his point.


                            1925


389    "Lettre: 1925." Mélanges, 1477. This is a fragment which
       states: "Quand on a passé sa vie à chercher le vrai, on
       s'aperçoit qu'on l'eût mieux employée à faire du bien."

390    "Lettre de retraite de la Commisssion internationale de co-
       opération intellectuelle: 27 juillet 1925." Archives de
       l'Unesco, C.I.C.I./C.A./lre Session/P.V.1. Also in Mélan-
       ges, 1476-1477. Here Bergson presents his regrets at his
       inability to attend sessions of the commission. He also
       discusses various suggestions regarding the affairs of the
       commission.


                            1926


391    "Lettre à I. Benrubi: 21 novembre 1926." Benrubi. Souve-
       nirs sur Henri Bergson, 110-111. Also in Mélanges, 1480.
       This is a discussion of Benrubi's Contemporary Thought of
       France.

1927

392    "Lettre à Léon Brunschvicg à l'occasion de la commémoration
       du deux cent cinquantième anniversaire de la mort de Spi-
       noza: 12 février 1927." Bulletin de la Société Française
       de Philosophie, 27 juin 1927, p. 26. Also in Ecrits et
       paroles, 3, 587-588; Mélanges, 1482-1483. Here Bergson
       characterizes Spinoza's theory of knowledge as "connais-
       sance intérieure."

393    "Lettre à de la Vallette-Montbrun, secrétaire général de
       l'Association des amis de Maine de Biran: 30 septembre
       1927." Revue Maine de Biran, 1, No. 1, 1929, 1-2. Also
       in Ecrits et paroles, 3, 589; Mélanges, 1484. Here Berg-
       son gives his very high opinion of Maine de Biran and his
       philosophy.

394    "Lettre à Wilfred Monod: 27 janvier 1927." W. Monod. Le
       Problème du bien, 2, p. 76. Also in H. Sunden. La Théo-
       rie bergsonienne de la religion, 13; Mélanges, 1481-1482.
       Here Bergson claims that the problem of God is a moral
       problem and discusses the possible relation between God
       and creation.

1928

395    L'Evolution créatrice. "Introduction par Kjell Strömberg.
       Discours de réception prononcé par Per Hallström lors de
       la remise du Prix Nobel de littérature à H. Bergson, le
       10 novembre 1928." La Vie et l'oeuvre de H. Bergson, par
       Jean Guitton. Guilde des Bibliophiles, collection des
       Prix Nobel de littérature. Paris: Presses du Compagnon-
       nage, 1962, 349. This is Bergson's Nobel Prize acceptance
       speech.

       TRANSLATION

396    L'evoluzione creatrice. Trans. L. Alano. Milano:
       Fabbri, 1966, 396 (I premi Nobel per la letteratura, 28).

397    "Lettre à I. Benrubi: 12 juin 1928." Benrubi. Souvenirs
       sur Henri Bergson, 112-114. Also in Mélanges, 1486-1487.
       Here Bergson congratulates Benrubi on his Philosophische
       Stroemungen in Frankreich. He also issues a warning con-
       cerning the difficulties involved in assigning "influence"
       to philosophers.

398     "Lettre à Fl. Delattre: 16 janvier 1928." <u>Revue philosophi-</u>
        <u>que de la France et de l'Etranger</u>, 1941, p. 134. <u>Mélanges</u>,
        1485. This is a brief fragment concerning Bergson's
        health.

399     "Lettre à V. Jankélévitch: 7 juillet 1928." Jankélévitch.
        <u>Bergson</u>, 1959, 253. Also in <u>Mélanges</u>, 1487. Here Berg-
        son agrees that there are similarities between his own
        philosophy and that of Spinoza.

400     "Lettre à L. Lévy-Bruhl: 22 novembre 1928." <u>Séances et Tra-</u>
        <u>vaux de l'Académie des Sciences Morales et Politiques</u>,
        1929, p. 374. Also in <u>Mélanges</u>, 1490. This letter is
        about the congratulations of the French Academy for Berg-
        son's Nobel Prize.

401     "Lettre au Duc de la Force: 22 novembre 1928." <u>Mélanges</u>,
        1491. Here Bergson thanks the French Academy for kind
        words concerning his Nobel Prize.


                                1929


402     "Lettre à Fl. Delattre: 11 mars 1929." <u>Revue de Philosophie</u>,
        mars 1941, 134. Also in <u>Mélanges</u>, 1493. This letter is
        about Bergson's health.


                                1930


403     "Lettre à Vladimir Jankélévitch: 6 août 1930." Vladimir Jan-
        kélévitch. <u>Bergson</u>. Paris: Félix Alcan, 1931, v; Nouvel-
        le édition, 1959, 253. Also in <u>Ecrits et paroles</u>, 3, 592;
        <u>Mélanges</u>, 1487. Here Bergson congratulates Jankélévitch
        on his book about him.


                                1931


404     "Lettre à Jeanne Hersch: 22 juillet 1931." <u>Archives de</u>
        <u>Psychologie</u>, 23 août 1931, 97. Also in <u>Mélanges</u>, 1498.
        In this letter, Bergson thanks Mlle. Hersch for her study
        of his philosophy.

405     "Lettre à Albert Kahn pour le 25e anniversaire de la fonda-
        tion du cercle 'Autour du monde': 12 juin 1931." Alain

Petit.   "Le Premier Elève de Bergson: Un Précurseur alsa-
cien de l'Unesco."  Revue Hommes et Mondes, novembre 1949,
418 et 422.  Also in Ecrits et paroles, 2, 593 (particielle-
ment); Mélanges, 1497-1498.  In these passages Bergson
discusses the importance of the exchange of students between nations.


1932


406    Les Deux Sources de la morale et de la religion.  Paris:
       Félix Alcan, 1932, 346.

407    Les Deux Sources de la morale et de la religion.  Genève:
       Skira, 1946, 310.

408    "Les Deux Sources de la morale et de la religion."  Edition
       du Centenaire, 981-1247.

       TRANSLATIONS

409    Die beiden Quellen der Moral und der Religion.  Trans.
       Eugen Lerch.  Jena: Diederichs, 1933.

410    Las dos fuentes de la moral y de la religión.  Montivi-
       deo: Ed. Claudio Garcia, 1944, 346.

411    Las dos fuentes de la moral y de la religión.  Trans.
       Miguel Gonzalez Fernandez.  Buenos Aires:  Ed. Sudameri-
       cana, 1946, 390.

412    Le due fonti della morale e della religione.  Trad. M.
       Vinciguerra.  Milano: Ed. di Comunita, 1947, 348; 2e ed.,
       1950, 352; 3e ed., 1962, 311.

413    L'obbligazione morale: De le due fonti della morale e
       della religione.  Trans. Luigi Pinto.  Napoli: Ediz.
       Glaux, 1961, 141.

414    The Two Sources of Morality and Religion.  Trans. Ashley
       Andra and Cloudesly Brereton with collaboration of
       W.-Horsfal Carter.  London: Macmillan and Co., 1935, 278.

415    Yaratici tekâmul den hayatin telâmülü.  Trans. Mustafa
       Sekip.  Istanbul: Devlet Matbaasi, 1934, 216.

416    "Lettre à Guy-Grand: 11 juin 1932."  Bulletin de l'Union
       pour la Vérité, 40, No. 7-8, avril-mai 1933, 331-332.

Also in Ecrits et paroles, 3, p. 597; Mélanges, 1504.
This is about talks on Bergson's Two Sources given at the
Union pour la vérité.

417    "Lettre à Xavier Léon: 28 mai 1932." Bulletin de la Société
Française de Philosophie, 32, No. 4, octobre 1932, 122-123.
Also in Mélanges, 1502-1503. This is a letter written on
the occasion of the Commémoration Jules Lachelier.

418    "Lettre à A. Suarès: 22 novembre 1932." Dietschy. Le Cas
Suarès, 282. Also in Mélanges, 1505. Here Bergson analyzes and comments positively on Suarès' writing.

419    "Lettre au directeur de Comoedia: 8 avril 1932." Comoedia,
8 avril 1932. Also in Mélanges, 1500. In this letter
Bergson denies that he has been reduced to publishing The
Two Sources of Morality and Religion at his own expense.

420    "Lettre-préface." Raoul Mourgue. Neurobiologie de l'hallucination. Bruxelles: Lamertin, 1932, 1-2. Also in Ecrits
et paroles, 3, 594-595; Mélanges, 1501-1502. In this
letter, Bergson discusses method in psychology.


1933


421    "Lettre à A. Suarès: 16 juillet 1933." Mossé-Bastide.
Bergson éducateur, 74. Also in Mélanges, 1507. This is
about the nature of art.

422    "Lettre au P. Blaise Romeyer: 24 mars 1933." Blaise Romeyer.
"Autour du problème de la philosophie chrétienne." Archives de Philosophie, 10, No. 4, 1934, 478. Also in Ecrits
et paroles, 3, 596; Mélanges, 1507. This is about the
issue of theodicy in The Two Sources.

423    "Letter to Raimundo Lida." Nosotros, 27, No. 295, 1933,
447-448.

424    "La Philosophie française." La Science française. Paris:
Larousse, 1933, 1-26. Also in Mélanges, 1157-1189. The
second version was written with the collaboration of E.
Le Roy.

1934

425   "Lettre à J. Chevalier: Fin 1934." Le Van, No. 169, janvier
      1935, 29. Also in Entretiens avec Bergson, 222-223; Mé-
      langes, 1518. This is about Chevalier's interpretation of
      Les Deux Sources. Bergson states: "Combien je souhaite
      que ces pages soient lues et méditées!"

426   "Lettre au Jury du Prix Nobel de la Paix: 9 janvier 1934."
      A. Heurgon-Desjardins. Paul Desjardins et les décades de
      Pontigny, 387-388. Also in Mélanges, 1509-1511. In this
      letter Bergson urges the candidacy of Paul Desjardins for
      the Nobel Peace Prize.

427   La Pensée et le mouvant: Essais et conférences. Paris:
      Félix Alcan, 1934, 322. The articles contained in this
      collection are: "Croissance de la vérité: Mouvement rétro-
      grade du vrai," "De la Position des problèmes," "Le Possi-
      ble et le réel," "L'Intuition philosophique," "La Percep-
      tion du changement," "Introduction à la métaphysique,"
      "La Philosophie de Claude Bernard," "Sur le Pragmatisme
      de William James: Vérité et réalité," and "La Vie et
      l'oeuvre de Ravaisson."

428   La Pensée et le mouvant: Essais et conférences. 12e éd.
      Paris: Presses Universitaires de France, 1941, 291.

429   La Pensée et le mouvant: Essais et conférences. Genève:
      Skira, 1946, 272.

      TRANSLATIONS

430   The Creative Mind. Trans. Mabelle L. Andison. New York:
      Philosophical Library, 1946, 307.

431   The Creative Mind. Trans. Mabelle L. Andison. New York:
      Greenwood Press, 1968, 307.

432   Denken und schöpferisches Werden: Aufsätze und Vortrage.
      Trans. Leonore Kottje. Meisenheim am Glan: Westkultur-
      verlag, 1948, 279. The introduction is by Friedrich
      Kottje.

433   An Introduction to Metaphysics: The Creative Mind.
      Trans. Mabelle L. Andison. Totowa, New Jersey: Little-
      field, Adams and Co., 1965, 252.

434    "Quelques mots sur la philosophie française et sur l'esprit
française." Entretiens philosophiques, Conférences radio-
diffusées du Poste National Radio-Paris. Paris: Imprimerie 111 rue du Mont-Cenis, 1934, 5-9. Also in Mélanges,
1513-1517. Bergson is claiming here that science, form,
and moral insight define French philosophy and the French
spirit.

1935

435    "L'Académie française vue de New York par un de ses membres."
Trois Siècles de l'Académie française: 1635-1935. Paris:
Firmin-Didot, 1935, 473-485. Also in Ecrits et paroles,
3, 606-615; Mélanges, 1529-1539. Bergson here discusses
American attitudes towards the Académie française.

436    "Lettre à Léon Bopp: 9 juillet 1935." Mélanges, 1519. In
this letter Bergson thanks Bopp for a copy of Esquisse
d'un traité du roman. Interesting remarks on aesthetics
and the mechanism of artistic production conclude Bergson's reflections.

437    "Lettre à Fl. Delattre: décembre 1935." Revue Philosophique de la France et de l'Etranger, mars 1941, 131. Also
in Mélanges, 1522. In this letter Bergson discusses mod-
esty in philosophy.

438    "Lettre à Fl. Delattre: décembre 1935." Revue Anglo-améri-
caine, 13, No. 5, juin 1936, 395-401. Also in Ecrits et
paroles, 3, 600-605; Mélanges, 1522-1528. In this letter
Bergson gives his (remarkably high) opinion of Samuel
Butler.

439    "Lettre à A. Suarès: 4 juillet 1935." Dietschy. Le Cas
Suarès, 84. Also in Mélanges, 1518. In this letter Bergson congratulates Suarès for his writings.

440    "Lettre à A. Suarès: 1er octobre 1935." Mélanges, 1521.
Bergson congratulates Suarès on the reception of an award.

441    "Lettre au P. Gorce: 16 août 1935." Sophia (Naples), 3,
1935. Also in La Croix, 21 septembre 1935, 3; Ecrits et
paroles, 3, 598-599; Mélanges, 1520-1521. In this letter
Bergson concurs with Gorce's interpretation of his thought,
and adds that he is able to accept the essentials of those
passages of Aquinas' philosophy which he has read.

1936

442     "Lettre à L. Bopp: 28 avril 1936." Mélanges, 1546. In this
        letter Bergson thanks Bopp for his "portrait de notre cher
        Thibaudet."

443     "Lettre à Jacques Chevalier: février 1936." "Publiée à la
        suite de l'article de Jacques Chevalier, "William James
        et Bergson," dans le receuil d'études, Harvard et la
        France, édité par les soins de la Revue d'Histoire Moderne,
        1936, 117-121." Also in Ecrits et paroles, 3, 617-620; Mé-
        langes, 1542-1545. In this letter Bergson gives his eval-
        uation of William James and states that James' "spiritual-
        ism" explains his pragmatism and pluralism.

444     "Lettre à Jeanne Hersch: 25 novembre 1936." Mélanges, 1570-
        1571. This is a discussion of Hersch's L'Illusion philo-
        sophique.

445     "Lettre à Jean Labadie: 12 février 1936." Jean Labadie.
        "Aux Frontières de l'au-delà." Choses vécues. Paris:
        Grasset, 1939, 7-8. Also in Ecrits et paroles, 3, 616;
        Mélanges, 1541. In this letter Bergson discusses the fu-
        ture of psychical research.

446     "Lettre à A. Suarès: 27 juillet 1936." Dietschy. Le Cas
        Suarès, 302. Also in Mélanges, 1553-1554. Here Bergson
        sees in Suarès' Valeurs an aesthetic, a philosophy, and a
        "morale."

447     "Lettre au professeur Spearman." Citée par R. Millet. Le
        Temps, 15 novembre 1936. Also in Ecrits et paroles, 3,
        642; Mélanges, 1571. In this letter Bergson agrees that
        he is the enemy of dry rationalism but not of the exer-
        cise of reason.

448     "Mes Missions 1917-1918: 24 août 1936." Hommes et Mondes,
        No. 12, juillet 1947, 359-375. Also in Ecrits et paroles,
        3, 627-641; Mélanges, 1554-1570. Here Bergson discusses
        his missions to the United States during World War I, his
        relations to Colonel House, Woodrow Wilson, and America's
        idealism.

449     "Quelques mots sur Thibaudet critique et philosophe." Nou-
        velle Revue Française, 47, juillet 1936, 7-14. Also in
        Ecrits et paroles, 3, 621-626; Mélanges, 1547-1553. In
        this brief essay Bergson lauds Thibaudet's critical meth-
        od, his originality, and his generosity.

1937

450     "Lettre à R. Jolivet: 1937." Studia Catholica, 14, No. 1,
        1938, 55-60. Also in Mélanges, 1579. Bergson insists in
        this brief letter that his thought does not support anti-
        substantialism.

451     "Lettre à A. Suarès: 1937." Dietschy. Le Cas Suarès, 303.
        Also in Mélanges, 1580. Bergson has kind words to say
        here concerning Suarès' writing.

452     "Lettre au Père A. D. Sertillanges: 19 janvier 1937." Citée
        à la suite de l'article d'A. D. Sertillanges. "Le Libre
        Arbitre chez Saint Thomas et chez M. Bergson." Vie Intel-
        lectuelle, 49, No. 1, 10 avril 1937, 268-269. Also in
        Ecrits et paroles, 3, 643-644; Mélanges, 1573-1574. In
        this letter Bergson discusses his philosophy and its rela-
        tionship to Thomism.

453     "Message au Congrès Descartes." Nouvelles Littéraires, No.
        778, 11 septembre 1937, 1. Also in Ecrits et paroles, 3,
        645-649; Mélanges, 1574-1579. Bergson here discusses René
        Descartes and his philosophy, as well as the part which
        philosophy must play in the modern world.

1938

454     "Lettre à Léon Bopp: 22 septembre 1938." Mélanges, 1582-
        1583. Bergson thanks Bopp for a copy of Liaisons du Monde.
        The "devenir" of L'Evolution créatrice, Bergson insists,
        does not suggest anarchism or revolution, for "...un prin-
        cipe d'explication n'est pas une maxime de conduite."

455     "Lettre à Milic Capek: 3 juillet 1938." Milic Capek. Berg-
        son and Modern Physics. Dordrecht, Holland, 1971, 401.
        Bergson agrees that his concepts of the physical world
        anticipated current ideas in physics.

456     "Lettre à Georges Guyau: 3 mars 1938." Mélanges, 1581. Berg-
        son congratulates Guyau on his reception into the French
        Academy.

457     "Lettre à A. Suarès: 17 mars 1938." Dietschy. Le Cas
        Suarès, 304. Also in Mélanges, 1581. In this letter
        Bergson defines the character of Suarès' determined opti-
        mism.

458     "Témoignage sur l'Angleterre." Le Figaro, 19 juillet 1938.
        Also in Ecrits et paroles, 3, 650; Mélanges, 1582.  Sooner
        or later, Bergson holds, France and England should become
        one nation.


                                1939


459     "Lettre à I. Benrubi: 15 juillet 1939."  Benrubi. Souvenirs
        sur Henri Bergson, 133.  Also in Mélanges, 1588-1589.
        Here Bergson discusses his writings, immediately prior to
        his death.  He denies the intention to write another book.

460     "Lettre à J. Chastenet: décembre 1939."  Le Temps, 8 janvier
        1940, p. 2, col 6.  Also in Le Temps, 13 janvier 1940,
        p. 2, col. 1-2; Mélanges, 1591.  In this letter Bergson
        reiterates his 1914 opinion of Bismarckian Germany and
        finds it applicable to the contemporary scene.

461     "Lettre à Halévy en souvenir de Péguy: 25 janvier 1939."
        J. Gaulmier.  Péguy et nous.  Beyrouth, 1944, 53-55; Le
        Temps, 25 janvier 1939; L'Aube, 12 janvier 1945; Feuillets
        de l'Amitié Charles Péguy, 30, 13-14; Etudes Bergsonien-
        nes, 8, 58-60.  Also in Ecrits et paroles, 3, 651-653;
        Mélanges, 1585-1587.  In this brief essay Bergson pays
        hommage to Péguy.

462     "Lettre à M. Nédoncelle: 1939."  Oeuvres philosophiques de
        Newman.  Paris: Aubier, 1945, 16-17.  Also in Mélanges,
        1592.  In this letter Bergson comments on Cardinal New-
        man's philosophical background--or lack of it.

463     "Lettre à B. Romeyer: 7 août 1939."  Archives de Philosophie,
        17, No. 1, 1947, 46.  Also in Mélanges, 1589.  Bergson
        here replies that no celebration of his eightieth birth-
        day should be attempted.

464     "Lettre à A. Suarès: 28 mai 1939."  Dietschy.  Le Cas Suarès,
        303.  Also in Mélanges, 1588.  Here Bergson congratulates
        Suarès for his moral and ethical concern.

465     "Lettre à l'Université de Lausanne: 1939."  A. Reymond.
        "Henri Bergson."  Gazette de Lausanne, 12 janvier 1941.
        Also in Mélanges, 1590.  Bergson thanks the University of
        Lausanne for the award of an honorary degree.

466     "Life and Matter at War; Reprint from April, 1915, Issue."
        Hibbert Journal, 38, No. 4, October 1939, 4-12.

467    "Une Pensée. 1939."  Mélanges, 1591.  Bergson here remarks
       briefly on the difficulty of doing philosophy.


                              1940


468    "Lettre à A. Billy: 1940 (?)."  Le Figaro, 3 août 1940.
       Also in Mélanges, 1593.  Bergson here recalls his years as
       a young professor at Clermont.


                   Fragments Without Dates


469    "Annotations sur un article de G. Maire."  J. Guitton.  Voca-
       tion..., 38.  Also in Mélanges, 1597.  Here Bergson dis-
       cusses his relations with Lachelier and Boutroux, and his
       opinion of Jaurès is that he is "éloquent et généreux."

470    "Lettre à A. O. Lovejoy."  Arthur Oncken Lovejoy.  The Rea-
       son, the Understanding, and Time.  Baltimore, Maryland:
       Johns Hopkins, 1961, 185-202.  In this letter Bergson ex-
       plains the basic characteristics of duration.

470a   "Sur L'Effort créatrice."  Le Figaro Littéraire, 11 janvier
       1941.  Also in Mélanges, 1597.  Here Bergson discusses the
       difficulties of embodying a creative idea.

# PART III


# WORKS CONCERNING BERGSON

471    ABBAGNO, Nicola. <u>Sorgenti irrazionali del pensiero</u>.
        Naples: F. Perella, 1923, 174. Bradley, Royce, Bergson,
        Gentile, and Aliotta are discussed in this study.

472    ABBOTT, Lyman. "Philosophy of Progress." <u>Outlook</u>, 103, No.
        8, 22 February 1913, 388-391.

473    ABERLY, J. "Review of <u>Les Deux Sources de la morale et de la
        religion</u> by Henri Bergson." <u>Lutheran Church Quarterly</u>, 8,
        1935, 419-420.

474    "Académie française: Réception de M. Henri Bergson: Discours
        de M. Bergson: Réponse de M. René Doumic." <u>Le Petit Temps</u>,
        25 janvier 1918.

475    ACKER, Leonardo van. "Centenário de Bergson: Depoimento."
        <u>Revista Brasileira de Filosofia</u>, 11, No. 41, 1961, 108-
        110. The author discusses the articles and books which
        he has written on Bergson, as well as those aspects in
        which he conceives Bergson's thought to be valuable. He
        concludes by mentioning two studies of Bergson recently
        published in Brazil.

476    ACKER, Leonardo van. <u>A filosofia bergsoniana: Gênese, evo-
        lução e estrutura gnoseológica do bergsonismo</u>. São Paulo:
        Livraria Martins Editôra, 1959, 200.

477    ACKER, Leonardo van. "Structure épistémologique et métho-
        dologique de la métaphysique bergsonienne." <u>Revista da
        Universidade Católica de São Paulo</u>, 10. Nos. 18-19, 1956,
        125-163. The author deals with Bergson's substantialism
        and with the complementarity which Bergson establishes
        between intuition and intellect. This study is published
        in the author's <u>A filosofia bergsoniana</u>.

478    ACKER, Leonardo van. <u>Structure épistémologique et méthodo-
        logique de la métaphysique bergsonienne</u>. São Paulo: Ed.
        da Revista da Universidade Católica de São Paulo, 1956.

479    ADES, Albert. <u>Adès chez Bergson: Reliques inconnues d'une
        amitié</u>. Paris: N. Fortin et ses fils, 1949, 159. This
        is a republication of three articles published in 1918.
        It includes an account of an interview with Bergson in
        March, 1918, and an exchange of letters concerning this
        interview. Bergson's political and social views are
        expressed in the interview.

480    ADES, Albert. "La Philosophie de Bergson dans la vie."
       Grande Revue, No. 2, 1918, 647-665; No. 3, 1918, 75-94;
       No. 4, 1918, 279-293.

481    ADOLPH, K. "Bergsons Philosophie." Pastor Bonus, 30, 1918,
       219-228.

482    ADOLPHE, Lydie. "Bergson et l'élan vital." Etudes Bergso-
       niennes, 3, 1952, 79-138.

483    ADOLPHE, Lydie. "Bergson et la science d'aujourd'hui."
       Etudes Philosophiques, N.S. 14, No. 4, 1959, 479-488.
       According to the author, Bergson's philosophy is consis-
       tent with contemporary science. This is particularly
       true of quantum physics.

484    ADOLPHE, Lydie. "La Contemplation créatrice (Aristote, Plo-
       tin, Bergson)." Diss., Paris: 1951, 157.

485    ADOLPHE, Lydie. La Dialectique des images chez Bergson.
       Paris: Presses Universitaires de France, 1951, 308.

486    ADOLPHE, Lydie. "Emile Bréhier, 'Images plotiniennes, ima-
       ges bergsoniennes' (Discussion)." Etudes Bergsoniennes,
       2, 1949, 215-222.

487    ADOLPHE, Lydie. La Philosophie religieuse de Bergson.
       Paris: Presses Universitaires de France, 1946, 236. "Pré-
       face par Emile Bréhier."

488    ADOLPHE, Lydie. L'Univers bergsonien. Paris: Edit. du
       Vieux Colombier, 1955, 353. This work is an exposition
       of Bergson's philosophy of the sciences. It primarily
       emphasizes the natural sciences.

489    "Against Rationalism." London Times Literary Supplement,
       No. 3610, 7 May 1971, 530. This is a review of Bergson
       and the Evolution of Physics, edited by P. A. Y. Gunter.

490    AGOSTI, Vittorio. "Di alcune pubblicazioni del centenario
       bergsoniano." Humanitas, 14, No. 11, 1959, 837-842.

491    AGUIRRE, Alicia Rumayor. "La conciencia: Psicofenómeno e
       intencionalidad: Revisión del tema a través de Henri Berg-
       son." Diss., Labastida (Monterrey, México), 1966, 87.

492    AHLBERG, Alf. Psykologiens historia: D. 2. Fran Spinoza
       till Bergson. Stockholm: Natur und Kultur, 1951, 133.

493    AICHELE, Ronald B. "Russell on 'The Theory of Continuity'."
       Dianoia, 5, Spring 1969, 1-11.  The author discusses the
       mathematical theory of motion, Bergson's objections to it,
       and Russell's defense.

494    AIMEL, Georges.  "Individualisme et philosophie bergso-
       nienne." Revue de Philosophie, 12, No. 6, juin 1908, 582-
       593.

495    AKELY, Lewis Ellsworth.  "Bergson and Science." Philosophi-
       cal Review, 24, No. 3, May 1915, 270-287.  The author
       holds that: "Science may possibly have something to learn
       from a great modern philosophy such as that of Bergson."
       (270).  The author stresses the place of intuition in sci-
       ence and the need for a new philosophy of science educa-
       tion.

496    ALAIN.  Les Arts et les dieux.  Ed. Georges Bénézé.  Paris:
       Gallimard, 1958, 1488.  Bergson's disciples are discussed
       on pages 63 and 1195.

497    ALAIN.  Cahiers de Lorient.  Vol. 2.  Paris: Gallimard,
       1964, 332.  Bergson, Colette, Maeterlinck, Maurras, and
       Rolland are discussed in this book.

498    ALAIN.  Propos.  Ed. Maurice Savin.  Paris: Gallimard, 1956,
       1370.  Bergson is discussed on page 614.

499    ALAIN.  Propos 1906-1936.  Vol. 2.  Ed. S. S. de Sacy.
       Paris: Gallimard, 1970, 1408.

500    "A La Recherche de l'esthétique à travers les oeuvres de
       Bergson, Proust, Malraux." Arts, No. 509, 1955, 3.  This
       is a review of André and Jean Brincourt.  Les Oeuvres et
       les lumières.

501    ALAVOINE, Maurice.  "Quelques Remarques sur une origine com-
       mune de la magie et de la religion selon Bergson." Revue
       de la Méditerranée, 8, No. 4, 1950, 421-440; No. 5, 1950,
       553-571; No. 6, 1950, 694-716.

502    ALAVOINE, Maurice.  "Signification actuelle de Bergson."
       Revue de la Méditerranée, 19, Nos. 4-5, juillet-octobre
       1959, 272-287.

503    ALBANESE, Vincenzo.  "H. Bergson e la renascita religiosa."
       Studia Patavina, 14, 1967, 427-435.

504    ALBERINI, Coriolano.  "Curso intensivo sobre el Bergsonismo."
       Humanidades, 6, 1923, 318-319.  This is an outline of a
       course.  It includes an introduction, an account of Berg-
       son's philosophy and critics, and a conclusion.

505    ALDERISIO, Felice.  "Review of Les Deux Sources de la morale
       et de la religion by Henri Bergson."  Nuova Rivista Sto-
       rica, 18, 1934, 629-633.

506    ALESSANDRI, A.  "Review of Liberté ou libération? by M. A.
       Lahbabi."  Revue Philosophique de la France et de l'Etran-
       ger, 84, No. 3, 1959, 416-417.

507    ALEXANDER, Hartley B.  "Socratic Bergson."  Mid-West Quarter-
       ly, No. 4, October 1913, 32-43.

508    ALEXANDER, Hartley Burr.  "Socratic Bergson."  Nature and
       Human Nature.  Chicago: Open Court, 1923, 301-318.

509    ALEXANDER, Ian W.  Bergson: Philosopher of Reflection.  Lon-
       don: Bowes and Bowes Publishers Limited; New York: Hillary
       House, 1957, 109 (Studies in Modern European Literature
       and Thought).  This is an excellent short study of Berg-
       son's philosophy.  It draws parallels between Bergson's
       thought and behaviorism and phenomenology, and argues
       against irrationalist interpretations of Bergson.

510    ALEXANDER, Ian W.  "Review of Les Etudes Bergsoniennes, Vol.
       1.  Floris Delattre: Bergson et Proust.  Henri Gouhier:
       Maine de Biran et Bergson."  French Studies, 3, No. 2,
       April 1949, 175-176.

511    ALEXANDER, Ian W.  "Review of Les Etudes Bergsoniennes, Vol.
       II, 1949."  French Studies, 3, No. 4, 1949, 373-374.

512    ALEXANDER, Ian W.  "Review of Ruskin et Bergson: De L'Intui-
       tion esthétique à l'intuition métaphysique by Floris Delat-
       tre."  French Studies, 2, No. 1, 1948, 98-99.

513    ALEXANDER, Samuel.  "Freedom."  Proceedings of the Aristote-
       lian Society, N.S. 14, 1913-1914, 322-354.  Freedom and
       "durée" are discussed on pages 329-336; mind and neural
       processes on page 341.

514    ALEXANDER, Samuel.  "Review of Matière et mémoire by Henri
       Bergson."  Mind, 22, No. 24, October 1897, 572-573.

515    ALEXANDER, Samuel.  Space, Time and Deity: The Gifford Lec-
       tures at Glasgow 1916-1918.  2 vols.  London: Macmillan

and Co., 1920.  Bergson's concept of time is discussed on
pages i, 36, 44, 140; the spatialization of time on page
148; Bergson and Heraclitus on page 150; not-being on page
199; motion as unitary on page 321; change on page 329;
the intensity of sensations in Vol. 2, page 1621.

516    ALIOTTA, Antonio.  The Idealistic Reaction Against Science.
       Trans. W. Agnes McCaskill.  London: Macmillan and Co.,
       Ltd., 1914, 483.  Cf. "Bergson's Doctrine of Intuition,"
       127-137.  The author is critical of Bergson's "exaggera-
       tions," particularly as concerns the failings of the in-
       tellect.

517    ALIOTTA, Antonio.  "La misura in psycologia sperimentale."
       Diss. Florence, 1905, 253.

518    ALIOTTA, Antonio.  Le origini dell'irrazionalismo contem-
       poraneo.  Naples: Perella, 1927, 326.

519    ALIOTTA, Antonio.  La reazione idealistica contro la scienza.
       Palermo: Casa editrice "Optima," 1912, 526.

520    ALLEMAND, J.  "Henri Bergson."  Existences, 1, No. 4, 1935,
       5-7.

521    ALLIEGRO, Ciro.  Conoscenza di Dio secondo H. Bergson.
       Diss., Pnt. Univ. Gregoriana, 1939, 80.  Roma: Via Reggio
       Emila 34, 1939.

522    ALMEIDA, Vieira de.  "Bergson: Esboço de análise."  Colóquio,
       2, No. 10, 1960, 52-56.

523    ALPERN, Henry.  The March of Philosophy.  New York: Dial,
       1913, 381.  Bergson is discussed on pages 301-318.

524    ALQUIE, Ferdinand.  "Bergson et la Revue de Métaphysique et
       de Morale."  Revue de Métaphysique et de Morale, 47, No.
       4, 1941, 315-328.  The author is largely critical of Berg-
       son.

525    ALTMANN, Bruno.  "Henri Bergson, Stammvater der Naziphilo-
       sophie?"  Das Wort, 3, No. 3, 1938, 119-124.

526    ALTMANN, Bruno.  "Bergsons Welterfolg."  Die Aehre, 19-20,
       1914-1915.

527    ALTMANN, Bruno.  "Judentum und Christentum: Henri Bergson
       und der Kirchenhistoriker, Loisy."  Judische Rundschau,
       29, No. 23, 1934, 6ff.

528   ALVAREZ ARROYO, Jesús.  "La sustancialidad del tempo en
      Bergson."  Salmanticensis, 16, 1969, 299-327.

529   ALVES, Garcia J.  "O dualismo metodologico na psicología
      contemporánea."  Revista Portuguesa de Filosofia, 12, No.
      1, 1956, 14-28.  The author argues that for Bergson a
      dualism of objects and of methods need not lead to a dual-
      ism of kinds of knowledge.

530   ALZAMORA VALDES, Mario.  "Bergson o el renacimiento de la
      sabiduria."  Mercurio Peruano, 23, No. 168, marzo 1941,
      111-114.

531   AMADO-LEVY-VALENSI, Eliane.  "Bergson et le mal: Y a-t-il
      un pessimisme bergsonien?"  Actes du Xe Congrès des Socié-
      tés de Philosophie de Langue Française (Congrès Bergson).
      Paris: Armand Colin, 1, 1959, 7-11.  This study deals with
      Bergson's conception of the problem of evil, both in those
      works in which it is treated explicitly and in those in
      which it is approached but not designated as such.  The
      author concludes with an analysis of the pessimism-opti-
      mism contrast at the heart of Bergson's thought.

532   AMADO-LEVY-VALENSI, Eliane.  "Table ronde: Morale."  Actes
      du Xe Congrès des Sociétés de Philosophie de Langue Fran-
      çaise (Congrès Bergson).  Paris: Armand Colin, 2, 1959,
      237-257.

533   AMBACHER, Michel.  "Intelligence physicienne de la matière
      et expérience philosophique de la matérialité dans la
      philosophie naturelle de Bergson."  Actes du Xe Congrès
      des Sociétés de Philosophie de Langue Française (Congrès
      Bergson).  Paris: Armand Colin, 1, 1959, 13-16.  The prob-
      lem of matter is often obscured in Bergson's philosophy
      by the brilliance which surrounds his treatment of life,
      evolution, and religion.  Nonetheless, the problem is
      approached in The Two Sources, Matter and Memory, and
      elsewhere.  The author suggests an interpretation of Berg-
      son's concept of matter.

534   AMES, Van Meter.  "Kumar: Bergson and the Stream of Con-
      sciousness Novel."  Journal of Aesthetics and Art Criti-
      cism, 22, No. 3, 1964, 347.  This is a review.

535   AMIDOU, Philip R.  "Memory and Duration in Bergson: A Study
      of Terminology in Matter and Memory and Introduction to
      Metaphysics."  Diss., St. Louis, 1968.

536   "A Monsieur Henri Bergson." Revue de Métaphysique et de
      Morale, 41, No. 4, 1939, 557-558.

537   ANASTASIADIS, Ilias K. Savigny, Thering, Bergson. Athènes:
      1916, 40.

538   ANCELOT-HUSTACHE, Jeanne. Een doopsel van begeerte: Henri
      Bergson, 1859-1941. Antwerpen: Hoogland, Frankrijklei,
      1954, 16. "Vertaald door Kor. Van Miert."

539   ANDERSON, James F. "Bergson, Aquinas, and Heidegger on the
      Notion of Nothingness." The Nature of Philosophical En-
      quiry. Proceedings of the American Catholic Philosophical
      Association. Ed. George F. McLean and V. Voorhies. Wash-
      ington, D.C.: Catholic University of America, 1967, 143-
      148.

540   ANDERSON, James F. "Teilhard's Christianized Cosmology."
      Heythrop Journal, 13, No. 1, January 1972, 63-67. The
      author casts light on Teilhard de Chardin's evolutionism
      by referring to two philosophers, Blondel and Bergson, who
      influenced him.

541   ANDRES, Cyril Bruyn. Life, Emotion, and Intellect. London
      and Leipsic: Fisher Unwin, 1913, 95.

542   ANDREU, Pierre. "Bergson et Sorel." Etudes Bergsoniennes,
      2, 1949, 225-226. The author examines Sorel's interpreta-
      tion of Bergson as an essentially religious philosopher.
      This article is followed by an unpublished passage by
      Sorel, "La Trilogie de l'esprit."

543   ANDREU, Pierre. "Bergson et Sorel." Etudes Bergsoniennes,
      3, 1962, 43-78.

544   ANDREU, Pierre. "Bergson et la théorie des mythes chez
      Sorel." La Nef, 4, No. 32, juillet 1947, 51-58. This ar-
      ticle is reprinted from Andreu's Notre Maître, Monsieur
      Sorel, "La Trilogie de l'esprit."

545   ANDREU, Pierre. "Discussion of 'Bergson et Sorel'." Etudes
      Bergsoniennes, 3, 1962, 170-180.

546   ANGELI, A. M. de. "L'influsso della filosofia di Bergson
      sull'estetica Proustiana." Diss., Universita cattolica
      del Sacre Cuore de Milan, 1966.

547    ANGIOLETTI, Biovanni Batista. Scrittori d'Europa. Milano:
       Libr. d'Italia, 1928, 185. Bergson is discussed on pages
       61-71.

548    ANQUIN, Nimio de. "El bergsonismo: Analogía de la exper-
       iencia." Sol y Luna, Año 4, No. 6, julio 1941, 13-62.

549    ANSELME, F. "Review of Bergson éducateur by R.-M. Mossé-
       Bastide." Nouvelle Revue Pédagogique, 11, 1956, 334-340.

550    ANTAL, Illés. "Bergson und Schopenhauer." Drittes Jahrbuch
       der Schopenhauer Gesellschaft, 1914, 3-15.

551    Anthologie des philosophes français contemporains. Ed.
       Arnaud Dandieu. Paris: Editions du Saggitaire, 1931,
       533. Twenty-two philosophers, including Poincaré, Durk-
       heim, Bergson, and Meyerson, are presented in this anthol-
       ogy.

552    ANTONELLI, E. "Bergson et le mouvement social contemporain."
       Neue Schweizer Rundschau, 1912, 627-635, 809-816. This
       study is devoted to a discussion of Bergson and syndical-
       ism, Marxism, and neo-Catholicism.

553    ANTONELLI, E. Bergson et le mouvement social contemporain.
       Zürich: Wissen und Leben, 1913.

554    ANTONELLI, Maria Teresa. "La filosofia in Henri Bergson."
       Rivista rosminiana, 60, No. 1, 1966, 37-67.

555    ANTONI, Carlo. "Henri Bergson." Vite de pensatori. Torino:
       Ediz. Radio Italiana, 1956, 96.

556    ANTONIADE, C. "Filosofia lui Henri Bergson." Studii filo-
       sofice, 5, No. 1, 1910, 24-59; No. 2, 1910, 113-169. This
       article is in Rumanian.

557    ARABI-DARKAOUI, Assad. Essai sur l'idée de pureté chez
       Bergson. Damas, Syria: Impr. de l'Université, 1963, 178.

558    ARBELET, Claire. Magnificat du soir: Journal. Paris:
       Beauchesne, 1965, 138.

559    ARBOUR, Roméo. "Le Bergsonisme dans la littérature fran-
       çaise." Revue Internationale de Philosophie, 13, No. 2,
       1959, 220-248. This article is an analysis of the aesthe-
       tic latent in Bergson's works. It deals with the fortui-
       tous convergence of Bergson and symbolism and the literary

polemics circa 1910.  Bergson's influence is diffuse and
enduring.  His disciples included Péguy, Proust, Ch. Du
Bos, and Thibaudet.

560    ARBOUR, Roméo.  Henri Bergson et les lettres françaises.
       Paris: Corti, 1956, 456.

561    ARDAO, Arturo.  La filosofía en el Uruguay en el siglo XX.
       México and Buenos Aires: Fondo de Cultura Economica, 1956,
       193.  Bergson is discussed on pages 56-60, 88-89, and 167-
       170.

562    ARDIGO, Roberto.  "Un  pretesa pregiudiziale contro il posi-
       tivismo."  Rivista di filosofia e scienzi affini, 18, Nos.
       1-2, 1908, 1-46.  Reprinted in Ardigó's collected works,
       Volume 10.  Bergson and others are criticized for failure
       to understand science and scientific philosophy.

563    "Are Americans Money Worshippers?  Bergson's Opinion."  Out-
       look, 117, No. 4, September 1917, 119.

564    ARGAN, Giulio Carlo.  "Da Bergson a Fautrier."  Aut Aut, No.
       55, gennaio 1960, 10-23.

565    ARMSTRONG, A. C.  "Bergson, Berkeley, and Philosophical In-
       tuition."  Philosophical Review, 23, No. 4, July 1914,
       430-438.  Bergson's interpretation of Berkeley is dis-
       cussed in this article.

566    ARMSTRONG, A. C. "The Philosophy of Bergson."  Methodist
       Magazine, 96, 1914, 839-850.

567    ARON, Raymond.  "Note sur Bergson et l'histoire."  Etudes
       Bergsoniennes, 4, 1956, 41-51.

568    AROUET, François.  (See POLITZER, Georges).

569    ARRAIZA, I.  "Dios en la filosofia de Henri Bergson."
       Ecclesiastica Xaveriana, 10, No. 1, 1960, 8-140.

570    ARREGUI, Cristina.  "Cuatro filósofos contemporáneos frente
       al problema de la immortalidad: H. Bergson, Max Scheler,
       Louis Lavelle, A. Wenzl."  Cuadernos Urugayos de Filosofía,
       1, No. 1, 1961, 109-137.

571    ARRUDA, Aniz de.  "Review of Matière et mémoire and Duration
       and Simultaneity by Henri Bergson."  Revista Portuguesa de
       Filosofia, 22, 1966, 212-213.  This is a review of the

English translation of <u>Duration</u> <u>and</u> <u>Simultaneity</u> and the
72nd printing of <u>Matière</u> <u>et</u> <u>mémoire</u>.

572    ARSLAN, Emin. "Un recuerdo de Bergson." <u>El</u> <u>Mundo</u>, enero
1941.

573    ASKOWITH, II. "Dr. Miller's Article on Bergson." <u>New</u> <u>Repub-</u>
<u>lic</u>, 26, No. 337, 18 May 1921, 356-357. This is a letter
to the editor defending Bergson.

574    ASMODEE. "Silhouette: Henri Bergson." <u>Revue</u> <u>Française</u>, 19e
Année, No. 2, 1er juin 1924.

575    ASNAOUROW, Félix. "Progresos de la psicología." <u>Nosotros</u>,
16, No. 152, enero 1922, 55-59. This brief article concerns the importance of the unconscious mind in the functioning of human personality. The discovery of the unconscious and its function is credited to Janet, Binet, and
Bergson in France, and to Freud and his disciples. The
essay concludes with an account of Freud's disciple,
Alfred Adler.

576    ASSMUS, W. "Bergson: Advocat d. Intuitionsphilosophie:
Bergson und sein Kritik d. Intellectualismus." <u>Unter</u> <u>dem</u>
<u>Banne</u> <u>des</u> <u>Marxismus</u>, 2, No. 1, 1928, 8-43.

577    ATKINSON, John Keith. "<u>Les</u> <u>Caves</u> <u>du</u> <u>Vatican</u> and Bergson's
<u>Le</u> <u>Rire</u>." <u>Publications</u> <u>of</u> <u>the</u> <u>Modern</u> <u>Language</u> <u>Association</u>
<u>of</u> <u>America</u>, 84, No. 2, March 1969, 325-328.

578    AUBRUN, Charles-Vincent. "La Critique littéraire et Bergson." <u>Mélanges</u> <u>littéraires</u> <u>et</u> <u>historiques</u>. Poitiers:
Publications de l'Université, 1946, 232-239.

579    "The Author of 'Creative Evolution'." <u>Spectator</u>, 166, No.
5871, 10 January 1941, 27. This is an obituary article.

580    AVELING, Francis. <u>Directing</u> <u>Mental</u> <u>Energy</u>. London: University of London Press, 1927, 276.

581    AVORD, René. "Réflexions sur la philosophie bergsonienne."
<u>France</u> <u>Libre</u>, 2, No. 7, mai 1941, 42-54. This is a Résis-
tance publication.

582    AXELOS, K. "Review of <u>L'Univers</u> <u>bergsonien</u> by Lydie Adolphe.
<u>Revue</u> <u>Philosophique</u> <u>de</u> <u>la</u> <u>France</u> <u>et</u> <u>de</u> <u>l'Etranger</u>, 84, No.
3, 1959, 411.

583    BABBIT, Irving.  "Bergson and Rousseau."  Nation, 95, No.
       2472, 1912, 452-455.

584    BABYNIN, B. N. "Философия Бергсона." Вопросы фило-
       софии и психологии, 22, № 3, 1191, 251-290; № 4,
       1911, 472-516.

585    BACH, Salomon.  Depuis Renan: Propos bergsoniens.  Toulouse:
       "Poésie," 1910, 109.

586    BACHELARD, Gaston.  L'Activité rationaliste de la physique
       contemporaine.  Paris: Presses Universitaires de France,
       1951, 223.  Bergson is discussed on pages 54-58.

587    BACHELARD, Gaston.  L'Air des songes: Essai sur l'imagina-
       tion du mouvement.  Paris: Librairie José Corti, 1943, 307.
       "Philosophie cinématique et philosophie dynamique," 289-
       302.  The author holds that: "...d'autres images, prises
       dans leurs aspects matériels et dans leurs aspects dyna-
       miques, pourraient offrir au bergsonisme des motifs d'ex-
       plication plus appropriés." (290).

588    BACHELARD, Gaston.  La Dialectique de la durée.  Paris:
       Boivin, 1936, 170.  This is a thoroughgoing critique of
       the Bergsonian concept of duration as "continuous" and
       "full."  The author argues that duration contains discon-
       tinuities and is best understood as a dialectic movement
       between being and non-being.

589    BACHELARD, Gaston.  L'Intuition de l'instant.  Paris: Stock,
       1932, 129.  The author opposes the conceptions of Roupnel
       to those of Bergson.

590    BACHELARD, Gaston.  Les Intuitions atomistiques.  Paris:
       Boivin et Cie., 1933, 162.

591    "Background to Bergson: A Study in Genealogy."  Tablet, 194,
       12 November 1949, 313.

592    BADI', Amir Mehdi.  L'Illusion de l'extensibilité infinie
       de la vérité: Vol. 2.  Vers une connaissance objective.
       Lausanne: Payot, 1960, 159.  This study includes criti-
       cisms of Bergson and Fichte.

593    BAEUMKER, Claus.  "Philosophie."  Philosophisches Jahrbuch
       der Görresgesellschaft, 25, No. 1, 1912, 1-23.

594    BAHM, Archie J.  Philosophy: An Introduction.  New York:
       John Wiley and Sons, 1953, 441; Ch. 11, "Intuitionism,"

142-151. This is an exposition of Bergson's philosophy, primarily his epistemology, with comparisons to naïve realism.

595    BAILLET, Dom Louis. "Lettres de Dom Louis Baillet à Joseph Lotte, présentées par C.-Th. Quoniam." Feuillets de l'Amitié Charles Péguy, No. 54, septembre 1956, 19-36.

596    BAILLOT, A. "Bergson et Schopenhauer." Mercure de France, 208, 15 décembre 1928, 513-529.

597    BAISNEE, Jules A. "Bergson's Approach to God." New Scholasticism, 10, No. 2, April 1936, 116-144. The author holds that Bergson, in spite of his virtues, fails to meet the charges of pantheism and agnosticism.

598    BAKER, Alberto E. Iniciación a la filosofía: Desde Sócrates a Bergson. 7 Ed. Barcelona: Apollo, 1942, 180.

599    BALCAR, A. "Zaklady Bersonovy filosoficike soustavy." Filosoficka revue, No. 3, 19, 74-78; No. 4-5, 1946, 112-115. This essay surveys the foundation of Bergson's system from a Thomist viewpoint.

600    BALCAR, Otokar. Prameny náboženství v pojeti Henri Bergsona a ve světle ethnologie: Kritická studie. Kroměříž, Czechoslovakia: Karel Kryl, 1948.

601    BALDWIN. "Mysticism and Mechanics." The Journal of Philosophy, 43, No. 24, 1932, 680-681. This is an abstract of a talk on Bergson.

602    BALDWIN, James Mark. "Intuition." American Year Book. New York and London: Appleton and Company, 1912, 673-674. This is a brief, general account of Bergson's thought.

603    BALFOUR, Arthur J. "Creative Evolution and Philosophic Doubt." Hibbert Journal, 10, Part 1, October 1911, 1-23. Reprinted in Living Age, 271, No. 3511, 2 December 1911, 515-527. Cf. also Revue de Métaphysique et de Moral, 20, juillet 1912, 27.

604    "Mr. Balfour's Objection to Bergson's Philosophy." Current Literature, 51, No. 6, December 1911, 659-661. "When a former Prime Minister of England is in controversy with the leading philosophic thinker of our day over the deepest questions of human life and destiny, it behooves all the world to listen." (659). The author's account of Lord Balfour's objections is, however, superficial.

605    BALMER, W. T. "Bergson and Eucken in Mutual Relation."
       London Quarterly Review, 122, No. 3, July 1914, 84-99.

606    BALSILLIE, David. An Examination of Professor Bergson's Phi-
       losophy. London: Williams and Nordgate, 1912, 228.

607    BALSILLIE, David. "Professor Bergson on Time and Free Will."
       Mind, 20, No. 79, July 1911, 357-378. Reprinted as Chap-
       ter I of An Examination of Professor Bergson's Philosophy.

608    BALTHASAR, Hans Urs Von. "La Philosophie de la vie chez
       Bergson et chez les Allemands modernes." Henri Bergson.
       Ed. Béguin and Thévenaz, 264-270. The author explores the
       profound influence of Bergson on the German "Philosophers
       of Life," especially Scheler and Klages.

609    BALTHASAR, Nicholas. "La Philosophie moderne et sa criti-
       que." Revue Néo-scolastique de Philosophie, 2e Sér., 31,
       No. 21, février 1929, 53-80. The author follows Decoster
       in criticism of criteriological principles in Descartes,
       Spinoza, Kant, Fichte, Hegel, and Bergson.

610    BALTHASAR, Nicholas. "Le Problème de Dieu d'après la philo-
       sophie nouvelle." Revue Néo-scolastique de Philosophie,
       14, No. 4, novembre 1907, 449-489; 15, No. 1, février 1908,
       90-124.

611    BALZ, Albert G. A. "Review of Mind-Energy by Henri Berg-
       son." The Journal of Philosophy, 18, No. 23, 1921, 634-
       643.

612    BANDAS, Rudolph G. "The Bergsonian Conception of Science
       and Philosophy." New Scholasticism, 2, No. 3, July 1928,
       215-235. Bergson's distinction between intuition and in-
       tellect is untenable, according to the author.

613    BANFI, Antonio. Studia sulla filosofia del novecento. Roma:
       Editori Riuniti, 1965, 570. This study includes an essay
       on Bergson's "pragmatic idealism."

614    BANHOS, Alfonso. "Bergson e o pensamento moderno." Etudios,
       febrero-marzo 1941.

615    "Banning of Bergson." Independent, 79, No. 3423, 20 July
       1914, 85-86.

616    BARALT, Luis A. "Bergson y la muerte." Sustancia, 2, Nos.
       7-8, septiembre 1941, 344-346.

617    BARATA VIANNA, Sylvio.  "Bergson e a duração real."
       Kriterion, 12, Nos. 49-50, 1959, 310-326.

618    BARATONA, A.  "L'ultimo libro di Bergson."  Rivista de filo-
       sofia, Anno 4, No. 3, 1912.

619    BARATZ, Léon.  Bergson et ses rapports avec le catholicisme
       et le judaïsme.  Monte Carlo: L'auteur, 7 rue Bel Respiro,
       1955, 4.

620    BARATZ, Léon.  Deux "Juifs-chrétiens": Henri Bergson et
       J.-J. Bernard.  Monte Carlo: L'auteur, 7 rue Bel Respiro,
       1947, 6.

621    BARD, Joseph.  "Tradition and Experiment."  Royal Society of
       Literature of the United Kingdom, London, Essays by Di-
       verse Hands, N.S. 21, 1944, 103-124.  Bergson and Proust
       are dealt with in this essay.

622    BARETT, C. "Review of Les Deux Sources de la morale et de la
       religion by Henri Bergson."  Philosophical Review, 43, No.
       1, January 1934, 1-6.

623    BARISCH, Theodor.  "Henri Bergson und das Problem des Ko-
       mischen: Eine Vorstudie."  Beitrage zur deutschen und nor-
       dischen Literatur.  Berlin: Akademie Verlag, 1958, 377-
       391.  "Festgabe für Leopold Magon zum 70. Geburtstag."

624    BARLOW, Michel.  Henri Bergson.  Paris: Editions Universi-
       taires, 1966, 128 (Classiques du XXe Siècle, 83).  This is
       an account of Bergson's thought for the general reader.

625    BARON, Roger.  "Intuition bergsonienne et intuition sophia-
       nique."  Etudes Philosophiques, 18, No. 4, 1963, 439-442.

626    BARR, Nann Clark.  "The Dualism of Bergson."  Philosophical
       Review, 22, No. 6, 1912, 629-652.  The author argues that
       Bergson seeks to overcome his dualism in the mutual depen-
       dence of life and matter.  But for a real synthesis life
       and matter must be processes constitutive of a self.

627    BARREAU, Hervé.  "Bergson et Zénon d'Elée."  Revue Philoso-
       phique de Louvain, 3e Sér., 67, No. 94, mai 1969, 267-
       284; No. 95, août 1969, 389-430.  Bergson successively
       presented four reports of Zeno's arguments, especially of
       the Achilles.  His interpretation differs from that of the
       neo-Kantians (Renouvier, Evellin) and from that of the
       historians of mathematics (Tannery, Milhaud) who were his

contemporaries.  It is metaphysical and proceeds in oppos-
ing space that is divisible and duration and motion that
are indivisible.  Zeno is right, according to Bergson, in
denouncing the contradictions of common sense and scientific thought.  Both agree in attributing indivisible unity
to true beings.  Bergsonism is hence an Eleatism, not an
Eleatism of rest (Parmenides) but an Eleatism of motion.

628    BARRETT, William.  Irrational Man: A Study in Existential
       Philosophy.  New York: Doubleday and Company, Inc., 1958,
       278.  Bergson and existentialism are discussed on pages
       13 and 100.

629    BARS, Henri.  "Bergson et l'humanité."  L'Eveil des Peuples,
       10 avril 1938.

630    BARS, Henri.  La Littérature et sa conscience.  Paris: Gras-
       set, 1963, 380.  Claudel, Bremond, Barrès, Bergson, and
       others are treated in this study.

631    BARTH, Hans.  "Bergson und Sorel."  Jahrbuch der Schweizer-
       ischen Philosophische Gesellschaft, 1, 1941, 66-77.

632    BARTHELEMY, Madeleine.  "Esquisse d'une étude sur la philo-
       sophie bergsonienne et la vocation de l'unité."  Revue de
       Métaphysique et de Morale, 60, No. 1-2, 1955, 58-68.

633    BARTHELEMY-MADAULE, Madeleine.  "Actualité de Bergson."
       Etudes Philosophiques, 14, No. 4, 1959, 479-488.

634    BARTHELEMY-MADAULE, Madeleine.  "Autour du Bergson de M.
       Jankélévitch."  Revue de Métaphysique et de Morale, 55,
       No. 4, 1960, 511-524.  This is a highly laudatory review
       of Jankélévitch's Bergson.

635    BARTHELEMY-MADAULE, Madeleine.  Bergson.  Paris: Presses
       Universitaires de France, 1968, 122.  This is a more aca-
       demic treatment of Bergson than the author's earlier Berg-
       son, published in 1967.

636    BARTHELEMY-MADAULE, Madeleine.  Bergson: Adversaire de Kant:
       Etude critique de la conception bergsonienne du kantisme,
       suivie d'une bibliographie kantienne.  Paris: Presses Uni-
       versitaires de France, 1966, 276.  "Préface de Vladimir
       Jankélévitch."

637    BARTHELEMY-MADAULE, Madeleine.  Bergson et Teilhard de Char-
       din.  Paris: Editions du Seuil, 1963, 685.

638    BARTHELEMY-MADAULE, Madeleine. "Bergson et Teilhard de Chardin." La Parole attendue. Ed. Pierre Teilhard de Chardin et al. Paris: Editions du Seuil, 1964, 116-131 (Cahiers de Pierre Teilhard de Chardin, No. IV).

639    BARTHELEMY-MADAULE, Madeleine. Bergson und Teilhard de Chardin: Die Anfänge eine neuen Welterkenntnis. Trans. L. Hafliger. Olten and Freiburg im Breisgau: Walter, 1970, 783.

640    BARTHELEMY-MADAULE, Madeleine. "Introduction à la méthode chez Bergson et Teilhard de Chardin." Actes du Xe Congrès des Sociétés de Philosophie de Langue Française (Congrès Bergson). Paris: Armand Colin, 1, 1959, 211-216. Bergson and Teilhard de Chardin felt, from the beginning, the same need to return to the great metaphysical questions, to discover a being ("être") which does not deceive. The author analyzes the direction and the method which each philosopher utilized.

641    BARTHELEMY-MADAULE, Madeleine. "Introduction à un rapprochement entre Bergson et Teilhard de Chardin." Etudes Bergsoniennes, 5, 1960, 65-85.

642    BARTHELEMY-MADAULE, Madeleine. "Lire Bergson." Etudes Bergsoniennes, 8, 1968, 85-120. This is a criticism of Gilles Deleuze (Le Bergsonisme, P.U.F., 1966) concerning intuition as a method of "division," memory as "virtual coexistence," and the distinction between "superhuman" and "inhuman." The author raises interesting questions.

643    BARTHELEMY-MADAULE, Madeleine. "Table ronde: Vie et évolution." Actes du Xe Congrès des Sociétés de Philosophie de Langue Française (Congrès Bergson). Paris: Armand Colin, 2, 1959, 91-117.

644    BARUZI, Jean. "Emile Bréhier, 'Images plotiniennes, images bergsoniennes'." Etudes Bergsoniennes, 2, 1949, 215-222. The author participates here with several philosophers in a discussion of Bergson and Plotinus.

645    BARUZI, Jean. "Le Point de rencontre de Bergson et de la mystique." Recherches Philosophiques, 2, 1932-1933, 301-316.

646    BARUZI, Joseph. "Jean Hyppolite, 'Henri Bergson et l'existentialisme'." Etudes Bergsoniennes, 2, 1949, 208-215. The author participates here with several philosophers in a discussion of Bergson and existentialism.

647    BARUZI, Joseph. La Volonté de métamorphose. Paris: Grasset,
       1911, 202. Bergson's influence is found throughout this
       book.

648    BARZIN, Betty. "Bergson et Vichy." Nation, 152, No. 8, 22
       February 1941, 223. This article discusses relations be-
       tween Bergson and the Vichy government and Husserl and the
       German government.

649    BARZIN, Marcel. "L'Intuition bergsonienne." Académie
       Royale de Belgique. Bulletin de la Classe des Lettres et
       des Sciences Morales et Politiques, 45, Nos. 10-11, 1959,
       527-534.

650    BARZIN, Marcel. "Table ronde: Matière, causalité, discon-
       tinu." Actes du Xe Congrès des Sociétés de Philosophie de
       Langue Française (Congrès Bergson). Paris: Armand Colin,
       2, 1959, 121-142.

651    BASTIDE, Georges. "Table ronde: Esthétique." Actes du Xe
       Congrès des Sociétés de Philosophie de Langue Française
       (Congrès Bergson). Paris: Armand Colin, 2, 1959, 193-210.

652    BASTIDE, Georges. "Table ronde: Unité, unicité, dialogue."
       Actes du Xe Congrès des Sociétés de Philosophie de Langue
       Française (Congrès Bergson). Paris: Armand Colin, 2, 1959,
       281-302.

653    BASU, P. S. Bergson et le Vedânta. Montpellier: Librairie
       Nouvelle, 1930, 147.

654    BATAILLON, Marcel. "Discours au Collège de France." Bulle-
       tin de la Société Française de Philosophie, 54, No. 1,
       janvier-mars 1960, 11-20.

655    BATAILLON, Marcel. "A Tribute to Bergson on the Occasion of
       the Bergson Centennial in Paris, 1959." The Bergsonian
       Heritage. Ed. Thomas Hanna. New York and London: Colum-
       bia University Press, 1962, 105-118. This is a discussion
       of Bergson as a teacher.

656    BATAULT, Georges. "La Philosophie de M. Bergson." Mercure
       de France, 72, No. 258, 16 mars 1908, 193-211.

657    BATE, Walter Jackson. Negative Capability: The Intuitive
       Approach in Keats. Harvard Honors Thesis in English, Num-
       ber 13. Cambridge, Massachusetts: Harvard University
       Press, 1939, 11-24. Bate compares Keats' distinction be-

tween "Imagination" and the "logical faculty" to Bergson's distinction between intuition and intellect.

658   BATTAGLIA, Felice. "Bergson e la storia." Giornale di metafisica, 12, No. 2, 1957, 180-182. This is a note on articles by Polin and Aron in Etudes Bergsoniennes, 4 (1956).

659   BATTAGLIA, Félice. "Introduction: Synthèse des travaux du congrès." Actes du Xe Congrès des Sociétés de Philosophie de Langue Française (Congrès Bergson). Paris: Armand Colin, 2, 1959, 305.

660   BATTAGLIA, Otto Forst de. "Les Origines d'Henri Bergson." Le Figaro Littéraire, 4, No. 193, 31 décembre 1949, 6.

661   BAUDOUIN, Charles. "Epiméthée et Prométhée: Recherche d'un dénominateur commun entre les diverses bipolarités bergsoniennes." Actes du Xe Congrès des Sociétés de Philosophie de Langue Française (Congrès Bergson). Paris: Armand Colin, 1, 1959, 17-22. According to the author, all the polarities inherent in Bergson's philosophy (mathematical time and lived time, intelligence and intuition, etc.) can be likened to the opposition between two brothers, Prometheus (the inspired soul) and Epimetheus (the conformist mind).

662   BAUDOUIN, Charles. "Review of La Pensée et le mouvant by Henri Bergson." Scientia, 58, No. 12, 1935, 369-437.

663   BAUDOUIN, Charles. "Table ronde: Liberté." Actes du Xe Congrès des Sociétés de Philosophie de Langue Française (Congrès Bergson). Paris: Armand Colin, 2, 1959, 167-189.

664   BAUHOFER, Oskar. "Review of Les Deux Sources de la morale et de la religion by Henri Bergson." Theologie der Gegenwart, 38, 1934, 156.

665   BAUMKER, Claus. "Über die Philosophie von Henri Bergson." Philosophisches Jahrbuch der Gutberletgesellschaft, 25, 1912, 1-23.

666   BAUSOLA, A. "Review of Bergson éducateur by R.-M. Mossé-Bastide." Rivista di filosofia neoscolastica, 49, No. 5-6, 1957, 559-561.

667   BAYART, Pierre. Une Application du bergsonisme à la science économique et comptable. Paris: Librairie du "Recueil Sirey," 1929, 16. "Extrait de la Revue d'Economie Politique, No. 5, 1929."

668    BAYER, Raymond.  "L'Esthétique de Bergson."  Revue Philoso-
       phique de la France et de l'Etranger, 131, Nos. 3-4, mars-
       août 1941, 244-318.  This is a well-known inquiry into
       Bergson's aesthetics, stressing both the strengths and
       weaknesses of Bergson's position.  Bergson, according to
       the author, fails to stress the place of technical ele-
       ments in art.

669    BAYER, Raymond.  L'Esthétique de Bergson.  Paris: Presses
       Universitaires de France, 1943, 75.

670    BAYER, Raymond.  "L'Esthétique de Bergson."  Etudes Berg-
       soniennes.  Paris: Presses Universitaires de France, 1943,
       124-198.

671    BAYER, Raymond.  "Recent Esthetic Thought in France."  Phil-
       osophic Thought in France and the United States.  Ed. Mar-
       vin Farber.  Albany, New York: State University of New
       York Press, 1968, 267-278.  Bergson is discussed on pages
       271-272.

672    BAYET, Albert.  "Morale bergsonienne et sociologie."  Anna-
       les Sociologiques, Série C, Fascicule 1, 1935, 1-51.  This
       is an analysis of the Two Sources.

673    BAYLAC, Jacques.  "La Philosophie de M. Bergson."  Bulletin
       de Littérature Ecclésiastique, 11, No. 5, octobre 1909,
       329-341.

674    BAZAILLAS, Albert.  Musique et inconscience: Introduction à
       la psychologie de l'inconscient.  Paris: Félix Alcan, 1908,
       320.  The author gives a highly aesthetic account of Berg-
       son's philosophy.

675    BAZAILLAS, Albert.  "La Philosophie de M. Bergson."  Renais-
       sance Politique et Littéraire, 21 février 1914.

676    BAZAILLAS, Albert.  La Vie personnelle: Etude sur quelques
       illusions de la vie intérieure.  Paris: Félix Alcan, 1905,
       305.  The author's psychology is influenced by Bergson,
       though at points he is critical of Bergson's philosophy.

677    BEAUCHATAUD, G. and LE SENNE, René.  "Le Caractère et l'écri-
       ture d'Henri Bergson."  Graphologie, No. 30, avril 1948,
       3-11.

678    BECHARA HERNANDEZ, J.  "La filosofiá de Bergson."  Universi-
       dad de Antioquia (Colombia), Ser. 6, Año 15, Nos. 94-95,
       1949, 209-220.

679    BECHER, Erich. "Review of Materie und Gedächtnis by Henri
       Bergson." Literarisches Centralblatt für Deutschland, 61,
       No. 28, 9 Juli 1910, 917-918.

680    BECK, Heinrich. "Henri Bergsons Erkenntnistheorie." Diss.,
       Leipsic, 1921, 89.

681    BECKER, H. "Review of Les Deux Sources de la Morale et de la
       religion by Henri Bergson." Annals of the American Acad-
       emy of Political and Social Science, 164, 1933, 270.

682    BECKER, Kenneth L. "Review of Duration and Simultaneity by
       Henri Bergson." Modern Schoolman, 47, No. 1, 1969, 121.
       This is an appreciative but brief review.

683    BECQUEREL, Jean. "Critique de l'ouvrage Durée et simultané-
       ité." Bulletin Scientifique des Etudiantes de Paris, 10,
       No. 2, mars-avril 1923, 18-29.

684    BEER, François-Joachim. "Souvenir sur Henri Bergson." Arts,
       No. 20, 15 juin 1945, 3.

685    BEGUIN, Albert. "Note conjointe sur Bergson et Péguy." Hen-
       ri Bergson. Ed. Béguin and Thévenaz, 321-327.

686    BEGUIN, Albert. "Péguy et Bergson." Feuillets de l'Amitié
       Charles Péguy, No. 30, octobre 1952, 3-7.

687    BEGUIN, Albert and THEVENAZ, Pierre. "Avant-propos." Henri
       Bergson. Ed. Béguin and Thévenaz, 7-12. The author cites
       points of similarity and difference between Bergson and
       Péguy. Péguy was more "Christian" than Bergson and did
       not share the latter's optimism.

688    BEHLER, Ernst. "Der Beitrag Henri Bergsons zur Gegenwarts-
       philosophie." Hochland, 55, No. 5, 1962-1963, 417-429.

689    BELIN-MILLERON, Jean. "Dynamique de la différenciation et
       équivalence: En marge de la fabulation et de l'élan vital."
       Actes du Xe Congrès des Sociétés de Philosophie de Langue
       Française (Congrès Bergson). Paris: Armand Colin, 1, 1959,
       23-25. Bergson urges us to enlarge the schemas by which
       we translate reality. To enter into the path opened by
       Bergson is to construe the results of our observations
       under the heading of the multiple and the cosmic. The au-
       thor presents the results of an inquiry into collective
       thought, then observations on the dynamic of natural
       forms.

690 BELIN-MILLERON, Jean. "Table ronde: Matière, causalité, discontinu." _Actes du Xe Congrès des Sociétés de Philosophie de Langue Française_ (Congrès Bergson). Paris: Armand Colin, 2, 1959, 121-142.

691 BELLON, L. "De tweebronnen van den Godsdienst volgens H. Bergson." _Studia Catholica_, 8, 1931-1932.

692 BELOT, Gustave. "Un Nouveau Spiritualisme." _Revue Philosophique de la France et de l'Etranger_, 44, No. 8, août 1897, 183-199. The author sees a danger of materialism in _Matter and Memory_.

693 BELOT, Gustave. "Une Théorie nouvelle de la liberté." _Revue Philosophique de la France et de l'Etranger_, 30, No. 10, octobre 1890, 360-392. This is an appreciative review of _Time and Free Will_.

694 BELTRAN DE HEREDIA, Benito. "Henri Louis Bergson: Un príncipe del espíritu: Resonancias de un centenario." _Verdad y Vida_, 17, 1959, 729-746.

695 BEMOL, Maurice. _Essai sur l'orientation des littératures de langue française au XXe siècle_. Paris: Nizet, 1960, 338. Bergson's literary influence is discussed on pages 132-137.

696 BEMOL, Maurice. _Paul Valéry_. Paris: Les Belles Lettres, 1949, 454. Bergson and Valéry are discussed on pages 426-427.

697 BENAVIDES, C. "Simpatias filosofias de William James." _Pensamiento_, 16, No. 63, 1960, 317-330. This essay discusses the influence on James of several philosophers, including Bergson.

698 BENDA, Julien. "A Propos de 'La Philosophie française'." _Mercure de France_, 112, No. 417, 1915, 186-188. The author holds that Bergson does not understand French philosophy, with its rationalistic devotion to clear and distinct ideas.

699 BENDA, Julien. _Belphégor: Essai sur l'esthétique de la présente société française_. Paris: Emile Paul, 1918, 214. This is one of many books and articles by Benda devoted in part or as a whole to criticism of Bergson's philosophy.

700 BENDA, Julien. _Le Bergsonisme ou une philosophie de la mobilité_. Paris: Mercure de France, 1912, 134.

701    BENDA, Julien. La Crise du rationalisme. Paris: Edit. du
       Club Maintenant, 1949, 125.

702    BENDA, Julien. "Une Méprise sur l'intuition bergsonienne."
       Revue du Mois, 7, No. 5, 10 mai 1912, 575-580.

703    BENDA, Julien. "Un Phénomène moderne: La Volonté concilia-
       trice." Etudes Philosophiques, N.S. 4, No. 3, juillet-
       décembre 1949, 310-318.

704    BENDA, Julien. Une Philosophie pathétique. Paris: Cahiers
       de la Quinzaine, 1913, 139 (Série 15, Cahier 2). This is
       a thoroughgoing criticism of Bergson's philosophy.

705    BENDA, Julien. "Le Procès du rationalisme." La Pensée,
       N.S. No. 7, avril-juin 1946, 100-103.

706    BENDA, Julien. De Quelques Constantes de l'esprit humaine:
       Critique du mobilisme contemporain. (Bergson, Brunschvicg,
       Boutroux, Le Roy, Bachelard, Rougier). Paris: Gallimard,
       1950, 213.

707    BENDA, Julien. "Réponse au défenseur de bergsonisme." Mer-
       cure de France, 204, 1er juillet 1913, 5-41; 16 juillet
       1913, 283-309.

708    BENDA, Julien. Sur Le Succès du bergsonisme: Précédé d'une
       réponse au défenseurs de la doctrine. Paris: Mercure de
       France, 1914, 250. This study contains "Une Philosophie
       pathétique."

709    BENEZE, Georges. "Bergson et la mémoire-image." Actes du
       Xe Congrès des Sociétés de Philosophie de Langue Française
       (Congrès Bergson). Paris: Armand Colin, 1, 1959, 27-29.
       This is a critical study of Bergson's theories of habit
       memory and memory image, a distinction used by him to
       prove the existence of a psychological unconscious.

710    BENEZE, Georges. "Table ronde: Durée et mémoire." Actes
       du Xe Congrès des Sociétés de Philosophie de Langue Fran-
       çaise (Congres Bergson). Paris: Armand Colin, 2, 1959,
       41-61.

711    BENGE, Frances. "Bergson y Prado." Cuadernos Americanos,
       147, No. 4, 1966, 116-123.

712    BENITO Y DURAN, Angel. "San Augustín y Bergson: La concien-
       cia psicológia punto de partida de metafísicas divergen-
       tes." Augustinus, 14, No. 1, 1914, 1969, 95-134.

713   BENNETT, C. A. "Bergson's Doctrine of Intuition." Philo-
      sophical Review, 25, No. 1, January 1916, 45-48.

714   BENRUBI, Isaac. Bergson: Estudio sobre su doctrina: Selec-
      ción de textos. Trans. Demetrio Nanez. Buenos Aires:
      Ed. Sudamericana, 1942, 225. This book was published un-
      der the name Jacques Benrubi.

715   BENRUBI, Isaac. "H. Bergson." Deutsche-französische Rund-
      schau, 2, 1929, 1018-1026.

716   BENRUBI, Isaac. "Henri Bergson." Die Zukunft, 18, No. 36,
      4 Juni 1910, 318-322.

717   BENRUBI, Isaac. "Review of Henri Bergsons Intuitive Philo-
      sophie by Albert Steenbergen." Revue Philosophique de la
      France et de l'Etranger, 69, No. 2, février 1910, 204-206.
      This is a critical review which defends Bergson while
      tending to concur with certain of Steenbergen's criticisms.

718   BENRUBI, Isaac. The Contemporary Thought of France. Trans.
      E. B. Dickes. London: Williams and Nordgate, 1926, 214.

719   BENRUBI, Isaac. "Un Entretien avec Bergson: Fragment de
      journal." Henri Bergson. Ed. Béguin and Thévenaz, 365-
      371. The author describes a visit with Bergson in Decem-
      ber, 1934. The significance of Bergson's essay "Le Pos-
      sible et le réel" is discussed, along with Bergson's
      intellectual development.

720   BENRUBI, Isaac. "Eucken und Bergson." Technik, 3, No. 1,
      1932, 26-27. This article was published under the name
      Jacques Benrubi.

721   BENRUBI, Isaac. Philosophische Strömungen der Gegenwart in
      Frankreich. Leipsic: Meiner, 1928, 529.

722   BENRUBI, Isaac. "Review of Quellen der Moral und der Reli-
      gion by Henri Bergson." Deutsche-Französische Rundschau,
      5, 1932, 773-778. This is a review of Les Deux Sources.

723   BENRUBI, Isaac. "La Renaissance de la philosophie en
      France." Revue de Métaphysique et de Morale, 19, No. 4,
      juillet 1911, 499-503. This article also appears in Atti
      del IV Congresso Internazionali di Filosofia, 1912.

724   BENRUBI, Isaac. "Die Renaissance des Idealismus in Frank-
      reich." Deutsche Rundschau, 149, October-Dezember 1911,
      388-406.

725    BENRUBI, Isaac. Les Sources et les courants de la philoso-
       phie contemporaine en France. 2 vols. Paris: Félix
       Alcan, 1933, 1058. Bergson is discussed in Vol. 2, on
       pages 741-938.

726    BENRUBI, Isaac. Souvenirs sur Henri Bergson. Paris: Dela-
       chaux et Niestle, 1942, 135. The author recounts the sub-
       stance of numerous conversations with Bergson over the
       course of many years.

727    BENRUBI, Jacques. (See BENRUBI, Isaac).

728    BENSE, Max. Die Philosophie. Frankfurt am Main: Suhrkamp,
       1951, 466. Zwischen den beiden Kriegen. 1. Bd. Bergson,
       Benda, and Mounier are discussed in this section.

729    BENTLEY, Eric. The Life of Drama. London: Methuen, 1965,
       371.

730    BERGER, Gaston. "The Different Trends of Contemporary
       French Philosophy." Philosophy and Phenomenological Re-
       search, 7, No. 1, 1946, 1-11. Bergson is discussed on
       pages 2 and 6.

731    BERGER, Gaston. "Discours à la Sorbonne." Bulletin de la
       Société Française de Philosophie, 54, No. 1, janvier-
       mars 1960, 21-25.

732    BERGER, Gaston. "Discours inaugural du Congrès." Actes du
       Xe Congrès des Sociétés de Philosophie de Langue Fran-
       çaise (Congrès Bergson). Paris: Armand Colin, 2, 1959,
       9-11.

733    BERGER, Gaston. "La Philosophie d'Henri Bergson." Cahiers
       du Sud, No. 233, mars 1941, 165-171.

734    BERGER, Gaston. "Le Progrès de la réflexion chez Bergson et
       chez Husserl." Henri Bergson. Ed. Béguin and Thévenaz,
       257-263. The author compares Bergson and Husserl, both of
       whom he characterizes as Cartesian. According to the au-
       thor, Bergson's and Husserl's thought both end in insur-
       mountable difficulties. Bergson is left with the untena-
       bility of a purely felt present, and Husserl with the in-
       accessibility of an absolute verity.

735    BERGER, Gaston. "Table-ronde." Nouvelles Littéraires, No.
       1677, 22 octobre 1959, 1 et 5-6.

736    BERGER, Gaston.  "Table ronde: Matière, causalité, discon-
       tinu."  Actes du Xe Congrès des Sociétés de Philosophie
       de Langue Française (Congrès Bergson).  Paris: Armand
       Colin, 2, 1959, 121-142.

737    BERGER, Gaston.  "A Tribute to Bergson on the Occasion of
       the Bergson Centennial in Paris, 1959."  The Bergsonian
       Heritage.  Ed. Thomas Hanna.  New York and London: Colum-
       bia University Press, 1962, 119-123.  The author holds
       that Bergson's message prepares us to meet our present
       technological problems.

738    BERGERON, André.  "L'Autoposition du moi par la conscience
       morale."  Dialogue, 97, No. 11, 1964, 105-111.  Brun-
       schvicg, Lavelle, Blondel, Sartre, Bergson, and others
       are discussed in this study of the development of the hu-
       man self.

739    "Bergson."  Kinotechnik, 10, 1928, 68.

740    "Bergson and the Art World."  Art World, 2, No. 2, May 1917,
       106-109.

741    "Bergson and Balfour Discuss Philosophy."  Review of Reviews,.
       44, No. 1, January 1912, 107-108.

742    "Review of Bergson and the Evolution of Physics.  Ed. and
       Trans. with Intro. P. A. Y. Gunter."  Choice, 7, No. 7,
       September 1970, 887.

743    "Bergson and Psychical Research."  Unpopular Review, 1, No.
       1, 1914, 63-111.  This is a general discussion of psychi-
       cal research with brief references to Bergson.

744    "Bergson au Panthéon."  Le Figaro, 99, No. 127, 13 janvier
       1945, 2.  This article describes a dispute over whether
       Bergson's remains should be placed in the Panthéon.

745    "Bergson Centenary, 1859-1959."  Discovery, 12, December
       1959, 507.  This is a centenary memoir.

746    "Bergson devant cinq philosophes d'aujourd'hui."  Nouvelles
       Littéraires, No. 1677, 22 octobre 1959.  Jean Brun, Gaston
       Berger, Gabriel Marcel, Henri Gouhier, and Dominique Jani-
       caud discuss Bergson and his present relevance.

747    "Bergson Died a Roman Catholic."  Christian Century, 58, No.
       5, 29 January 1941, 139-140.  This article comments on
       Raïssa Maritain's claims concerning Bergson's baptism.

748    "Bergson Dies in Paris." Christian Century, 58, No. 3, 15
       January 1941, 76-77.

749    "Bergson Elected Member of the French Academy." New York
       Times, 13 February 1914, 4, col. 2.

750    "Bergson et le bergsonisme." Chronique des Lettres Fran-
       çaises, 5, 1927, 264-265.

751    "Bergson et la vie contemplative: Lettre d'une prieure du
       Carmel." Nouvelles Littéraires, No. 322, 15 décembre
       1928, 4.

752    "Bergson in English." Nation (New York), 92, No. 2400, 29
       juin 1911, 648-649. This is a review of Matter and Memo-
       ry, translated by N. M. Paul and W. S. Palmer and of Cre-
       ative Evolution, translated by Arthur Mitchell. An essen-
       tially critical review, it develops interesting compari-
       sons of Bergson, James, and Pillon.

753    "Bergson Looking Backward." Literary Digest, 50, No. 1292,
       23 January 1915, 149-150. This is an account of Bergson's
       interpretation of German militarism.

754    "Bergson on Germany's Moral Force." Literary Digest, 49,
       No. 1287, 19 December 1914, 1223.

755    "Bergson Reported Catholic." The American Hebrew, 141, No.
       9, 16 July 1937, 18.

756    "Bergson Returns to Realism." America, 54, No. 2, 19 Octo-
       ber 1935, 28.

757    "Bergson Thanks America." New Republic, 13, No. 164, Decem-
       ber 1917, 207-209. This is a speech by Bergson to the
       American and English Red Cross, 28 October 1917, delivered
       in Paris.

758    "M. Bergson and a Critic." Spectator, 108, No. 4359, 13
       January 1912, 61. This is a review of Laughter and of
       J. M. Stewart's Critical Exposition.

759    "M. Bergson and Others." Spectator, 106, No. 4323, 1911,
       689-690. This is an impressionistic review of Matter and
       Memory and Creative Evolution.

760    "M. Bergson et le caractère quotidien de la philosophie."
       Spectateur, décembre 1911.

761   "M. Bergson Retires." Living Age, 310, No. 4026, 3 September 1921, 617.

762   "Henri Bergson." Coenobium, 4, 1910, 141.

763   "Henri Bergson." Documents de la Vie Intellectuelle, 1, No. 4, 20 janvier 1930, 38-40. This was originally published in Nouvelles Littéraires, 15 December 1928.

764   "Henri Bergson." Synthèses, 5, No. 4-5, 1946, 244-247.

765   "Henri Bergson." London Times Literary Supplement, 40, No. 2033, 18 January 1941, 27, 36. This is an obituary.

766   "Henri Bergson: Echo der Zeitungen z. Bergsons 70. Geburtstag." Das literarische Echo, 31, No. 3, 1929, 152.

767   Henri Bergson: Essais et témoignages. Ed. Albert Béguin and Pierre Thévenaz. Neuchâtel: La Baconnière, 1943, 373 (Les Cahiers du Rhône).

768   Henri Bergson: Exposition du centenaire: Paris (21 mai-juillet) 1959. Paris: Bibliothèque Nationale, 1959, 56. "Catalogue par Simone Pétremont et Gérard Willemetz. Préface par Julien Cain."

769   "Bergson's New Idea." Current Literature, 47, No. 6, December 1909, 650-651.

770   "Bergson's New Idea of Evolution." Literary Digest, 46, No. 9, 1 March 1913, 454.

771   "Bergson's New Message on Dynamic Religion." Literary Digest, 116, 19 August 1933, 18.

772   "Bergson's Reception in America." Current Opinion, 54, No. 3, March 1913, 226.

773   "Bergson's Wonder-Working Philosophy." Current Literature, 50, No. 5, May 1911, 518-520. This article contains reviews of Creative Evolution, translated by Arthur Mitchell; Matter and Memory, translated by N. M. Paul and W. S. Palmer; and Time and Free Will, translated by F. L. Pogson.

774   "M. Bergson's Philosophy." London Times Literary Supplement, 34, No. 1744, 4 July 1935, 426. This is a review of La Pensée et le mouvant.

775    "Henri Bergsons Weg zu Thomismus." Hochland, 34, No. 2,
       1937, 174-175.

776    BERL, Emmanuel. A Contretemps. Paris: Gallimard, 1969, 215.
       Surrealism and Barrès, Bergson, Breton, Foucault, Merleau-
       Ponty, and others are discussed in this book.

777    BERL, Emmanuel. "Cinquante ans après." Nouvelles Litté-
       raires, No. 1677, 22 octobre 1959, 6.

778    BERL, Emmanuel. Mort de la morale bourgeoise, 1929. Paris:
       Pauvert, 1965, 175.

779    BERL, Emmanuel. "Les Sources de la morale et de la reli-
       gion." Europe, 19, No. 114, 1932, 318-323. This is a
       highly critical review of Les Deux Sources.

780    BERL, Heinrich. "Bergson." Menorah, 10, No. 7-8, 1932,
       317-318. This is an account of a visit with Bergson.

781    BERMANN, Gregorio. "Las orientaciones de la filosofía
       contemporánea." Nosotros, 11, No. 99, julio 1917, 428.

782    BERNARDIS, P. de. "La Philosophie nouvelle et le problème
       religieux." Annales de Philosophie Chrétienne, 4e Série,
       16, mai-juin 1913.

783    BERNARD-MAITRE, Henri. "Autour de la pensée d'Henri Berg-
       son." Revue de Synthèse, 91, No. 57-58, janvier-juin 1970,
       133-135.

784    BERNE-JOFFROY, A. "Valéry et les philosophes." Revue de
       Métaphysique et de Morale, 44, No. 1, 1959, 72-95. The
       author argues on pages 91-95 that Valéry and Bergson
       differ profoundly.

785    BERNSTEIN, Herman. "Henri Bergson." Celebrities of Our
       Time. New York: Lawren, 1924, 143-153.

786    BERNSTEIN, Herman. With Master Minds. New York: Univer-
       sity Series Publishing Co., 1913, 243.

787    BERROD, P. "La Philosophie de l'intuition." Revue Philo-
       sophique de la France et de l'Etranger, 74, No. 9, sep-
       tembre 1912, 283-289.

788    BERRUETA, Juan Dominguez. "L'Intuition bergsonienne." Nou-
       velles Littéraires, No. 322, 15 décembre 1928, 3.

789    BERTELOOT, Joseph. "Humanitarisme et 'bergsonisme'."
       Etudes par des Pères de la Compagnie de Jésus, 72e Année,
       223, 5 avril 1935, 29-47.

790    BERTEVAL, W. "Bergson et Einstein." Revue Philosophique de
       la France et de l'Etranger, 132, No. 1, 1942-1943, 17-28.
       This is an attempt to reconcile Bergson and Einstein. It
       is translated, with an introduction, in Bergson and the
       Evolution of Physics, Ed. P. A. Y. Gunter, 214-227.

791    BERTEVAL, W. "Réflexions sur quelques points de la philoso-
       phie de M. Bergson." Revue de Théologie et de Philosophie,
       22, No. 90, 1934, 34-50.

792    BERTHELOT, René. "Discussion: Sur la nécessité, la finalité,
       et la liberté chez Hegel." Bulletin de la Société Fran-
       çaise de Philosophie, 7, No. 2, avril 1907, 119-140.
       Bergson is discussed on pages 136-138. This article is
       reprinted, with changes, in Evolutionisme et platonisme.

793    BERTHELOT, René. "L'Espace et le temps chez les physiciens."
       Revue de Métaphysique et de Morale, 17, No. 6, juin 1910,
       774-775.

794    BERTHELOT, René. Evolutionisme et platonisme: Mélanges
       d'histoire de la philosophie et d'histoire des sciences.
       Paris: Félix Alcan, 1908, 326. Bergson is discussed on
       pages 131-138.

795    BERTHELOT, René. Un Romantisme utilitaire: Etude sur le
       mouvement pragmatiste. Vol. 2. Le Pragmatisme chez Berg-
       son. Paris: Félix Alcan, 1913, 364. This is an exposi-
       tion of Bergson's philosophy followed by a lengthy cri-
       tique of Bergson's basic contentions in mathematics, phys-
       ics, biology, and psychology.

796    BERTOCCI, Angelo Philip. Charles Du Bos and English Litera-
       ture: A Critic and his Orientation. New York: Columbia
       University Press, 1949, 285. This study contains many
       references to Bergson and Du Bos. See its index.

797    BERTON, Jean. "Review of Les Deux Sources de la morale et
       de la religion by Henri Bergson." Etudes Théologiques et
       Religieuses, 7e Annee, No. 4, 1932, 325-326.

798    BESNIER, Charles. "Sur Bergson 'perdu et retrouvé'." Nou-
       velle Revue Pédagogique, 15 mai 1960.

799    BESSE, Clément. "Lettre de France: Pour l'intellectualisme."
       Revue Néo-scolastique de Philosophie, 14, No. 3, août 1907,
       281-303.

800    BETANCOUR, Cayetano. "Henri Bergson." Universidad Católica
       Boliviarana, 6, Nos. 19-20, 1941, 177-208.

801    BEURLIER, E. "Review of Essai sur les données immédiates
       by Henri Bergson." Bulletin Critique, 2e Sér., 10, 1er
       juillet 1892.

802    BEVILACQUA, Giulio. "Bergson e l'esperienza mistica." Hu-
       manitas, 14, No. 11, 1959, 771-778.

803    BEYER, Friedrich. "Bergsons Rückkehr zu Wildentum." Der
       Türmer, 17, No. 1, Oktober 1914, 107-109. This article
       contains a reply to Bergson's criticisms of the German
       mentality and the German war-machine.

804    BEYER, Thomas Percival. "Creative Evolution and the Woman's
       Question." Educational Review, 47, No. 1, January 1914,
       22-27.

805    BHATTACHARYA, A. C. Sri Aurobindo and Bergson: A Synthetic
       Study. Gyanpur, India: Jagabandhu Prakashan, 1972, 282.

806    BIAGIONI, L. "Giovanni Papini: Begegnung mit Henry Bergson."
       Zeitschrift für Religions und Geistesgeschichte, 4, No. 4,
       1952, 371-374.

807    BIBESCO. "L'Anémone et l'asphodèle." Nouvelles Littéraires,
       No. 1677, 22 octobre 1959, 1 et 6.

808    "Bibliographie de Bergson." Documents de la Vie Intellec-
       tuelle, 1, No. 4, 20 janvier 1930, 69-72.

809    "Bibliographie des ouvrages relatifs à Bergson." Documents
       de la Vie Intellectuelle, 2, No. 5, 20 février 1930, 278-
       279.

810    "Bibliographie des ouvrages relatifs à Bergson." Documents
       de la Vie Intellectuelle, 3, No. 3, 20 juin 1930, 583-588.

811    BIGELOW, Gordon E. "A Primer of Existentialism." College
       English, 23, No. 3, December 1961, 171-178. This study
       treats of Bergson along with many other thinkers (Sartre,
       Camus, Marcel, etc.).

812    BILLY, André.  "Review of Henri Bergson by Jacques Cheva-
       lier."  L'Oeuvre, No. 4799, 20 novembre 1928, 4.

813    BILLY, André.  "La Conversion de Bergson."  Le Figaro Litté-
       raire, 17 octobre 1959, 4.

814    BILLY, André.  "M. Pouget, Bergson et l'enfer."  Le Figaro
       Littéraire, 30 octobre 1954, 2.

815    BILLY, André.  "Réorganisons le Panthéon."  Le Figaro, 119,
       No. 133, 20 janvier 1945, 1.  This article concerns a sug-
       gestion that Bergson's remains be buried in the Panthéon.

816    BILLY, André.  "Une Réponse d'Henri Bergson à l'enquête du
       'Figaro'."  Le Figaro, 116, No. 74, 15 mars 1941, 4.

817    BINET, Alfred.  L'Ame et le corps.  Paris: Flammarion, 1926,
       286.  Bergson's theory of perception is discussed on page
       48; Bergson's influence on Binet on pages 85-87n; Bergson
       and Berkeley on the brain on pages 234-235; Bergson and
       Binet on the function of the brain on pages 236-241 and
       268.

818    BINET, Alfred.  "H. Bergson: Note sur la conscience de l'ef-
       fort intellectuel."  Année Psychologique, 8, 1901, 471-
       478, 492.

819    BINET, Alfred.  "Une Enquête sur l'évolution de l'enseigne-
       ment de la philosophie."  Année Psychologique, 14, 1908,
       229-230.

820    BISSON, L.-A.  "Proust, Bergson, and George Eliot."  Modern
       Language Review, 40, No. 2, April 1945, 104-114.  The au-
       thor discusses the influence of Bergson as well as George
       Eliot on Proust.

821    BJORKMAN, Edwin.  "Henri Bergson: The Philosopher of Actual-
       ity."  Forum, 46, No. 3, September 1911, 268-276.  This
       article is a very general discussion of Bergson's philoso-
       phy.

822    BJORKMAN, Edwin.  "Henri Bergson: Philosopher or Prophet?"
       Review of Reviews, 54, No. 2, August 1911, 250-252.

823    BJORKMAN, Edwin.  "Is There Anything New Under the Sun?"
       Forum, 46, No. 1, July 1911, 11-21.  The author gives a
       very "popularized" account of Bergson's thought.

824    BJORKMAN, Edwin.  Is There Anything New Under the Sun?  New
       York and London: Kennerly, 1911, 259.

825    BJORKMAN, Edwin.  Voices of Tomorrow: Critical Studies of
       the New Spirit in Literature.  New York and London:
       Kennerly, 1913, 328.  Bergson is discussed on pages 205-
       223.

826    BLACKLOCK, W.  "Bergson's Creative Evolution."  Westminster
       Review, 177, No. 2, March 1912, 343-347.

827    BLANCH, Robert J.  "The Synchronized Clocks of Bergson and
       Rousseau."  Revue des Langues Vivantes, 33, No. 5, 1967,
       489-492.

828    BLANCHARD, Pierre.  "Philosophie et vie spirituelle."  Actes
       du Xe Congrès des Sociétés de Langue Française (Congrès
       Bergson).  Paris: Armand Colin, 1, 1959, 31-34.  The au-
       thor argues that Bergson's philosophy is prophetic.  With
       almost Biblical accents, it recalls man to his destiny
       and humanity to its function.

829    BLANCHE, Robert.  "Review of Bergson and the Evolution of
       Physics.  Ed. and Trans. with Intro. P. A. Y. Gunter."
       Journal de Psychologie Normale et Pathologique, 68, No. 1,
       janvier-mars 1971, 106-107.

830    BLANCHE, Robert.  "Review of L'Intellectualisme de Bergson
       by Léon Husson."  Journal de Psychologie Normale et Patho-
       logique, 44, 1947, 246-247.  The author finds merit in
       Husson's approach and in his interpretation of Bergson.

831    BLANCHE, Robert.  "Psychologie de la durée et physique du
       champ."  Journal de Psychologie Normale et Pathologique,
       44, No. 3, 1951, 411-424.  This article is translated with
       introduction in Bergson and the Evolution of Physics, Ed.
       P. A. Y. Gunter, 105-120.

832    BLANCHOT, Maurice.  Faux pas.  Paris: Gallimard, 1943, 366.
       Proust, Camus, Mallarmé, Bergson, and others are discussed
       in this book.

833    BLANCHOT, Maurice.  "Symbolism and Bergson."  Yale French
       Studies, 2, No. 2, 1949, 63-66.

834    BLANCO, J. E.  "Cinco lecciones sobre Bergson."  Studium,
       3, Nos. 7-8, 1959, 149-160.  This article contains an in-

troduction, a short biography of Bergson, and a bibliography.

835    BLANCO, J. E.    "Cinco lecciones sobre Bergson: Lección segunda." Studium, 4, Nos. 9-10, 1960, 3-17.  Blanco analyzes Quid Aristoteles de loco senserit and the Essai.

836    BLESZYNSKI, K.  "Ostatnia pracn Wl. Dawida o Bergsonie." Krytyka, 16, No. 5, 1914, 143-150.

837    BLOCH, Marc-André.  "Sens et postérité de l'Essai."  Actes du Xe Congrès des Sociétés de Philosophie de Langue Française (Congrès Bergson).  Paris: Armand Colin, 1, 1959, 35-38.  With the Essai, the author holds that French philosophy assigned itself for the first time to the task of recovering what Bergson termed "les données immédiates de la conscience," or what his successors would call "expérience préobjective" or "expérience à l'état naissant." Bergson provided a model of a style of philosophizing which is still felt in a sector of French philosophy.

838    BLOCH, Marc-André.  "Table ronde: Sources et histoire du bergsonisme." Actes du Xe Congrès des Sociétés de Philosophie Française (Congrès Bergson).  Paris: Armand Colin, 2, 1959, 213-233.

839    BLONDEL, Charles.  La Conscience morbide: Essai de psychopathologie générale.  Paris: Félix Alcan, 1914, 342.  The author's psychology is strongly influenced by Bergson.

840    BLONDEL, Charles.  La Psychographie de Marcel Proust.  Paris: Vrin, 1932, 195.  Bergson and Proust are discussed on 167 and 184-187.

841    BLONDEL, Maurice.  "La Philosophie ouverte." Henri Bergson. Ed. Béguin and Thévenaz, 73-90.  The author examines Bergson's philosophical method and concept of intuition.  He is both respectful and critical of the conclusions to which Bergson's method leads, particularly as concerns religious philosophy.

842    BLUM, Eugène.  "Le IIe Congrès international de philosophie: Genève, 4-8 septembre 1904." Revue Philosophique, 58, No. 11, novembre 1904, 509-519.  This article contains an account of Bergson's critique of psycho-physical parallelism on pages 509-510.

843    BLUM, Jean. "La Philosophie de M. Bergson et la poésie sym-
       boliste." Mercure de France, 73, No. 222, 15 septembre
       1906, 201-207.

844    BOAS, George. "Bergson (1859-1941) and His Predecessors."
       Journal of the History of Ideas, 20, No. 4, October-
       December 1959, 503-514. According to the author, Berg-
       son's originality lies in the use he made of his prede-
       cessors' ideas.

845    BOBROMSKA, K. "Bergsonizm ozyli filozofja zmiennosoi pôdrug
       J. Bendy." Przeglad Filozoficzny, 18, No. 3, 1914, 374-
       384.

846    BOCHENSKI, Innocentius M. La Philosophie contemporaine en
       Europe. Trans. F. Vaudon. Paris: Payot, 1951, 252.

847    BODE, Boyd Henry. "Review of Creative Evolution by Henri
       Bergson, translated by A. Mitchell." American Journal of
       Psychology, 23, No. 2, April 1912, 333-335.

848    BODE, Boyd Henry. "Review of L'Evolution créatrice by Henri
       Bergson." Philosophical Review, 17, No. 1, January 1908,
       84-89.

849    BOER, Jesse De. "A Critical Study of Bergson's Theory of
       Change, Duration, and Causality." Diss., Harvard, 1942

850    BOER, Jesse De. "A Critique of Continuity, Infinity, and
       Allied Concepts in the Natural Philosophy of Bergson and
       Russell." The Return to Reason. Ed. John Wild. Chicago:
       Henry Regnery Company, 1953, 373, 92-124. This paper pre-
       sents an analytical and critical study of the Bergson-
       Russell conflict. It deals with Bergson's treatment of
       Zeno's paradoxes, Russell's critique of Bergson, and Rus-
       sell's concepts of time and motion.

851    BOER, Tjitze J. de. "De filosofie van Henri Bergson."
       Beweging, 3, 1909, 225-244.

852    BOGDANOVITCH, R. "L'Idée de durée chez Bergson et chez Mar-
       cel Proust." Notre Temps, 3 juillet 1932, 208-213.

853    BOINE, Giovanni. "La novità di Bergson." Nuova ontologia,
       Ser. 5, 173, No. 1025, 1914, 24-37.

854    BOINE, Giovanni. La novità di Bergson. Roma: Nuova Antolo-
       gia, 1918, 16.

855    BOIS, Elie-Joseph. "A La Recherche du temps perdu." Le
       Temps, NO. 19124, 13 novembre 1932, 2. Bois' article
       contains Proust's denial of Bergson's influence.

856    BOJINOFF, Assen. Ist eine Metaphysik des Absoluten möglich?
       Die zwei Grundtypen aller Metaphysik: (Gegen) Antike Skep-
       sis, Positivismus, Henri Bergson, Hans Driesch. Sofia:
       Tschiepeff, 1928, 148.

857    BOLL, Marcel. Attardés et précurseurs. Paris: Chiron,
       1922, 283. This study contains a critical discussion of
       Bergson and Boutroux.

858    BOLL, Marcel. "Sur La Durée, la liberté, et autres 'intui-
       tions'." Mercure de France, 122, 1er février 1919, 385-
       410.

859    BONHOFF, K. "Aus Bergsons Hauptwerken." Protestantische
       Monatshefte, 17, 1913, 168-181.

860    BONHOMME, Mary Bernard. "Educational Implications of Berg-
       son's Philosophy." Catholic Educational Review, 45, No.
       10, December 1947, 615-616.

861    BONHOMME, Mary Bernard. Educational Implications of the
       Philosophy of Henri Bergson. Washington, D.C.: Catho-
       lic University of America Press, 1944, 208. "In the
       light of Catholic educational philosophy, one conclusion
       is unavoidable. Despite its many fine qualities and the
       genuine good will of its author, Bergsonism, like all
       modern philosophies, is exclusivistic. It is not based
       on a complete conception of reality." (183). The author
       gives a very general, rather minimal account of Bergson's
       philosophy of education.

862    BONHOMME, Mary Bernard. "Educational Implications of the
       Philosophy of Henri Bergson." Diss., Catholic University
       of America, 1947.

863    BONKE, H. "Bergsons Bedeutung." Unsere Welt, 9, 1917, 85-
       92.

864    BONKE, H. Plagiator Bergson: Membre de l'Institut. Char-
       lottenburg, Sweden: Huth, 1915, 47.

865    BONNARD, André. Le Mouvement antipositiviste contemporain
       en France. Diss., Grenoble, 1936. Paris: Jel, 1936, 227.

866   BONNEFON, Daniel and Charles. Les Ecrivains modernes de la France. Paris: Fayard, 1927, 715.

867   BONNET, Christian L. "Review of The Creative Mind by Henri Bergson." Modern Schoolman, 23, No. 4, May 1946, 222-223.

868   BONNET, Henri. Alphonse Darlu: Le Maître de philosophie de Marcel Proust. Paris: Nizet, 1961, 139. "Darlu et Bergson" are discussed on pages 79-82.

869   BONNET, Henri. "A Propos des théories de M. Bergson." Société Nouvelle, 2e Série, 46, No. 4, octobre 1912, 26-37. The author is highly critical of Bergson's theories.

870   BONNET, Henri. "Bergson et Proust." Actes du Xe Congrès des Sociétés de Philosophie de Langue Française (Congrès Bergson). Paris: Armand Colin, 1, 1959, 39-43. The author argues that the analogies between Bergson and Proust are most numerous at the level of the exploration of the unconscious mind. This is not a matter of influence. Both seek felt experience. Both have a similar starting point. They differ at the level of interpretations and conceptions.

871   BONNET, Henri. Le Progrès spirituel dans l'oeuvre de Marcel Proust: Vol. 2. L'Eudémonisme esthétique de Proust. Paris: Vrin, 1949, 293. Bergson and Proust are discussed on pages 212-236.

872   BONNET, Henri. "Table ronde: Durée et mémoire." Actes du Xe Congrès des Sociétés de Philosophie de Langue Française (Congrès Bergson). Paris: Armand Colin, 2, 1959, 41-61.

873   BONUS, Arthur. "Bergson muß es wissen!" März, 7, No. 3, 5 September 1914, 312-314. This article is a criticism of Bergson's attack on the German mentality and German militarism.

874   BOPP, Léon. "Bergson et Thibaudet." Henri Bergson. Ed. Béguin and Thévenaz, 341-348. The author examines both the Bergsonian and the non-Bergsonian aspects of the literary criticism of Albert Thibaudet.

875   BORDEAUX, Henry. "Les Dernières Années d'Henri Bergson." Revue des Deux Mondes, N.S. Année 11, No. 22, 15 novembre 1958, 220-226.

876    BORDEAUX, Henry.  "Dernière Visite à Bergson."  L'Académie
       française en 1914: Histoire d'une candidature.  Paris:
       Edit. d'histoire et d'art, 1946, 78-86.

877    BORDEAUX, Henry.  Histoire d'une vie: Vol. 3.  La Douceur
       de vivre menacée 1909-1914.  Paris: Plon, 1956, 367.  This
       book contains a section on Bergson, among many others.

878    BORDEAUX, Henry.  Histoire d'une vie: Vol. 10.  Voyages d'un
       monde à l'autre: 1931-1936.  Paris: Plon, 1964, 354.
       Barrès, Bergson, Maurras, Bremond, Anna de Noailles, and
       others are discussed in this book.

879    BOREL, Emile.  "L'Evolution de l'intelligence géométrique."
       Revue de Métaphysique et de Morale, 15, No. 6, 1907, 747-
       754.  Borel charges Bergson with neglecting non-Euclidean
       geometry and giving a static picture of the human intel-
       lect.

880    BOREL, Emile.  "Lettre à l'éditeur (Discussions)."  Revue de
       Métaphysique et de Morale, 16, No. 2, 1908, 244-245.
       Borel finds himself in essential agreement with Bergson as
       regards "l'intelligence géométrique."

881    BORGESE, Giuseppe Antonio.  Studî di letterature moderne.
       Milano: Fratelli Treves, 1915, 383.

882    BORNE, Etienne.  Passion de la vérité.  Paris: Fayard, 1962,
       251.  The second chapter of this work is on Pascal, Berg-
       son, and Blondel.

883    BORNE, Etienne.  "Simples Notes de poétique bergsonienne."
       Henri Bergson.  Ed. Béguin and Thévenaz, 135-140.  The au-
       thor holds that Bergson's philosophy contains a recogniz-
       able poetic.  He claims that for Bergson art is neither
       a servile imitation of reality nor an escape into illusion,
       but a kind of knowledge.  For Bergson the beautiful is an
       allusion to an invisible reality of which nature is the
       visible symbol.

884    BORNE, Etienne.  "Spiritualité bergsonienne et spiritualité
       chrétienne."  Etudes Carmélitaines, 17, No. 2, octobre
       1932, 157-184.  This article contains a critique of Les
       Deux Sources.  The author holds that Bergson brings over
       into the realm of morals and religion ideas which have no
       value except in aesthetics.

885    BORNE, Etienne.  "Sur Les Philosophies de la vie et de l'action (Bergson et Blondel)."  Recherches et Débats, No. 10, 1955, 133-165.

886    BORNECQUE, Jacques-Henry.  "Une Source du Rire de Bergson." Revue Universelle, N.S. 42, 25 septembre 1942, 304-311.

887    BORNHAUSEN, Karl.  "Die Philosophie H. Bergsons und ihre Bedeutung für den Religionsbegriff."  Zeitschrift für Theologie und Kirche, 6, No. 6, 1910, 39-77.

888    BORNSTEIN, Benedykt.  "Kant i Bergson."  Przeglad Filozoficzny, 16, No. 2-3, 1913, 129-199.

889    BORNSTEIN, Benedykt.  Kant i Bergson: Studyum o zasadniczym problemacie teoryi.  Warsaw: Wende, 1913.

890    BOROS, Ladislas.  The Moment of Truth: Mysterium Mortis. London: Bruns and Oates, 1965, 201.  The author treats of death in Bergson, Blondel, Marcel, and others.

891    BOS, Camille.  "Contribution à la théorie psychologique du temps."  Revue Philosophique de la France et de l'Etranger, 50, No. 12, décembre 1900, 594-610.

892    BOSANQUET, Bernard.  "On a Defect in the Customary Logical Formulation of Inductive Reasoning."  Proceedings of the Aristotelian Society, N.S. 11, 1910-11, 24-40.  The author pursues a careful criticism of Bergson's concept of the intellect.  "With tautological identity as the principle of intelligence, all systematic coherence, between term and term, equally as between judgment and judgment, inevitably vanishes."  (31-32).

893    BOSANQUET, Bernard.  "The Prediction of Human Conduct: A Study in Bergson."  International Journal of Ethics, 21, No. 1, October 1910, 1-15.  In this address delivered at University College, Cardiff, Bosanquet attempts to make clear to a general audience Bergson's position on certain questions.

894    BOSANQUET, Bernard.  The Principle of Individuality and Value.  London: Macmillan, 1912, 409.  Bergson is discussed on pages 32-34, 54n, 94, 102n, 107n, 134, 137, 150, 168n, 172, 177n, 204-208, 230, 259, and 355.

895    BOTTI, Luigi.  "Mentre Bergson é messo all'indice."  Rassegna nazionale, 198, 1914.  This article is a study of Olgiati's Filosofia de Henri Bergson.

896    BOUCAUD, Charles.  "L'Histoire de droit et la philosophie de
       M. Bergson."  Revue de Philosophie, 4, No. 2, ler mars
       1904, 229-306.

897    BOUCHE, J.  "La Philosophie de M. Bergson."  Questions ecclé-
       siastiques, 6, février 1913.

898    BOUGLE, Célestin.  Les Maîtres de la philosophie universi-
       taire en France.  Paris: Maloine, 1938, 112.

899    BOUGLE, Célestin.  "Syndicalistes et Bergsoniens."  Revue du
       Mois, 6, No. 4, 10 avril 1909, 403-416.

900    BOUGLE, M.  "Bergson y Durkheim."  La Nación, 4 septiembre
       1928.

901    BOULANGER, Maurice.  "Cervantès et Bergson."  Lettres Ro-
       manes, 1, No. 4, novembre 1947, 277-296.

902    BOULE, L.  "Les Localizations cérebrales et la philosophie
       spiritualiste."  Revue des Questions Scientifiques, 3e
       Sér., 23, 1913, 192-228, "et à suivre."

903    BOUQUET, A. C.  "Review of Les Deux Sources de la morale et
       de la religion by Henri Bergson."  Cambridge Review, 56,
       1933-1935, 308-310.

904    BOURDEAU, Jean.  La Philosophie affective: Nouveaux cou-
       rants et nouveaux problèmes de la philosophie contempo-
       raine: Descartes et Schopenhauer, W. James et M. Bergson,
       M. Th. Ribot et Alf. Fouillée, Tolstoi et Leopardi.  Paris:
       Félix Alcan, 1912, 181.

905    BOURQUIN, Constant, Ed.  Comment doivent écrire les philo-
       sophes?  Ce qu'en pensent: M. Henri Bergson, MM. André
       Lalande et Ernest Sellière, Antoine Albalat (et autres).
       Paris: Editions du Monde Nouveau, 1923, 166.

906    BOURQUIN, Constant.  Julien Benda: Ou, Le Point de vue de
       Sirius.  Paris: Editions du Siècle, 1925, 250.  The intro-
       duction is by Jules de Gaultier.

907    BOURQUIN, Constant.  "Sur La Prétention philosophique du
       symbolisme."  Belles-lettres, 3, No. 28, octobre 1921,
       337-349.

908    BOUVIER, Robert.  "Review of Les Etudes Bergsoniennes.  Vol-
       ume III."  Erasmus, 6, Nos. 13-14, 1953, 449-452.

909    BOVIATSIS-DESCHAMPS, Renée. "Le Bergsonisme est-il un hu-
       manisme?" Diss., Montpellier, 1948, 195. The author
       holds that Bergson envisaged man as capable, by his own
       capacities, of becoming semi-divine.

910    BOYD, W. "Review of L'Evolution créatrice by Henri Bergson."
       Review of Theology and Philosophy, 3, No. 10, October 1907,
       249-251.

911    BOYER, Charles. "Bergson et l'immortalité de l'âme." Gior-
       nale di metafisica, 14, No. 6, novembre-dicembre 1959,
       753-758. For Bergson experience renders probable the in-
       dependence of the soul with respect to the body, after
       whose dissolution it (the soul) could continue to subsist
       --though it is not possible to prove the soul's immortali-
       ty. Bergson rests his case primarily on the retention and
       recall of memories.

912    BOYER, Charles. "Il pensiero religioso di Bergson." Humani-
       tas, 14, No. 11, 1959, 779-784.

913    BRAILEANU, T. "Review of Les Deux Sources de la morale et
       de la religion by Henri Bergson." Revista de pedagogia,
       2, Nos. 1-2, 1935, 111-117.

914 ·  BRAMBILA, Antonio. "Anotaciones críticas sobre el Dios de
       Bergson." Luminar, 2, No. 4, Otoño, 1938, 22-62.

915    BRASILLACH, Robert. Les Quatre Jeudis: Images d'avant-
       guerre. Paris: Edit. Balzac, 1944, 519. Bergson is dis-
       cussed on pages 62-69.

916    BRAUN, O. "Review of Materie und Gedächtnis by Henri Berg-
       son." Archiv für Gesamte Psychologie, 15, No. 4, 1915,
       13-15.

917    BRAUNSCHVIG, Marcel. La Littérature française contemporaine
       étudiée dans les textes (1850-1925). Paris: Armand Colin,
       1926, 356. The first section of this book contains selec-
       tions from Bergson and many others.

918    BRAVO, C. "Duración y intuición en la filosofía de Henri
       Bergson." Estudios, 59, No. 321, 1938, 233-254.

919    BREHIER, Emile. "Review of Bergson, maître de Péguy by
       André Henry." Etudes Bergsoniennes, 1952, 3, 213-214.

920    BREHIER, Emile. "Emile Brehier. 'Images plotiniennes,
       images bergsoniennes'." Etudes Bergsoniennes, 2, 1949,

215-222. This is a discussion between Bréhier and several other philosophers of his article, "Images plotiniennes, images bergsoniennes."

921    BREHIER, Emile.  "Henri Gouhier.  'Maine de Biran et Bergson'."  Etudes Bergsoniennes, 2, 1949, 198-199.  The author argues that Bergson and Maine de Biran are entirely different in their approach and conclusions.

922    BREHIER, Emile.  Histoire de la philosophie: Vol. 2.  La Philosophie moderne: 2e Partie.  Paris: Presses Universitaires de France, 1945, 1206.  Bergson is discussed on pages 1023-1034.

923    BREHIER, Emile.  "Hommage à Bergson."  Revue des Deux Mondes, N.S. 2, No. 10, 15 mai 1949, 368-370.

924    BREHIER, Emile.  "L'Idéalisme de L. Brunschvicg."  Revue Philosophique de la France et de l'Etranger, 136, Nos. 1-3, 1946, 1-7.  Bréhier stresses similarities between Brunschvicg and Bergson.

925    BREHIER, Emile.  "Images plotiniennes, images bergsoniennes."  Etudes Bergsoniennes, 2, 1949, 107-128.

926    BREHIER, Emile.  "Liberté et métaphysique."  Revue Internationale de Philosophie, 2, No. 5, 1948, 1-13.  Bergson and others are treated in this study.

927    BREHIER, Emile.  Notice sur la vie et les oeuvres de M. Bergson.  Paris: Firmin-Didot, 1946, 31.

928    BREHIER, Emile.  "Notice sur la vie et les travaux d'Henri Bergson."  Etudes de philosophie moderne.  Paris: Presses Universitaires de France, 1965, 129-144.

929    BREHIER, Emile.  "La Philosophie d'Henri Bergson."  Revue Hebdomadaire des Cours et des Conférences, 20, No. 2, 2 mai 1912, 337-346.  This is a lecture which was given at the Université d'Oviedo, 28 March 1912.

930    BREMOND, A.  "Réflexions sur l'homme dans la philosophie de Bergson."  Archives de Philosophie, 17, No. 1, 1947, 122-148.

931    BREMOND, Henri.  "L'Américanisme de W. James."  Revue de France, 4, No. 21, 1er novembre 1924, 181-188.

932    BRERETON, Cloudesley. "Bergson on Morality and Religion."
       Contemporary Review, 148, No. 408, 1935, 369-373. This is
       a review of The Two Sources.

933    BRETON, Stanislas. "La Notion de puissance et la critique
       contemporaine." Sophia, 17, No. 3-4, 1949, 290-293. The
       author cites criticisms of the concept of potential ("puis-
       sance") by Bergson, Hamelin, N. Hartmann, Sartre, and La-
       velle.

934    BRIACH, R. "Bergsons Entwicklung Theorie." Kosmos, 49,
       1914.

935    BRICOUT, J. "M. Bergson à l'Index." Revue du Clergé Fran-
       çais, 20e Année, No. 474, 15 août 1914, 451ff.

936    BRIDOUX, André. Le Souvenir. Paris: Presses Universitaires
       de France, 1954, 90.

937    BRINCOURT, André and Jean. Les Oeuvres et les lumières: A
       La Recherche de l'esthétique à travers Bergson, Proust,
       Malraux. Paris: La Table Ronde, 1955, 222.

938    BRINKGREVE, M.-R.-J. "Bergson." Tijdschrift voor Wijs-
       begeerte, 20, No. 2, 1926, 211-226.

939    BRISSON, Pierre. Vingt ans de Figaro: 1938-1958. Paris:
       Gallimard, 1959, 273. Bergson and many others are treated
       in this book.

940    BROAD, Charley Dunbar. "Note on Achilles and the Tortoise."
       Mind, 23, No. 86, April 1913, 318-319. The author insists:
       ". . . it is important even at this time of day to settle
       the controversy finally, because it and Zeno's other para-
       doxes have become the happy hunting-ground of Bergsonians
       and like contemners of the human intellect." (318).

941    BROCK, F. H. Cecil. "Implications of Bergson's Philosophy."
       Proceedings of the Aristotelian Society, N.S. 26, 1925-
       1926, 279-298.

942    BROCKDORF, Cay von. Die Wahrheit über Bergson. Berlin:
       Curtuis, 1916, 55.

943    BROGLIE, Louis de. "Les Conceptions de la physique contem-
       poraine et les idées de Bergson sur le temps et le mouve-
       ment." Revue de Métaphysique et de Morale, 48, No. 4,
       1941, 241-257. This article is translated, with an intro-

duction, in Bergson and the Evolution of Physics, Ed.
P. A. Y. Gunter, 45-62.  The author argues that Bergson's
ideas closely resemble and foreshadow those of quantum
physics.

944   BROGLIE, Louis de.  Physics and Microphysics.  New York:
      Pantheon Books, 1955, 282.  "Concepts of Contemporary Phys-
      ics and the Ideas of Bergson on Time and Motion" occurs in
      abridged form on pages 186-193.

945   BROGLIE, Louis de.  Physique et microphysique.  Paris: Albin
      Michel, 1947, 371.  "Les Idées de Bergson sur le temps et
      le mouvement" is found on pages 191-211.

946   BROPHY, Liam.  "The Anguish of Henri Bergson."  Social Jus-
      tice Review, 53, August 1959, 110-119.  According to the
      author a conflict between Jewish background and Catholic
      faith is evident in Bergson's later years.

947   BROWN, A. Barratt.  "Intuition."  International Journal of
      Ethics, 24, No. 3, 1913-14, 282-293.  This is a discussion
      of the meaning of intuition, including a critical compari-
      son of Bergson's concept of intuition with that of F. H.
      Bradley.

948   BROWN, William.  "The Philosophy of Bergson."  Church Quar-
      terly Review, 74, No. 2, April 1912, 126-142.  This is a
      review of Time and Free Will, Matter and Memory, Creative
      Evolution, Stewart's Critical Exposition of Bergson's Phi-
      losophy, and Balsillie's Examination of Professor Berg-
      son's Philosophy.

949   BROWN, William.  Suggestion and Mental Analysis.  London:
      University of London Press, 1922, 167.  Bergson is dis-
      cussed on pages 127-167.

950   BROWNING, Douglas.  Philosophers of Process.  New York:
      Random House, 1965, 346.  The introduction is by Charles
      Hartshorne.  A selection from Bergson is presented on
      pages 2-56.

951   BRUCE, H. Addington.  "The Soul's Winning Fight with Sci-
      ence."  American Magazine, 77, No. 3, March 1914, 21-26.
      James, Bergson, Lodge, and others are discussed in this
      article.

952   BRUCH, Jean-Louis.  "Die Bergson-Forschung in Frankreich."
      Antares, 5, No. 2, 1957, 31-32.

953    BRUCH, Jean-Louis. "Vingt Ans après la mort de Bergson."
       Culture Française, No. 5, octobre-décembre 1961.

954    BRUCKER, Ted J. "Finality in the Philosophy of Henri Berg-
       son." Diss., St. Louis, 1967.

955    BRUERS, Antonio. Pensatori antichi c moderni. Roma: Bardi,
       1936, 308. Bergson is discussed on pages 283-295.

956    BRUERS, An. "Il principio di creazione del Bergson e la
       metapsichica." Luce e ombra, 15, No. 6, 1915.

957    BRUN, Jean. "Bergson: Philosophe de la coïncidence." Cri-
       tique, 16, No. 157, 1960, 535-552.

958    BRUN, Jean. "Table-ronde." Nouvelles Littéraires, No. 1677,
       22 octobre 1959, 1 et 5-6.

959    BRUNELLO, Bruno. "Review of La Pensée et le mouvant by
       Henri Bergson." Giornale critico della la filosifia ita-
       liana, 16, No. 1, 1935, 78-81.

960    BRUNET, Georges. "Autour de Pascal: II. Une Page retrouvé
       de Bergson." Revue d'Histoire Littéraire de la France, 47,
       No. 2, 1947, 169-171.

961    BRUNING, Walthar. "La filosofia irracionalista de la histo-
       ria en la actualidad." Revista de Filosofía, 5, No. 2,
       1958, 3-17. Nietzsche, Bergson, and Klages are discussed
       in this study of irrationalist philosophies of history.

962    BRUNNER, Fernand. "Table ronde: Morale." Actes du Xe Con-
       grès des Sociétés de Philosophie de Langue Française (Con-
       grès Bergson). Paris: Armand Colin, 2, 1959, 237-257.

963    BRUNO, Antonio. Religiosita perenne. Bari: Laterza e
       Figli, 1947, 121. Chapter five, entitled "Bergson posi-
       tiva e negativa dell'attavismo," is found on pages 76-81.

964    BRUNSCHVICG, Léon. "Bergson et l'intelligence." Documents
       de la Vie Intellectuelle, 2, No. 5, 20 février 1930, 246-
       254. This article was originally in Progrès de la con-
       science dans la philosophie occidentale. Vol. 2, Chs.
       21-22.

965    BRUNSCHVICG, Léon. "H. Bergson: Lauréat du Prix Nobel."
       Revue de Paris, 25e Année, No. 23, 1er décembre 1928,
       671-686.

966     BRUNSCHVICG, Léon.  "Henri Bergsons Philosophie."  Revue
        Rhénane, 9, No. 4, 1929, 4-12.

967     BRUNSCHVICG, Léon.  "Le Bergsonisme dans l'histoire de la
        philosophie."  Nouvelles Littéraires, No. 322, 15 décem-
        bre 1928, 1, 6.

968     BRUNSCHVICG, Léon.  "Evolution de la pensée française."  La
        Nef, 1, No. 2, août 1944, 36-54.

969     BRUNSCHVICG, Léon.  "L'Idéalisme contemporain."  Biblio-
        thèque du Congrès international de philosophie: Philoso-
        phie générale et métaphysique.  Paris: Armand Colin, 1900,
        39-57.

970     BRUNSCHVICG, Léon.  L'Idéalisme contemporain.  Paris: Félix
        Alcan, 1905, 185.

971     BRUNSCHVICG, Léon.  "La Philosophie nouvelle et l'intellec-
        tualisme."  Revue de Métaphysique et de Morale, 9, 1901,
        433-478.

972     BRUNSCHVICG, Léon.  Le Progrès de la conscience dans la phi-
        losophie occidentale.  Paris: Félix Alcan, 1927, II, 441.
        Part 4 is entitled "La Philosophie de la conscience de
        Condillac à Bergson."

973     BRUNSCHVICG, Léon.  "La Vie intérieure de l'intuition."
        Henri Bergson.  Ed. Béguin and Thévenaz, 181-186.  The au-
        thor discusses the often surprising, always creative de-
        velopment of Bergson's thought.  We must study Bergson,
        he holds, by avoiding the temptation to enclose Bergson's
        thought in a system.

974     BRUZIO, Filippo.  "Scienza e filosofia bergsoniana."  Ras-
        segna d'Italia, 2, 1947, 89-93.

975     BUBER, Martin.  Hinweise: Gesammelte Essays.  Zürich: Manes-
        se Verlag, Conzett und Huber, 1953, 220-228.  This was
        first published in 1943.  It contains a chapter on Bergson.

976     BUBER, Martin.  "The Silent Question: About Henri Bergson
        and Simone Weil."  Judaism, 1, No. 2, April 1952, 99-105.

977     BUCCAZO.  "L'Intellectualisme de M. Bergson."  Parthénon, 3,
        5 août 1913.

978     BUJEAU, L.-V.  L'Oeuvre de J.-H. Fabre et la psychologie de
        l'insecte.  Paris: Presses Universitaires de France, 1940,

98.  Bergson's definition of instinct is discussed on page 3; the association of ideas (images) in animals on page 48; animal intelligence on page 54; insect intelligence on page 56; insect language on page 57.  See also pages 59, 65, and 75 for other discussions of Bergson's thought.

979    BUNGE, C.  "El pragmatismo."  Nosotros, 9, No. 75, julio 1915, 17-19.

980    BUNGE, Mario.  Intuition and Science.  Englewood Cliffs, New Jersey: Prentice-Hall, Inc., 1942.  The author criticizes Bergson's concept of intuition on pages 12-17.

981    BURAND, Georges.  "L'Origine scolastique de la théorie de la perception extérieure de Bergson."  Entretiens Israélites, janvier 1914.

982    BURGELIN, Pierre.  "Le Social et la nature chez Bergson."  Actes du Xe Congrès des Sociétés de Philosophie de Langue Française (Congrès Bergson).  Paris: Armand Colin, 1, 1959, 45-47.  Bergson's reticence and use of metaphor make interpretation of his text a delicate matter.  A case in point is the term "nature" in Les Deux Sources, which Burgelin attempts to define.

983    BURGELIN, Pierre.  "Table ronde: Morale."  Actes du Xe Congrès des Sociétés de Philosophie de Langue Française (Congrès Bergson).  Paris: Armand Colin, 2, 1959, 237-257.

984    BURGERS, Antoon.  "De houding van Bergson en Merleau-Ponty t.o.v. de wetenschappen."  Tijdschrift voor Filosofie, 27, No. 2, June 1965, 262-297.

985    BURKILL, T. A.  "L'Attitude subjectiviste et ses dangers de Descartes à Bergson."  Revue Philosophique de la France et de l'Etranger, 149, No. 3, 1959, 325-337.  The author argues that Bergson's reduction of all reality to pure duration seems as arbitrary as Descartes' logico-mathematical cosmology.

986    BURKILL, T. A.  "Henri Bergson."  Nature, 147, 8 February 1941, 168-169.  This is an obituary notice.

987    BURLOUD, Albert.  De La Psychologie à la philosophie.  Paris: Hachette, 1950, 238.  Bergson and psychological method are discussed on pages 26-30; "durée" on pages 79-89; instinct on pages 92-93; biology on pages 104-107.  See also pages 118, 135, 203, and 205.

988     BURNET, Etienne. <u>Essences</u>. Paris: Seheur, 1929, 252.
        Bergson and Proust are discussed on pages 165-252.

989     BURNS, Cecil Delisle. "Bergson: A Criticism of his Philoso-
        phy." <u>North American Review</u>, 197, No. 688, March 1913,
        364-370. The author proposes various criticisms of "in-
        tuition."

990     BURROUGHS, John. "A Prophet of the Soul." <u>Atlantic Month-
        ly</u>, 113, No. 1, January 1913, 120-132.

991     BURROUGHS, John. "Sundown Papers." <u>Last Harvest</u>. New York:
        Houghton Mifflin, 1922, 264-288.

992     BURY, R. de. "Les Confidences de M. Bergson avec M. Gremil."
        <u>Mercure de France</u>, 108, 15 mars 1914, 397-398.

993     BURZIO, Filippo. "Bergson e il problema della natura."
        <u>Agorã</u>, Anno 2, No. 8, 1947.

994     BURZIO, Filippo. "Cinque maestri." <u>Ritratti</u>. Torino:
        Ribet, 1929.

995     BUSCH, Joseph F. <u>Bergson of Betoomd élan rhythme de schep-
        ping</u>. Amsterdam: Bech, 1939, 255.

996     BUSCH, Joseph F. "Einstein et Bergson, convergence et di-
        vergence de leurs idées." <u>Proceedings of the Tenth Inter-
        national Congress of Philosophy</u>. Amsterdam: North-Holland
        Publishing Co., 1959, 872-875. This article is translated,
        with introduction, in <u>Bergson and the Evolution of Physics</u>,
        Ed. P. A. Y. Gunter, 208-214.

997     BUSCH, Joseph F. "Het gouden jaar van Bergson." <u>Synthèse</u>,
        4, No. 1, 1939, 42-51.

998     BUSH, W. T. "The Bergson Lectures." <u>Columbia University
        Quarterly</u>, 15, No. 3, June 1913  254-257.

999     BUSSY, Gertrude Carman. "Typical Recent Conceptions of Free-
        dom." Diss., Northwestern, 1917.

1000    BUSTOS-FIERRO, Raul. "Spencer en Bergson." <u>Homenaje a Berg-
        son</u>. Córdoba, Argentina: Imprenta de la Universidad, 1936,
        97-122.

1001    BUTTY, Enrique. "La duración de Bergson y el tiempo de Ein-
        stein." <u>Cursos y Conferencias</u>, Año 5, No. 5, agosto 1936,

449-489; No. 7, octubre 1936, 681-706; No. 8, noviembre
1936, 825-845; No. 10, enero 1937, 1020-1052; No. 11, febrero 1937, 1203-1228; No. 12, marzo 1927, 1327-1362.
This examination of the relations between Einstein's and
Bergson's concepts of time consists of seven chapters,
entitled: 1. Objectividad scientifica; 2. Movimiento, espa-
cio y tiempo; 3. Duración y tiempo; 4. El tiempo físico;
5. El tiempo de la teoría de la relatividad; 6. Los tiem-
pos multiples de Einstein y el tiempo universal; 7. El
universo de Minkowski y la duración universal.

1002    C., E. G.   "Review of Bergson e São Tomaz o conflicto entre
a intuição e a inteligencia by Sebastian Tauzan."
Sapientia, 1, No. 3, enero-marzo 1947, 93-96.

1003    C., J.   "Collège de France: Cours de M. Bergson sur l'idée
de cause." Revue de Philosophie, 1, No. 3, avril 1901,
358-388.

1004    C., M. F.   "Review of Les Deux Sources de la morale et de la
religion by Henri Bergson." Rivista di psicologia, 28,
1932, 347.

1005    CADIN, Francesco.   "Heidsieck e la dottrina bergsoniana
dello spazio." Rivista di filosofia neoscolastica, 51,
Nos. 5-6, 1959, 529-534.

1006    CAHUET, Albéric.   "Ceux qui auront connu trois guerres:   Les
Récents Octogénaires de l'Académie." Illustration, 97,
No. 5046, 18 novembre 1939, 308.

1007    CAIN, Julien.   "Bergson président de la Commission internationale de coopération intellectuelle." American Philosophical Society Proceedings, N.S. 104, No. 4, August 1960,
404-407.

1008    CAIRNS, Dorion.   "Bergson and Vichy: Reply with Rejoinder."
Nation, 152, No. 13, 29 March 1931, 391-392.   This article
concerns the treatment of Husserl by the Germans and of
Bergson by the Vichy French.

1009    CAIROLA, Giuseppi.   "Bergson e Spinoza." Rivista di filosofia, 40, No. 4, 1949, 406-418.   This article is republished in Scritti, Torino, 1954, 67-82.

1010    CALCAGNO, Alberto.   "Henri Bergson e la cultura contemporaneo." Rivista filosofica, 4, No. 4, luglio-ottobre 1912,
407-431.   This article maintains that the paradoxical suc-

cess of Bergson's philosophy is due to its apparent success in providing a new synthesis of nature and spirit, so
long and so unhappily separated since their union in Creek
thought.

1011    CALDERON, Francisco García.  "Bergson: Crítico de la civi-
lización occidental."  La Nación, 19 novembre 1939, Sec.
II, 1, Col, 1.

1012    CALDERON, Francisco García.  "Dos filósofos franceses: Bergson y Boutroux."  El Comercio, 5 mayo 1907.

1013    CALDERON, Francisco García.  "El filósofo francés: Henri
bergson."  Universidad, 2, No. 9, 1936, 4-5.

1014    CALDERON, Francisco García.  "Los proyectos de un filósofo."
La Nación, 1921.

1015    CALDWELL, Dr. William.  Pragmatism and Idealism.  London:
A. and C. Black, 1913, 268.  Chapter 9 is entitled "Pragmatism and Idealism in the Philosophy of Bergson" and appears on pages 234-261.

1016    CALIFANO, Joseph J.  "Bergson's Concept of Motion."  Thomist,
34, No. 4, 1970, 555-567.  The author argues that Bergson's concept of motion is distinct from his concept of
duration and close to that of Aquinas.

1017    CALKINS, Mary Whiton.  "Henri Bergson: Personalist."  Philosophical Review, 21, No. 6, November 1912, 666-675.  The
author protests against the "abstractness" of many evalua-
tions of Bergson.

1018    CALKINS, Mary Whiton.  The Persistent Problems of Philosophy:
An Introduction to Metaphysics Through the Study of Modern
Systems.  New York: Macmillan, 1925, 601.  Bergson is dis-
cussed on pages 437-441.

1019    CALLOT, Emile.  "Review of La Dialectique de la durée by G.
Bachelard."  Revue de Philosophie, 37, No. 2, 1937, 164-
170.  This is a review article.  The author explains that
the originality of Bachelard's thought can be seen by com-
paring it with Bergson's.  For Bergson duration is continuous.  For Bachelard, duration (conceived as a dialectic
between being and non-being) has basic discontinuities.

1020    CALLOT, Emile.  Von Montaigne zu Sartre.  Meisenheim und
Wien: Westkulturverlag Von Hain, 1953, 206.

1021 CALO, Giovanni. Il problema delle libertà nel pensiero contemporaneo. Milano: Sandron, 1907, 228.

1022 CAMBON, G. "L'ombra di Bergson e la letteratura contemporanea." L'ultima, Anno 5, maggio-giugno 1950.

1023 CAMILUCCI, Marcello. "La madre di Bergson." L'osservatore
romano, 28 settèmbre 1960.

1024 CAMINOS, Irene Enriqueta. "La libertad como problema psico-
lógico: Bergson y Santo Tomás." Actas del Primer Congreso Argentino de Psicologia, 1, 1955, 177-184.

1025 CAMON AZNAR, José. La idea del tiempo en Bergson y el im-
presionismo: Contestación de S. Zuazo Ugalde. Madrid:
Aguirre, 1956, 69.

1026 CAMPANALE, Domenico. "Scienza e metafisica nel pensiero di
H. Bergson." Problemi epistemologici da Hume all'ultimo
Wittgenstein. Bari: Adriatica Editrice, 1961, 424. Berg-
son is discussed on pages 156-198.

1027 CAMPANALE, Domenico. "Scienza e metafisica nel pensiero di
Henri Bergson." Rassegna di scienze filosofiche, 7. No.
2, 1964, 137-167; Nos. 3-4, 1964, 306-333.

1028 CAMPBELL, Clarence A. "Bergson's Doctrine of Freedom."
Diss., Washington (St. Louis), 1926.

1029 CAMPBELL, Clarence A. "Review of The Two Sources of Morality and Religion by Henri Bergson." Philosophy, 11, No.
41, January 1936, 98-102. This is a critical, balanced
review.

1030 CANGUILHEM, Georges. "Commentaire au 3e chapitre de L'Evolution créatrice." Bulletin de la Faculté des Lettres de
Strasbourg, 1943, 126-143, 199-214, "et à suivre." This
is an excellent, very careful analysis of the third chapter of Creative Evolution, relating Bergson's thought to
recent biology.

1031 CANGUILHEM, Georges. "Le Concept et la vie." Revue Philosophique de Louvain, 64, T.S. No. 82, mai 1966, 193-223.

1032 CANIVEZ, André. "Bergson et Lagneau." Actes du Xe Congrès
des Sociétés de Philosophie de Langue Française (Congrès
Bergson). Paris: Armand Colin, 1, 1959, 49-52. The author stresses both the points of contact and the differ-

ences between Bergson and Lagneau.  Neither proposed doctrines.  Each proposed a kind of difficult philosophical
life, Lagneau with rudeness, Bergson with art and finesse.

1033   CANIVEZ, André.  "Table ronde: Unité, unicité, dialogue."
       Actes du Xe Congrès des Sociétés de Philosophie de Langue
       Française (Congrès Bergson).  Paris: Armand Colin, 2,
       1959, 281-302.

1034   CANNABRAVA, Euryalo.  Descartes e Bergson.  São Paulo:
       Eidôra Amigosdo Livra, 1942, 208.

1035   CANTECOR, G.  "La Philosophie nouvelle et la vie de l'es-
       prit."  Revue Philosophique de la France et de l'Etranger,
       55, No. 3, mars 1903, 252-277.  This article is a criti-
       que of Bergson from a Kantian viewpoint.

1036   CANTIN, Stanislas.  "H. Bergson et le problème de la liber-
       té."  Laval Théologique et Philosophique, 10, No. 1, 1945,
       71-102.

1037   CANTIN, Stanislas.  "Henri Bergson et le problème de la li-
       berté."  Diss., Laval, 1949, 102.

1038   CAPEK, Milič.  "Review of Bergson and the Evolution of Phys-
       ics, Ed. and Trans. with Intro. P. A. Y. Gunter."  Process
       Studies, 2, No. 2, Summer 1972, 149-159.

1039   CAPEK, Milič.  Bergson and Modern Physics.  New York: Human-
       ities Press; Dordrecht, Holland: Reidel Publishing Company,
       1971, 414  (Vol. 7, Boston Studies in the Philosophy of
       Science, Synthese Library).  This is an excellent analysis
       of Bergson's insights into the problems and basic concepts
       of contemporary physics.

1040   CAPEK, Milič.  Bergson a tendance současné fysiki.  Prague:
       Facultas Philosophica Universitates Carolinae pragensis,
       1937-1938, 160 (Práce z vědeckých ustavů, No. 47).  This
       is a dissertation.  The author argues that Bergson's
       thought coincides with the tendencies of modern physics.

1041   CAPEK, Milič.  "Bergson et l'esprit de la physique contem-
       poraine."  Actes du Xe Congrès des Sociétés de Philosophie
       de Langue Française (Congrès Bergson).  Paris: Armand
       Colin, 1, 1959, 53-56.

1042   CAPEK, Milič.  "La Genèse idéal de la matière chez Bergson;
       la structure de la durée."  Revue de Métaphysique et de

Morale, 57, No. 3, 1952, 325-348.  This is an account of
Bergson's philosophical cosmogony.

1043    CAPEK, Milič.  The Philosophical Impact of Contemporary
        Physics.  New York: Van Nostrand Company, Inc., 1961, 414.
        Bergson and modern physics are discussed on the following
        pages:  13-16; 51; 56; 115; 120; 126-133; 140; 154; 157;
        160-161; 163; 173; 180; 186; 194-200; 202-205; 207-209;
        213; 220; 241; 271; 271-273; 275; 286; 287-288; 316; 331;
        337; 339; 340; 350; 357-358; 368-369; 372; 374; 388; 391;
        395.

1044    CAPEK, Milič.  "Process and Personality in Bergson's
        Thought."  Philosophical Forum, 18, 1959-1960, 25-42.
        "If the dynamic and incomplete universe is the only place
        in which human action can be meaningfully called 'action,'
        then certain polarity within the universe is necessary to
        save ethical judgments from becoming inconsequential emo-
        tive reactions."  (41-42).  The author argues that Berg-
        son's philosophy provides a framework in which moral judg-
        ments and moral action have meaning.

1045    CAPEK, Milič.  "La Signification actuelle de la philosophie
        de James."  Revue de Métaphysique et de Morale, 67, No. 3,
        1962, 291-321.  Section V of this article is entitled
        "James et Bergson: Les Influences réciproques," 308-315.

1046    CAPEK, Milič.  "Stream of Consciousness and 'durée réelle'."
        Philosophy and Phenomenological Research, 20, No. 3, March
        1950, 331-353.  The author provides a very clear and very
        perceptive analysis of the similarities and differences
        between Bergson and William James.

1047    CAPEK, Milič.  "Table ronde: Physique."  Actes du Xe Congrès
        des Sociétés de Philosophie de Langue Française (Congrès
        Bergson).  Paris: Armand Colin, 2, 1959, 65-87.

1048    CAPEK, Milič.  "La Théorie bergsonienne de la matière et la
        physique moderne."  Revue Philosophique de la France et de
        l'Etranger, 143, Nos. 1-3, janvier-mars 1953, 28-59.  This
        article is translated, with an introduction, in Bergson
        and the Evolution of Physics, Ed. P. A. Y. Gunter, 297-
        330.  It is the best short general survey of Bergson's
        philosophy of physics and its contemporary significance.

1049    CAPEK, Milič.  "La Théorie biologique de la connaissance
        chez Bergson et sa signification actuelle."  Revue de Méta-
        physique et de Morale, 64, No. 2, 1959, 194-211.

1050    CAPEK, Milic.  "Time and Eternity in Royce and Bergson."
        Revue Internationale de Philosophie, 79-80, Nos. 1-2,
        1967, 22-45.  Royce's ultimate failure to "take time seri-
        ously" and his abortive attempts to do so are discussed
        in this article, which includes many comparisons of Royce
        and Bergson.

1051    CAPPELLAZZI, A.  "Il pensiero filosofico e la filosofia di
        Bergson."  Scuola cattolica, 2 Ser., 5, No. 6, 1914.

1052    CARAMELLA, Santino.  Enrico Bergson.  Milano: Athena, 1925,
        112.

1053    CARBONARA, Cleto.  Morale e religione nella filosofia de En-
        rico Bergson.  Napoli: Perella, 1934, 69.

1054    CARBONARA, Cleto.  "Morale e religione nella filosofia di H.
        Bergson."  Logos, 16, Nos. 2, 3, e 4, 1933.  This is a
        review article concerning Les Deux Sources.

1055    CARBONARA, Cleto.  Pensatori moderni: L. Brunschvicg, H.
        Bergson, B. Croce, A. Aliotta.  Napoli: Libreria Scien-
        tifica Editrice, 1972, 290.  Bergson's philosophy of re-
        ligion is discussed on pages 121-210.

1056    CARDONE, Domenico Antonio.  "Ce que je dois à Bergson."
        Actes du Xe Congrès des Sociétés de Philosophie de Langue
        Française (Congrès Bergson).  Paris: Armand Colin, 1, 1959,
        57-58.  The encounter with Bergson's thought revealed to
        Cardone the means of attaining the absolute.  Cardone
        claims that man can become the God of our planet in real-
        izing a community of love and through this community at-
        tain the secret reason of creative evolution.

1057    CARDONE, Domenico Antonio.  "Il concetto della natura ed il
        valore dell'umanità nella filosofia de H. Bergson."  Rivis-
        ta internazionale de filosofia del diritto, 10, No. 2,
        1930.

1058    CARDONE, Domenico Antonio.  "La disindividualizzione nella
        cultura moderna e il problema della civiltà morale, alla
        memoria de H. Bergson."  Richerche filosofiche, 5, No. 1,
        1951, 4-15.

1059    CARDONE, Domenico Antonio.  "Tempo obbietivo e tempo unico
        nella filosofia di H. Bergson."  Logos, 17, No. 1, 1934,
        1-16.  The author compares Bergson's position with Kant's.

1060    CARLILE, William W.  "Perception and Intersubjective Inter-
        course."  Mind, 21, No. 84, October 1912, 508-521.  On
        page 513 the author discusses James Ward's views with
        reference to Bergson.

1061    CARLINE, Armando.  La vita dello spirito.  Florence: Valec-
        chi, 1921, 225.  This study deals with Bergson, Blondel,
        Croce, and Gentile.

1062    CARNUS, J.  "The Rise of French Personalism."  Personalist,
        34, No. 3, 1953, 261-268.  This article discusses the re-
        lations between Bergson, Maine de Biran, and personalism.

1063    CARR, Herbert Wildon.  "Review of Bergson for Beginners by
        Darcy B. Kitchen."  Mind, 23, No. 92, October 1914, 612-
        163.

1064    CARR, Herbert Wildon.  "Review of Le Bergsonisme by Albert
        Thibaudet."  Mind, 33, No. 131, July 1924, 332-334.  This
        review contains an interesting mention of Bergson's philo-
        sophical endeavors circa 1924.  Otherwise it is a humdrum
        review.

1065    CARR, Herbert Wildon.  "Review of Henri Bergson: An Account
        of his Life and Philosophy by Algot Ruhe and Nancy Mar-
        garet Paul."  Mind, 24, No. 93, January 1915, 117-119.

1066    CARR, Herbert Wildon.  Henri Bergson: The Philosophy of
        Change.  Port Washington, New York: Kennikat, 1970, 91.

1067    CARR, Herbert Wildon.  "Bergson's Theory of Instinct."  Pro-
        ceedings of the Artistotelian Society, N.S. 10, 1909-10,
        93-114.  This article is an account of Bergson's theory
        of instinct.  The author attempts to meet specific objec-
        tions to Bergson's theory on pages 111-114.

1068    CARR, Herbert Wildon.  "Bergson's Theory of Knowledge."
        Proceedings of the Aristotelian Society, N.S. 9, 1908-
        09, 41-60.  This study is an account of Bergson's episte-
        mology as developed in L'Evolution créatrice.  It also
        contains a reply by Bergson to criticisms of the work.

1069    CARR, Herbert Wildon.  "Bergson's Theory of Memory."  Athe-
        naeum, No. 4567, 8 May 1915, 427-429; No. 4568, 15 May
        1915, 448-450.  This article is a report of a lecture
        given by the author at King's College, London, on 5 May
        1915.

1070    CARR, Herbert Wildon. Changing Backgrounds in Religion and
        Ethics. London: Macmillan and Co., Ltd., 1927, 224. Carr
        attempts to build a religious and ethical philosophy on
        the foundation of Bergsonian evolutionism.

1071    CARR, Herbert Wildon. "The Concept of Mind Energy." Mind,
        29, No. 113, 1920, 1-10. The author presents a rather
        windy exposition of Bergson's Mind-Energy.

1072    CARR, Herbert Wildon. "Review of The Ethical Implications
        of Bergson's Philosophy by Una Bernard Sait." Mind, 24,
        No. 93, January 1915, 119-120.

1073    CARR, Herbert Wildon. The General Principle of Relativity.
        London: Macmillan and Co., Ltd., 1920. The author dis-
        cusses Bergson's and Russell's concepts of motion and con-
        tinuity on pages 34-39.

1074    CARR, Herbert Wildon. "L'Interaction de l'esprit et du
        corps." Revue de Métaphysique et de Morale, 25, No. 1,
        janvier 1918, 25-59.

1075    CARR, Herbert Wildon. "Life and Logic." Mind, 22, No. 88,
        October 1913, 484-492. This is a defense of Bosanquet's
        criticisms of Bergson in The Principle of Individuality
        and Value.

1076    CARR, Herbert Wildon. "Life and Matter." Personalist, 8,
        No. 1, January 1927, 5-24.

1077    CARR, Herbert Wildon. "Review of Modern Science and the Il-
        lusions of Professor Bergson by Hugh S. R. Elliot." Mind,
        21, No. 84, October 1912, 579-581. The author is highly
        critical of Elliot's criticisms of Bergson.

1078    CARR, Herbert Wildon. "Review of Nella intelligenza
        dell'espressione by Leone Vivante." Mind, 32, No. 125,
        January 1923, 367. In this review Vivante's and Bergson's
        concepts of memory are discussed.

1079    CARR, Herbert Wildon. "The Philosophical Aspects of Freud's
        Theory of Dream Interpretation." Mind, 23, No. 91, July
        1914, 321-334. A comparison of Bergson's and Freud's con-
        cepts of dreams is made on pages 324-325.

1080    CARR, Herbert Wildon. "The Philosophy of Bergson." Hibbert
        Journal, 9, Part 2, July 1910, 873-883.

1081    CARR, Herbert Wildon.  "Review of The Philosophy of Bergson
        by A. D. Lindsay."  Mind, 20, No. 80, October 1911, 560-
        566.

1082    CARR, Herbert Wildon.  The Philosophy of Change: A Study of
        the Fundamental Principles of the Philosophy of Bergson.
        London: Macmillan and Co., Ltd., 1941, 216.

1083    CARR, Herbert Wildon.  "Review of Pragmatism and Idealism
        by William Caldwell."  Mind, 23, No. 90, April 1914, 268-
        271.  Bergson and pragmatism are discussed on pages 270-
        271.

1084    CARR, Herbert Wildon.  "The Problem of Simultaneity."  Pro-
        ceedings of the Aristotelian Society, Supplementary Vol-
        ume, 2, 1923, 15-25.  The author is in essential agreement
        with Bergson's position in Duration and Simultaneity.

1085    CARR, Herbert Wildon.  The Problem of Truth.  London and
        Edinburgh: T. C. and E. C. Jack, 1913, 93.  Chapter seven
        is on Bergson and Croce.

1086    CARR, Herbert Wildon.  "Reply to Bertrand Russell."  Ber-
        trand Russell.  The Philosophy of Bergson.  Cambridge:
        Bowes and Bowes, 1914, 36.

1087    CARR, Herbert Wildon.  The Scientific Approach to Philosophy.
        London: Macmillan and Co., Ltd., 1924, 278.

1088    CARR, Herbert Wildon.  "The Theory of Psycho-physical Paral-
        lelism as a Working Hypothesis in Psychology."  Proceed-
        ings of the Aristotelian Society, N.S. 11, 1910-11, 129-
        143.  This is a criticism of the theory of mind-body paral-
        lism based on Bergson's "Le Paralogisme psychophysiologi-
        que."

1089    CARR, Herbert Wildon.  "Time" and "History" in Contemporary
        Philosophy: With Special Reference to Bergson and Croce.
        London: Milford, Oxford University Press, 1918, 19 (Pro-
        ceedings of the British Academy, VIII, 20 March 1918).
        The author claims that from different standpoints Berg-
        son and Croce reach a closely similar dynamic conception
        of reality.

1090    CARR, Herbert Wildon.  "What Does Bergson Mean by Pure Per-
        ception?"  Mind, 28, No. 108, October 1918, 472-474.  The
        author replies to an earlier discussion of the same topic
        by Mr. Harward.

1091    CARR, Herbert Wildon.  "What Does Bergson Mean by Pure Per-
        ception?"  Mind, 26, No. 113, January 1920, 123.  This is
        a further reply to Mr. Harward.

1092    CARRASQUILLA, Tomas.  "Punctos de vista: Bergson."  Atenea,
        Año 18, No. 187, enero 1941, 1-3.

1093    CARUS, Paul.  "The Anti-intellectual Movement of Today."
        Monist, 22, No. 3, July 1912, 397-404.

1094    CASARES, Carlos Alberto.  Leyendo a Bergson: Al margen del
        libro Les Deux Sources de la morale et de la religion.
        Buenos Aires: Imprenta Amorrortu, 1933, 53.

1095    CASARES, Tomás D.  "Bergson."  Criterio, 1, No. 39, 29 no-
        viembre 1928, 268-269.

1096    CASAS, M.  "Bergson y el sentido de su influencia en Améri-
        ca."  Humanitas, 8, No. 12, 1959, 95-108.

1097    CASAUBON, Juan A.  Aspectos del bergsonismo.  Buenos Aires,
        1946.

1098    CASO, Antonio.  Filosofiá de la intuición.  México: The Au-
        thor, 1914, 11.

1099    CASO, Antonio.  Filosofiá francesa contemporánea.  México,
        1917.

1100    CASO, Antonio.  Problemas filosóficos.  México: Porrúa her-
        manos, 1915, 296.  The chapter in this work entitled "La
        filosofía de la intuición" concerns Bergson's philosophy.

1101    CASSIRER, Ernst.  "Henri Bergsons etik och religionsfilo-
        sofi."  Judisk Tidskrift, 14, No. 1, 1941, 13-18.

1102    CASSIRER, Ernst.  An Essay on Man.  New Haven, Connecticut:
        Yale University Press, 1944, 237.  Bergson is discussed
        on pages 88, 89ff, 102ff, and 107.

1103    CASTELLANI, Leonardo.  "Bergson."  Humanidades (Salta), Año
        3, No. 7.  Though at least four journals entitled Humani-
        dades have been published in this century, I have been
        unable to locate one published at Salta.  It has, there-
        fore, been impossible to find further information on this
        item.

1104    CASTELLANI, Leopoldo.  "Henri Bergson frente a Kant y Santo
        Tomás."  Tribuna Católica, 7, No. 2, 1921, 190-204.

1105    CASTELLANO, Torres F.  "La crisis del idealismo."  Criterio, 7, No. 324, 17 mayo 1934, 60.

1106    CASTRO, Antonio.  Algunas anotaciones a la logica viva. Montevideo, 1914.  The author develops Thomist criticisms of Bergson and Vas Ferreyra.

1107    CATEL, Paola.  Péguy e Bergson.  Saggio: Casale Monferrato, 1935, 8.

1108    CATHERIN-NOLLACE, Jeanne.  Le Cinéisme.  Paris: Edit. Universitaires, 1964, 203.

1109    CATTAUI, Georges.  "Bergson, Kierkegaard and Mysticism." Trans. A. Dru.  Dublin Review, 192, No. 1, January 1933, 70-78.

1110    CATTAUI, Georges.  "Ce Bergson qui fut des nôtres."  Journal de Genève , 26-27 février 1966.

1111    CATTAUI, Georges.  "Henri Bergson: His Work and Influence." Colosseum, 3, No. 4, December 1936, 272-286.

1112    CATTAUI, Georges.  Marcel Proust.  Paris: Juliard, 1952, 287.  Bergson and Proust are discussed on pages 48, 127, 137, 170, 181-182, 188, 205, 207-208, 221, 258, and 259.

1113    CATTAUI, Georges.  "Témoignage."  Henri Bergson.  Ed. Béguin and Thévenaz, 120-131.  The author gives an account of talks with Bergson from 1932-1938, concerning such topics as Charles Péguy, Jacques Maritain, Marcel Proust, Hyppolite Taine, Christianity, and the future of Europe.

1114    CATTAUI, Georges and MADAULE, Jacques, Eds.  Entretiens sur Paul Claudel.  Paris and La Haye: Mouton, 1968, 333.

1115    CAVADI, Rosa.  "L'apprendimento genuino del tempo nella metafisica de H. Bergson."  Teoresi, 21, No. 1, 1966, 45-96.

1116    CAVAGNA, Giordano Bruno.  La dottrina conoscenza in Enrico Bergson.  Napoli: Instituto Edit. del Mezzogiorno, 1966, 317.

1117 CAVARNOS, Constantine.  A Dialogue Between Bergson, Aristotle and Philologus.  Cambridge, Massachusetts: The Author, 1950, 60.  Perennial problems of change, knowledge and the structure of reality are approached in this book at an introductory level.

1118   CAZAMIAN, Louis. "Bergson on Ethics and Religion." Univer-
       sity of Toronto Quarterly, 4, No. 2, January 1935, 139-157.
       Cazamian gives a general account of Les Deux Sources.

1119   CELIDE, G. "Philosophe à la mode." Gazette de France, ler
       février 1914.

1120   CELIDE, G. "Le Sorcier d'Israël." Gazette de France, 22
       février 1914.

1121   CELTUS. "Bergson et la politesse." Le Figaro, 117, No. 46,
       24 février 1942, 1.

1122   CEPEDA I, Manuel Eduardo. "La teoriá filosófica de Bergson."
       Annales Universidad Central del Ecuador, 83, No. 338,
       1954, 65-73.

1123   CERESOLE, P. "Le Parallélisme psycho-physiologique et l'ar-
       gument de M. Bergson." Archives de Psychologie, 5, No. 2,
       1906, 112-120. The author holds that to refute parallel-
       ism by Bergson's argument one must show that as a matter
       of fact the external world may be modified without modi-
       fication of the nervous system.

1124   CERIANI, Grazioso. "Enrico Bergson." Civiltà cattolica,
       92, No. 2, 1941, 113-126.

1125   CERIANI, Grazioso. "Henri Bergson (+ 1941)." Scuola ca-
       tolica, 69, No. 2, 1941, 112-126; No. 3, 243-259. This
       is an obituary notice.

1126   CESSELIN, Félix. La Philosophie organique de Whitehead.
       Paris: Presses Universitaires de France, 1950, 248. Berg-
       son's and Whitehead's similarities are discussed on pages
       64-65, 88-89, 104-105, 128-129, 172-173, 178-179, 200-201,
       204, and 205.

1127   CHAHINE, Osman Eissa. "La Durée créatrice dans la philoso-
       phie de Bergson." Diss., Paris, 1956, 190.

1128   CHAIX-RUY, Jules. "Bergson parvient-il à éliminer toute
       réference au néant?" Actes du Xe Congrès des Sociétés
       de Philosophie de Langue Française (Congrès Bergson).
       Paris: Armand Colin, 1, 1959, 59-62. Bergson's critique
       of the idea of nothing seems decisive. But has Bergson
       completely exorcized this concept? Can it be eliminated
       by philosophical reflection? The author ponders these
       questions.

1129    CHAIX-RUY, Jules.  "L'Exigence morale dans la philosophie
        d'Henri Bergson."  Giornale di metafisica, 14, No. 6,
        1959, 766-783.  An increasing moral exigency constitutes,
        the author holds, one of the most marked traits of Berg-
        son's thought.  At the level of human history, Bergson
        teaches in The Two Sources that we assist in an evolution
        of the law which culminates in Christian morality, the
        most open morality in existence.

1130    CHAIX-RUY, Jules.  "I molteplici orientamenti della filo-
        sofia bergsoniana."  Humanitas, 14, No. 11, 1959, 800-
        821.

1131    CHAIX-RUY, Jules.  El superhombre: De Nietzsche a Teilhard
        de Chardin.  Trans. D. R. Duch.  Salamanca: Ed. Sígueme,
        1968, 311.

1132    CHAIX-RUY, Jules.  The Superman: From Nietzsche to Teilhard
        de Chardin.  Notre Dame and London: University of Notre
        Dame Press, 1969, 229.

1133    CHAIX-RUY, Jules.  Le Surhomme: De Nietzsche à Teilhard de
        Chardin.  Paris: Éditions du Centurion, 1965, 349.

1134    CHAIX-RUY, Jules.  "Table ronde: Néant et existentialisme."
        Actes du Xe Congrès des Sociétés de Philosophie de Langue
        Française (Congrès Bergson).  Paris: Armand Colin, 2, 1959,
        145-164.

1135    CHAIX-RUY, Jules.  "Vitalité et élan vital: Bergson et
        Croce."  Etudes Bergsoniennes, 5, 1960, 143-167.

1136    CHALLAYE, Félicien.  Bergson.  Paris: Mellottée, 1929.

1137    CHALLAYE, Félicien.  "Bergson vu par les Soviets."  Preuves,
        4, No. 44, octobre 1954, 62-63.

1138    CHALLAYE, Félicien.  "Immortalité et existentialisme."  Syn-
        thèses, No. 128, janvier 1957, 286-296.

1139    CHALLAYE, Félicien.  Metodologiá de las ciencias.  Barcelona:
        Ed. Labor, 1935, 220.  Bergson's views are discussed on
        pages 148, 166, and 203.

1140    CHALLAYE, Félicien.  Philosophie scientifique et philosophie
        morale.  Paris: Nathan, 1923, 652.

1141    CHALLAYE, Félicien.  Psychologie et métaphysique.  Paris:
        Nathan, 1925, 766.

1142    CHALLAYE, Félicien.  "Le Syndicalisme révolutionnaire."
        Revue de Métaphysique et de Morale, 15, No. 1, janvier
        1907, 103-127; No. 2, mars 1907, 256-272.

1143    CHALLAYE, Félicien.  Syndicalisme révolutionnaire et syndi-
        calisme réformiste.  Paris: Félix Alcan, 1909, 156.

1144    CHAMBERS, Connor J.  "Henri Bergson, Zenon, y la disensión
        académica."  Diálogos, 7, No. 4, 1971, 17-38.

1145    CHAMPIGNY, Robert.  "Position philosophique de la liberté."
        Revue de Métaphysique et de Morale, 64, No. 2, 1959, 225-
        235.  Bergson, Ruyer, and Sartre are compared.

1146    CHAMPIGNY, Robert.  "Proust, Bergson and Other Philosophers."
        Proust: A Collection of Critical Essays.  Ed. René Girard.
        New Jersey: Prentice-Hall, Inc., 1962, 122-131.  This was
        published originally as "Temps et reconnaissance chez
        Proust et quelques philosophes," PMLA, 1958.

1147    CHAMPIGNY, Robert.  "Temps et reconnaissance chez Proust et
        quelques philosophes."  Publications of the Modern Lan-
        guage Association of America, 73, No. 1, March 1958, 129-
        135.  According to the author Proust differed with Berg-
        son over many significant poins.

1148    CHANDLER, A.  "M. Bergson's 'Two Sources'."  Theology, 30,
        No. 3, March 1935, 136-146.

1149    CHANYSHEV, A. N. Философия Анри Бергсона. Москва:
        Издательство Московского университета, 1960, 54.
        (Pamphlet).

1150    CHAPELAN, Maurice.  "Le Fonds Bergson à la bibliothèque
        Doucet."  Le Figaro Littéraire, 19, No. 945, 28 mai 1964,
        10.  This concerns the creation of a Bergson library in
        Paris.

1151    CHAPPELL, Vere C.  "Time and Zeno's Arrow."  Journal of Phi-
        losophy, 59, No. 8, 12 April 1962, 197-213.  This article
        is republished, with an introduction, in Bergson and the
        Evolution of Physics, Ed. P. A. Y. Gunter, 253-274.  The
        author argues that reductio ad absurdam disproofs of
        Zeno's arguments cannot be used to establish any concept
        of time, Bergson's included.

1152    CHARLIER.  "Compte rendu de l'intellectualisme de L. Husson."
        L'Education Nationale, 2, No. 5, 29 janvier 1948, 14.
        This is a brief review.

1153    CHARPENTIER, Jacques.  "Henri Bergson."  Mercure de France,
        229, 15 juillet 1931, 369-372.

1154    CHARTIER, E.  "Discussion de Bergson's 'paralogism psycho-
        physiologique'."  Revue de Métaphysique et de Morale, 12,
        No. 6, 1904, 1027-1037.

1155    CHATTELUN, Maurice.  "De L'Expérience musicale à l'essen-
        tialisme bergsonien."  Actes du Xe Congres des Sociétés de
        Philosophie de Langue Française (Congrès Bergson).  Paris:
        Armand Colin, 1, 1959, 63-66.  The author evokes Bergso-
        nian views which a musician could be led to consider
        through examining the relations of these views to music.

1156    CHATTELUN, Maurice.  "Table ronde: Esthétique."  Actes du Xe
        Congrès des Sociétés de Philosophie de Langue Française
        (Congrès Bergson).  Paris: Armand Colin, 2, 1959, 193-210.

1157    CHAUCHARD, Paul.  "Evolution matérialiste et fixisme onto-
        logique dans la création évolutive."  Actes du Xe Congrès
        des Sociétés de Philosophie de Langue Française (Congrès
        Bergson).  Paris: Armand Colin, 1, 1959, 67-70.  If, on
        the scientific level, one cannot be a "fixiste" in the
        classical sense of the word, the author holds, at the lev-
        el of philosophy the fact of evolution agrees equally well
        with either an evolutionary explanation or a certain
        "fixiste" thesis.  Until Bergson, evolution appeared a
        purely mechanistic concept.

1158    CHAUCHARD, Paul.  "Table ronde: Vie et évolution."  Actes du
        Xe Congrès des Sociétés de Philosophie de Langue Française
        (Congrès Bergson).  Paris: Armand Colin, 2, 1969, 91-117.

1159    CHAUMEIX, André.  "Henri Bergson."  Revue des Deux Mondes,
        111, 8e période, No. 61, 1er février 1941, 345-355.  This
        essay is a tribute to Bergson written soon after his death.

1160    CHAUMEIX, André.  "Les Critiques du rationalisme: A Propos
        des idées de M. Bergson et M. William James."  Revue Heb-
        domadaire, 19e Année, No. 1, 1er janvier 1910, 1-33.

1161    CHAUMEIX, André.  "Hommage à Bergson."  Revue des Deux Mon-
        des, N.S. 2, No. 10, 15 mai 1949, 371-375.

1162    CHAUMEIX, André.  "La Philosophie de M. Bergson."  Journal
        des Débats, 24 mai 1908, 1027-1032.  This article is re-
        printed in Pragmatisme et modernisme.  Ed. J. Bourdeau.
        Paris: Félix Alcan, 221-236.

1163   CHAUMEIX, André. "Le Souvenir d'Henri Bergson." Candide,
       27, No. 2, 15 janvier 1941.

1164   CHAUMEIX, André and LE ROY, Edouard. Séance de l'Académie
       française du 18 octobre 1945: Discours de réception de M.
       Edouard Le Roy: Réponse de M. André Chaumeix. Paris:
       Perrin, 1946, 63.

1165   CHAUVY, Michel. Intériorité: Trois Cheminements vers l'in-
       tériorité: Plotin, Saint Augustin, Bergson. Montreux,
       Suisse: Payot, 1957, 28.

1166   CHAVEZ, Ezequiel. "El pensamiento filosófico de Enrique
       Bergson con referencia a los acontecimientos culminantes
       de la época y el momento actual de la vida en el mondo."
       Luminar, 2, No. 4, 1941.

1167   CHERNOWITZ, Maurice. "Bergson's Influence on Marcel Proust."
       Romantic Review, 27, No. 1, 1936, 45-60. This is a review
       of Bergson und Proust by Jäckel.

1168   CHEVALIER, Irénée. "L'Expérience mystique." Henri Bergson.
       Ed. Béguin and Thévenaz, 105-120. The author considers
       Bergson's theory of mysticism in its relations to the con-
       cept of the "élan vital" and the teachings of the Chris-
       tian mystics.

1169   CHEVALIER, Jacques. Bergson. Paris: Plon, 1926, 317. This
       is a well-known comprehensive account of Bergson's philos-
       ophy.

1170   CHEVALIER, Jacques. "Bergson." El Escorial, 2, 1941, 317-
       318.

1171   CHEVALIER, Jacques. Bergson et le père Pouget. Paris:
       Plon, 1954, 80. The preface is by François Mauriac.

1172   CHEVALIER, Jacques. "Bergson et son époque." Revue Hebdo-
       madaire des Cours et des Conférences, 27, No. 8, 1926;
       673-681; No. 9, 1926, 18-26; No. 10, 1926, 142-148; No. 11,
       1926, 193-202; No. 13, 1926, 308-417; No. 14, 1926, 552-
       560; No. 15, 1926, 596-607. The articles appear in the au-
       thor's Bergson.

1173   CHEVALIER, Jacques. "Bergson et les sources de la morale."
       Cadences. Paris: Plon, 1939, 374.

1174    CHEVALIER, Jacques.  "Bergson nous parle... ."  Le Figaro
        Littéraire, 14, No. 680, 2 mai 1959, 1, 7; No. 681, 9 mai
        1959, 1, 5-6, 8.

1175    CHEVALIER, Jacques.  "Bergson vu par Jacques Chevalier."
        Nouvelles Littéraires, No. 1677, 22 octobre 1959, 2.

1176    CHEVALIER, Jacques.  Bergson y el Padre Pouget.  Trans. José
        A. Míquez.  Madrid: Aguilar, 1959, 92.

1177    CHEVALIER, Jacques.  "M. Bergson et les sources de la mora-
        le."  Revue des Deux Mondes, 8e Sér., 9, No. 10, 15 mai
        1932, 384-395.  This is a review of Les Deux Sources de la
        morale et de la religion.

1178    CHEVALIER, Jacques.  "Enrique Bergson: 1859-1941."  Sciencia
        Tomista, 40, 1941, 146.  This is an obituary article.

1179    CHEVALIER, Jacques.  Henri Bergson.  Authorized Trans.
        Lilian A. Clare.  New York: Macmillan, 1928, 351.

1180    CHEVALIER, Jacques.  Henri Bergson.  Trans. L. Clare, 1928;
        rpt. Freeport, New York: AMS Press, 1969, 351.

1181    CHEVALIER, Jacques.  Henri Bergson.  Trans. E. Zazo.
        Brescia, Italy: Morcelliana, 1937, 173.  "Pref. di Ch.
        Boyer."  2nd ed, 1947.

1182    CHEVALIER, Jacques.  "Henri Bergson."  Les Grands Courants
        de la pensée mondiale contemporaine: IIIe Partie: Por-
        traits. I.  Paris: Fischbacher, 1964, 820.  See pages 123-
        152.

1183    CHEVALIER, Jacques.  Henri Bergson: Suivi de pages inédites
        et de l'histoire du 7e fauteuil: Portrait de Bergson par
        Henri de Nolhac: Bibliographie: Autographe.  Paris: Ser-
        vant, 1928, 103.  This is a Nobel Prize commemorative.

1184    CHEVALIER, Jacques.  "Chevalier parle de Bergson."  Esprit,
        9, No. 97, février 1941, 259.

1185    CHEVALIER, Jacques.  "Ciò che la filosofia deve a Bergson."
        Humanitas, 14, No. 11, 1959, 785-791.

1186    CHEVALIER, Jacques.  "Comment Bergson échappa à l'Index."
        Le Figaro Littéraire, 9 mai 1959, 5-6.

1187    CHEVALIER, Jacques.  "Comment Bergson a trouvé Dieu."  Henri
        Bergson.  Ed. Béguin and Thévenaz, 91-96.  The author

traces the development of Bergson's thought to its culmi-
nation in a philosophy of religion.  Letters to the author
from Bergson dealing with the terms "classic" and "Greco-
Latin" are quoted in part.

1188   CHEVALIER, Jacques.  "Comment Bergson a trouvé Dieu."  Revue
des Deux Mondes, N.S. Année 4, No. 20, 15 octobre 1951,
604-618.

1189   CHEVALIER, Jacques.  "Comment Bergson a trouvé le Dieu."
Cadences II.  Paris: Plon, 1951, 70-88.

1190   CHEVALIER, Jacques.  "Comó Bergson encontró a Dios."  Revista de Filosofia (Madrid), 11, No. 43, 1952, 539-557.

1191   CHEVALIER, Jacques.  "Le Continu et le discontinu."  Proceedings of the Aristotelian Society, Supplementary Volume, 4, 1924, 174-196.  Also in Annales de l'Université de
Grenoble, N.S. 2, No. 1, 1924.  The author argues, in
Bergsonian fashion, that: "La continuité que nous présente
l'univers en sa totalité, et dans chacune de ses parties
distinctes, individualisées, est la continuité d'un rythme... ."  (196).  Continuity is thus to be understood in
terms of duration.

1192   CHEVALIER, Jacques.  Conversaciones con Bergson.  Trans.
José A. Miquez.  Madrid: Aguilar, 1960, 420.

1193   CHEVALIER, Jacques.  "De Descartes à Bergson et à Maurice
Blondel."  Revue Politique et Littéraire, Revue Bleue, 75e
Année, No. 4, 20 février 1937, 131-133.

1194   CHEVALIER, Jacques.  "Discussion avec Jacques Maritain sur
'Aristote et Bergson'."  Les Lettres, 8, No. 4, 1er avril
1920, 79-118.

1195   CHEVALIER, Jacques.  "Entretiens avec Bergson."  Table Ronde,
No. 137, mai 1959, 9-28.

1196   CHEVALIER, Jacques.  Entretiens avec Bergson.  Paris: Plon,
1959, 315.

1197   CHEVALIER, Jacques.  "Entretiens avec Bergson: Extraits du
volume du même titre."  Humanitas, 14, No. 11, 1959, 843-
852.

1198   CHEVALIER, Jacques.  Histoire de la pensée: Vol. 4.  La Pensée moderne de Hegel à Bergson.  Paris: Flammarion, 1966,
756.  "Texte posthume revu et mis au point par Léon Husson."

1199    CHEVALIER, Jacques. Historia del pensamiento: El pensamien-
        to moderno de Hegel a Bergson. Trans. and Preface José
        A. Miquez. Madrid: Aguilar, 1968, 733. This posthumous
        text was edited by Léon Husson.

1200    CHEVALIER, Jacques. "Hoe Bergson God heeft gevonden." Het
        Schild, 20, 1939, 372-373.

1201    CHEVALIER, Jacques. L'Idée et le réel. Grenoble: Arthaud,
        1932, 173. This book consists of four articles previously
        published in La Nouvelle Journée, Les Annales de l'Univer-
        sité de Grenoble, Les Mélanges Hauriou, and Proceedings of
        the Aristotelian Society.

1202    CHEVALIER, Jacques. "L'Intellectualisme d'Henri Bergson."
        Nouvelles Littéraires, No. 322, 15 décembre 1928, 5.

1203    CHEVALIER, Jacques. Les Maîtres de la pensée française:
        Bergson. Paris: Plon, 1926, 317. "Nouvelle édition revue
        et augmentée." Paris: Plon, 1934, 357.

1204    CHEVALIER, Jacques. "La Morale de Bergson." Le Van, No.
        169, mai 1932, 28-29. This is a review of Les Deux
        Sources. It is included in Chevalier's Bergson.

1205    CHEVALIER, Jacques. "L'Opinion de M. Jacques Chevalier."
        Documents de la Vie Intellectuelle, 2, No. 5, 20 février
        1930, 256-261. This article was originally published in
        Nouvelles Littéraires, 15 décembre 1928.

1206    CHEVALIER, Jacques. "La Portée métaphysique de la pensée
        bergsonienne." Documents de la Vie Intellectuelle, 3, No.
        3, 20 juin 1930, 562-568. This was originally Chapter VII
        in Bergson.

1207    CHEVALIER, Jacques. "Le Souvenir de Bergson." Ecrits de
        Paris, octobre 1960, 103-112. "Entretien à la radio cana-
        dienne, avec Odette Lutgen."

1208    CHEVALIER, Jacques. La Vie de l'esprit. Grenoble: Arthaud,
        1932, 96.

1209    CHEVALLEY, Abel. "Letter from France." Saturday Review of
        Literature, 6, No. 29, 8 February 1930, 720. This note
        concerns the influence of Bergson on literature.

1210    CHEYDLEUR, Frédéric D. "Essai sur l'évolution des doctrines
        de M. Georges Sorel." Diss., Grenoble, 1914, 599.

1211    CHIAPELLI, Allesandro.  Della critica al nuovo idealismo.
        Torino: Fratelli Boca, 1910, 300.

1212    CHIAPELLI, Alessandro.  "L'energia spirituale: A proposito
        del nuovo libro di Enrico Bergson." Nuova antologia, Ser.
        6, 205, No. 3, 1 marzo 1920, 3-13.  This is a review.

1213    CHIAPPELLI, Allesandro.  Idee e figure moderne.  Ancona:
        Puccini e Figli, 1912, 175.  Spencer, Tolstoi, James, Berg-
        son, and others are discussed in this study.

1214    CHIAPPELLI, Alessandro.  "Les Tendances vives de la philoso-
        phie contemporaine." Revue Philosophique de la France et
        de l'Etranger, 69, No. 3, mars 1910, 217-248.

1215    CHIDE, Alphonse.  "Autour Du Problème de la connaissance."
        Revue Philosophique de la France et de l'Etranger, 67,
        No. 12, décembre 1909, 581-604.

1216    CHIDE, Alphonse.  L'Idée de rythme.  Digne, France: Chaspoul,
        1905, 184.

1217    CHIDE, Alphonse.  Le Mobilisme moderne.  Paris: Félix Alcan,
        1908, 292 (Bibliothèque de Philosophie Contemporaine).

1218    CHIDE, Alphonse.  "Pragmatisme et intellectualisme." Revue
        Philosophique de la France et de l'Etranger, 65, No. 4,
        avril 1908, 367-388.

1219    CHORON, Jacques.  "Bergson, Klages, Simmel: La Mort et les
        'philosophies de la vie'." La Mort et la pensée occiden-
        tale.  Trans. M. Manin.  Paris: Payot, 1969, 181-183.

1220    CHRISTOFLOUR, Raymond.  "Bergson et la conception mystique
        de l'art." Henri Bergson.  Ed. Béguin and Thévenaz, 157-
        169.  The author examines passages in Laughter and The Two
        Sources of Morality and Religion for their implications
        for Bergson's concept of art.  He concludes that for Berg-
        son art, like other basic human activities, has a reli-
        gious goal.

1221    CHURCH, Margaret.  "Bergson's 'durée' in Modern English and
        American Literature." Diss., Duke, 1949.

1222    CITOLEUX, Marc.  "Le Bergsonisme et l'expérience mystique."
        Revue Universitaire, 42e Année, No. 1, janvier 1933, 35-
        41.  This is a review of Les Deux Sources.

1223    CITOLEUX, Marc. "La Philosophie de la vie et le bergsonis-
        me." Mercure de France, 281, No. 950, 15 janvier 1938,
        225-258.

1224    CIUSA, Niso. Inchiesta sul bergsonismo. Sassari, Italy:
        Tip. Gallizzi, 1953, 111.

1225    CLAESSENS, François. "Bergson en Proust: Wijsgeer en dich-
        ter." Streven, 2, No. 1, 1948, 318-320. This essay is on
        Delattre's Bergson et Proust.

1226    CLEMENT, André. "La Conception du hasard chez Lévy-Bruhl et
        la critique qui en fit Bergson." Diss., Laval, 1954.

1227    CLEUGH, Mary Frances. Time and Its Importance in Modern
        Thought. Rpt. London: Metheun, 1937, 308. New York:
        Russell and Russell, 1970, 308. The author prefaces his
        study by stating that: "Bergson, Alexander, McTaggart, and
        Dunne have given us something fresh to think about and to
        take us farther than St. Augustine deemed possible."
        Bergson is dealt with especially on pages 108-127.

1228    CLOUARD, Henri. Histoire de la littérature française: Du
        Symbolisme à nos jours (1885-1914). Paris: Albin Michel,
        1949, 665. The chapter entitled "Bergson libérateur" is
        an appreciative account of Bergson as a writer and of his
        literary influence.

1229    CLOUTIER, Paul P. " A Bergsonian Analysis of the Humor of
        Anatole France." Dissertation Abstracts International,
        32, 1971, 911A. The author analyzes the humor of Anatole
        France by means of Bergson's theory of laughter.

1230    CLUNY, Claude Michel. "Le Temps de Bergson." Lettres Fran-
        çaises, No. 1249, 18-24 septembre 1968, 13.

1231    COCHET, Marie-Anne. L'Intuition et l'amour: Essai sur les
        rapports métaphysiques de l'intuition et de l'instinct
        avec l'intelligence et la vie. Paris: Perrin, 1920, 263.

1232    COCKERELL, T. D. A. "The New Voice of Philosophy?" Dial,
        51, No. 607, 1 October 1911, 253-255. This is a review of
        Creative Evolution.

1233    COHEN, Josué J. "La Morale bergsonienne." Revue des Confé-
        rences Françaises en Orient, 2, No. 18, 1938, 593-601.

1234    COHEN, Robert Joseph. Morale individualiste ou morale so-
        ciale: Henri Bergson ou Josué Jéhouda. Paris: La Colonne
        Vendôme, 1950, 47. The preface is by Henri Baruk.

1235    COIGNET, Clarisse. De Kant à Bergson: Réconciliation de la
        religion et de la science dans un spiritualisme nouveau.
        Paris: Félix Alcan, 1911, 155.

1236    COIGNET, Clarisse. "Kant et Bergson." Revue Chrétienne,
        4e Sér., 1, No. 7, juillet 1904, 27-41.

1237    COIGNET, Clarisse. "La Vie d'après M. Bergson." Bericht
        über den III. internationalen Kongress für Philosophie
        zu Heidelberg. Hrsg. von Th. Elsenhans. Heidelberg:
        Carl Winters Universität Buchhandlung, 1909, 358-364.

1238    COIMBRA, Leonardo. O criacionismo: Esboço de um sistema
        filosófico. Pôrto: Biblioteca da Renascença, 1912, 311.

1239    COJAZZI, Antonio. "Il Croce de fronte a Socrate e a Berg-
        son." Città de vita, 7, 1952, 654-661.

1240    COLIN, Pierre. "Bergson et l'absolu." De La Connaissance
        de Dieu. Paris and Bruges: Desclée de Brouwer, 1959, 113-
        124.

1241    COLLETTI, Giovanni. I fondamenti logico-metafisici del
        Bergsonismo, e altri scritti. Padova: Cedam, 1964, 104.

1242    COLLETTI, Giovanni. "Psicologia o filosofia in Bergson?"
        Sophia, 32, Nos. 3-4, 1964, 320-331.

1243    COLLIN, Lucien. "Bergson: Un Homme de chrétienté." Améri-
        que Française, 10, No. 6, 1952, 58-60.

1244    COLLIN, Lucien. "Mon Maître, Bergson." Amérique Française,
        11, No. 3, mai-juin 1953, 35-37.

1245    COLLINS, James. A History of Modern European Philosophy.
        Milwaukee: Bruce, 1954, 954. Bergson is discussed on
        pages 809-848.

1246    COLOMBO, Yoseph. "Un concetto bergsoniano in antichi testi
        ebraici." Studi di letteratura, storia e filosofia in
        onore di Bruno Revel. Firenze: Leo S. Olschki editore,
        1965, 201-205.

1247    COLONNA, Louis.  "M. Bergson et son enseignement."  Revue
        Hebdomadaire des Cours et des Conférences, 22, No. 8, 5
        mars 1914, 798-809.

1248    COLUM, Mary M.  "Writers and Human Rights."  Forum, 93, No.
        1, January 1935, 19-24.  This article discusses Bergson,
        Lippman, and democracy.  It also includes a review of The
        Two Sources.

1249    COLUMER, A.  "De Bergson à Bonnot: De Bergson au banditisme."
        L'Action d'art, 1913.

1250    "Committees for Intellectual Cooperation."  Current History,
        24, No. 3, June 1926, 413-415.

1251    CONCHE, Marcel.  "Sur La Critique bergsonienne de l'idée de
        néant."  Actes du Xe Congrès des Sociétés de Langue Fran-
        çaise (Congrès Bergson).  Paris: Armand Colin, 1, 1959,
        71-75.  It is argued in this article that the metaphysical
        concept of "nothing" is a pseudo-idea.

1252    CONCHE, Marcel.  "Table ronde: Néant et existentialisme."
        Actes du Xe Congrès des Sociétés de Philosophie de Langue
        Française (Congrès Bergson).  Paris: Armand Colin, 2, 1959,
        145-164.

1253    CONSTANT, Léonard.  "Cours de M. Bergson sur l'histoire de
        l'idée de temps."  Revue de Philosophie, 4, No. 1, janvier
        1904, 105-111.  The author provides a summary of Bergson's
        course on the history of the concept of time.

1254    CONTE, Alberto.  "O mundo objectivo na filosofía intuicionis-
        ta de Bergson."  Sustancia, 2, Nos. 7-8, septiembre 1941,
        334-343.

1255    COOKE, Harold P.  "Ethics and New Intuitionists."  Mind, 22,
        No. 85, January 1913, 82-86.

1256    COPLESTON, Frederick Charles.  "Bergson and Intuition."
        Modern Schoolman, 11, No. 3, March 1934, 61-65.  This is
        an analysis of Bergson's concept of "intuition."  Several
        different meanings of the term are defined.

1257    COPLESTON, Frederick Charles.  "Bergson on Morality."  Pro-
        ceedings of the British Academy, 41, 1955, 247-266.

1258    COPLESTON, Frederick Charles.  "Henri Bergson."  The Month,
        177, No. 1, January-February 1941, 47-57.

1259    COPLESTON, Frederick Charles. Friedrich Nietzsche: Philoso-
         pher of Culture. London: Burnes and Oates, 1942, 205-213.
         Copleston compares Bergson's mysticism and Nietzsche's su-
         perhumanism.

1260    COPLESTON, Frederick Charles. "Review of Roots of Bergson's
         Philosophy by Ben-Ami Scharfstein." Hibbert Journal, 42,
         No. 167, 1944, 286-288.

1261    COR, Raphaël. Essais sur la sensibilité contemporaine:
         Nietzsche: De M. Bergson à M. Bazaillas: M. Claude Debussy.
         Paris: Falque, 1912, 209.

1262    COR, Raphaël. "De La Morale bergsonienne à l'immoralisme."
         Mercure de France, 258, No. 881, 1935, 225-246. The au-
         thor feels that Bergson is a dangerous freethinker.

1263    COR, Raphaël. De La Morale bergsonienne à l'immoralisme.
         Paris: Mercure de France, 1935, 23.

1264    CORBIERE, Charles. "Le Dieu de M. Bergson." Revue de Théo-
         logie et des Questions Religieuses, 19e Année, No. 2, 1er
         mars 1910, 176-187.

1265    COREY, Charles E. "Bergson's Intellect and Matter." Philo-
         sophical Review, 22, No. 5, 1913, 512-519. According to
         the author, Bergson is primarily interested in division
         and analysis; the work of integration is seldom done with
         equal care so that a distinction of a kind is apt to ap-
         pear, later in his system, as one of degree only.

1266    CORNU, Auguste. "Bergsonianism and Existentialism." Philo-
         sophic Thought in France and the United States; Ed.
         Marvin Farber. Albany, New York: State University of New
         York Press, 1968, 813. See pages 151-168. Cornu pro-
         vides a Marxist interpretation of Bergson.

1267    CORRANCE, Henry C. "Bergson's Idea of God." Quest, 9, No.
         1, January 1917, 340-342. This is a discussion of Prof.
         Radhakrishnan's gravamen against Bergson's philosophy.

1268    CORRANCE, Henry C. "Bergson's Philosophy and the Idea of
         God." Hibbert Journal, 12, No. 46, January 1914, 374-
         388. The author argues that at this date Bergson neither
         affirms nor denies the reality of God.

1269    COSTA, João Cruz. "O itinerário de Bergson." Kriterion,
         13, No. 51-52, 1960, 1-8.

1270   COSTA DE BEAUREGARD, Olivier. "Essai sur la physique du temps: Son Equivalence avec l'espace; son irréversibilité." Actes du Xe Congrès des Sociétés de Philosophie de Langue Française (Congrès Bergson). Paris: Armand Colin, 1, 1959, 77-80. The author deals with the law of equivalence between space and time and its apparent antinomy, so deeply felt by Bergson. He deals with, in particular, the problem of the insertion of minds into the material cosmos and the problem of the irreversibility of time.

1271   COSTA DE BEAUREGARD, Olivier. La Notion du temps: Equivalence avec l'espace. Paris: Herman, 1963, 207. The author urges that Einstein has opened the way toward a reconciliation of physics' time-quantity and Bergson's time-quality.

1272   COSTA DE BEAUREGARD, Olivier. "Le Principe de la relativité et la spatialisation du temps." Revue des Questions Scientifiques, 5e Série, No. 1, 1949, 38-65. The author concludes that Bergsonian aspects of time remain to be treated by science. This article is translated, with an introduction, in Bergson and the Evolution of Physics, Ed. P. A. Y. Gunter, 227-250.

1273   COSTA DE BEAUREGARD, Olivier. "Quelques aspects de l'irréversibilité du temps dans la physique classique et quantique." Revue des Questions Scientifiques, 5e Série, No. 2, 20 avril 1952, 171-191. The author argues that time is irreversible, but that past, present, and future co-exist. This article is translated, with an introduction, in Bergson and the Evolution of Physics, Ed. P. A. Y. Gunter, 77-105.

1274   COSTA DE BEAUREGARD, Olivier. Le Second Principe de la science du temps. Paris: Editions du Seuil, 1963, 152.

1275   COSTA DE BEAUREGARD, Olivier. "Table ronde: Physique." Actes du Xe Congrès des Sociétés de Philosophie de Langue Française (Congrès Bergson). Paris: Armand Colin, 2, 1959, 65-87.

1276   COSTELLOE, Karin (née Stephen). "An Answer to Mr. Bertrand Russell's Article on the Philosophy of Bergson." Monist, 24, No. 1, January 1914, 145-155.

1277   COSTELLOE, Karin (née Stephen). "Complexity and Synthesis: A Comparison of the Data and Philosophical Methods of Mr. Russell and M. Bergson." Proceedings of the Aristotelian

Society, N.S. 15, 1914-1915, 271-303.  This is a very carefully thought out analysis which is critical of Russell.

1278    COSTELLOE, Karin (née Stephen).  "What Bergson Means by 'Interpenetration'."  Proceedings of the Aristotelian Society,
13, 1912-1912, 131-155.  It is argued here that the notion
of interpenetration is absolutely essential to Bergson's
philosophy.

1279    COSTER, Sylvain de.  "Bergson et Varendonck."  Revue de
l'Université Libre de Bruxelles, 43, No. 3, 1937-1938,
295-303.

1280    COTNARNEANU, Léon, Ed.  Suites françaises: Par Henri Bergson,
le duc de Broglie, Jules Cambon.  New York: Brentano's,
1945.  This is a collection of articles from Le Figaro.

1281    COTRANEI, Giulio.  "Henry Bergson e il pensiero biologico."
Idea, 1, No. 24, 1949, 4.

1282    COUCHOUD, Paul-Louis.  "La Métaphysique nouvelle: Matière
et mémoire de M. Bergson."  Revue de Métaphysique et αe
Morale, 10, 1902, 225-243.  This essay is a generally lau-
datory account of Bergson's philosophical method.

1283    COUTURAT, Louis.  "Contre Le Nominalisme de M. Le Roy."
Revue de Métaphysique et de Morale, 8, No. 1, janvier
1900, 87-93.  The author criticizes Le Roy's concept of
measurement and of number, including Cantorian infinite
numbers.  M. Le Roy was a well known disciple of Bergson.

1284    COUTURAT, Louis.  "Etudes sur l'espace et le temps de MM.
Lechalas, Poincaré, Delboeuf, Bergson, L. Weber, et Evellin."  Revue de Métaphysique et de Morale, 4, 1896, 646-
669.

1285    COUTURE, Léonce.  "Review of Essai sur les données immédiates by Henri Bergson."  Polybiblion, 2e Série, 31 (Partie
littéraire), 1890, 303-304.

1286    COVIELLO, Alfredo.  "Henri Bergson."  Sustancia, Año 2, No.
6, marzo 1941, 305-306.

1287    COVIELLO, Alfredo.  "Bibliographia bergsoniana."  Sustancia,
2, Nos. 7-8, 1941, 394-440.

1288    COVIELLO, Alfredo.  Critica bibliográfica y análisis cultural.  Tucumán, Argentina: Septentrion, 1938.  Bergson is

discussed on pages 24, 40, 101, 104, 115, 117, 143, 280, 293, 301; evolution on page 101; intuition on pages 98, 132; and intuitionism on page 107.

1289    COVIELLO, Alfredo. La essencia de la contradicción. Tucumán, Argentina: Septentrion, 1939. Bergson is discussed on pages 75, 76, 81, 85, 87, 88, 97, 105, and 161.

1290    COVIELLO, Alfredo. "La influencia de Bergson in America." Sustancia, Nos. 7-8, septiembre 1941, 375-393.

1291    COVIELLO, Alfredo. El proceso filosófico de Bergson y su bibliografía. Tucumán, Argentina: La Raza, 1941, 119. This is a biographical-critical sketch and bibliography formerly published in Sustancia. This version contains additional materials.

1292    COX, Marian. "Bergson's Message to Feminism." Forum, 49, No. 5, May 1913, 548-559. The author states: " . . . a definite message is in his insistent demand that we turn away from the intellectualism of life to life itself, and this also is the aim of feminism." (548).

1293    "Review of Creative Evolution by Henri Bergson. Authorized Trans. by Arthur Mitchell." Athenaeum, 1, No. 4355, April 1911, 411-412.

1294    "Review of Creative Evolution by Henri Bergson. Authorized Translation by Arthur Mitchell." Bookman (New York), 34, No. 2, October 1911, 206.

1295    "Review of Creative Evolution by Henri Bergson." Lancet, 181, 10 February 1912, 1710-1711.

1296    "Review of Creative Evolution by Henri Bergson." Saturday Review (London), 91, No. 2901, 3 June 1911, 695-686.

1297    "Review of 'Creative Evolution and the Philosophic Doubt' by Arthur J. Balfour in Hibbert Journal." Revue de Métaphysique et de Morale, 20, No. 4, 1912, Supplément, 27-29.

1298    CRESCINI, Angelo. "La molteplicità nella filosofia del Bergson." Rivista de filosofia neoscolastica, 53, No. 5, 1961, 414-419. This article considers the problem of the one and the many in Bergson.

1299    CRESPI, Angelo. "Balfour e Bergson alle prese." Coenobium, 6, No. 10, 1911.

1300    CRESPI, Angelo. "Lo spirito della filosofia de Bergson: I.
        L'analisi bergsoniana." Cultura contemporanea, 4, Nos.
        7-8, 10-11, 1912.

1301    CRESPI, Attilio. "La metafisica di H. Bergson." Coenobium,
        2, No. 5, 1908, 46-51.

1302    CRESSON, André. Bergson, sa vie, son oeuvre: Avec Un Exposé
        de sa philosophie. Paris: Presses Universitaires de
        France, 1941, 160. This work contains passages quoted
        from Bergson's writings.

1303    CRESSON, André. H. Bergson: Liste des articles et des oeu-
        vres. Paris: Presses Universitaires de France, 1941, 158.

1304    CRESSON, André. Les Courants de la pensée philosophique
        française. 2 Vols. Paris: Armand Colin, 1927, 210 and
        212. French philosophic thought from Montaigne to Berg-
        son is discussed in this study. The discussion of Bergson
        is short.

1305    CRESSON, André. La Position actuelle des problèmes philo-
        sophiques. Paris: Stock, 1924, 127.

1305a   CRISTIANI, Aldo Horacio. "Duración y tiempo en Bergson."
        Cuadernos de filosofía, 10, No. 1, enero-julio 1970, 121-
        135.

1306    CRISTIANI, Léon. Le Problème de Dieu et le pragmatisme.
        Paris: Bloud et Cie., 1908, 62.

1307    "Review of Critical Exposition of Bergson's Philosophy by
        J. M. Stewart." International Journal of Ethics (Ethics),
        23, No. 1, January 1913, 211-216.

1308    "Review of Critical Exposition of Bergson's Philosophy by
        J. M. K. Stewart." London Quarterly Review, 118, No. 2,
        April 1912, 358-359.

1309    CROCE, Benedetto. "Note Concerning Bergson's Philosophy."
        Critica, 27 Juli 1929, 276. The author maintains that
        Bergson again took up a critique of abstract intelligence
        already begun by Hegel. But Hegel went beyond intuition
        through his "concept of the concept." Croce and Bergson
        conversed on this topic at the Congrès de Bologne in 1911.

1310    CROCE, Benedetto. "Noterelle di estetica: 3. Bergson e
        Taine." Critica, 10, No. 6, 1912, 479-481.

1311    CRONAN, Edward P. "Bergson and Free Will." New Scholas-
        ticism, 11, No. 1, January 1937, 1-57. The author agrees
        with Bergson that free will is an observable fact, that
        physical determinism is an unproved assumption, and that
        the attempt to measure psychic life is too often only a
        measurement of external causes. But he shows that Berg-
        son's refutation of choice is invalid. Bergson's errors
        are due to an anti-intellectual prejudice, a mistaken in-
        sistence that time and space are mutually exclusive cate-
        gories, and to the practice of fitting facts to his pre-
        conceived idea of duration.

1312    CRUTCHER, Roberta. Personality and Reason. London: Favil
        Press, 1931, 178. The preface is by H. Wildon Carr. The
        author combines Bergson's vitalism with Carr's monadology
        to produce a theory of personality.

1313    CRUZ-HERNANDES, Miguel. "Bergson et Unamuno." Actes du Xe
        Congrès des Sociétés de Philosophie de Langue Française
        (Congrès Bergson). Paris: Armand Colin, 1, 1959, 81-83.
        Bergson was for Unamuno the greatest contemporary philoso-
        pher. In the midst of positivistic scientism Bergson's
        thought involved a spiritualistic restoration which meri-
        ted the supreme title "quixotic."

1314    CUENOT, Lucien. Invention et finalité en biologie. Paris:
        Flammarion, 1942, 259. Bergson is discussed on pages 23,
        29, 31, 35, 39, 156-158, and 193.

1315    CUIDAD, Mario. Bergson y Husserl: Diversidad en coinciden-
        cia. Ediciones de los Anales de la Universidad de Chile,
        Serie Negra, No. 8, 1960, 43.

1316    CUNNINGHAM, Gustavus Watts. "Bergson's Concept of Duration."
        Philosophical Review, 23, No. 6, November 1914, 525-539.

1317    CUNNINGHAM, Gustavus Watts. "Bergson's Concept of Finality."
        Philosophical Review, 23, No. 6, 1914-1915, 648-663.

1318    CUNNINGHAM, Gustavus Watts. "Bergson's Doctrine of Intui-
        tion; Reply to M. W. Landes." Philosophical Review, 33,
        No. 6, November 1924, 604-606.

1319    CUNNINGHAM, Gustavus Watts. A Study in the Philosophy of
        Bergson. New York: Longmans, Green and Co., 1916, 212.

1320    CURTUIS, Ernst Robert. Die Literarischen Wegbereiter des
        Neuen Frankreich. Potsdam: Kiepenheur, 1923, 344. See

the introduction for a statement of the influence of Bergson on French literature before 1914.

1321   CUVILLIER, Armand. "Bergson et le message de l'Orient." Nouvelles Littéraires, No. 1005, 7 novembre 1946.

1322   CUVILLIER, Armand. "Les Courants irrationalistes dans la philosophie contemporaine." Cahiers Rationalistes, 6, No. 35, mars–avril 1936, 45-82.

1323   D'ABRO, Arthur. Bergson ou Einstein. Paris: Gaulon, 1927, 320. This is a polemic directed against Bergson's criticisms of relativity theory.

1324   D'ABRO, Arthur. The Evolution of Scientific Thought. New York: Dover Publications, 1927, 481. Bergson's criticisms of Einstein are declared erroneous on pages 214-217.

1325   DAL SASSO, A. "Le sorgenti della morale e della religione in Bergson." Rivista di filosofia neoscolastica, 23, No. 6, 1932. This is a review of Les Deux Sources.

1326   D'AMATO, Ferdinando. Il pensiero di Enrico Bergson. Città di Castello: Casa Ed. il Solco, 1921, 390.

1327   DAMBSKA, Izydora. "Sur Quelques Idées communes à Bergson, Poincaré et Eddington." Actes du Xe Congrès des Sociétés de Philosophie de Langue Française (Congrès Bergson). Paris: Armand Colin, 1, 1959, 85-89. Eddington is often very close to Bergson, the author holds, when it comes to questions of methodology concerning the structure of science. Eddington is close to the moderate conventionalism of Poincaré, and it is through this concept that he rejoins Bergson's concept of science.

1328   DAMBSKA, Izydora. "Table ronde: Physique." Actes du Xe Congrès des Sociétés de Philosophie de Langue Française (Congrès Bergson). Paris: Armand Colin, 2, 1959, 65-87.

1329   DAMI, Aldo. "L'Intelligence et le 'discontinu'." Henri Bergson. Ed. Béguin and Thévenaz, 233-238. The author concludes that Bergson is an essentially literary figure whose ideas are in no way confirmed by modern physics and mathematics. He concedes, however, that Bergson did maintain some interest in the exact sciences.

1330   D'AMORE, Benedetto. "La filosofia davanti al problema dell'esistenza di Dio ne Les Deux Sources di Enrico Bergson." Sapienza, 4, No. 2, 1951, 248-263.

1331   DAN, C. "Determinism and Creation in Bergson's Philosophy."
       Revista de Filozofie, 12, No. 12, 1965, 1587-1603. This
       article is in Rumanian.

1332   DANCKERT, Werner. "Impressionistische Gehalte in der Philo-
       sophie Bergsons." Deutsche Vierteljahrsschrift für Liter-
       aturwissenschaft, 7, No. 1, 1929, 154-156.

1333   D'ANTONIO, F. "La dottrina di Bergson e il diritto penale."
       Rivista penale, Anno 109, No. 1-2, 1928.

1334   D'ARCY, Charles F. God and Freedom in Human Experience.
       London: Edward Arnold, 1915, 312. D'Arcy is strongly in-
       fluenced by Bergson.

1335   D'ARCY, M. C. "Henri Bergson." Tablet, 177, 11 January
       1941, 29.

1336   D'ARMAGNAC, Christian. "De Bergson à Teilhard: La Nature,
       l'homme et Dieu." Etudes, 320, février 1964, 167-177.
       This is a review of Barthélemy-Madaule, Bergson et Teil-
       hard de Chardin and Gouhier, Bergson et le Christ des Evan-
       giles.

1337   "Datos biográficos sobre Bergson." La Prensa, enero 1926.

1338   D'AUREC, Pierre. "De Bergson spencérien à l'auteur de l'Es-
       sai." Archives de Philosophie, 17, No. 1, 1947, 102-121.
       Bergson's early intellectual development is chronicled in
       this article.

1339   DAURIAC, Lionel. "Le Mouvement bergsonien." Revue Philoso-
       phique de la France et de l'Etranger, 75, No. 4, avril
       1914, 400-414. This is a review of books on Bergson by
       Benda, Segond, Wilbois, Schrecker, and Le Roy.

1340   DAURIAC, Lionel. "Review of La Philosophie bergsonienne by
       Jacques Maritain." Revue Philosophique de la France et de
       l'Etranger, 77, No. 6, 1914, 631-634.

1341   DAURIAC, Lionel. "Quelques Réflexions sur la philosophie de
       M. H. Bergson." Année Philosophique, 17, 55-72. This is
       a penetrating study. The author compares Bergson with
       Kant and Ried.

1342   DAURIAC, Lionel. "Review of Le Rire by Henri Bergson."
       Revue Philosophique de la France et de l'Etranger, 50,
       No. 12, décembre 1900, 665-670.

1343    DAUZATS, Charles. "Réception de M. Henri Bergson à l'Acadé-
        mie." Le Figaro, 3e Sér., 64, No. 25, 25 janvier 1918, 3.

1344    DAVAL, Roger. Histoire des idées en France. Paris: Presses
        Universitaires de France, 1953, 128. This study includes
        a section on Bergson.

1345    DAVENSON, Henri. "Bergson et l'histoire." Henri Bergson.
        Ed. Béguin and Thévenaz, 205-213. The author explores the
        influence of Bergson's philosophy on the philosophy of
        history in France. In one respect, he explains that Berg-
        son's philosophy has been felt as liberating his contempo-
        raries from a preoccupation with history. Yet Bergson's
        philosophy leads us to view history as a living discipline
        which can enrich our present and future.

1346    DAVID, J. Wł. "O intuicyi w filozofii." Krytyka, 13, Nos.
        3-4, September-October 1911, 92-101, 166-173. This is re-
        published as O intuicyi w filozofii Bergsona. Kraków:
        Gebethner, 1911.

1347    DAVID, J. Wł. "Okolo Bergsonismu." Krytyka, 14, No. 12,
        1912, 344-353; 15, Nos. 1-2, 1912, 1-10; No. 3, 1912, 99-
        111; No. 4, 1912, 181-189; No. 5, 1912, 239-252; No. 6,
        1912, 311-326.

1348    DAVIDSON, W. T. "Bergson in England." London Quarterly Re-
        view, 117, No. 1, January 1912, 123-126.

1349    DAVIES, John C. "Thibaudet and Bergson." Journal of the
        Australian Universities Language and Literature Associa-
        tion, No. 9, 1959, 48-59. This article presents Thibau-
        det's debt to Bergson. It includes a bibliography.

1350    DAVIS, William H. "Review of Bergson and the Evolution of
        Physics. Ed. and Trans. P. A. Y. Gunter." Southern Hu-
        manities Review, 5, No. 1, Winter 1971, 88-89.

1351    DAVY, Georges. "Henri Bergson: 1859-1941." Revue Universi-
        taire, 9, No. 4, 1941, 243-255; No. 5, 1941, 321-336.

1352    DAVY, Georges. "Les Sentiments sociaux et les sentiments
        moraux." Nouveau Traité de psychologie. Vol. 6. Ed.
        Georges Dumas. Paris: Félix Alcan, 1939, 153-240. Berg-
        son's views on moral obligation are discussed on pages
        201-203 and also on 235n.

1353    DAYAN, Maurice. "L'Inconscient chez Bergson." Revue de Métaphysique et de Morale, 70, No. 3, 1965, 287-324. This is a careful and valuable study.

1354    DEBIDOUR, V. H. "Review of Entretiens avec Bergson by Jacques Chevalier." Bulletin des Lettres, 22e Année, No. 216, 15 mars 1960, 103-104.

1355    DE CARVALHO, A. Mosca. "O paradoxo fundamental do tempo e a filosofia de H. Bergson." Estudos, 3, No. 1-2, 1943, 32-38.

1356    DECAUDIN, Michel. Henri Bergson. Guilde du Livre, 1964, 402.

1357    DECLOUX, S. "Review of Bergson: Il profondo e la sua espressione by Vittorio Mathieu." Revue Philosophique de Louvain, 3e Série, 56, No. 51, août 1958, 525-526.

1358    DECORTE, Marcel. "Les Origines ravaissoniennes du bergsonisme." New Scholasticism, 8, No. 2, April 1934, 103-151.

1359    DECOSTER, Paul. Acte et synthèse: Esquisse d'une critique de la pensée pure. Bruxelles: Lamertin, 1928, 158.

1360    DECOSTER, Paul. "La Philosophie de M. Bergson." Pages Amies, No. 6, 20 janvier 1908.

1361    DECOSTER, Paul. La Réforme de la conscience. Bruxelles: Lamertin, 1919, 91.

1362    DEDEYAN, Charles. "Bergson et Du Bos." Table Ronde, No. 208, mai 1965, 79-90. This is a chapter from the author's book on Du Bos. It traces certain influences on Du Bos by Bergson.

1363    DEDEYAN, Charles. Le Cosmopolitisme littéraire de Charles Du Bos: La Maturité de Charles Du Bos (1914-1927). Vol. 2. Paris: Société d'Edit. d'Enseignement Supérieur, 1966, 732.

1364    DE DONADIO, Delia M. "Acerca de las nociones de posibilidad y de nada en Bergson." Diálogos, 3, No. 5, 1966, 83-99.

1365    DE FRANCESCO, Dian Angelo. "La 'Professione del tragico'." Letteratura moderne, 1, No. 1, 1951, 94-98.

1366     DE GAULLE, Charles.  The Edge of the Sword.  Trans. G. Hop-
         kins.  New York: Criterion Books, 1960, 128.  Bergson is
         discussed on pages 16-17 and 20-21.

1367     DEGUY, Michel.  "Essai de prolongement du Rire."  Nouvelle
         Revue Française, 11, No. 1, janvier 1963, 177-180.

1368     DEHOVE, Henri Charles.  La Théorie bergsonienne de la morale
         et de la religion.  Lille, France: S.I.L.I.C., 1933, 105.

1369     DEJARDIN, André.  "Bergson aux frontières du catholicisme."
         Synthèse, 4, No. 47, avril 1950, 192-195.

1370     DE KADT, J.  "Bergson."  De Fakkel, 1940.

1371     DELACROIX, Gilbert.  "La Réception de M. Bergson par M. Dou-
         mic."  Revue Hebdomadaire, N.S. 14e Année, No. 5, 2 février
         1918, 132-134.

1372     DELACROIX, Henri.  Les Grandes Formes de la vie mentale.
         Paris: Félix Alcan, 1934, 187.  The author's psychology is
         influenced by Bergson, especially his theory of the func-
         tion of the body and his theory of memory.

1373     DELACROIX, Henri.  Le Langage et la pensée.  Paris: Félix
         Alcan, 602.  New Edition, Félix Alcan, 1930, 624.  Bergson
         is discussed on page 449.

1374     DELAGE, Yves.  "Sur La Nature du comique."  Revue du Mois,
         20, No. 118, 10 août 1919, 337-354.  Delage holds in op-
         position to Bergson that laughter arises through percep-
         tion of disharmony between cause and effect.

1375     DE LAGUNA, Theodore.  "Review of La Pensée et les nouvelles
         écoles anti-intellectualistes by Alfred Fouillée."  Jour-
         nal of Philosophy, 9, No. 16, 1 August 1912, 498-500.
         Bergson is discussed on page 500.

1376     DELANEY, C. F.  "Bergson on Science and Philosophy."  Pro-
         cess Studies, 2, No. 1, Spring 1972, 29-43.  The author
         analyzes the differences between and the interdependence
         of science and philosophy in Bergson's philosophy by com-
         paring Bergson's position with Kant's.  He concludes by
         suggesting criticisms by C. S. Pierce of the concept of
         intuition.

1377     DELATTRE, Floris.  "Review of 'An Approach to Bergson' by
         Zygmunt Hladki."  Etudes Bergsoniennes, 3, 217-218.

1378    DELATTRE, Floris. "Review of Approach to Metaphysics by
        E. W. F. Tomlin." Etudes Bergsoniennes, 2, 1949, 265-
        269. Delattre is critical of Tomlin's dismissal of Berg-
        son.

1379    DELATTRE, Floris. "Bergson et Proust, accords et dissonan-
        ces." Etudes Bergsoniennes, 1, 1948, 1-127.

1380    DELATTRE, Floris. "Le Bergsonisme et la littérature." Re-
        vue de l'Enseignement des Langues Vivantes, 29, No. 6,
        juin 1922, 252-257.

1381    DELATTRE, Floris. "Les Dernières Années de Bergson." Etu-
        des Bergsoniennes. Paris: Presses Universitaires de
        France, 1942, 5-18.

1382    DELATTRE, Floris. "Les Dernières Années d'Henri Bergson."
        Revue Philosophique de la France et de l'Etranger, 131,
        Nos. 2-3, mars-août 1941, 125-138.

1383    DELATTRE, Floris. "La Durée bergsonienne dans le roman de
        Virginia Woolf." Revue Anglo-américaine, 9, No. 2, 1932,
        97-108. The author argues that both Bergson and William
        James influenced Woolf.

1384    DELATTRE, Floris. Feux d'automne: Essais choisis. Paris:
        Didier, 1950, 284. "Avant-propos de Maurice Le Breton."

1385    DELATTRE, Floris. "Floris Delattre, 'Henri Bergson et l'An-
        gleterre' (Discussion)." Etudes Bergsoniennes, 2, 1949,
        199-208. This is a résumé of Delattre's previous article
        on Bergson and Great Britain, with additional insights.
        Bergson knew Britain as Victorian Britain.

1386    DELATTRE, Floris. "Review of 'La Liberté' by Léon Husson."
        Etudes Bergsoniennes, 3, 218-219.

1387    DELATTRE, Floris. "La Personnalité d'Henri Bergson et l'An-
        gleterre." Revue de Littérature Comparée, 7, No. 2, avril-
        juin 1927, 300-315.

1388    DELATTRE, Floris. Ruskin et Bergson: De L'Intuition esthé-
        tique à l'intuition métaphysique. Oxford: Clarendon
        Press, 1947, 27. This is the Zaharoff Lecture for 1947.

1389    DELATTRE, Floris. "Samuel Butler et le bergsonisme: Avec
        Deux Lettres inédites d'Henri Bergson." Revue Anglo-amé-
        ricaine, 13, No. 5, 1935-1936, 385-405. Significant dif-
        ferences between Bergson and Butler are pointed out here.

1390    DELATTRE, Floris. "William James bergsonien." Revue Anglo-
        américaine, 1, No. 2, 1923-24, 135-144.

1391    DELATTRE, Floris. William James bergsonien. Paris: Presses
        Universitaires de France, 1924, 34.

1392    DELAUNAY, Louis. "Henri Bergson et Plotin." Revue des Fa-
        cultés Catholiques de l'Ouest, 27, 1918, 344-362, 622-645.

1393    DELAUNAY, Louis. Monsieur Bergson et Plotin. Angers:
        Siraudeau, 1919, 43.

1394    DELAY, Jean. Les Dissolutions de la mémoire. Paris: Presses
        Universitaires de France, 1942, 152. "Préface de Pierre
        Janet." Bergson's concept of memory is discussed on pages
        5 and 8-13; Bergson's concept of amnesia on 43-75. Berg-
        son's "durée" is characterized as mere "temps autistique"
        on pages 99-100 and 111-113.

1395    DELAY, Jean. "Table ronde: Durée et mémoire." Actes du Xe
        Congrès des Sociétés de Philosophie de Langue Française
        (Congrès Bergson). Paris: Armand Colin, 2, 1959, 41-61.

1396    DELAY, Jean. "Table ronde: Psychologie, phénoménologie, in-
        tuition." Actes du Xe Congrès des Sociétés de Philosophie
        de Langue Française (Congrès Bergson). Paris: Armand
        Colin, 2, 1959, 15-37.

1397    DELBOS, Victor. "Matière et mémoire, étude critique." Re-
        vue de Métaphysique et de Morale, 5, 1897, 353-389.

1398    DELEDALLE, Gerard. L'Existentiel: Philosophes et littéra-
        tures de l'existence. Paris: Lacoste, 1949, 291. Sartre,
        Marcel, Camus, Bergson, and others are discussed in this
        study.

1399    DELEDALLE, Gerard. "Un Inédit de John Dewey: Spencer et
        Bergson." Revue de Métaphysique et de Morale, 70, No. 3,
        1965, 325-333. In this essay John Dewey gives an analysis
        of the close relations between Spencer's and Bergson's
        thought.

1400    DELEUZE, Gilles. "Bergson (1859-1941)." Les Philosophes
        célèbres: Ouvrage publié sous la direction de Maurice
        Merleau-Ponty. Paris: Editions d'Art Lucien Mazenod, 1956,
        292-299.

1401    DELEUZE, Gilles. Le Bergsonisme. Paris: Presses Universi-
        taires de France, 1966, 120.

1402    DELEUZE, Gilles. "La Conception de la différence chez Berg-
        son." Etudes Bergsoniennes, 4, 1956, 77-112.

1403    DELFGAAUW, Bernard. "Bergson et la philosophie existentiel-
        le." Actes du Xe Congrès des Sociétés de Philosophie de
        Langue Française (Congrès Bergson). Paris: Armand Colin,
        1, 1959, 91-96. Existential philosophers, the author
        holds, have in general a very low opinion of Bergson.
        Nonetheless their philosophies are very close to Bergson's
        on at least three points: the importance of choice, the
        unity of time, and affectivity.

1404    DELFGAAUW, Bernard. "Table ronde: Néant et existentialisme."
        Actes du Xe Congrès des Sociétés de Philosophie de Langue
        Française (Congrès Bergson). Paris: Armand Colin, 2,
        1959, 145-164.

1405    DELFGAAUW, Bernard. Twentieth-Century Philosophy. Trans.
        N. D. Smith. Albany, New York: Magi Books, 1969, 172.
        Bergson is discussed in "The Philosophy of Evolution,"
        93-102.

1406    DELFGAAUW, Bernard. Die Wijsbegeerte van de 20e Eeuw.
        Baarn, Holland: Uitgeverij het Wereldvenster, 1957, 198.

1407    DELFOUR. "Le Style de M. Bergson." L'Univers, 19 avril
        1911.

1408    DELHOMME, Jean. "Durée et vie dans la philosophie de Berg-
        son." Etudes Bergsoniennes, 2, 1949, 131-190.

1409    DELHOMME, Jean. "Review of 'Les Rapports de Dieu et le mon-
        de dans la philosophie de Bergson' by Henri Gouhier."
        Etudes Bergsoniennes, 3, 215-217.

1410    DELHOMME, Jean. Vie et conscience de la vie: Essai sur Berg-
        son. Paris: Presses Universitaires de France, 1954, 195.

1411    DELHOMME, Jeanne. "L'Exercice de la pensée et ses condi-
        tions dans la philosophie d'Henri Bergson." Etudes Berg-
        soniennes, 3, 152-158. This is a résumé of a talk by Del-
        homme followed by a discussion between Delhomme and sever-
        al other philosophers.

1412    DELHOMME, Jeanne. "Nietzsche et Bergson: La Représentation
        de la vérité." Etudes Bergsoniennes, 5, 1960, 39-62.

1413    DELHOMME, Jeanne. "Note sur Bergson et la musique." Revue
        Musicale, 26, No. 210, janvier 1952, 89-91.

1414    DELHOMME, Jeanne.  "Le Problème de l'intériorité: Bergson et
Sartre."  Revue Internationale de Philosophie, 48, No. 2,
1959, 201-219.  The author argues that Bergson and Sartre
bypass the Kantian distinction between matter and form to
recover the unity of the empirical and the transcendental,
of consciousness and self, and of experience and thought.
But Bergson identifies consciousness and spirit ("esprit"),
conceiving philosophy as metaphysics.  Sartre conceives
consciousness as the negative dimension of the being of
the subject and as the starting-point of an ontology of
nothingness.

1415    DELLA SETA, U.  "L'intuizione della filosofia de Enrico
Bergson."  Ultra, 6, 1912.

1416    DELLE PIANE, Arístides L.  "Henri Bergson."  Revista Nacional Literatura-Arte-Ciencia, 13, No. 39, marzo 1941, 364-
411.

1417    DELLE PIANE, Arístides L.  Henri Bergson.  Montevideo: Talleres gráficos de institutos penales, 1941, 57.

1418    DELLE PIANE, Arístides L.  La filosofía y su enseñanza.
Montevideo, 1916.  Bergson and pragmatism are discussed in
this book.

1419    DELMER, Gerrard.  De La Mémoire à l'intuition.  Bruxelles:
Ed. de la Phalange, 1937, 285.

1420    DELTEIL, Joseph.  "Bergsonisme grammatical ou la pêche à la
ligne."  Nouvelles Littéraires, No. 313, 13 octobre 1928,
1-2.

1421    DELVOLVE, Jean.  "L'Influence de la philosophie de M. Bergson.  I."  Mouvement Socialiste, 29, 230, avril 1911, 267-
268.

1422    DEMIASHKEVICH, Michael John.  "The Educational Implications
of Bergson's Theory of Knowledge."  Educational Adminis-
tration and Supervision, 17, February 1931, 128-138.

1423    DEMIASHKEVICH, Michael John.  An Introduction to the Philosophy of Education.  New York: American Book Company, 1935,
449.  The educational philosophy of Bergson is examined on
pages 149-155.  The author concludes that the basic principles of Bergson's pedagogy are that intellectual effort
must be strong and methodical and that it must seek high
quality in its results.

1424 DE MIRO D'AJETA, Vittorio. Il drama del pensiero nella filosofia de Enrico Bergson. Napoli: Tip. Laurenziana, 1963,
85.

1425 DENES, Tibor. "Bergson et Proust." Bulletin de la Société
des Amis de Marcel Proust et des Amis de Combray, No. 11,
1961, 411-417.

1426 DENNERT, E. "Bergson als Plagiator." Unsere Welt, 8, 1916,
217ff.

1427 DEPRUN, Jean. L'Union de l'âme et du corps chez Malebranche,
Biran et Bergson: Notes prises au cours de Merleau-Ponty à
l'Ecole normale supérieure: (1947-1948). Paris: Vrin,
1968, 131.

1428 DERINS, Françoise. "En Marge du bergsonisme." La Nef, 5,
No. 41, avril 1948, 135-136. The author discusses problems with Mlle. Lafranchi's thesis on Bergson at the Sorbonne.

1429 DERINS, Françoise. "Hommage national à Henri Bergson."
Etudes Bergsoniennes, 1, 1948, 177-179. This article was
originally published in La Nef, June 1947.

1430 DE ROUVILLE, M. "Review of Les Deux Sources de la morale et
de la religion by Henri Bergson." Vragen van den Dag, 48,
1933.

1431 DERSELBE. La Science positive et les philosophes de la liberté. 1900.

1432 DESAYMARD, Joseph. H. Bergson à Clermont-Ferrand. Clermont-
Ferrand: Bellet, 1910, 40. This mémoire was published
originally in Bulletin Historique et Scientifique de l'Auvergne, 30 May 1910, 204-216, and June 1910, 243-267.

1433 DESAYMARD, Joseph. La Pensée de Bergson. Paris: Mercure de
France, 1912, 78.

1434 DESAYMARD, Joseph. "La Pensée d'Henri Bergson." Vieille
Auvergne, mars 1913.

1435 DESCAVES, Pierre. "Autour des 'posthumes' de Valéry et de
Bergson." Erasme, 1re Année, 1946, 411-413.

1436 DESCAVES, Pierre. "De Bergson à Valéry." Gavroche, 3, 13
septembre 1945.

1437   DESCHOUX, Marcel.  "Brunschvicg et Bergson."  Revue Interna-
       tionale de Philosophie, 5, No. 15, 1951, 100-114.

1438   DESCOQS, Pedro.  Praelectiones Theologiae Naturalis.  Vol. 2.
       Paris: Beauchesne, 1935, 725.  Section V, Chapter 4 is en-
       titled "Argumentum ex experientia mystica H. Bergson" (375-
       411).  The author argues that Bergson, though a great psy-
       chologist, was not a great metaphysician.

1439   DESHAYES, Marius Louis.  Dialogues bergsoniens.  Niort,
       France: Imp. Soulisse-Martin, 1934, 85.

1440   DESHAYES, Marius Louis.  La Foi bergsonienne.  Compiègne,
       France: Imprimerie de Compiègne, 1948, 37.

1441   DESPRECHINS, Emile.  "M. Bergson et le féminisme."  Femme
       Belge, 5, No. 8, janvier 1922, 763-766.

1442   DE STEFANO, R.  "Metafisica e scienza positiva in Bergson."
       Richerche filosofiche, 5, No. 1, 1951, 16-30.

1443   DESTERNES, Jean.  "Grèce: Kazantzakis nous parle de Bergson
       et d'Istrati."  Nouvelles Littéraires, No. 1068, 13 févri-
       er 1948, 5.  Kazantzakis speaks here of Bergson's influ-
       ence on him.

1444   DEUSTUA, Alejandro O.  "La actividad estetica."  Revista de
       Filosifia (Buenos Aires), 8, No. 2, marzo 1922, 208-220.
       The author opposes Bergson's aesthetic theories to those
       of Charles Lalo.

1445   DEUSTUA, Alejandro O.  "Libertad y axiologia."  Sustancia, 2,
       Nos. 7-8, septiembre 1941, 327-328.

1446   "Review of Les Deux Sources de la morale et de la religion
       by Henri Bergson."  Biblioteca Sacra, 91, No. 3, octubre
       1933, 456-460.

1447   "Review of Les Deux Sources de la morale et de la religion
       by Henri Bergson."  Journal des Débats, 39, Pt. 1, 8 avril
       1932, 557-559.

1448   "Review of Les Deux Sources de la morale et de la religion
       by Henri Bergson."  Journal of Nervous and Mental Disease,
       77, No. 4, March 1933, 452-454.  This review contains some
       interesting comparisons of Bergson and Freud.

1449   "Review of Les Deux Sources de la morale et de la religion
       by Henri Bergson."  Monist, 44, No. 1, 1934, 158.

1450   DEVAUX, André-A.  "A L'Occasion du centenaire de la nais-
       sance d'Henri Bergson: Signification et exigences de la
       vocation philosophique chez Bergson."  Revue de Synthèse,
       3e Série, 80, Nos. 13-14, janvier-juin 1959, 3-30.

1451   DEVAUX, Andre-A.  "Aspects de la pédagogie de Bergson."
       Synthèses, 15e Année, No. 171, août 1960, 44-56.

1452   DEVAUX, André-A.  "Bergson et Teilhard de Chardin."  Cahiers
       Universitaires Catholiques, No. 2, novembre 1964, 116-120.

1453   DEVAUX, André-A.  "La Connexion entre liberté et vocation
       dans la philosophie de Bergson."  Actes du Xe Congrès des
       Sociétés de Philosophie de Langue Française (Congrès Berg-
       son).  Paris: Armand Colin, 1, 1959, 97-101.  For Bergson
       liberty is a fact, and can be known without proofs, sim-
       ply by the experience we have of ourselves.  Devaux at-
       tempts to show that this fact reveals another, that of
       "personal vocation" felt as an appeal to each man to re-
       alize the ideal self which he bears within him.

1454   DEVAUX, André-A.  "La Métaphysique de Bergson et le chris-
       tianisme."  Table Ronde, No. 172, mai 1962, 105-115.  This
       article concerns Gouhier's Bergson et Le Christ des Evan-
       giles.

1455   DEVAUX, André-A.  "Michel Lecointe: La Matière biblique dans
       la 'Note sur M. Bergson et la philosophie bergsonienne' et
       la 'Note conjointe sur M. Descartes et la philosophie car-
       tésienne' de Charles Péguy."  Feuillets de l'Amitié Char-
       les Péguy, No. 138, 15 février 1968, 26-27.

1456   DEVAUX, André-A.  "Le Mystique et le philosophe selon Berg-
       son."  Giornale di metafisica, 14, No. 6, 1959, 766-783.
       Bergson holds, according to the author, that in the mysti-
       cal experience the person coincides with supra-intellec-
       tual emotion without losing his own identity.  The universe
       is renewed by the mystics, who are the conscious instru-
       ments of God.

1457   DEVAUX, André-A.  "Table ronde: Liberté."  Actes du Xe Con-
       grès des Sociétés de Philosophie de Langue Française (Con-
       grès Bergson).  Paris: Armand Colin, 2, 1959, 167-189.

1458   DEVAUX, Philippe.  "Le Bergsonisme de Whitehead."  Revue In-
       ternationale de Philosophie, 15, Nos. 56-57, 1961, 217-
       236.

1459    DEVAUX, Philippe. "Table ronde: Sources et histoire du
        bergsonisme." Actes du Xe Congrès des Sociétés de Philo-
        sophie de Langue Française (Congrès Bergson). Paris:
        Armand Colin, 2, 1959, 213-233.

1460    DEVAUX, Philippe. De Thales à Bergson. Liège, Belgium:
        Sciences et Lettres, 1955, 607. Bergson's position is
        discussed on pages 523, 528, 556, 559, 560-573, and 584.

1461    DEVIVAISE, Charles. "Présence de Bergson." Etudes Philoso-
        phiques, N.S. 4, No. 1, janvier-mars 1949, 45-49.

1462    DEVIVAISE, Charles. "Table ronde: Psychologie, phénoménolo-
        gie, intuition." Actes du Xe Congrès des Sociétés de Phi-
        losophie de Langue Française (Congrès Bergson). Paris:
        Armand Colin, 2, 1959, 15-37.

1463    DE VLEESCHAUWER, H.-J. "De voorges-chiedenis van het Berg-
        sonisme." Vlaamsche Arbeid, 1925-1926, 20-21.

1464    DEWEY, John. "Bergson on Instinct." New Republic, 83, No.
        1073, 1935, 200-201. This is a review of The Two Sources.
        Dewey states that: "One who finds nothing sound in the
        philosophical foundations may nevertheless learn a great
        deal from Bergson's clear and informed discussion of these
        matters." (201).

1465    DEWEY, John. "Introduction." A Contribution to a Bibliogra-
        phy of Henri Bergson. New York: Columbia University Press,
        1913, ix-xii.

1466    DEWEY, John. "Perception and Organic Action." The Journal
        of Philosophy, 9, No. 24, November 1912, 645-668. Dewey,
        in this essay, makes a critical analysis of Bergson's the-
        ory of perception, as expressed in Matter and Memory.

1467    DEWEY, John. "Spencer and Bergson." Ed. with a French
        translation by Gérard Deledalle. Revue de Métaphysique et
        de Morale, 70, No. 3, 1965, 325-333. In this article
        Dewey analyzes the close relations between Spencer's and
        Bergson's thought.

1468    D'HAUTEFEUILLE, François. "Bergson et Spinoza." Revue de
        Métaphysique et de Morale, 65, No. 4, 1960, 463-474.

1469    D'HAUTEFEUILLE, François. "La Critique par Henri Bergson de
        l'idée de néant." Revue de Métaphysique et de Morale, 64,
        No. 2, 1959, 212-224.

1470   D'HAUTEFEUILLE, François. "Le Développement de la philosophie de Bergson et la poésie contemporaine." Ecrits de Paris, février 1959, 73-78.

1471   D'HAUTEFEUILLE, François. Le Privilège de l'intelligence. Paris: Editions Brossard, 1923, 251. The author proposes a different concept of intuition than Bergson; he also makes some interesting criticisms of Bergson's version of intuition.

1472   D'HAUTEFEUILLE, François. "Schopenhauer, Nietzsche et Bergson." Archives de Philosophie, 28, No. 4, octobre-décembre 1965, 553-556.

1473   D'HENDECOURT, Marie-Madeleine. "Métaphysique et mystique chez Bergson et Laberthonnière." Actes du Xe Congrès des Sociétés de Philosophie de Langue Française (Congrès Bergson). Paris: Armand Colin, 1, 1959, 149-152. This essay explores the spiritual initiatives of Bergson and Laberthonnière, stressing the analogies between Bergsonian intuition and the "laborious intuition" of charity of Laberthonnière.

1474   D'HENDECOURT, Marie-Madeleine. "Table ronde: Religion." Actes du Xe Congrès des Sociétés de Philosophie de Langue Française (Congrès Bergson). Paris: Armand Colin, 2, 1959, 261-278.

1475   DHORME, Edouard. "Review of Les Deux Sources de la morale et de la religion by Henri Bergson." Revue de l'Histoire des Religions, 109, 1934, 220-227.

1476   DHUROUT, E. Claude Bernard: Extraits de son oeuvre: Avec un exposé de sa philosophie: Emprunté à l'oeuvre d'H. Bergson. Paris: Félix Alcan, 1939, 140. Bergson's essay on Claude Bernard is republished in this book on pages 19-32.

1477   DIBBLEE, George Binney. Instinct and Intuition: A Study in Mental Duality. London: Faber and Faber, 1929, 394. The author states that: "Dating back to . . . Descartes I must acknowledge my immense obligations to many philosophers of the French school, of whom I can only mention the most modern: MM. Henri Bergson, Maurice Blondel, and my friend M. Jacques Chevalier . . . ." (8). There are numerous references to Bergson throughout. See especially pages 8, 16, 33, 41, 55, 63, 102, 104, 127, 182, 205, 230, 238, 265, 283, 300, 365, and 372.

1478    DIENES, V. and P.  "Bermerkungen zur Metaphysik Bergsons."
        Husz. szás, 1910.  (Ungar. Sprache).

1479    DIMITROFF, Emanouil P.  Estetikata na Bergsona.  Sofia:
        Kameñ del, 1948, 92.  This book surveys Bergson's aesthet-
        ics.

1480    DIMITROFF, Emanouil P.  Filosofsky Stoudii.  Sofia, 1937,
        102.  Dimitroff's book includes chapters on Bergson and
        vitalism.

1481    DIMNET, Ernest.  "The Meaning of M. Bergson's Success."  Sat-
        urday Review (London), 116, No. 3045, 7 March 1914, 300.

1482    DINGLE, Herbert.  "Introduction."  Duration and Simultaneity.
        Indianapolis, Indiana: Bobbs-Merrill, 1965, xv-lxii.  The
        author defends Bergson's criticism of relativity theory
        while rejecting Bergson's "psychological" starting-point.

1483    DINGLE, Reginald J.  "Henri Bergson."  Nineteenth Century,
        129, No. 768, February 1941, 128-134.  This is an obit-
        uary article.

1484    DISTELLO, A.  "Hamelin, Bergson e Brunschvicg."  Richerche
        filosofiche, 5, No. 1, 1951, 31-34.  It is argued here
        that Bergsonism is historicism.

1485    DIVE, Pierre.  Les Interprétations physiques de la théorie
        d'Einstein.  "2e édition, revue et augmentée."  Paris:
        Dunod, 1945, 80.  "Préface de M. Ernest Esclangon.  Avec
        le facsimile d'un autographe d'Henri Bergson.

1486    Dj., M.  "Necrolog: Henri Bergson."  Analeli Facultatii de
        drept, Annul 2, Nr. 2-3-4, 3pp.  This article was pub-
        lished in Bucharest.

1487    DOBZHANSKY, Theodosius Grigorievich and BOESIGER, Ernest.
        Essais sur l'évolution.  Paris: Masson et Cie., 1968, 182
        (Collection "Les Grands Problèmes de la Biologie, No. 9).
        Bergson is discussed on pages 2, 6, and 145-148.  Chapter
        7, which is entitled "L'Evolution créatrice," appears on
        pages 145-165.  The authors reject Bergson's vitalism but
        argue that evolution is "creative."

1488    DODSON, George Rowland.  Bergson and the Modern Spirit: An
        Essay in Constructive Thought.  Boston: American Unitarian
        Association, 1913, 296.

1489    DOLLARD, Stewart E.   "Bergson and the Communion of Saints."
        America, 53, 25 May 1935, 163.  This is a review of The
        Two Sources.

1490    DOLLARD, Stewart E.   "Bergsonian Metaphysics and God."
        Diss., St. Louis, 1934.

1491    DOLLARD, Stewart E.   Bergsonian Metaphysics and God.  Ann
        Arbor, Michigan: University Microfilms, 1940, 236.

1492    DOLLARD, Stewart E.   "Bibliographic Footnote."  Modern
        Schoolman, 20, No. 1, November 1942, 27-36.

1493    DOLLARD, Stewart E.   "A Summary of Bergsonism."  Modern
        Schoolman, 20, No. 1, November 1942, 27-36.  Dollard pro-
        duces a succinct summary of Bergson's thought with suita-
        ble Thomistic criticisms.

1494    DOLLARD, Stewart E.   "Two Schools of Becoming."  Modern
        Schoolman, 6, No. 3, March 1930, 47-49.  The author com-
        pares Bergson and Heraclitus.

1495    DOLLEANS, Edouard.   "Conversation avec Bergson sur la jus-
        tice."  La Nef, 4, No. 32, juillet 1947, 61-62.

1496    DOLLEANS, Edouard.   "L'Influence d'Henri Bergson à travers
        les lettres françaises."  Etudes Bergsoniennes, 2, 1949,
        228-237.  This essay examines the influence of Bergson on
        Charles Du Bos, Joseph Baruzi, and others.

1497    DOLLEANS, Edouard.   "Review of L'Intelligence créatrice and
        'Le Message de Bergson' by Henry Mavit."  Etudes Bergso-
        niennes, 2, 1949, 257-264.

1498    DOLLEANS, Edouard.   "Review of Ruskin et Bergson: De L'In-
        tuition esthétique à l'intuition métaphysique by Floris
        Delattre."  Etudes Bergsoniennes, 1, 1948, 188-200.  This
        review is laudatory.

1499    DOLSON, Grace Neal.   "Review of De Kant à Bergson by C.
        Coignet."  Philosophical Review, 21, No. 3, May 1912,
        380-381.

1500    DOLSON, Grace Neal.   "The Philosophy of Henri Bergson."
        Philosophical Review, 19, No. 6, November 1910, 579-596;
        20, No. 1, January 1911, 46-48.

1501    DOMENACH, Jean-Marie. "Essais." Esprit, 16e Année, No. 131,
        mars 1947, 528-530. Péguy and Bergson are discussed in
        this essay.

1502    DONADILLE, Marc. Essai sur le problème moral à propos des
        "Deux Sources de la morale et de la religion" de M. Henri
        Bergson. Genève: S.N.D. Ed., 1936, 160.

1503    DONADILLE, Marc. "Essai sur le problème moral à propos des
        'Deux Sources de la morale et de la religion' de M. Henri
        Bergson." Diss., Genève, 1936, 4 (Résumé).

1504    D'ORS, Eugenio. "Allo, Madrid!" Nouvelles Littéraires, No.
        322, 15 décembre 1928, 3.

1505    DORWARD, Alan. "Review of The Misuse of the Mind by Karen
        Stephen." Mind, 32, No. 125, January 1923, 100-103.

1506    DOUGLAS, George William. "Christ and Bergson." North Amer-
        ican Review, 197, No. 689, April 1913, 433-444.

1507    DOUMIC, René. "Bergson vu par René Doumic." Nouvelles Lit-
        téraires, No. 1677, 22 octobre 1959, 2.

1508    DOUMIC, René. "Réponse à Bergson." Journal Officiel de la
        République Française, 10, No. 5, 26 janvier 1918, 966-970.
        This is a talk given on the occasion of Bergson's recep-
        tion into the Académie française.

1509    DOUMIC, René. Séance de l'Académie française du 24 janvier
        1918: Discours de réception de M. Henri Bergson: Réponse
        de M. René Doumic. Paris: Perrin et Cie., 1918, 79.

1510    DRAGHICESCO, D. "L'Influence de la philosophie de M. Berg-
        son. V." Mouvement Socialiste, 30, No. 235, novembre
        1911, 266-269.

1511    DRAGHICESCO, Demetrio. "Dios y la immortalidad en la filo-
        sofía de Bergsón." Luminar, 2, No. 4, Otoño, 1938, 9-21.

1512    DRESDEN, Samuel. Bezonken avonturen: Essays. Amsterdam:
        Meulenhoff, 1949, 189. Bergson, Proust, Valéry, and Camus
        are discussed in this work.

1513    DRESDEN, Samuel. "Les Idées esthétiques de Bergson." Etudes
        Bergsoniennes, 4, 1956, 55-75.

1514    DRESDEN, Samuel. "Het religieuze spiritualisme van Henri
        Bergson." Annalen van het Genootschap voor Wetenschappel-

ijke Philosophie, 22, 1953, 27-42. This essay was first
printed in Algemeen Nederlands Tijdschrift voor Wijsbegeerte, 1952.

1515    DRESDEN, Samuel. "Het religieuze spiritualisme van Henri
Bergson." Algemeen Nederlands Tijdschrift voor Wijsbegeerte, 45, No. 2, 1952, 89-104.

1516    DREVER, James. Instinct in Man. Cambridge, Massachusetts:
University Press, 1917, 316. Bergson's views on instinct
are discussed on pages 82-110. "Instinct is the 'life impulse' becoming conscious as determinate conscious impulse."
(88).

1517    DREYFUS, Robert. Souvenirs sur Marcel Proust. Paris: Grasset, 1926, 341. Memory in Bergson and Proust is discussed
on pages 287-292.

1518    DRIESCH, Hans. "Bergson, der biologische Philosoph." Zeitschrift für den Ausbau der Entwicklungslehre, 2, Nos. 1-2,
1908, 48-55.

1519    DRIESCH, Hans. The History and Theory of Vitalism. Trans.
C. K. Ogden. London: Macmillan and Co., Ltd., 1914, 239.
Bergson is discussed on pages 66-92, 132-137, and 162-163.

1520    DRIESCH, Hans. The Science and Philosophy of the Organism.
2nd ed. London: A. and C. Black, 1929, 344. Bergson and
convergent evolution are discussed on pages 182-183; Matter and Memory on 219; Bergson on mind and brain on 309;
and Driesch and Bergson on "élan vital" on 328.

1521    DROUIN, Marcel. "Fragments philosophiques de la mémoire, du
jugement, de l'action: Ribot, Bergson, Hamelin." Revue de
Métaphysique et de Morale, 53, No. 1, 1948, 1-25. Hamelin
gives us a better concept of "l'esprit" than does Bergson,
according to the author.

1522    DUBOIS, Jacques. "Trois Interprétations classiques de la
définition aristotélicienne du temps: 3. Un Dialogue avec
Kant et Bergson: Henri Carteron." Revue Thomiste, 61, No.
3, 1961, 399-429. The first two sections of this article
appeared in earlier issues of the Revue Thomiste and are
not concerned directly with Bergson.

1523    DUBOIS-DUMEE, J.-P. "Péguy: Ecrivain bergsonien." La Nef,
3, No. 25, décembre 1946, 75-83.

1524    DU BOS, Charles. Approximations. 7 vols. Paris: Plon-
        Nourrit, 1922, 266; Crés et Cie., 1927, 238; Le Rouge et
        le Noir, 1929, 316; Corrêa, 1930, 327; Corrêa, 1932, 326;
        Corrêa, 1934, 448; Corrêa, 1947, 420. Du Bos' literary
        criticism is thoroughly impregnated with Bergson's thought.

1525    DU BOS, Charles. "Begegnung mit Bergson." Merkur, 4, No.
        8, 1950, 854-861.

1526    DU BOS, Charles. "Bergson vu par Charles Du Bos." Nouvel-
        les Littéraires, No. 1677, 22 octobre 1959, 2.

1527    DU BOS, Charles. Cours inédit sur Bergson, donné devant un
        auditoire privé les 20 février, 23 février et 2 mars 1922.
        Archives de Mme. C. Du Bos.

1528    DU BOS, Charles. Journal: 1924-1925. Paris: Corrêa, 1948,
        460. Bergson is discussed on pages 63-68. This article
        first appeared in Revue de Paris, October, 1946.

1529    DUBRAY, C. A. "The Philosophy of Henri Bergson." Bulletin
        of the Catholic University of Washington, 20, April 1914,
        317ff.

1530    DUBRAY, Paul. "Bergson et son influence sur la littérature
        contemporaine." Zeitschrift für Französischen und En-
        glischen Unterricht, 31, No. 5, 1932, 269-274.

1531    DUBRAY, Paul. "Bergson et son influence sur le néo-catho-
        licisme littéraire." Zeitschrift für Französischen und
        Englischen Unterricht, 32, No. 3, 1933, 131-136.

1532    DUCASSE, Pierre. "Review of Les Deux Sources de la morale
        et de la religion by Henri Bergson." Revue de Synthèse,
        4, octobre 1932, 173-182.

1533    DUCKWORTH, Colin. "Albert Thibaudet: Poète bergsonien."
        Revue des Sciences Humaines, N.S. No. 88, 1957, 461-468.

1534    DUGAS, L. "La Logique des sentiments." Nouveau Traité de
        psychologie. Vol. 6. Ed. Georges Dumas. Paris: Félix
        Alcan, 1939, 1-114. Bergson and morality are discussed on
        pages 107-113.

1535    DUGGAN, G. H. Evolution and Philosophy. Wellington, New
        Zealand: A. H. and A. W. Reed, 1949, 227. The first sec-
        tion (of three) contains criticisms of Bergson's evolu-
        tionary theories.

1536    DUHAMEL, Georges. "Un Entretien sur la vie." Le Figaro,
        117e Année, No. 81, 4-5 avril 1942, 3.

1537    DUJOVNE, León. "Bergson." Síntesis, 2, No. 20, enero 1929,
        201-211.

1538    DUJOVNE, León. "Bergson o el discípulo de su propra filo-
        sofía." La Nación, 9 febrero 1941.

1539    DUJOVNE, León. "La energía espiritual." Síntesis, 1, No.
        12, mayo 1928, 117. This is a note concerning the Spanish
        translation of L'Energie spirituelle published in Madrid
        in 1928.

1540    DUJOVNE, León. La filosofía de la historia de Neitzsche a
        Toynbee. Buenos Aires: Edición Galatea-Nueva Visión, 1957,
        203. The author maintains that Bergson, with Spengler,
        constituted the all-important influence on Toynbee.

1541    DUJOVNE, León. "Moral, religión y arte en la obra de Berg-
        son." La Nación, 9 marzo 1941.

1542    DUJOVNE, León. "Un numéro de 'Les Nouvelles Littéraires'
        dedicado a Bergson." Síntesis, 2, No. 22, marzo 1929,
        117-119.

1543    DUJOVNE, León. "El problema de la personalidad en Bergson."
        Logos, Año 1, No. 1, 1941.

1544    DUMANI, Georges. "Henri Bergson ou un philosophe entre deux
        défaites." Revue du Caire, 5e Annee, No. 48, novembre
        1942, 17-32.

1545    DUMAS, Georges. "Les Expressions préalables." Nouveau Trai-
        té de psychologie. Vol. 3. Ed. Georges Dumas. Paris:
        Félix Alcan, 1933, 84-292. Bergson's theory of laughter
        is discussed on pages 256-258 and 269-271.

1546    DUMAS, Georges. "Introduction à la psychologie." Nouveau
        Traité de psychologie. Vol. 1. Ed. Georges Dumas. Paris:
        Félix Alcan, 1920, 335-366. Bergson and the history of
        French psychology are discussed on pages 342-350, 355-356,
        and 362.

1547    DUMAS, Georges. "La Symbolisation." Nouveau Traité de Psy-
        chologie. Vol. 4. Ed. Georges Dumas. Paris: Félix Alcan,
        1934, 264-338. Bergson's concept of symbolization is dis-
        cussed on pages 306-311.

1548   DUMESNIL, Georges.  "La Sophistique comtemporaine."  Amitié
       de France, février-avril, mai-juillet, août-octobre 1912.

1549   DUMESNIL, Georges.  La Sophistique contemporaine: Petit Exa-
       men de la philosophie de mon temps: Métaphysique, science,
       morale, religion.  Paris: Beauchesne, 1912.  The author
       presents many criticisms of Bergson and Bergsonism.

1550   DUMONTET, Georges.  "Morality and Religion in the Philosophy
       of Henri Bergson: Exposition and Critique."  Diss., Har-
       vard, 1944, 320.

1551   DUNAN, Renée.  "Autour d'Einstein."  Monde Nouveau, 4, Nos.
       19-20, 15 septembre et 1er octobre 1922, 290-295.  Berg-
       son is discussed on pages 290-291.

1552   DUNAN, Renée.  "Bergson contre Einstein."  Vie des Lettres,
       No. 1, janvier 1923.

1553   DUNBAR, Harry B.  "The Impact of the Ecole Normale Supé-
       rieure on Selected Men of Letters of France."  Disserta-
       tion Abstracts, 23, No. 2, August 1962, 630.

1554   DUNN, Oliver C.  "A Study of Bergson's Theory of Morality."
       Diss., Cornell, 1937.

1555   DUNNE, M. A.  "Plato and Bergson: A Comparison and a Con-
       trast."  American Catholic Quarterly Review, 40, No. 159,
       July 1915, 442-449.

1556   DUPRAT, Em.  "Estudios de filosofía contemporánea: La filo-
       sofía de H. Bergson."  Cultura Española, Año 3, No. 1,
       1908, 185-202; No. 2, 1908, 567-584.

1557   DUPRAT, Em.  "La filosofía francesa en 1907."  Nosotros, 2,
       No. 15, octubre 1908, 156-160.  The author discussed Crea-
       tive Evolution and its impact.

1558   DUPRAT, Em.  "La filosofía francesa en 1908."  Nosotros, 3,
       Nos. 2-3, julio y agosto 1909, 324-328.

1559   DUPRAT, Guillaume-Léonce.  "La Spatialité des faits psychi-
       ques."  Revue Philosophique de la France et de l'Etranger,
       63, No. 5, 1907, 492-501.

1560   DUQUE, Baldomero Jiménez.  "El problema mistico."  Revista
       Española de Teleogía, 2, No. 4, octubre-diciembre 1942,
       617-647.

1561    DURANT, William James. Contemporary European Philosophers:
        Bergson, Croce, and Bertrand Russell. Girard, Kansas:
        Haldeman-Julius Company, 1925, 64.

1562    DURANT, William James. Die großen Denker. Zürich: Orell
        Füssli, 1929, 557. Bergson is discussed on pages 427-444.

1563    DURANT, Will. Van Sokrates tot Bergson: Hoofdfiguren uit de
        geschiedenis van het denken. "Vert. door Helena C. Pos
        (Herdruk III: Van Spencer tot Bergson)." Amsterdam: Em
        Querido, 1962, 191.

1564    DURBAN, William. "The Philosophy of Henri Bergson." Homi-
        letic Review, 63, No. 1, January 1912, 20-23.

1565    DWELSHAUVERS, Georges. "M. Bergson et la méthode intuitive."
        Revue du Mois, 4, No. 9, 10 septembre 1907, 336-350.
        This article also appeared in Samedi, No. 44, 1907. The
        author considers the problem of method in psychology.

1566    DWELSHAUVERS, Georges. "Evolution et durée dans la philoso-
        phie de Bergson." Revue de l'Université de Bruxelles, 18,
        No. 1, octobre 1912, 21-66.

1567    DWELSHAUVERS, Georges. "De L'Intuition dans l'acte de l'es-
        prit." Revue de Métaphysique et de Morale, 16, No. 1,
        janvier 1908, 55-65. This article was reprinted in La
        Synthèse mentale.

1568    DWELSHAUVERS, Georges. "L'Intuition du spirituel." Revue
        de Philosophie, 31, No. 3, 1931, 327-394.

1569    DWELSHAUVERS, Georges. Les Mécanismes subconscients. Paris:
        Félix Alcan, 1925, 146.

1570    DWELSHAUVERS, Georges. La Psychologie française contempo-
        raine: La Psychologie de Bergson. Paris: Félix Alcan,
        1920, 256.

1571    DWELSHAUVERS, Georges. "Raison et intuition: Etude sur la
        philosophie de M. Bergson." Belgique Artistique et Litté-
        raire, 1re Année, 1905, 185-199, 316-331; 2e Année, 1906,
        17-35.

1572    DWELSHAUVERS, Georges. "Raison et intuition: Etude sur la
        philosophie de M. Bergson." Revue Hebdomadaire des Cours
        et des Conférences, 15, No. 4, 1906-07, 175-181; No. 8,
        1906-07, 366-374; No. 10, 1906-07, 462-471; No. 13, 1906-

07, 585-590; No. 16, 1906-07, 732-736; No. 17, 1906-07, 804-809.

1573    DWELSHAUVERS, Georges. "Recherches expérimentales sur la pensée implicite." Revue de Philosophie, 28, No. 3, 1928, 217-255.

1574    DWELSHAUVERS, Georges. La Synthèse mentale. Paris: Félix Alcan, 1908, 276. This study, like most of Dwelshauver's writings, is strongly influenced by Bergson.

1575    DWELSHAUVERS, Georges. Traité de psychologie. Paris: Payot, 1934, 606. Bergson and Wm. James are discussed on page 17; Bergson and introspective psychology on pages 34-35; Bergson and Watson on page 39; Bergson and Ravaisson on habit on pages 134-138; "durée psychologique" on pages 399-400 and 407-408; and Bergson on memory on pages 431, 542, 570-581, and 589.

1576    DYRSSEN, Carl. Bergson und die Deutsche Romantik. Marburg, Germany: Elwert, 1922, 56.

1577    DYSERINCK, Hugo. "Die Briefe Henri Bergsons an Graf Hermann Keyserling." Deutsche Vierteljahrsschrift für Literaturwissenschaft und Geistesgeschichte, 34, No. 1, 1960, 535-552; No. 2, 1960, 169-188.

1578    E., P. "En días de dolor para Francia se apagó la vida del gran filósofo Henri Bergson." La Gaceta, 6 enero 1941.

1579    EBACHER, Roger. "Existence historique et temporalité selon Bergson." Laval Théologique et Philosophique, 25, No. 2, 1969, 208-233.

1580    EBACHER, Roger. La Philosophie dans la cité technique: Essai sur la philosophie bergsonienne des techniques. Québec: Laval University Press; Paris: Bloud et Gay, 1968, 242.

1581    ECKSTEIN, Jerome. "Bergson's Views on Science and Metaphysics: Reconsidered." Philosophical Quarterly (India), 38, No. 3, 1965, 163-179. Bergson's attitude towards science has been misunderstood. The author compares Bergson and Dewey and stresses their similiarities.

1582    ECKSTEIN, Jerome. "Interestedness and non-Interestedness: Two Approaches to Knowledge." Diss., Columbia, 1961.

1583    EDGELL, Beatrice. Theories of Memory. Oxford: University
        Press, 1924, 174. An essay entitled "The Conception of
        Memory in the Philosophy of M. Bergson" appears on pages
        114-133. The author stresses parallels between Bergson
        and Samuel Butler.

1584    "Editorial." New York Times, 22 February 1914, Sect. 5, p.
        4, col. 1.

1585    "Editorial." New York Times, 7 January 1941, 22, col. 2.

1586    EDMAN, Irwin. "Henri Bergson." Nation, 152, No. 3, 18 Jan-
        uary 1941, 76-77. This is an obituary article. It was
        used as a preface to the Modern Library edition of Crea-
        tive Evolution.

1587    EDMAN, Irwin. "Henri Bergson." Sustancia, 2, Nos. 7-8,
        septiembre 1941, 329-333.

1588    EDMAN, Irwin. "Lo que nos ha dejado Bergson." Ultra, marzo
        1941 (Havana). This is a Castillian version of an article
        in Nation, January 1941.

1589    EDMAN, Irwin. "Review of The Two Sources of Religion and
        Morality by Henri Bergson." Journal of Philosophy, 32,
        No. 14, 1935, 387-388. The author concludes that: "Mr.
        Bergson's book is in the best sense provocative."

1590    EICHTHAL, Eugène d'. "Des Rapports de la mémoire et de la
        métaphysique." Revue Philosophique de la France et de
        l'Etranger, 85, Nos. 3-4, mars-avril 1918, 177-201. This
        is a criticism of Bergson's concept of memory.

1591    EINSTEIN, Albert. "A Propos de la déduction relativiste de
        Meyerson." Revue Philosophique de la France et de l'Etran-
        ger, 105, Nos. 3-4, mars-avril 1928, 161-166. Einstein
        agrees with Meyerson and Bergson that time should not be
        spatialized.

1592    EINSTEIN, Albert. "Foreword." Louis de Broglie. Physics
        and Microphysics. New York: Pantheon Books, 1955, 7.
        Einstein states: "I found the consideration of Bergson's
        and Zeno's philosophy from the point of view of the newly
        acquired concepts highly fascinating." (7).

1593    EINSTEIN, Albert. "Remarques sur la théorie de la relativi-
        té." Bulletin de la Société Française de Philosophie, 20,
        No. 3, juillet 1822, 102-113. Also in Ecrits et paroles,

3, 497-503; Mélanges, 1340-1347; Translated, with an Introduction, in Bergson and the Evolution of Physics, Ed.
P. A. Y. Gunter, 133. Relativity deals, Einstein holds,
with objective reality, not subjective time. When it
comes to objective reality there are many time series,
not one, as Bergson holds.

1594   "Das einzige mögliche Weltreligion: H. Bergson." Deutsche
Rundschau, 63. Jahrg., No. 3, 1937, 211.

1595   EISLER, Rudolf. Philosophen-lexikon. Berlin: Siegfried
Müller und John, 1912, 889. Bergson is discussed on pages
57-60.

1596   ELLACURIA, Ignacio. "Religión y religiosidad en Bergson:
II. La religión estática, sus formas: Crítica." Revista
de Orientación y Cultura, 16, No. 159, 1961, 205-212.

1597   ELLENGERGER, Henri F. The Discovery of the Unconscious.
New York: Basic Books, 1970, 932. Bergson's knowledge of
hypnotism is discussed on page 168; his critique of
thought-reading under hypnosis on page 172; his similarities with Von Schubert on page 262; Bergson's prophecies
on research into the unconscious mind on page 321; his relationships with Pierre Janet on pages 336, 354-355, 376,
394, and 400; his relationships with Alfred Binet on page
355; his similarities to Alfred Adler on page 624; his relationship to Paul Haberlin on page 623; and his relations
with C. G. Jung on page 818. For other references see the
index.

1598   ELLIOT, Hugh S. R. Modern Science and the Illusions of Professor Bergson. London: Longmans, Green and Company, 1912,
257. The author is highly critical. He assumes a mechanistic view of science and denies that Bergson's philosophy has any foundation in fact.

1599   EMERY, Léon. De Montaigne à Teilhard de Chardin via Pascal
et Rousseau. Lyon: Cahiers Libres, 1965, 144.

1600   EMERY, Léon. "Vers Le Point oméga?" Polarité du symbole.
Paris: Les Etudes Carmélitaines chez Desclée de Brouwer,
1960, 75-93. The author deals in this essay with Bergson
and Teilhard de Chardin.

1601   EMMENS, Wilko. Das Raumproblem bei H. Bergson. Leiden:
Brill, 1931, 223.

1602    EMMET, Dorothy M.  "Some Reflections Concerning M. Bergson's 'Two Sources of Morality and Religion'."  Proceedings of the Aristotelian Society, N.S. 34, 1933-1934, 231-248.

1603    ENOCH, Maurice.  "Réception de M. Henri Bergson à l'Académie française: Biographie."  Larousse Mensuel, 4, No. 134, avril 1918, 409-410.

1604    ERCKMANN, R.  "Bergson und Hanns Hörbiger."  Schlüssel zum Weltgeschehen, 4, 1928, 364-369.

1605    ESCHBACH, V.  "Henri Bergson."  Kölnische Volkszeitung, 20 Januar 1910.

1606    "Review of Essai sur les données immédiates de la conscience by Henri Bergson."  Revue Philosophique de la France et de l'Etranger, 19, 1890, 518-538.

1607    ESSER, P. H.  Levensaspecten: Essays Over Bergson, Pascal, Kierkegaard en Dostoievsky.  Zutphen: Ruys, 1946, 130.

1608    ESSERTIER, Danier.  Philosophes et savants français du XXe siècle: Extraits et notices.  Paris: Félix Alcan, 1929, 251.

1609    ETCHEVERRY, Auguste.  "La Durée bergsonienne."  Actes du Xe Congrès des Sociétés de Philosophie de Langue Française (Congrès Bergson).  Paris: Armand Colin, 1, 1959, 103-106. The theory of duration, the author holds, is at the heart of Bergson's doctrine; it is on this foundation that his entire metaphysics rests.  The awareness of lived time constitutes the ultimate source of his intuitive method.

1610    ETCHEVERRY, Auguste.  "Table ronde: Durée et mémoire."  Actes du Xe Congrès des Sociétés de Philosophie de Langue Française (Congrès Bergson).  Paris: Armand Colin, 2, 1959, 41-61.

1611    "Etudes bergsoniennes."  Revue Philosophique de la France et de l'Etranger, Nos. 3-4, mars-août 1941, 121-342.

1612    Etudes Bergsoniennes.  Paris: Albin Michel, 1948, Vol. 1, 220.  Bergson and Proust, and Bergson and Maine de Biran are discussed in this issue.

1613    Etudes Bergsoniennes.  Paris: Albin Michel, 1949, Vol. 2, 273.  Bergson's Latin thesis, Bergson and Plotinus, Bergson and England, and Bergson and existentialism are discussed in this issue.

1614   Etudes Bergsoniennes. Paris: Albin Michel, 1952, Vol. 3,
       219.  Bergson's concept of evil and his relations with
       Sorel and Dauriac are discussed in this issue.

1615   Etudes Bergsoniennes. Paris: Presses Universitaires de
       France, 1956, Vol. 4, 254.  Bergson's philosophy of his-
       tory, Bergson's aesthetics, and Bergson and Péguy are dis-
       cussed in this issue.

1616   Etudes Bergsoniennes. Paris: Presses Universitaires de
       France, 1960, Vol, 5, 220.  Valéry, Neitzsche, Teilhard
       de Chardin, Edouard Le Roy, Croce, Kant, and others are
       discussed in this issue in relation to Bergson.

1617   Etudes Bergsoniennes. Paris: Presses Universitaires de
       France, 1961, Vol. 6, 212.  Several of Bergson's essays
       are published here: "La Conscience et la vie," "Fantômes
       de vivants," "Le Rêve," "L'Effort intellectuel," "Le Pos-
       sible et le réel," and "La Perception du changement."  The
       table of contents of the Edition du Centenaire also ap-
       pears here.

1618   Etudes Bergsoniennes. Paris: Presses Universitaires de
       France, 1966, Vol. 7, 231.  Summaries of "The Nature of
       the Soul" and "The Nature of Personality," lectures by
       Bergson delivered in Britain in 1911 and 1914, are pub-
       lished in this issue, along with articles on Bergson's
       philosophy of religion and his relations with Albert Thi-
       baudet.

1619   Etudes Bergsoniennes. Paris: Presses Universitaires de
       France, 1968, Vol. 8, 175.  Letters between Bergson and
       Péguy are published in this issue, which also contains an
       essay on Spinozist themes in Bergson's thought and various
       talks given at the unveiling of a Bergson plaque at the
       Panthéon.

1620   Etudes Bergsoniennes. Paris: Presses Universitaires de
       France, 1970, Vol. 9, 232.  Bergson's mission to Spain in
       1916, talks given in Madrid entitled "L'Ame humaine" and
       "La Personnalité" are presented here, along with materials
       pertaining to Bergson and Charles Du Bos.

1621   "Review of Eucken and Bergson by Mrs. E. Hermann."  Indepen-
       dent, 74, No. 3350, 13 February 1913, 368-370.

1622   Eucken (Rudolph), Bergson (Henri) en Russell (Bertrand):
       Filosofische Gegenschriften.  Haarlem: De Toorts, 1963,

397. "Ingeleid door R. F. Beerling en B. Delfgaauw. Vert. van Henri Bergson: Gerard Wijdeveld."

1623    EUCKEN, Rudolph, BERGSON, Henri, and RUSSELL, Bertrand. Filosofische Gegenschriften. "(...Vert. van Henri Bergson, Gerard Wijdeveld en A. Moreno...). Ingeleid door H. F. Beerling en B. Delfgaauw (Pantheon der winnaars van de Nobelprijs voor litteratuur)." Haarlem: De Toorts, 1963, 664.

1624    EUCKEN, Rudolph. Main Currents of Modern Thought. Trans. Meyrick Booth. London and Leipsic: Unwin, 1912, 488. Bergson and Lodge are discussed on pages 185-189.

1625    EVANS, Serge. "La Vie et l'intelligence." Renaissance Contemporaine, 24 juin 1913.

1626    EVELLIN, François. Infini et quantité: Etude sur le concept de l'infini en philosophie et dans les sciences. Paris: Baillière, 1880. This work was utilized by Bergson in writing Time and Free Will.

1627    "Review of L'Evolution créatrice by Henri Bergson." Hibbert Journal, 6, No. 1, January 1908, 435-442.

1628    "Review of L'Evolution créatrice by Henri Bergson." Nation, 89, 30 September 1909, 298-300.

1629    EWALD, Oscar. "Philosophy in Germany in 1911." Philosophical Review, 21, No. 5, September 1912, 499-526. Bergson is discussed on pages 523-525.

1630    "Review of Examination of Professor Bergson's Philosophy by David Balsillie." Revue de Métaphysique et de Morale, 20, No. 4, 1912, Supplément, 25.

1631    FABRE, Lucien. "Au Sujet du Valéry de Thibaudet." Nouvelle Revue Française, 19, No. 12, décembre 1923, 662-676. The author discusses Bergson's influence on Thibaudet on pages 671-672.

1632    FABRE-LUCE, Alfred. Journal 1951. Paris: Amiot-Dumont, 1951, 420. This entry deals with Bergson, plus many others.

1633    FABRE-LUCE DE GRUSON, Françoise. "Actualité de l'esthétique bergsonienne." Actes du Xe Congrès des Sociétés de Philosophie de Langue Française (Congrès Bergson). Paris:

Armand Colin, 1, 1959, 107-110.  This essay is a reply to
R. Bayer's article on Bergson's theory of art (1942).
Bergson systematically eliminated all technical consider-
ations from the nature of art, while for Bayer art is
above all a matter of "technique."

1634    FABRE-LUCE DE GRUSON, Françoise.  "Bergson: Lecteur de Kant."
        Etudes Bergsoniennes, 5, 1960, 171-190.

1635    FABRE-LUCE DE GRUSON, Françoise.  "Sens commun et bon sens
        chez Bergson."  Revue Internationale de Philosophie, 13,
        No. 2, 1959, 187-200.  According to the author, Bergson's
        dialectic between common sense ("sens commun") and good
        sense ("bon sens") presupposes a primary dissociation of
        their functions, according to which the judiciary element
        of good sense makes up for the mistakes of common sense.
        Bergson attempts to elicit again the agreement of minds
        at the level of good sense.  While common sense bases it-
        self on the prejudices natural to the intelligence, good
        sense appropriates the pure apprehensions of intuition.
        To make good sense prevail over common sense is to affirm
        the superiority of the immediate, of movement, and of pro-
        gress over their contraries.

1636    FABRE-LUCE DE GRUSON, Françoise.  "Table ronde: Esthétique."
        Actes du Xe Congrès des Sociétés de Philosophie de Langue
        Française (Congres Bergson).  Paris: Armand Colin, 2,
        1959, 193-210.

1637    FABRIS, Matteo.  La filosofia sociale di Henri Bergson.
        Bari, Italy: Resta, 1966, 262.

1638    FAGUET, Emile.  "Un Historien du symbolisme."  La Revue,
        Sér. 6, 24e Année, Vol, C, 1er janvier 1913, 37-47.  This
        article concerns Tancrède de Visan and Bergson.

1639    FAGUET, Emile.  Propos de théâtre: Troisième Série.  Paris:
        Société Française d'Imprimerie et de Librairie, 1906, 376.
        Bergson's theory of laughter is discussed on pages 343-
        374.  This essay was published first in Journal des Débats,
        26 September 1904 and was republished 3 October 1904.

1640    FALKENFELD, Hellmuth.  "Das Verhältnis von Zeit und Realität
        bei Kant und Bergson."  Diss., Humboldt (Berlin), 1918, 48.

1641    FARAL, Edmond and LE ROY, Edouard.  Hommage national à Hen-
        ri Bergson à la Sorbonne, le 13 mai 1947.  Paris: Firmin-
        Didot, 1947, 10.

1642   FARGES, Albert. Le Cerveau, l'âme et les facultés. 6e éd.
       Paris: Berche et Tralin, 1900, 491.

1643   FARGES, Albert. "La Cosmologie bergsonienne." Revue du
       Clergé Française, 15 mars 1913.

1644   FARGES. Albert. "L'Erreur fondamentale de la philosophie
       nouvelle." Revue Thomiste, 17, No. 2, mars-avril 1909,
       182-197; No. 3, mai-juin 1909, 299-312.

1645   FARGES, Albert. Etudes philosophiques pour vulgariser les
       théories d'Aristote et de Saint Thomas et montrer leur ac-
       cord avec les sciences: I. Théorie fondamentale de l'acte
       et la puissance ou du mouvement: Le Devenir, sa causalité,
       sa finalité: Avec La Critique de la philosophie "nouvelle"
       de MM. Bergson et Le Roy, ou du modernisme philosophique.
       Paris: Berche et Tralin, 1909-1910, 443.

1646   FARGES, Albert. "La Notion bergsonienne du temps." Revue
       Néo-scolastique de Philosophie, 19, No. 75, 1912, 337-378.

1647   FARGES, Albert. La Philosophie de M. Bergson, professeur au
       Collège de France: Exposé et critique. Paris: Maison de
       la Bonne Presse, 1912, 491.

1648   FARGES, Albert. La Philosophie de M. Bergson, professeur au
       Collège de France: Exposé et critique. 2e éd. Paris:
       Impr. Feron-Vrau, 1914, 527. This edition includes re-
       plies to critics.

1649   FARGES, Albert. "Le Problème de la contingence d'après M.
       Bergson." Revue Pratique d'Apologétique, 8, No. 86, 15
       avril 1909, 115-122.

1650   FARGES, Albert. "Le Sens commun et son amputation par
       l'école bergsonienne." Revue Néo-scolastique de Philoso-
       phie, 21, No. 84, novembre 1914-1919, 440-479.

1651   FATONE, Vincente. "Review of Les Deux Sources de la morale
       et de la religion by Henri Bergson." Verbum, 26, No. 83,
       1933, 107-110.

1652   FATUD, Jean-Marie. "Roman Ingarden: Critique de Bergson."
       For Roman Ingarden: Nine Essays in Phenomenology. Ed.
       Anna-Teresa Tymieniecka. S-Gravenhage: Martinus Nijhoff,
       1959, 7-28.

1653   FAUCONNET, Charles-André. "Review of Bergson by Félicien
       Challaye." Erasmus, 3, No. 17-18, 1950, 547-550.

1654    FAVARGER, Charles. "Durée et intuition." Revue de Théolo-
        gie et de Philosophie, 3e Série, 10, No. 3, 1960, 169-187.
        This talk was given at the Congrès Bergson of the Société
        romande de philosophie.

1655    FAVARGER, Charles. "Review of Henri Bergson by Günther
        Pflug." Revue de Théologie et de Philosophie, 3e Série,
        10, No. 3, 1960, 257-258.

1656    FAVARGER, Charles. "Review of La Dialectique des images
        chez Bergson by Lydie Adolphe." Revue de Théologie et de
        Philosophie, 3e Série, 4, No. 1, 1954, 84-85.

1657    FAVARGER, Charles. "Review of L'Univers bergsonien by Lydie
        Adolphe." Revue de Théologie et de Philosophie, 3e Série,
        6, No. 2, 1956, 147-149.

1658    FAVILLE, A. "Review of L'Intellectualisme de Bergson by
        Léon Husson." Revue Philosophique de Louvain, 3e Série,
        4, No. 4, novembre 1949, 527-529.

1659    FAWCETT, Edward Douglas. "Matter and Memory." Mind, 21, No.
        82, April 1912, 201-232. This is a discussion of Berg-
        son's mind-body dualism, with special emphasis on the "spa-
        tiality" of matter.

1660    FAWCETT, Edward Douglas. "Review of Time and Free Will by
        Henri Bergson." Quest, 2, 1911, 492-496.

1661    FEDI, R. "Lo spiritualismo de Enrico Bergson." Bilychnis,
        Anno 20, No. 2, 1929.

1662    FELDMAN, Valentin. L'Esthétique française contemporaine.
        Paris: Félix Alcan, 1936, 139. The romantic realism of
        Basch, "illuminism" of Bergson, "rationalistic realism" of
        Souriau, etc. are discussed in this essay.

1663    FENART, Michel. Les Assertions bergsoniennes. Paris: Vrin,
        1937, 362.

1664    FERLOV, Knud. "De Kierkegaard à Bergson." Nouvelles Litté-
        raires, No. 322, 15 décembre 1928, 3.

1665    FERNANDAT, René. "Bergson et Valéry." Vie Intellectuelle,
        14, Nos. 8-9, août-septembre 1946, 122-146.

1666    FERNANDEZ, Julio César. "Henri Bergson's Message: A Philos-
        ophy for Today." Américas, 15, No. 8, August 1963, 10-12.

1667    FERNANDEZ, Ramon. "Henri Bergson." Nouvelle Revue Fran-
        çaise, 55, No. 325, 1941, 470-473.

1668    FERNANDEZ, Ramon. Itinéraire français. Paris: Editions du
        Pavois, 1943, 480. The influence of Bergson on Thibaudet
        is discussed on pages 36-55.

1669    FERNANDEZ, Ramon. "Review of La Pensée et le mouvant by H.
        Bergson." Nouvelle Revue Française, 22, No. 250, 1er juil-
        let 1934, 135-136.

1670    FERRAR, W. "Review of L'Evolution créatrice by Henri Berg-
        son." Commonwealth, December 1909, 636-637.

1671    FERRATER MORA, José. Diccionario de filosofía. 3e ed.
        Buenos Aires: Ed. Sudamericana, 1958, 1047.

1672    FERRATER MORA, José. Introducción a Bergson. Buenos Aires:
        Ed. Sudamericana, 1946, 64.

1673    FERRATER MORA, José. "Introducción a Bergson." Cuestiones
        disputadas: Ensayos de filosofía. Madrid: Revista de Oc-
        cidente, 1955, 113-150.

1674    FERRI, Luigi. "Review of Essai sur les donnees immédiates
        de la conscience by Henri Bergson." Rivista italiana di
        filosofia, 5, No. 2, marzo-aprile 1890, 248-249.

1675    FERRO, Carmelo. "Bergson davanti a Cristo." Vita e pen-
        siero, 35, No. 1, gennaio 1952.

1676    FESSARD, Gaston. La Méthode de réflexion chez Maine de
        Biran. Paris: Bloud et Gay, 1938, 153.

1677    FESTUGIERE, A. J. "Religion statique et mysticisme en Grèce
        d'après un ouvrage récent." La Vie Spirituelle, 34,
        Suppl., 1933, 89-102.

1678    FEUER, Lewis S. "Review of Le Bergsonisme: Une Mystifica-
        tion philosophique by Politzer." Philosophy and Phenome-
        nological Research, 8, No. 3, 1947-1948, 470-472.

1679    FEULING, Daniel Martin. "Bergson und der Thomismus." Jahr-
        buch für Philosophie und spekulative Theologie, 25, 1913,
        33-55.

1680    FIGUEROA, Ernesto L. Bergson: Exposición de sus ideas fun-
        damentales. La Plata, Argentina: Biblioteca Humanidades,
        1930, 299.

1681     FILHO, Candido Mota.  "Centenário de Bergson: Depoimento."
         Revista Brasileira de Filosifia, 11, No. 41, 1961, 106-
         107.  The author describes Bergson's influence on his phi-
         losophy and mentions articles which he has written con-
         cerning Bergson.

1682     FILIASI CARCANO, P.  "Review of Bergson by Lorenzo Giusso."
         Giornale critico della filosofia italiano, 5, No. 1, 1951,
         145-152.

1683     FILLOUX, Jean-Claude.  La Mémoire.  Paris: Presses Universi-
         taires de France, 1949, 128.  Bergson is discussed on
         pages 6-7, 15, 24, 34-36, 44-45, 72-73, 100, and 107-120.

1684     FINNABOGASON, Gundnmur.  L'Intelligence sympathique.  Paris:
         Félix Alcan, 1913, 244.  The author's psychology is strong-
         ly influenced by Bergson.

1685     FISER, Emeric.  Le Symbole littéraire: Essai sur la signi-
         fication du symbole chez Wagner, Baudelaire, Mallarmé,
         Bergson et Marcel Proust.  Paris: Corti, 1941, 225.

1686     FITCH, Girdler B.  "The Comic Sense of Flaubert in the Light
         of Bergson's Le Rire."  Publications of the Modern Lan-
         guage Association of America, 55, No. 2, June 1940, 511-
         531.

1687     FITE, Warner.  The Living Mind.  New York: Dial, 1930, 317.
         Bergson is discussed on pages 99-103, 146, and 154-156.

1688     FLEISCHMANN, Wolfgang B.  "Conrad's Chance and Bergson's
         Laughter."  Renascence, 14, No. 2, Winter 1961, 66-71.

1689     FLEURIOT DE LANGLE, Paul.  Les Sources du comique dans la
         "Farce de Maître Pathelin."  Angers: Librairie du Roi René,
         1926, 31.

1690     FLEURY, René-Albert.  Bergson et la quantité.  Paris: Copy-
         Odéon, 1940, 8.

1691     FLEWELLING, Ralph Tyler.  "Bergson and Personalism."  Perso-
         nalist, 14, No. 2, April 1933, 81-92.  The author argues
         that Bergson's philosophy has a close affinity with perso-
         nalism.

1692     FLEWELLING, Ralph Tyler.  Bergson and Personal Realism.  New
         York and Cincinnati, Ohio: The Abingdon Press, 1920, 304.

1693   FLEWELLING, Ralph Tyler.  "Bergson: A Philosopher of Free-
       dom."  Personalist, 22, No. 2, April 1941, 189-190.

1694   FLEWELLING, Ralph Tyler.  "Bergson, Ward and Eucken in Their
       Relation to Bowne."  Methodist Magazine, 96, 1914, 374-
       383.

1695   FLORENCE, Jean.  "M. Bergson et Renouvier."  Phalange, 8,
       No. 86, 1913, 97-104.

1696   FLORENCE, Jean.  "Nature et méthode de la philosophie."
       Phalange, 7, 20 juillet 1912, 1-15.

1697   FLORENCE, Jean.  "La Philosophie de M. Bergson, jugée par M.
       Lasserre."  Phalange, 5, No. 51, 20 septembre 1910, 218-
       269.  This article concerns Pierre Lasserre's articles in
       L'Action Française on Bergson.

1698   FLORENCE, Jean.  "Réponse à M. Julien Benda."  Phalange, 7,
       20 septembre 1912, 278-285.

1699   FLORIAN, Mircea.  Der Begriff der Zeit bei Henri Bergson.
       Diss., Greifswald, 1914, 126.  Greifswald, Germany: Brun-
       cken and Co., 1914.

1700   "Floris Delattre on Bergson's Catholicism."  New York Times,
       7 December 1941, 33, col. 3.

1701   FLOURNOY, Théodore.  La Philosophie de William James.  Paris:
       Saint-Blaise, 1911, 219.

1702   FONDANE, Benjamin.  "Bergson, Freud y los dioses."  Sur, Año
       5, No. 15, 1935.

1703   FONDANE, Benjamin.  La Conscience malheureuse.  Paris: Denoël
       et Steele, 1936, 306.  Nietzsche, Gide, Bergson, Husserl,
       Heidegger, Kierkegaard, and Chestov are dealt with in this
       study of the "unhappy consciousness."

1704   FONSEGRIVE, George.  "De Taine à Péguy."  Correspondant, 10
       novembre 1916, 529-534.

1705   FONTANA, Paul.  "Cours de M. Bergson au Collège de France:
       Théories de la volonté."  Revue de Philosophie, 11, No. 7,
       juillet 1907, 70-91; No. 10, octobre 1907, 407-427.

1706   FOREST, Aimé.  "L'Existence selon Bergson."  Archives de
       Philosophie, 17, No. 1, 1947, 81-101.

1707    FOREST, Aimé. "Histoire de la philosophie." Revue Thomiste,
        50, No. 1, 1950, 231-241. The author reviews books on
        Bergson by Husson and Gouhier.

1708    FOREST, Aimé. "La Méthode idéaliste." Revue Néo-scolasti-
        que de Philosophie, 2e Sér., 37, No. 43, août 1934, 178-
        201. This study concerns the problems of contemporary
        French idealism. It deals with the debt of Bergson and
        Boutroux to Ravaisson.

1709    FOREST, Aimé. "La Réalité concrète chez Bergson et chez
        Saint Thomas." Revue Thomiste, N.S. 16, No. 77, mai-juin
        1933, 368-398.

1710    FORNASARI, Archimedes. "A Critical Study of Henri Bergson's
        Two Sources of Morality and Religion." This is an unpub-
        lished work written in 1964 at the Catholic University of
        America. The author defends Bergson against anti-intel-
        lectualism and pantheism, but criticizes his notion of
        final cause.

1711    FORSTER, H. "Henri Bergson." Overland, N.S. 71, No. 3,
        April 1918, 358.

1712    FORSYTH, T. M. "Bergson's and Freud's Theories of Laughter:
        A Comparison and a Suggestion." South African Journal of
        Science, 23, 1926, 987-995.

1713    FORSYTH, T. M. "Creative Evolution in its Bearings on the
        Idea of God." Philosophy, 25, No. 94, July 1950, 195-208.
        The author holds: "Foundational for the whole doctrine of
        Creative Evolution is the philosophy of Bergson, and the
        principle has been one of the most prominent in philosophy,
        ever since the publication of his epoch-making book bear-
        ing that title." (195).

1714    FORT, Joseph Barthélemy. Samuel Butler (1835-1902): Etude
        d'un caractère et d'une intelligence. Bordeaux: Impri-
        merie Bière, 1934, 515. The author deals with Bergson and
        Butler in this study.

1715    FORTI, Edgard. "La Psychologie bergsonienne et les survi-
        vances actuelles de l'associationisme." Revue de Méta-
        physique et de Morale, 30, No. 4, octobre-décembre 1923,
        509-537. The author defends Bergson's approach to psy-
        chology against that of E. Rignano and H. Piéron.

1716   FOSTER, Frank Hugh.  "Some Theistic Implications of Berg-
       son's Philosophy."  American Journal of Theology, 22, No.
       2, April 1918, 274-299.

1717   FOSTER, Steven.  "Bergson's 'Intuition' and Whitman's 'Song
       of Myself'."  Texas Studies in Literature and Language, 6,
       No. 3, 1964, 376-387.

1718   FOUILLEE, Alfred.  "L'Influence de la philosophie de M. Berg-
       son. II."  Mouvement Socialiste, 29, No. 230, avril 1911,
       269.

1719   FOUILLEE, Alfred.  Le Mouvement idéaliste et la réaction con-
       tre la science positive.  Paris: Félix Alcan, 1896, 331.
       Bergson is discussed on pages 198-206.

1720   FOUILLEE, Alfred.  La Pensée et les nouvelles écoles anti-
       intellectualistes.  Paris: Félix Alcan, 1911, 415.

1721   FOUKS, Léon.  "Note sur la dialectique bergsonienne et le
       judaïsme."  Actes du Xe Congrès des Sociétés de Philoso-
       phie de Langue Française (Congrès Bergson).  Paris: Armand
       Colin, 1, 1959, 111-113.  During his last years Bergson
       found himself increasingly attracted to Christianity and,
       by contrast, seems to have ignored Judaism.  Nonetheless,
       the author holds, there are striking analogies between his
       conceptions and those of Israel, whose unique faith is an
       ardent quest for God.

1722   FOUKS, Leon.  "Table ronde: Durée et mémoire."  Actes du Xe
       Congrès des Sociétés de Philosophie de Langue Française
       (Congrès Bergson).  Paris: Armand Colin, 2, 1959, 41-61.

1723   FOUKS, Léon.  "Table ronde: Morale."  Actes du Xe Congrès
       des Sociétés de Philosophie de Langue Française (Congrès
       Bergson).  Paris: Armand Colin, 2, 1959, 237-257.

1724   FOUKS, Léon.  "Table ronde: Religion."  Actes du Xe Congrès
       des Sociétés de Philosophie de Langue Française (Congrès
       Bergson).  Paris: Armand Colin, 2, 1959, 261-278.

1725   FOWLIE, Wallace.  Age of Surrealism.  Bloomington, Indiana:
       Indiana University Press, 1950, 215.  The influence of
       Bergson on surrealism is discussed on pages 19-20, 86, and
       104.

1726   FRAENKL, Pavel.  "Bergsons betydning for europeisk littera-
       tur i vårt århundre: Et idéhistorisk panorama."  Samtiden,
       68, No. 8, 1959, 485-496.

1727    FRAGUEIRO, Alfredo.  "El intuicionismo bergsoniano en la
        filosifía del Derecho."  Homenaje a Bergson.  Córdoba, Ar-
        gentina: Imprenta de la Universidad, 1936, 159-178.

1728    FRAISSE, Simone.  "Review of Péguy entre Juarès et l'église
        by André Robinet."  Revue d'Histoire Littéraire de la
        France, 70e Année, No. 1, 1970, 153-155.

1729    FRANCASTEL, Pierre.  "Bergson et Picasso."  Mélanges 1945:
        Vol 4.  Etudes philosophiques.  Paris: Les Belles Lettres,
        1946, 200-203.

1730    FRANCHESI, Gustavo J.  "En la muerte de Enrique Bergson."
        Criterio, Año 13, No. 678, 27 febrero 1941, 197-201.

1731    FRANCIA, Ennio.  "Caratteri della 'recherche' nella let-
        teratura francese."  Humanitas, Anno 6, No. 7, luglio
        1951, 752-765.  This study is concerned with Bergson,
        Gide, Mauriac, and Proust.

1732    FRANCK, Henri.  Lettres à quelques amis.  Paris: Grasset,
        1926, 303.  "Préface d'André Spire."  Bergson is discussed
        on pages 83, 84, 85, 90, and 141.

1733    FRANK, Simon.  "L'Intuition fondamentale de Bergson."  Henri
        Bergson.  Ed. Béguin and Thévenaz, 187-195.

1734    FRANKE, L.  "Review of Les Deux Sources de la morale et de
        la religion by Henri Bergson."  Blätter für deutsche Phi-
        losophie, 8, 1935, 221.

1735    FREE, Lincoln Forrest.  "The Philosophical and Educational
        Views of Henri Bergson."  Diss., New York, 1940.

1736    FREIRE, Antonio.  "O pensamento de deus de Nikos Kazant-
        zakis."  Revista Portuguesa de Filosofia, 26, No. 1, 1970,
        92-109.

1737    FRENKIAN, A. M.  "Libertatea si determinismul la Bergson
        fatã de stinta modernã."  Revista de Pedagogie, 1938, 215-
        243.

1738    FRESSIN, Augustin.  La Perception chez Bergson et chez Mer-
        leau-Ponty.  Paris: Société d'Editions d'Enseignement Su-
        périeure, 1967, 399.

1739    FREUD, Sigmund.  Wit and its Relation to the Unconscious.
        New York: Moffat, Yard and Company, 1916, 383.  References
        to Bergson's Laughter may be found on pages 301-360.

1740    FRIEDMAN, G.  "A Propos d'un livre sur Bergson."  Europe,
        27, 1931, 281-285.

1741    FRIEDMAN, Maurice.  "Bergson and Kazantzakis."  To Deny Our
        Nothingness: Contemporary Images of Man.  London: Victor
        Gollancz, Ltd., 1967, 63-79.

1742    FRIEDMAN, Melvin.  "William James and Henri Bergson: The
        Psychological Basis."  Stream of Consciousness: A Study in
        Literary Method.  New Haven, Connecticut: Yale University
        Press; London: Geoffrey Cumberlege, Oxford University
        Press, 1955, 74-98.

1743    FRITZSCHE, Richard.  "Review of Materie und Gedächtnis and
        Einführung in die Metaphysik by Henri Bergson and Henri
        Bergsons intuitive Philosophie by Steenbergen."  Viertel-
        jahrschrift für wissenschaftliche Philosophie und Sozio-
        logie, 34, No. 4, 1910, 353-357.

1744    FROST, S. E., Jr.  Masterworks of Philosophy: Digests of 11
        Great Classics.  Garden City, New York: Doubleday, 1946,
        757.  Selections from Creative Evolution are quoted on
        pages 725-757.

1745    FRUTOS, Eugenion.  "El primer Bergson en Antonio Machado."
        Revista de Filosofía, 19, Nos. 73-74, 1960, 117-168.  The
        influence of Bergson on the poet Machado is discussed in
        this article.

1746    FULTON, James Street.  "Bergson's Religious Interpretation
        of Evolution."  Rice Institute Pamphlet, 43, No. 3, 1956,
        14-27.  This essay discusses Bergson's position in The Two
        Sources of Morality and Religion.  The author argues that
        in this book Bergson no longer describes evolution as a
        mere emergence of novelty, but as the increase of value,
        progress, and spiritual significance.  The author provides
        a brief but penetrating account of moral obligation and
        static religion.

1747    G., H.  (Henri Gouhier?).  "Entretien avec E. Le Roy, suc-
        cesseur de Bergson au Collège de France."  Nouvelles Lit-
        téraires, No. 322, 15 décembre 1928, 6.

1748    G., L.  "Bergson and the Evolution of Physics, Ed. and Trans.
        with Intro. P. A. Y. Gunter."  Review of Metaphysics, 25,
        No. 1, September 1971, 140-141.

1749    GABRIEL, José.  "De Socrates à Bergson."  Argentina Libre,
        2, 23 enero 1941.

1750    GABRIEL, L.  "Evolution und Zeitbegriff von H. Bergson zu
        Teilhard de Chardin."  Wissenschaft und Weltbild, 15, 1962,
        31-36.

1751    GAGEY, Jacques.  Gaston Bachelard ou la conversion à l'ima-
        ginaire.  Paris: Rivière et Cie., 1969, 303.  Bergson,
        Brunschvicg, Lautréamont, Roupnel, and Sartre are dealt
        with in this study in relation to Bachelard.

1752    GAGNEBIN, Samuel.  "A L'Occasion du centenaire de Bergson
        (18 octobre 1859-3 janvier 1941)."  Studia Philosophica,
        19, 1959, 87-118.  This article concerns the Bergson con-
        ference of the Société romande de philosophie (Swiss)
        held 12-13 September 1959.

1753    GAGNEBIN, Samuel.  A L'Occasion du centenaire de Bergson (18
        octobre 1859-3 janvier 1941).  Bâle, Switzerland: Verlag
        für Recht und Gesellschaft, 1959, 32.  This article ap-
        peared originally in Studia Philosophica, 19, 1959.

1754    GAGNEBIN, Samuel.  "Hommage à Edouard Le Roy."  Revue de Thé-
        ologie et de Philosophie, 3e Sér., 5, 1955, 202-217.

1755    GAGNEBIN, Samuel.  "Note sur la méthode dans la philosophie
        de Bergson."  Henri Bergson.  Ed. Béguin and Thévenaz,
        222-226.  The author discussed Bergson's philosophical
        method, which he terms "experimental."  Because he did not
        sufficiently realize the importance of the intellect, the
        author holds, Bergson is not able to resolve his sharp op-
        positions between quality and quantity, duration and space,
        memory and perception.

1756    GAGNEBIN, Samuel.  La Philosophie de l'intuition: Essai sur
        les idées de M. Edouard Le Roy.  St. Blaise, France: Foyer
        Solidariste, 1912, 240.  The first third of the book is
        devoted to the philosophy of Bergson.  It is reviewed in
        Revue de Philosophie, 12, 7 août 1912.

1757    GALEFFI, Romano.  "O cômico em Bergson."  Revista Brasileira
        de Filosofia, 8, No. 32, 1958, 416-444.  This is an analy-
        sis of Chapter I, Le Rire.

1758    GALEFFI, Romano.  La filosofia di Bergson.  Roma: Instituto
        Statale dei Sordomuti, 1949, 191.  This is a thesis.

1759    GALEFFI, Romano.  "Presença de Bergson."  Anais do III Con-
        gresso Nacional de Filosofia.  São Paulo: Instituto Bra-
        sileiro de Filosofia, 1960, 425-445.

1760    GALEFFI, Romano. Presença de Bergson. Salvador, Brazil:
        Publicações da Universidade da Bahia, 1961, 82.

1761    GALIMBERTI, Andrea. "Au Sujet d'un mot de Bergson." Actes
        du Xe Congrès des Sociétés de Philosophie de Langue Fran-
        çaise (Congrès Bergson). Paris: Armand Colin, 1, 1959,
        115-117. In explicating a sentence asserted by Bergson
        in 1911 ("No philosopher had had more than one idea.") the
        author examines the way in which Bergson conceives his
        theory of man's world and his civilization, and the part
        which he assigns there to ideas.

1762    GALIMBERTI, Andrea. "Table ronde: Unité, unicité, dialo-
        gue." Actes du Xe Congrès des Sociétés de Philosophie de
        Langue Française (Congrès Bergson). Paris: Armand Colin,
        2, 1959, 281-302.

1763    GALLAGHER, Idella J. "Bergson on Closed and Open Morality."
        New Scholasticism, 42, No. 3, Winter 1968, 48-71. This is
        a thoughtful analysis of Bergson's two kinds of morality.

1764    GALLAGHER, Idella J. "Moral Obligation in the Philosophy of
        Henri Bergson." Diss., Marquette, 1963.

1765    GALLAGHER, Idella J. Morality in Evolution: The Moral Phi-
        losophy of Henri Bergson. The Hague: Martinus Nijhoff,
        1970, 112.

1766    GALLAGHER-PARKS, Mercedes. "Art et réalité: Etude pour une
        esthétique psychologique et bergsonienne." Deuxième Con-
        grès internationale d'esthétique et de science de l'art.
        Vol. 1. Paris: Félix Alcan, 1937, 75-79.

1767    GALLEGOS ROCAFULL, J. M. "De Bergson a Tomás de Aquino."
        Latino-américa, 3, 1951, 457-459. This is a review of
        Maritain's book, De Bergson à Thomas d'Aquin.

1768    GALLI, Luis Alejandro. "Materialismo y espiritualismo."
        Criterio, 6, No. 303, diciembre 1933, 374.

1769    GALLY, Henriette. Ruskin et l'esthétique intuitive. Paris:
        Vrin, 1933, 353. Chapter three concerns Ruskin and Berg-
        son.

1770    GALPERINE, Charles. "Conversation sur Claudel et Bergson."
        Entretiens sur Paul Claudel. Ed. Georges Cattaui and
        Jacques Madaule. Paris and La Haye: Mouton, 1968, 141-
        152.

1771   GALY, R.  "Le Temps et la liberté chez Kant et chez Bergson."
       Etudes Philosophiques, 16, No. 3, juillet-septembre 1961,
       281-284.

1772   GANNE, Pierre.  "Bergson et Claudel."  Henri Bergson.  Ed.
       Béguin and Thévenaz, 294-301.  The author compares Bergson
       and Claudel at length, terming Bergson a "poet" and Clau-
       del a "philosopher."  He finds their ideas and personal
       development to be basically similar.

1773   GAOS, Joaé.  "Bergson, ségun su autobiografía filosófica."
       Homenaje a Bergson.  Imprenta Universitaria México, 1941,
       7-48.

1774   GAOS, José.  Dos exclusivas del hombre: La mano y el tiempo.
       México: Fondo de Cultura Económica, 1945, 189.  This book
       consists of five lectures developing the thesis that the
       human hand and human time are unique in nature.

1775   GARCEZ, Maria Dulce Nogueira.  Do significado da contribui-
       ção de Bergson para e psicologia e a educação contemporâ-
       neas.  Univ. de S. Paulo, Faculd. de Filosofia, Boletim
       n. 184, Psicologia educacional n. 4, 1957, 242.

1776   GARCIA, J. Alvez.  "O dualismo metodologico na psicologia
       contemporânea."  Revista Portuguesa de Filosofia, 12, No.
       1, 1956, 14-20.

1777   GARCIA BACCA, Juan David.  "Bergson o el tiempo creador."
       Cuadernos Americanos, 26, No. 2, marzo-abril 1946, 89-128.

1778   GARCIA BACCA, Juan David.  Nueve grandes filosofos contempo-
       raneos y sus temas: Vol. 1.  Bergson, Husserl, Unamuno,
       Heidegger, Scheler, Hartmann.  Caracas: Imprenta Nacional,
       1947, 316.  Bergson is discussed on pages 9-51.

1779   GARCIA CAFFARENA, Judit G.  "Bipolaridad: Leit Motiv berg-
       soniano."  Universidad de Santa Fe, 64, No. 1, 1965, 127-
       138.

1780   GARCIA MORENTE, Manuel.  "Review of Le Bergsonisme by Albert
       Thibaudet."  Revista de Occidente, 4, No. 2, abril 1924,
       120-123.

1781   GARCIA MORENTE, Manuel.  "Europa en decadencia?"  Revista de
       Occidente, Año 1, No. 2, agosto 1923, 177.

1782   GARCIA MORENTE, Manuel.  La filosofía de Henri Bergson: Con
       el discurso pronunciado por M. Bergson en la Residencia de

Estudiantes el 10 de mayo de 1916. Madrid: Publicaciones
de la Residencia de Estudiantes, 1917, 150.

1783    GARDINER, H. N. "Mémoire et reconnaissance." Psychological
Review, 3, No. 3, September 1896, 578-580.

1784    GARDNER, Martin. Relativity for the Million. New York:
Macmillan, 1962, 182. The author discusses Bergson and
Einstein on pages 120-125.

1785    GARNETT, A. Campbell. "Review of Les Deux Sources de la morale et de la religion by Henri Bergson." International
Journal of Ethics, 63, No. 2, January 1933, 232-233.

1786    GARRIGOU-LAGRANGE, Reginald. Le Sens commun, la philosophie
de l'être et les formules dogmatiques. Paris: Desclée De
Brouwer et Cie., 1909, 350. The author asserts that Bergson's philosophy is an "evolutionary monism."

1787    GARRITY, Robert John. "Finality in the Philosophy of Henri
Bergson." Diss., Duquesne, 1964.

1788    GASPARINI, Duilio. "Maritain e Bergson: Trent-anni dopo."
Studia patavina, 8, No. 4, 1961, 490-500.

1789    GATES, R. Ruggles. "Evolutionism of Bergson." Monist, 25,
No. 4, October 1915, 537-555.

1790    GATTI, Pasquale. "Philosophy of Language." Logos, 12, Nos.
2, 3 e 4, 1926. Against Bergson and Croce, Gatti holds
that language is a valid expression of thought.

1791    GAUCHE, M. "Autour d'Henri Bergson." Belgique Artistique
et Littéraire, 34, 1914, 332-341.

1792    GAUDEAU, B. "La Philosophie de M. Bergson détruit la liberté." L'Univers, 16 juin 1912.

1793    GAULTIER, Jules de. "Le Réalisme du contenu." Revue Philosophique de la France et de l'Etranger, 69, No. 1, janvier
1910, 39-64. This essay deals with problems of continuity
and discontinuity in Bergson.

1794    GAULTIER, Paul. "Henri Bergson." Revue Politique et Littéraire, Revue Bleue, 56e Année, No. 10, 1918, 297-302; No.
11, 1918, 331-336; No. 12, 1918, 360-365; No. 13, 1918,
389-394; No. 14, 1918, 428-431; No. 15, 1918, 469-472.

1795    GAULTIER, Paul.  Les Maîtres de la pensée française.  Paris:
        Payot et Cie., 1921, 271.  Henri Bergson is discussed on
        pages 96-197.

1796    GAULTIER, Paul.  "L'Oeuvre philosophique de M. Emile Bou-
        troux."  Revue des Deux Mondes, 11, No. 6, 15 octobre
        1912, 837-871.

1797    GAULTIER, Paul.  La Pensée contemporaine: Les Grands Pro-
        blemes.  Paris: Hachette, 1911, 312.

1798    GAUTHIER, E.  "Is Bergson a Monist?"  Philosophical Quarter-
        ly, 19, No. 4, 1945.

1799    GEBERT, K.  "Philosophie der Innerwelt: Deutsche Übertragg.
        der Philosophie Bergsons."  Das 20. Jahrhundert, No. 48,
        November 1908.

1800    GEIGER, L. B.  "Review of La Pensée et le mouvant by Henri
        Bergson."  Revue des Sciences Philosophiques et Religieu-
        ses, 24, 1935, 312.

1801    GEMELLI, Agostino.  "Henri Bergson e la néoscolastica itali-
        ana."  Rivista di filosofia neoscolastica, 7, No. 2, 1915.
        This is a review of Olgiati, La filosofia de Henri Bergson.

1802    GEMELLI, Agostino.  "Henri Bergson und die italien. Neuschol-
        lastik."  Philosophisches Jahrbuch der Görres-Gesellschaft,
        27, 1914, 441-460.

1804    GENETTE, Gérard.  Figures: Essais.  Paris: Edit. du Seuil,
        1966, 269.

1805    GENTA, Jordán B.  "Comentario sobre el libro Homenaje a
        Bergson editado por el Instituto de Filosofía de la Uni-
        versidad de Córdoba (R.A.)."  Nosotro, 1, No. 1, julio
        1936, 466-468.

1807    GENTILE, Giovanni.  "Review of L'Energie spirituelle by H.
        Bergson."  Critica, 18, No. 1, 1920, 107-112.

1808    GENTILE, Giovanni.  "Review of La Pensée et le mouvant by
        Henri Bergson."  Leonardo, Anno 6, No. 7-8, 1935, 339-340.

1809    GENTILE, Giovanni.  "Il pensiero di Enrico Bergson secondo
        Ferdinando D'Amato."  Critica, 20, No. 1, 1922, 42-44.

1810    GEORGE, André.  "Bergson et la déshumanisation de la science."
        Nouvelles Littéraires, No. 957, 6 décembre 1945, 5.  This

article recounts the proceedings of the first meeting of
"Les Amis de Bergson." The basic subject discussed was
the danger to man posed by his technology, as symbolized
by the recently exploded atomic bomb. De Broglie, Le Roy,
Marcel, and others entered into the discussion. Bergson,
it was concluded, remains an optimist about technology.

1811    GEORGE, André. "Bergson et Einstein." Documents de la Vie
Intellectuelle, 1, No. 4, 20 janvier 1930, 52-60. This
essay recapitulates the Bergson-Einstein debate.

1812    GEORGE, André. "Bergson et les livres récents de M. Edouard
Le Roy." Documents de la Vie Intellectuelle, 1, No. 4,
20 janvier 1930, 60-64. This article is signed "A. G.".

1813    GEORGE, André. "Bergson et Thibaudet." Documents de la Vie
Intellectuelle, 3, No. 3, 20 juin 1930, 578-582.

1814    GEORGE, André. "La Confrontation Teilhard-Bergson." Nouvelles Littéraires, No. 1878, 29 août 1963, 3.

1815    GEORGE, André. "Le Temps, la vie et la mort." La Vie Intellectuelle, 43, No. 1, 1946, 121-146. The author explains
that Bergson's notion of biological time is verified by
research into physiological clocks by Pierre Lecomte du
Noüy.

1816    GEORGES-MICHEL, Michel. En Jardinant avec Bergson, en jun-
glant avec Kipling, en chassant le crocodile avec Sara
Bernhardt, en boxant avec Maeterlinck... . Paris: Albin
Michel, 1926, 349. This book contains an interview with
Henri Bergson.

1817    GERMAN, Terence Joseph. "Bergson's Individual-Communal
Morality." Diss., St. Louis, 1969.

1818    GERRARD, Thomas John. "Bergson and Divine Fecundity."
Catholic World, 98, No. 581, August 1913, 631-648.

1819    GERRARD, Thomas John. "Bergson and Finalism." Catholic
World, 98, No. 579, June 1913, 374-382.

1820    GERRARD, Thomas John. "Bergson and Freedom." Catholic
World, 97, No. 578, May 1913, 222-231.

1821    GERRARD, Thomas John. Bergson: An Exposition and Criticism
From the Point of View of Saint Thomas Aquinas. London:
Herder, 1914, 208. The author is thoroughly critical of
Bergson.

1822    GERRARD, Thomas John.  "Bergson, Newman and Aquinas."  Cath-
       olic World, 96, No. 576, March 1912, 748-762.

1823    GERRARD, Thomas John.  "Bergson's Philosophy of Change."
       Catholic World, 96, No. 574, January 1913, 433-448.

1824    GERRARD, Thomas J.  "Bergson's Philosophy of Change: His
       Intuitive Method."  Catholic World, 96, No. 575, February
       1913, 602-616.

1825    GHEREA, J. D.  Le Moi et le monde.  Paris: Vrin, 1939, 475.
       The author argues that ideas and immediate "durée" are the
       materials out of which the self and the world are con-
       structed.

1826    GHEREA, J. D.  "Le Problème de la connaissance et les
       durées."  Revue de Métaphysique et de Morale,  43, No. 1,
       janvier 1936, 89-111.  The author explains his method as
       follows: "Nous avons commencé, cette fois, par décomposer
       le 'temps' en ses durées, et c'est la multiplicité de
       celles-ci qui est à la base de l'analyse aboutissant à la
       conscience impersonelle... ."  (111).  The author offers
       many criticisms of intuitionism.

1827    GIBSON, A. Boyce.  "Review of Bradley and Bergson by R.
       Loomba."  Australasian Journal of Psychology and Philos-
       ophy, 19, No. 1, 1941, 76-78.

1828    GIBSON, A. Boyce.  "The Intuition of Bergson."  Quest, 3,
       No. 1, January 1911.

1829    GIBSON, A. Boyce.  "Mystic or Pragmatist?"  Australasian
       Journal of Psychology and Philosophy, 25, No. 1, 1947, 81-
       103.  This is a review of The Creative Mind.  The author
       draws interesting parallels between Bergson, pragmatists,
       and positivists.

1830    GIBSON, A. Boyce.  "Review of The Two Sources of Morality
       and Religion by Henri Bergson."  Australasian Journal of
       Psychology and Philosophy, 15, No. 1, 1937, 65-75.  This
       is a thoughtful and generally laudatory review.

1831    GIBSON, W. R.  "The Intuition of Bergson."  Quest, 2, 1910,
       201-228.

1832    GIESSLER.  "Review of 'L'Effort intellectuel' by Henri Berg-
       son."  Zeitschrift für Psychologie und Physiologie der
       Sinnesorgane, 32, 1903, 128-129.

1833   GIESSLER. "Review of 'Le Rêve' by Henri Bergson." Zeit-
       schrift für Psychologie und Physiologie der Sinnesorgane,
       29, 1902, 231. The author is critical of Bergson's con-
       cept of laughter.

1834   GILBERT, Pierre. "Sur La Critique du bergsonisme." Revue
       Critique des Idées et des Livres, 24, No. 140, 10 février
       1914, 374-375.

1835   GILLOUIN, René. Henri Bergson: Choix de textes avec étude
       du système philosophique. Paris: Louis-Michaud, 1910,
       222.

1836   GILLOUIN, René. "Les Dernières Années d'un sage: Bergson
       vivant." Ecrits de Paris, mars 1969, 55-62.

1837   GILLOUIN, René. "Un Humaniste de notre temps." Ecrits de
       Paris, février 1969, 48-57.

1838   GILLOUIN, René. Idées et figures d'aujourd'hui. Paris:
       Grasset, 1912, 267. The concluding chapter of this book
       concerns Henri Bergson.

1839   GILLOUIN, René. "L'Influence de la philosophie de M. Berg-
       son. VII." Mouvement Socialiste, 31, No. 238, février
       1912, 132-133.

1840   GILLOUIN, René. La Philosophie de M. Bergson. Paris:
       Grasset, 1911, 187.

1841   GILLOUIN, René. "La Philosophie de M. Bergson." Parthénon,
       1, No. 1, octobre 1911.

1842   GILLOUIN, René. "La Philosophie de M. Henri Bergson."
       Monde Nouveau, 4e Année, No. 19-20, 1922, 164-171; No. 21,
       1922, 357-364; No. 22, 1922, 29-37.

1843   GILLOUIN, René. "La Philosophie de M. Henri Bergson."
       L'Olivier, 3e Année, No. 1, janvier 1914, 3-13.

1844   GILLOUIN, René. "La Philosophie de M. Henri Bergson."
       Revue de Paris, 18e Année, No. 19, 1er octobre 1911, 528-
       558; No. 20, 15 octobre 1911, 847-875.

1845   GILLOUIN, René. "Réflexions sur Bergson et le bergsonisme."
       Monde Nouveau, 10, No. 11, janvier-février 1929, 808-816.

1846   GILSON, Etienne. "Review of Bergson et le Christ des Evan-
       giles by Henri Gouhier." Etudes Bergsoniennes, 7, 1966,

221-227.  This essay was first published in Les Nouvelles
Littéraires, 25 January 1962, under the title "L'Itinéraire d'Henri Bergson."  It is an extremely favorable review, which cites Chapter V, "Une Christologie philosophique," as a masterpiece.

1847    GILSON, Etienne.  "Bergson: Le Privilège de l'intelligence."
        Etudes Bergsoniennes, 8, 1968, 170-173.

1848    GILSON, Etienne.  "Review of Le Bergsonisme by Albert Thi-
        baudet."  Revue Philosophique de la France et de l'Etran-
        ger, 39, No. 5, septembre-octobre 1925, 308-310.

1849    GILSON, Etienne.  "La Gloire de Bergson."  Tribune de Genève,
        29 mai 1947.

1850    GILSON, Etienne.  "The Glory of Bergson."  Thought, 22, No.
        87, December 1947, 577-584.

1851    GILSON, Etienne.  Hommage public à Henri Bergson, Panthéon,
        le...11 mai 1967.  Paris: Firmin-Didot, 1967, 6.

1852    GILSON, Etienne.  "L'Itinéraire d'Henri Bergson."  Nouvelles
        Littéraires, No. 1795, 25 janvier 1962, 1 et 9.  This is
        a review of Bergson et le Christ des Evangiles by Henri
        Gouhier.

1853    GILSON, Etienne.  Le Philosophe et la théologie.  Paris:
        Fayard, 1960, 263.

1854    GILSON, Etienne.  The Philosopher and Theology.  New York:
        Random House, 1962, 237.  Bergsonians and war are discussed
        on pages 23-24 and 44-46; "The Bergson Affair" on pages
        107-131; and Bergson and Thomism on pages 155-173.  Berg-
        son is declared not to be a Christian on pages 133-152.

1855    GILSON, Etienne.  "Le Privilège de l'intelligence."  Nouvel-
        les Littéraires, No. 2071, 11 mai 1967, 3.  This is an ad-
        dress delivered at the dedication of the Bergson plaque at
        the Panthéon.

1856    GILSON, Etienne.  "Souvenir de Bergson."  Revue de Métaphy-
        sique et de Morale, 64, No. 2, avril 1959, 129-140.

1857    GILSON, Etienne.  "Table ronde: Religion."  Actes du Xe Con-
        grès des Sociétés de Philosophie de Langue Française (Con-
        grès Bergson).  Paris: Armand Colin, 1959, 2, 261-278.

1858    GILSON, Etienne.  "Table ronde: Sources et histoire du berg-
        sonisme."  Actes du Xe Congres des Sociétés de Philosophie
        de Langue Française (Congrès Bergson).  Paris: Armand
        Colin, 2, 1959, 213-233.

1859    GINSBURG, Benjamin.  "Bergson's Creative Ethics."  Nation,
        136, No. 3537, 19 April 1933, 452-453.  This is an account
        of Bergson's positon in Les Deux Sources.

1860    GIRAUD, Victor.  Le Miracle français: Trois Ans après.
        Paris: Hachette, 1918, 362.

1861    GIRONELLA, Juan Roïg.  "Ensayo de filosofía religiosa."
        Revista de Filosofía, 4, No. 1, enero-marzo 1945, 197-
        203.

1862    GIROUX, Laurent.  "Bergson et la conception du temps chez
        Platon et Aristote."  Dialogue, 10, No. 3, 1971, 479-503.
        The author agrees with Bergson's account of Plato's con-
        cept of time but criticizes Bergson's account of Aristot-
        le's account of time.  An analysis of Book Four of Aris-
        totle's Physics shows that units of time, not units of
        space, are Aristotle's means of measuring time.  Moreover,
        for Aristotle time varies according to the kind of motion
        which is to be measured.

1863    GIUSSO, Lorenzo.  Bergson.  Milano: Bocca, 1949, 239.

1864    GIUSSO, Lorenzo.  "La conquista dell'assoluto in Bergson."
        Giornale d'Italia, 34, 1 aprile 1934.

1865    GIUSTI, Roberto Fernando.  "Una amistad entre filósofos."
        Literatura y vida.  Buenos Aires: Nosotros, 1939, 374.
        This is a commentary on the James-Bergson correspondence.

1866    GIUSTI, Roberto Fernando.  "Una amistad entre filósofos."
        La Prensa, 7 enero 1934, Sec. II.

1867    GIVORD, Robert.  "L'Idée de néant est-elle une pseudo-idée?"
        Actes du Xe Congrès des Sociétés de Philosophie de Langue
        Française (Congrès Bergson).  Paris: Armand Colin, 1, 1959,
        119-122.  This is an analysis of Bergson's critique of the
        idea of nothingness.  In spite of Bergson's critique, the
        author holds that if one considers only the logical uni-
        verse of significations, the idea of nothingness exists
        mentally just as well as other ideas.  Moreover, Bergson
        did not see the entire significance of his critique and
        did not understand that metaphysics, in the last analysis,
        is nothing but this critique taken to the limit.

1868    GIVORD, Robert.  "Table ronde: Néant et existentialisme."
        Actes du Xe Congrès des Sociétés de Philosophie de Langue
        Française (Congrès Bergson).  Paris: Armand Colin, 2, 1959,
        145-164.

1869    GLENDENNING, Nigel.  "The Philosophy of Henri Bergson in the
        Poetry of Antonio Machado."  Revue de Littérature Comparée,
        36, No. 1, 1962, 53-70.

1870    GOBLOT, Edmond.  "A Propos de la philosophie de Bergson."
        Le Volume, 24, No. 34, 18 mai 1912, 537-539.

1871    GODME, J. P.  "Henri Bergson ou l'angélisme expérimental."
        Cahiers d'Occident, 2e Sér., 2, No. 1, 1928, 118-147.
        This article compares Bergson and Pascal.  It is highly
        critical.

1872    "God's Instrument."  Catholic World, 165, No. 990, Septem-
        ber 1947, 556-557.  This is an excerpt from The Two Sour-
        ces, with introductory comments.

1873    GOETZ, Philip Becker.  "Bergson."  Open Court, 26, No. 9,
        September 1912, 572.  This is a poem.

1874    GOLDSCHMIDT, Victor.  "Le Vide pythagoréan et le nombre chez
        Bergson."  Revue Philosophique de la France et de l'Etran-
        ger, 94, No. 2, 1969, 259-266.

1875    GOLDSTEIN, Julius.  "Henri Bergson und die Sozialwissen-
        schaft."  Archiv für Sozialwissenschaft und Sozialpolitik,
        31, No. 1, Juli 1910, 1-22.

1876    GOLDSTEIN, Julius.  "Henri Bergson und der Zeitlosigkeits-
        idealismus."  Literaturblatt der Frankfurter Zeitung, 2
        Mai 1909.

1877    GOMEZ ROBLEDO, Antonio.  "Reflexiones sobre Bergson."
        Abside, 5, Nos. 4-5, abril 1941, 223-242.

1878    GOMULICKI, Bronislaw R.  "The Development and Present Status
        of the Trace Theory of Memory."  British Journal of Psy-
        chology Monograph Supplements, 29, 1953, 94.  Bergson's
        influence on McDougall is discussed on pages 30-31; his
        concepts of habit memory and pure memory on page 61.

1879    GONZALES SANCHEZ, Gustavo.  "Bergson y nosotros."  Revista
        Javeriana, 54, No. 269, 1960, 638-645; No. 270, 1960, 714-
        719; 55, No. 271, 1961, 41-46.

1880    GONZALO CASAS, Manuel. "Bergson y el sentido de su influ-
        encia en América." Humanitas, 7, No. 12, 1959, 95-108.
        A Latin American Bergson bibliography is given on pages
        103-108.

1881    GONZALO CASAS, Manuel. "Bibliographia bergsoniana in Spagna
        e nell'America latina." Giornale di metafisica, 14, No. 6,
        1959, 866-872.

1882    GOOSENS, Werner. "La Théodicé de M. H. Bergson: A Propos
        d'un ouvrage récent." Collationes Grandavenses, 22, 1935,
        113-118, 172-176.

1883    GORCE, Matthieu-Maxime. "Le Néo-réalisme bergsonien-tho-
        miste." Sophia, 3, No. 1, gennaio-febbraio 1935, 35-47,
        145-160. The author argues that the philosophies of imma-
        nence, as presented by Le Roy and Blondel, have tried to
        find in the idealism of Bergson a new apologetic and an
        attractive way to the heart of Christianity, but they have
        failed. Bergson is not Aquinas.

1884    GORSEN, Peter. "Ahnherr des modernen Denkens: Der lange
        missverstandene Philosoph Henri Bergson." Die Welt der
        Literatur, 1, No. 19, 26 November 1964, 641.

1885    GORSEN, Peter. Zur Phänomenologie des Bewusstseinsstroms:
        Bergson, Dilthey, Husserl, Simmel und die lebensphiloso-
        phischen Antinomien. Bonn: Bouvier, 1966, 243.

1886    GOTTLIEB, N. "D'Une Erreur fondamentale dans Les Deux Sour-
        ces de M. Bergson." Revue des Etudes Juives, 96, No. 1,
        1933, 1-22.

1887    GOUHIER, Henri. "Autour du bergsonisme." Revue d'Histoire
        de la Philosophie et d'Histoire Générale de la Civilisa-
        tion, N.S. No. 7, 15 juillet 1934, 279-285. This is a re-
        view of books on Bergson by Jolivet, Rideau, Penido, Metz,
        and Lacombe.

1888    GOUHIER, Henri. "Avant-propos." Henri Bergson: Mélanges.
        Paris: Presses Universitaires de France, 1972, vii-xxiii.

1889    GOUHIER, Henri. Bergson et le Christ des Evangiles. Paris:
        Fayard, 1961, 222.

1890    GOUHIER, Henri. "Bergson et Claudel." Ed. Georges Cattaui
        and Jacques Madaule. Entretiens sur Paul Claudel. Paris
        and La Haye: Mouton, 1968, 135-140.

1891    GOUHIER, Henri. Bergson e il Cristo dei Vangeli. Milano:
        I.P.L., 1968, 220.

1892    GOUHIER, Henri. "Bergson et le Fonds Dauriac de la Biblio-
        thèque Victor Cousin." Etudes Bergsoniennes, 3, 19, 195-
        198. The author examines the relations between Dauriac
        and Bergson.

1893    GOUHIER, Henri. "Bergson et l'histoire des idées." Revue
        Internationale de Philosophie, 3, No. 10, 1949, 407-433.

1894    GOUHIER, Henri. "Bergson et la philosophie du christianis-
        me." Revue de Théologie et de Philosophie, 3e Sér., 10,
        No. 1, 1960, 1-22.

1895    GOUHIER, Henri. "Le Bergsonisme dans l'histoire de la phi-
        losophie française." Revue des Travaux de l'Académie des
        Sciences Morales et Politiques, 4e Sér., 112e Année, 1er
        semestre, 1959, 183-200.

1896    GOUHIER, Henri. "Le Bergsonisme et l'histoire de la philo-
        sophie (Position de questions)." L'Homme et l'Histoire
        (Actes du VIe Congrès des Sociétés de Philosophie de Lan-
        gue Française). Paris: Presses Universitaires de France,
        1952, 385-388.

1897    GOUHIER, Henri. "La Conversion de Maine de Biran au plato-
        nisme." Revue des Sciences Philosophiques et Théologiques,
        2, 1941.

1898    GOUHIER, Henri. "L'Esprit du bergsonisme." Rencontres, 1,
        No. 5, 1941, 87-103.

1899    GOUHIER, Henri. "Review of 'L'Intuition bergsonienne' by
        R.-M. Mossé-Bastide." Etudes Bergsoniennes, 2, 1949, 250-
        251.

1900    GOUHIER, Henri. "Maine de Biran et Bergson." Etudes Berg-
        soniennes, 1, 1948, 131-173.

1901    GOUHIER, Henri. "Les Rapports de Dieu et le monde dans la
        philosophie d'Henri Bergson." Der Mensch vor Gott: Fest-
        schrift für Theodor Steinbüchel zu seinem 60. Geburtstag.
        Dusseldorf: Patmos-Verlag, 1948, 291-302.

1902    GOUHIER, Henri. "Table-ronde." Nouvelles Littéraires, No.
        1677, 22 octobre 1959, 1 et 506.

1903    GOUHIER, Henri. "Table ronde: Esthétique." Actes du Xe
        Congrès des Sociétés de Philosophie de Langue Française
        (Congrès Bergson). Paris: Armand Colin, 2, 1959, 193-210.

1904    GOUHIER, Henri. "Table ronde: Liberté." Actes du Xe Con-
        grès des Sociétés de Philosophie de Langue Française (Con-
        grès Bergson). Paris: Armand Colin, 2, 1959, 167-189.

1905    GOUHIER, Henri. "Review of La Théorie bergsonienne de la
        religion by Hjalmar Sunden." Etudes Bergsoniennes, 2,
        1949, 244-250. The author takes issue with supposed "in-
        fluences" on Bergson. In general, he is appreciative.

1906    GOUHIER, Henri. "Vingt Ans après." Nouvelles litteraires,
        No. 1677, 4 février 1960, 4. This is a review of Berg-
        son's Oeuvres and Ecrits et paroles and Jankélévitch's
        Bergson.

1907    GOUHIER, Henri and ROBINET, André, Eds. Henri Bergson:
        Oeuvres: Edition du centenaire. Paris: Presses Univer-
        sitaires de France, 1959, 1602. Professor Robinet's "Ap-
        parat critique" and "Notes historiques" are found on pages
        1485-1539 and 1541-1578 respectively. Professor Gouhier's
        "Introduction" is found on pages vii-xxx.

1908    GOUIRAN, Emilio. "Henri Bergson: Precisiones." Sustancia,
        2, Nos. 7-8, septiembre 1941, 357-358.

1909    GOUIRAN, Emilio. "Un punto de vista sobre la filosofía Berg-
        soniana: Charles Péguy." Homenaje a Bergson. Córdoba,
        Argentina: Imprenta de la Universidad, 1936, 54-64.

1910    GOULD, F. J. "Bergson and Balfour." Literary Guide and
        Rationalist Review, N.S. No. 185, November 1911, 163-164.

1911    GRAHAM, J. W. "A Negative Note on Bergson and Virginia
        Woolf." Essays in Criticism, 6, No. 1, 1956, 70-74.

1912    GRAMONT, Elisabeth de. Souvenirs du monde de 1890 à 1940.
        Paris: Grasset, 1966, 452.

1913    GRAMZOW, Otto. "Bergson." Westermanns illustrierte deut-
        sche Monatshefte, 69, No. 8, August 1915, 795-800.

1914    GRANDJEAN, Frank. Esquisse d'une pédagogie inspirée du
        bergsonisme. Genève: Atar, 1917, 31. This essay was pub-
        lished originally in Bulletin de la Société Pédagogique
        Genevoise.

1915   GRANDJEAN, Frank. La Raison et la vue. Paris: Félix Alcan,
       1920, 374. This is a critique of the influence of the
       sense of sight on the formation of human reason. The in-
       fluence of Bergson on this study is both apparent and pro-
       fessed.

1916   GRANDJEAN, Frank. Une Révolution dans la philosophie.
       Genève: Atar, 1913, 168.

1917   GRAPPE, André. "Bergson et le symbole." Actes du Xe Con-
       grès des Sociétés de Philosophie de Langue Française (Con-
       grès Bergson). Paris: Armand Colin, 1, 1959, 123-129.  No
       aspect of Bergson's philosophy has been more disparaged
       than his symbolism. Is this attitude valid?  The author
       analyzes Bergson's concept of symbolism and compares it
       with Bergson's concept of the image.

1918   GRAPPE, André. "Pradines et Bergson." Revue Philosophique
       de la France et de l'Etranger, 155, No. 1, 1965, 103-110;
       156, No. 4, 1966, 478-496; 158, No. 3, 1967, 371-384.

1919   GRAPPE, André. "Table ronde: Psychologie, phénoménologie,
       intuition." Actes du Xe Congres des Sociétés de Philoso-
       phie de Langue Française (Congrès Bergson). Paris: Armand
       Colin, 2, 1959, 15-37.

1920   GRAY, Carlo. "Intuizionismo bergsoniano e intuizione
       dell'essere rosminiana." Rivista rosminiana, 21, Nos. 1
       et 4, 1927.

1921   GREEN, Frederick Charles. The Mind of Proust: A Detailed
       Interpretation of "A La Recherche du temps perdu." Cam-
       bridge, England: Cambridge University Press, 1949, 546.
       Bergson's influence on Proust is discussed on pages 494-
       546.

1922   GREGH, Fernand. L'Age d'or: Souvenirs d'enfance et de jeu-
       nesse. Paris: Grasset, 1947, 335. The author describes
       Bergson's visits with the Prousts on pages 153-158.

1923   GREGH, Fernand. "Bergson et Proust." Journal de Genève,
       27 juillet 1941.

1924   GREGOIRE, Franz. "La Collaboration de l'intuition et de
       l'intelligence." Revue Internationale de Philosophie,
       3, No. 3, 1949, 392-406.

1925   GREGOIRE, Franz. L'Intuition selon Bergson: Etude critique.
       Louvain: Nauwelaerts, 1947, 127.

1926    GREGOIRE, Franz.  L'Intuition selon Bergson: Fasc. 2.  Com-
        plément sur la fidélité de Bergson aux documents mysti-
        ques.  Louvain: Université, 1950, 106.

1927    GREGOIRE, Franz.  "Réflexions sur l'étude critique des phi-
        losophies intuitionnistes: Le Cas de l'élan vital chez
        Bergson."  Revue Philosophique de Louvain, 3e Sér., 45,
        Nos. 6-7, mai-août 1947, 169-187.  The author explores
        Bergson's claimed intuition of (1) self, (2) evolutionary
        factor, and (3) God.  He validates 1 and 3, but claims
        that 2 is an inference.

1028    GREGORY, J.  "Dreams as Psychical Explosions."  Mind, 25,
        No. 98, April 1916, 193-205.  The author proposes criti-
        cisms of Bergson's theory of dreams.

1929    GREMIL, M.  "Figures du temps présent: M. Henri Bergson."
        La Dépêche de Toulouse, 16 février 1914.

1930    GRENET, Paul.  "Racines bergsoniennes de l'existentialisme."
        Actes du Xe Congrès des Sociétés de Philosophie de Langue
        Française (Congrès Bergson).  Paris: Armand Colin, 1, 1959,
        131-134.  The author holds that Bergson's philosophy con-
        tains several positions very close to those of the exis-
        tentialists: the priority of existence over possibility,
        the identification of existence with liberty, and the sep-
        aration of reality into two zones: the in-itself, identi-
        cal, inert, passive, and the for-itself, always other,
        free, empty.  Nonetheless, Bergson is not an existential-
        ist.  He possesses a conviction which transfigures these
        propositions: the refusal of all real negativity.

1931    GRENET, Paul.  "Table ronde: Néant et existentialisme."
        Actes du Xe Congrès des Sociétés de Philosophie de Langue
        Française (Congrès Bergson).  Paris: Armand Colin, 2, 1959,
        145-164.

1932    GRIMALDI, Nicholas.  "Matière et tradition."  Revue de Méta-
        physique et de Morale, 76, No. 2, avril-juin 1971, 167-
        195.  Matter is an "attribute of time"; it is a resistance
        to the future and a conservation of the present.  This es-
        say includes an interpretation of both Bergson's and Leib-
        niz' concept of matter.

1933    GRIVET, Jules.  "Henri Bergson: Esquisse philosophique."
        Etudes par des Pères de la Compagnie de Jesus, 121, 5
        octobre 1909, 31-50; 20 novembre 1909, 454-478; 124, 20
        juillet 1910, 153-184.

1934    GRIVET, Jules. "La Théorie de la personne d'après Henri
        Bergson." Etudes par des Pères de la Compagnie de Jésus,
        129, No. 4, 1911, 449-485.

1935    GRONAU, Gotthard. Henri Bergson: Ein Beitrag zur Philoso-
        phie der Gegenwart. Wolfenbüttel, Germany: Ernst Fischer,
        1914, 38.

1936    GRONAU, Gotthard. "Henri Bergson: Ein Beitrag zur Philoso-
        phie der Gegenwart." Wissenschaftliche Beilag zum Jahres-
        bericht des Städtischen Lyzeums Fräulein-Marien Schule zu
        Rüstringen. Oldenburg, Germany, 1914.

1937    GROOT, Herko. Het mysterie van de tijd. Assens, Denmark:
        Van Gorcum, 1958, 100. This essay includes a discussion
        of Kant and Bergson.

1938    GROOT, M. "'La Durée' een sleutel tot de filosofie van Berg-
        son." Brandpunt, 1, 1946.

1939    GROOT, M. "Einstein, Bergson, Freud." Het Baken, 2, 1946.

1940    GROSSMAN, I. "Бакунин и Бергсон." Заветы, No. 5,
        1914, 47-62.

1941    GROSSE, Ernst. "Review of Le Rire by Henri Bergson." Deut-
        sche Literaturzeitung, 21, No. 1, 1901, 13-14.

1942    GROZEFF, Grozu. "Intouitziata spored Bergson." Filossofski
        Pregled, 10, No. 3, 1938, 255-266.

1943    GROZEV, Grozyu P. Bergsonisme et matérialisme dialectique.
        София: Наука и изкуство, 1950, 145. Bergson's psychol-
        ogy is viewed by the author as a "form of bourgeois sub-
        jective-idealist psychology" and his views of heredity and
        development are seen as "idealistic and anti-scientific."
        The psychology of Pavlov is in decisive opposition to the
        Bergsonian introspective, subjective concept of conscious-
        ness. According to Pavlov consciousness is the highest
        neural activity, conditioned by the action of the external
        world.

1944    GRUBB, Edward. The Religion of Experience. London: Headley
        Brothers, Ltd., 1919, 202. Chapter IV concerns Bergson
        and intuition.

1945    GRUNSKY, Hans Alfred. "Bergson." Das Reich, 2, No. 21,
        1941, 13.

1946    GSELL, Paul. "Bergson est-il passé de mode?" Revue Mondi-
        ale, 187, 15 décembre 1928, 355-374.

1947    GSELL, Paul. "La Vraie Pensée d'Henri Bergson." Revue Mon-
        diale, 11e Sér., 27e Année, 15 février 1926, 349-369.

1948    GUASTELLA, Cosmo. L'infinito. Palermo: Libreria Interna-
        zionale, Alberto Reber, 1912, 172. Criticisms of Berg-
        son's concept of continuity are offered on pages 121-123
        and 129.

1949    GUERIN, Pierre. "Aristote, Bergson et Brunschvicg vus par
        Laberthonnière." Revue de l'Histoire de la Philosophie
        Religieuse, 25, No. 1, 1945, 52-70.

1950    GUEROULT, Martial. "Bergson en face des philosophes." Etu-
        des Bergsoniennes, 5, 1960, 9-35.

1951    GUEROULT, Martial. "Bergson en face des philosophes."
        Revista Brasileira de Filosofia, 1, No. 3, 1951, 239-254.

1952    GUEROULT, Martial. "Perception, idée, objet, chose chez G.
        Berkeley: La Formule bergsonienne." Revue Philosophique
        de la France et de l'Etranger, 143, No. 2, avril 1953,
        181-200. This article examines Bergson's interpretation
        of George Berkeley's philosophy.

1953    GUERRERO, F. "Review of Les Deux Sources de la morale et de
        la religion by Henri Bergson." Estudios Ecclesiasticos,
        12, No. 2, abril 1933, 251-268.

1954    GUIEYSSE, Charles. "La Métaphysique de M. Bergson." Pages
        Libres, No. 355, 19 octobre 1907, 405-412; No. 356, 20 oc-
        tobre 1907, 413-419.

1955    GUILLAUME, Edouard. "La Question du temps, d'après M. Berg-
        son." Revue Générale des Sciences, 33, 30 octobre 1922,
        573-582. This is an expository account of Durée et simul-
        tanéité.

1956    GUILLAUME, Henri. "Face à Juarès, Bergson et l'Eglise: Peu
        à peu, Péguy s'éclaire." Le Monde des Livres, No. 7482,
        1er février 1969, 1-2.

1957    GUILLAUME, Paul. La Psychologie de la forme. Paris: Fla-
        marrion, 1937, 236. Bergson, functionalism, and the
        "Gestalt" are discussed on pages 215-218.

1958    GUISAN, Gilbert, et al., Eds.  "Hommage à Arnold Reymond,
        1874-1958."  Etudes de Lettres, 3e Sér., 11, 1969, 74-126.
        This journal is published in Lausanne.

1959    GUITRY, Sacha.  Quatre Ans d'occupation.  Paris: L'Elan,
        1947, 555.  The author discusses an encounter with Bergson
        on page 120.

1960    GUITTON, Jean.  "Bergson et Loisy."  Actes du Xe Congrès des
        Sociétés de Philosophie de Langue Française (Congrès Berg-
        son).  Paris: Armand Colin, 1, 1959, 135-137.  The author
        evokes some memories and offers some thoughts concerning
        the relations between Bergson and Loisy, in particular
        their positions with regard to the religious problem and
        Christianity.

1961    GUITTON, Jean.  "Bergson et Loisy."  Revue de Paris, 66e
        Année, No. 12, décembre 1959, 27-39.

1962    GUITTON, Jean.  "Esquisse pour un portrait d'Henri Bergson."
        Table Ronde, No. 145, 1960, 57-71.  This sketch of Bergson
        begins from personal reminiscences.  Bergson had great
        charm, but was by no means a "conversationalist."  Irony,
        modesty, and economy were basic to his character.  Candor
        and ingenuity appeared to him to be dispositions towards
        genius.

1963    GUITTON, Jean.  The Guitton Journals 1952-1955.  Trans.
        Frances Forrest.  London: Harvill Press, 1963, 320.
        "Bergson's House" is discussed on pages 260-264 and "Berg-
        son's Testament" on pages 224-226.

1964    GUITTON, Jean.  "Jeanne Bergson."  Le Figaro, 7 décembre
        1961.

1965    GUITTON, Jean.  Journal.  Vol. 1.  Paris: Plon, 1968, 315.
        The following articles on Bergson appear here: "Prix No-
        bel," 60-65; "Sur La Mère de Bergson," 152-155; "Le Testa-
        ment de Bergson," 227-228; "La Maison de Bergson," 261-265;
        and "Bergson, Bréhier, Brunschvicg," 268-273.

1966    GUITTON, Jean.  "La Mère de Bergson."  Le Figaro Littéraire,
        28 mai 1960, 4.

1967    GUITTON, Jean.  Profils parallèles.  Paris: Fayard, 1969,
        496.  Teilhard and Bergson are discussed on pages 401-
        457.

1968    GUITTON, Jean. Regards sur la pensée française, 1870-1940:
        Leçons de captivité. Paris: Beauchesne, 1968, 253.

1969    GUITTON, Jean. "Souvenirs sur les relations de M. Loisy et
        de M. Bergson." Mémorial J. Chaine. Lyon: Facultés Ca-
        tholiques, 1950, 187-202.

1970    GUITTON, Jean. "Table ronde: Religion." Actes du Xe Cong-
        grès des Sociétés de Philosophie de Langue Française (Con-
        gres Bergson). Paris: Armand Colin, 2, 1959, 261-278.

1971    GUITTON, Jean. La Vocation de Bergson. Paris: Gallimard,
        1960, 263.

1972    GUNDOLF, Ernst. "Die Philosophie Henri Bergsons." Jahrbuch
        für die geistige Bewegung, 3, 1912, 32-92.

1973    GUNN, John Alexander. "Bergson and Einstein." Australasian
        Journal of Psychology and Philosophy, 4, No. 3, 1926, 215-
        218. This is a review of Durée et simultanéité. The au-
        thor disagrees with both Einstein and Bergson over the na-
        ture of time.

1974    GUNN, John Alexander. Bergson and His Philosophy. London:
        Methuen and Co., Ltd., 1920, 190.

1975    GUNN, John Alexander. "Great Thinkers, II. Henri Bergson."
        Australasian Journal of Psychology and Philosophy, 3, No.
        4, 1925, 277-286. Much interesting historical comment is
        contained in this article.

1976    GUNN, John Alexander. Modern French Philosophy: A Study of
        Development Since Comte. New York: Dodd, Mead and Company,
        1922; London: Fisher Unwin, 1923, 358. The preface is by
        H. Bergson.

1977    GUNN, John Alexander. The Problem of Time. London: Allen
        and Unwin, Ltd., 1929, 460.

1978    GUNN, John Alexander. "Time and Modern Metaphysics." Aus-
        tralasian Journal of Psychology and Philosophy, 4, No. 4,
        1926, 258-267. Guyau, Bergson, Alexander, Broad, Russell,
        Cassirer, and Whitehead are considered in this article.

1979    GUNTER, Pete Addison Yancey, Ed. and Trans. Bergson and the
        Evolution of Physics. Knoxville, Tennessee: University of
        Tennessee Press, 1969, 348. This is a collection of es-
        says concerning Bergson's philosophy of physics. It is

introduced by the editor's essay on Bergson's philosophical method, which, it is argued, is <u>pro</u> and not <u>anti</u>-scientific

1980    GUNTER, Pete Addison Yancey.   "Bergson's Reflective Anti-intellectualism."  <u>Personalist</u>, 47, No. 1, 1966, 43-60. The author defends Bergson against the dual charges of anti-intellectualism and an anti-scientific attitude. Bergson's intuition is reflection and is intended to be scientifically fruitful.

1981    GUNTER, Pete Addison Yancey.   "Bergson's Theory of Matter and Modern Cosmology."  <u>Journal of the History of Ideas</u>, 32, No. 4, October-December 1971, 525-542.  According to the author, Bergson's theory of matter foreshadows developments in contemporary cosmology.

1982    GUNTER, Pete Addison Yancey.   "The Heuristic Force of <u>Creative Evolution</u>."  <u>Southwest Journal of Philosophy</u>, 1, No. 3, 1970, 111-118.  The author argues that Bergson's biological theories remain potentially fruitful and suggest mathematical interpretations of evolutionary processes.

1983    GUNTER, Pete Addison Yancey.   "Nietzschean Laughter."  <u>Sewanee Review</u>, 76, No. 3, Summer 1963, 493-506.  This article contains criticisms of Bergson's theory of laughter.

1984    GUNTER, Pete Addison Yancey.   "Temps biologique et développement biologique."  <u>Cahiers de l'Association Lecomte du Noüy</u>, 3, Spring 1971, 16-22.  The author argues that new discoveries in embryology suggest the validity of Bergson's and Lecomte du Noüy's concepts of biological time.

1984a   GUNTER, Pete Addison Yancey.   "The Unity of Intuition and the Understanding in Bergson."  Diss., Yale, 1963, 269. The author argues that: "Intuition and discursive understanding must be conceived to constitute a functioning unity, a unity in which these two modes of judgment work together to create a continual 'expansion' of knowledge."

1985    GUNTER, Pete Addison Yancey.   "Whitehead, Bergson, Freud: Suggestions Toward a Theory of Laughter."  <u>Southern Journal of Philosophy</u>, 4, No. 2, 1966, 55-60.  This article contains criticisms of Bergson's concept of laughter.

1986    GURVITCH, Georges.   "Deux Aspects de la philosophie de Bergson: Temps et liberté."  <u>Revue de Métaphysique et de Morale</u>, 65, No. 3, 1960, 307-316.

1987   GURVITCH, Georges.  "La Philosophie sociale de Bergson."
       Renaissance, 1, No. 2, 1943, 81-94.

1988   GURVITCH, Georges.  "La Philosophie sociale de Bergson."
       Revue de Métaphysique et de Morale, 53, No. 3, 1948, 294-
       306.

1989   GURVITCH, Georges.  The Spectrum of Social Time.  Dordrecht,
       Netherlands: Reidel, 1964, 152.  Bergson's social philoso-
       phy is discussed on pages 18-25 and Bergson's influence on
       Gurvitch, on pages ix-x.

1990   GURVITCH, Georges.  La Vocation actuelle de la sociologie.
       Paris: Presses Universitaires de France, 1950, 607.  "La
       Théorie sociologique de Bergson" is discussed on pages
       554-567.

1991   GURWITSCH, Aron.  The Field of Consciousness.  Pittsburgh,
       Pennsylvania: Duquesne University Press, 1964, 427.  Berg-
       son's concept of qualitative multiplicity is discussed on
       pages 140-143.  For other references, see the index.

1992   GURWITSCH, Aron.  "Die französische Metaphysik der Gegenwart:
       H. Bergson."  Archiv für systematische Philosophie, N.S.
       9, No. 4, 1903, 463-490.

1993   GURWITSCH, A. Философские исследования и очерки.
       Москва: Труд, 1913, 311.

1994   GUSDORF, Georges.  " Mémoire et personne: Vol. 1.  La Mémoire
       concrète.  Paris: Presses Universitaires de France, 1951,
       258.  Bergson is discussed on pages 17-21, 27-28, 32-36,
       77-81, 98-99, 144-145, and 248-249.

1995   GUSDORF, Georges.  Mémoire et personne: Vol. 2.  La Dialec-
       tique de la mémoire.  Paris: Presses Universitaires de
       France, 1951, 280.  Bergson is discussed on pages 300-301,
       308, 352-357, 439-441, 462-463, 464-468, 490-491, and 541-
       544.

1996   GUSDORF, Georges.  "Le Sens du présent."  Revue de Métaphy-
       sique et de Morale, 53, No. 3, 1948, 265-293.  Piéron,
       Janet, and Bergson are discussed in this article.

1997   GUTHRIE, Hunter.  "Bergson Sought the Truth and Found it
       Before the End."  America, 64, No. 16, 25 January 1941.
       427-428.

1998    GUY, Alain. "Le Bergsonisme en Amérique latine." Caravelle:
        Cahiers du Monde Hispanique et Luso-brésilien, 1, No. 1,
        1963, 121-139.

1999    GUY, Alain. "El Congreso Bergson: París, 17-20 de mayo de
        1959." Espíritu, 8, No. 1959, 194-195.

2000    GUY, Alain. "O Congresso 'Bergson'--17-20 de maio de 1959."
        Revista Portuguesa di Filosofia, 15, 1959, 417-419.

2001    GUY, Alain. "José Vasconcelos et Bergson." Actes du Xe
        Congrès des Sociétés de Philosophie de Langue Française
        (Congrès Bergson). Paris: Armand Colin, 1, 1959, 139-143.
        The author holds that the aesthetic and Christian monism
        of the Mexican philosopher Vasconcelos is an original and
        audacious "refraction" of Bergsonism. Vasconcelos thought
        he had surpassed Bergson at more than one point.

2002    GUY, Alain. "Table ronde: Sources et histoire du bergsonis-
        me." Actes du Xe Congrès des Sociétés de Philosophie de
        Langue Française (Congrès Bergson). Paris: Armand Colin,
        2, 1959, 213-233.

2003    GUY-GRAND, Georges. "M. Bergson et la civilisation moderne."
        Mercure de France, Sér. moderne 236, 15 juin 1932, 513-
        531. This article is a review of Les Deux Sources.

2004    GUY-GRAND, Georges. "Un Grand Philosophe de la vie: M.
        Bergson." La Vie, 1, 4 mai 1912.

2005    GUY-GRAND, Georges. La Philosophie syndicaliste. Paris:
        Grasset, 1911, 237. Bergson is discussed on pages 34-41,
        123-124, 144-147, and elsewhere.

2006    GUY-GRAND, Georges. Le Procès de la démocratie. Paris:
        Armand Colin, 1911, 326. The materials which make up this
        book were published in Revue de Métaphysique et de Morale
        in January, March, July, and September 1910.

2007    GUYOT, Charly. "Notes sur Bergson et les lettres fran-
        çaises." Revue Internationale de Philosophie, 13, No. 2,
        1959, 249-271. The author holds that Péguy transposed cer-
        tain "simple ideas" of Bergson onto the sociological and
        historical level. Proust is nearer to Bergson than Péguy,
        thanks to a common Ruskinian affiliation.

2008    GUYOT, Charly. "Péguy et Bergson." Revue d'Histoire de Phi-
        losophie Religieuse, 13e Année, No. 2, 1950, 273-289.

2009    GUZZO, Agosto. "Bergson: Il profonde e la sua espressione." Archivo di filosofia, 23, No. 1, 1954, 257-259. This is a review of Mathieu's Bergson.

2010    H., D. Z. "Thibaudet, or, the Critic as Mediator." Yale French Studies, 2, No. 3, 1949, 74-78. The influence of Bergson on Thibaudet is discussed on pages 77-78.

2011    HABICHT, Rob. Henri Bergson und das deutsche Typenlustspiel. Leipsic: Heitz, 1936.

2012    HAERSOLTE, R. A. V. van. "Enkele raakpunten van Bergson met de exacte wetenschappen." Algemeen Nederlands Tijdschrift voor Wijsbegeerte en Psychologie, 52, No. 1, 1959-1960, 12-23. Bergson reproaches the devotees of natural science for not having sufficiently taken account of duration. But he was wrong to transpose onto an ontological level the superiority of "lived time" over "time-space." The author considers the resolution of the paradox of Achilles in the light of this distinction.

2013    HAGAN, Robert Alfred. "The Person and Bergson's Metaphysics." Diss., St. Louis, 1967.

2014    HAGE, Kamal el. La Valeur du langage chez Bergson. Beyrouth, Lebanon: Publications de l'Université Libanaise, 1971, 146. This is a continuation of the author's thesis.

2015    HAGE, Kamal el. "La Valeur du langage chez Henri Bergson: Exposé et critique." Diss., Paris, 1949, 206.

2016    HAGER, Wilhelm. Bergson als Neu-Romantiker mit besonderer Berücksichtigung von M. Maeterlinck. München: Frölich, 1916, 81. This is an inaugural dissertation.

2017    HAGSTRAND, Yngve. Forskande filosofi det Bergsonska tänkandet och den moderna fysiken. Lund, Sweden: Gleerup, 1962, 141. "Företal av Alf Nyman."

2018    HALDA, Bernard. "Bergson et Du Bos." Etudes Bergsoniennes, 9, 1970, 157-200.

2019    HALDANE, John Burdon Sanderson. The Causes of Evolution. London and New York: Longmans, Green and Co., 1932, 234. Bergson is discussed on pages 166-168.

2020    HALEVY, Daniel. Charles Péguy et les Cahiers de la Quinzaine. Paris: Payot, 1919, 267.

2021   HALL, D. L.  "Abstract of 'Bergson's Theory of Matter and
       Modern Cosmology' by P. A. Y. Gunter." Process Studies,
       2, No. 2, Summer 1972, 172.  This article is more a review
       than an abstract.

2022   HAMILTON, George Rostrever.  Bergson and Future Philosophy.
       London: Macmillan and Co., Ltd., 1921, 152.

2023   HAMMOND, Albert L.  "Some Alleged Incapacities of Intellect."
       Philosophical Review, 34, No. 6, November 1925, 557-559.

2024   HAMPSHIRE, Stuart.  "Philosophy in France."  New Statesman,
       55, No. 1402, 25 January 1958, 109-110.

2025   HANNA, Thomas.  "The Bergsonian Heritage."  The Bergsonian
       Heritage.  Ed. Thomas Hanna.  New York and London: Colum-
       bia University Press, 1962, 1-31.

2026   HANSEN, Valdemar.  "Henri Bergson: Et Tilbageblik."  Nordisk
       Tidskrift, 17, No. 4, 1941, 264-269.

2027   HARPER, James Wilson.  Christian Ethics and Social Progress.
       London: James Nisbet and Co., 1912, 285.  This study con-
       tains chapters on Bergson.

2028   HARRIS, Marjorie S.  "Bergson and the Art of Life."  Person-
       alist, 14, No. 2, April 1933, 107-118.

2029   HARRIS, Marjorie S.  "Bergson's Conception of Freedom."
       Philosophical Review, 62, No. 5, September 1933, 511-520.

2030   HART, Thomas N.  "God in the Ethico-religious Thought of
       Henri Bergson."  Thomist, 32, No. 3, July 1968, 333-365.
       The author argues that Bergson opposes a supra-human to
       an infra-human ethic.  The ordinary ethic is bypassed.

2031   HARWARD, J.  "What Does Bergson Mean by Pure Perception?"
       Mind, Vol. 27, No. 106, 1918, 203-207.  The author asserts:
       "On pages 26-30 of Matter and Memory Bergson considers
       'how conscious perception may be explained.'  It is very
       difficult to assign any precise meaning to the contents of
       these pages." (203).

2032   HARWARD, J.  "What Does Bergson Mean by Pure Perception?"
       Mind, Vol. 28, No. 112, 1919, 463-470.  This is a response
       to H. Wildon Carr's reply to Harward's earlier discussion.
       It seems to me a good reply.

2033   HASLEY, Louis. "Humor in Literature; a Definition." The
       CEA Critic, 32, No. 5, February 1970, 10-11.

2034   HASSELMANN, Karl B. "Das Problem der Willensfreiheit, unter
       besonderer Berücksichtigung der Theorien Münsterbergs,
       Bergsons und Joels." Diss., 1923, 159.

2035   HASTOUPIS, A. P. "Bergson and his Religious Philosophy."
       Θεολογια (Athens), 23, 1952, 596-603.

2036   HAUSHEER, Herman. "Bergson's Critique of Scientific Psy-
       chology." Philosophical Review, 36, No. 5, September 1927,
       450-461. The author suggests that Bergson is similar to
       Rickert in opposing the scientific faith that science can
       comprehend the whole universe with its concepts. The psy-
       chical is free and creative. It displays two aspects:
       directly or by refraction through space. No psychological
       datum ever appears twice the same. The psychical is not a
       quantity and hence cannot be measured. It is subjective
       and cannot be an object. Its inner nature can be grasped
       by intuition, but not by symbols and concepts.

2037   HAUSHEER, Herman. "Thought Affinities of Bergson and Schel-
       ling." Personalist, 14, No. 2, April 1933, 93-106. Berg-
       son and Schelling show close affinities, according to the
       author. Bergson adds an empirical foundation to Schel-
       ling's speculations.

2038   HAVET, Jacques. "French Philosophical Tradition Between the
       Two Wars." Philosophic Thought in France and the United
       States. Ed. Marvin Farber. Albany, New York: State Uni-
       versity of New York Press, 1968, 3-30. Bergson and Blon-
       del are discussed on pages 5-8.

2039   HAYEN, André. "La Réflexion est dialogue." Actes du Xe
       Congrès des Sociétés de Philosophie de Langue Française
       (Congrès Bergson). Paris: Armand Colin, 1, 1959, 145-147.

2040   HAYEN, André. "Table ronde: Liberté." Actes du Xe Congrès
       des Sociétés de Philosophie de Langue Française (Congrès
       Bergson). Paris: Armand Colin, 2, 1959, 167-189.

2041   HAYEN, André. "Table ronde: Unité, unicité, dialogue."
       Actes du Xe Congrès des Sociétés de Philosophie de Langue
       Française (Congrès Bergson). Paris: Armand Colin, 2,
       1959, 281-302.

2042   HAYTSCHEK, Aloisia. "Henri Bergsons Theorie des Komischen."
       Diss., Wien, 1938, 207.

2043    HEATH, Louise Robinson. The Concept of Time. Chicago: University of Chicago Press; London: Cambridge University Press, 1936, 235. This is a historical study of the development of the concept of time, culminating in a discussion of the reality of time. References to Bergson are found throughout.

2044    HEATON, David M. "Two French Philosophical Sources of T. W. Hulme's Imagism." Dissertation Abstracts International, 31, 1970, 759A.

2045    HEBERT, Marcel. "M. Bergson et son affirmation de l'existence de Dieu." Revue de l'Université de Bruxelles, 17, Nos. 8-9, mai-juin 1912, 609-616. This essay concerns Bergson's mention of God in Creative Evolution. It was also published in Coenobium, June 1912, 1-7.

2046    HEBERT, Marcel. M. Bergson et son affirmation de l'existence de Dieu. Brüssel: Weißenbruch, 1912, 8. This appeared first in Revue de l'Université de Bruxelles, May-June 1912.

2047    HEBERT, Marcel. Le Pragmatisme: Etude de ses diverses formes, anglo-américaines, françaises et italiennes et de sa valeur religieuse. 1-2 éds. Paris: Emile Nourry, 1908, 105, 168. Chapter four of this study concerns Bergson.

2048    HEBRARD, Dom. La Vie intérieure: Esquisse d'une philosophie religieuse de la vie intérieure et de l'action. Paris: Beauchesne, 1918, 596.

2049    HEIDSIECK, François. "Bergson et l'histoire de la philosophie." L'Homme et l'histoire (Actes du Vie Congrès des Sociétés de Philosophie de Langue Française). Paris: Presses Universitaires de France, 1952, 389-394.

2050    HEIDSIECK, François. Henri Bergson et la notion d'espace. Paris: Le Cercle du Livre, 1957, 196.

2051    HEIDSIECK, François. "La Notion d'espace chez Bergson." Diss., Paris, 1955, 196.

2052    HEIDSIECK, François. "Table ronde: Physique." Actes du Xe Congrès des Sociétés de Philosophie de Langue Française (Congrès Bergson). Paris: Armand Colin, 2, 1959, 65-87.

2053    HEINTZ, Joseph-Walter. "La Notion de conscience chez William James et Henri Bergson." Diss., Paris, 1950.

2054    HELLMAN, Winfried. "Der Begriff der Zeit bei Henri Bergson."
         Philosophia Naturalis, 4, No. 1, 1957, 126-139.

2055    HELMS, Paul. Fra Plato til Bergson: Idealistisk Taenken
         gennem Tiderne. Copenhagen: Madsen, 1919, 276.

2056    HENDEL, Charles W. "The Achievement of Bergson." Univer-
         sity of Toronto Quarterly, 10, No. 3, April 1941, 269-282.
         This is a highly affirmative assessment of Bergson's phi-
         losophy.

2057    HENGSTENBERG, Hans Eduard. "Henri Bergson in Deutschland."
         Die Besinnung, 5, 1950, 248-254.

2058    HENRY, André. Bergson, maître de Péguy. Paris: Editions
         Elzévir, 1948, 328.

2059    HENRY, André. "Review of Henri Bergson et les lettres fran-
         çaises by Romeo Arbour." Feuillets de l'Amitié Charles
         Péguy, No. 65, juin 1958, 35-36.

2060    HENRY, André. "Quelques Aspects du bergsonisme de Péguy
         d'après les notes de 1914." Etudes Bergsoniennes, 4, 1956,
         113-115.

2061    HENRY, J. "Bergsonisme et morale." Revue Néo-scolastique
         de Philosophie, 25, No. 98, mai 1923. The author con-
         cludes that Bergsonism leads, not to anarchy, but to the
         individual's contributing to the march of evolution as a
         whole.

2062    HENRY, Mary. "Péguy's Debt to Pascal." L'Esprit créateur,
         No. 2, 1962, 55-65.

2063    HENSLOW, George. "M. Bergson's Creative Evolution." Lancet,
         182, 17 February 1912, 456. The author cites others who
         have dealt with the "new teleology" other than Bergson,
         namely, Henslow himself, H. H. Church, and Alfred Russell
         Wallace. This is a letter to the editor.

2064    "La herencia moral de la filosofía Griega." Criterio, 9,
         No. 456, noviembre 1936, 292. This is a comment on a book
         by Enrique Molina.

2065    HERMAN, D. J. "Finality in the Philosophy of Henri Bergson."
         Dissertation Abstracts International, 29, No. 7, 1968,
         2302A.

2066   HERMANN, E. Eucken and Bergson: Their Significance for
       Christian Thought. London: James Clark and Co., 1912, 244.

2067   HERMANT, Abel. "Review of L'Energie spirituelle by Henri
       Bergson." Le Figaro, 3e Sér., 65, No. 179, 29 juin 1919,
       4.

2068   Hermit of Prague (Pseud.). "Review of Modern Science and
       the Illusions of Professor Bergson by Hugh S. R. Elliot."
       Bedrock, 1, No. 3, July 1912, 277-280.

2069   HEROUX, Jean. "La Liberté humaine dans Bergson." Le Canada
       Français, 31, 1943-1944, 430-443.

2070   HERR, Lucien. "Review of Essai sur les données immédiates
       de la conscience by Henri Bergson." Revue Critique, N.S.
       30, No. 52, 29 décembre 1890, 517-519. This is a brief
       mention, along with several other books.

2071   HERSCH, Jeanne. "Les Images dans l'oeuvre de M. Bergson."
       Archives de Psychologie, 23, No. 90, 1932, 97-130. Images
       provide an invaluable means of understanding Bergson's
       thought. The author studies the different sorts of ima-
       gery used in each of Bergson's major works to date. An ap-
       pendix gives several examples of images.

2072   HERSCH, Jeanne. "L'Obstacle du langage." Henri Bergson.
       Ed. Béguin and Thévenaz, 214-221. The author examines and
       criticizes Bergson's conception of the function of lan-
       guage and concludes that Bergson's philosophical language
       is not sufficiently "profoundly created."

2073   HERSCH, Jeanne. "Souplesse bergsonienne." Labyrinthe: Jour-
       nal Mensuel des Lettres et des Arts, 2, No. 13, 6 août
       1945.

2074   HERTE, François. "Bergson." Revue du Néo-positivisme (Edi-
       tion spéciale), 5, 15 mai-juin 1925, 92-144.

2075   HERTRICH, Charles. Le Génie de Bergson. St.-Etienne: Edit.
       des Flambeaux, 1940, 14.

2076   HERTRICH, Charles. "Qu'est-ce que la vie? d'après Bergson.
       St.-Etienne: Edit. des Flambeaux, 1942, 24.

2077   HESS, Gerhard. Französische Philosophie der Gegenwart.
       Berlin: Junker und Dünnhaupt, 1933, 95. This study of re-
       cent French philosophy begins with a section on Bergson.

2078    HESS, M. Whitcomb.  "Bergson and Greek Mysticism."  Personal-
        ist, 17, No. 4, 1936, 377-383    The author uses this essay
        largely as an opportunity to express his own views.  He
        mentions Bergson's position as an unjustifiable anti-intel-
        lectualism and holds that Bergson failed to understand
        Aristotle, Plotinus, and Greek mysticism.

2079    HESSEN, Johannes.  Die Philosophie des 20. Jahrhunderts.
        Rottenburg, Germany: Bader, 1951, 190.  Bergson and exis-
        tentialism are discussed in this history of twentieth cen-
        tury philosophy.

2080    HEYMANS, Gérard.  "Les Deux Mémoires de M. Bergson."  Année
        Psychologique, 19, 1913, 66-74.  The author proposes cri-
        ticisms of Bergson's concept of memory.  He denies Berg-
        son's dualistic conclusions.

2081    HEYMANS, Gérard.  "Les Deux Mémoires de Bergson."  Gessamel-
        te Kleinere Schriften zur Philosophie und Psychologie: Vol.
        2.  Allgemeine Psychologie, Ethik und Aesthetik.  Den Haag,
        Netherlands: Nijhoff, 1927, 291-330.

2082    HEYMANS, Gérard.  "Een Nederlandsch boek over Bergson door
        Hoogveld: Di Nieuwe Wijsbegeerte."  Gids, Ser. 4, 33, No.
        1, 1916, 161-171.

2083    HEYMANS, Gérard.  "Die philosophie van Henri Bergson."  Tijd-
        schrift voor Wijsbegeerte, 5, No. 2, 1912, 205-238.

2084    HEYMANS, Gérard.  "Review of Le Rire by Henri Bergson."
        Zeitschrift fur Psychologie und Physiologie des Sinnesor-
        gane, 25, 1901, 155-156.  This is an expository, congratu-
        latory review.  It is very brief.

2085    HEYNE, Ranier.  "Georges Sorel und der autoritäre Staat des
        20. Jahrhunderts."  Archiv des öffentlichen Rechts, 29,
        Nos. 2-3, 1938, 129-177, 257-309.

2086    HIBBEN, John Gries.  "The Philosophical Aspects of Evolu-
        tion."  Philosophical Review, 18, No. 2, March 1910, 113-
        116.

2087    HICKS, G. Dawes.  "The Nature of Willing."  Proceedings of
        the Aristotelian Society, 13, 1912-1913, 27-65.  This es-
        say calls attention to "certain fundamental considerations
        in the psychology of volition that have important bearing
        upon the positions . . . of James and Bergson."  The na-
        ture of volition does not entail anti-intellectualism, ac-
        cording to the author.

2088   HICKS, G. Dawes. "Survey of Recent Philosophical and Theo-
       logical Literature: Philosophy." Hibbert Journal, 10, No.
       2, January 1912, 477-488. Recent Bergson literature is
       discussed on pages 479-480.

2089   HILPERT, Constantin. "Die Unterscheidung der intuitiven
       Erkenntnis von der Analys bei Bergson." Diss., Breslau,
       1915, 98.

2090   HIROFUGI, T. "A Study of Mind and Matter in Bergson's Phi-
       losophy." Mem. Osaka Kyoiku University, 10, 1967, 135-140.
       The text of this article is in Japanese.

2091   HIRSCH, Charles-Henry. "Review of 'Le Rire' by Henri Berg-
       son." Mercure de France, 34, No. 4, avril 1900, 223-227.

2093   HIRSCH, L. "Kämpfer gegen Materialismus und Intellektualis-
       mus für das 75. Jahre Bergsons." C.V. Zeitung Blätter für
       Deutschtum und Judentum, 13, No. 41, 1934.

2094   HIRSCHBELD, Peter. "Proust und Bergson." Zeitschrift für
       Ästhetik und allgemeine Kunstwissenschaft, 23, No. 2, 1929,
       165-184.

2095   HLADKI Zygmunt. "An Approach to Bergson." Hibbert Journal,
       47, No. 1, October 1948, 71-78.

2096   HOCKING, William Ernest. "Bergson." Types of Philosophy.
       New York: Scribner's, 1929, 188-212.

2097   HOCKING, William Ernest. The Meaning of God in Human Expe-
       rience. New Haven, Connecticut: Yale University Press;
       London: Henry Frowde, 1912, 586. Bergson, logic, and
       space are discussed on pages 80-89.

2098   HOCKING, William Ernest. "Significance of Bergson." Yale
       Review, N.S. 3, No. 1, 1913-1914, 303-326.

2099   HOEBER, F. "Erlebnis der Zeit und Willensfreiheit: Versuche
       über Bergsons intuitive Philosophie." Die weissen Blätter,
       4, No. 12, 1916, 185-198.

2100   HOERNLE, R. F. A. "The Analysis of Volition: Treated as a
       Study of Psychological Principles and Methods." Proceed-
       ings of the Aristotelian Society, N.S. 13, 1912-1913. 156-
       189. Bergson is discussed on pages 163-167 and 180-181.

2101   HOFFDING, Harald. Henri Bergson's filosofi. Kopenhagen:
       Glyendal, 1914, 70.

2102    HOFFDING, Harald. Lehrbuch der Geschichte der neueren Phi-
        losophie. Leipsic: Reisland, 1907, 286. This study con-
        tains a critique of L'Essai sur les données immédiates.

2103    HOFFDING, Harald. Modern Philosophers and Lectures on Berg-
        son. London: Macmillan, 1915, 317. This is an exposition
        and criticism of Bergson's basic theses. The author holds:
        " . . . Bergson rather paves the way towards a sort of ar-
        tistic perception than towards a higher science." (238).
        The "Lectures on Bergson" occur on pages 229-302; notes,
        on 313-317.

2104    HOFMANN, H. "Review of 'World of Dreams' by Henri Bergson."
        Harvard Divinity Bulletin, 25, No. 10, October 1960, 26-
        27.

2105    HOGARTH, Henry. "Bergson's Spiritual Pilgrimage." Hibbert
        Journal, 51, No. 200, October 1952, 63-66. Bergson is
        Catholicized in this article.

2106    HOLK, Lambertus Jacobus van. De beteekenis van Bergson voor
        de philosophische theologie. Leiden, Netherlands:
        Sijthoff, 1921, 175.

2107    HOLLARD, A. "Review of L'Evolution créatrice by Henri Berg-
        son." Foi et vie, 10, No. 18, 16 septembre 1907, 545-550.

2108    Homenaje a Bergson. Córdoba, Argentina: Imprenta de la Uni-
        versidad, 1936, 189. Instituto de Filosofía.

2109    Homenaje a Bergson. México: Imprenta Universitaria, 1941,
        188. Universidad Nacional Autonoma de México, Centro de
        Estudios Filosoficos de la Facultad de Filosofía y Letras.

2110    "Hommage à Bergson: Allocution de Stanislas Sicé, Emile Bré-
        hier, André Chaumeix." Revue des Deux Mondes, N.S. 2, No.
        10, 15 mai 1949, 364-375.

2111    "Hommage à Henri Bergson." Chronique des Lettres Françaises,
        7, 1929, 94-106.

2112    HONIGSHEIM, Paul. "Bergson et Neitzsche dans la nouvelle
        littérature française." Zeitschrift für Sozialforschung,
        3, 1934, 409-415.

2113    HOOGVELD, J. Die nieuwe Wijsbegeerte: Een studie over Berg-
        son. Utrecht, Netherlands: Dekker and van de Vegt, 1915,
        194.

2114   HOOKHAM, George.  "Further Notes on Bergson's Philosophy."
       National Review, 69, No. 350, April 1912, 325-336.

2115   HOOKHAM, George.  "Professor Bergson as a Critic of Darwin."
       National Review, 69, No. 349, March 1912, 100-118.

2116   HOPPENOT, Henri.  "Le Cours de M. Bergson."  Bulletin de la
       Semaine, 8, No. 6, 8 février 1911, 71-72.  This is an ac-
       count of Bergson's lectures on personality delivered at
       the Collège de France.

2117   HORKHEIMER, Max.  "Zur Henri Bergsons Metaphysik der Zeit."
       Zeitschrift für Sozialforschung, 3, 1934, 321-342.

2118   HORNE, Alistair.  The Price of Glory.  New York: St. Mar-
       tin's Press, 1963, 371.  Bergson and French militarism are
       discussed on page 11.

2119   HORNE, James R.  "Bergson's Mysticism Compared with Agape
       and Eros."  Hibbert Journal, 55, No. 4, July 1957, 363-
       372.  The author argues that Bergson tried to fit Agape
       into a metaphysical system too limited to appropriate it.

2120   HOUWENS POST, Hendrik.  Bergson: De Philosophie der Intuïtie.
       Den Haag, Netherlands: Leopolds Uitg. Maatsch., 1940, 95.

2121   HOWARTH, Herbert.  Notes on Some Figures Behind T. S. Eliot.
       London: Chatto and Windus, 1965, 396.

2122   HOWLETT, Jacques.  "Fragilité bergsonienne."  Lettres Nou-
       velles, 7e Année, No. 14, 3 juin 1959, 2-4.

2123   HUBENER, Gustav.  "Husserl, Bergson, George."  Die Güldenkam-
       mer, 3, 1913, 212-221.

2124   HUBERT, Judd D.  "The Influence of H. Bergson on Contempora-
       ry Esthetics (in France)."  Diss., Columbia, 1949.

2125   HUBSCHER, Arthur.  "Bergson."  Von Hegel zu Heidegger.
       Stuttgart: Reclam, 1961, 278.

2126   HUDSON, David.  "Three French Philosophers."  Circle Maga-
       zine, No. 1, January 1964, 10.

2127   HUGEL, Baron Friedrich von.  Eternal Life: Its Implications
       and Applications.  Edinburgh: Clark, 1912, 443.  Bergson
       is discussed on pages 288-302 and elsewhere.

2128    HUISMAN, Denis. "Bergson existe-t-il?." <u>Carrefour</u>, No. 767, 27 mai 1959, 21.

2129    HUISMAN, Denis. "Y a-t-il une esthétique bergsonienne?" <u>Actes</u> <u>du</u> <u>Xe</u> <u>Congrès</u> <u>des</u> <u>Sociétés</u> <u>de</u> <u>Philosophie</u> <u>de</u> <u>Langue</u> <u>Française</u> (Congrès Bergson). Paris: Armand Colin, 1, 1959, 153-155. Bergson did not write a treatise on aesthetics. Nonetheless, it can be said that the eight volumes of his work are eight books on the philosophy of art. The author holds that intuition is for Bergson aesthetic in all its manifestations. Bergson's thought is a vast aesthetic of perception.

2130    HULME, Thomas Ernest. "Mr. Balfour, Bergson, and Politics." <u>New</u> <u>Age</u>, N.S. 10, 9 November 1911, 38-40. This is a letter.

2131    HULME, Thomas Ernest. "Bax on Bergson." <u>New</u> <u>Age</u>, N.S. 9, 3 August 1911, 328-330.

2132    HULME, Thomas Ernest. "Bergson and Bax." <u>New</u> <u>Age</u>, N.S. 5, 22 July 1909, 259. This is a letter.

2133    HULME, Thomas Ernest. "Bergson in English." <u>Cambridge</u> <u>Magazine</u>, 1, 27 April 1912, 265. This is a letter.

2134    HULME, Thomas Ernest. "Bergson in English." <u>Cambridge</u> <u>Magazine</u>, 1, 18 May 1912, 353. This is a letter.

2135    HULME, Thomas Ernest. "Bergsonism." <u>New</u> <u>Age</u>, N.S. 10, 23 November 1911, 46-47. This is a letter.

2136    HULME, Thomas Ernest. "Bergsonism." <u>New</u> <u>Age</u>, N.S. 10, 23 November 1911, 94. This is a letter.

2137    HULME, Thomas Ernest. "Bergsonism in Paris." <u>New</u> <u>Age</u>, N.S. 9, 22 July 1911, 189-190. This is a letter.

2138    HULME, Thomas Ernest. <u>Further</u> <u>Speculations</u>. Ed. Sam Hynes. Minneapolis, Minnesota: University of Minnesota Press, 1955, 226. The editor discusses Hulme's Bergsonism on pages xii-xiv; Hulme's notes on Bergson are given on pages 28-63.

2139    HULME, Thomas Ernest. "The New Philosophy." <u>New</u> <u>Age</u>, N.S. 5, 1 July 1909, 198-199.

2140    HULME, Thomas Ernest. "Searchers After Reality: I. Bax." <u>New</u> <u>Age</u>, N.S. 5, 29 July 1909, 265-266.

2141    HULME, Thomas Ernest. <u>Speculations</u>: <u>Essays</u> <u>on</u> <u>Humanism</u> <u>and</u>
        <u>the</u> <u>Philosophy</u> <u>of</u> <u>Art</u>. Ed. Herbert Read. London: Rout-
        ledge and Kegan Paul, Ltd., 1949, 271. The foreward is by
        Jacob Epstein. The following chapters on Bergson occur on
        the following pages: "Bergson's Theory of Art," 143-169;
        "The Philosophy of Intensive Manifolds," 173-214.

2142    HUNEKER, James Gibbons. <u>The</u> <u>Pathos</u> <u>of</u> <u>Distance</u>. New York:
        Scribner's, 1913, 394. Bergson is characterized as the
        playboy of western philosophy on pages 367-385.

2143    HUNEKER, James Gibbons. "The Playboy of Western Philosophy."
        <u>Forum</u>, 49, No. 3, March 1913, 257-268.

2144    HUNT, Harriet E. <u>The</u> <u>Psychology</u> <u>of</u> <u>Auto-education</u>: <u>Based</u> <u>on</u>
        <u>the</u> <u>Interpretation</u> <u>of</u> <u>Intellect</u> <u>Given</u> <u>by</u> <u>Henri</u> <u>Bergson</u> <u>in</u>
        <u>his</u> "<u>Creative</u> <u>Evolution</u>": <u>Illustrated</u> <u>in</u> <u>the</u> <u>Work</u> <u>of</u> <u>Maria</u>
        <u>Montessori</u>. Syracuse, New York: Bardeen, 1912, 82.

2145    HUSBAND, Mary Gilliland. "Review of <u>L'Evolution</u> <u>créatrice</u>
        by Henri Bergson." <u>International</u> <u>Journal</u> <u>of</u> <u>Ethics</u>, 22,
        No. 4, July 1912, 462-467. This review gives a very gen-
        eral account of Bergson's position in <u>L'Evolution</u> <u>créa-</u>
        <u>trice</u>.

2146    HUSSON, Léon. "Les Aspects méconnus de la liberté bergso-
        nienne." <u>Actes</u> <u>du</u> <u>4e</u> <u>Congrès</u> <u>des</u> <u>Sociétés</u> <u>de</u> <u>Philosophie</u>
        <u>de</u> <u>Langue</u> <u>Française</u>. Neuchâtel, Switzerland: La Bacon-
        nière, 1949, 373-391.

2147    HUSSON, Léon. "Les Aspects méconnus de la liberté bergso-
        nienne." <u>Etudes</u> <u>Bergsoniennes</u>, 4, 1956, 157-201.

2148    HUSSON, Léon. "Le Centenaire d'Henri Bergson." <u>Cahiers</u>
        <u>Français</u>, 13, No. 44, 1959, 8-13.

2149    HUSSON, Léon. "Le Développement de la conception de l'intel-
        ligence chez Bergson." <u>Bulletin</u> <u>Ecole</u> <u>Pratique</u> <u>de</u> <u>Psycho-</u>
        <u>logie</u> <u>et</u> <u>de</u> <u>Pédagogie</u>, 6, No. 4, 1952, 301-313.

2150    HUSSON, Léon. <u>L'Intellectualisme</u> <u>de</u> <u>Bergson</u>: <u>Genèse</u> <u>et</u> <u>dé-</u>
        <u>veloppement</u> <u>de</u> <u>la</u> <u>notion</u> <u>bergsonienne</u> <u>d'intuition</u>. Paris:
        Presses Universitaires de France, 1947, 240.

2151    HUSSON, Léon. "La Portée lointaine de la psychologie bergso-
        nienne." <u>Actes</u> <u>du</u> <u>Xe</u> <u>Congrès</u> <u>des</u> <u>Sociétés</u> <u>de</u> <u>Philosophie</u>
        <u>de</u> <u>Langue</u> <u>Française</u> (Congrès Bergson). Paris: Armand
        Colin, 1, 1959, 157-162. In studying Bergson's theory of

pure memory the author wishes to show how Bergson's psychology surpasses the formulas within which psychology is
usually imprisoned and how it can still renew the reflections of contemporary thinkers.

2152    HUSSON, Léon. "Renée Boviatis-Deschamps. Le Bergsonisme
est-il un humanisme? Thèse présentée à la Faculté des Lettres de Montpellier, 195 pages dactylographiées, 1948."
Etudes Bergsoniennes, 2, 1949, 251-256. This is an appreciative review, which, however, criticizes the author's
failure to deal with the step by step development of Bergson's thought. Bergson did not intend men to become
"gods," in Husson's opinion.

2153    HUSSON, Léon. "Signification et limites de la critique de
l'intelligence chez Bergson." Actes du XIe Congrès internationale de philosophie. XIII. Histoire de la philosophie moderne et contemporaine. Louvain: Nauwelaerts;
Amsterdam: North-Holland Publishing Co., 1953, 174-179.

2154    HUSSON, Léon. "Table ronde: Durée et mémoire." Actes du
Xe Congrès des Sociétés de Philosophie de Langue Française
(Congrès Bergson). Paris: Armand Colin, 2, 1959, 41-61.

2155    HUSSON, Léon. "Table ronde: Liberté." Actes du Xe Congrès
des Sociétés de Philosophie de Langue Française (Congrès
Bergson). Paris: Armand Colin, 2, 1959, 167-189.

2156    HUSSON, Léon. "Table ronde: Matière, causalité, discontinu."
Actes du Xe Congrès des Sociétés de Philosophie de Langue
Française (Congrès Bergson). Paris: Armand Colin, 2, 1959,
121-142.

2157    HUSSON, Léon. "Table ronde: Morale." Actes du Xe Congrès
des Sociétés de Philosophie de Langue Française (Congrès
Bergson). Paris: Armand Colin, 2, 1959, 237-257.

2158    HUSSON, Léon. "Table ronde: Psychologie, phénoménologie,
intuition." Actes du Xe Congrès des Sociétés de Philosophie de Langue Française (Congrès Bergson). Paris: Armand
Colin, 2, 1959, 15-37.

2159    HUSSON, Léon. "Y a-t-il de l'intellectualisme chez Bergson?
Réponse à M. J. Benda." Etudes Philosophiques, N.S. 5,
No. 2, avril-juin 1950, 233-239.

2160    HUXLEY, Julian S. "Mind Considered From the Point of View
of Biology." Journal of Philosophical Studies (Philoso-

phy), 2, No. 7, July 1927, 330-348.  Bergson is discussed
on pages 33, 343-344, and 346-347.

2161   HYPPOLITE, Jean.  "Aspects divers de la mémoire chez Bergson."  Revue Internationale de Philosophie, 3, No. 10,
1949.

2162   HYPPOLITE, Jean.  "Du Bergsonisme à l'existentialisme."
Mercure de France, 306, No. 2, mai-août 1959, 403-416.

2163   HYPPOLITE, Jean.  "Du Bergsonisme à l'existentialisme."
Universidad Nacional.  Cuyo, Actas primero Congreso nacional de Filosofía, 1, 1949, 442-455.

2164   HYPPOLITE, Jean.  "Discours à l'Ecole Normale Supérieure."
Bulletin de la Société Française de Philosophie, 54, No.
1, janvier-mars 1960, 7-9.

2165   HYPPOLITE, Jean.  "Emile Bréhier, 'Images plotiniennes, images bergsoniennes'."  Etudes Bergsoniennes, 2, 1949, 215-
222.  The author participates here with several philosophers in a discussion of Bergson and Plotinus.

2166   HYPPOLITE, Jean.  "Jean Hyppolite, 'Henri Bergson et l'existentialisme'."  Etudes Bergsoniennes, 2, 1949, 208-215.
The author participates here with several philosophers in
a discussion of Bergson and existentialisme.

2167   HYPPOLITE, Jean.  Sens et existence dans la philosophie de
Merleau-Ponty.  Oxford: Clarendon University Press, 1963,
26.  References to Bergson and Merleau-Ponty are found in
this study.

2168   HYPPOLITE, Jean.  "Table ronde: Néant et existentialisme."
Actes du Xe Congrès des Sociétés de Philosophie de Langue
Française (Congrès Bergson).  Paris: Armand Colin, 2, 1959,
145-164.

2169   HYPPOLITE, Jean.  "Table ronde: Unité, unicité, dialogue."
Actes du Xe Congrès des Sociétés de Philosophie de Langue
Française (Congrès Bergson).  Paris: Armand Colin, 2, 1959,
281-302.

2170   HYPPOLITE, Jean.  "A Tribute to Bergson on the Occasion of
the Bergson Centennial in Paris, 1959."  The Bergsonian
Heritage.  Ed. Thomas Hanna.  New York and London: Columbia University Press, 1962, 103, 106.  This essay discusses Bergson's contribution to the Collège de France.

2171    HYPPOLITE, Jean. "Vie et philosophie de l'histoire chez
        Bergson." Universidad nacional. Cuyo, Actas primero Con-
        greso nacional de Filosofía, 2, 1949, 915-921.

2172    IBERICO, Mariano. "Bergson y Freud." Revista de Filosofía,
        Año 13, No. 3, 1927, 375-378. The author discusses assump-
        tions which Bergson and Freud have in common, namely, the
        importance of instinct and the unconscious mind in human
        behavior and development.

2173    IBERICO, Mariano. "La filosofía de Bergson." Sustancia, 2,
        Nos. 7-8, septiembre 1941, 351-356.

2174    IBERICO, Mariano. Une filosofía estética. Lima, 1922.
        This study contains a chapter entitled "Bergson." It was
        originally the author's thesis, completed in 1919.

2175    IBERICO, Mariano. Perspectivas sobre el tema del tiempo.
        Lima: Universidad Nacional Mayor de San Marcos, 1958, 195.

2176    IBERICO, Mariano. "El viaje del espíritu." Humanidades, 19,
        No. 1, 76-91. Bergson is discussed on pages 84-89.

2177    IBERICO, Rodrígues Mariano. "La filosofía de Bergson."
        Letras, No. 20, 1941, 307-316.

2178    IBERICO Y RODRIGUEZ, Mariano. La filosofía de Enrique Berg-
        son. Lima, 1916.

2179    IMBART DE LA TOUR, Pierre. "Le Pangermanisme et la philoso-
        phie de l'histoire: Lettre à M. Henri Bergson." Revue des
        Deux Mondes, 6e Sér., 30, No. 3, 1er décembre 1915, 481-
        520.

2180    IMBART DE LA TOUR, Pierre. Le Pangermanisme et la philoso-
        phie de l'histoire: Lettre à M. Bergson. Paris: Perrin,
        1916, 76.

2181    INGARDEN, Roman. "Intuicja i inteleck u Henryka Bergsona."
        Z badań nad filosofia współczena. Warzawa: Pánstwowe
        Wydawnictwo Naukowe, 1963, 664.

2182    INGARDEN, Roman. "L'Intuition bergsonienne et le problème
        phénoménologique de la constitution." Actes du Xe Con-
        grès des Sociétés de Philosophie de Langue Française (Con-
        grès Bergson). Paris: Armand Colin, 1, 1959, 163-166.
        The author examines the analogies between Bergson's intui-
        tion of pure duration and the theories of Kant and above

all Husserl.   Certain differences between these philosophers are also made apparent.

2183    INGARDEN, Roman.   "Intuition und Intellekt bei Henri Bergson."  Jahrbuch für Philosophie und phänomenologische Forschung, 5, 1922, 285-461.   It is an excellent, carefully
thought out study of Bergson's critique of intellectual
analysis and of Bergson's concept of duration.

2184    INGARDEN, Roman.   "Table ronde: Psychologie, phénoménologie,
intuition."  Actes du Xe Congrès des Sociétés de Philosophie de Langue Française (Congrès Bergson).   Paris: Armand
Colin, 2, 1959, 15-37.

2185    INGARDEN, Roman.   "Table ronde: Unité, unicité, dialogue."
Actes du Xe Congrès des Sociétés de Philosophie de Langue
Française (Congrès Bergson).   Paris: Armand Colin, 2, 1959,
281-302.

2186    INGARDEN, Roman.   Time and Modes of Being.   Trans. H. R.
Michejda.   Springfield, Illinois: Charles C. Thomas, 1964,
170.   Bergson is discussed on pages 36, 67, 115, 122, 127,
144, and 148.

2187    INGE, William Ralph.   The Philosophy of Plotinus.   London,
New York: Longmans, Green, and Co., 1918, I, 270.   Bergson's concept of time is discussed on pages 174-177; Bergsons's concept of consciousness on pages 242-244.

2188    INGENIEROS, José.   "Encuesta sobre cooperación intelectual."
Revista de Filosofía, 9, No. 4, julio 1923, 1-11.

2189    "Review of 'Introduction à la métaphysique' by Henri Bergson.  Jeunesse Laïque, No. 37, 1905, 223-232.

2190    IRIARTE, Joaquín de.   "Review of Nueve grandes filósofos contemporáneos y sus temas by J. David García Bacca."  Razón
y Fe, 140, No. 620-621, 1949, 235.

2191    IRIARTE, Joaquín de.   "El sentido espiritualista de la filosofía de Bergson."  Razón y Fe, 122, No. 2, 1941, 196-210.

2192    IRWIN, Jean McQueen.   "Bergson and Gestalt Psychology: Cor-
ollary Critiques of Scientific Method in Psychology."  Psychological Bulletin, 38, No. 8, October 1941, 739.   This
is an abstract of a paper given at the twenty-first meeting of the Western Psychological Association.

2193    ISAACHSEN-DUDOK VAN HEEL, Valborg. "Henri Bergson." Groot-
        Nederland, 17, 1919.

2194    ISAYE, Gaston. "Bergson et Teilhard de Chardin." Actes du
        Xe Congrès des Sociétés de Philosophie de Langue Française
        (Congrès Bergson). Paris: Armand Colin, 1, 1959, 167-169.
        The author studies the role of Bergson's intuition (con-
        ceived as both reflective and synthesizing intuition) in
        three of Teilhard de Chardin's affirmations: the question
        of the "within," the question of finality, and the ques-
        tion of "ultra-reflexion."

2195    ISAYE, Gaston. "Table ronde: Liberté." Actes du Xe Congrès
        des Sociétés de Philosophie de Langue Française (Congrès
        Bergson). Paris: Armand Colin, 2, 1959, 167-189.

2196    ISAYE, Gaston. "Table ronde: Vie et évolution." Actes du
        Xe Congrès des Sociétés de Philosophie de Langue Française
        (Congrès Bergson). Paris: Armand Colin, 2, 1959, 91-117.

2197    "Is the Bergson Philosophy that of a Charlatan?" Current
        Literature, 52, No. 2, February 1912, 198-199. The au-
        thor provides a balanced assessment of Bergson's popular-
        ity.

2198    ISWOLSKY, Hélène. Au Temps de la lumière. Montréal: Edit.
        de l'Arbre, 1945, 260.

2199    ITURRIOZ, J. "El cristianismo de Bergson." Estudios, No.
        132.

2200    ITURRIOZ, J. "El cristianismo de Bergson." Razón y Fe, 43,
        No. 127, 1943, 243-256.

2201    ITURRIOZ, J. "El cristianismo de Bergson." Vida Contempo-
        ráneo, 6, No. 113, 1945.

2202    IVANOFF. Les Deux Aspects du bergsonisme. Paris: Croville-
        Morant, 1929, 15.

2203    IZQUIERDO, G. "El esfuerzo intelectual segun H. Bergson."
        Revista de Aragón, 3, No. 2, februario 1902.

2204    JACKEL, Kurt. Bergson und Proust: Eine Untersuchung über
        die weltanschaulichen Grundlagen von "A La Recherche du
        temps perdu." Breslau: Priebatsch, 1934, 129.

2205    JACKS, Lawrence Pearsall. The Alchemy of Thought. New York:
        Holt, 1911; London: Williams and Nordgate, 1910, 349.

2206    JACKS, Lawrence Pearsall.  "M. Bergson as Liberator."  Hib-
        bert Journal, 33, No. 1, October 1934, 55-68.  This is a
        review of La Pensée et le mouvant by Henri Bergson.

2207    JACOB, B.  "La Philosophie d'hier et celle d'aujourd'hui."
        Revue de Métaphysique et de Morale, 6, 1989, 170-201.

2208    JACOB, Jean and WEILER, Maurice.  Ecrivains français du
        vingtième siècle: Textes choisis.  Paris: Belin, 1966, 375.

2209    JACOBSON, Leon.  "Translator's Preface."  Duration and Si-
        multaneity.  Indianapolis, Indiana: Bobbs-Merril, 1965,
        190, v-xi.

2210    JACOBSSON, Malte.  Henri Bergson's intuitions filosofi.
        Lund, Sweden: Lindstedt, 1911, 40.

2211    JACOBY, Gunther.  "Bergson, Pragmatism and Schopenhauer."
        Monist, 22, No. 3, October 1912, 593-611.

2212    JACOBY, Gunther.  "Bergson und A. Schopenhauer."  Interna-
        tionale Monatsschrift für Wissenschaft, 10, 1916, 454-479.

2213    JACOBY, Gunther.  "Review of Einführung in die Metaphysik by
        Henri Bergson; and Henri Bergsons intuitive Philosophie by
        Albert Steenbergen."  Archiv für die gesamte Psychologie,
        18, 1910, 19-20.

2214    JACQUEMONT, P.  "M. Bergson à l'Académie française."  La
        France Illustrée, 2 février 1918.

2215    JACQUES, E.  "Review of L'Univers bergsonien by Lydie
        Adolphe."  Revue Philosophique de Louvain, 3e Sér., 54,
        No. 43, 1956, 508-509.

2216    JAENSCH, E. R. and KRETZ, Adalbert.  "Strukturpsychologische
        Erlauterungen zur philosophischen Zeitlehre, insbesondere
        bei Bergson und Proust."  Zeitschrift für Psychologie und
        Psychologie der Sinnesorgane I.  Abtlg.: Zeitschrift für
        Psychologie, 124, No. 1, 1932, 55-92.

2217    JAGER, Georg.  "Das Verhältnis Bergsons zu Schelling."
        Diss., Leipsic, 1917, 64.

2218    JAGU, Chanoine Armand.  "Hommage à Bergson: Le Savant,
        l'écrivain, l'artiste."  Mémoires de l'Académie des Sci-
        ences, Belles-Lettres et Arts d'Angers, 1960.

2219    JAHN, M. Franz. Das Problem des Komischen. Potsdam, Germany: Astein, 1905, 130.

2220    JAKI, Stanley L. "Review of Bergson and the Evolution of Physics. Ed. and Trans. with Intro. P. A. Y. Gunter." Zygon, 7, No. 2, June 1972, 138-139.

2221    JALOUX, Edmond. Avec Marcel Proust. Paris et Genève: La Palatine, 1953, 153. The influence of Bergson on Proust is discussed on pages 19-20 and 23.

2222    JALOUX, Edmond. "Henri Bergson." Le Gaulois, 24 janvier 1918.

2223    JALOUX, Edmond. L'Esprit des livres. Paris: Plon, 1923, 257. Bergson is discussed on pages 101-107.

2224    JAMES, Henry. The Letters of William James. Boston: Little, Brown and Company, 1926, 384. This collection includes correspondence later published in Perry's Thought and Character of William James.

2225    JAMES, William. "Bradley or Bergson?" Journal of Philosophy, 7, No. 2, 20 January 1910, 29-33.

2226    JAMES, William. "A Great French Philosopher at Harvard." Nation, 90, No. 2335, 31 March 1910, 312-314.

2227    JAMES, William. "The Philosophy of Bergson." Hibbert Journal, 7, No. 3, April 1909, 562-577. This essay is reprinted as "Bergson and His Critique of Intellectualism," as Lecture VI in A Pluralistic Universe. New York: Longmans, Green and Company, 1919, 223-272.

2228    JAMES, William. Philosophie de l'expérience. Trans. E. Le Brun and M. Paris. Paris: Flammarion, 1910, 368.

2229    JAMES, William. Le Pragmatisme. Trans. E. Le Brun. Paris: Flammarion, 1968, 251. This book contains an introduction by Henri Bergson.

2230    JAMIL, Khwija Moinud-Din. Nietzsche and Bergson. Rajshahi, Pakistan: International Printing Firm, 1959, 173.

2231    JAMIL, Khwija Moinud-Din. "Nietzsche and Bergson in the Domain of Moral Philosophy." Diss., Paris, 1953, 133.

2232    JANEFF, Janko. "Das Leben und das Überlegendige: Eine kri-
        tische Untersuchung der Metaphysik Bergsons." Diss.,
        Heidelberg, 1924, 99.

2233    JANET, Pierre. L'Evolution de la mémoire et de la notion du
        temps. Paris: Chahine, 1928, 619. Bergson is discussed
        on pages 23, 26-27, and 144; Bergson and Janet on pages 155-
        159; Bergson's concept of memory on pages 195-202; the con-
        cept of the present on pages 305-310; Bergson and Blondel
        on page 461; Bergson and Einstein on pages 486-487; Berg-
        son and science on pages 516-518, 584, 600, 602, and 604.

2234    JANET, Pierre. "La Psychologie de la croyance et le mysti-
        cisme." Revue de Métaphysique et de Morale, 43, No. 4,
        1936, 507-532; 44, No. 2, 1937, 369-410.

2235    JANET and SEAILLES. Histoire de la philosophie: Les Pro-
        blèmes et les écoles (Supplément: Période contemporaine,
        par Parodi, Tisserand, Dugas, Dorolle et Abel Rey). Paris:
        Delagrave, 1929, 240. Bergson, Durkheim, Hamelin, Lagneau,
        William James, Couturat, and others are treated in this
        study.

2236    JANKELEVITCH, Vladimir. "Avec L'Ame toute-entière." Bulle-
        tin de la Société Française de Philosophie, 54, No. 1,
        janvier-mars 1960, 55-62.

2237    JANKELEVITCH, Vladimir. Bergson. Paris: Félix Alcan, 1931,
        300. Instead of confining himself to a simple exposition,
        the author tries to recover the genesis and framework of
        Bergson's thought by a reconstruction of ideas. He places
        special emphasis on the critical interpretation of con-
        cepts of matter.

2238    JANKELEVITCH, Vladimir. "Bergson et le judaïsme." Mélanges
        de philosophie et de littérature juives. Vol. 1. Paris:
        Presses Universitaires de France, 1957, 64-94.

2239    JANKELEVITCH, Vladimir. Henri Bergson. Trans. F. Gonzales
        Arambura. Xalapa, México, 1962, 379.

2240    JANKELEVITCH, Vladimir. Henri Bergson. Paris: Presses Uni-
        versitaires de France, 1959, 299. This is a thoroughgoing
        rewrite of the author's earlier Bergson. It is one of the
        best general works on Bergson.

2241    JANKELEVITCH, Vladimir. "Henri Bergson: Totalidades orgáni-
        cas." La Palabra y el Hombre, 20, No. 4, 1961, 561-581.

2242    JANKELEVITCH, Vladimir. "Bergsonisme et biologie: à propos
d'un ouvrage récent." Revue de Métaphysique et de Morale,
36, No. 2, avril-juin 1929, 253-256. This is a review of
Introduction biologique à l'étude de la neurologie et de
la psychopathologie by Von Monakow and Mourgue.

2243    JANKELEVITCH, Vladimir. "De La Simplicité." Henri Bergson.
Ed. Béguin and Thévenaz, 170-178. The author describes
Bergson's throught as an ettempt to attain an ultimately
simple insight, and thereby overcome the complexities
which the intelligence has artificially introduced.

2244    JANKELEVITCH, Vladimir. "Deux Philosophes de la vie: Bergson, Guyau." Revue Philosophique de la France et de
l'Etranger, 97, No. 6, juin 1924, 402-449.

2245    JANKELEVITCH, Vladimir. "Les Deux Sources de la morale et
de la religion d'après Bergson." Revue de Métaphysique et
de Morale, 40, No. 1, 1933, 101-117. This is a highly appreciative review.

2246    JANKELEVITCH, Vladimir. "N'écoutez pas ce qu'ils disent,
regardez ce qu'ils font." Revue de Métaphysique et de Morale, 64, No. 2, 1959, 161-162. The author claims that
central to Bergson's philosophy is the necessity to "s'en-
gager."

2247    JANKELEVITCH, Vladimir. "L'Optimisme bergsonien." Evidences, No. 16, janvier 1951, 1-4.

2248    JANKELEVITCH, Vladimir. "Prolégomènes au bergsonisme." Revue de Métaphysique et de Morale, 35, No. 4, octobre-décembre 1928, 437-490.

2249    JANKELEVITCH, Vladimir. "Prolégomènes au bergsonisme."
Documents de la Vie Intellectuelle, 1, No. 4, 20 janvier
1930, 40-62.

2250    JANKELEVITCH, Vladimir. "A Tribute to Bergson on the Occasion of the Bergson Centennial in Paris, 1959: With the
Whole Soul." The Bergsonian Heritage. Ed. Thomas Hanna.
New York and London: Columbia University Press, 1952, 155-
166. The author insists that: "Bergsonism is a maximalist
philosophy . . . . For Bergson there are only utter totalities, organic totalities; no vacuum comes to deplete the
positive fullness in which we live; all that exists is complete, viable, all-sufficient to itself." (156).

2251    JANICAUD, Dominique. Une Généalogie du spiritualisme fran-
        çais: Aux Sources du bergsonisme: Ravaisson et la méta-
        physique. The Hague: Martinus Nijhoff, 1969, 276. This
        excellent study traces the sources of Bergson's thought in
        Ravaisson. A bibliography occurs on pages 277-285.

2252    JANICAUD, Dominique. "Table-ronde." Nouvelles Littéraires,
        No. 1677, 22 octobre 1959, 1 et 5-6.

2253    JANSSENS, Edgar. "Review of 'Raison et intuition: Etude sur
        la philosophie de M. Henri Bergson' by Georges Dwelshau-
        vers." Revue Néo-scolastique de Philosophie, 14, No. 1,
        février 1907, 140-142.

2253    JAQUES, R. S. "The Significance of Bergson for Recent Po-
        litical Thought and Movements in France." Royal Society
        of Canada Proceedings and Transactions, 3rd Series, 26,
        1932, Section ii, 5-12.

2254    JARLOT, G. "Personne et humanité: Deux sources?" Archives
        de Philosophie, 12, No. 1, 1936, 1-65. This study con-
        cerns Les Deux Sources de la morale et de la religion by
        Henri Bergson.

2255    JARY, Jacques. "Ce que nous devons au bergsonisme." Renais-
        sance Politique, Littéraire et Artistique, 2, février 1914,
        28-29. This is a comment on an article by T. de Visan
        which appeared in the February 1914 issue of Temps Présent.

2256    JEANNIERE, René. "La Théorie des concepts chez M. Bergson
        et M. James." Revue de Philosophie, 17, No. 12, décembre
        1910, 578-598.

2257    JEANSON, Francis. Signification humaine du rire. Paris:
        Editions du Seuil, 1950, 213. Bergson's concept of laugh-
        ter is discussed on pages 33-41 and throughout.

2258    JENNINGS, H. S. "Moderne Wissenschaft und die Illusion von
        Bergson von H. Elliot." Archiv für Hydrobiologie, 9, 1913,
        648-655.

2259    JERPHAGNON, Lucien. De La Banalité: Essai sur l'Ipséité et
        sa durée vécue: Durée personnelle et co-durée. Paris:
        Vrin, 1965, 426.

2260    JERPHAGNON, Lucien. "Entre La Solitude et la banalite: Phi-
        losophie bergsonienne du banal." Revue de Métaphysique et
        de Morale, 67, No. 3, 1962, 322-329.

2261    JERUSALEM, William. _Einleitung in die Philosophie._ Vienna
       and Leipsic: Braumiller, 1913, 402.

2262    JERUSALEM, William. _Introduction to Philosophy._ Trans.
       C. F. Saunders. London: Macmillan, 1911, 402.

2263    JETTE, Emile. "L'Illusion bergsonienne et la perception ex-
       térieure." _Carnets Viatoriens_, 12, No. 4, 1947, 266-276.

2264    JETTE, Emile. "La Perception chez Bergson." Diss., Laval,
       1943, 147.

2265    JEVONS, Frank Byron. _Personality._ London: Methuen and Co.,
       1913, 171. Bergson is discussed on pages 78-124 and else-
       where. The views of Hume, James, Bergson, and others are
       criticized in this study.

2266    "The Jewishness of Bergson." _Literary Digest_, 46, No. 13,
       29 March 1913, 712.

2267    JHA, A. "Notes on the Nature of Comic Laughter." _Calcutta
       Review_, 180, No. 1, July 1966, 62-69. Beckett, Bergson,
       and Ionesco are discussed in this essay.

2268    JIMINEZ LUQUE, Baldomero. "El valor noético del misticismo
       bergsoniano." _Spes Nostra_, 1, No. 1, 1944, 25-36.

2269    JOAD, Cyril Edward Mitchinson. "Henri Bergson." _New States-
       man and Nation_, 21, No. 516, 11 January 1941, 33-34. This
       is an obituary notice.

2270    JOAD, Cyril Edward Mitchinson. _Great Philosophies of the
       World._ New York: Robert M. McBride and Co., 1933, 79.
       Bergson is discussed in Chapter VI, which is entitled "The
       Philosophy of Change," 114-123.

2271    JOAD, Cyril Edward Mitchinson. "The Problem of Free Will
       in the Light of Recent Developments in Philosophy." _Pro-
       ceedings of the Aristotelian Society_, N.S. 23, 1922-1923,
       121-140. The author maintains that: "For Bergson this re-
       ality is a continuous flow or change. It is a pure becom-
       ing without marks or features of any kind, the distinc-
       tions and individuations we discern in it being due to the
       discriminating, selecting and cutting-up operations of our
       intellect . . . . Beyond the "élan vital" there is no-
       thing." (125).

2272    JOEL, Karl. "Neues Denken." _Neue Rundschau_, 21, No. 2,
       1910, 549-588.

2273   JOERGENSEN, Joergen Fr.  Henri Bergson's Filosofi i omrids.
       Kjoebenhavn: Forf., 1917, 88.

2274   JOHANNET, R.  "Discussion avec J. Maritain et Joseph de Ton-
       quédec sur Bergson."  Les Lettres, 8, No. 2, 1er février
       1920, 24-32.

2275   JOHANNET, René.  "De Tardieu à Bergson."  Ecrits de Paris,
       No. 189, janvier 1961, 45-57.

2276   JOHNSON, Patricia J.  "Bergson's Le Rire: Game Plan for Ca-
       mus' L'Etranger?"  French Review, 47, No. 1, October 1973,
       46-56.  The author finds the influence of Bergson's theory
       of laughter in Camus' novel The Stranger.

2277   JOHNSTON, Charles.  "Where Bergson Stands."  Harper's Weekly,
       57, No. 2934, 15 March 1913, 16.  The author offers a gen-
       eral account of Bergson's philosophy.

2278   JOHNSTONE, James.  "Does the Demonstration of Physical Con-
       tinuity in the Germ-Plasms of Successive Generations of
       Animal Organisms Also Demonstrate the Transmission of Men-
       tal Characters?"  Proceedings of the Aristotelian Society,
       Supplementary Volume, 4, 1924, 130-137.

2279   JOHNSTONE, James.  The Philosophy of Biology.  Cambridge,
       England: University Press, 1914, 391.  This study is a
       thoroughgoing attempt to apply Bergson's philosophy to the
       basic problems and concepts of biology.

2280   JOLIVET, Régis.  "Bergson et le bergsonisme."  L'Année Théo-
       logique, 2, 1941, 253-264.

2281   JOLIVET, Régis.  "Bergson et le bergsonisme."  Doctor Com-
       munis, 13, No. 1, 1960, 49-75.

2282   JOLIVET, Régis.  "Critique de la critique bergsonienne de
       l'idée du néant exposée dans l'ouvrage de Le Roy."  Le Pro-
       blème de Dieu."  Archives de Philosophie, 8, No. 2, 1931,
       75-83.

2283   JOLIVET, Régis.  "De L'Evolution créatrice aux Deux Sources."
       Revue Thomiste, N.S. 16, No. 77, mai-juin 1933, 347-367.

2284   JOLIVET, Régis.  Essai sur le bergsonisme.  Paris: Vitté,
       1931; Lyon: Vitté, 1932, 162.

2285    JOLIVET, Régîs.  "L'Intuition intellectuelle et le problème
de la métaphysique."  Archives de Philosophie, 11, 1934,
No. 2, 97-111.

2286    JOLIVET, Régîs.  "Le Mouvement philosophique en France en
1926-1927."  New Scholasticism, 2, No. 2, April 1928, 138-
161.  Bergson and psychology are discussed on pages 148-
149.

2287    JOLIVET, Régîs.  "Le Nouveau Livre de M. Bergson: Les Deux
Sources de la morale et de la religion."  Revue Apologétique, 54, No. 561, juin 1932, 641-662.

2288    JOLIVET, Régîs.  "Philosophie chrétienne et bergsonisme."
Revue des Sciences Religieuses, 15, No. 1, 1935, 28-43.

2289    JOLIVET, Régîs.  "Réflexions sur le déclin du bergsonisme
dans les années d'après-guerre."  Actes du Xe Congrès des
Sociétés de Philosophie de Langue Française (Congrès Bergson).  Paris: Armand Colin, 1, 1959, 171-175.  The author
argues that the decline of Bergsonism is due to criticisms
of Bergson's psychology and to the emergence of existential doctrines.  Bergson combined existential elements in
his doctrine, but these never went beyond the abstract level of a conceptual analysis.

2290    JOLIVET, Régîs.  "Thomisme et bergsonisme."  Studia Catholica, 14, No. 1, 1938, 43-60.

2291    JOLL, James.  "Le Président Soleil."  New York Review of
Books, 7, No. 8, 17 November 1966, 18.  Bergson's influence on Charles DeGaulle is mentioned in this article.

2292    JONES, H. Gordon.  "Bergson et l'évolution: L'Evolution créatrice."  Trans. Pierre Hilleman.  Revue Positiviste Internationale, 8, No. 5, 1er octobre 1913, 311-320.  This article appeared originally in Positivist Review, 1 August
1912.  The author examines the biological doctrines of
L'Evolution créatrice.  He concedes that extreme forms of
mechanism and finalism cannot account for evolution but
denies that Bergson's "élan vital" can explain cellular
differentiation, evolutionary convergence, or the wholeness of life.

2293    JONES, Joseph.  "Emerson and Bergson on the Comic."  Comparative Literature, 1, No. 1, 1949, 63-72.

2294    JONES, Tudor.  The Spiritual Ascent of Man.  London: University of London Press, 1916.

2295   JONES, William Thomas. "Working Philosophy of Life." Dis-
       covery, 4, No. 11, November 1923, 287-290.

2296   JORDAN, Bruno. "Kant and Bergson." Monist, 22, No. 3, July
       1912, 404-414.

2297   JOUHAUD, Michel. "Edouard Le Roy, le bergsonisme et la phi-
       losophie réflexive." Etudes Bergsoniennes, 5, 1960, 87-
       139. This is a review of Le Roy's Essai d'une philosophie
       première. Part 1 is entitled "The Structure of Le Roy's
       Thought" and Part 2, "Le Roy and Bergson." The author con-
       cludes: "...si la matière de l'oeuvre reste bergsonienne,
       sa forme, c'est-à-dire son mouvement d'ensemble, s'inspire
       davantage de Lachelier." (129).

2298   JOURDAIN, Philip E. B. "Review of L'infinito by Cosmo
       Guastella." Mind, 22, No. 87, July 1913, 438-439.

2299   JOURDAIN, Philip E. B. "Logic, M. Bergson and Mr. H. G.
       Wells." Hibbert Journal, 10, No. 4, July 1912, 835-845.

2300   JOURNET, C. "Autour d'Henri Bergson." Nova et Vetera, 33,
       No. 4, 1958, 262-278. Chevalier, Sertillanges, and the
       Maritains are dealt with in this study.

2301   JOUSSAIN, André. "Bergson et la pensée juive." Ecrits de
       Paris, septembre 1955, 75-81.

2302   JOUSSAIN, André. "Bergsonisme et marxisme." Ecrits de Pa-
       ris, No. 137, avril 1956, 50-55. The author argues that
       Bergson is neither a revolutionary like Sartre nor, as cer-
       tain Russian commentators insist, a reactionary conserva-
       tive. Unlike the revolutionary, Bergson believes in the
       conservation of the past and tradition. Unlike the reac-
       tionary, he believes in creativity and the openness of the
       future.

2304   JOUSSAIN, André. "Le Conscient, l'inconscient dans leur rap-
       port avec la durée pure chez Bergson." Archives de Philo-
       sophie, 22, No. 1, janvier-mars 1959, 5-23.

2305   JOUSSAIN, André. "Edouard Schuré et la renaissance de l'idé-
       alisme romantique." Revue Politique et Littéraire, Revue
       Bleue, 49e Année, No. 1, 1er juillet 1911, 21-26.

2306   JOUSSAIN, André. Esquisse d'une philosophie de la nature.
       Paris: Félix Alcan, 1921, 197.

2307    JOUSSAIN, André. "L'Expansion du bergsonisme et la psycho-
        logie musicale." Revue Politique et Littéraire, Revue
        Bleue, 50e Année, No. 24, 15 juin 1912, 758-763.

2308    JOUSSAIN, André. "L'Idée de l'inconscient et l'intuition de
        la vie." Revue Philosophique de la France et de l'Etran-
        ger, 71, No. 5, mai 1911, 467-493. Bergson is discussed
        on pages 487-489.

2309    JOUSSAIN, André. "Review of La Philosophie de l'intuition:
        Essai sur les idées de M. Edouard Le Roy by Samuel Gagne-
        bin." Revue Philosophique de la France et de l'Etranger,
        74, No. 8, août 1912, 191-193.

2310    JOUSSAIN, André. "Le Possible et le réel chez Bergson."
        Archives de Philosophie, 23, No. 4, octobre-décembre 1960,
        512-521.

2311    JOUSSAIN, André. Romantisme et religion. Paris: Félix Al-
        can, 1910, 179.

2312    JOUSSAIN, André. "Schopenhauer et Bergson." Archives de
        Philosophie, 26, No. 4, octobre-décembre 1963, 71-89.

2313    JOUSSAIN, André. "Le Testament de Bergson." Ecrits de Pa-
        ris, novembre 1954, 75-77.

2314    "Jugements sur Bergson." Documents de la Vie Intellectuelle,
        1, No. 4, 20 janvier 1930, 35-72; No. 5, 20 février 1930,
        245-279; 3, No. 3, 20 juin 1930, 541-588. This is a se-
        ries of articles and passages on Bergson. Most of them
        have been published elsewhere.

2315    JULES-BOIS, H. A. "Bergson the Magician." Catholic World,
        152, No. 912, March 1941, 673-681. The author concludes
        that: "The fundamentals of Bergson's philosophy are neo-
        Platonic or Eleatic, in no way Christian or Catholic."
        (674).

2316    JUNCO, Alfonso. "La conversión de Bergson." America Espa-
        ñola, 12, No. 42-43, 1941, 291-295.

2317    JUNOD, Robert. "Roses de Noël." Henri Bergson. Ed. Béguin
        and Thévenaz, 49-55. The author praises Bergson, compar-
        ing his inspiration to the laborious methods of the asso-
        ciationist Taine. Bergson's philosophy, he concludes,
        will endure.

2318    JUREVICS, Paulis.  "Andrijs Bergsons."  Lielās personības, 2,
        1937, 408-448.

2319    JUREVICS, Paulis.  Henri Bergson: Eine Einführurung in seine
        Philosophie.  Freiburg, Germany: Alber, 1949, 268.

2320    JUREVICS, Paulis.  "Deux Philosophes de la conscience: Teich-
        müller et Bergson."  Archiv für spiritualistische Philoso-
        phie und ihre Geschichte, 1, 1940, 273-307.

2321    JUREVICS, Paulis.  "Divi apzinas filozofi: G. Teichmullers
        un H. Bergson."  Celi, 7, 1937, 21-53.

2322    JUREVICS, Paulis.  Le Problème de la connaissance dans la
        philosophie de Bergson.  Paris: Vrin, 1930, 278.

2323    K., A.  "Review of Bergson: Exposición de sus ideas fondamen-
        tales by Ernesto L. Figueroa."  Humanidades, 22, 1930, 241-
        242.

2324    KAHL-FURTHMANN, G.  "Henri Bergson: Das Lachen."  Philoso-
        phischer Literaturanzeiger, 3, No. 3, 1951, 103-105.

2325    KAHN, Sholom J.  "Henri Bergson's Method."  Antioch Review,
        5, No. 3, 1945, 440-441.

2326    KALLEN, Horace M.  "James, Bergson and Mr. Pitkin."  The
        Journal of Philosophy, 7, No. 13, 23 June 1910, 353-357.
        The author defends William James' interpretation of Berg-
        son.

2327    KALLEN, Horace M.  "James, Bergson, and Traditional Meta-
        physics."  Mind, 23, No. 90, April 1914, 207-239.  The
        author argues that Bergson is a proponent of "traditional
        metaphysics," with its system-building tendencies, its
        distinction between appearance and reality, and its assump-
        tion that reality is "compensatory."  James, he insists,
        is not.

2328    KALLEN, Horace M.  "Review of Laughter: An Essay on the Mean-
        ing of the Comic by Henri Bergson."  The Journal of Philos-
        ophy, 9, No. 11, 23 May 1912, 303-305.

2329    KALLEN, Horace M.  "La Methode de l'intuition et la méthode
        pragmatiste."  Revue de Métaphysique et de Moral, 29, No.
        1, janvier-mars 1922, 35-62.  The author contrasts Berg-
        son's philosophy, with its appeal to direct intuition, and
        pragmatism, for which knowledge is "indirect."

2330    KALLEN, Horace M.  William James and Henri Bergson: A Study
        in Contrasting Theories of Life.  Chicago: University of
        Chicago Press, 1914, 248.

2331    KANN, Albert.  Henri Bergson und meine Ideen.  Vienna:
        Selbstverlag, 1935, 246.  The author claims to have ante-
        dated Bergson's ideas in The Two Sources.

2332    KANNING, Fritz.  "Rationales und intuitives Erkennen nach
        Henri Bergson.  I.  Rationale Grundbegriffe."  Diss.,
        Tübingen, 99.

2333    KANTERS, Robert.  "De Bergson à Bourvil."  Table Ronde, 1re
        Année, No. 5, mai 1948, 840-843.

2334    KAPLAN, Francis.  "Le Christianisme de Bergson."  Evidences,
        No. 19, mai-juin 1951, 12-17.

2335    KAPPSTEIN, Theodor.  "Philosoph als Nobelpreisträger."  C. V.
        Zeitung Blätter für Deutschtum und Judentum, 7, 1928, 675.

2336    KAUFMAN, Alvin H.  "Elan Vital, Nisus and Creativity as
        Treated in the Thought of Henri Bergson, S. Alexander, and
        A. N. Whitehead."  Diss., Boston, 1952.

2337    KAUL, C.  "Henri Bergson und das Baal Schem."  Der Morgen,
        12, 1936, 307-309.

2338    KAULINS, Jānis.  "Vai A. Bergsons, Kā apzinas filozofs,
        pielīdzinams G. Teichmilleram?"  Celi, 8, 1938, 406-415.
        This is a critique of Jurevics' article, "Divi apzinas
        filosofi."  The author asks if Bergson is really like
        Teichmüller.

2339    KAYATTA, George N.  "Comic Elements in Montaigne's Essais
        in the Light of Bergson's Le Rire."  Dissertation Ab-
        stracts International, 32, 1971, 408A.

2340    KAYSER, Rudolf.  "Der neue Bergson."  Neue Rundschau, 46,
        Pt. 2, 1933, 141-143.

2341    KAZANTZAKIS, Helen.  Nikos Kazantzakis: A Biography Based on
        his Letters.  New York: Simon and Schuster, 1968, 589.
        Bergson's relations to Kazantzakis are discussed on pages
        58, 400, 444, 459, 490, and 561.

2342    KEELING, Stanley V.  "Bergson: Some Recent Appreciations in
        Philosophy in France."  Journal of Philosophical Studies,

4, No. 15, July, 1929, 379-386. This is a review both of an edition of Nouvelles Littéraires dedicated to Bergson and of writings by Chevalier. It contains interesting comments on the fate of Bergsonism in England.

2343   KEELING, Stanley V. "The Latest Phase of M. Bergson's Philosophy." Philosophy (Journal of Philosophical Studies), 7, No. 27, July 1932, 327-331. This is a largely expository account of Les Deux Sources.

2344   KEELING, Stanley V. "Philosophy in France: Some Afterthoughts of M. Bergson." Philosophy, 10, No. 39, July 1935, 355-359. This is a review of La Pensée et le mouvant. It is largely expository.

2345   KEHR, Theodor. "Bergson und die Problemen von Zeit und Dauer." Archiv für die gesamte Psychologie, 26, No. 1, 1913, 137-154.

2346   KELLER, Adalb. V. "Die Philosophie des Lebens." Wissen und Leben, 7, 1913, 89-97, 194-284, 292-305.

2347   KELLER, Adolph. Eine Philosophie des Lebens. Jena: Diederichs, 1914, 46.

2348   KELLEY, John Joseph. "Bergson's Mysticism: A Philosophical Exposition and Evaluation of Bergson's Concept of Mysticism." Diss., Fribourg, 1954, 151.

2349   KELLEY, John Joseph. Bergson's Mysticism: A Philosophical Exposition and Evaluation of Bergson's Concept of Mysticism. Fribourg, Germany: Saint Martin's Press, 1954, 151.

2350   KERLER, Dietrich Heinrich. "Bergson's Bildertheorie und das Problem des Verhältnisses zwischen Lieb une Seele." Vierteljahrsschrift für wissenschaftliche Philosophie, 152, 1916, 349-362.

2351   KERR, Walter. Tragedy and Comedy. New York: Simon and Schuster, 1967, 355. Bergson is discussed on pages 152, 175, 186, 196, 198, 243, 244, 246, and 272.

2352   KEYSERLING, Herman Von. "Bergson." Beilage zur Allgemeinen Zeitungen, No. 35, 28 November 1908.

2353   KHOLOPOV, I. "К вопросу о природе интуиции." Вопросы философии и психологии, 23, № 5, 1912, 667-703.

2354    KHOROSHKO, V. "Философия Бергсона из точки зрения
        медика." Русская мысль, 26, № 2, 1915, 93–118.

2355    KIEFER, D. "Über Bergsons Philosophie." März, 7, No. 2,
        1914, 745–748.

2356    KINGSTON, F. Temple. French Existentialism: A Christian
        Critique. Toronto: University of Toronto Press, 1961, 221.
        Bergson and existentialism are discussed on pages 13, 81,
        82, 93, 146, 159, and 195.

2357    KINKEL, H. "Geist und Seele: Die Grundlagen der Anthropol-
        ogie bei Ludwig Klages." Philosophisches Jahrbuch der
        Görresgesellschaft, 46, No. 3, 1933, 175–200. The author
        examines the influence of Bergson and others on Klages.

2358    KINNEN, Edouard. "Bergson et nous." Revue Internationale
        de Philosophie, 14, No. 1, 1963, 68–91. This article con-
        sists of reflections inspired by the 1959 Congrès Bergson.

2359    KINNEN, Edouard. "Le Bergsonisme et les fondements philo-
        sophiques d'une civilisation humaniste." Diss., Paris,
        1959, 280. For a short résumé Cf. Annales de l'Université
        de Paris, 29e Année, No. 4, octobre-décembre 1959, 693–
        695.

2360    KINNEN, Edouard. "La filosofía social de H. Bergson." Re-
        vista de Filosofiía, 7, No. 1-2, 1960, 57–74.

2361    KITCHIN, Darcy Herworth. Bergson for Beginners. London:
        Allen and Company, Ltd., 1913, 225.

2362    KLAWITTER, Robert. "Henri Bergson and James Joyce's Fic-
        tional World." Comparative Literature Studies, 3, No. 4,
        1966, 429–437.

2363    KLEINER, Juljusz. "Z zagadnien bergsonizmu i romantyzmu."
        Przeglad Filozoficzny, 24, No. 2, 1920, 140–148.

2364    KLEMPERER, Victor. Geschichte der französischen Literatur.
        Vol 5. Leipsic: Teubner, 1931, 382. Chapter X, entitled
        "Bergson: Die gewahrte Form," appears on page 190.

2365    KLEMPERER, Victor. Geschichte der französischen Literatur:
        Der Ausgleich. Leiden, Germany: Teubner, 1931, 190. This
        study contains seventy pages devoted to Bergson.

2366    KLIMKE, Fr.  "Bergson: Die Philosophie des Lebens."  Stimmen
der Zeit, 89, 1915, 223-236.

2367    KLIMKE, Fr.  "Plagiator Bergson: Ein Kulturfrage."  Stimmen
der Zeit, 90, 1916, 422.

2368    KNIGHT, George Wilson.  "Bergson and Shakespeare."  London
Times Literary Supplement, 28, No. 1407, 17 January 1929,
44.  Close similarities between Bergson and Shakespeare
are stressed in this essay.

2369    KNUDSEN, Peter.  "Ist Bergson ein Plagiator Schopenhauers?"
Archiv für Geschichte der Philosophie, 32, No. 1, 1919,
89-107.

2370    KNUDSEN, Peter.  "Die Bergsonische Philosophie in ihrem Verhältnis zu Schopenhauer."  Jahrbuch der Schopenhauer Gesellschaft, 16, 1928, 3-44.

2371    KOCH, Artur.  "Das Zweierlie-Vorurteil im Bergsonischen In-
tuismus."  Diss., Greifswald, 1922, 163.

2372    KODIS, J.  "Philosophie de Bergson."  Przeglad Filozoficzny,
1, No. 4, 1908.

2373    KODIS, J.  "Die schöpferische Evolution von Bergson."
Przeglad Filozoficzny, 2, 1909.  (Pöln. Sprache).

2374    KOHLER, Joseph.  "Bergson und die Rechtwissenschaften."  Archiv für Rechts und Wirtschaft-Philosophie, 7, No. 1, 1913,
56-69.

2375    KONCZEWSKI, C.  "La Pensée inverbale, ralentie et accélérée:
De La Mémoire créatrice."  Revue de Métaphysique et de Morale, 74, No. 1, janvier-mars 1969, 91-105.

2376    KOORT, Alfred.  Kaasaegset filosofiat I.  Tartu, Soviet
Union: Akdeemilin Kooperativ, 1938, 127.  This book contains a section on Bergson.

2377    KOPPER, Joachim.  "Review of Pour connaître la pensée de
Bergson by François Meyer."  Philosophischer Literaturanzeiger, 3, No. 6, 1951, 262-266.

2378    KOPPNANG, Ole.  "Etiske verdieri Henri Bergsons filosofi."
Spektrum, 3, No. 2, 1948, 30-37.

2379    KORN, Alejandro.  "Bergson."  Obras.  La Plata, Argentina:
Universidad Nacional de La Plata, 1939, 2, 11-30.

2380    KORN, Alejandro.  "Bergson en la filosofía contemporánea."
        Homenaje a Bergson.  Córdoba, Argentina: Imprenta de la
        Universidad, 1937, 3-12.

2381    KORN, Alejandro.  De San Augustin a Bergson.  2nd ed.
        Buenos Aires: Nova, 1959, 154.  The introduction is by
        Juan Carlos Torchia Estrada.

2382    KORN, Alejandro.  "Filosofía Argentina."  Nosotros, 21, Nos.
        219-220, agosto 1927, 61.

2383    KORN, Alejandro.  Filósofos y sistemas.  Buenos Aires: Edi-
        torial Claridad, 1937, 182.  This book includes a study of
        Bergson and contemporary philosophy.

2384    KOSTYLEV, N. "Ле-Дантек и Бергсон." Вестник Евро-
        пы, 261, 1910, 89.

2385    KRAKOWSKI, Edouard.  "L'Avènement du bergsonisme: Génie et
        tradition."  Grande Revue, 137, No. 3, février 1932, 566-
        574; 138, No. 3, mars 1932, 57-72; No. 4, avril 1932, 267-
        282; No. 5 mai 1932, 428-450.

2386    KRAKOWSKI, Edouard.  "Bergson et les philosophes de l'héro-
        'isme."  Mercure de France, 247, 1er novembre 1933, 513-528.

2387    KRAKOWSKI, Edouard.  "Bergson et Plotin."  Documents de la
        Vie Intellectuelle, 3, No. 3, 20 juin 1930, 582-583.  This
        study was published originally in Une Philosophie de
        l'amour et de la beauté.  Paris: de Boccard, 1929, 236-237.

2388    KRAKOWSKI, Edouard.  L'Esthétique de Plotin et son influ-
        ence.  Paris: de Boccard, 1929, 272.  The author asserts
        that the influence of Plotinus extends to Biran, Ravaisson,
        and Bergson.

2389    KRAKOWSKI, Edouard.  "L'Intuition antique et son destin mo-
        derne: Platon, Plotin et les contemporains."  Mercure de
        France, 221, No. 770, 15 juillet 1930, 317-358.  Bergson's
        influence on French literature is discussed on pages 353-
        356.

2390    KRAKOWSKI, Edouard.  La Philosophie: Gardienne de la cité,
        de Plotin à Bergson.  Paris: Ed. du Myrtle, 1946, 292.

2391    KRAKOWSKI, Edouard.  "Platon, Plotin, et les contemporains."
        Mercure de France, 221, 770, 15 juillet, 317-358.

2392    KRAMER, F.  "Bergsonische Intuitionsphilosophie: Bedeutung
        d., für d. moderne Schule." Pädagogische Rundschau, 2,
        No. 1, 1926, 34.

2393    KRAUSE, Franz.  "Wo sucht Bergson, Die beiden Quellen der
        Moral und der Religion." Die Drei, 15, No. 1, 1932, 27-
        32.

2394    KREMER-MARIETTI, Angèle.  "Bergson métaphysicien de la ma-
        tière." Actes du Xe Congrès des Sociétés de Philosophie
        de Langue Française (Congrès Bergson). Paris: Armand Co-
        lin, 1, 1959, 177-181. The function of "matter" in Berg-
        son's philosophy cannot be resolved simply by distinguish-
        ing living from non-living matter.  The author discusses
        criteria given by Bergson for an integral knowledge of
        matter and his theories concerning perception, which is
        the insertion of spirit in matter.

2395    KREMER-MARIETTI, Angèle.  "Bibliographie: Une Idéalogie berg-
        sonienne." Etudes Bergsoniennes, 9, 1970, 209-227.

2396    KREMER-MARIETTI, Angèle.  "L'Explication bergsonienne."
        Etudes Bergsoniennes, 7, 1966, 184-192.  The author as-
        serts that: "L'Explication métaphysique, dans l'esprit du
        bergsonisme, au contraire, au lieu d'identifier rationalité
        et réalité, impliquerait l'objet et tendrait en le recou-
        vrant tout entier à ne laisser aucun vide entre la pensée
        et la réalité." (182).

2397    KREMER-MARIETTI, Angèle.  Les Formes du mouvement chez Berg-
        son. Le Puy, France: Cahiers du Nouvel Humanisme, 1953,
        126.

2398    KREMER-MARIETTI, Angèle.  "Intuition et durée dans quelques
        ouvrages récents sur Bergson." Etudes Bergsoniennes, 8,
        1968, 159-167.  This is a review of Bergson et les méta-
        morphoses de la durée by André Robinet; Bergson et les ni-
        veaux de la réalité by Georges Mourelos; and Bergsonisme
        by Gilles Deleuze.

2399    KREMER-MARIETTI, Angèle.  "Table ronde: Matière, causalité,
        discontinu." Actes du Xe Congrès des Sociétés de Philoso-
        phie de Langue Française (Congrès Bergson). Paris: Armand
        Colin, 2, 1959, 121-142.

2400    KRONENBERG, Moritz.  "Bergson und Hegel." Das literarische
        Echo, 16, No. 13, 1914, 877-881.

2401    KRONER, Richard.  "Henri Bergson."  Logos (Tübingen), 1, No.
        1, 1910, 125-150.

2402    KUCHARSKI, Paul.  "Sur Le Point de départ de la philosophie
        de Bergson."  Archives de Philosophie, 17, No. 1, 56-80.

2403    KUDIELKA, E.  "Der 'andere' Bergson: Zum Gedenken anläßlich
        der 100. Wiederkehr seines Geburtstages."  Wissenschaft
        und Weltbild, 12, No. 4, 1959, 622-628.

2404    KUKI, Shuzo.  "Bergson au Japon."  Nouvelles Littéraires,
        No. 322, 15 décembre 1928, 6.

2405    KUMAR, Shiv Kumar.  "Bergson and Proust's 'Souvenir involun-
        taire'."  Canadian Modern Language Review, 16, No. 2, 1959,
        7-10.

2406    KUMAR, Shiv Kumar.  "Bergson and Stephen Dedalus' Aesthetic
        Theory."  Journal of Aesthetics and Art Criticism, 16, No.
        1, 1957-1958, 124-127.

2407    KUMAR, Shiv Kumar.  "Bergson and the Stream of Consciousness
        Novel."  Diss., Cambridge, 1954.

2408    KUMAR, Shiv Kumar.  Bergson and the Stream of Consciousness
        Novel.  London: Blackie, 1962; New York: New York Universi-
        ty Press, 1963, 174.

2409    KUMAR, Shiv Kumar.  "Bergson's Theory of the Novel."  Modern
        Fiction Studies, 6, No. 4, Winter 1960, 325-336.

2410    KUMAR, Shiv Kumar.  "Bergson's Theory of the Novel."  Modern
        Language Review, 56, No. 2, April 1961, 172-179.  The au-
        thor argues that Bergson provides a theoretical basis for
        the stream of consciousness novel.

2411    KUMAR, Shiv Kumar.  "Dorothy Richardson and Bergson's 'Mé-
        moire par excellence'."  Notes and Queries, 6, No. 1, 1959,
        14-19.

2412    KUMAR, Shiv Kumar.  "Dorothy Richardson and the Dilemma of
        Being Versus Becoming."  Modern Language Notes, 74, No. 6,
        June 1959, 494-501.  Parallels and disagreements between
        Richardson and Bergson are analyzed in this article.

2413    KUMAR, Shiv Kumar.  "Joyce and Bergson's 'mémoire pure'."
        Osmania Journal of English Studies, 1, No. 1, 1961, 55-60.

2414    KUMAR, Shiv Kumar.  "Joyce's 'Epiphany' and Bergson's 'L'Intuition philosophique'."  Modern Language Quarterly, 20, No. 1, March 1959, 27-30.

2415    KUMAR, Shiv Kumar.  "Memory in Virginia Woolf and Bergson." University of Kansas Review, 26, No. 3, Spring 1960, 235-239.

2416    KUMAR, Shiv Kumar.  Virginia Woolf and Bergson's 'durée'. Hoshiarpur, India: Vishveshvaranand Book Agency, 1957, 17.

2417    KUMAR, Shiv Kumar.  "Virginia Woolf and Bergson's 'Mémoire par excellence'."  English Studies, 41, No. 5, October 1960, 313-318.

2418    KUNTZE, F.  "Bergson und das Not der Gegenwart."  Die Westmark, Rheinische Monatsschrift, 1, 1920, 35-43.

2419    KURRIS, Frans.  "Le Bergsonisme d'Albert Thibaudet."  Etudes Bergsoniennes, 7, 1966, 139-178.  The author studies the influence of Bergson on the most important French literary critic "d'entre les deux guerres."  Thibaudet, however, was not in all respects Bergsonian.

2420    KURRIS, Frans.  Kerngedachten van Henri Bergson.  Roermond, Netherlands: Romen, 1968, 129.

2421    LACHELIER, Jules.  Oeuvres.  Paris: Félix Alcan, 1933, I, 219; II, 244.

2422    LACHIEZE-REY, Pierre.  "Blondel et Bergson."  Etudes Philosophiques, 7, No. 5, 1952, 383-386.  It is argued here that Blondel substituted an "élan spirituel" for Bergson's "élan vital."

2423    LACOMBE, Olivier; GOUHIER, Henri; BARTHELEMY-MADAULE, Mme.; and LE BLOND, R. P.  "Bergson et le Christ des Evangiles." Recherches et Débats, No. 43, juin 1963, 161-196.

2424    LACOMBE, Roger-E.  La Psychologie bergsonienne: Etude critique.  Paris: Félix Alcan, 1933, 324.  Cf. lengthy review, Revue de Métaphysique et de Morale, 61, No. 1, 1934, 7-9. The author denies that the arguments and facts brought forward by Bergson support the conception of life which he proposes.  Bergson has not succeeded in justifying the two central theses of his psychology.  His critique of parallelism is not convincing and his conception of the deeper mental life has not been established.

2425    LACROIX, Jean. "Henri Bergson." Esprit, No. 96, janvier
        1941, 182-184.

2426    LACROIX, Jean. "Henri Bergson." Le Monde, No. 1102, 4-10
        décembre 1969, 11.

2427    LACROIX, Jean. "L'Intuition, méthode de purification."
        Henri Bergson. Ed. Béguin and Thévenaz, 196-204. The au-
        thor examines Bergson's conceptions of intuition and of
        philosophical method. He rejects anti-intellectual inter-
        pretations of Bergson's intuition and concludes that Berg-
        son's method involves a laborious effort to transcend con-
        ventional concepts.

2428    LACROIX, Jean. "La Pensée engagée." Esprit, 9, No. 96,
        1941, 182-184.

2429    LACROIX, Jean. "La Philosophie: Ravaisson et Bergson." Le
        Monde, No. 7877, 13 mai 1960, 16. Also in Le Monde hebdo-
        madaire, No. 1128, 4-10 juin 1970, 13.

2430    LACROIX, Marcel. "M. Bergson et les origines de la morale
        et de la religion." Le Correspondant, 104e Année, No.
        1672, 25 mai 1932, 481-491. This is a review of Les Deux
        Sources.

2431    LACROIX, Maurice. "Rolland, Péguy, Bergson." Résistances,
        13 janvier 1945.

2432    LA DOW, Stanley V. "Bergson's View of Mysticism." Theos-
        ophy Quarterly, 30, No. 118, October 1932, 108-119. This
        is a review of Les Deux Sources.

2433    LAFILLE, Pierre. André Gide, romancier. Paris: Hachette,
        1954, 595. A comparison of Bergson and Gide is found on
        pages 402-405.

2434    LAFONTAINE, Albert-P. La Culture française: La Philosophie
        de Bergson. Paris: Vrin, 1924, 80. This is a general sur-
        vey of Bergson's thought.

2435    LAFRANCE, Guy. "Bergson et la philosophie scientifique."
        Proceedings of the VIIth Inter-American Congress of Philos-
        ophy, 2, 348-354.

2436    LAFRANCE, Guy. "Continuité et absolue nouveauté dans la du-
        rée bergsonienne." Dialogue, 7, No. 1, June 1968, 94-101.
        The author states his intentions as follows: "Comment, en

effet, Bergson réussit-il à concilier, au sein d'une même réalité, deux éléments en apparence aussi opposés que la continuité et l'absolue nouveauté?  Telle est la question que nous voulons élucider dans cet article."  (98).

2437   LAFRANCHI, Genevieve.  "Du Niveau psychologique de l'intuition bergsonienne."  Actes du Xe Congrès des Sociétés de Philosophie de Langue Française (Congrès Bergson).  Paris: Armand Colin, 1, 1959, 183-184.  The author holds that it is possible, thanks to reference points of a psychological order, for Bergson to pass from a metaphysical intuition to a lucidly controlled mystical or contemplative intuition.

2438   LAFRANCHI, Geneviève.  "La Méthode de Bergson: De La Position du problème métaphysique."  Diss., Paris, 1948.

2439   LAFRANCHI, Geneviève.  "Table ronde: Psychologie, phénoménologie, intuition."  Actes du Xe Congrès des Sociétes de Philosophie de Langue Française (Congrès Bergson).  Paris: Armand Colin, 2, 1959, 15-37.

2440   LA HARPE, Jean de.  "Souvenirs personnels."  Henri Bergson. Ed. Béguin and Thévenaz, 357-364.  The author describes a visit with Bergson in September 1936.  Among the subjects discussed were: the influence of Cournot and others on Bergson; the significance of certain of Bergson's critics; and the import of psychoanalysis.

2441   LAHBIBI, Modamed Aziz.  Liberté ou libération?: A Partir des libertés bergsoniennes.  "Préf. de M. de Gandillac." Paris: Editions Montaigne, 1956, 254.  The author argues that Bergson's identification of liberty with subjectivity makes it impossible to understand how liberty can be active in a social context.  Real liberty has as its conditions both supports in human reality and a location in external liberty.

2442   LAIRD, John.  "Review of La Pensée et le mouvant: Essais et Conférences by Henri Bergson."  Mind, 43, No. 172, October 1934, 518-526.  This is a thoughtful, penetrating review.

2443   LAIRD, John.  Recent Philosophy.  London: Thornton Butterworth, Ltd., 1936, 256.  Chapter V is entitled "The Pragmatists and Bergson," 84-107.

2444   LALANDE, André.  Les Illusions évolutionnistes.  Paris: Félix Alcan, 1930, 464.

2445    LALANDE, André. "Philosophy in France, 1905." Philosophi-
        cal Review, 15, No. 3, May 1906, 241-266.

2446    LALANDE, André. "Philosophy in France, 1907." Philosophi-
        cal Review, 19, No. 4, July 1910, 241-266.

2447    LALANDE, André. "Philosophy in France, 1907: I. Philosophy
        in the Universities." Philosophical Review, 17, No. 3,
        May 1908, 291-306.

2448    LALANDE, André. "Philosophy in France, 1911." Philosophi-
        cal Review, 21, No. 3, 1912, 279-302.

2449    LALANDE, André. "Philosophy in France, 1912." Philosophi-
        cal Review, 22, No. 4, July 1913, 357-374.

2450    LALANDE, André. "Philosophy in France, 1924." Philosophi-
        cal Review, 34, No. 6, November 1925, 5333-557. Bergson
        is discussed on pages 533-534.

2451    LALANDE, André. "Philosophy in France, 1932." Philosophi-
        cal Review, 43, No. 1, 1934, 1-26. Bergson's Les Deux
        Sources, too compact for a résumé, is declared a remark-
        ably rich and original book in this article.

2452    LALANDE, André. "Philosophy in France, 1933-1934." Philo-
        sophical Review, 44, No. 1, January 1935, 1-23. This ar-
        ticle includes a brief account of La Pensée et le mouvant.

2453    LALANDE, André. "La Psychologie, ses divers objets et ses
        méthodes." Revue Philosophique de la France et de l'Etran-
        ger, 87, Nos. 3-4, mars-avril 1919, 117-221.

2454    LALANDE, André. "La Psychologie, ses divers objets et ses
        méthodes." Nouveau Traité de psychologie. Vol. 1. Ed.
        Georges Dumas. Paris: Félix Alcan, 1930, 367-419. Berg-
        son's influence on introspective psychology is discussed
        on pages 380-382.

2455    LALANDE, André. "Review of Les Sources et les courants de
        la philosophie contemporaine en France by J. Benrubi."
        Revue Philosophique de la France et de l'Etranger, 117,
        No. 2, 1934, 285-291.

2456    LALANDE, André. Vocabulaire technique et critique de la phi-
        losophie. 2 Vols. Paris: Félix Alcan, 1926, 1065.

2457    LALANDE, André. Vocabulaire technique et critique de la phi-
        losophie. Paris: Presses Universitaires de France, 1947,

1280. "Cinquième édition, augmentée d'un grand nombre d'articles nouveaux." Bergson's concept of "immédiat" is discussed on pages 460-462; "inconnaissable," on 473; "intuition," on 528; and "liberté," on 545.

2458   LALO, Charles. "Promesses et carences de l'esthétique bergsonienne." Revue de Metaphysique et de Morale, 47, No. 4, 1941, 301-314. The author states: "...Bergson ne s'est jamais arrêté devant ces difficultés inhérentes à son système—sauf en matière d'esthétique. De cette surprenante exception nous avons tenté de donner ici quelques raisons principales." (314).

2459   LALOU, René. "Review of Bergson et Proust by Floris Delattre." Nouvelles Littéraires, No. 1087, 1er juillet 1948, 8.

2460   LALOU, René. Histoire de la littérature française contemporaine. Paris: Presses Universitaires de France, 1947, 447. Bergson and Péguy are discussed on pages 322-323 and 333.

2461   LAMEERE, Jean. "Table ronde: Esthétique." Actes du Xe Congrès des Sociétés de Philosophie de Langue Française (Congrès Bergson). Paris: Armand Colin, 2, 1959, 193-210.

2462   LANCZI, E. "Bemerkungen zur Metaphysik Bergsons." Husz. száz, 1910. (Ungar. Sprache).

2463   LANDES, Margaret W. "A Suggested Interpretation of Bergson's Doctrine of Intuition." Philosophical Review, 33, No. 5, September 1924, 450-462.

2464   LANDORMY, Paul Charles Reed. "Remarques sur la philosophie nouvelle et sur ses rapports avec l'intellectualisme." Revue de Métaphysique et de Morale, 9, 1901, 478-486. The author insists that Bergson is anti-intellectual, M. Le Roy notwithstanding.

2465   LANDQUIST, John. "Henri Bergson." Ord och Bild, 20, 1911, 541-550. Also in Revue Scandinave, 2, 1911.

2466   LANDQUIST, John. Henri Bergson: En populär framställing av hans filosofi. Trans. L. Welhaven. Oslo: Aas and Wahls, 1928, 79.

2467   LANDQUIST, John. "Interview with Bergson." Living Age, 315, No. 4085, 21 October 1922, 222-224. This article was pub-

lished in Vienna Neue Freie Presse, 19 August 1922. The
article contains interesting remarks on the philosophy of
history.

2468    LANESSAN, Jean Marie de. Transformation et créationisme.
Paris: Félix Alcan, 1914, 349.

2469    LANGEVIN, Paul. "L'Evolution de l'espace et du temps." Revue de Métaphysique et de Morale, 19, No. 4, 1911, 455-466.
This article is an analysis of the paradoxes of the Special Theory of Relativity. Possibly it influenced Bergson's attitudes in Duration and Simultaneity.

2470    LANSON, Gustave. "Sur Le Rire de Bergson." Essais de méthode, de critique et d'histoire littéraire. Paris: Hachette,
1965, 497, 459-463.

2471    LANTIERI, Simon. "Table ronde: Esthétique." Actes du Xe
Congrès des Sociétés de Philosophie de Langue Française
(Congrès Bergson). Paris: Armand Colin, 2, 1959, 193-210.

2472    LAPIERRE, J. W. "Vers Une Sociologie concrète." Esprit,
19e Année, No. 184, novembre 1951, 720-730. Levi-Strauss
and Bergson are discussed in this essay.

2473    LAPORTE, Jean. "Maine de Biran et Bergson." Revue de
France, 4, No. 15, 1er août 1924, 620-625.

2474    LAPORTE, Jean. "La Métaphysique bergsonienne et l'expérience mystique." Revue de France, 8, No. 24, 15 décembre
1928, 725-733.

2475    LAPORTE, Jean. "La Philosophie religieuse de Bergson." Revue Politique et Littéraire, Revue Bleue, 70e Année, No.
23, 3 décembre 1932, 719-726. This is a review of Les
Deux Sources.

2476    LAPORTE, Jean. "Témoignage." Nouvelles Littéraires, No.
322, 15 décembre 1928, 4.

2477    LAPRADE, Jacques de. "Autour de Bergson." Arts, No. 176,
23 juillet 1948, 2.

2478    LAPRADE, Jacques de. "Bergson et Proust." Arts, No. 177, 6
août 1948, 2.

2479    LARAGUETA, J. "La Liberté dans la philosophie d'Henri Bergson." Actes du Xe Congrès des Sociétés de Philosophie de

Langue Française (Congrès Bergson).  Paris: Armand Colin,
1, 1959, 339-342.  Is there for consciousness a causality
which is, the author asks, not only contingent and open to
variability but also free in the sense of a possible op-
tion between different directions?  What is Bergson's position in this regard?  The definition of liberty has its
reality in human life, the author concludes.

2480   LARBAUD, Valéry.  "Charles Péguy: A Propos de son cahier sur
       M. Bergson et la philosophie bergsonienne."  Feuillets de
       l'Amitié Charles Péguy, No. 72, juin 1959, 2-5.  This is a
       translation of an article from The New Weekly, 4 July 1914.

2481   LAROCK, V.  "Les Deux Morales selon Bergson."  Synthèse, 20,
       Nos. 236-237, 1966, 13-22.

2482   LARRABEE, Harold A.  Henri Bergson: Selections.  New York:
       Appleton-Century-Crofts, 1949, 160.

2483   LARRABEE, Harold A.  "Review of La Pensée et le mouvant by
       Henri Bergson."  International Journal of Ethics, 45, No.
       1, October 1934-1935, 117-118.

2484   LARROSA, Juan R.  "Del filósofo Bergson al Mariscal Joffre."
       La Nación, 8 septiembre 1918.

2485   LARROYO, Francisco.  El existencialismo: Sus fuentes y direc-
       ciones.  México: Editorial Stylo, 1951, 227.  Bergson,
       Blondel, Sartre, Marcel, and others are dealt with in
       this study.

2486   LARSSON, Hans.  Intuitions problemet: Särskilt med hänsyn
       till Henri Bergsons teori.  Stockholm: Bonnier, 1925, 80.

2487   LA SELLE, Mgr. H. de.  Un Duel à quatre: Saint Thomas, Kant,
       Bergson, Sartre.  Vion, France: La Chapelle du Chêne, 1954,
       62.

2488   LASH, Kenneth.  "A Theory of the Comic as Insight."  Journal
       of Philosophy, 45, No. 5, February 1948, 113-121.

2489   LASSERRE, Pierre.  "Le Destin de Bergson."  Nouvelles Litté-
       raires, No. 294, 2 juin 1928, 1.

2490   LASSERRE, Pierre.  Faust en France et autres études.  Paris:
       Calmann-Lévy, 1929, 235.  Bergson is discussed on pages
       120-131.

2491    LASSERRE, Pierre. "La Philosophie de M. Bergson." L'Action
        Française, 6, août et septembre 1910.

2492    LASSERRE, Pierre. "Que nous veut Bergson?" L'Action Fran-
        çaise, 6, No. 173, 22 juin 1913, 3-4.

2493    LASSON, Adolf. "Henri Bergson." Deutsche Literaturzeitung,
        31, No. 22, 28 Mai 1910, 1364-1366. This article is a re-
        port of an address on Bergson by Adolf Lasson.

2494    LATANZI, Lamberto. "Un sabio, un articulo y un libro."
        Criterio, Año 14, No. 682, 27 marzo 1941, 299-302.

2495    "Latest of Philosophers: Three Works Which Have Given Berg-
        son Wide Repute Among the World Thinkers." New York Times
        Review of Books, 60, No. 19, 566, 20 August 1911, 503.
        This is a review of Time and Free Will, Matter and Memory,
        and Creative Evolution.

2496    LATTRE, Alain de. "Une Ontologie de la précarité: Jeanne
        Delhomme." Revue Philosophique de la France et de l'Etran-
        ger, 149, No. 3, 1959, 381-394. This article includes a
        discussion of the relations between Delhomme and Bergson.

2497    LATTRE, Alain de. "Remarques sur l'intuition comme prin-
        cipe régulateur de la connaissance chez Bergson."
        Etudes Bergsoniennes, 7, 1966, 195-215. "De l'intuition
        comme retour à une intimité inédite et secrète, il n'est
        pas une fois question; l'intuition, constante dans Matière
        et Mémoire, n'intervient qu'à titre de principe directeur,
        de règle et de référence permanente par rapport à quoi
        peut être discerné et dégagé le sens des analyses qui sont
        effectuées par ailleurs et dont les résultats sont con-
        signés." (210). An excellent treatment of Matter and Mem-
        ory is given on pages 211-214.

2498    "Laughter." Edinburgh Review, 285, No. 440, April 1912, 383-
        404. Five books on the subject of laughter are discussed
        in this review. Bergson's views are discussed on pages
        392-397.

2499    "Review of Laughter: An Essay on the Meaning of the Comic by
        Henri Bergson." North American Review, 195, June 1912,
        859-861.

2500    LAURENT, Jacques. "Mèches à vendre." La Parisienne, No. 9,
        septembre 1953, 1304-1337. This study deals with Bergson,
        Courteline, Giraudoux, and others.

2501   LAURILLA, Kaarle Sanfrid. La Théorie du comique de M. Henri
       Bergson. Helsinki: Libr. academ., 1929, 66 (Suomalaisen
       Tiedeakatemian toimituksia, sarja B. nid. 23, No. 2).
       This study is a criticism of Bergson's concept of laughter.

2502   LAVELLE, Louis. "Bergson: El hombre y el filósofo." La
       Nación (Buenos Aires), 6 abril 1941, Sec.II, pág. 4, Col.
       1. Also in Le Temps, 7 January 1941.

2503   LAVELLE, Louis. "Henri Bergson." France Libre, I, No. 4,
       1941, 347-353. Also in Le Temps, 7 January 1941.

2504   LAVELLE, Louis. "Henri Bergson: L'Homme et le philosophe."
       Le Temps, 7 janvier 1941.

2505   LAVELLE, Louis. Du Temps et de l'éternité. Paris: Editions
       Montaigne, 1945, 447.

2506   LAVELLE, Louis. "L'Homme et le philosophe." Henri Bergson.
       Ed. Béguin and Thévenaz, 39-48. The author considers var-
       ious respects in which both the openness of the future and
       the memory of the past combine to constitute Bergson's
       "duration." The author concludes that Bergson's criti-
       cisms of the intelligence are directed only against ab-
       stractions which distance us from life.

2507   LAVELLE, Louis. Leçon inaugurale faite au Collège de France,
       le 2 décembre 1941. Paris: L'Artisan du Livre, 1942, 52.

2508   LAVELLE, Louis. "Obituary." France Libre, No. 4, février
       1941, 347-353. This is a Résistance publication.

2509   LAVELLE, Louis. "La Pensée religieuse de Bergson." Revue
       Philosophique de la France et de l'Etranger, 131, Nos. 3-
       8, mars-août 1941, 139-174.

2510   LAVELLE, Louis. La Philosophie française entre les deux
       guerres. Paris: Aubier, 1942, 275. Bergson is discussed
       on pages 89-112.

2511   LAVELLE, Louis. "Le Rythme du temps." Le Temps, 77, No.
       27547, 1938, 3.

2512   LA VIA, Luigi. "Possibilità di sviluppi tra dualismo e con-
       creto nella considerazione bergsoniana del tempo e della
       coscienza." Teoresi, 21, 1966, 194-237.

2513   LAZAREFF, Pierre. "French Spirit vs. Nazi Peace." Decision,
       1, No. 3, March 1941.

2514    LAZAREV, A. "Философия Бергсона." Мысль и слово,
        1,1917, 177-214.

2515    LAZAREV, Adolf-M. Vie et connaissance: Essais traduits du
        russe par B. Schloezer. Paris: Vrin, 1948, 136. "Préface
        de Nicolas Berdiaeff."

2516    LAZZARINI, Renato. "Bergson e noi: X Congresso della So-
        cietà di filosofia di lingua francese, Parigi, 17-19 mag-
        gio 1959." Filosofia, 10, No. 4, 1959, 642-643.

2517    LAZZARINI, Renato. "Intention et intuition dans la méthodo-
        logie philosophique de Bergson." Actes du Xe Congrès des
        Sociétés de Philosophie de Langue Française (Congrès Berg-
        son). Paris: Armand Colin, 1, 1959, 195-189. One finds
        in Bergson, the author holds, a double methodological pro-
        cedure: the "méthodique des choses," in which mind adapts
        itself to things in order to manipulate them, and the "mé-
        thodique propre au sujet spirituel," in which the mind en-
        ters into the essences of things conceived as so many dura-
        tions.

2518    LAZZARINI, Renato. "Table ronde: Psychologie, phénoménolo-
        gie, intuition." Actes du Xe Congrès des Sociétés de Phi-
        losophie de Langue Française (Congrès Bergson). Paris:
        Armand Colin, 2, 1959, 15-37.

2519    LAZZARINI, Renato. "Table ronde: Sources et histoire du
        bergsonisme." Actes du Xe Congrès des Sociétés de Philoso-
        phie de Langue Française (Congrès Bergson). Paris: Armand
        Colin, 2, 1959, 213-233.

2520    LAZZERONI, V. "La psicologia di Henri Bergson." Sophia, 10,
        No. 2-3, 1942, 275-289; No. 4, 1942, 424-439. This very
        careful study of Bergson's psychology is republished in
        Studi e ricerche di psicologia attuale, edited by A. Marzi
        e collaboratori. Firenze: Instituto de Psicologia
        dell'Universita di Firenze, 1947.

2521    LEBACQZ, Joseph. De L'Identique au multiple: Le Problème
        des universaux reconsidéré à la lumière du bergsonisme et
        des philosophies existentialistes. Louvain: Editions
        Nauwelaerts; Paris: Beatrice-Nauwelaerts, 1968, 164 (Bibli-
        othèque de la Faculté de philosophie et lettres de Namur,
        fasc. 43).

2522    LE BIDOIS, Robert. "Autour du Prix Nobel: H. Bergson, écri-
        vain." Flambeau, 12, No. 1, 1929, 73-88; No. 2, 1929, 152-
        153.

2523    LE BOUTILLIER, Cornelia. Religious Values in the Philosophy
        of Emergent Evolution. New York: Columbia University
        Press, 1938, 104.

2524    LEBREC, Jean. Joseph Malègue romancier et penseur: Avec des
        documents idédits. Paris: Dessain et Tolra, 1969, 462.
        This study contains references to Bergson.

2525    LEBRETON, Jules. L'Encyclique et la théologie moderniste.
        Paris: Beauchesne, 1908, 802.

2526    LE BRETON, Maurice. La Personnalité de William James.
        Paris: Hachette, 1929, 383. James and Bergson are dis-
        cussed on pages 151-164.

2527    LE BRUN, Philip. "T. S. Eliot and Henri Bergson." Review
        of English Studies, 18, No. 70, 1967, 149-161; No. 71,
        1967, 172-286. Bergson exercised an unacknowledged influ-
        ence on Eliot, according to the author.

2528    LECHALAS, Georges. Etude sur l'espace et le temps. Paris:
        Félix Alcan, 1896, 201. 2e éd. Paris: Félix Alcan, 1909,
        327.

2529    LECHALAS, Georges. "Matière et mémoire: D'Après un nouveau
        livre de M. Bergson." Annales de Philosophie Chrétienne,
        N.S. 26, 1897, 146-164, 314-334.

2530    LECHALAS, Georges. "Le Nombre et le temps dans leur rapport
        avec l'espace, à propos de Les Données immédiates." Anna-
        les de Philosophie Chrétienne, N.S. 23, 1890, 516-540.

2531    LECHAT, Paul-Hubert. "Influence de Bergson sur l'évolution
        de la pensée contemporaine." Actes du Xe Congrès des So-
        ciétés de Philosophie de Langue Française (Congrès Berg-
        son). Paris: Armand Colin, 1, 1959, 191-194. Bergson's
        influence, the author holds, is felt in diverse fields
        (psychology, literary criticism). In metaphysics itself a
        Bergsonism of intention, if not of fact, is paralleled by
        intellectualist philosophies.

2532    LECHAT, Paul-Hubert. "Table ronde: Sources et histoire du
        bergsonisme." Actes du Xe Congrès des Sociétés de Philoso-
        phie de Langue Française (Congrès Bergson). Paris: Armand
        Colin, 2, 1959, 213-233.

2533    LECLERE, Albert. "Le Mouvement catholique kantien en
        France." Kant-studien, 7, No. 2, 1902, 300-363. This ar-
        ticle contains references to Bergson and his followers.

2534    LECLERE, Albert. _Pragmatisme, modernisme, protestantisme._
        Paris: Bloud et Cie., 1909, 296.

2535    LE DANTEC, Félix. "La Biologie de M. Bergson." _Revue du
        Mois,_ 4, No. 8, août 1907, 230-241. This essay is repub-
        lished as Chapter VI of Le Dantec, _Science et Conscience._

2536    LE DANTEC, Félix. _Contre la métaphysique: Question de métho-
        de._ Paris: Félix Alcan, 1912, 255.

2537    LE DANTEC, Félix. "Review of _L'Evolution créatrice_ by Henri
        Bergson." _Revue du Mois,_ 4, No. 8, août 1907, 351-354.
        The author gives a critique of Bergson's biology.

2538    LE DANTEC, Félix. "Réflexions d'un philistin sur la méta-
        physique." _Grande Revue,_ 62, No. 13, 10 juillet 1910, 1-
        16.

2539    LE DANTEC, Félix. _Science et conscience: Philosophie du XXe
        siècle._ Paris: Flammarion, 1908, 328. The author devel-
        ops various criticisms of Bergson's philosophy in Chapter
        6 of this work.

2540    LEE, Harold N. "Bergson's Two Ways of Knowing." _Tulane
        Studies in Philosophy,_ 8, 1959, 50-59. Bergson's most im-
        portant contribution to philosophy, the author holds, is
        his insistence on the continuity of concrete duration.
        Bergson's distinction between intellect and intuition, how-
        ever, downgrades the intellect. The author reinterprets
        the meanings of intellect and intuition so as to escape
        anti-intellectualism.

2541    LEFEVRE, Frédéric. "Table ronde: Esthétique." _Actes du Xe
        Congrès des Sociétés de Philosophie de Langue Française_
        (Congrès Bergson). Paris: Armand Colin, 2, 1959, 193-210.

2542    LEFEVRE, J. "L'Evolution créatrice de Bergson: Notes criti-
        ques de biologie." _Pensée Catholique,_ No. 81, 1962, 18-
        58. This is a thoroughgoing criticism of Bergson's biol-
        ogy.

2543    LEGENDRE, Maurice. "M. Bergson et son _Evolution créatrice._"
        _Bulletin de la Semaine,_ 6 mai 1908.

2544    LEGENDRE, Maurice. "L'Influence de la philosophie de M.
        Bergson. IV." _Mouvement Socialiste,_ 30, No. 233, juillet-
        août 1911, 120-123.

2545    LEGENDRE, Maurice.  "Remarques sur le nouveau livre de M.
        Bergson, L'Energie spirituelle."  Les Lettres, 8, No. 1,
        ler janvier 1920, 1-15.

2546    LEGENDRE, Maurice.  "Réponse."  Les Lettres, 8, No. 3, ler
        mars 1920, 55-60; No. 4, ler avril 1920, 79-118.  The au-
        thor replies to criticisms of his review of L'Energie spi-
        rituelle.

2547    LEHMANN, Gerhard.  Geschichte der Philosophie: Vol. 10.  Die
        Philosophie im ersten Drittel des XX. Jahrhunderts.  Ber-
        lin: de Gruyter and Co., 1957, 128.  Bergson is discussed
        in this book along with Nietzsche, Klages, Palágyi, and
        Losskij, under the heading "Irrationalismus und Intuition-
        ismus."

2548    LEHRMANN, Chanan.  Bergsonisme et judaïsme: Cours professé à
        l'Université de Lausanne.  Genève: Editions Union, 1937,
        120.

2549    LEIBRICH, Louis.  "Iphigénie en Tauride à la lumière de la
        philosophie d'aujourd'hui."  Etudes Germaniques, 4e Année,
        No. 2-3, avril-septembre 1949, 129-138.  This essay deals
        with Bergson and several other contemporary philosophers.

2550    LEIGHTON, J. A.  "On Continuity and Discreteness."  Journal
        of Philosophy, Psychology and Scientific Methods, 7, No. 9,
        28 April 1910, 231-238.

2551    LELIEVRE, Charles.  "Bergson et les deux bases de la morale."
        Christianisme Social, 46e Année, No. 1, janvier-février
        1933, 55-72.  This is a review of Les Deux Sources.

2552    LEMAITRE, Charles.  "Bergsonisme et métaphysique."  Revue
        Néo-scolastique de Philosophie, 2e Sér., 35, No. 40, novem-
        bre 1933, 516-538; 36, No. 42, mai 1934, 5-28; No. 43,
        août 1934, 153-177.  This essay deals with Bergson and
        Aquinas.  It would be natural for Bergson to infer God's
        existence from the contingency of nature, but Le Maître
        holds that Les Deux Sources disappoints us in this respect.

2553    LEMASSON, Emile.  Histoire de la philosophie: Une Doctrine,
        le bergsonisme: Exposé historique.  Paris: Beauchesne,
        1935, 130.

2554    LENOBLE, Eugène.  "Bergson."  Revue du Clergé Français, 69,
        No. 416, 15 mars 1912, 715-725.  This is a review of Berg-
        son's "L'Intuition philosophique."

2555    LENOBLE, Eugène. "H. Bergson." Dictionnaire pratique des connaissances religieuses. Vol. 1. Paris: Letouzey, 1925, 750-759.

2556    LENOBLE, Eugène. "Review of L'Evolution créatrice by Henri Bergson." Revue du Clergé Français, 53, No. 316, 15 janvier 1908, 180-208.

2557    LENOIR, Raymond. "A Propos d'Henri Bergson." Synthèses, 2e Année, No. 7, 1947, 81-84.

2558    LENOIR, Raymond. "Bergson, à propos d'un ouvrage récent." Revue de Synthèse, 1, No. 2, 1931, 257-263. This is a review of Jankélévitch's Bergson.

2559    LENOIR, Raymond. "Bergsonisme et sociologie." Revue de Métaphysique et de Morale, 45, No. 2, 1938, 255-268.

2560    LENOIR, Raymond. "Henri Bergson au Meeting d'Oxford." Revue Philosophique de la France et de l'Etranger, 149, No. 3, 1959, 339-343.

2561    LENOIR, Raymond. "La Prévision et la nouveauté." Revue de Métaphysique et de Morale, 28, No. 2, janvier-mars 1921, 100-103. The author provides an account of Bergson's talk given at the "Meeting d'Oxford" which, minimally rewritten, became the article "Le Possible et le réel."

2562    LENOIR, Raymond. "Réflexions sur le bergsonisme." Nouvelle Revue Française, 13, No. 12, 1er décembre 1919, 1077-1089.

2563    LENOIR, Raymond et al. La Tradition philosophique et la pensée française. Paris: Félix Alcan, 1922. This collection contains an article by René Gillouin on Bergson.

2564    LEON, P. "Review of Les Deux Sources de la morale et de la religion by Henri Bergson." Mind, 39, No. 164, October 1932, 485-495. This is a critical but appreciative review.

2565    LEOTARD, Georges. En Marge de Bergson: Essai sur la matérialité de la mémoire. Dilbeck: Editions Marguerite, 1938, 191.

2566    LEOTARD, Georges. Etudes philosophiques: Introduction au bergsonisme ou l'univers de Monsieur Henri Bergson. Bruxelles: Editions Marguerite, 1942, 88.

2567    LEPERCQ, Daniel. "La Philosophie bergsonienne." Revue de la Jeunesse, 5e Année, No. 10, 25 février 1914, 543-554.

2568   LERCH, Emil.  "Bergson in ein Nuß."  <u>Volk</u> <u>und</u> <u>Heimat</u>, 5, No.
       2, 1929.

2569   LERCH, Eugen.  "Henri Bergson."  <u>Das</u> <u>Buch</u>, 3, No. 2, 1951,
       5-16.

2570   LEROUX, Emmanuel.  "Témoignage."  <u>Nouvelles</u> <u>Littéraires</u>, No.
       322, 15 décembre 1928, 4.

2571   LEROY, André-Louis.  "Review of <u>Bergson</u> by I. W. Alexander."
       <u>Revue</u> <u>Philosophique</u> <u>de</u> <u>la</u> <u>France</u> <u>et</u> <u>de</u> <u>l'Etranger</u>, 149, No.
       3, 1959, 412-415.

2572   LEROY, André-Louis.  "Le Congrès Bergson (17-20 mai 1959)."
       <u>Revue</u> <u>Philosophique</u> <u>de</u> <u>la</u> <u>France</u> <u>et</u> <u>de</u> <u>l'Etranger</u>, 149, No.
       3, 1959, 379-380.  The author states that the method of
       "table ronde" was a happy innovation and that the discus-
       sion of Bergson's philosophy of religion at the Congrès
       Bergson was impassioned.

2573   LEROY, André-Louis.  "Influence de la philosophie berkley-
       enne sur la pensée continentale."  <u>Hermathena</u>, 82, No. 2,
       novembre 1953, 27-48.

2574   LE ROY, Edouard.  "A Propos de l'intuition bergsonienne."
       <u>Revue</u> <u>du</u> <u>Mois</u>, 13, No. 78, 10 juin 1912, 733-735.  Le Roy
       replies to Julien Benda's criticisms of Bergson's concept
       of intuition.

2575   LE ROY, Edouard.  <u>Bergson</u>.  Trans. Carlos Rahola.  Barcelona:
       Ed. Labor, 1932, 204.

2576   LE ROY, Edouard.  "Bergson vu par Edouard Le Roy."  <u>Nouvel-</u>
       <u>les</u> <u>Littéraires</u>, No. 1677, 22 octobre 1959, 2.

2577   LE ROY, Edouard.  "Comment se pose le problème de Dieu."  <u>Re-</u>
       <u>vue</u> <u>de</u> <u>Métaphysique</u> <u>et</u> <u>de</u> <u>Morale</u>, 15, No. 2, 1907, 129-
       178; No. 4, 1907, 470-523.

2578   LE ROY, Edouard.  "De La Valeur objective des lois physi-
       ques."  <u>Bulletin</u> <u>de</u> <u>la</u> <u>Société</u> <u>Française</u> <u>de</u> <u>Philosophie</u>, 1
       (Séance du 28 mars 1901), 1901, 5-32.

2579   LE ROY, Edouard.  "Une Enquête sur quelques traits majeurs
       de la philosophie bergsonienne."  <u>Archives</u> <u>de</u> <u>Philosophie</u>,
       17, No. 1, 1947, 7-21.

2580   LE ROY, Edouard.  <u>L'Exigence</u> <u>idéaliste</u> <u>et</u> <u>le</u> <u>fait</u> <u>de</u> <u>l'évo-</u>
       <u>lution</u>.  Paris: Boivin et Cie., 1927, 270.

2581    LE ROY, Edouard. L'Expérience de l'effort et de la grâce chez Maine de Biran. Paris: Boivin et Cie., 1934, 441.

2582    LE ROY, Edouard. "Hommage à Henri Bergson." La Nef, 4, No. 32, juillet 1947, 47-50. Bergson's scrupulous scientific preparation is discussed on pages 47-48.

2583    LE ROY, Edouard. The New Philosophy of Henri Bergson. Trans. Vincent Benson. New York: Holt and Company; London: Williams and Nordgate, 1913, 235.

2584    LE ROY, Edouard. Les Origines humaines et l'évolution de l'intelligence. Paris: Boivin et Cie., 1938, 375.

2585    LE ROY, Edouard. "Les Paradoxes de la relativité sur le temps." Revue Philosophique de la France et de l'Etranger, 62, No. 1-2, 1937, 10-47; No. 3-4, 1937, 194-245.

2586    LE ROY, Edouard. La Pensée intuitive: Vol. 1. Au delà du discours. Paris: Boivin et Cie., 1929, 204.

2587    LE ROY, Edouard. La Pensée intuitive: Vol. 2. Invention et vérification. Paris: Boivin et Cie., 1930, 297.

2588    LE ROY, Edouard. Une Philosophie nouvelle: Henri Bergson. Paris: Félix Alcan, 1914, 210.

2589    LE ROY, Edouard. "Une Philosophie nouvelle: M. Henri Bergson: I. La Méthode. II. La Doctrine." Revue des Deux Mondes, 6e période, 7, 1er février 1912, 551-580; 15 février 1912, 800-833.

2590    LE ROY, Edouard. "Philosophy in France, 1907: I. Philosophy in the Universities. II. Philosophy of Religion." Philosophical Review, 17, No. 3, May 1908, 291-315.

2591    LE ROY, Edouard. "Un Positivisme nouveau." Revue de Métaphysique et de Morale, 9, 1901, 138-153.

2592    LE ROY, Edouard. "Réponse à M. Couturat." Revue de Métaphysique et de Morale, 8, 1900, 223-233. The author replies to Couturat's criticism of "Science et philosophie."

2593    LE ROY, Edouard. "Science et philosophie." Revue de Métaphysique et de Morale, 7, 1899, 375-425, 503-562, 708-731; 8, 1900, 37-72.

2594    LE ROY, Edouard. "Sur La Logique de l'invention." Revue de Métaphysique et de Morale, 13, No. 2, 1905, 193-223.

2595    LE ROY, Edouard.  "Sur Quelques Objections adressées à la
        Nouvelle Philosophie."  Revue de Métaphysique et de Morale,
        9, 1901, 292-327;, 407-432.

2596    LE ROY, Edouard and CHAUMEIX, André.  Séance de l'Académie
        française du 18 octobre 1945: Discours de réception de M.
        Edouard Le Roy: Réponse de M. André Chaumeix.  Paris: Per-
        rin, 1946, 63.

2597    LE ROY, Edouard and FARAL, Edmond.  Hommage national à Henri
        Bergson à la Sorbonne, le 13 mai 1947.  Paris: Firmin-
        Didot, 1947, 10.

2598    LE ROY, Georges.  "La Pensée bergsonienne et le christianis-
        me."  Actes du Xe Congrès des Sociétés de Philosophie de
        Langue Française (Congrès Bergson).  Paris: Armand Colin,
        1, 1959, 195-199.  Bergson's philosophy cannot be counted,
        the author holds, among the specifically Christian philos-
        ophies; too many difficulties prevent this.  Between Berg-
        son's conclusions and the teachings of Christianity is
        there consonance or dissonance?

2599    LE ROY, Georges.  "Table ronde: Religion."  Actes du Xe Con-
        grès des Sociétés de Philosophie de Langue Française (Con-
        grès Bergson).  Paris: Armand Colin, 2, 1959, 261-278.

2600    LERSCH, Philipp.  "Grundsätliches zur Lebensphilosophie."
        Blätter für deutsche Philosophie, 9, No. 4, 1936; 10, Nos.
        1 and 2, 1937.  Bergson, pragmatism, and Schelling are
        dealt with in this study.

2601    LERSCH, Philipp.  Lebensphilosophie der Gegenwart.  Berlin:
        Junker und Dünnhaupt, 1932, 98.  Bergson, Dilthey, Scheler,
        Keyserling, and their philosophies are discussed in this
        study of the "Philosophy of Life."

2602    LE SAVOUREUX, H.  "Bergsonisme et neurologie."  Nouvelle Re-
        vue Française, 22, No. 251, 1er août 1934, 201-227.  This
        is a highly critical account of Bergson's position with
        regard to neurology.

2603    LE SAVOUREUX, H.  Bergsonisme et neurologie.  Paris: Nouvel-
        le Revue Française, 1934, 27.  The author argues that Pro-
        fessor Marie's theories (which are becoming dated anyhow)
        do not support Bergson's theories.  Bergson's theory of
        aphasia is purely metaphysical and devoid of scientific
        value.

2604   LE SENNE, René. "Le Bergsonisme et la morale." Revue de Paris, 39, No. 14, 15 juillet 1932, 411-422. This is a review of Les Deux Sources.

2605   LE SENNE, René. Introduction à la philosophie. Paris: Presses Universitaires de France, 1949, 476. "Avant-propos de L. Lavelle." Hamelin, Bergson, and others are discussed in this study.

2606   LE SENNE, René. Introduction à la philosophie. Paris: Presses Universitaires de France, 1970, 604. "Cinquième édition augmentée et mise au jour par Edouard Morot-sir et Paule Levert." Chapter three, "L'Intuitionisme bergsonien," appears on pages 178-223.

2607   LE SENNE, René. "L'Intuition morale d'après Bergson." Revue Philosophique de la France et de l'Etranger, 131, Nos. 2-3, mars-août 1941, 219-243.

2608   LE SENNE, René. "L'Intuition morale d'après Bergson." Etudes Bergsoniennes. Paris: Presses Universitaires de France, 1943, 98-123.

2609   LE SENNE, René. Traité de caractérologie. Paris: Presses Universitaires de France, 1941, 523.

2610   LE SENNE, René and BEAUCHATAUD, G. "Le Caractère et l'écriture d'Henri Bergson." Graphologie, No. 30, avril 1948, 3-11. This article contains an analysis of Bergson's handwriting.

2611   LESTIENNE, R. "Caractères de la durée physique." Scientia, 107, 1972, 77-89. The author examines the relations between the time of consciousness and that of physical processes. He distinguishes two kinds of physical time and raises the question whether physical time is irreversible.

2612   LEVASTI, Arrigo. Bergson e la religione. Roma: Edizion del Tripode, 1951, 20. This essay was published originally in Tripode, No. 12, settèmbre 1951.

2613   LEVEQUE, Raphael. "Retour sur 'l'intellectualisme bergsonien'." Actes du Xe Congrès des Sociétés de Philosophie de Langue Française (Congrès Bergson). Paris: Armand Colin, 1, 1959, 201-204. Bergson is not an "intellectualist," the author holds. For, from the intellectualist perspective, philosophy is a laborious effort. For Bergson, however, philosophy has an intrinsic grace. Once we have

mounted to the source, we have only to consent to the movement with which we are impelled.

2614    LEVI, Albert William. "Substance, Process, Being: A White-
headian-Bergsonian View." Journal of Philosophy, 55, No.
18, 29 August 1958, 749-761.

2615    LEVI, Adolfo. "La filosofia dell'esperienza: La filosofia
dell'intuizione indifferenziata (Bergson e James)." Rivista di psicologia applicata, 7, No. 1, gennaio-febbraio
1911, 47-75.

2616    LEVI, Adolfo. L'Indeterminismo della filosofia francese
contemporanea: La filosofia della contingenza. Firenze:
Bernardo Seeber, 1905, 300. Bergson is discussed in this
book on pages 81-125.

2617    LEVI, Adolfo. Sulle ultime forme dell'indeterminismo francese. Firenze: Civelli, 1903.

2618    LEVI, Adolfo. "L'ultime libre di Henri Bergson." Rivista
di filosofia, 27, No. 2, 1936, 173-176. This is a review
of La Pensée et le mouvant.

2619    LEVINE, Louis. "The Philosophy of Bergson." New York Times,
22 February 1914, Sect. 5, p. 4, col. 1.

2620    LEVINE, Louis. Syndicalism in France. New York: Columbia
University, 1914, 299. The irrationalist influence of
Bergson's ideas on the French Syndicalist movement is dis-
cussed in this study.

2621    LEVINE, Menache. "Al ha' comi o al ha' enouchi." Haaretz,
24 December 1937, 10. These are notes on the Hebrew translation of Laughter.

2622    LEVRON, Jacques. "Bergson: Professeur de littérature à Angers, 1882-1883." Nouvelles Littéraires, No. 1014, 9 janvier 1947, 6. This note concerns Bergson's courses on
Rousseau and on literary criticism.

2623    LEVI-STRAUSS, Claude. Totemism. Trans. R. Needham. Boston:
Beacon Press, 1963, 116. Bergson, totemism, and intuition
as method in anthropology are discussed in chapter V, "Totemism From Within," which appears on pages 92-104.

2624    LEVI-STRAUSS, Claude. Le Totémisme aujourd'hui. Paris:
Presses Universitaires de France, 1962, 156. Bergson is
discussed on pages 92-103.

2625   LEVY-BRUHL, Henri.  "Histoire et bergsonisme."  Revue de Syn-
       thèse, 19-59, 1940-1945, 141-149.

2626   LEVY-BRUHL, Lucien.  "Bergson vu par L. Lévy-Bruhl."  Nouvel-
       les Littéraires, No. 1677, 22 octobre 1959, 2.

2627   LEVY-BRUHL, Lucien.  "Henri Bergson à l'Ecole normale."  Nou-
       velles Littéraires, No. 322, 15 décembre 1928, 1.

2628   LEVY-BRUHL, Lucien.  "Revue critique de l'Essai, anonyme."
       Revue Philosophique de la France et de l'Etranger, 29, No.
       5, mai 1890, 519-538.  This is a thoroughgoing, perceptive
       analysis.

2629   LEWIS, Clarence Irving.  "Bergson and Contemporary Thought."
       University of California Chronicle, 16, No. 2, 1914, 181-
       197.

2630   LEWIS, Wyndham.  Time and Western Man.  New York: Harcourt,
       Brace and Company, 1928, 400; London: Chatto and Windus,
       1927, 487.  Highly critical references to Bergson are giv-
       en throughout this largely literary study.

2631   LEWKOWITZ, Albert.  "Zur Religionsphilosophie der Gegenwart:
       II.  Philosophie des Lebens: Darwin, Bergson, Simmel."
       Monatsschrift für Geschichte und Wissenschaft des Juden-
       tums, 66, No. 10-12, 1922, 250-268.

2632   LEWKOWITZ, Julius.  Die Philosophie H. Bergsons: Veröffent-
       lichung der wissenschaftlichen Vereinung jüdischer Lehrer
       und Lehrerinnen zu Berlin.  Berlin: Poppelauer, 1914, 16.

2633   LIBBY, Malanchthon F.  "The Continuity of Bergson's Thought."
       University of Colorado Studies, 9, No. 4, September 1913,
       147-202.

2634   LICHTIGFELD, A.  "The Survival of the Soul: 1.  A Reflection
       about the Survival of the Soul in the Thought of Macmurray,
       Bergson, Jaspers.  2.  The Survival-Hypothesis in Modern
       Thought."  Filosofia, 16, Suppl. al No. 4, novembre 1965,
       753-762.

2635   LICORISH, R. F.  "Bergson's Creative Evolution and the Ner-
       vous System in Organic Evolution."  Lancet, 182, 10 Febru-
       ary 1912, 391-392.  Lamarckian criticisms of Bergson are
       proposed in this article.

2636   LIDA, Raimundo.  "Bergson: Filósofo del lenguaje."  Nosotros,
       27, No. 282, septiembre 1933, 5-49.

2637    LIICEANU, G.  "On Intellectualist Interpretations of Berg-
        son's Intuitionism."  Revista de Filozofie, 13, No. 6,
        1965, 795-801.  The author holds that the richness of the
        real leads Bergson to transcend the conditions of elemen-
        tary logic; but his is wrong to search for the solution in
        a zone opposed to reason.  This article is in Rumanian.

2638    LINDSAY, Alexander Dunlap.  The Philosophy of Bergson.  Lon-
        don: Dent and Sons, Ltd., 1911, 247.

2639    LINDSAY, Alexander Dunlap.  The Philosophy of Bergson.  1911
        rpt.  New York: Kennikat Press, 1968, 247.

2640    LINN, Pierre.  "Return of Bergson."  Commonweal, 17, No. 1,
        2 November 1932, 14-17.  This is a review of Les Deux Sour-
        ces.

2641    LINS, Ivan.  "Bergson: Un filósofo da 'Belle-époque'."  Re-
        vista do Livro, 50, No. 19, 1960, 19-33.

2642    LION, Ferdinando.  Lebensquellen französischer Metaphysik:
        Descartes, Rousseau, Bergson.  Hamburg: Claasen und Go-
        verts; Zürich: Europa-Verlag, 1949, 128.

2643    LION, Fernand.  Cartesio, Rousseau e Bergson: Saggio di sto-
        ria vitalista della filosofia.  Milano: Bompiani, 1949,
        183.

2644    LIPPMANN, Walter.  "Bergson's Philosophy."  New York Times
        Review of Books, 62, No. 20, 021, Part 6, 17 November 1912,
        665-666.  This is a review of An Introduction to Metaphys-
        ics.

2645    LIPPMANN, Walter.  "The Most Dangerous Man in the World."
        Everybody's Magazine, 27, No. 1, July 1912, 100-101.  The
        author proposes that: "Bergson is not so much a prophet as
        a herald in whom the unrest of modern times has found a
        voice."  (100).

2646    LIPPMANN, Walter.  "Most Dangerous Man in the World."  Satur-
        day Review of Literature, 30, No. 34, 23 August 1947.
        This essay is reprinted from Everybody's Magazine, July
        1912.

2647    LISSARAGUE, Salvador.  "El perfil de la convivencia en Berg-
        son."  Revista Internacional de Sociología, 20, 1962, 149-
        157.

2648    LLERA, Humberto Pinera.  Filosofía de la vida y filosofía
        existencial: Ensayos.  Cuba: La Havane, 1952, 228.

2649    LODGE, Sir Oliver.  "Balfour and Bergson."  Hibbert Journal,
        10, No. 2, January 1912, 290-307.  This article is re-
        printed in Sir Oliver Lodge, Modern Problems.  New York:
        George H. Doran Company, 1912, 26-57.

2650    LODGE, Sir Oliver.  "Bergson's Intuitional Philosophy Jus-
        tified."  Current Literature, 52, No. 4, April 1912, 443-
        445.

2651    LODGE, Sir Oliver.  Modern Problems.  London: Methuen; New
        York: Doran, 1912, 348.  An essay entitled "Balfour and
        Bergson" appears on pages 26-57.

2652    LOISY, Alfred Dirmin.  George Tyrrell et Henri Bergson.
        Paris: Nourry, 1936, 205.

2653    LOISY, Alfred Dirmin.  Y a-t-il deux sources de la religion
        et de la morale?  Paris: Nourry, 1933, 204.  The author
        holds that each of Bergson's proposed "sources" is a dif-
        ferent aspect of the same thing.  This study is polite but
        highly critical.

2654    LONG, Wilbur.  "Heterodoxy of Henri Bergson."  Personalist,
        29, No. 1, January 1948, 60-72.

2655    LOOMBA, Ram Murti.  Bradley and Bergson: A Comparative Study.
        Lucknow, India: Upper India Publishing House, 1937, 187.

2656    LOSSKI, N.  "Недостатки гноссологии Бергсона и вли-
        яние их на его метафизику."  Вопросы философии и
        психологии, 24, № 118, 1913, 224-235.

2657    LOSSKI, N.  Интуитивная философия.  Петербург: Изда-
        тельство "Учитель", 1922, 109.

2658    LOSSKY, Nickolai.  L'Intuition, la matière et la vie.  Paris:
        Félix Alcan, 1928, 177.  A sketch of Bergsonian theory of
        perception is given on pages 23-24; his concept of symbol-
        ism on page 49.

2659    LOTTE, Joseph.  "Henri Bergson: L'Evolution créatrice."  La
        Renaissance catholique au début du XXe siècle.  Ed. L.-A.
        Maugendre.  Paris: Beauchesne, 1963, 89-92.  This article
        is reprinted from Messager de la Vendée, 11 and 18 August
        1907.

2660    LOTTE, Joseph. "Lettre du 10 nov. 1912 à la Revue de la Jeunesse." Bulletin des Professeurs Catholiques de l'Université, 25 juin 1913.

2661    LOTTE, Joseph. Lettres et entretiens. Paris: L'Artisan du Livre, 1927, 215 (Cahiers de la Quinzaine, 18e Série, 1er cahier). Letters and talks concerning Bergson are given on pages 119-120 and 154-155.

2662    LOTTE, Joseph. "Une Philosophie de la vie." La Renaissance catholique au début du XXe siècle. Ed. L.-A. Maugendre. Paris: Beauchesne, 1963, 294, 119-128. This article is reprinted from Journal de Coutances, 6 and 26 July 1910.

2663    LOVECCHIO, A. "E. Bergson e la sua ultima opera." Ricerche filosofiche, Anno 2, No. 3-4, 1932. This is a review of Les Deux Sources.

2664    LOVEDAY, Thomas. "Review of L'Evolution créatrice by Henri Bergson." Mind, 17, No. 67, July 1908, 402-408.

2665    LOVEJOY, Arthur Oncken. Bergson and Romantic Evolutionism. Berkeley, California: University of California, 1914, 61.

2666    LOVEJOY, Arthur Oncken. "The Meaning of Vitalism." Science, 33, No. 851, January-June 1911, 610-614. Bergson's "psycho-vitalism" is discussed on page 614.

2667    LOVEJOY, Arthur Oncken. "The Metaphysician of the Life-Force." Nation, 89, No. 2309, 30 September 1909, 298-301. This is a review of L'Evolution créatrice.

2668    LOVEJOY, Arthur Oncken. "The Paradox of the Time-Retarding Journey." Philosophical Review, 60, No. 1, January 1931, 48-68; No. 2, April 1931, 152-167. In this essay Lovejoy concurs with Bergson's criticisms of both the general and special theories of relativity and defends Bergson against d'Abro.

2669    LOVEJOY, Arthur Oncken. "The Practical Tendencies of Bergsonism, I and II." International Journal of Ethics, 53, No. 3, April 1913, 253-275; No. 4, July 1913, 419-443. This is a thoroughgoing criticism of Bergson and his followers, with special emphasis on the relations between Bergson's thought and both syndicalism and Roman Catholic "modernism."

2670    LOVEJOY, Arthur Oncken.  "The Problem of Time in Recent
        French Philosophy: I.  Renouvier and Recent Temporalism."
        Philosophical Review, 21, No. 1, January 1912, 10-31.

2671    LOVEJOY, Arthur Oncken.  "The Problem of Time in Recent
        French Philosophy: II.  Temporalism and Anti-intellectual-
        ism: Bergson."  Philosophical Review, 21, No. 3, May 1912,
        322-343.  The author argues that Bergson's concept of time
        is paradoxical and makes him an extreme anti-intellectual.
        But Bergson also has a quantitative conception of time,
        which is more acceptable.

2672    LOVEJOY, Arthur Oncken.  "The Problem of Time in Recent
        French Philosophy: III.  Time and Continuity: Pillon,
        James."  Philosophical Review, 21, No. 4, September 1912,
        527-545.  According to the author, Pillon's notion of time,
        with which Lovejoy agrees, eliminates Bergson's "difficul-
        ties" and agrees with one of James' three concepts of time.

2673    LOVEJOY, Arthur Oncken.  The Reason, the Understanding, and
        Time.  Baltimore, Maryland: Johns Hopkins Press, 1961, 210.
        See especially "Bergson on 'Real Duration'," 185-202, for
        a letter from Bergson and criticisms of "real duration."
        Bergson's views are discussed at several points in this
        study.

2674    LOVEJOY, Arthur Oncken.  "Schopenhauer as an Evolutionist."
        Monist, 21, No. 2, April 1911, 195-222.  References to
        Bergson may be found in this article.

2675    LOVEJOY, Arthur Oncken.  "Some Antecedents of the Philoso-
        phy of Bergson."  Mind, 22, No. 88, October 1913, 465-492.
        Ravaisson, Lionel Dauriac, and G. Noël were precursors of
        Bergson, according to the author.

2676    LOVEJOY, Arthur Oncken.  The Thirteen Pragmatisms.  Balti-
        more, Maryland: Johns Hopkins Press, 1963, 290.  Bergson's
        influence on William James is discussed in "William James
        as Philosopher" on pages 105-188.  This essay was first
        published in International Journal of Ethics, 1911.

2677    LOVEJOY, Arthur Oncken.  "Review of William James and Henri
        Bergson: A Study in Contrasting Theories of Life by Horace
        M. Kallen."  Nation, 100, No. 2597, 1915, 388-390.

2678    LOW, Sidney.  "Mr. Balfour in the Study."  Edinburgh Review,
        216, No. 442, October 1912, 257-278.  Bergson is discussed
        on pages 268-271.

2679    LOWE, Victor. "The Influence of Bergson, James, and Alexan-
        der on Whitehead." Journal of the History of Ideas, 10,
        No. 2, 1949, 267-296. The author argues that very little
        influence was exerted by Bergson on A. N. Whitehead.

2680    LOWE, Victor. Understanding Whitehead. Baltimore, Mary-
        land: Johns Hopkins Press, 1962, 398. The influence of
        Bergson on Whitehead is discussed on pages 257-263.

2681    LUARD, Trant Bramston. Incarnation: A Monologue in Verse.
        London: Centaur Press, 1934, 22. This work is based on
        the English translation of Henri Bergson's L'Evolution cré-
        atrice.

2682    LUBAC, E. Esquisse d'un système de psychologie rationnelle.
        Paris: Félix Alcan, 1904, 245. "Préface par Henri Berg-
        son." This is a Bergsonian psychology.

2683    LUBAC, Henri de. "Deux thèses de doctorat sur Bergson."
        Etudes, 216, 5 août 1933, 306-313. This is a largely fa-
        vorable review of Rideau's Les Rapports de la matière et
        de l'esprit dans le bergsonisme and his Le Dieu de Bergson.

2684    LUBAC, Jean. La Valeur du spiritualisme. Paris: Grasset,
        1912, 337.

2685    LUCE, Arthur Aston. Bergson's Doctrine of Intuition. New
        York and Toronto: The Macmillan Co., 1922, 112.

2686    LUCHAIRE, Julien. "Bergson à Genève." Nouvelles Littérai-
        res, No. 322, 15 décembre 1928, 4.

2687    LUCQUES, Claire. "Le Présent supplément d'âme." Actes du
        Xe Congrès des Sociétés de Philosophie de Langue Française
        (Congrès Bergson). Paris: Armand Colin, 1, 1959, 205-209.

2688    LUCQUES, Claire. "Table ronde: Morale." Actes du Xe Con-
        grès des Sociétés de Philosophie de Langue Française (Con-
        grès Bergson). Paris: Armand Colin, 2, 1959, 237-257.

2689    LUQUET, J. Idées générales de psychologie. Paris: Félix
        Alcan, 1906, 295.

2690    LUX, Jacques. "Nos Philosophes: M. Henri Bergson." Revue
        Politique et Littéraire, Revue Bleue, 5e Série, 6, No. 22,
        ler décembre 1906, 703-704.

2691  LYMAN, Eugene W.  "Bergson's Philosophy of Religion."  Review of Religion, 1, No. 3, March 1937, 249-269.  This is an analysis and exposition of The Two Sources.

2692  M., F.  "Henri Bergson è morto cattolico?"  La Civiltà cattolica, 92, No. 3, 1941, 537-538.

2693  M., P.  "Le Rire: Conférence de M. Bergson."  Moniteur de Puy-de-Dôme, 21 février 1884.  Also in Mélanges, 313-315.

2694  MAC CALLUM, H. R.  "Review of Bergson by V. Jankélévitch."  International Journal of Ethics, 42, No. 4, July 1932, 501-503.  This is an excellent review.

2695  MACASKILL, John.  "Bergson and a Philosophical Peace."  Calcutta Review, 2nd Ser., 6, No. 3, April 1918, 215-222.

2696  MACASKILL, John.  "Intellect and Intuition: A Footnote to Bergson and Bradley."  Contemporary Review, 108, No. 7, July 1915, 91-99.  The author cites interesting similarities between the two thinkers.

2697  MAC DONALD, M. S.  "Review of L'Effort intellectuel by Henri Bergson."  Philosophical Review, 11, No. 4, July 1902, 416-417.

2698  MADECO, Sílvio de.  "Centenário de Bergson: Depoimento."  Revista Brasileira de Filosofia, 11, No. 41, 1961, 112-113.  The author states the reasons that led him to study Bergson.  He explains the basic concepts covered in his writings and the nature of Bergson's influence on Brazilian philosophy.

2699  MACEDO, Sílvio de.  Intuição e linguagem em Bergson e Heidegger.  Maceió, Brazil, 1966, 112.

2700  MACINTOSH, Douglas C.  "Bergson and Religion."  Biblical World, 41, No. 1, January 1913, 34-40.

2701  MACQUARRIE, John.  Twentieth-Century Religious Thought.  New York and Evanston, 1963, 415.  Vitalism and Bergson are discussed on pages 170-173.

2702  MACWILLIAM, John.  Criticism of the Philosophy of Bergson.  Edinburgh: Clark, 1928, 336.

2703  MADAULE, Jacques.  Reconnaissances.  Paris: Desclée de Brouwer, 1943, 111, 422.  Bloy, Fournier, Rivière, Bergson, and Martin du Gard are discussed in this book.

2704    MADAULE, Jacques. Reconnaissances III. Paris: Desclée de
        Brouwer, 1946, 423.

2705    MADAULE, Jacques and CATTAUI, Georges, Eds. Entretiens sur
        Paul Claudel. Paris and La Haye: Mouton, 1968, 333.

2706    MADINIER, Gabriel. Conscience et mouvement: Etude sur la
        philosophie française de Condillac à Bergson. Paris: Pres-
        ses Universitaires de France, 1938, 481.

2707    MADINIER, Gabriel. Conscience et mouvement: Etude sur la
        philosophie française de Condillac à Bergson. Louvain:
        Nauwelaerts; Paris: Béatrice-Nauwelaerts, 1967, 482. The
        preface is by Aimé Forest.

2708    MAES, J.-D. "Bergsons Godsdienstphilosophie." Thomistisch
        Tijdschrift, 2, 1932.

2709    MAEZTU, Ramiro de. "La moral de Bergson." La Prensa, 11
        septiembre 1932, Sec. II, Col. 1 (Suppl.).

2710    MAGNAT, G.-E. "Portraits graphologiques: Deux Philosophes:
        Henri Bergson et Louis Lavelle." Une Semaine Dans le Mon-
        de, 26 juin 1948. This article contains an analysis of
        Bergson's handwriting.

2711    MAGNIN, E. "Un Colloquio con H. Bergson." Rivista di filo-
        sofia neoscolastica, 25, No. 1, enero 1933, 109-114.
        This article recounts a conversation between Magnin and
        Bergson concerning The Two Sources of Morality and Reli-
        gion. It contains some interesting comments on philosoph-
        ical method.

2712    MAGNIN, E. "Entretien avec M. Bergson." Vie Catholique,
        10, No. 432, 7 janvier 1933, 1-2.

2713    MAILLARD, Pierre. "Henri Bergson." Philosophisches Jahr-
        buch der Görresgesellschaft, 5, 1947, 409-412.

2714    MAIORANA, María-Teresa. "Bergson et les penseurs ibéro-amé-
        ricains." Actes du Xe Congrès des Sociétés de Philosophie
        de Langue Française (Congrès Bergson). Paris: Armand Co-
        lin, 1, 1959, 217-220. The author recounts the situation
        in Spanish-American philosophy at the time of Bergson's
        influence and indicates briefly those authors who felt
        Bergson's influence and contributed to independent philo-
        sophical thought in Latin America.

2715    MAIORANA, María-Teresa. "Bergson y el misticismo cristiano."
        Criterio, 33, No. 1373, 1961, 94-96.

2716    MAIORANA, María-Teresa. "Comentarios deshilvanados a una
        lectura de Bergson: Las dos fuentes de la religión y la
        moral." Criterio, 29, Nos. 1266-1270, 1956, 769-772.

2717    MAIRE, Gilbert. "Un Ami d'Henri Bergson: Joseph Desaymard."
        Etudes Bergsoniennes, 3, 158-159. This is a résumé of
        Maire's talk on Bergson and Desaymard followed by a dis-
        cussion.

2718    MAIRE, Gilbert. "Les Années de Bergson à Clermont-Ferrand."
        Glanes, 2, mars-avril 1949.

2719    MAIRE, Gilbert. "Les Années de Bergson à Clermont-Ferrand
        avant les Données immédiates de la conscience." Proceed-
        ings of the Tenth International Congress of Philosophy.
        Amsterdam: North-Holland Publishing Company, 1949, 1207-
        1209.

2720    MAIRE, Gilbert. Aux Marches de la civilisation occidentale:
        Henri Bergson, etc. Paris: Baudinière, 1929, 224.

2721    MAIRE, Gilbert. "Review of 'Bergson et bergsonisme'. Archi-
        ves de Philosophie, 17, Cahier I." Etudes Bergsoniennes,
        1, 1948, 200-213. This is a review of an issue of the Ar-
        chives de Philosophie dedicated to Bergson, his thought,
        and his influence. E. Le Roy, B. Romeyer, P. Kucharski,
        A. Forest, P. d'Aurec, A. Bremond, and A. Ricour contribu-
        ted to the issue. The reviewer explains that the issue
        testifies to a remarkable effort by Catholic philosophy to
        grasp the essentials of Bergson's philosophy.

2722    MAIRE, Gilbert. "Bergson et l'élan vital." Age Nouveau, 13,
        No. 2, février-mars 1959, 71-75.

2723    MAIRE, Gilbert. Bergson mon maître. Paris: Grasset, 1935,
        230. The author gives personal recollections of Bergson
        and traces the development of his own Bergsonism.

2724    MAIRE, Gilbert. "Henri Bergson et la défense de la civili-
        sation." Civilisation, 1, No. 1, 1959, 10-12.

2725    MAIRE, Gilbert. "Henri Bergson: Son Oeuvre." Nouvelle Re-
        vue Critique, 10, 1926.

2726    MAIRE, Gilbert. Henri Bergson: Son Oeuvre. Paris: Nouvelle
        Revue Critique, 1928, 72.

2727    MAIRE, Gilbert. "Bergsoniens contre Bergson." La Revue,
        6e Sér., 106, 1er février 1914, 316-330.

2728    MAIRE, Gilbert. "Le Bergsonisme dans la pensee sorélienne."
        Fédération, novembre 1947, 17-18.

2729    MAIRE, Gilbert. "Bergsonisme et fédéralisme." Fédération,
        décembre 1949.

2730    MAIRE, Gilbert. "Intuition et phénoménologie." Une Régres-
        sion mentale d'Henri Bergson à Jean-Paul Sartre. Paris:
        Grasset, 1959, 101-111.

2731    MAIRE, Gilbert. "Jean Hyppolite. 'Henri Bergson et l'exis-
        tentialisme'." Etudes Bergsoniennes, 2, 1949, 208-215.
        The author participates here with several philosophers in
        a discussion of Bergson and existentialism.

2732    MAIRE, Gilbert. "Un Jugement littéraire récent sur Henri
        Bergson." Etudes Bergsoniennes, 2, 1949, 238-243. This
        is a review of Clouard, Histoire de la littérature fran-
        çaise. "Pour la première fois, à ma connaissance, un phi-
        losophe est dignement étudié dans une oeuvre strictement
        littéraire et par un pur littérateur." (243).

2733    MAIRE, Gilbert. "Le Philosophe Bergson tel que je l'ai con-
        nu." France Illustration, 7, No. 279, 17 février 1951,
        190.

2734    MAIRE, Gilbert. "La Philosophie de Georges Sorel." Cahiers
        du Cercle Proudhon, 2, No. 2, mars-avril 1912, 57-81.
        This article contains part of a letter from Bergson ex-
        plaining his relationship to Sorel.

2735    MAIRE, Gilbert. "Philosophie et biologie." Documents de la
        Vie Intellectuelle, 1, No. 4, 20 janvier 1930, 66-67.
        This article also appears in Aux Marches de la civilisa-
        tion occidentale, Badin, 1929.

2736    MAIRE, Gilbert. "Rencontre de Bergson." Etudes Bergsonien-
        nes, 9, 1970, 201-208.

2737    MAIRE, Gilbert. "Systèmes philosophiques d'écoles littérai-
        res: L'Utilisation du contresens." Revue Critique des
        Idées et des Livres, 20, No. 117, 25 février 1913, 430-444.

2738    MAIRE, Gilbert. William James et le pragmatisme religieux.
        Paris: Denoël et Steele, 1933, 287.

2739    MAISONNEUVE, L. "Review of L'Evolution créatrice by Henri
        Bergson." Polybiblion, 2e Série, 71 (Partie Littéraire),
        1907, 405-406.

2740    MAISONNEUVE, L. "Review of Matière et mémoire by Henri Berg-
        son." Polybiblion, 2e Série, 45 (Partie Littéraire), 1897,
        497-499.

2741    MAITRA, Shishir Kumar. The Neo-Romantic Movement in Contem-
        porary Philosophy. Calcutta: The Book Company, 1922, 268.
        This study deals with Nietzsche, Chamberlain, Keyserling,
        and Bergson. It is highly critical.

2742    MAITRA, Sisirkumar. "Rabandrinath Tagore and Bergson." Cal-
        cutta Review, 3rd Ser., 17, No. 3, May-June 1926, 189-205.

2743    MAIZIERE, G. "Une Philosophie moderne: M. Bergson." Le Gau-
        lois, 1912.

2744    MALAGARRIGA, Carlos. "Bergson." La Nación, Suppl., 11 no-
        viembre 1928.

2745    MALAGARRIGA, Carlos. "Bergson." La Nación, Sec. II, 3, 18
        noviembre 1928.

2746    MALAGARRIGA, Carlos. "Filosofía bergsoniana y Catolicismo."
        Nosotros, 21, No. 221, octobre 1927, 5-13.

2747    MALAGARRIGA, Carlos. "Notas lexicológicas de un traductor."
        Nosotros, 24, No. 253, junio 1930, 322-338. This is a re-
        view of the Spanish translation of Creative Evolution,
        Madrid, 1912.

2748    MALAGARRIGA, Carlos. "Significado de la evolución por Henri
        Bergson." Atlantida, 9, No. 27, marzo 1913, 348-379. See
        the note on page 475.

2749    MALINOW, Carlos A. "Finalidad y determinismo en los siste-
        mas evolutivos de Pierre Teilhard y Henri Bergson." Diá-
        logos, 2, No. 4, 1965, 111-131.

2750    MALLOY, Joseph I. "Death of Noted French Philosopher."
        Catholic World, 152, No. 911, February 1941, 620-621.

2751    MAMELET, A. "L'Idée de rythme par A. Chide." Revue de Méta-
        physique et de Morale, 14, No. 5, juillet 1906, 733-745.

2752   MAÑACH, Jorge.  "En el centenario de Bergson."  Revista de
       la Biblioteca Nacional Jose Martí, 1, Nos. 1-4, 1959, 18-
       41.

2753   MANACORDA, Guido.  I contrafforti.  Brescia, Italy: Morcel-
       liana, 1935, 330.  A chapter entitled "L'Ultimo Bergson"
       appears on pages 241-245.

2754   MANDEL, A.  "Bergson et la question."  Monde Juif, 14e Année,
       No. 85-86, 1959.

2755   MANGOLD, F.  "Bergsons Begriff d. Komischen erarbeitet a.
       Molières Komodien."  Zeitschrift für französische Sprache
       und Literatur, 30, No. 1, 1931, 1-11.

2756   MARACHE, Theodore Jr.   "Bergson and Free Will."  Personal-
       ist, 20, No. 1, 1939, 21-28.

2757   MARBLE, Annie Russell.  "Henri Bergson: Thinker and Teacher."
       Nobel Prize Winners in Literature, 1901-1931.  New York:
       Appleton-Century, 1932, 313-326.

2758   MARC, Alexandre.  "Le Temps et la personne."  Recherches
       Philosophiques, 4, 1934-1935, 127-149.

2759   MARCEL, Gabriel.  "Les Amis de Bergson."  La Nef, 4, No. 31,
       1947, 176.

2760   MARCEL, Gabriel.  "Henri Bergson et le problème de Dieu."
       L'Europe Nouvelle, 15, No. 742, 30 avril 1932, 558-559.
       This is a review of Les Deux Sources.

2761   MARCEL, Gabriel.  "Bergsonism and Music."  Reflections on
       Art.  Ed. Susanne K. Langer.  Baltimore, Maryland: Johns
       Hopkins Press, 1958, 142-151.

2762   MARCEL, Gabriel.  "Bergsonisme et musique."  Revue Musicale,
       6e Année, No. 5, 1er mars, 1925, 220-229.

2763   MARCEL, Gabriel.  "Carence de la spiritualité."  Documents
       de la Vie Intellectuelle, 3, No. 3, 20 juin 1930, 574-
       578.  This article appeared originally in Nouvelle Revue
       Française, March 1929.

2764   MARCEL, Gabriel.  "Charles Du Bos: In Memoriam."  Etudes par
       des Pères de la Compagnie de Jésus, 240, 5-20 septembre
       1939, 449-455.  Also in Hommage à Charles Du Bos.  Paris:
       Plon, 1945, 165-171.

2765    MARCEL, Gabriel. "Clairière." Nouvelles Littéraires, No.
        322, 15 décembre 1928, 3.

2766    MARCEL, Gabriel. "Les Conditions dialectiques de la philo-
        sophie de l'intuition." Revue de Métaphysique et de Mora-
        le, 20, No. 5, 1912, 638-652.

2767    MARCEL, Gabriel. "Discours sur Bergson." Bulletin de la
        Société Française de Philosophie, 54, No. 1, janvier-mars
        1960, 27-32.

2768    MARCEL, Gabriel. "En Mémoire de Bergson." Temps Présent,
        9, No. 21, 12 janvier 1945, 6.

2769    MARCEL, Gabriel. "Floris Delattre, 'Henri Bergson et l'An-
        gleterre'." Etudes Bergsoniennes, 2, 1949, 199-208. The
        author participates here with several philosophers in a
        discussion of Bergson and Great Britain.

2770    MARCEL, Gabriel. "Grandeur de Bergson." Henri Bergson.
        Ed. Béguin and Thévenaz, 29-38. The author stresses the
        openness of Bergson's thought and its emphasis on authen-
        tic experience. He suggests that Bergson's intuition
        achieves its true value only through the dialectic by
        which it is tested.

2771    MARCEL, Gabriel. "Review of La Pensée et le mouvant by
        Henri Bergson." Europe Nouvelle, 17, No. 1, 30 juin 1934,
        662-663.

2772    MARCEL, Gabriel. "Table-ronde." Nouvelles Littéraires, No.
        1677, 22 octobre 1959, 1 and 5-6.

2773    MARCEL, Gabriel. "A Tribute to Bergson on the Occasion of
        the Bergson Centennial in Paris, 1959." The Bergsonian
        Heritage. Ed. Thomas Hanna. New York and London: Colum-
        bia University Press, 1962, 124-132. According to the
        author, Bergson is distinguished through his attachment
        to "authentic experience."

2774    MARCHIOLI, E. "L'anima e l'evoluzione secondo Bergson."
        Critica sociale, No. 8, 1912.

2775    MARCK, Siegfried. "Philosophie." Nord und Sud, 37, No. 5,
        Mai 1913, 201-213.

2776    MARCOTTE, Marcel. "Histoire de la philosophie: Bergson."
        L'Enseignement Secondaire au Canada, 28, No. 4, octobre
        1948, 47-55.

2777    MARIETTI, Angèle. "Le Bergsonisme dans la perspective d'une
        théorie du même et autre." Revue Moderne des Arts et de
        la Vie, 56, No. 11, ler novembre 1955, 21-22.

2778    MARIN, F. "Sur L'Origine des espèces." Revue Scientifique,
        4e Sér., 16, No. 19, 1901, 577-588. This is an early at-
        tempt to apply Bergsonism to biology, prior to Creative
        Evolution.

2779    MARITAIN, Jacques. "Bergsonian Morality and the Problem of
        Supra-Morality." Moral Philosophy. New York: Scribner's,
        1964, 418-447.

2780    MARITAIN, Jacques. Bergsonian Philosophy and Thomism.
        New York: Greenwood Press, 1968, 383.

2781    MARITAIN, Jacques. "The Bergsonian Philosophy of Morality
        and Religion." Redeeming the Time. London: Centenary
        Press, 1946, 74-100.

2782    MARITAIN, Jacques. "Bergsonisme et métaphysique." Chroni-
        ques (huitième numéro de). Paris: Plon, 1929, 5-131.

2783    MARITAIN, Jacques. "Bergsonisme et métaphysique." Le Ro-
        seau d'Or, 24, No. 6, 1929, 5-131.

2784    MARITAIN, Jacques. "Bergsonismo y metafísica." Criterio,
        2, No. 70, 1929, 297-301; No. 71, 1929, 329-332; No. 72,
        1929, 361-363; No. 74, 1929, 425-429.

2785    MARITAIN, Jacques. "Bergsons Metaphysik und Moral." Philo-
        sophisches Jahrbuch der Görresgesellschaft, 58, No. 3,
        1948, 179-210. This is a translation from De Bergson à
        Thomas d'Aquin.

2786    MARITAIN, Jacques. De Bergson a Santo Tomás de Aquino: En-
        sayos de metafísica y de moral. Buenos Aires: Club de Le-
        tores, 1946, 254.

2787    MARITAIN, Jacques. De Bergson à Thomas d'Aquin: Essais de
        métaphysique et de morale. New York: Edit. de la Maison
        Française, 1944, 269.

2788    MARITAIN, Jacques. De Bergson à Thomas d'Aquin: Essais de
        métaphysique et de morale. Paris: Hartmann, 1947, 333.

2789    MARITAIN, Jacques. De Bergson a Tommaso d'Aquino: Saggio di
        metafisica e morale. Verone, Italy: Mondadori, 1946, 300.

2790    MARITAIN, Jacques. "Les Deux Bergsonismes." Revue Thomiste,
        20, No. 4, juillet-août 1912, 433-450.

2791    MARITAIN, Jacques. Les Deux Bergsonismes. Toulouse, France:
        Edition Privat, 1912.

2792    MARITAIN, Jacques. "Discussion avec Jacques Chevalier sur
        'Aristote et Bergson'." Les Lettres, 8, No. 4, 1er avril
        1920, 79-118.

2793    MARITAIN, Jacques. "Discussion avec de Tonquédec et R. Jo-
        hannet sur Bergson." Les Lettres, 8, No. 2, 1er février
        1920, 24-32.

2794    MARITAIN, Jacques. "L'Ethique bergsonienne et le problème
        de la supra-morale." La Philosophie morale. Paris: Gal-
        limard, 1960, 518-554.

2795    MARITAIN, Jacques. "L'Evolutionnisme de M. Bergson." Revue
        de Philosophie, 19, Nos. 9-10, septembre-octobre 1911, 467-
        540.

2796    MARITAIN, Jacques. L'Evolutionnisme de M. Bersgson. Mont-
        ligeon, France: Imprimerie-Librairie de Montligeon, 1911,
        76. "Extrait de la Revue de Philosophie, octobre 1911."

2797    MARITAIN, Jacques. Metafísica de Bergson: Freudismo y psico-
        analisis. Trans. M. A. Berraz. Buenos Aires: Intituto de
        Filosofía, 1938, 73.

2798    MARITAIN, Jacques. "The Metaphysics of Bergson." Redeeming
        the Time. London: Centenary Press, 1946, 46-73.

2799    MARITAIN, Jacques. "La Métaphysique du bergsonisme." Docu-
        ments de la Vie Intellectuelle, 3, No. 3, 20 juin 1930,
        568-574. This essay was published originally in La Méta-
        physique bergsonienne, 2nd. ed.

2800    MARITAIN, Jacques. "L'Opinion de M. Jacques Maritain."
        Documents de la Vie Intellectuelle, 2, No. 5, 20 fevrier
        1930, 261-271. This essay was published originally in
        "Bergsonisme et métaphysique," Le Roseau d'Or.

2801    MARITAIN, Jacques. La Philosophie bergsonienne: Etudes cri-
        tiques par Jacques Maritain. Paris: M. Rivière et Cie.,
        1914, 477. This is a determined criticism of Bergson's
        philosophy by a Catholic philosopher. The superiority of
        Aquinas' views is stressed.

2802    MARITAIN, Jacques. La Philosophie bergsonienne: Etudes cri-
        tiques par Jacques Maritain. 2-3e ed. Paris: Librairie
        Tequi, 1930, 1948. The third edition of this work is re-
        vised and enlarged.

2803    MARITAIN, Jacques. Quatre Essais sur l'esprit dans sa con-
        dition charnelle. Paris: Desclée de Brouwer, 1939, 267.

2804    MARITAIN, Jacques. Ransoming the Time. New York: Scrib-
        ner's, 1943, 322. Chapter 2 is entitled "The Metaphysics
        of Bergson."

2805    MARITAIN, Jacques. Redeeming the Time. London: Centenary
        Press, 1943. Bergson's metaphysics are discussed in chap-
        ter 3 of this book.

2806    MARITAIN, Jacques. "Remarques sur l'intuition bergsonienne
        de la durée." Miscellanea Philosophica R. P. Josepho
        Gredt. Romae: S.A.L.E.R. Herder, 1938, 73-80. This vol-
        ume of essays is Vols. 7-8 of Studia Anselmiana.

2807    MARITAIN, Jacques. "Santo Tomás y Henri Bergson en los
        estilos de la ética." Columna, No. 8, 1937, 66-67.

2808    MARITAIN, Jacques. "Sur L'Ethique bergsonienne." Revue de
        Métaphysique et de Morale, 64, No. 2, 1959, 141-140. The
        author argues that Bergson's error was to term "moral" a
        system of social pressures which is infra-moral.

2809    MARITAIN, Jacques and Raïssa. "Notre Maître perdu et re-
        trouvé." Revue Dominicaine, 47, No. 2, février 1941, 61-
        68.

2810    MARITAIN, Raïssa. Adventures in Grace: Sequel to 'We Have
        Been Friends Together.' New York and Toronto: Longmans,
        Green and Co., 1945, 262.

2811    MARITAIN, Raïssa. "Henri Bergson." Commonweal, 32, No. 13,
        17 January 1941, 317-319. In this article Raïssa Maritain
        makes controversial claims concerning Bergson and Catholi-
        cism.

2812    MARITAIN, Raïssa. "Henri Bergson." Nova et Vetera, 14e An-
        née, No. 1, 1941, 3-12.

2813    MARITAIN, Raïssa. "Henri Bergson." Catholic Digest, 5, No.
        3, March 1941, 7-10. This is a short version of articles
        and discussions in Commonweal, 1941.

2814    MARITAIN, Raïssa. "Henri Bergson: Souvenirs." Henri Berg-
        son. Ed. Béguin and Thévenaz, 349-356. The author re-
        counts reports concerning Bergson during his later years.
        She claims that Bergson was baptised sometime after 1932.
        She also recounts a visit with Bergson in 1936 or 1937.

2815    MARITAIN, Raïssa. "Bergson's Christianity." Commonweal,
        34, No. 19, 29 August 1941, 446-447.

2816    MARITAIN, Raïssa. "Discussion of Bergson." Commonweal, 33,
        No. 20, 7 March 1941, 492-494; No. 24, 4 April 1941, 601.

2817    MARITAIN, Raïssa. Les Grandes Amitiés: Les Aventures de la
        grâce. Paris: Desclée de Brouwer, 1944, 262.

2818    MARITAIN, Raïssa. Les Grandes Amitiés: Souvenirs. Paris:
        Desclée de Brouwer, 1941, 228.

2819    MARITAIN, Raïssa. Die großen Freundschaften: Begegnungen
        mit Henri Bergson, Léon Bloy, Jacques Maritain, Pierre van
        der Meer de Walcheren, Charles Péguy. Trans. B. Schluter
        and G. G. Meister. Heidelberg: Kerle, 1954, 451.

2820    MARITAIN, Raïssa. "Souvenirs." La Relève, Sér. 5, mars
        1941, 161-187. This article is republished in Henri Berg-
        son, edited by Béguin and Thévenaz, 349-356.

2821    MARITAIN, Raïssa. We Have Been Friends Together. Trans.
        J. Kernan. New York and Toronto: Longman's, Green and Co.,
        1942, 208. Bergson is discussed on pages 79-103.

2822    "Maritain on Bergson's Catholicism." New York Times, 13 Jan-
        uary 1941, p. 18, col. 8.

2823    MARKRICH, William Louis. "Hay Bergsonismo en la filosofía de
        José Enrique Rodó?" University of Washington Abstracts of
        Thesis and Faculty Bibliography, 8, 1944, 58.

2824    MARKS, Marcus M. "Hour with Dr. Henri Bergson: Discussion
        of Study and Travel Plan for College Students." Review of
        Reviews, 70, No. 5, November 1924, 505-506.

2825    MARMY, Emile. "Hommage à Henri Bergson." Monatsschrift d.
        Schweiz. Studentverein, 85, 1940-1941, 267.

2826    MARNEFF, J. "Bergson's and Husserl's Concepts of Intuition."
        Philosophical Quarterly, 23, No. 3, 1960, 169-180. The au-
        thor argues that we must use Husserl's method while main-
        taining Bergson's realism.

2827    MAROT, Jean.  "Le Cours de M. Bergson."  Renaissance Politi-
        que et Littéraire, 2, 31 janvier 1914.

2828    MARQUET, Urbain.  "Bergson, novitas florida... ."  Actes du
        Xe Congrès des Sociétés de Philosophie de Langue Française
        (Congrès Bergson).  Paris: Armand Colin, 1, 1959, 221-223.
        The author holds that the intellectualist climate in which
        Bergson lived and wrote excluded from thought a function
        of reason which can be termed inspiration.  Inspiration
        can be defined through its contrast with external pressure.
        In his "novitas florida" Bergson introduces us to a re-
        newed fecundity.

2829    MARQUET, Urbain.  "Table ronde: Psychologie, phénoménologie,
        intuition."  Actes du Xe Congrès des Sociétés de Philoso-
        phie de Langue Française (Congrès Bergson).  Paris: Armand
        Colin, 2, 1959, 15-37.

2830    MARSHALL, Henry Rutgers.  "Retentiveness and Dreams."  Mind,
        25, N.S. 98, April 1916, 207-202.  The author considers
        the views of Marshall, Freud, and Bergson on dreaming.

2831    MARTIN, Auguste.  "Le Dossier Bergson-Péguy."  Etudes Berg-
        soniennes, 8, 1968, 3-60.  This article contains correspon-
        dence between Bergson, Péguy, Joseph Lotte, and others.

2832    MARTIN, S.  "Bergson: Creative Evolution."  Princeton Theo-
        logical Review, 10, No. 1, January 1912, 116-118.

2833    MARTINETTI, Pietro.  La Libertà.  Milano: Libreria editrice
        Lombarda, 1928.

2834    MARTINEZ, Pas Enriqu.  "Dios en la filosofía de Henri Berg-
        son."  Homenaje a Bergson.  Córdoba, Argentina: Imprenta
        de la Universidad, 1936, 123-138.

2835    MARTINEZ, Paz Enrique.  Dios en la filosofía de Henri Berg-
        son.  Córdoba, Argentina: Imprenta de la Universidad, 1936,
        21.

2836    MARTINEZ, Raúl.  "El problema de la religión en Bergson."
        Homenaje a Bergson.  Córdoba, Argentina: Imprenta de la
        Universidad, 1936, 179-189.

2837    MARTINS, Diamantino.  "A memoria de Bergson."  Broteria, 34,
        No. 3, março 1942, 241-248.

2838    MARTINS, Diamantino.  "Bergson ante la mística cristiana."
        Manresa, 15, No. 2, 1943, 97-106.

2839    MARTINS, Diamantino. <u>Bergson</u>: <u>A</u> <u>intuição</u> <u>como</u> <u>método</u> <u>na</u>
<u>metafísica</u>. Porto: Tavares Martins, 1946, 327.

2840    MARTINS, Diamantino. <u>Bergson</u>: <u>La</u> <u>intuición</u> <u>como</u> <u>método</u> <u>en</u>
<u>la</u> <u>metafísica</u>. Trans. José H. López. Madrid: Bolanos y
Aquilar, 1943, 322.

2841    MARTINS, Diamantino. "La filosofía bergsoniana." <u>Revista</u>
<u>de</u> <u>Filosofía</u>, 2, No. 3, 1943, 315-346.

2842    MASCI, Filippo. "L'idealismo indeterminista." <u>Naples</u> <u>Aca-</u>
<u>demia</u> <u>di</u> <u>Scienze</u> <u>Moral</u> <u>e</u> <u>Politiche</u>, 30, No. 1, 1899, 35-
184.

2843    MASON, Joseph Warren Teets. "The Bergson Method Confirmed."
<u>North</u> <u>American</u> <u>Review</u>, 197, No. 686, January 1913, 90-104.

2844    MASON, Joseph Warren Teets. <u>Creative</u> <u>Freedom</u>. New York and
London: Harper and Brothers, 1926, 538. This book pre-
sents itself as a history of human spiritual evolution.
The author explains: "Readers of this book, familiar with
Bergson's writings, will realize how much the author owes
to him." (xii).

2845    MASON, Joseph Warren Teets. "Las influencias de Bergson en
el Japón." <u>La</u> <u>Prensa</u>, 12 noviembre 1939, Sec. 111.

2846    MASON, Joseph Warren Teets. "Professor Bergson's Principle."
<u>Nation</u>, 93, No. 2402, July 1911, 13. This is a letter to
the editor criticizing a review of <u>Matter</u> <u>and</u> <u>Memory</u>.

2847    MASON, Joseph Warren Teets. "Renacimiento del bergsonismo
en Los Estados Unidos." <u>La</u> <u>Prensa</u>, 5 mayo 1939, Sec. II.

2848    MASSIS, Henri. "A L'Ocasion du centenaire de la naissance
d'Henri Bergson: Proust et Bergson." <u>Revue</u> <u>de</u> <u>la</u> <u>Méditer-</u>
<u>ranée</u>, 19, No. 4-5, juillet-octobre 1959, 263-271.

2849    MASSIS, Henri. "Un Art de vivre." <u>Arts</u>, No. 776, 25-31 mai
1960, 1,3.

2850    MASSIS, Henri. "M. Henri Bergson ou le modernisme philosophique." <u>Cahiers</u> <u>d'Occident</u>, 2e Sér., 2, No. 4, 1928, 161-
170. This is a series of notes on Bergson's philosophy
written originally in December, 1913.

2851    MASSIS, Henri. "Les Cours du Collège de France." <u>Candide</u>,
27, No. 2, 14 janvier 1941.

2852 MASSIS, Henri. "La declinación del bergsonismo." Criterio, Año 1, No. 15, junio 1929, 457-460.

2853 "Massis, Henri. 'La declinación del bergsonismo'." Humani- dades, 19, 1929, 276. This is a brief mention of Massis' article in Criterio.

2854 MASSIS, Henri. Maurras et notre temps: Entretiens et souve- nirs. Paris: Plon, 1961, 452. "Edit. définitive augm. de documents inédits."

2855 MASSIS, Henri. "La Philosophie de M. Bergson critiquée par Pie X." Le Temps, No. 19044, 25 août 1913, 3.

2856 MASSIS, Henri. "Proust et Bergson." Revue de la Méditerra- née, 19, Nos. 92-93, 1959, 363-371.

2857 MASSON-OURSEL, Paul. "Henri Bergson et l'Inde." Revue de l'Histoire des Religions, No. 123, mars-juin 1941, 193-200. The author states that: "Notre conclusion sera que Bergson, malgré les allusions qu'il y a faites dans les Deux Sour- ces, prêta peu d'intérêt à l'expérience indienne." (200).

2858 MASSON-OURSEL, Paul. "L'Inde n'a-t-elle connu qu'un mysti- cisme incomplet? (Les Deux Sources et la mystique indien- ne)." Revue de Métaphysique et de Morale, 60, No. 3, juil- let-septembre 1933, 355-362. The author holds, against Bergson, that certain varieties of Indian mysticism de- serve to be called "complete."

2859 MASSON-OURSEL, Paul. "Mystique et logique: I. Ingénuité naturelle ou torsion? II. Logique bergsonienne." Revue Philosophique de la France et de l'Etranger, 131, Nos. 3- 8, mars-août 1941, 176-181.

2860 MASSON-OURSEL, Paul. "Mystique et logique: I. Ingénuité naturelle ou torsion? II. Logique bergsonienne." Etudes Bergsoniennes. Paris: Presses Universitaires de France, 1942, 55-61.

2861 MASUI, Jacques. "Sur Un Hommage à Bergson." Cahiers du Sud, No. 242, janvier 1942, 43-53.

2862 MASUR, Gerhard. "Bergson y la evolución creadora." Educa- ción, Ser. 1-2, No. 1, julio-agosto 1941, 25-31.

2863 MASUR, Gerhard. Prophets of Yesterday: Studies in European Culture 1890-1914. London: Weidenfeld and Nicholson, 1963, 482.

2864    MATCHINSKI, Mathhias.  "Image scientifique du monde: Son ca-
        ractère 'Cinémato-graphique' d'après Bergson et principe
        de causalité."  Actes du Xe Congrès des Sociétés de Philo-
        sophie de Langue Françsise (Congrès Bergson).  Paris: Ar-
        mand Colin, 1, 1959, 225-228.  What attitude should a sci-
        entist or philosopher have towards Bergson's celebrated
        critique of the cinematographic, atomizing scientific
        mind?  The author argues that the sciences can approach
        the ideal of continuity presented by Bergson and that the
        problem of the cinematographic image of the world is bound
        up in science with the problem of causality.

2865    MATCHINSKI, Mathhias.  "Table ronde: Matière, causalité, dis-
        continu."  Actes du Xe Congrès des Societés de Philosophie
        de Langue Française (Congrès Bergson).  Paris: Armand Co-
        lin, 2, 1959, 121-142.

2866    MATCHINSKI, Matthias.  "Table ronde: Physique."  Actes du Xe
        Congrès des Sociétés de Philosophie de Langue Françaisc
        (Congrès Bergson).  Paris: Armand Colin, 2, 1959.

2867    MATHEWS, Dean.  "Review of The Two Sources of Morality and
        Religion by Henri Bergson."  Fortnightly Review, N.S. 137,
        No. 4, April 1935, 495-496.  This is a schematic but lau-
        datory review.

2868    MATHEWSON, Louise.  Bergson's Theory of the Comic in the
        Light of English Comedy.  Lincoln, Nebraska: University of
        Nebraska Press, 1920, 27 (University of Nebraska Studies
        in Language, Literature, and Criticism, No. 5).

2869    MATHIEU, Vittorio.  "Review of Henri Bergson by G. Pflug."
        Philosophische Rundschau, 7, Nos. 3-4, 1959, 242-246.

2870    MATHIEU, Vittorio.  Bergson: Il profundo e la sua espres-
        sione.  Torino: Edizione di Filosofia, 1954, 292.  The es-
        sential idea of this study is that of conceptualizing Berg-
        son's intuitions in order to render them technically use-
        ful and to submit them, in a certain fashion, to experi-
        mental tests.

2871    MATHIEU, Vittorio.  "Bergson technicien."  Revue Internatio-
        nale de Philosophie, 13, No. 48, 1959, 173-186.  The au-
        thor argues that Bergson employs an entirely conceptual
        technique in order to attain a non-conceptual object.
        This technique involves the realization that concepts and
        images are equally metaphorical.  Images, however, manage
        through their plurality to suggest a reality beyond all

images.  Bergson's thought is an exemplary testimony to the effort to surpass the intelligence by means of the intelligence itself.

2872    MATHIEU, Vittorio.  "Bibliografia bergsoniana in Francia (1945-1959)."  Giornale di metafisica, 14, No. 6, 1959, 835-852.

2873    MATHIEU, Vittorio.  "Bibliografia bergsoniana in Germania (1945-1959)."  Giornale di metafisica, 14, No. 6, 1959, 853-856.

2874    MATHIEU, Vittorio.  "Il duale in Bergson."  Filosofia, 2, No. 2, 1951, 229-252.

2875    MATHIEU, Vittorio.  "La durata."  Filosofia, 3, No. 1, 1952, 3-32.

2876    MATHIEU, Vittorio.  "Review of Ecrits et paroles by Henri Bergson."  Filosofia, 9, No. 3, 1958, 500-501.

2877    MATHIEU, Vittorio.  "Interpreti vecchi e nuovi di Bergson." Humanitas, 14, No. 11, 1959, 822-836.

2878    MATHIEU, Vittorio.  "Intorno a Bergson: Filosofo della religione."  Studia Patavina, 8, No. 1, 1961, 79-93.

2879    MATHIEU, Vittorio.  "La memoria e il profundo."  Filosofia, 3, No. 4, ottobre 1952, 507-528.

2880    MATHIEU, Vittorio.  "Scienza e metafisica in Bergson."  Giornale di metafisica, 14, No. 6, 1959, 784-798.  For Bergson, the author argues, science and philosophy study different aspects of reality.  Their methods are therefore different.  Philosophy, possessing its own method and object, will be scientific and will be able to progress indefinitely like science.  Bergson's thought in this regard shows originality.

2881    MATHIEU, Vittorio.  "Storicismo e bergsonismo."  Cultura e scuola, No. 7, marzo-maggio 1963, 151-157.

2882    MATHIEU, Vittorio.  "Tempo, memoria, eternità: Bergson e Proust."  Archivio di filosofia, 21, No. 1, 1958, 161-173.

2883    MATHIEU, Vittorio.  "Tempo, memoria, eternità: Bergson e Proust."  Il Tempo.  Padova: Cedam, 1958, 256.

2884    MATHIEU, Vittorio. "Il tempo ritrovato: Bergson e Einstein."
        Filosofia, 4, No. 4, 1953, 625-656.

2885    MATISSE, Georges. L'Eternelle Illusion: Les Métaphysiques
        de la vie et de l'esprit. Paris: Editions d'Art et d'His-
        toire, 1942, 771.

2886    MAURENTIUS, F. "Du Caractère humanisant de l'éducation ar-
        tistique." Nouvelle Revue Pédagogique, 5, No. 7, 1950,
        409-411.

2887    MAUROIS, André. "Henri Bergson." Grands Ecrivains du demi-
        siècle. Paris: Club du Livre du Mois, 1957, 103-123.

2888    MAUROIS, André. Choses nues: Chroniques. Paris: Gallimard,
        1963, 278. Bergson and many others are discussed in this
        book.

2889    MAUROIS, André. De Proust à Camus. Paris: Perrin, 1964,
        346. Henri Bergson is discussed on pages 45-64.

2890    MAUROIS, André. De Proust a Camus. Barcelona: Ediciones
        G. P., 1967, 307.

2891    MAUROIS, André. Etudes littéraires. Vol. 1. New York:
        Edit. de la Maison Française, 1941. Valéry, Gide, Proust,
        Bergson, Claudel, and Péguy are discussed in this study.

2892    MAUROIS, André. From Proust to Camus: Profiles of Modern
        French Writers. London: Weidenfeld and Nicholson, 1967,
        368.

2893    MAUROIS, André. "Un Grand Vivant." Nouvelles Littéraires,
        No. 1677, 22 octobre 1959, 1 et 5. Maurois' visits with
        Bergson are discussed in this article.

2894    MAUROIS, André. "Il y a 25 ans mourait Bergson." Historia,
        21, No. 1, janvier 1966.

2895    MAUROIS, André. Von Proust bis Camus. München and Zürich:
        Droemer, 1964, 304. This study contains a section on Berg-
        son.

2896    MAURY, Lucien. "Le Bergsonisme." Revue Politique et Litté-
        raire, Revue Bleue, 51e Année, No. 4, 25 janvier 1913, 120-
        123. This is a review of Benda's Bergsonisme.

2897    MAVIT, Henri. "Bergson et l'existence créatrice." Etudes
        Bergsoniennes, 3, 141-148.

2898   MAVIT, Henri. "Bergson et le langage du philosophe." Vie
       et Langage, 8e Année, No. 86, mai 1959, 257-260.

2899   MAVIT, Henri. L'Intelligence créatrice. Paris: Presses Uni-
       versitaires de France, 1939, 155 (Bibliothèque de Philoso-
       phie Contemporaine). Mavit's study is permeated with Berg-
       son's ideas.

2900   MAVIT, Henri. "Le Message de Bergson." Culture Humaine, 9,
       No. 9, août 1947, 481-501.

2901   MAVIT, Henri. "Table ronde: Esthétique." Actes du Xe Con-
       grès des Sociétés de Philosophie de Langue Française (Con-
       grès Bergson). Paris: Armand Colin, 2, 1959, 193-210.

2902   MAXENCE, Jean. Positions: Valeur de l'inquiétude: Henri
       Bergson: Nécessité d'un dogmatisme: Pour continuer Jacques
       Rivière: Hiérarchie de la connaissance. Paris: Saint-Mi-
       chel, 1930, 247.

2903   MAY, William Eugene. "The Reality of Matter in the Meta-
       physics of Bergson." International Philosophical Quarter-
       ly, 10, No. 4, 1970, 611-642. The author holds that a de-
       tailed examination of both Bergson's text and Plotinian
       heritage reveals that matter, though entirely dependent on
       spirit in order to endure, is real in the sense that it is
       an authentic meontic principle within enduring principles.

2904   MAY, William Eugene. "The Reality of Matter in the Philoso-
       phy of Henri Bergson." Dissertation Abstracts, 29, No. 9,
       March 1969, 3184A.

2905   MAYER, Charles L. Man: Mind or Matter? Trans. with Preface
       by Harold A. Larrabee. Boston: Beacon Press, 1951, 200.
       Criticisms of Bergson's position in Matter and Memory are
       developed on pages 86-88.

2906   MAYER, Hans. "Welt und Wirkung Henri Bergsons." Deutsche
       Literatur und Weltliteratur Reden und Aufsätze. Berlin:
       Rütten und Loening, 1957, 517-530.

2907   MAYER, Hans. "Welt und Wirkung Henri Bergsons." Literatur
       der Übergangzeit: Essays. Wiesbaden, Germany: Limes Ver-
       lag, 1949, 98-116.

2908   MAYER, Willy. "Über Störungen des 'wiederkennens': Eine
       kritische Untersuchung im Anschluß an Matiere et mémoire
       von Henri Bergson." Zeitschrift für Patho-psychologie,

1, Mai 1912, 603-639.  Bergson's theories of memory and perception are examined in this essay, which contains a criticism of Bergson's data, a search for verification by means of observations, a summary, and conclusion.

2909    MAYNIAL, Edouard.  Précis de la littérature française moderne et contemporaine (1715-1925).  Paris: Delagrave, 1926, 268.  Bergson is discussed on pages 228-229.

2910    MAZZANTINI, Carlo.  "Evidenza e problematicità dell'iniziativa nella filosofia morale di Enrico Bergson."  Giornale di metafisica, 14, No. 6, 1959, 799-817.  This is a critical interpretation of Bergson's conceptions of intellectual activity, with special emphasis on the problem of "initiative" as it is presented in The Two Sources.  Bergson considers "initiative" to be the essential attribute of humanity.

2911    MAZZANTINI, Carlo.  Filosofia perenne e personalità filosofiche.  Padova: Cedam, 1942, 334.  Bergson's philosophy of religion is discussed on pages 189-206.  This article was published formerly in Convivium, 1932.

2912    MAZZANTINI, Carlo.  "La morale e la religione secondo Bergson."  Convivium, 4, No. 5, 1932.  This is a review of Les Deux Sources.

2913    MAZZANTINI, Carlo.  "Review of La Pensée et le mouvant by Henri Bergson."  Rivista di filosofia neoscolastica, 27, 1935, 544-545.

2914    MAZZANTINI, Carlo.  "Il tempo come slancio vitale nell'intuitionismo di Bergson."  Il Tempo, Anno 18, 1962, 43-54.

2915    MCCABE, Joseph.  "The Anti-rationalism of Bergson."  Literary Guide and Rationalist Review, N.S. No. 184, October 1911, 147-149.

2916    MCCABE, Joseph.  Principles of Evolution.  Baltimore, Warwicke, and York, 1913, 264.  Criticisms of Bergson may be found on pages 247-253.

2917    MCEVOY, P.  "Idea of God in the Philosophy of Bergson."  Irish Ecclesiastical Records, 44, October 1934, 367-379.

2918    MCGILVARY, Evander Bradley.  "James, Bergson, and Determinism."  University of California Publications, Modern Philology Section (Gayley Anniversary Papers), 11, 1922, 23-30.

2919    MCGILVARY, Evander Bradley.  "Review of Philosophy and Berg-
        son by A. D. Lindsay and Critical Exposition of Bergson's
        Philosophy by J. McKellar Stewart."  Philosophical Review,
        21, No. 5, September 1912, 598-602.

2920    MCGILVARY, Evander Bradley.  "The Two Theories of Conscious-
        ness in Bergson."  Journal of Philosophy, 9, No. 13, 1912,
        354-355.

2921    MCMAHON, C. Patrick.  "The Concept of Matter in the Metaphys-
        ics of Bergson."  Dissertation Abstracts, 26, No. 8, Febru-
        ary 1966, 4731.

2922    MEAD, George Herbert.  Movements of Thought in the Nine-
        teenth Century.  Chicago: University of Chicago Press,
        1936, 518.  Bergson is discussed on pages 292-325 and 496-
        510.

2923    MECKAUER, Walter.  "Der Intuitionismus und seine Elemente
        bei Henri Bergson."  Diss., Breslau, 1916.  Leipsic:
        Meiner, 1917, 160.

2924    MEHL, Roger.  "The Situation of Religious Philosophy in
        France."  Philosophic Thought in France and the United
        States.  Ed. Marvin Farber.  Albany, New York: State Uni-
        versity of New York Press, 1968, 249-264.  Bergson is dis-
        cussed on pages 259-261.

2925    MEIN, Margaret.  Proust's Challenge to Time.  Manchester,
        England: Manchester University Press, 1962, 144.  Refer-
        ences to Bergson are found throughout this work, especial-
        ly on pages 78-93.

2926    MEISNER, E.  "Henri Bergson: Philosoph."  Geisteskultur, 42,
        1933, 72-77.

2927    MEISSNER, J. W.  "Spirit and Matter: The Psychological Para-
        dox."  Journal of Existentialism,  8, No. 30, 1967-1968,
        179-202.

2928    MELLOR, Stanley Alfred.  Religion as Affected by Modern Sci-
        ence and Philosophy.  London: Lindsey Press, 1914, 256.
        Bergson is discussed on pages 147-166.

2929    MELZI, Giuseppe.  "L'imortalità dell'anima nella filosofia
        di H. Bergson."  Rivista di filosofia neoscolastica, 42,
        No. 3, 1950, 238-255.

2930   MENDILOW, Adam Abraham. _Time and the Novel_. London: Peter
       Nevill, 1952, 244. The introduction is by J. Isaacs.

2931   MENDILOW, Adam Abraham. _Time and the Novel_. New York: Hu-
       manitas Press, 1965, 245. Bergson, Proust, Gide, and oth-
       ers are discussed in this study.

2932   MENNICKEN, Peter. "Die Philosophie Henri Bergsons und der
       Geist modernen Kunst." Diss., Köln, 1921, 116.

2933   MENSCH, L. "Review of _Le Rire_ by Henri Bergson." _Polybib-
       lion_, 2e Sér., 52 (Partie littéraire), 1900, 326-327.

2934   MENTRE, F. "Une Nouvelle Philosophie de la sensation." _Re-
       vue de Philosophie_, 33, Nos. 1-2, janvier-février 1933, 76-
       84. This study concerns the works of M. Pradines, "le dis-
       tingué disciple de Bergson."

2935   MERCANTI, P. _Il pensiero filosofico contemporaneo e la filo-
       sofia del Bergson_. Roma: Signorelli, 1915.

2936   MERCANTON, Jacques. "La Philosophie bergsonienne et le pro-
       blème de l'art." _Henri Bergson_. Ed. Béguin and Thévenaz,
       149-156. The author asserts that Bergson's philosophy is
       ideally suited to explicating the nature of art. He exam-
       ines aspects of Bergson's thought that lend themselves to
       such explications.

2937   MERCANTON, Jacques. _Poètes de l'univers_. Paris: Skira,
       1947, 230. Bergson is discussed on pages 209-216. Valéry
       is also discussed in this study.

2938   MERCANTON, Jacques. "Une Visite à Bergson." _Labyrinthe.
       Journal Mensuel des Lettres et des Arts_, 2, No. 13, 13 oc-
       tobre 1945, 6.

2939   MERCIER, André. "Table ronde: Physique." _Actes du Xe Con-
       grès des Sociétés de Philosophie de Langue Française_ (Con-
       grès Bergson). Paris: Armand Colin, 2, 1959, 65-87.

2940   MERCIER, Désiré. "Vers L'Unité." _Revue Néo-scolastique de
       Philosophie_, 20e Année, No. 3, 1913, 253-278. The author
       views Bergson as a monist and pantheist.

2941   MEREDITH, J. C. "Critical Side of Bergson's Philosophy."
       _Westminster Review_, 167, No. 1, February 1912, 194-206.

2942   MERLAN, Philip. "A Certain Aspect of Bergson's Philosophy."
       _Philosophy and Phenomenological Research_, 2, No. 4, June

1942, 529-545.  "Bergson's great discovery is, that it is
not only with our instincts, that we serve, but that even
our intellectual life is service . . . ."  Merlan's article contains interesting comments on the sources of Bergson's optimism.

2943    MERLAN, Philip.  "Le Problème de l'irrationalisme dans les
Deux Sources de Bergson."  Revue Philosophique de la France et de l'Etranger, 149, No. 3, juillet-septembre 1959,
305-319.  The author concludes: "Parce qu'il n'y a pas de
dualisme dans toutes les autres branches de ses speculations philosophiques.  Tout y est harmonie; il en est ainsi de l'intellect et de l'intuition.  L'irrationalité elle-
même n'est que la rationalité en devenir."  (319).

2944    MERLEAU-PONTY, Maurice.  "Bergson se faisant."  Eloge de la
philosophie et autres essais.  Paris: Gallimard, 1953, 288-
308.

2945    MERLEAU-PONTY, Maurice.  "Discours sur Bergson."  Bulletin
de la Société Française de Philosophie, 54, No. 1, 1940,
35-45.

2946    MERLEAU-PONTY, Maurice.  Eloge de la philosophie: Leçon inaugurale faite au Collège de France, le 15 janvier 1953.
Paris: Gallimard, 1953, 93.

2947    MERLEAU-PONTY, Maurice.  Résumés de cours: Collège de France,
1952-1960.  Ed. C. Lefort.  Paris: Gallimard, 1968, 182.
Bergson's philosophy of nature is discussed on pages 109-
111.

2948    MERLEAU-PONTY, Maurice.  Signes.  Paris: Gallimard, 1960,
439.  "Bergson se faisant" is on pages 221-249.

2949    MERLEAU-PONTY, Maurice.  Signs.  Trans. R. C. McCleary.
Evanston, Illinois: Northwestern University Press, 1964,
355.  "Bergson in the Making," which is on pages 182-191,
appeared originally in Bulletin de la Société Française
de Philosophie.

2950    MERLEAU-PONTY, Maurice.  "A Tribute to Bergson on the Occasion of the Bergson Centennial in Paris, 1959."  The Bergsonian Heritage.  Ed. Thomas Hanna.  New York and London:
Columbia University Press, 1962, 133-149.  This is a general, highly appreciative survey of Bergson's thought.

2951    MERLEAU-PONTY, Maurice.  L'Union de l'âme et du corps chez
Malebranche, Biran et Bergson: Notes prises au cours de

Maurice Merleau-Ponty à l'Ecole normale supérieure (1947-1948). Ed. Jean Duprun. Paris: Vrin, 1968, 136.

2952    MESNARD, Paul. "Catholicisme et bergsonisme." Revue Apologétique, 55, Nos. 4-5, avril-mai 1933, 546-557.

2953    MESNARD, Pierre. "La Doctrine de l'héroïsme moral considéré comme clef de voûte de la philosophie bergsonienne." Actes du Xe Congrès des Sociétés de Philosophie de Langue Française (Congrès Bergson). Paris: Armand Colin, 1, 1959, 227-233. Bergson's doctrine of moral heroism is the justification of his entire doctrine of liberty, the author holds, since at this level liberty becomes creative of superior ideas.

2954    MESNARD, Pierre. "Table ronde: Morale." Actes du Xe Congrès des Sociétés de Philosophie de Langue Française (Congrès Bergson). Paris: Armand Colin, 2, 1959, 237-257.

2955    MESSAUT, Jourdain. "Autour des Deux Sources." Revue Thomiste, N.S. 16, No. 77, 1933, 466-502.

2956    MESSER, August. "Bergsons 'intuitive' Philosophie." Zeitschrift für christliche Erzeigwiss, 7, 1914, 74ff.

2957    METALNIKOV, S. "Les Facteurs psychiques de l'evolution." Revue de Synthèse, 16, No. 2, 1938, 107-119.

2958    METZ, André. "L'Ame et le corps d'après Bergson." Revue de Philosophie, 32, No. 1, janvier 1932, 7-35.

2959    METZ, André. Bergson et le bergsonisme. Paris: Vrin, 1933, 253. The author is highly critical of both Bergson and Bergsonism.

2960    METZ, Andre. "Bergson et la notion d'espace." Archives de Philosophie, 28, No. 3, 1965, 439-444. This is a review of Heidsieck's Henri Bergson et la notion d'espace stressing the importance of relativity theory.

2961    METZ, André. "Bergson, Einstein et les relativistes." Archives de Philosophie, 22, No. 3, juillet 1959, 369-384. The author argues that Edouard Le Roy played a significant role in the error which Bergson made in interpreting relativity. In 1937 Le Roy published an article rectifying Bergson's error. Moreover, Bergson's conception of duration can be shown to harmonize with Einstein's conception of time and to complete it. But Bergson misunderstood Ein-

stein's conception of time, in part because he confused
relativity with relativism.

2962    METZ, André. "Bergson et Meyerson." Actes du Xe Congrès
des Sociétés de Philosophie de Langue Française (Congrès
Bergson). Paris: Armand Colin, 1, 1959, 235-237. The author reviews Meyerson's bibliography and quotes at length
from Bergson's review of Meyerson's Identity and Reality.

2963    METZ, André. "Un Dernier Mot d'André Metz." Revue de Phi-
losophie, 31, No. 4, 1924, 440. This is the author's fi-
nal reply to Bergson, including Albert Einstein's opinions.
It is translated, with an introduction, in Bergson and the
Evolution of Physics, Ed. and Trans. with Intro. P. A. Y.
Gunter, 189-190.

2964    METZ, Andre. "Un Prochain Ouvrage sur Bergson." Documents
de la Vie Intellectuelle, 1, No. 4, 20 janvier 1930, 67-68.

2965    METZ, André. "Relativité et relativisme." Revue Philosophique de la France et de l'Etranger, 51, Nos. 1-2, janvier-
février 1926, 63-87. This essay is a criticism of Duration and Simultaneity.

2966    METZ, André. La Relativité: Exposé élémentaire des théories
d'Einstein et réfutation des erreurs contenues dans les ouvrages les plus notoires. Paris: Chiron, 1923, 156. The
preface is by Jean Becquerel. In the second part of this
book Metz criticizes critics of relativity theory, including Bergson.

2967    METZ, André. "Réplique à M. André Metz." Revue de Philosophie, 31, No. 4, 1924, 437-439. The author replies to
Bergson's criticisms. This essay is translated, with an
introduction, in Bergson and the Evolution of Physics, Ed.
P. A. Y. Gunter, 186-189.

2968    METZ, André. "Le Temps d'Einstein et la philosophie: A Propos de l'ouvrage de M. Bergson, Durée et simultanéité."
Revue de Philosophie, 31, No. 1, 1924, 56-58. This criticism of Bergson's thought is translated, with an introduction, in Bergson and the Evolution of Physics, Ed. P. A. Y.
Gunter, 135-265.

2969    METZ, André. Temps, espace, relativité. Paris: Beauchesne,
1937, 211. Bergson is discussed on pages 69, 79, and 82-
89.

2970    MEYER, François. Pour connaître la pensée de Bergson. Gre-
        noble: Bordas, 1944, 124.

2971    MEYER, Hans. "Die Lebensphilosophie in Frankreich: Henri
        Bergson." Geschichte der abendländischen Weltanschauung.
        Vol. 5. Die Weltanschauung der Gegenwart. Wurzburg, Ger-
        many: Schöningh, 1949, 245-266.

2972    MEYERSON, Emile. "Dans la lignée des grands créateurs."
        Nouvelles Littéraires, No. 322, 15 décembre 1928, 1.

2973    MEYERSON, Emile. De L'Explication dans les sciences. Paris:
        Payot, 1927, 784. Bergson is mentioned on pages 32, 191,
        198, 220, 333, 511, 512, 527, 586, 674, and 681.

2974    MEYERSON, Emile. Identité et réalité. 2e éd. Paris: Félix
        Alcan, 1912, 242.

2975    MEYERSON, Emile. Identity and Reality. London: Allen and
        Unwin; New York: Macmillan, 1930, 495. Bergson's concept
        of absolute motion is discussed on page 131; his ideas con-
        cerning the ether on page 257; on the relativity of sense
        qualities on page 296; on the electromagnetic theory of
        light on page 296; on memory on pages 354-355; on the "seg-
        mentation of reality" on pages 356-357; on constants and
        variables on pages 436-440.

2976    MEYERSON, Emile. Identity and Reality. Trans. Kate Loewen-
        berg. New York: Dover Publications, 1942, 495. Bergson
        is discussed on pages 131, 153, 257, 292, 295-296, 307,
        354-357, 361, 366, 378, 384, 433, and 436.

2977    MICHAUD, Guy. Message poétique du symbolisme. Paris: Nizet,
        1947. Vol. 3, L'Univers poétique, contains an essay enti-
        tled "Bergson philosophe du temps perdu." It appears on
        pages 486-492.

2978    MIEVILLE, Henri. "La Philosophie religieuse de Bergson:
        Questions de méthode." Studia Philosophica, 19, 1959,
        173-192. The author argues that Bergson's shift from a
        biological monism to a theistic position involves changes
        in his methodology.

2979    MIEVILLE, Henri. La Philosophie religieuse de Bergson: Ques-
        tions de méthode. Basel, Switzerland: Verlag für Recht
        und Ges., 1959, 20. This essay is reprinted from Studia
        Philosophica.

2980    MIGNARD. "Automatisation et spontanéité: Pathologie mentale et psychologie bergsonienne." Journal de Psychologie Normale et Pathologique, 11, 1914, 199-220.

2981    MIKUMO, Natsumi. "Essay on the Moral and Religious Philosophy of Bergson and Blondel." Philosophy, No. 32, 1956, 4-6. This article is in Japanese.

2982    MILET, Albert. "Les Cahiers du P. Marechal: Sources, doctrines et influences subies." Revue Néo-scolastique de Philosophie, 2e Sér., 43, No. 67-68, 1940-1945, 225-251. Bergson is discussed on pages 238-241.

2983    MILHAUD, Jean. A Bergson: La Patrie reconnaissante. Paris: Imprimerie nationale, 1967, 78. "Texte précédé d'une lettre de M. André Maurois...à Jean Milhaud. Post-face de M. Jean Guitton." This is an account of successful efforts to place a plaque dedicated to Bergson in the Panthéon.

2984    MILLAS, Jorge. "Goethe en Bergson." Asomante, 5, No. 4, oct.-dic. 1949, 104-116.

2985    MILLER, Dickinson S. "Mr. Bergson's Theories: What is Their Importance?" New Republic, 26, No. 333, 20 April 1921, 242-246. This is a highly critical review of Mind-Energy.

2986    MILLER, Lucius Hopkins. "Bergson and Religion." Biblical World, N.S. 46, No. 5, November 1915, 285-293.

2987    MILLER, Lucius Hopkins. Bergson and Religion. New York: Henry Holt and Company, 1916, 275.

2988    MILLER, Lucius Hopkins. "The Religious Implications of Bergson's Doctrine Regarding Intuition and the Primacy of Spirit." The Journal of Philosophy, 12, No. 23, 1915, 617-632. The author holds that Bergson's thought leads to the primacy of spirit and hence to a religious outlook.

2989    MILLET, Raymond. "Révision de quelques jugements sur la pensée de Bergson." Le Temps, No. 26323, 23 septembre 1933, 4.

2990    MILLOT, Albert. "L'Intérêt pédagogique de la doctrine de Bergson." Etudes Bergsoniennes. Paris: Presses Universitaires de France, 1942, 199-222.

2991    MILLOT, Albert. L'Intérêt pédagogique de la doctrine de Bergson. Paris: Presses Universitaires de France, 1943,

24. This article was first published in the Revue Philosophique de la France et de l'Etranger, 1941.

2992    MILLOT, Albert. "L'Intérêt pédagogique de la doctrine de Bergson." Revue Philosophique de la France et de l'Etranger, 131, Nos. 3-8, mars-aout 1941, 218-243.

2993    MILLOT, Albert. La Théorie bergsonienne de l'obligation morale et ses conséquences pédagogiques. Paris: Editions des Cours Jarach, 1932, 16. This essay was first published in Littérature, Philosophie, Pédagogie, July 1932.

2994    MILORADOVICH, K. M. "Два учения о времени: Канта и Бергсона." Журнал Министерства Народного Просвещения, No. 18, 1913, 323-329.

2995    MIN, Anselm Kyongsuk. "An Evolutionary View of Religion: Henri Bergson." Diss., St. Louis, 1967.

2996    MINKOWSKI, Eugène. "Les Idées de Bergson en psychopathologie." Nouvelles Littéraires, No. 324, 29 décembre 1928, 7.

2997    MINKOWSKI, Eugène. "Les Idées de Bergson en psychopathologie." Recueil d'articles 1923-1965. Paris: Librairie Le Livre Psychologique; Lille, France: Librairie Le Furet du Nord, 1965, 43-46.

2998    MINKOWSKI, Eugène. "L'Irrationnel: Donnée immédiate." Revue Philosophique de la France et de l'Etranger, 84, No. 3, 1959, 289-304. The transcendance of becoming, as an immediate datum of consciousness, consists in what is most immanent in it and in what follows from it. The author has reached this conclusion by proceeding along the path traced out by Bergson, though he has deviated from Bergson's thought in part through his adherence to Bleuler. These "infidelities," however, are only the expression of a dialogue.

2999    MINKOWSKI. Eugène. Lived Time: Phenomemological and Psychopathological Studies. Evanston, Illinois: Northwestern University Press, 1970, 455. This is an application of Bergsonian ideas--with certain additional insights--to the problems of psychopathology.

3000    MINKOWSKI, Eugène. "Métaphore et symbole." Cahiers Internationaux de Symbolisme, No. 5, 1964, 47-55. This essay deals with the function of symbolism in Bergson and Bachelard.

3001   MINKOWSKI, Eugène. "La Pure Durée et la durée vécue."
       Actes du Xe Congrès des Sociétés de Philosophie de Langue
       Française (Congres Bergson). Paris: Armand Colin, 1, 1959,
       239-241. The terms "pure duration" and "felt duration"
       are employed by Bergson in both Time and Free Will and Cre-
       ative Evolution. What encompasses these two ideas? How
       are they related?

3002   MINKOWSKI, Eugène. La Schizophrénie: Psychopathologie des
       schizoïdes et des schizophrènes. Paris: Payot, 1927, 268.

3003   MINKOWSKI, Eugène. La Schizophrénie: Psychopathologie des
       schizoïdes et des schizophrènes. Paris: Desclée de
       Brouwer, 1954, 254.

3004   MINKOWSKI, Eugène. "Sur Le Chemin d'une psychologie formel-
       le." Tijdschrift voor Philosophie, 12, No. 3, 1950, 504-
       530. Minkowski holds that a new category ("le vécu")
       should be added by psychology to its categories "conscient"
       and "inconscient." This essay was originally written in
       1938.

3005   MINKOWSKI, Eugène. "Table ronde: Durée et mémoire." Actes
       du Xe Congrès des Sociétés de Philosophie de Langue Fran-
       çaise (Congrès Bergson). Paris: Armand Colin, 2, 1959,
       41-61.

3006   MINKOWSKI, Eugène. "Table ronde: Morale." Actes du Xe Con-
       grès des Sociétés de Philosophie de Langue Française (Con-
       grès Bergson). Paris: Armand Colin, 2, 1959, 237-257.

3007   MINKOWSKI, Eugene. "Table ronde: Psychologie, phénoménolo-
       gie, intuition." Actes du Xe Congrès des Sociétés de Phi-
       losophie de Langue Française (Congrès Bergson). Paris:
       Armand Colin, 2, 1959, 15-37.

3008   MINKOWSKI, Eugène. "Table ronde: Sources et histoire du
       bergsonisme." Actes du Xe Congrès des Sociétés de Philo-
       sophie de Langue Française (Congrès Bergson). Paris: Ar-
       mand Colin, 2, 1959, 213-233.

3009   MINKOWSKI, Eugène. Le Temps vécu: Etudes phénoménologiques
       et psychopathologiques. Paris: d'Arthey, 1933.

3010   MINKOWSKI, Eugène. Vers Une Cosmologie: Fragments philoso-
       phiques. 1-2 éds. Paris: Aubier, 1936, 1967, 263.

3011   MIRABENT, F. "A Propósito de Bergson." Revista de Ideas
       Estéticas, 2, No. 8, 1944, 79-89.

3012    MIROGLIO, Abel. "Table ronde: Matière, causalité, discon-
        tinu." Actes du Xe Congrès des Sociétés de Philosophie de
        Langue Française (Congrès Bergson). Paris: Armand Colin,
        2, 1959, 121-142.

3013    MIROGLIO, Abel. "Trois Réfutations du parallélisme psycho-
        physiologique." Revue Philosophique de la France et de
        l'Etranger, 42, Nos. 11-12, novembre-décembre 1937, 215-
        254.

3014    MIROGLIO, Abel and Yvonne-Delphée. "Réflexions sur les Deux
        Sources de la morale et de la religion." Revue Philosophi-
        que de la France et de l'Etranger, 117, No. 1, janvier-fé-
        vrier 1934, 50-103.

3015    "Mise à l'Index des oeuvres de Bergson." Acta Apostolicae
        Sedis, 12  June 1914, 314-315. Also in Mélanges, 1089.
        Time and Free Will, Matter and Memory, and Creative Evolu-
        tion are in this proclamation placed on the Roman Catholic
        "Index."

3016    MISIAK, Henry K. The Philosophical Roots of Scientific Psy-
        chology. New York: Fordham University Press, 1961, 142.
        Bergson's criticisms of associationism are mentioned on
        page 99; the influence of Bergson on psychology is men-
        tioned on pages 116-118 and 123.

3017    MITCHELL, Arthur. "Review of L'Evolution créatrice by Henri
        Bergson." Journal of Philosophy, Psychology, and Scientif-
        ic Methods, 5, No. 22, 22 October 1908, 603-612.

3018    MITCHELL, Arthur. "Review of La Pensée et le mouvant by Hen-
        ri Bergson." Philosophical Review, 45, No. 1, 1935, 94-95.

3019    MITCHELL, Arthur. Studies in Bergson's Philosophy. Law-
        rence, Kansas: University Press, 1914, 115.

3020    MITCHELL, Arthur. "Studies on Bergson." Bulletin of the
        University of Kansas, 20, No. 4, 1915, 1-115.

3021    "Review of Modern Science and the Illusions of Professor
        Bergson by Hugh S. R. Elliot." Contemporary Review, 101,
        No. 6, June 1912, 905-906.

3022    MOISANT, Xavier. "Dieu dans la philosophie de M. Bergson."
        Revue de Philosophie, 6, No. 5, mai 1905, 495-518. The au-
        thor indicates how Bergson argues from the experience of
        duration to the existence of God.

3023   MOISANT, Xavier.  "La Notion de multiplicité dans la philo-
       sophie de Bergson."  Revue de Philosophie, 2, No. 6, juin
       1902, 447-465.  Bergson's position is virtually identical
       with scholasticism's, according to the author.

3024   MOKIEVSKI, P. "Философия Анри Бергсона." Русское
       богатство, 6,1909, 153-158.

3025   MOLINA, Enrique.  "El espíritu según Bergson."  Revista de
       Filosofía, 3, No. 2, marzo 1917, 203-214.

3026   MOLINA, Enrique.  La filosofía de Bergson.  Santiago, Chile:
       Imprenta Barcelona, 1916, 128.

3027   MOLINA, Enrique.  Dos filósofos contemporáneos: Guyau, Berg
       son.  1-2 ed.  Santiago, Chile: Nascimento, 1925, 1948,
       389.

3028   MOLINA, Enrique.  "La verdad y el método de Bergson."  Revis-
       ta de Filosofía, 2, No. 6, noviembre 1916, 321-341.

3029   MOLINA, Garmendia (Enrique).  "Scienza e filosofia nel pen-
       siero di Henri Bergson."  Annuario Liceo-ginnasio Giovanni
       Plana in Alessandria, 1929-1934.

3030   MOLINA, Garmendia (Enrique).  Proyecciones de la intuición:
       Nuevos estudios sobre la filosofía bergsoniana.  Santiago,
       Chile: Prensas de la Universidad de Chile, 1935.

3031   MOMIGLIANO, Attilio.  "L'origine del comico."  Cultura filo-
       sofica, 3, No. 4, 1909, 406-433.

3032   MONAKOW, Constantin von and MOURGUE, Raoul.  Introduction
       biologique à l'étude de la neurologie et de la psychopa-
       thologie: Intégration et désintégration de la fonction.
       Paris: Félix Alcan, 1928, 420.  This book applies Berg-
       sonian ideas to neurology and psychopathology.

3033   MONDAIN, G.  "Remarques sur la théorie matérialiste."  Foi
       et Vie, 11, No. 12, 15 juin 1908, 369-373.

3034   MONK, Arthur W.  "Was Bergson an Irrationalist?"  Calcutta
       Review, 180, No. 2, August 1966, 89-93.

3035   MONOD, Wilfred.  Quelques Philosophes de France.  Libourne,
       France: Gélix, 1941, 55.  A chapter on Bergson is included
       in this book.

3036    MONROE, Warner. "The Vital Impulse and Spiritual Aspiration." Ethics, 59, No. 3, April 1949, 201-210.

3037    MONROE, Warner. "The Vital Impulse as a Basis for Morality: A Critical Development of Bergson's Position." Diss., Washington at Seattle, 1948.

3038    MONTAGNE, H.-A. "Bergson et ses plus récents commentateurs." Questions Actuelles, 114, No. 20, 17 mai 1913, 631-638. This essay was first published in Revue Thomiste, 1913.

3039    MONTAGUE, William Pepperell. Great Visions of Philosophy: Varieties of Speculative Thought in the West From the Greeks to Bergson. La Salle, Illinois: Open Court, 1950, 484 (Paul Carus Lectures, 4th Series). Chapter 23, entitled "Bergson and a World on the March," appears on pages 412-426.

3040    MONTCHEUIL, Y. de. "Review of Le Dieu de Bergson by Rideau." Revue Apologétique, 55, No. 7, août 1933, 129-143.

3041    MONTCHEUIL, Y. de. "Une Thèse de philosophie religieuse sur Bergson." Revue Apologétique, 56, No. 6, juillet 1933, 5-25.

3042    MONTFORT, Eugène. Vingt-cinq ans de littérature française. Vol. 1. Paris: Librairie de France, 1922, 389. Bergson is discussed on pages 108-113.

3043    MONTIANI, Oddino. Bergson e il suo umanismo integrale. Padova: Cedam, 1957, 307.

3044    MONTIERO PACHECO, Maria Cândida de Costa Reis. "A dimensão temporal definidora duma antropologia em S. Gregório de Nissa e Bergson." Actas da Assembleia Internacional de Estudios Filosóficos. Braga, Portugal: Faculdade de Filosofia, 1969, 153-164.

3045    MONTIERO PACHECO, Maria Cândida da Costa Reis. "A dimensão temporal definidora duma antropologia em S. Grégorio de Nissa e Bergson." Revista Portuguesa de Filosofia, 25, Nos. 3-4, 1969, 153-164.

3046    MOON, H. Kay. "Alejandro Casona and Henri Bergson." Symposium Unamuno, 55, 1966, 345-359.

3047    MOORE, Addison W. "Bergson and Pragmatism." Philosophical Review, 21, No. 4, July 1912, 397-414. The author argues

that Bergson is not a pragmatist.  He suggests many criticisms of Bergson from a pragmatist standpoint.

3048     MOORE, Charles Leonard.  "The Return of the Gods."  Dial, 53,
         No. 634, 16 November 1912, 371-372.

3049     MOORE, Jared S.  "Duration and Value."  Philosophical Review,
         22, No. 3, 1913, 304-306.  The author argues that an analo-
         gy between Bergson's theories and Munsterberg's view of
         the relations between metaphysics and psychology may be ap-
         plied to the problem of time.  Time is psychologically dis-
         crete; but from the standpoint of value it is continuous.

3050     MOORE, John Morrison.  Theories of Religious Experience with
         Special Reference to James, Otto, and Bergson.  New York:
         Round Table Press, 1938, 253.

3051     MORANDI, F.  "Il Congresso dellà Società di Filosofia di Lin-
         gua Francesi: Bergson et Nous."  Gregorianum, 41, No. 1,
         1960, 78-79.

3052     MOREAU, Joseph.  "Table ronde: Matière, causalité, disconti-
         nu."  Actes du Xe Congrès des Sociétés de Philosophie de
         Langue Française (Congrès Bergson).  Paris: Armand Colin,
         2, 1959, 121-142.

3053     MOREAU, Joseph.  "Table ronde: Sources et histoire du berg-
         sonisme."  Actes du Xe Congrès des Sociétés de Philosophie
         de Langue Française (Congrès Bergson).  Paris: Armand Co-
         lin, 2, 1959, 213-233.

3054     MOREAU, Pierre.  "Review of Henri Bergson et les lettres
         françaises by Roméo Arbour."  Revue d'Histoire Littéraire
         de la France, 58, No. 2, avril-juin 1958, 249-259.

3055     MOREAU, Pierre.  "Review of Henri Bergson et les lettres
         françaises by Roméo Arbour."  Revue de Littérature Compa-
         rée, 37, No. 3, 1963, 480-483.

3056     MORESCO, Gino.  "Intellectualismo y espiritualidad."  Cri-
         terio, 2, No. 79, 5 septiembre 1929, 11.

3057     MORGAN, Charles.  "Bergson und die Maritains oder die Frei-
         heit vom Materialismus."  Von der Freiheit des Geistes:
         Essays.  Ed. Gerd van Bebber and Ernst Sander.  Stuttgart:
         Dt. Verl.-Anst., 1956, 173-180.

3058    MORGAN, Conwy Lloyd. Instinct and Experience. New York:
        Macmillan; London: Methuen, 1912, 299. See especially
        Chapter VII, "The Philosophy of Instinct," 204-240.

3059    MORIES, A. "Bergson and Mysticism." Westminster Review,
        177, No. 3, June 1912, 687-689.

3060    MORKOVSKY, Mary Christine. "Bergson's Exorcism of the Phan-
        tom of Nothingness." Modern Schoolman, 48, No. 2, 1971,
        135-150. The ideas of nothing and of possibility are nec-
        essary for practical knowledge. But, the author holds,
        intellectualist philosophies that reach reality only by
        passing through them reduce spontaneity to rearrangement
        and freedom to determinism. Negation, possibility, and
        necessity are for Bergson always subordinate to and de-
        rived from creatively evolving duration.

3061    MORKOVSKY, Mary Christine. "Crystallized Creativity: Berg-
        son's View of Customs." Humanitas, 7, No. 1, Spring 1971,
        37-48. The author argues that for Bergson, creativity gen-
        erates customs. The view that customs generate or account
        for creativity is false.

3062    MORKOVSKY, Mary Christine. "Intellectual Analysis in Berg-
        son's Theory of Knowing." Journal of the History of Phi-
        losophy, 10, No. 1, January 1972, 43-54. For Bergson, in-
        tellectual analysis is a necessary condition of the most
        valuable kind of knowledge, the intuition of duration.
        The author examines Bergsonian analyses of the human self
        and life. These follow a brief outline Bergson gives of
        his method in Creative Evolution.

3063    MORKOVSKY, Theresa Clare. "Freedom in Henri Bergson's Meta-
        physics." Dissertation Abstracts, 27, No. 9, March 1967,
        3084A.

3064    MORLAND, Jacques. "Une Heure chez M. Bergson." L'Opinion,
        4e Année, No. 33, 19 août 1911, 241-242. This article is
        quoted in Mercure de France, 93, 16 septembre 1911, 413ff.

3065    MOROT-SIR, Edouard. "What Bergson Means to us Today." The
        Bergsonian Heritage. Ed. Thomas Hanna. New York and Lon-
        don: Columbia University Press, 1962, 35-53. The author
        suggests points at which Bergson's philosophy can have fu-
        ture impact on biological and sociological thought and on
        psychology.

3066     MORRA, Gianfranco. "Morale della pressione e morale
         dell'aspirazione secondo Bergson." Ethica, 2, No. 1, 1963,
         41-53.

3067     MORRIS, Charles William. Six Theories of Mind. Chicago:
         University of Chicago Press, 1932, 337. Chapter I is en-
         titled "Mind as Process: Hegel, Bradley, Bosanquet, Berg-
         son, Gentile."

3068     MORRISON, David. "The Treatment of History by Philosophers."
         Proceedings of the Aristotelian Society, N.S. 14, 1913-
         1914, 291-321. Bergson and individual personality are dis-
         cussed on pages 308-311.

3069     MORROW, Carolyn. "An Analysis of 'Poema de un dia': The Phi-
         losophy of Bergson in Machado's Concept of Time." Romance
         Notes, 11, No. 2, 1960, 149-153. The author discusses the
         influence of Bergson on Machado.

3070     MORSE, Samuel French. "Wallace Stevens, Bergson, Pater."
         ELH, 31, No. 1, March 1964, 1-34.

3071     MORSELLI, Emilio. Un nuovo idealismo: H. Bergson. Udine:
         Tosoline e Jacob, 1900.

3072     MORSIER, Edouard de. Silhouettes d'hommes célebres: Bergson,
         al. Genève: Editions du Mont-Blanc, 1947, 135.

3073     MORUZZI, G. "Bergson e la scienza." Studium, 50, No. 1,
         1954, 3-10.

3074     MOSCHETTI, Andrea Mario. "S. Agostino e il bergsonismo."
         S. Agostino e le grandi correnti della filosofia agosti-
         niana: Atti del Congresso Italiano di Filosofia Agostinia-
         na, Roma 20-23 ottobre 1954. Macerata, Italy: Edizioni
         Agostiniane, 1956, 271-277.

3075     MOSSE-BASTIDE, Rose-Marie. "Review of Adès chez Bergson: Re-
         liques inconnues d'une amitié by A. Adès." Revue Philoso-
         phique de la France et de l'Etranger, 84, No. 3, 1959, 403-
         406.

3076     MOSSE-BASTIDE, Rose-Marie. Bergson éducateur. Paris: Pres-
         ses Universitaires de France, 1955, 465. This book is an
         excellent study of Bergson's concept of education, in the
         broadest sense, and of Bergson's life and opinions.

3077     MOSSE-BASTIDE, Rose-Marie. Bergson et Plotin. Paris: Pres-
         ses Universitaires de France, 1959, 422. The author ar-

gues that Bergson and Plotinus share the same approach to metaphysics through psychological experience, an identical concept of creative causality, and the same description of the means of salvation.  But for Bergson ecstasy is not a "point of arrival."

3078    MOSSE-BASTIDE, Rose-Marie.  "Bergson et Spinoza."  Revue de Métaphysique et de Morale, 54, No. 1, 1949, 67-82.

3079    MOSSE-BASTIDE, Rose-Marie.  "Bibliographie des questions d'enseignement et d'éducation."  Bergson éducateur.  Paris: Presses Universitaires de France, 1955, 449-450.  This bibliography contains references to articles and books in which Bergson's educational ideas are discussed.  It is very brief.

3080    MOSSE-BASTIDE, Rose-Marie, Ed.  Ecrits et paroles.  Paris: Presses Universitaires de France, 1957-1959, 3 vols., 665 (Bibliothèque de Philosophie Contemporaine).  This is a relatively complete collection of talks, reports, letters, and other writings by Bergson.

3081    MOSSE-BASTIDE, Rose-Marie.  "Introduction à la traduction, Quid Aristoteles de Loco Senserit par Henri Bergson."  Etudes Bergsoniennes, 2, 1949, 9-25.

3082    MOSSE-BASTIDE, Rose-Marie.  "L'Intuition bergsonienne."  Revue Philosophique de la France et de l'Etranger, 138, Nos. 4-6, avril-juin 1948, 195-206.  Several aspects of intuition are discussed by the author.

3083    MOSSE-BASTIDE, Rose-Marie.  "Table ronde: Esthétique."  Actes du Xe Congrès des Sociétés de Philosophie de Langue Française (Congrès Bergson).  Paris: Armand Colin, 2, 1959, 193-210.

3084    MOSSE-BASTIDE, Rose-Marie.  "Table ronde: Psychologie, phénoménologie, intuition."  Actes du Xe Congrès des Sociétés de Philosophie de Langue Française (Congrès Bergson).  Paris: Armand Colin, 2, 1959.

3085    MOSSE-BASTIDE, Rose-Marie.  "Table ronde: Sources et histoire du bergsonisme."  Actes du Xe Congrès des Sociétés de Philosophie de Langue Française (Congrès Bergson).  Paris: Armand Colin, 2, 1959, 213-233.

3086    MOSSE-BASTIDE, Rose-Marie.  "La Théorie bergsonienne de la connaissance et ses rapports avec la philosophie de Plotin." Actes du Xe Congrès des Sociétés de Philosophie de Langue Française (Congrès Bergson). Paris: Armand Colin, 1, 1959, 243-247. This study stresses the influence of Plotinus' theories concerning the participation of the self in the universality of beings and being on the development of Bergson's thought. Our duration can intensify and enlarge itself so as to coincide with eternity.

3087   MOSSE-BASTIDE, Robert. "L'Idée de lieu chez Aristote." Etudes Bergsoniennes, 2, 1949, 29-104. This is a French translation of Bergson's Latin thesis, Quid Aristoteles de Loco Senserit.

3088   MOUBRAY, G. A. de C. de. "Bergson and Swedenborg." New Church Magazine, 71, No. 2, April-June 1952, 23-26.

3089   MOUNIER, Emmanuel. "Henri Bergson." Temps Nouveau, 17 janvier 1941. This is apparently a Résistance publication published in Moscow.

3090   MOUNIER, Emmanuel. "Péguy: Médiateur de Bergson." Henri Bergson. Ed. Béguin and Thévenaz, 311-320. The author examines Péguy's advocacy of Bergson's philosophy. Péguy's originality, the author holds, lay in applying Bergson's philosophy beyond the limits of the university "ivory tower."

3091   MOURELOS, Georges. Bergson et les niveaux de la réalité. Paris: Presses Universitaires de France, 1964, 256.

3092   MOURGUE, Raoul. "Bergson et la biologie du système nerveux." Nouvelles Littéraires, No. 322, 15 décembre 1928, 5.

3093   MOURGUE, Raoul. "Une Découverte scientifique: La Durée bergsonienne." Revue Philosophique de la France et de l'Etranger, 120, No. 4, novembre 1935, 350-367.

3094   MOURGUE, Raoul. Une Découverte scientifique: La Durée bergsonienne. Paris: Félix Alcan, 1935, 18. This is reprinted from Revue Philosophique de la France et de l'Etranger, 1935.

3095   MOURGUE, Raoul and VON MONAKOW, Constantin. Introduction biologique à l'étude de la neurologie et de la psychopathologie, intégration et désintégration de la fonction. Paris: Félix Alcan, 1928, 420. This book applies Bergsonian ideas to neurology and psychology.

3096    MOURGUE, Raoul. "Néo-vitalisme et sciences physiques." Re-
        vue de Métaphysique et de Morale, 25, No. 4, 1918, 419-
        431.

309     MOURGUE, Raoul. Neurobiologie de l'hallucination: Essai sur
        une variété particulière de désintégration de la fonction.
        Bruxelles: Lamertin, 1932, 416. "Lettre-préface d'Henri
        Bergson."

3098    MOURGUE, Raoul. "Le Point de vue neuro-biologique dans
        l'oeuvre de M. Bergson et les données actuelles de la sci-
        ence." Revue de Métaphysique et de Morale, 27, No. 1, jan-
        vier-mars 1920, 27-70.

3099    MOUTSOPOULOS, E. "La Critique du platonisme chez Bergson."
        Etudes Bergsoniennes, 9, 1970, 123-156.

3100    MUELLER, Gustav. "Review of Les Deux Sources de la morale
        et de la religion by Henri Bergson." Books Abroad, 8, No.
        4, October 1934, 425. According to the author, Bergson
        approves the inevitability of war. This is a cursory,
        curt review.

3101    "La Muerte de Henri Bergson." Filosofía y Letras, Universi-
        dad Autónoma de México, No. 1, enero-marzo 1941.

3102    MUIRHEAD, J. "M. Bergson's New Work on Morals and Religion."
        Hibbert Journal, 31, No. 1, October 1932, 1-11. This is a
        summary, with critical remarks, of Les Deux Sources.

3103    MUIRHEAD, J. "Philosophy of Bergson." Hibbert Journal, 9,
        No. 4, July 1911, 895-907. This is a review of Time and
        Free Will, Matter and Memory, and Creative Evolution.

3104    MULFORD, Henry Jones. "What is Intuition?" Monist, 26, No.
        2, 1926, 307-312.

3105    MULLEN, Mary Domenica. Essence and Operation in the Teaching
        of St. Thomas and in some Modern Philosophies. Washington,
        D.C.: Catholic University of America Press, 1941, 119.

3106    MÜLLER, Aloys. Problem des absoluten Raumes und seine Be-
        ziehung zum allgemeinen Raumproblem. Braunschweig, Ger-
        many: Vieweg und Sohn, 1911, 154. Bergson is discussed
        on page 56 and following.

3107    MÜLLER, Claus G. "Henri Bergson." Das jüdische Gemeinde-
        blatt, 4, No. 42, 1949, 7.

3108    MÜLLER, Ernst. "Henri Bergson." Archiv für systematische Philosophie, N.S. 18, No. 2, 1912, 185-194.

3109    MULLER, Herbert J. Science and Criticism. New Haven, Connecticut: Yale University Press, 1943, 495.

3110    MULLER, Herbert J. Science and Criticism. New York: George Braziller, Inc., 1956, 303. Bergson is discussed on pages 246-250 and 260.

3111    MULLER, Jean. "Henri Bergson, philosophe d'une renaissance ou ce que nous devons à Bergson." Renaissance Contemporaine, 24 avril 1911, 409-416.

3112    MULLER, Maurice. "Un Aspect de la théorie bergsonienne de la physique." Henri Bergson. Ed. Béguin and Thévenaz, 227-232. The author concludes that the physical theories encountered by Bergson in the course of his philosophy do not constitute an essential part of his philosophy.

3113    MULLER, Peter J. "Review of Duration and Simultaneity by Henri Bergson." Review of Metaphysics, 9, No. 4, 1965-1966, 804-805.

3114    MÜLLER-FREIENFELS, Richard. The Evolution of Modern Psychology. Trans. B. Wolfe. New Haven, Connecticut: Yale University Press, 1936, 513. Bergson is discussed on pages 54, 90-94, 102, 140, 257, 263-266, 323, 484, and 489.

3115    MÜLLER-FREIENFELS, Richard. Irrationalismus: Umrisse einer Erkenntnislehre. Leipsic: Felix Meiner, 1922, 300. This is an epistemological study which reaches conclusions very close to Bergson's. There are, however, some interesting divergences.

3116    MÜLLER-FREIENFELS, Richard. "Review of Materie und Gedächtnis by Henri Bergson." Zeitschrift für Psychologie und Physiologie des Sinnesorgane, 56, No. 1-2, 1910, 126-129.

3117    MÜLLER-FREIENFELS, Richard. "Die Philosophie Bergsons als Ausdruck französischer Mentalität." Zwiebelfisch, 20, No. 11-12, 1928, 399-404.

3118    MUNNYNCK, Marc de. "Henri Bergsons Philosophie." Schweizerische Rundschau, 31, 1930, 909-924, 995-1011.

3119    MUNNYNCK, Marc de. "Examen de la philosophie bergsonienne." Revue Catholique des Idées et des Faits, No. 1, 24 janvier, 1930, 9-13.

3120    MUNNYNCK, Marc de.    "Examen de la philosophie bergsonienne."
        Documents de la Vie Intellectuelle, 3, No. 3, 20 juin 1930,
        542-562.  This was originally in Revue Catholique des
        Idées et des Faits, 1930.

3121    MURATORE, Margherita.    "Review of Péguy entre Juarès, Berg-
        son et l'église by André Robinet."  Studi francesi, No. 40,
        1970, 119-121.

3122    MURE, G. R. G.    "Change, II."  Philosophy, 9, No. 36, 1934,
        450-464.  Bergson and modern physics are discussed on pa-
        ges 451-452 and problems in interpreting Bergson on page
        456.

3123    MURET, T.    "L'Intuition comme principe d'une raison concrète
        et d'une philosophie de l'histoire dans l'oeuvre de Berg-
        son."  Diss., Paris, 1970.

3124    MURILLO, Roberto E.    "Bergson y el problema de la educación."
        Revista de Filosofía de la Universidad de Costa Rica, 4,
        Nos. 15-16, 1965, 351-359.

3125    MURILLO ZAMORA, Roberto.    Communicación y lenguaje en la fi-
        losofía de Bergson.  San José, Costa Rica: Ciudad univer-
        sitaria Rodrigo Facio, 1965, 129.

3126    MURILLO ZAMORA, Roberto.    "La Notion de causalité dans la
        philosophie de Bergson."  Diss., Strasbourg, 1967, 196.

3127    MURILLO ZAMORA, Roberto.    La Notion de causalité dans la
        philosophie de Bergson.  San José, Costa Rica: Ciudad uni-
        versitaria, 1968, 127.  This is reprinted from Revista de
        Filosofía de la Universidad de Costa Rica, 1968.

3128    MYERS, Henry Alonzo.    "Analysis of Laughter."  Sewanee Re-
        view, 43, No. 4, October 1935, 452-463.

3129    MYERSON, Ignace.    "Les Images."  Nouveau Traité de psycholo-
        gie.  Vol. 2.  Ed. Georges Dumas.  Paris: Félix Alcan,
        1932, 541-606.  Bergson, James, and the concept of the
        image are discussed on pages 554-557.

3130    N., M.    "Les Derniers Moments de Bergson."  Le Figaro Litté-
        raire, 119, No. 121, 6 janvier 1945, 2.

3131    N., R.    "Review of La Pensée et le mouvant by Henri Bergson."
        Revue Mabillon, 25, No. 100, octobre-décembre 1935, 1.

3132   NABERT, Jean. L'Expérience intérieure de la liberté. Paris: Presses Universitaires de France, 1924, 334.

3133   NABERT, Jean. "Les Instincts virtuels et l'intelligence dans Les Deux Sources de la morale et de la religion." Journal de Psychologie Normale et Pathologique, 31, 1934, 309-332. This is a penetrating analysis of the function of mystical intuition in Bergson's philosophy of religion.

3134   NABERT, Jean. "L'Intuition bergsonienne et la conscience de Dieu." Revue de Métaphysique et de Morale, 48, No. 4, 1941, 283-300.

3135   NAGEL. "Bergsons Rede." Die übersinnliche Welt. Berlin, 1914, 94-109.

3136   NAMER, Emile. "Review of Bergson: Il profondo e la sua espressione by Vittorio Mathieu." Revue Philosophique de la France et de l'Etranger, 84, No. 3, 1959, 411-412.

3137   NAMER, Emile. "Le Message de Giordano Bruno et d'Henri Bergson." Actes du Xe Congrès des Sociétés de Philosophie de Langue Française (Congrès Bergson). Paris: Félix Alcan, 1, 1959, 250-254. Both Bergson and Bruno, the author holds, were placed at a turning point in history, Bruno at the birth of Copernicus' system, Bergson at the birth of the general theory of relativity. In spite of the disparity between the problems and the times, both ally themselves with the Pythagorean tradition according to which mathematics and science lead both to philosophical intuition and religious thought.

3138   NAMER, Emile. "Table ronde: Sources et histoire du bergsonisme." Actes du Xe Congrès des Sociétés de Philosophie de Langue Française (Congrès Bergson). Paris: Félix Alcan, 2, 1959, 213-233.

3139   NANAJIVAKO, Bhikklau. "Karma: The Ripening Fruit." Main Currents, 29, No. 5, September-October 1972, 28-36. Karma (activity) designates in Indian philosophies the "ripening fruit" of vital processes. It corresponds to the need of a new categorial term in modern philosophy for phenomena inadequately interpreted through mechanical activity. Bergson speaks of the free action as ripening fruit. Heidegger continues to extend the range of its existential significance.

3140     NANCE, John.  "Are we Developing a New Faculty, the Aware-
        ness of Becoming?"  Hibbert Journal, 45, No. 2, January
        1947, 147-152.

3141     NARSY, R.  "Review of L'Energie spirituelle by Henri Berg-
        son."  Journal des Débats, 11 août 1919.

3142     NATHANSON, William.  "Spinoza and Bergson."  Guardian, 1, No.
        2, December 1924, 15-16.

3143     NAVARTE, Cástor.  "Razón y vida en el pensamiento de Berg-
        son."  Razón y Fe, 7, No. 1-2, 1960, 27-56.

3144     NAVILLE, Pierre.  "Après Bergson."  Cahiers du Sud, No. 271,
        1945, 319-366.

3145     NEDELJKOVIC, Dragoljub.  "Romain Rolland et Stefan Zweig."
        Diss., Strasbourg, 581.

3146     NEDELJKOVIC, D. Анри Бергсон: прилог критици са-
        временог интуиционизма и друштвеног мистицизма.
        Скопље, "Славија", 1939, 184. (In Serbian).

3147     NEDONCELLE, Maurice.  "Quelques Aspects de la causalité chez
        Bergson."  Actes du Xe Congrès des Sociétés de Philosophie
        de Langue Française (Congrès Bergson).  Paris: Félix Alcan,
        1, 1959, 255-260.  The author studies the idea of cause in
        Bergson's thought, including its principal aspects (the
        causality of matter, personal causality, and interpersonal
        causality) and their significance for a philosophy of in-
        tersubjectivity.

3148     NEDONCELLE, Maurice.  "Quelques Aspects de la causalité chez
        Bergson."  Explorations personnalistes.  Paris: Aubier Mon-
        taigne, 1970, 243-249.  This article appeared originally
        in Actes du Xe Congrès des Sociétés de Philosophie de Lan-
        gue Française (Congrès Bergson), 1959.

3149     NEDONCELLE, Maurice.  "Table ronde: Matière, causalité, dis-
        continu."  Actes du Xe Congrès des Sociétés de Philosophie
        de Langue Française (Congrès Bergson).  Paris: Félix Alcan,
        2, 1959, 121-142.

3150     NELSON, Alvin F.  The Development of Lester Ward's World
        View.  Fort Worth, Texas: Branch-Smith, Inc., 1968, 67.
        Similarities between Ward and Bergson are discussed on pa-
        ges 65-67.

3151    NERY, José de Castro.  "Centenário de Bergson: Depoimento."
        Revista Brasileira de Filosofia, 11, No. 41, 1961, 111-
        112.  The author briefly considers the influence of Berg-
        son on his thought.

3152    NEVE, Paul.  Le Pragmatisme et la philosophie de M. Bergson.
        Louvain: Institut supérieur de philosophie, 1912, 38.
        This study is reprinted from Annales de l'Institut Supé-
        rieur de Louvain.

3153    "New Conception of God as Creative Evolution."  Current Lit-
        erature, 51, No. 2, August 1911, 182-183.  This is a re-
        view of articles on Bergson in England.

3154    NEWMAN, Rabbi L. I.  "Tribute to Bergson."  New York Times,
        19 January 1941, 34, col. 8.

3155    "Nicholas Murray Butler Medal Awarded to Henri Bergson in
        Recognition of his Two Sources of Morality and Religion."
        Journal of Philosophy, 37, No. 13, 20 June 1940, 364.

3156    NICOL, Eduardo.  Historicismo y existencialismo: La tempo-
        ralidad del ser y la razón.  México: Colegio de México,
        1950, 375.  Bergson, Marcel, Sartre, and others are dis-
        cussed in this study.

3157    NICOL, Eduardo.  "La marcha de Bergson hacia lo concreto:
        Mysticismo y temporalidad."  Homenaje a Bergson.  Imprenta
        Universitaria México, 1941, 49-80.

3158    NICOLARDOT, Firmin.  A Propos de Bergson: Remarques et es-
        quisses.  Paris: Vrin, 1921, 174.

3159    NICOLARDOT, Firmin.  Flore de Gnose: Laggrond, Pellis et
        Bergson: Complément de l'étude intitutlée "Un Pseudonyme
        bergsonien?"  Paris: L'Auteur, 1924, 136.  The author con-
        cludes that L'Univers, la force et la vie was not written
        by Bergson but by Auguste Glardon and E. Pellis.

3160    NICOLARDOT, Firmin.  Un Pseudonyme bergsonien?  Ou le pré-
        sage inaperçu.  Paris: Vrin, 1923, 242.  The author sug-
        gests that a book entitled L'Univers, la force et la vie,
        published in 1884, under the pseudonym A. Laggrond, is an
        early work by Bergson.

3161    NIEL, André.  "Vers Un Humanisme cosmologique: De Bergson à
        Teilhard de Chardin et J. Huxley."  Critique, 11e Année,
        No. 106, 1956, 220-229.

3162    NIEVA, R. "Notio Synthetica Temporis Apud Henri Bergson."
        Homenaje a Bergson. Córdoba, Argentina: Imprenta de la
        Universidad, 1936, 139-157.

3163    NISO, Ciusa. Inchiesta sul bergsonismo. Sassari, Italy:
        Galizzi, 1953, 111.

3164    NJOG-MOUELLE, Ebénézer. "Bergson et l'idée de profondeur."
        Diss., Paris, 1967, 213.

3165    NOAILLES, Anna, Comtesse de. "Bergson vu par Anna de Noail-
        les." Nouvelles Littéraires, No. 1677, 22 octobre 1959, 1.

3166    NOAILLES, Anna, Comtesse de. "La Renommée d'Henri Bergson."
        Nouvelles Littéraires, No. 322, 15 décembre 1928, 1.

3167    "Nobel Prize for Literature for 1927." London Mercury, 19,
        No. 108, December 1928, 124.

3168    NODET, Victor. Les Agnoscies: La Cécité psychique en parti-
        culier. Paris: Félix Alcan, 1899, 220.

3169    NOEL, Léon. "Bulletin d'épistémologie: Le Pragmatisme."
        Revue Néo-scolastique de Philosophie, 14, No. 2, mai 1907,
        220-243.

3170    NOEL, Léon. La Conscience du libre-arbitre. Louvain: Insti-
        tut supérieur de philosophie; Paris: Lethielleux, 1899,
        288.

3171    NOGUE, J. "Le Symbolisme spatial de la qualité." Revue Phi-
        losophique de la France et de l'Etranger, 51, Nos. 7-8,
        juillet-août 1926, 70-106; Nos. 9-10, octobre-novembre
        1926, 267-298. The author defends spatial symbolization
        of consciousness.

3172    NOON, William T. "Modern Literature and the Sense of Time."
        Thought, 33, No. 131, 1958-1959, 571-603. The author in-
        cludes Beckett, Bergson, and Proust in his survey of tem-
        poralist literature.

3173    NORDMANN, Charles. "L'Ame immortelle, M. Bergson et la bio-
        logie." L'Illustration, 85, Pt. 2, 15 octobre 1927, 416-
        418.

3174    NORDMANN, Charles. Notre Maître le temps: Les Astres et les
        heures: Einstein ou Bergson? Paris: Hachette, 1924, 223.

3175     NORDMANN, Charles.  The Tyranny of Time: Einstein or Bergson?
         Trans. E. E. Fournier d'Albe.  London: Unwin, Ltd., 1925,
         216.

3176     NOULET, Emilie.  "Bergson et Valéry."  Lettres Françaises,
         1, No. 3, janvier 1948, 31-51.

3177     NOULET, Emilie.  "Bergson y Valéry."  Homenaje a Bergson.
         Imprenta Universitaria México, 1941, 81-106.

3178     NOULET, Emilie.  "Une Doctrine de vie."  Alphabet critique:
         1924-1964.  Bruxelles: Presses Universitaires de Bruxelles,
         1964, 106-114.  The original version, in Spanish, was pub-
         lished in Cuadernos Americanos, January-February 1944.

3179     NOULET, Emilie.  "Valéry et la philosophie."  Flambeau, 10,
         No. 3, 1927, 195-208.  Parallels between Bergson and Valé-
         ry are developed on pages 199-208.

3180     "Les Nouveaux Elus à l'Académie française."  Revue Hebdoma-
         daire des Cours et des Conférences, N.S. 10, No. 8, 21
         février 1914, 4 pp. (no pagination).

3181     NUNEZ, E.  "O sentido do tempo no homem."  Journal Brasilei-
         ro Psiquiatria, 4, No. 2, 1955, 198-212.  The author dis-
         cusses the experience of time in Minkowski, Binswanger,
         Bergson, Heidegger, and modern psychiatry.

3182     NUÑEZ, Horacio Rogué.  "El tema de Dios en Bergson."  Revis-
         ta de la Universidad Nacional de Córdoba, 41, No. 1, 1954,
         7-71; No. 3-4, 1954, 497-563.

3183     NYMAN, Alf.  Evidence logique et évidence géométrique.  Lund,
         Sweden: Gleerup, 1959, 120.  The author explores attempts
         by F. A. Lange, K. Kroman, and H. Bergson to reduce logi-
         cal evidence to spatial evidence.

3184     NYMAN, Alfred.  "Einstein-Bergson-Vaihinger."  Annalen der
         Philosophie, 6, 1927, 178-204.  The author considers dif-
         ferent interpretations of relativity theory, including
         Bergson's.

3185     NYQUIST, Finn.  "Evolusjonen etter Bergson og sporsmalet
         transcendens."  Samtiden, 69, No. 10, 1951, 672-680.  This
         study explores the concept of evolution according to Berg-
         son and the problem of transcendance.

3186     NYS, Désirée.  La Notion du temps.  2e éd.  Louvain: Insti-
         tut supérieur de philosophie, 1913, 308.

3187    "Obituary." _American Journal of Sociology_, 56, No. 6, March 1941, 734.

3188    "Obituary." _Current Biography Yearbook_. New York: Wilson, 1941, 976, 73.

3189    "Obituary." _Publisher's Weekly_, 139, No. 3, 11 January 1941, 148.

3190    "Obituary." _School and Society_, 53, No. 1359, 11 January 1941, 50.

3191    "Obituary." _Time_, 37, No. 2, 13 January 1941, 32.

3192    "Obituary." _Wilson Library Bulletin_, 15, No. 2, February 1941, 454.

3193    "Obituary Article." _New York Times_, 6 January 1941, 15, col. 1.

3194    O'BRIEN, James F.   "Zeno's Paradoxes of Motion: Analysis of Aristotle, Russell, Bergson." _Modern Schoolman_, 40, No. 1, January 1963, 105-137.

3195    OESTERREICHER, John M.   "Henri Bergson and the Faith." _Thought_, 22, No. 87, December 1947, 635-678.

3196    OESTERREICHER, John M.   _Muren storten in: Zeven Joodse filosofen de weg naar Christus_. Haarlem: Standaardboekerij, 1954, 411.

3197    OESTERREICHER, John M.   _Sept Philosophes juifs devant le Christ_. Paris: Cerf, 1955, 616.  Bergson, Spinoza, Brunschvicg, and other Jewish thinkers are analyzed by the author in terms of their attitudes towards Christ and Christianity.

3198    OESTERREICHER, John M.   _Walls are Crumbling: Seven Jewish Philosophers Discover Christ_. New York: Devin-Adair, 1952, 393.

3199    O'KEEF, D.   "Bergson's Critical Philosophy." _Irish Theological Studies_, No. 2, April 1913, 178-189.

3200    OLDEWELT, H. M. J.   "1859-Bergson-1959." _Algemeen Nederlands Tijdschrift voor Wijsbegeerte en Psychologie_, 52, 1, 1959-1960, 1-12.

3201   OLDEWELT, H. M. J.  "De psychologische ondergrond van Berg-
       son's wijsbegeerte."  Synthèse, 3, No. 2, 1941, 49-61.  A
       résumé of this article, in French, may be found in volume
       3, no. 3 of Synthèse on pages 99-100.

3202   OLGIATI, Francesco.  "Il concetto di sostenza."  Rivista di
       filosofia neoscolastica, 21, No. 3, maggio-agosto 1929.
       The author analyzes the concept of substance in Locke,
       Berkeley, Hume, Mill, Taine, and Bergson.

3203   OLGIATI, Francesco.  "La filosofia bergsoniana e il realis-
       mo."  Relazioni e comunicazioni al X Congresso nazionale
       di filosofia.  Milano: Vita e Pensiero, 1935.

3204   OLGIATI, Francesco.  "La filosofia bergsoniana e il realis-
       mo."  Revista di filosofia neoscolastica, Suppl. 27, 1935,
       59-70.

3205   OLGIATI, Francesco.  La filosofia de Enrico Bergson.  Tori-
       no:  Fratelli Boca, 1914, 317.

3206   OLGIATI, Francesco.  "La morte di Henri Berrgson."  Revista
       di filosofia neoscolastica, Anno 33, No. 1, 1941, 86-94.

3207   O'NEILL, James C.  "An Intellectual Affinity: Bergson and
       Valéry."  Publications of the Modern Language Association,
       66, No. 2, March 1951, 49-64.  There are similarities, but
       no influences, between Bergson and Valéry, according to
       the author.

3208   O'NEILL, James C.  "Philosophy and Criticism: Bergson and
       Thibaudet."  Modern Language Quarterly, 11, No. 4, Decem-
       ber 1950, 492-497.  The author claims that Thibaudet was a
       Bergsonian, Professor Spitzer's opinions notwithstanding.

3209   ORGAZ, Raúl A.  "Los fundamentos sociológicos de la moral de
       Bergson."  Homenaje a Bergson.  Córdoba, Argentina: Impren-
       ta de la Universidad, 1936, 33-52.

3210   ORGAZ, Raúl A.  "La sociología en la moral de Bergson."  Cur-
       sos y Conferencias, Año 4, No. 5, 1936.

3211   ORTEGAT, Paul.  Intuition et religion.  Louvain: Institut su-
       périeur de philosophie à l'Université catholique, 1947,
       248.  The author lumps Bergson, Le Roy, and existential-
       ists together under the same heading (intuitionism).  He
       is highly critical of "intuitionism."

3212    OSORIO OSORIO, Alberto. "Etude sur la pensée religieuse de
Bergson et d'Unamuno." 2 vols. Diss., Bordeaux, 167, 386.

3213    OSORIO OSORIO, Alberto. "Ideas sobre el humanismo espiritualista de Bergson." Lotería, 14, No. 161, 1969, 19-21.

3214    OSTERTAG, H. "Bergson." Neue kirchliche Zeitschrift, 25,
1913, 991-1006.

3215    OSUEGADA, Raul. El problema de la libertad y personalidad
en la temática bergsoniana. Guatemala: Universidad de San
Carlos de Guatemala, Facultad de Humanidades, 1949, 80.
The author argues as follows. Bergson holds that reason
is capable of comprehending extension or substance but
that duration or becoming can only be understood intuitive-
ly. The conclusions of reason are deterministic, while
those of intuition are vitalistic or creative. Although
indeterminacy or incipient creativity is characteristic of
all life, it is only in man that it is coupled with the
ability to react in terms of past experience. This reaction in terms of the totality of one's experience is personality.

3216    OTT, Emil. Henri Bergson: Der Philosoph moderner Religion.
Berlin and Leipsic: Teubner, 1914, 131. This is from
Natur und Geisteswelt, 480.

3217    OTTAVIANO, Carmelo. "Bergson e il realismo." Sophia, 4, No.
1, 1936, 104-107. This article contains a letter from
Bergson to R. P. Gorce.

3218    OULMONT, Charles. Bergson. Trans. José Marinho. Lisboa:
Editorial Inquérito, 1943, 70.

3219    OVINK, Bernard Jan Hendrik. Henri Bergson. Baarn, Netherlands, 1920 (Denkers [Groote], 4th Ser., No. 1).

3220    OXENSTIERNA, Gunnar Gabriel. Tids-och intuitionsproblem i
Bergsons filosofi. Uppsala, Sweden: Akademisk avhandlung,
1926, 153.

3221    OYARZUN, Luis. "La idea de inspiración en Bergson." Revista de Filosofía, 6, No. 2-3, 1959, 73-83.

3222    PAASEN, Carl Richard van. De antithisen in de philosophie
van Henri Bergsons. Haarlem: Kleijnenberg and Co., 1923,
128.

3223     PACOTTE, Julian. La Logique et l'empirisme intégral. Paris:
         Hermann and Co., 1935, 56. Views of Bergson and Poincaré
         are discussed in this study.

3224     PACOTTE, Julian. La Pensée mathématique contemporaine.
         Paris: Félix Alcan, 1925, 126. The author concludes that
         Bergson's metaphysics best conforms to the spirit of con-
         temporary mathematical physics.

3225     PALACIOS, Juan-Miguel. "L'Accueil fait à Bergson par la
         presse espagnole." Etudes Bergsoniennes, 9, 1970, 114-
         121. This essay describes Bergson's reception by the Span-
         ish press during his mission to Spain in 1916.

3226     PALACIOS, Juan-Miguel. "Circonstances du voyage espagnol."
         Trans. Michel Gauthier. Etudes Bergsoniennes, 9, 1970,
         7-10.

3227     PALACIOS, Juan-Miguel. "Traductions en espagnol d'oeuvres
         d'Henri Bergson." Etudes Bergsoniennes, 9, 1970, 122.
         This is a bibliography of the Spanish translations of Berg-
         son's writings.

3228     PALANTE, Georges. "L'Influence de la philosophie de M. Berg-
         son. III." Mouvement Socialiste, 29, No. 230, avril 1911,
         270-271.

3229     PALANTE, Georges. "Sur Le Succès du bergsonisme." Mercure
         de France, Sér. moderne 116, 16 juillet, 1016, 306-308.
         This is a review of Benda's Sur Le Succès du bergsonisme.

3230     PALCOS, Alberto. "José Ortega y Gasset: El sentido de la
         filosofía." Nosotros, 10, No. 88, agosto 1916, 204.

3231     PALGON, Rudolf. Die Weltanschauung Henri Bergsons. Breslau,
         Germany: Priebatsch, 1929, 148.

3232     PALHORIES, Fortuné. Vies et doctrines des grands philoso-
         phes. Paris: Lanore, 1929, 111, 399. The final sections
         of this book are on James, Nietzsche, and Bergson.

3233     PALIARD, Jacques. Intuition et réflexion: Esquisse d'une
         dialectique de la conscience. Paris: Félix Alcan, 1925,
         464. This study is an attempted resolution of the "oppo-
         sition entre Bergson et Hamelin" concerning the nature of
         thought.

3234     PALLIERE, Aimé. Bergson et le judaïsme. Paris: Félix Alcan,
         1932, 43.

3235    PALMER, William Scott. "Life and the Brain." Contemporary
        Review, 96, No. 10, October 1909, 474-484. This review
        considers mind-brain and life-matter relations in Creative
        Evolution.

3236    PALMER, William Scott. "Presence and Omnipresence: A Chris-
        tian Study Aided by the Philosophy of Monsieur Bergson."
        Contemporary Review, 93, No. 6, June 1908, 734-742. This
        study extends Bergson's thought to religious experience.

3237    PALMER, William Scott. "Thought and Instinct." Nation, 5,
        5 June 1909, 341-342.

3238    PALUMBO, Enrique. "La intuición bergsoniana." en "Lógica y
        metafísica: Una introducción al estudio del problema de la
        causalidad." Cursos y Conferencias, 3, No. 9, marzo 1934,
        908-911.

3239    PANGE, Jean de. Journal: 1931-1933. Paris: Grasset, 1967,
        412.

3240    PAOLI, J. Défilé entre La Bruyère et Bergson. Göteborg,
        Sweden: Wettergren and Kerber, 1939, 58 (Göteborgs Högsko-
        las arsskrift, No. 2). This study attempts an explanation
        of certain social ideas in La Bruyère's Caractères by ref-
        erence to Bergson's writings.

3241    PAPADOPOULO, Alexandre. Un Philosophe entre deux défaites:
        Henri Bergson entre 1870 et 1940. Le Caire, Egypt: Edi-
        tions de la Revue du Caire, 1942, 420.

3242    PAPINI, Giovanni. "Begegnung mit Henri Bergson." Zeit-
        schrift für Religions und Geistesgeschichte, 4, No. 4,
        1952, 371-374.

3243    PAPINI, Giovanni. "Bergson vu par Giovanni Papini." Nouvel-
        les Littéraires, No. 1677, 22 octobre 1959, 2.

3244    PAPINI, Giovanni. Bli amanti di sofia: 1902-1918. Firenze:
        Vallecchi, 1942, 365. Bergson and others are discussed in
        this book.

3245    PAPINI, Giovanni. "Mes Rencontres avec Bergson." Nouvelles
        Littéraires, No. 322, 15 décembre 1928, 3.

3246    PAPINI, Giovanni. Passato remoto: 1885-1914. Firenze:
        L'Arco, 1948, 279. Bergson, Gourmont, Péguy, Rolland,
        Sorel, LeCardonnel, and others are dealt with in this book.

3247   PAPINI, Giovanni.  Sul pragmatismo: Saggi e ricerche.  Mila-
       no: Milanese, 1913, 163.

3248   PAPINI, Giovanni.  Stroncature.  3rd ed.  Firenze: Librería
       della voce, 1918, 398.  Bergson and Croce are discussed on
       pages 51-56.

3249   PAQUETTE, Guy.  "Le Fait social chez Bergson."  Diss., Paris,
       1969.

3250   PARAF, Pierre.  "H. Bergson et V. Basch."  Fraternité, 12
       janvier 1945.

3251   PARAF, Pierre.  "De Jules Romains à Henri Bergson."  La Ré-
       publique, 12 septembre 1937.

3252   PARAIN-VIAL, Jeanne.  "Bergson et la 'philosophia perennis'."
       Actes du Xe Congrès des Sociétés de Philosophie de Langue
       Française (Congrès Bergson).  Paris: Armand Colin, 1, 1959,
       261-266.  Though Bergson often stresses his opposition to
       traditional philosophy, the author argues, he nonetheless
       coincides at several points with the 'philosophia perennis.'
       Three points of coincidence are: the theory of knowledge,
       the philosophy of being, and moral philosophy.

3253   PARAIN-VIAL, Jeanne.  "Table ronde: Unité, unicité, dialogue."
       Actes du Xe Congrès des Sociétés de Philosophie de Langue
       Française (Congrès Bergson).  Paris: Armand Colin, 2, 1959,
       281-302.

3254   PARIENTE, J. C.  "Bergson et Wittgenstein."  Revue Interna-
       tionale de Philosophie, 23, Nos. 88-89, 1969, 183-204.

3255   "A Paris et ailleurs: Sous la Coupole: Renfort pour le dic-
       tionnaire: Peur des mots: Bergson et la politesse: Berg-
       son et Rembrandt."  Nouvelles Littéraires, No. 951, 25 oc-
       tobre 1945.

3256   PARKER, DeWitt H.  Experience and Substance.  Ann Arbor,
       Michigan: University of Michigan Press, 1941, 371.  Berg-
       son is discussed on pages 22, 26, 67, 136, 138-139, 145,
       and 171n.

3257   PARKER, George Frederick.  "Duration and Method in the Phi-
       losophy of Henri Bergson."  Dissertation Abstracts, 20, No.
       5, November 1959, 1828.

3258    PARKES, Henry Bramford. Pragmatic Test: Essays in the History of Ideas. San Francisco, California: Colt Press, 1941, 240. This study includes an essay on Bergson.

3259    PARKES, Henry Bramford. "The Tendencies of Bergsonism." Scrutiny, 4, No. 4, March 1936, 407-424.

3260    PARODI, Dominique. "M. Bergson et la morale." Enseignement Public, 102, No. 1, janvier 1933, 1-20. This article is a review of Les Deux Sources.

3261    PARODI, Dominique. "La Durée et la matière." Revue de Métaphysique et de Morale, 48, No. 4, 1941, 258-265.

3262    PARODI, Dominique. "Intuition et raison." Revue de Métaphysique et de Morale, 19, No. 4, juillet 1911, 555-559.

3263    PARODI, Dominique. "Review of La Pensée et le mouvant by Henri Bergson." Revue de Synthèse, 10, No. 2, 1935, 211-222.

3264    PARODI, Dominique. La Philosophie contemporaine en France: Essai de classification des doctrines. Paris: Félix Alcan, 1919, 302 (Bibliographie de Philosophie Contemporaine).

3265    PARODI, Dominique. "La Philosophie française de 1918 à 1925." Revue Philosophique de la France et de l'Etranger, 15, Nos. 11-12, novembre-décembre 1925, 359-383.

3266    PARODI, Dominique. "Review of Le Rire by Henri Bergson." Revue de Métaphysique et de Morale, 9, No. 2, mars 1901, 224-236.

3267    PARODI, Dominique. "Les Tendances de la philosophie contemporaine en France." Petit Messager Belge, No. 421, 1908, 50-51.

3268    PARPAGNOLI, Guido. "Henri Bergson." Argentina Libre, 2, enero 1941.

3269    PARR, Susan Dale Resneck. "'And by Bergson, Obviously': Faulkner's The Sound and the Fury, As I Lay Dying and Absalom, Absalom! From a Bergsonian Perspective." Dissertation Abstracts International, 32, 1971, 6996A. The author, pointing out Faulkner's stated indebtedness to Bergson, shows that Bergsonian concepts explain a great deal in Faulkner's writings.

3270     PARSONS, Edmund. _Time Devoured: A Materialistic Discussion of Duration_. London: George Allen and Unwin, 1964, 132. Bergson is discussed on pages 94-97.

3271     PASQUALI, Antonio. _Fundamentos gnoseológicos para una ciencia de la moral: Ensayo sobre la formación de una teoría del conocimiento moral en las filosifías de Kant, Lequier, Renouvier y Bergson_. Caracas: Universidad Central de Venezuela, 1963, 150.

3272     PASTORI, Paolo. "Bergson e Sorel." _Dialoghi_, Anno 16, No. 4-5, 1948, 129-169.

3273     PASTUSKA, J. _Filozofja religje H. Bergsona_. 1936.

3274     PATRI, Aimé. "Actualité ou déclin du bergsonisme." _Paru_, No. 32, 1947, 93ff.

3275     PAUL, Nancy Margaret and RUHE, Algot Henrik Leonard. _Henri Bergson: An Account of his Life and Philosophy_. London: Macmillan, 1914, 245.

3276     PAULHAN, François. "Contemporary Philosophy in France." _Philosophical Review_, 9, No. 1, January 1900, 42-69.

3277     PAULUS, Jean. "Les Deux Directions de la psychologie bergsonienne: Behaviorisme et introspection dans _Matière et mémoire_." _Tijdschrift voor Philosophie_, 6, Nos. 3-4, 1944, 297-332. This is a very penetrating analysis of Bergson's theory of mind-body interaction.

3278     PAULUS, Jean. "Les Deux Directions de la psychologie bergsonienne et la méthode introspective de l'_Essai_." _Tijdschrift voor Philosophie_, 5, No. 1, 1943, 85-140. The author effects an excellent analysis of Bergson's psychology.

3279     PAULUS, Jean. _Le Problème de l'hallucination et l'évolution de la psychologie d'Esquirol à Pierre Janet_. Paris: Droz, 1941, 198 (Bibliothèque de la Faculté de philosophie et lettres de l'Université de Liège, Fasc. 91). Bergson is discussed on pages 14n, 19, 66, 110, 117, 141, 151n, 153, 155, 163, and 164.

3280     PAVAN, A. "Maritain e Bergson." _Revista di filosofia neoscolastica_. 64. aprile-junio 1972, 265-287.

3281     PECKHAM, George William. _Logic of Bergson's Philosophy_. Diss., Columbia, 1917. New York: Columbia University

Press, 1917, 68.  The author is highly critical of Bergson's dualistic tendencies.  This dissertation was super-
vised by John Dewey.

3282   PEGNES, Thomas M.  "Review of L'Evolution créatrice by Henri
       Bergson."  Revue Thomiste, 16, No. 3, mai-juin 1908, 137-
       163.

3283   PEGUY, Charles.  "Bergson vu par Charles Péguy."  Nouvelles
       Littéraires, No. 1677, 22 octobre 1959, 1 et 2.

3284   PEGUY, Charles.  "Deux Lettres à Bergson."  Esprit, 21e An-
       née, No. 200, février 1953, 337-338.

3285   PEGUY, Charles.  Nota conjunta sobre Descartes y la filoso-
       fía cartesiana sequida de una nota sobre Bergson y la filo-
       sofía bergsoniana.  Buenos Aires: Emecé, 1946, 349.  The
       critical introduction is written by Carmen R. L. de Gándara.

3286   PEGUY, Charles.  Note conjointe: Note sur M. Bergson et la
       philosophie bergsonienne: Note conjointe sur M. Descartes
       et la philosophie cartésienne.  Paris: Gallimard, 1935, 318.

3287   PEGUY, Charles.  Note sur M. Bergson et la philosophie berg-
       sonienne.  Paris: 8, rue de la Sorbonne, 1914, 105.
       Cahiers de la Quinzaine, 8e cahier, 15e Série.

3288   PEGUY, Charles.  "Note sur M. Bergson et la philosophie berg-
       sonienne."  Grande Revue, 84, No. 8, 25 avril 1914, 613-
       631.

3289   PEGUY, Charles.  Note sur M. Bergson et la philosophie berg-
       sonienne.  Paris: Emile Paul, 1914, 101.

3290   PEGUY, Charles.  "Note sur M. Bergson et la philosophie berg-
       sonienne."  Oeuvres complètes.  Vol. 9.  Oeuvres posthumes.
       Paris: Nouvelle Revue Française, 1924, 335.

3291   PEGUY, Charles.  Note sur M. Bergson et la philosophie berg-
       sonienne: Note sur Descartes et la philosophie cartésienne.
       Paris: Nouvelle Revue Française, 1935, 323.

3292   PEGUY, Charles.  "Un Témoignage inédit de Péguy."  Henri
       Bergson.  Ed. Béguin and Thévanaz, 13-15.

3293   PALADAN, Joséphin.  "L'Impressionisme philosophique: Le Berg-
       sonisme."  Soleil, 22 août 1912.

3294    PELCA, G.  "M. Henri Bergson à l'Académie: L'Eloge d'Emile
        Ollivier: La Réception de M. Bergson: La Réponse de M. Dou-
        mic."  Le Gaulois, 26 janvier 1918.  This is an account of
        Bergson's reception into the Académie française.

3295    PELEGER, André.  "Le Bergsonisme en pratique."  Le Penseur,
        9, No. 4, 1912, 137-140; No. 6, 1912, 217-222; No. 7, 1912,
        260-264.  This is a rather satirical look at Bergson's phi-
        losophy.

3296    PELIKAN, Jaroslav.  "Bergson Among the Theologians."  The
        Bergsonian Heritage.  Ed. Thomas Hanna.  New York and Lon-
        don: Columbia University Press, 1962, 54-73.  Pelikan's es-
        say recounts the influence of Bergson on church historians
        H. Richard Niebuhr and Alfred Loisy.

3297    PELLE-DOUEL, Yvonne.  "Bergson und unser Jahrhundert."  Stim-
        men der Zeit, 168, No. 5, Mai 1961, 116-127.

3298    PEMBERTON, Harrison J.  "The Problem of Personal Identity
        with Special Reference to Whitehead and Bergson."  Diss.,
        Yale, 1953.

3299    PEÑA Y PRADO, Juan Manuel.  "Bergson y el problema de la me-
        moria."  Diss., Arequipa, Peru, 1921.

3300    PENIDO, Maurilio Teixeira-Leite.  Dieu dans le bergsonisme.
        Paris: Desclée de Brouwer, 1934, 261.

3301    PENIDO, Maurilio Teixeira-Leite.  La Méthode intuitive de M.
        Bergson: Essai critique.  Paris: Félix Alcan, 1918, 220.

3302    PENIDO, Maurilio Teixeira-Leite.  "Réflexion sur la théodicée
        bergsonienne."  Revue Thomiste, N.S. 16, No. 77, mai-juin
        1933, 426-452.

3303    "Review of La Pensée et le mouvant by Henri Bergson."  Ras-
        segna italiana, 17, 1934, 827.

3304    "Review of La Pensée et le mouvant by Henri Bergson."  Revue
        de Métaphysique et de Morale (Supplément), 41, No. 4, octo-
        bre 1934, 1.

3305    "Review of La Pensée et le mouvant by Henri Bergson."  Revue
        Mabillon, 26, 1934.

3306    PENTIMALLI, Giuseppi.  Bergson: La dottrina della durata
        reale e i suoi precedenti storici.  Torino: Fratelli Boca,
        1920, 190.

3307    PEPPER, Stephen C.  "The Development of Contextual Aesthetics." Antioch Review, 28, No. 2, 1968, 169-185.

3308    PEREGO, Luigi. La dinamica dello spirito nella conoscenza:
Saggio di critica e sintesi nel neo-dualismo gnoseologico
del Bergson. Bologna: Zanichelli, 1925, 140.

3309    PEREIRA RODRIGUEZ, José. Paginas escogidas de filosofía:
Platon, Kant, Bergson. Montivideo: Monteverde y Cia.,
1940, 115.

3310    PERELMAN, Chaim.  "Synthèse des travaux du Congrès." Actes
du Xe Congrès des Sociétés de Philosophie de Langue Française (Congrès Bergson). Paris: Armand Colin, 1959, 305-
313.

3311    PERNOT, C.  "Spiritualisme et spiritisme chez Bergson."
Revue de l'Enseignement Philosophique, 14, No. 3, 1964, 1-
24.  This is a study of Bergson's attitude towards psychical research.

3312    PERRY, Ralph Barton.  "Notes on the Philosophy of Henri Bergson." Journal of Philosophy, 8, No. 25, 7 December 1911,
673-682; No. 26, 21 December 1911, 713-721.  Perry pursues
a thoroughgoing criticism of Bergson's position, with special emphasis on Bergson's "irrationalism."

3313    PERRY, Ralph Barton. Philosophy of the Recent Past: An Out-
line of European and American Philosophy since 1860.  New
York: Scribner's, 1925, 230.  The chapter entitled "The
Impulse to Life: Bergson" is found on pages 174-182.

3314    PERRY, Ralph Barton. Present Philosophical Tendencies.  New
York: Longmans, Green, and Co., 1912, 383.  A section entitled "Immediatism vs. Intellectualism" is on pages 222-
241; Bergson's concept of law is criticized on pages 255-
254; Bergson's theory of mind is discussed on pages 299-
301.  These criticisms are largely taken from the Journal
of Philosophy, 1911.

3315    PERRY, Ralph Barton. The Thought and Character of William
James.  Boston: Little, Brown and Company, 1935, Vol. 1,
825, Vol. 2, 768.  In volume one Bergson is discussed on
pages 458, 461, 468, 652, 688.  In volume two Bergson is
discussed on pages 201, 386, 404, 437-438, 482, 496, 498,
537-538, 544, 551, 564, 566-68, 576, 581, 589-590, 599-
636, 642-643, 650, 654-655, 664, 666, 683, 696, 744, 754,

757, and 762-763.  Correspondence between James and Bergson may be found on pages 605-633.

3316   PERRY, Ralph Barton.  "William James et M. H. Bergson: Lettres, 1902-1910."  Revue des Deux Mondes, 8e Sér., 17, No. 20, 15 octobre 1933, 783-823.

3317   "La Personnalité d'Henri Bergson et l'Angleterre."  Chronique des Lettres Françaises, 5, 1927, 703-705.

3318   PETIT, Agénor.  M. Bergson et le rationalisme.  Prague: Impr. d'E. Grégr et fils, 1921, 24.  This study is followed by a letter from Bergson.

3319   PETIT, Henri.  "Review of Entretiens avec Bergson by Jacques Chevalier."  Nouvelles Littéraires, No. 1677, 22 octobre 1959, 2-3.

3320   PETRONE, Igino.  I limiti del determinismo scientifico: Saggio.  Modena, Italy: Vincenzie Nipoti, 1900, 139.

3321   PETRONE, Igino.  I limiti del determinismo scientifico: Saggio.  2nd ed.  Roma: Società di Cultura, 1903, 144.

3322   PETROVICI, J.  "Le Dynamisme contemporain."  Revue Politique et Littéraire, Revue Bleue, 71e Année, No. 12, 17 juin 1933, 356-359; No. 13, 1er juillet 1933, 401-405.

3323   PETRUCCIANO, Mario.  "Intuizionismo ed ermetismo."  Idea, 2, No. 41, 1950, 2.

3324   PFISTER, Charles.  "Bergson, élève de l'Ecole normale."  Nouvelles Littéraires, No. 322, 15 décembre 1928, 4.

3325   PFLUG, Günther.  Henri Bergson: Quellen und Konsequenzen einer Induktiven Metaphysik.  Berlin: Walter de Gruyter und Ges., 1959, 393.  Pages 116-129 are translated, with an introduction, in Bergson and the Evolution of Physics, Ed. P. A. Y. Gunter on pages 190-208 under the title "Inner Time and the Relativity of Motion."

3326   PHILIBERT, M.  "Les Conceptions métaphysiques de Lagneau et Bergson."  Revue de l'Enseignement Philosophique, 12, No. 4, 1962, 1-14.

3327   PHILIPPE, Oscar.  "Table ronde: Néant et existentialisme."  Actes du Xe Congrès des Sociétés de Philosophie de Langue Française (Congrès Bergson).  Paris: Armand Colin, 2, 1959, 145-164.

3328    PHILONENKO, Alexis.  "Bergson et la philosophie: Etude cri-
        tique sur l'interprétation de P. Trotignon."  Archives de
        Philosophie, 33, No. 1, 1970, 73-95.  This is a study of
        P. Trotignon's L'Idée de vie chez Bergson et la critique
        de la métaphysique.

3329    PHILONENKO, Alexis.  "Bergson: Le Rêve: Etude d'un texte de
        L'Energie spirituelle."  Cahiers de Philosophie, 2, No. 7,
        1964, sans pagination.  "Edités par le Groupe d'études de
        philosophie de la Faculté des lettres de Paris."

3330    "Philosopher in Eclipse: Henri Bergson and the Jet of Life."
        London Times Literary Supplement, No. 2033, 18 January
        1941, 27-36.  This is an obituary notice.

3331    "Philosophie de Bergson."  Revue de la Solidartité, juillet
        1911.

3332    "The Philosophy of Henri Bergson."  Quarterly Review, 216,
        No. 430, 1912, 152-177.  This is a survey of Bergson's ma-
        jor writings.

3333    "Review of The Philosophy of Poetry by Henri Bergson."  Clas-
        sical Bulletin, 39, No. 1, January 1963, 46.

3334    "Photograph of Bergson."  Scientific Monthly, 28, No. 6,
        June 1929, 571.

3335    PIAGET, Jean.  "Lettre."  Revue de Théologie et de Philoso-
        phie, 9, No. 1, 1959, 44.  Here Piaget asserts the posi-
        tive influence of Creative Evolution on his genetic epis-
        temology.

3336    PIAT, Clodius.  Insuffisance des philosophies de l'intuition.
        Paris: Plon-Nourrit et Cie., 1908, 319.

3337    PIAZZA, Elena.  "Il problema morale e religioso in H. Berg-
        son."  Sapienza, 13, Nos. 5-6, 1961, 459-478.

3338    PICARD, Gaston.  "Au Temps où naissait la gloire d'Henri
        Bergson."  Le Figaro Littéraire, 17 novembre 1928.

3339    PICARD, Gaston and TAUTAIN, Gustave-Louis.  "Enquête sur M.
        Henri Bergson et l'influence de sa pensée sur la sensibi-
        lité contemporaine."  Grande Revue, 83, No. 3, 10 février
        1914, 544-560; 25 février 1914, 744-760; 84, No. 5, 10
        mars 1914, 111-128; No. 6, 25 mars 1918, 309-328; No. 7,
        10 avril 1914, 513-528.

3340    PICCIOTO, Robert S.   "Meditaciones rurales de una mentalidad
        urbana: El tiempo, Bergson y Manrique en un poema de Anto-
        nio Machado."  Torre, 12, Nos. 45-46, 1964, 141-150.

3341    PICHL, K.  "Bergson und seine Nachfolger."  Wissenschaft und
        Weltbild, 5, No. 9, 1952, 304-314.

3342    PICLIN, Michel.  "Bergson et la transcendance."  Revue Phi-
        losophique de la France et de l'Etranger, 95, No. 4, 1970,
        445-469.  This article considers Bergson's concept of the
        transcendance of God, contrasting Bergson's position with
        that of classical Christian theology.  The transcendance
        of God, according to Bergson, is a transcendance "vis a
        tergo."  The unity of God is situated behind us, in the
        past, not in the future.

3343    PIECHAUD, Louis.  "La Maison de Bergson."  Nouvelles Litté-
        raires, No. 927, 10 mai 1945.

3344    PIEROLA, Raul Alberto.  "Imaginación y conciencia artística
        en la filosofía de Bergson."  Philosophia, 25, No. 25,
        1962, 55-58.

3345    PIERON, Henri.  "Remarques sur la théorie de la relativité."
        Bulletin de la Société Française de Philosophie, 22, No. 3,
        juillet 1922, 102-113.  Also in Ecrits et paroles, 3, 497-
        503; Mélanges, 1340-1347.  This item is translated, with
        an introduction, in Bergson and the Evolution of Physics,
        Ed. P. A. Y. Gunter, 133-135.

3346    PIERRE-QUINT, Léon.  "Bergson et Marcel Proust: Fragments
        d'une étude."  Henri Bergson.  Ed. Béguin and Thévenaz,
        328-340.  The author argues that Marcel Proust simply
        transposed Bergson's vision of the world into literature.

3347    PIERRE-QUINT, Léon.  "Review of Les Deux Sources de la mora-
        le et de la religion by Henri Bergson."  Revue de France,
        12e Année, No. 10, 15 mai 1932, 324-347.  This is a very
        personal and laudatory review.

3348    PIERRE-QUINT, Leon.  "Un Effort pour dominer l'absurde."
        Revue de Paris, 75, No. 4, 1948, 68-78.

3349    PIERRE-QUINT, Léon.  "Entretien avec Bergson."  Revue de Pa-
        ris, 65, No. 8, septembre 1958, 120-129.

3350    PIERRE-QUINT, Léon.  Marcel Proust: L'Homme, sa vie, son
        oeuvre.  Paris: Editions du Sagittaire, 1925, III.  Berg-
        son is discussed on page 33.

3351   PIERRE-QUINT, Léon.  "Le Prix Nobel à Bergson."  Revue de
       France, 8e Année, No. 24, 15 décembre 1928, 701-708.

3352   PIGNATO, Luca.  "Durata e storia nel pensiero de Bergson."
       Dialogo, 3, No. 1, 1966, 109-117.

3353   PIGNATO, Luca.  "Durata e storia tramonto di Bergson."  Ita-
       lia letteraria, Anno 10, No. 80, 1934, 1-2.  This is a re-
       view of La Pensée et le mouvant by Henri Bergson.

3354   PIGNATO, Luca.  "L'estetica mistica di Enrico Bergson."
       Bilychnis, Anno 20, No. 2, 1929.

3355   PIGNATO, Luca.  L'ottocento francesi: L'estetica mistica di
       Bergson.  Palermo: Ciclope, 1929, 140.

3356   PILLON, François.  "Review of Essai sur les données immédi-
       ates de la conscience by Henri Bergson."  Année Philoso-
       phique, 1, 1890, S.E. Suppl. 133.

3357   PILLON, François.  "Review of L'Evolution créatrice by Henri
       Bergson."  Année Philosophique, 19, 1907, 182-184.

3358   PILLON, François.  "Review of Matière et mémoire by Henri
       Bergson."  Année Philosophique, 7, 1896, 190-192.

3359   PILLON, François.  "Review of Le Rire by Henri Bergson."
       Année Philosophique, 11, 1900, 135-138.

3360   PILZECKER, A.  "Mémoire et reconnaissance."  Zeitschrift für
       Psychologie und Physiologie des Sinnesorgane, 13, 1897,
       229-232.  This is a review of Bergson's article in the Re-
       vue Philosophique.

3361   PIMENOFF, L. L.  "Freedom in the World-Soul: A Plea for Berg-
       sonianism."  Monist, 30, No. 3, July 1920, 460-473.

3362   PINA, António Ambrósio.  "O problema do método no intuicio-
       nismo de Bergson."  Filosofia, 6, No. 1, 1959, 11-27.

3363   PINCHEREL, Salvatore.  "Il calcolo delle probabilità e l'in-
       tuizione."  Scientia, 10, No. 6, 1916, 417-426.  A French
       translation of this article is given on pages 193-203.

3364   PINTO, Luigi.  "Introduction" to the Italian translation of
       Les Deux Sources de la morale et de la religion.  Napoli:
       Ediz. Claux, 1961, 141.

3365    PIOLI, G.  "Tendenze religiose nella filosofia del Bergson e la condamna dell' 'Indice'."  Bilychnis, 3, No. 8, 1914.

3366    PITKIN, Walter B.  "James and Bergson: Or, Who is against Intellect?"  Journal of Philosophy, 7, No. 9, 28 April 1910, 225-231.  The author argues that Bergson's and James' anti-intellectualisms differ profoundly.  Bergson does not reject conceptual thought.

3367    PITKIN, Walter B.  "Time and Pure Activity."  Journal of Philosophy, 11, No. 19, 10 September 1914, 521-526.

3368    "Plagiator Bergson."  Monatshefte d. Comeniusgesellschaft für Kultur und Geistesleben, N.S. 7, 1915, 185ff.

3369    "Une Plaque Bergson au Panthéon."  Le Monde, No. 6856, 27 janvier 1967, 8.

3370    PLAYNE, Caroline.  Bergson and Free Will.  London: Headley, 1915.

3371    PLEKHANOV, G. "Анри Бергсон." Современный мир, 3, № 2, 1909, 118-122.

3372    PLEKHANOV, Georges.  "Sur L'Evolution créatrice d'Henri Bergson (Trad. par Jean Deprun)."  Pensée, N.S. No. 80, juillet-août 1958, 103-107.

3373    PLINVAL, Georges de.  "Il y a dix ans mourait Henri Bergson."  Ecrits de Paris, janvier 1951, 91-96.

3374    POLIMENI, E.  "Bergson and the Church."  Tablet, 177, 22 February 1941, 156.

3375    POLIMENI, E.  "Bergson and Péguy."  Tablet, 177, 15 February 1941, 136.

3376    POLIMENI, E.  "Call to Heroism: The Tribute of Charles Péguy to Henri Bergson."  The Month, 178, Nos. 9-10, September-October 1941, 462-466.

3377    POLIN, Raymond.  "Bergson philosophe de la création."  Etudes Bergsoniennes, 5, 1960, 193-213.

3378    POLIN, Raymond.  "Henri Bergson et le mal."  Etudes Bergsoniennes, 3, 7-40.  According to the author, evil is for Bergson a positive reality and coincides with matter.

3379    POLIN, Raymond. "Henri Bergson et le mal." Etudes Bergso-
        niennes, 3, 180-191. This is a résumé of Polin's talk fol-
        lowed by a discussion, with several philosophers, of Berg-
        son's concept of evil.

3380    POLIN, Raymond. "Review of L'Intellectualisme de Bergson:
        Genèse et développement de la notion bergsonienne d'intui-
        tion by Léon Husson." Etudes Bergsoniennes, 1, 1948, 214-
        217. The author is critical of Husson's definition of "in-
        tellect."

3381    POLIN, Raymond. "Y a-t-il chez Bergson une philosophie de
        l'histoire?" Etudes Bergsoniennes, 4, 1956, 7-40.

3382    POLITZER, Georges. Le Bergsonisme: Une Mystification philo-
        sophique. Paris: Les Revues, 1929, 128. This edition was
        published under the pseudonym François Arouet. This is a
        thoroughgoing Marxist critique of Bergson, particularly as
        regards its social and political implications.

3383    POLITZER, Georges. Le Bergsonisme: Une Mystification philo-
        sophique. 2e éd. Paris: Editions Sociales, 1947, 112.

3384    POLITZER, Georges. La Fin d'une parade philosophique: Le
        Bergsonisme. Paris: Les Revues, 1928, 120. This is a
        Marxist critique of Bergson. The author insists that Berg-
        sonism is a rationalization of bourgeoise interests.

3385    POLITZER, Georges. La Fin d'une parade philosophique: Le
        Bergsonisme. Paris: Pauvert, 1968, 191.

3386    POMAR, Felipe C. del. "Los 'ismos' en la pintura contempo-
        ránea." Cursos y Conferencias, 3, No. 5, noviembre 1933,
        451.

3387    POORTMAN, J. J. "H. Bergson en die parapsychologie." Tijd-
        schrift voor Parapsychologie, 13, 1941, 51-66.

3388    POORTMAN, J. J. "Henri Bergson en die parapsychologie." De
        grondparadox en andere voordrachten en essays. Assens,
        Denmark: Van Gorcum, 1961, 38-53.

3389    "Portrait of Bergson." Current History, 29, No. 4, January
        1929, 604. This article concerns the award of a Nobel
        Prize to Bergson.

3390    "Portrait of Bergson." Outlook, 126, 29 December 1920, 767.
        This is a review of Mind-Energy.

3391   "Portrait of Bergson." Scholastic, 29, No. 5, 17 October
       1936, 21.

3392   "Portrait of Bergson." United Nations World, 5, No. 4,
       April 1951, 42-43. Bergson is discussed in this article
       on the French mentality.

3393   POS, Hendrik Josephus. "Henri Bergson in memoriam." Alge-
       meen Nederlands Tijdschrift voor Wijsbegeerte en Psychol-
       ogie, 38, Nos. 3-4, 1946, 71-76.

3394   POS, Hendrik Josephus. Uren met Bergson. Baam, Netherlands:
       Hollandia, 1940, 192.

3395   POUILLON, Jean. Temps et roman. Paris: Gallimard, 1946,
       277.

3396   POULAIN, Dorothy. "Monsieur Pouget: A Christian Socrates."
       Catholic World, 181, No. 1085, August 1955, 326-331.

3397   POULET, Georges. "Bergson et le thème de la vision panora-
       mique des mourants." Revue de Théologie et de Philosophie,
       10, No. 1, 1960, 23-41. Bergson's psychology of attention
       is analyzed in this searching study.

3398   POULET, Georges. La Distance intérieure. Paris: Plon, 1952,
       357.

3399   POULET, Georges. Etudes sur le temps humain. Edinburgh:
       University Press, 1949, 407. Bergson's influence is
       found throughout this study of man's sense of time.

3400   POULET, Georges. Etudes sur le temps humain. Paris: Plon,
       1950, 409.

3401   POULET, Georges. Studies in Human Time. Baltimore, Mary-
       land: Johns Hopkins Press, 1956, 323.

3402   POULTON, E. B. "Darwin and Bergson on the Interpretation of
       Evolution." Bedrock, 1, No. 2, April 1912, 48-65.

3403   POUSSA, Narciso. Bergson y el problema de la libertad.
       Buenos Aires: Editorial Schapire, 1948.

3404   PRABHAVANANDA, Swami. "Buddha and Bergson." Vedanta for
       the Western World. Ed. Christopher Isherwood. Hollywood,
       California: Marcel Rodd Co., 1948, 288-293.

3405    PRADINES, Maurice. "Spiritualisme et psychologie chez Henri Bergson." Revue Philosophique de la France et de
l'Etranger, 131, Nos. 3-8, 1941, 182-217.

3406    PRADINES, Maurice. "Spiritualisme et psychologie chez Henri Bergson." Etudes Bergsoniennes. Paris: Presses Universitaires de France, 1943, 62-97.

3407    PRAGER, Hans. "Henri Bergsons metaphysische Grundanschau-
ung." Archiv für systematische Philosophie, 16, No. 3,
1910, 310-320.

3408    PRAGER, Hans. "Schriften von Henri Bergson." Zeitschrift
für Philosophie und philosophische Kritik, 145, No. 1,
1912, 88-93.

3409    PRAJS, Lazare. Péguy et Israël. Paris: Nizet, 1970, 217.
The introduction is by Pierre Moreau.

3410    "Premio Nobel a Bergson." La Prensa, 14 noviembre 1928.

3411    PREVOST, Jean. Les Caractères. Paris: Albin Michel, 1948,
346. Barrès, Bergson, Bourget, Claudel, and others are
discussed in this book.

3412    PREVOST, Jean. "Review of 'L'Intuition philosophique' by
Henri Bergson." Nouvelle Revue Française, 16, No. 183,
1er décembre 1928, 860-862.

3413    PREZZOLINI, Giuseppe. Bergson. Firenze: Aldino, 1910, 4.

3414    PREZZOLINI, Giuseppe. "H. Bergson." Voce, Anno 3, No. 4,
6 gennaio 1910, 239-240.

3415    PREZZOLINI, Giuseppe. Del linguaggio come causa di errore:
H. Bergson. Firenze: Spinelli, 1904.

3416    PREZZOLINI, Giuseppe. "La filosofia di Enrico Bergson."
Rassegna contemporanea, 4, No. 11, 1908, 287-314.

3417    PREZZOLINI, Giuseppe. "Giorgio Sorel e il sindacalismo:
Le grandi teorie sindacaliste e la filosofia di E. Bergson." Bolletino filosofico, No. 2, 1909.

3418    PREZZOLINI, Giuseppe. La teoria sindacalista. Napoli: Francesco Perella, 1909, 338. Bergson is discussed on pages
281-335.

3419   PREZZOLINI, Giuseppe. Uomini 22 e città 3. Firenze: Val-
       lecchi, 1920, 313. Bergson is discussed on pages 41-66.

3420   PRICE, H. H. "Henri Bergson." Proceedings of the Society
       for Psychical Research, 46, Part 164, June 1941, 271-276.
       Bergson's theories of mind-body relations, of immortality,
       and of extra-sensory perception are discussed in this es-
       say.

3421   PRIDDIN, Deidre. The Art of the Dance in French Literature
       from Théophile Gautier to Paul Valéry. London: Black,
       1952, 176. Mallarmé, Lemaître, Noailles, Prévost, Valéry,
       Bergson, and others are discussed in this study.

3422   PRIGOGINE, I. "Evolution of Physics." Nature, 234, 19 No-
       vember 1971, 159-160. This is a review of Bergson and the
       Evolution of Physics, Ed. and Trans. with Intro. P. A. Y.
       Gunter.

3423   PRINGLE-PATTISON, Seth. The Idea of God in the Light of Re-
       cent Philosophy. Aberdeen, Scotland: University Press,
       1917, 423. Bergson is discussed on pages 366-385.

3424   PRINS, Adolphe. "L'Evolution et la conception matérialiste
       de l'univers." Revue de l'Université de Bruxelles, 13,
       No. 4, octobre 1907, 29-67.

3425   PRINS, D.-H. "Bergson over het wezen de moral en dat van
       den godsdienst." Theosophia, 1934.

3426   "Le Prix Nobel à M. Bergson." L'Action Française, 21e Année,
       No. 320, 15 novembre 1928, 4.

3427   PRO, Diego F. "La realidad espiritual y ontología." Alber-
       to Rouges. Argentina: Valles Calchaquiés, 1957, 386.

3428   "Professor Bergson at City College." Outlook, 103, No. 9,
       1 March 1913, 467.

3429   "Professor Bergson on Freewill." Spectator, 105, No. 4291,
       24 September 1910, 465-466. This is an exposition of Berg-
       son's position in Time and Free Will.

3430   "Professor Bergson on the Soul." Educational Review, 43, No.
       1, January 1912, 1-16. This is a summary of four lectures
       given by Bergson at the University of London. It is taken
       from a report in the London Times.

3431    "Professor Bergson's Concept of the Absolute." Contemporary
        Review, 103, No. 67, April 1913, 590-593. This is a re-
        view of Bergson's Introduction to Metaphysics.

3432    "Professor Henri Bergson." Open Court, 26, No. 9, September
        1912, 573.

3433    PROUST, Marcel. Correspondance générale. "Publiée par Ro-
        bert Proust et Paul Brach." Paris, I-IV, 1930-1936. See
        Volume III, page 195, for Marcel Proust's relation to Berg-
        son.

3434    PROUST, Marcel. "Lettre au Temps." Le Temps, No. 19124, 13
        novembre 1913, 2. This letter concerns the function of
        voluntary and involuntary memory in Bergson and Proust.
        Proust denies Bergson's influence.

3435    PROUST, Robert. "Marcel Proust intime." Nouvelle Revue
        Française, 20, No. 1, janvier 1923.

3436    PROUT, F. R. "Review of 'L'Intuition philosophique' by Hen-
        ri Bergson." Philosophical Review, 21, No. 2, March 1912,
        265.

3437    PRUDENCIO BUSTILLO, Ignacio. Al margen del bergsonismo.
        Sucre, Bolivia, 1913.

34 8    PRUDENCIO BUSTILLO, Ignacio. Ensayo de una filosofía jurí-
        dica. Sucre, Bolivia: Universidad de San Francisco Javier,
        1923.

3439    PRZYLUSKI, Jean. L'Evolution humaine. Paris: Presses Uni-
        versitaires de France, 1942, 268.

3440    PUCCIARELLI, Eugenio. "Bergson y la experiencia metafísica."
        Sustancia, 2, Nos. 7-8, septiembre 1941, 363-374.

3441    PUCCIARELLI, Eugenio. Bergson y la experiencia metafisica.
        Tucumán, Argentina: Editorial La Raza, 1941, 14. This
        pamphlet is reprinted from the September 1941 issue of
        Sustancia.

3442    PUCCIARELLI, Eugenio. "Dos actides frente al tiempo." Cua-
        dernos de filosofía, 10, No. 1, enero-junio 1970, 7-48.
        This article considers the relationship between time and
        man's participation in eternity. Bergson, Hamelin, Bache-
        lard, Lavelle, Guitton, and several other philosophers are
        discussed.

3443    PUCCIARELLI, Eugenio. "Espíritu y materia en Bergson." Re-
        vista de Pedagogía, Año 1, Nos. 4 y 5, 1942.

3444    PUCCIARELLI, Eugenio. Espiritu y materia en Bergson. 1939.

3445    PUCELLE, Jean. "L'Instant: Croisement de séries." Actes du
        Xe Congrès des Sociétés de Philosophie de Langue Française
        (Congrès Bergson). Paris: Armand Colin, 1, 1959, 267-269.

3446    PUGLIESI, Anna. "Henri Bergson tra Cattolici e Communisti."
        Ricerche filosofiche, 5, No. 1, 1951, 35-39. The author
        doubts Bergson's conversion to Catholicism and stresses
        similarities between the doctrines of Les Deux Sources
        and Communism.

3447    PUGLIESI, Anna. "Le Bergsonisme en Italie." Collaboration
        philosophique. Bologna: Mareggiani, 1958, 59-78.

3448    QUEIROZ, Amaro Xisto de. "A estética de Bergson." Kriteri-
        on, 6, Nos. 25-26, 1953, 315-319.

3449    QUERCY, Pierre. L'Hallucination: Vol. 2. Philosophes et
        mystiques. Paris: Félix Alcan, 1930, 381. Bergson's theo-
        ry of hallucination is analyzed on pages xxiii-xxvii and
        141-172.

3450    QUERCY, Pierre. "Remarques sur la théorie bergsonienne de
        l'aphasie sensorielle." Encéphale, 5e Année, 1925, 89-98.

3451    QUERCY, Pierre. "Remarques sur une théorie bergsonienne de
        l'hallucination." Annales Médico-psychologiques, 2, 1925,
        242-259. The author is highly critical of Bergson's theo-
        ry of hallucination. He holds that scientific facts do
        not verify this theory.

3452    QUEVEDO, J. F. "Síntesis de filosofia Bergsoniana." Proa,
        julio 1937, 4-5.

3453    QUICK, Oliver. "Bergson's Creative Evolution and the Indi-
        vidual." Mind, 22, No. 86, April 1913, 217-230. The au-
        thor discusses problems related to the "vital impetus."

3454    QUILES, Ismael. "La filosofía de la religión según Bergson."
        Ciencia y Fe, 3, No. 3, julio-diciembre 1947, 36-43.

3455    QUINTANILLA, Louis. "Bergsonisme et politique." Diss.,
        Johns Hopkins, 1938.

3456   QUINTANILLA, Louis. _Bergsonismo y política_. México and
Buenos Aires: Fondo de Cultura Económica, 1953, 205. The
introduction is by Samuel Ramos. This study concerns primarily Bergson and Georges Sorel.

3457   QUITO, Emérito S. "The Philosophy of Henri Bergson." _Uni-
tas_, 39, No. 1, 1966, 3-29.

3458   RABEAU, Gaston. "L'Expérience mystique et la preuve de
l'existence de Dieu." _Revue Thomiste_, N.S. 16, No. 77,
mai-juin 1933, 453-465.

3459   RABEAU, Gaston. "Fait psychologique et intuition." _Docu-
ments de la Vie Intellectuelle_, 2, No. 5, 1930, 271-277.
This study was published originally in _Réalité et relativi-
té_. Paris: Rivière, 1927, 191-200.

3460   RABIL, Albert. _Merleau-Ponty: Existentialist of the Social
World_. New York and London: Columbia University Press,
1967, 331. Bergson's concept of the function of the body
is discussed on pages 24-25; Merleau-Ponty, on pages 180-
187; Merleau-Ponty's theory of perception, on pages 180-
182. The author states: "Hence, two years before the writing of his first book, Merleau-Ponty apparently looked to
Bergson's theory of perception as one aiming at that 'am-
biguous' world to which his own thinking was directing
him." (183).

3461   RABOW, Hans. "Bericht über Neuerscheinunger der französi-
chen Philosophie." _Kantstudien_, 39, Nos. 3-4, 1934, 351-
352. This is a brief notice concerning _Les Deux Sources_.

3462   RADHAKRISHNAN, Sarvepalli. "Bergson and Absolute Idealism."
_Mind_, 28, No. 109, 1919, 41-53; No. 111, 1919, 275-296.
The author concludes that: "Bergsonism must have absolute
idealism as a foundation."

3463   RADHAKRISHNAN, Sarvapalli. "Bergson's Idea of God." _Quest_,
8, No. 4, October 1916, 1-8.

3464   RADHAKRISHNAN, Sarvapalli. "Is Bergson's Philosophy Monistic?" _Mind_, 25, No. 103, July 1917, 329-339. The author
views Bergson as a monist.

3465   RADKOWSKI, Tadeusz. "Henryk Bergson." _Tygodnik Warszawski_,
2, No. 3, 1946, 3-4.

3466    RAEYMAEKER, Louis de.  "Table ronde: Religion."  Actes du Xe
        Congrès des Sociétés de Philosophie de Langue Française
        (Congrès Bergson).  Paris: Armand Colin, 2, 1959, 261-278.

3467    RAGEOT, Gaston.  "Henri Bergson."  Revue de Paris, 25, No. 3,
        1er février 1918, 540-563.

3468    RAGEOT, Gaston.  "Henri Bergson."  Le Temps, No. 18263, 2
        juillet 1911, 3.

3469    RAGEOT, Gaston.  "Henri Bergson académicien."  Illustration,
        76, No. 3903, 2 février 1918, 103.

3470    RAGEOT, Gaston.  "Henri Bergson: L'Intuition."  Conferencia,
        2, octobre 1933, 423-435.

3471    RAGEOT, Gaston.  "Le Bergsonisme et le monde moderne."  Il-
        lustration, 86, Pt. 2, 24 novembre 1928, 597-598.

3472    RAGEOT, Gaston.  "Le Congrès international de psychologie."
        Revue Philosophique de la France et de l'Etranger, 60, No.
        7, juillet 1905, 67-87.  The author suggests that Bergson
        drew his concept of duration from the ideas of James and
        Ward.

3473    RAGEOT, Gaston.  "Correspondance avec M. Bergson sur sa rela-
        tion à M. W. James."  Revue Philosophique de la France et
        de l'Etranger, 50, No. 8, août 1905, 229-231.

3474    RAGEOT, Gaston.  "Review of L'Energie spirituelle by Henri
        Bergson."  Revue Hebdomadaire des Cours et des Conférences,
        28e Année, No. 51, 20 décembre 1919, 331-350.

3475    RAGEOT, Gaston.  "Una entrevista con Henri Bergson."  La
        Nación, 30 septiembre 1934.

3476    RAGEOT, Gaston.  "Review of L'Evolution créatrice by Henri
        Bergson."  Revue Philosophique de la France et de l'Etran-
        ger, 64, No. 7, juillet 1907, 73-85.  This is an apprecia-
        tive review of L'Evolution créatrice.

3477    RAGEOT, Gaston.  "Le Rôle historique du bergsonisme."  Le
        Temps, No. 22862, 13 mars 1924, 3.

3478    RAGEOT, Gaston.  Les Savants et la philosophie.  Paris:
        Félix Alcan, 1908, 179.  Chapter four, "La Métaphysique
        de la psychologie," concerns Bergson.

3479    RAGEOT, Gaston.  "Souvenirs d'un bergsonien."  Annales Poli-
         tiques et Littéraires, 72e Année, No. 2323, 1er décembre
         1928, 493-494.

3480    RALEA, Mihail.  Psihologie si vieata.  Bucuresti, Rumania:
         Fundatia p. lit. si artă, 1938, 298.  This work contains a
         section on Bergson and Einstein.

3481    RAMOS, Samuel.  "Concepto de la filosofía según Bergson."
         Homenaje a Bergson.  Imprenta Universitaria México, 1941,
         107-122.

3482    RAND, Benjamin, Ed.  Modern Classical Philosophers.  Boston:
         Houghton Mifflin Co., 1948, 892.  This book includes selec-
         tions from Bergson.

3483    RANGEL FRIAS, Raúl.  "Bergson."  Armas y Letras, 5, No. 5,
         mayo 1948, 5.

3484    RAO, P. Nagaraja.  "Bergson and Sankara."  Aryon Path, 12,
         No. 4, April 1941, 174-177.

3485    RAU, Enrique.  "El irracionalismo religioso de José Vascon-
         celos."  Criterio, 9, No. 450, 15 octubre 1936, 155, Col.
         la.

3486    RAUDIVE, Konstantin.  Der Chaosmensch und seine Überwindung.
         Memmingen: Dietrich, 1951, 400.  Valéry, Proust, Gide,
         Bergson, Mauriac, Péguy, Rolland, and others are treated
         in this study.

3487    RAUH, Frédéric.  "La Conscience du devenir."  Revue de Méta-
         physique et de Morale, 4, 1897, 659-681; 5, 1898, 38-60.

3488    RAUH, Frédéric.  De La Méthode dans la psychologie des senti-
         ments.  Paris: Félix Alcan, 1899, 397.

3489    RAUH, Frédéric.  "Sur La Position du problème du libre arbi-
         tre."  Revue de Métaphysique et de Morale, 12, No. 6, no-
         vembre 1904, 977-1006.

3490    RAUL VALLEJOS, M. A.  "El mundo especulativo de Henri Berg-
         son."  Universidad de San Carlos, No. 62, enero-abril 1964,
         113-119.

3491    RAVAGNAN, Luis M.  "La impresión de 'ya visto': Ensayo psi-
         cologico de H. Bergson."  Estudios, 27, No. 315, 27-76.
         This is a translation of Bergson's "Le Souvenir du pré-
         sent," with commentary.

3492    RAVAISSON-MOLLIEN, Félix. Testament philosophique et frag-
        ments précédés de la notice lue en 1904 par Henri Bergson.
        "Texte revu et présenté par Charles Devivaise." Paris:
        Boivin, 1933, 197.

3493    RAVERA, Rosa María. "Las ideas estéticas de Bergson." Uni-
        versidad, 31, No. 1, enero-marzo 1965, 127-150.

3494    RAYMOND, Marcel. "Bergson et la poésie récente: Notes pour
        une étude." Henri Bergson. Ed. Béguin and Thévenaz, 281-
        293. The author examines the influence of Bergson on the
        poets Péguy and Valéry.

3495    RAYMOND, Marcel. "Bergson et la Suisse romande." Actes du
        Xe Congrès des Sociétés de Philosophie de Langue Française
        (Congrès Bergson). Paris: Armand Colin, 1, 1959, 271-274.
        The author deals with Bergson's visits to French Switzer-
        land, his influence on philosophical thought there, and
        with the "pre-Bergsonian" character of the thought of
        Amiel and De Gourd.

3496    RAYMOND, Marcel. Génies de France. Neuchâtel, Switzerland:
        La Baconnière, 1942, 247. This study contains a section
        entitled "Bergson et la poésie récente."

3497    RAYMOND, Marcel. "Table ronde: Sources et histoire du berg-
        sonisme." Actes du Xe Congrès des Sociétés de Philosophie
        de Langue Française (Congrès Bergson). Paris: Armand
        Colin, 2, 1959, 213-233.

3498    RAYMOND, Marcel. "La Philosophie de l'intuition et la philo-
        sophie du concept." Etudes Franciscaines, 21, No. 2, juin
        1909, 669-687.

3499    RAYNER, Ernest A. "The Origin and Development of Persons."
        Philosophical Review, 25, No. 6, November 1916, 788-800.
        The author pursues a critique of both Bergson and Bosan-
        quet.

3500    READ, Herbert. Collected Essays in Literary Criticism.
        London: Faber and Faber, 1951, 381.

3501    REBOUL, Olivier. "La Création en art: Artiste et artisan:
        Alain, Bergson et Valéry." L'Homme et ses passions d'après
        Alain: Vol. 2. La Sagesse. Paris: Presses Universitaires
        de France, 1968, 69-74.

3502    RECK, Andrew J. "Bergson's Theory of Duration." Tulane
        Studies in Philosophy, 8, 1959, 27-47.

3503    RECOULY, Raymond. "Algunos recuerdos sobre H. Bergson." La
        Nación, noviembre 1924.

3504    "Redacción de 'El premio Nobel'." Síntesis, 2, No. 19, di-
        ciembre 1928, 117-118.

3505    REES, R. "Review of Les Deux Sources de la morale et de la
        religion by Henri Bergson." Adelphi, 10, 1933, 117-126.

3506    REGNIER, Marcel. "Le Congrès Bergson." Etudes par des
        Pères de la Compagnie de Jésus, 302, juillet-août 1959,
        128-130.

3507    REINEHR, Merle Jerome. "Self Creative Self in Henri Berg-
        son." Diss., St. Louis, 1964.

3508    REINKE, Johannes. Die Schaffende Natur: Mit Bezugnahme auf
        Schopenhauer und Bergson. Leipsic: Verlag von Quelle und
        Meyer, 1919, 153. Bergson is discussed on pages 111-129.

3509    REIN'L, Robert Lincoln Coffin. "Intuition and Analysis in
        Bergson's Theory of Knowledge." Diss., Harvard, 1940, 335.

3510    REISS, Françoise. "Quelle est la valeur actuelle de la pen-
        sée bergsonienne?" Arts, No. 724, 27 mai-2 juin 1959, 3.

3511    RENSI, Giuseppe. Raffigurazioni: Schizzi di uomini e di dot-
        trine. Modena, Italy: Guanda, 1934, 156. This study in-
        cludes a chapter on Bergson containing a vigorous critique
        of the distinction between instinct and intelligence.

3512    "Report of Bergson's Funeral." New York Times, 16 January
        1941, 21, col. 2.

3513    REULET-SANCHEZ, Aníbal. "Review of Bergsonismo y política
        by L. Quintanilla." Américas, 5, No. 7, July 1953, 36-37.
        The author observes: "For more than a quarter of a cen-
        tury, Bergson was the European philosopher most influen-
        tial in the Spanish American countries. But so far as I
        know, outside of a small sphere of intellectual anarchists
        Bergsonian philosophy found its warmest welcome among lib-
        eral and democratic elements . . . . And in Mexico,
        around 1910, it was the ideological battering ram used to
        start the attack on the Porfirio Díaz dictatorship . . . ."
        (37).

3514    REVEL, Jean-François. "D'Un Nouvel Eclectisme." Cahiers
        des Saisons, No. 19, Hiver 1960, 387-392.

3515    REVEL, Jean-François. _Pourquoi des philosophes?_ Paris: Pau-
        vert, 1954, 184. This study deals with Bergson, Sartre,
        Merleau-Ponty, and Lévi-Strauss.

3516    REVERDIN, Henri. "Table ronde: Liberté." _Actes du Xe Con-
        grès des Sociétés de Philosophie de Langue Française_ (Con-
        grès Bergson). Paris: Armand Colin, 2, 1959, 167-189.

3517    REVERDIN, Henri. "Table ronde: Religion." _Actes du Xe Con-
        grès des Sociétés de Philosophie de Langue Française_ (Con-
        grès Bergson). Paris: Armand Colin, 2, 1959, 261-278.

3518    REY, Abel. "Le Congrès international de philosophie, Bolo-
        gne, 6-11 avril 1911." _Revue Philosophique de la France
        et de l'Etranger_, 72, No. 7, juillet 1911, 1-22. The au-
        thor discusses Bergson's address on philosophical intui-
        tion.

3519    REY, Abel. "French Philosophy in 1926 and 1927." _Philo-
        sophical Review_, 37, No. 6, November 1928, 527-556. The
        author claims that Bergsonism and Scholasticism have large-
        ly given to French philosophy its present characteristics.

3520    REY, Abel. "L'Opinion de M. Abel Rey." _Documents de la Vie
        Intellectuelle_, 2, No. 5, 20 février 1930, 254-256. This
        essay is drawn from Janet's and Séailles' history of phi-
        losophy, 1928, 204-206.

3521    REY, Abel. "Philosophy in France, 1929." _Philosophical Re-
        view_, 40, No. 1, January 1931, 1-31. The author states
        that French philosophy continues to try to determine,
        through the transformation wrought by Bergson, the manner
        in which our intelligence apprehends reality. A trend to-
        wards earlier, classical philosophies is evident.

3522    REYLES, C. M. "Vida y estructura: El 'Homo Loquax'." _La
        Nación_, 1936.

3523    REYMOND, Arnold. "Henri Bergson et Maine de Biran." _Henri
        Bergson_. Ed. Béguin and Thévenaz, 248-256. The author
        compares Bergson and Maine de Biran. He explains that the
        thought of the two philosophers developed similarly.
        Both end by finding support for the activity of the indi-
        vidual self in the divine will.

3524    REYMOND, Arnold. "Notes sur Carnot et Bergson." _Revue Phi-
        losophique de la France et de l'Etranger_, 83, No. 3, 1958,
        371-372.

3525    REYMOND, Arnold-Frédéric. La Philosophie de M. Bergson et
le problème de la raison. Lausanne: Impr. coopérative "La
Concorde," 1913, 19.

3526    RIBIERO, Alvaro. Escritores doutrinados. Lisboa: Sociedade
de expansão cultural, 1965, 245. An essay on Bergson's
philosophy of language is included in this book.

3527    RIBY, Jules. "Lettres à Joseph Lotte: I. Avant-propos et
notes par Théo Quoniam." Feuillets de l'Amitié Charles
Péguy, No. 98, janvier 1963, 11-33.

3528    RIBY, Jules. "Lettres à Joseph Lotte: IV. Avant-propos et
notes par Théo Quoniam." Feuillets de l'Amitié Charles
Péguy, No. 102, août 1963, 2-19.

3529    RIBY, Jules. "Lettres à Joseph Lotte: V. Avant-propos et
notes par Théo Quoniam." Feuillets de l'Amitié Charles
Péguy, No. 104, 25 décembre 1963, 17-36.

3530    RIBY, Jules. "Lettres à Joseph Lotte: VI. Avant-propos et
notes par Théo Quoniam." Feuillets de l'Amitié Charles
Péguy, No. 105, 25 février 1964, 5-31.

3531    RIBY, Jules. "Lettres à Joseph Lotte: X. Avant-propos et
notes par Théo Quoniam." Feuillets de l'Amitié Charles
Péguy, No. 112, février 1965, 11-35.

3532    RIBY, Jules. "Lettres à Joseph Lotte: XI. Notes par Théo
Quoniam." Feuillets de l'Amitié Charles Péguy, No. 113,
avril 1965, 4-22.

3533    RICCABONI, Joseph J. "Bergson's Metaphysical Intuition and
Science." Journal of the History of Philosophy, 5, No. 2,
April 1967, 159-161. The author argues that Bergson's in-
tuition is "metaphysical" and therefore not intended--as
Mario Bunge insists--to be scientifically fruitful.

3534    RICE, C. "M. Bergson, Mystic." Blackfriars, 92, No. 3, 3
March 1933, 201-203. This is a review of Les Deux Sources.

3535    RICHARD, René. "Henri Bergson habla y concluye." La Nación,
1936.

3536    RICHARDSON, W. "The Jet of Life." Modern Churchman, 31, No.
3, 1941, 442-446.

3537    RICHLI-BIDAL, M.-L. Après le symbolisme: Retour à l'humain.
Paris: Presses Modernes, 1938, 240. A discussion of Berg-

son and the "unamiste" movement may be found on pages 78-91.

3538    RICHTER, Johannes Rudolf.  Intuition und intellectuelle Anschauung bei Schelling und Bergson.  Ohlau, Germany: Schles., 1929, 88.

3539    RICKERT, Heinrich.  Die Philosophie des Lebens.  Tübingen, Germany: Mohr, 1920, 196.

3540    RICKS, C. B.  "Frederic Harrison and Bergson."  Notes and Queries, 6, No. 5, May 1959, 175-178.  The author recounts various criticisms of Bergson's Introduction to Metaphysics by a British positivist.

3541    RICOEUR, Paul.  "Le Symbolisme et l'explication structurale."  Cahiers Internationaux de Symbolisme, No. 4, 1964, 81-96.  This study deals with symbolism in Bergson, Lévi-Strauss, F. de Saussure, and Sartre.

3542    RICOUR, Aimé.  "Morale et nature dans la philosophie morale de Bergson."  Archives de Philosophie, 17, No. 1, 1947, 149-171.

3543    RICOUR, Pierre.  "Aux Sources vives du bergsonisme: Qu'est-ce que philosopher?"  Bulletin des Etudes Françaises, 1, No. 1, avril 1941, 39-50.

3544    RIDEAU, Emile.  "Actualité de Bergson."  Etudes, 327, No. 6, décembre 1967, 638-653.

3545    RIDEAU, Emile.  "Bergson aujourd'hui."  Etudes, 302, Nos. 7-8, août 1959, 3-23.

3546    RIDEAU, Emile.  "Le Bergsonisme."  Nouvelle Revue Théologique, 69e Année, No. 6, juin 1937, 621-639; No. 7, juillet-août 1937, 733-754.

3547    RIDEAU, Emile.  "O Bergsonismo perante o mundo contemporâneo."  Brotéria, 24, No. 2, 1937, 121-127.

3548    RIDEAU, Emile.  Descartes, Pascal, Bergson.  Paris: Boivin, 1937, 246.

3549    RIDEAU, Emile.  Le Dieu de Bergson: Essai de critique religieuse.  Paris: Félix Alcan, 1932, 135.

3550  RIDEAU, Emile. "En relisant Les Deux Sources." Etudes par des Pères de la Compagnie de Jésus, 294, octobre 1957, 3-16.

3551  RIDEAU, Emile. "Matière et esprit chez Bergson." Revue Nouvelle, 16e Année, 31, No. 4, 15 avril 1960, 337-354. According to the author, matter is, for Bergson, generally, anything which disintegrates, analyzes, and dissociates.

3552  RIDEAU, Emile. Paganisme et christianisme. Tournai, France: Casterman, 1953, 254. This study treats of Bergson, along with many others.

3553  RIDEAU, Emile. Les Rapports de la matière et de l'esprit dans le bergsonisme. Paris: Félix Alcan, 1932, 182.

3554  RIEFSTAHL, Hermann. "Henri Bergsons Zeit und Freiheit." Philosophischer Literaturanzeiger, 3, No. 2, 1950, 67-71.

3555  RIEFSTAHL, Hermann. "Neue Bergson-Literatur." Zeitschrift für philosophische Forschung, 17, No. 1, 1963, 173-179.

3556  RIEFSTAHL, Hermann. "Die Philosophie Henri Bergsons und das Denken des 20. Jahrhunderts." Universitas, 15, No. 9, 1960, 981-988.

3557  RIGNANO, Eugenio. "Ce que la biologie doit à Bergson." Nouvelles Littéraires, No. 322, 15 décembre 1928, 3. The author holds that Bergson is responsible for broadening the concepts which biologists use to comprehend life.

3558  RIGNANO, Eugenio. "Ce qu la biologie doit à Bergson." Documents de la Vie Intellectuelle, 1, No. 4, 20 janvier 1933, 65-66. This article originally appeared in Nouvelles Littéraires, 1928.

3559  RIGNANO, Eugenio. The Psychology of Reasoning. New York: Harcourt, Brace and Co., Inc.; London: Kegan Paul, Trench Trubner and Co., Ltd., 1923, 325. Various references to Bergson's theory of dreams may be found on pages 40, 297, 303, and 310.

3560  RILEY, Woodbridge. "La Philosophie française en Amérique: III, Le Bergsonisme." Revue Philosophique de la France et de l'Etranger, 91, No. 1-2, 1921, 75-107; No. 3-4, 1921, 234-271.

3561  "Review of Le Rire: Essai sur la signification du comique by Henri Bergson." Wiener Zeitung, 1900.

3562    RIVAUD, Albert.  "La Pensée de Bergson et sa place dans
        l'histoire des idées."  Revue des Deux Mondes, 111, 8e pé-
        riode, No. 65, 15 juillet 1941, 158-184.  This is an ac-
        count of the development of Bergson's thought.

3563    RIVAUD, Albert.  "Remarques sur la durée."  Recherches Philo-
        sophiques, 3, 1933-1934, 19-33.

3564    RIVAUD, Albert.  Remarques sur la durée.  Paris: Boivin,
        1933-1934, 15.  This article appeared originally in Re-
        cherches Philosophiques.

3565    RIVERS, W. H. R.  Instinct and the Unconscious.  Cambridge
        University Press, 1920, 252.

3566    ROA, A.  "Bergson y el problema del conocimiento."  Estudios,
        59, No. 61, 1938, 34-43.

3567    ROBBERS, H.  "Henri Bergson."  Studien's Hertogenbosch, 1941,
        135.

3568    ROBBERS, H.  "Henri Bergson: 18 octobre 1859-5 janvier 1941."
        Studiën, 73, février 1941, 134-144.

3569    ROBERTAZZI, M.  "Review of La Pensée et le mouvant by Henri
        Bergson."  Convegno, 15 Anno, 1934, 150-153.

3570    ROBERTS, James Deotis.  "Bergson as a Metaphysical, Episte-
        mological, and Religious Thinker."  Journal of Religious
        Thought, 20, No. 2, 1963-1964, 105-114.

3571    ROBERTS, James Deotis.  Faith and Reason: A Comparative
        Study of Pascal, Bergson, and James.  Boston: Christopher
        Publishing House, 1962, 98.

3572    ROBINET, André, Ed.  Henri Bergson: Mélanges.  Paris: Pres-
        ses Universitaires de France, 1973, 1692.  "Notes des édi-
        teurs" are found on pages 1599-1629.  This collection of
        Bergson's writings was edited by Professor Robinet in col-
        laboration with Rose-Marie Mossé-Bastide, Martine Robinet,
        and Michel Gauthier.

3573    ROBINET, André.  Bergson et les métamorphoses de la durée.
        Paris: Seghers, 1965, 192.

3574    ROBINET, André.  "Le Bon Roi Dagobert est-il Juarès?"  Feuil-
        lets de l'Amitié Charles Péguy, No. 135, 1967, 29-30.
        This is a passage quoted from the author's Péguy entre
        Juarès, Bergson, et l'Eglise.

3575   ROBINET, André. "L'Espérance de la philosophie unique."
       Actes du Xe Congrès des Sociétés de Philosophie de Langue
       Française (Congrès Bergson). Paris: Armand Colin, 1, 1959,
       275-280.

3576   ROBINET, André. "Le Fonds Bergson de la Bibliothèque Dou-
       cet." Etudes Bergsoniennes, 7, 1966, 219-220. The author
       explains that a collection of certain of Bergson's letters,
       notes, manuscripts, and his personal library has been de-
       posited in the Bibliothèque Doucet in Paris.

3577   ROBINET, André. "Le Passage à la conception biologique: De
       La Perception, de l'image et du souvenir chez Bergson:
       Notes pour un commentaire du chapitre 11 de Matière et Mé-
       moire." Etudes Philosophiques, N.S. 15, No. 3, 1960, 375-
       388.

3578   ROBINET, André. Péguy entre Juarès, Bergson, et l'Eglise:
       Métaphysique et politique. Paris: Seghers, 1968, 351.

3579   ROBINET, André. "Péguy, lecteur de Bergson: Première rencon-
       tre." Etudes Bergsoniennes, 8, 1968, 63-81. This study
       is a description of the initial influence of Bergson on
       Péguy, with some interesting comments on the relations be-
       tween both men and Juarès.

3580   ROBINET, André. "Table ronde: Unité, unicité, dialogue."
       Actes du Xe Congrès des Sociétés de Philosophie de Langue
       Française (Congrès Bergson). Paris: Armand Colin, 2, 1959,
       281-302.

3581   ROBINET, André and GOUHIER, Henri, Eds. Henri Bergson:
       Oeuvres: Edition du Centenaire. Paris: Presses Universi-
       taires de France, 1959, 1602. Professor Robinet's "Appa-
       rat critique" and "Notes historiques" are found on pages
       1485-1539 and 1541-1578, respectively. Professor Gou-
       hier's "Introduction" is found on pages vii-xxx.

3582   ROBINET, André and Martine. "Henri Bergson et l'Angleterre."
       Etudes Bergsoniennes, 7, 1966, 5-136. This article con-
       tains a partial summary of "The Nature of the Soul" (a se-
       ries of lectures presented by Bergson at the University
       College, London, October, 1911) with press clippings, as
       well as a complete summary of "The Problem of Personality"
       (The Gifford Lectures, given by Bergson at Edinburgh,
       April-May, 1914) with press clippings. An interview with
       Bergson appears on pages 131-136.

3583    ROBINSON, Arthur.  "Review of A Critical Exposition of Berg-
        son's Philosophy by J. McKellar Stewart."  Mind, 23, No.
        91, July 1914, 443-444.

3584    ROBINSON, Arthur.  "Review of An Introduction to Metaphysics
        by Henri Bergson."  Mind, 23, No. 90, April 1914, 285.
        This is a review of T. E. Hulme's translation of the Intro-
        duction to Metaphysics.

3585    ROBINSON, Arthur.  "Memory and Consciousness."  Proceedings
        of the Aristotelian Society, 13, 1912-1913, 313-327.  Sev-
        eral interesting criticisms of Bergson's concepts of memo-
        ry and intelligence are offered by the author.

3586    ROBINSON, Arthur.  "The Philosophy of Bergson."  Modern
        Churchman, 3e Ser., 7, No. 3, March 1917.

3587    ROBINSON, Arthur.  "Review of The Philosophy of Change by
        H. Wildon Carr."  Mind, 24, No. 96, October 1915, 550-555.

3588    ROBLES, Oswaldo.  "Breve nota sobre la psicología y la antro-
        pología de Mr. Henri Bergson."  Homenaje a Bergson.  Im-
        prenta Universitaria México, 1941, 123-132.

3589    ROCHA, Zeferino.  "O misticismo na filosofia de Henri Berg-
        son."  Symposium, 1, Nos. 2-3, 1960, 105-120.

3590    ROCHE, Claude.  "La Notion d''autisme' chez Bergson."  Actes
        du Xe Congrès des Sociétés de Philosophie de Langue Fran-
        çaise (Congrès Bergson).  Paris: Armand Colin, 1, 1959,
        281-284.  By "autisme" is meant the most fundamental and
        most intimate part of the self.  It escapes the common con-
        ditions of knowledge.  The author discusses how, according
        to Bergson, it can be revealed and what its principal as-
        pects are.

3591    ROCHEDIEU, Edmond.  "La personalidad de Dios según Bergson."
        Luminar, 2, No. 4, Otoño 1938, 86-99.

3592    ROCHEDIEU, Edmond.  "La personalità de Dio in Bergson."  Re-
        ligio, 13, No. 5, 1937, 321-332.

3593    ROCHEDIEU, Edmond.  "L'Univers: Une Machine à faire des
        dieux."  Revue de Théologie et de Philosophie, N.S. 20, No.
        3, juillet 1932, 165-190.  This is a review of Les Deux
        Sources.

3594    ROCHOT, B.  "Sur Deux Livres d'Henri Bergson."  Revue de Syn-
        thèse, 33, No. 4, octobre-décembre 1963, 502-509.

3595    RODRIGUES, Gustave. Bergsonisme et moralité. Paris: Chiron, 1922, 156.

3596    ROELLENBLECK, Ewald. "Beitrag zur Theorie des Komischen: Mit besonderer Berücksichtigung von Bergson, Jean Paul, Lipps." Diss., Köln, 1922, 66.

3597    ROIG CIRONELLA, Juan. "La sumisión de los místicos al dogma enjuiciada por Bergson." Manresa, 17, No. 1, 1945, 44-56.

3598    ROLDAN, Sánchez Eleazar. "A propósito de Bergson." Revista de Filosofía, 14, No. 1, enero 1928, 117-123.

3599    ROLLAND, Edouard. "Le Dieu de Bergson." Sciences Ecclési- astiques, 14, No. 1, 1961, 83-98.

3600    ROLLAND, Edouard. La Finalité morale dans le bergsonisme. Paris: Beauchesne, 1937, 181.

3601    ROLLAND, Romain. "Unpublished letter to Jean-Pierre Dubois, 31 March 1942." A copy of this letter is retained in the archives of Mme. Romain Rolland. The letter concerns Pé- guy's Bergsonism.

3602    ROLLAND-GOSSELIN, Marie-Dominique. "Bergsonisme." Revue des Sciences Philosophiques et Théologiques, 8, No. 2, 1914, 308-312. This is a review of Bergson's address on parapsychology and of books on Bergson by Grandjean, Mari- tain, and Berthelot.

3603    ROLLAND-GOSSELIN, Marie-Dominique. "Bergsonisme." Revue des Sciences Philosophiques et Théologiques, 9, Nos. 1-2, janvier-avril 1920, 187-190. This is a review of L'Ener- gie spirituelle and of books on Bergson by Olgiati, Höff- ding, and Penido.

3604    ROLLAND-GOSSELIN, Marie-Dominique. "L'Intuitionisme berg- sonien et l'intelligence." Revue des Sciences Philosophi- ques et Théologiques, 7, No. 3, 1913, 389-411.

3605    ROMANELL, Patrick. "Bergson in Mexico: A Tribute to José Vasconcelos." Philosophy and Phenomenological Research, 21, No. 4, 1960-1961, 501-513. This study examines the Bergsonian period in Mexican philosophy (1910-1925) and the influence of Bergson on Vasconcelos.

3606    ROMANELL, Patrick. "Bergson no México: Um tribute a José Vasconcelos." Revista Brasileira de Filosofia, 10, No. 3, 1960, 373-383.

3607    ROMANELL, Patrick.  La formación de la mentalidad mexicana.
        México: Colegio de México, 1954, 238.  "Presentación de
        José Gaos."  References to Bergson may be found throughout
        this study of the Mexican mind.

3608    ROMANELL, Patrick.  Making of the Mexican Mind.  Lincoln,
        Nebraska: University of Nebraska Press, 1952, 213.

3609    ROMANELL, Patrick.  "Le Monisme esthétique de José Vascon-
        celos."  Revista de Filosofía, 64, No. 2, abril 1935.  The
        author explains that by renewing neoplatonic Christianity
        through Bergson, Vasconcelos achieves a religious monism.

3610    ROMER, A.  "Review of Die beiden Quellen der Moral und der
        Religion by Henri Bergson."  Archiv für die gesamte Psy-
        chologie, 96, 1934, 570.

3611    ROMERO, Francisco.  Sobre la filosofía en América.  Buenos
        Aires: Raigal, 1952, 135.

3612    ROMERO, Francisco.  "Temporalismo."  Nosotros, 5, No. 50-51,
        1940, 329-355.  Dilthey, Husserl, Bergson, and Heidegger
        are examined in this study.

3613    ROMEYER, Blaise.  "Autour du bergsonisme."  Archives de Phi-
        losophie, 16, No. 2, 1946, 1-45 (Supplément).

3614    ROMEYER, Blaise.  "Autour du problème de la philosophie chré-
        tienne."  Archives de Philosophie, 10, No. 1, 1933, 45-64.

3615    ROMEYER, Blaise.  "Caractéristiques religieuses du spiritu-
        alisme de Bergson."  Archives de Philosophie, 17, No. 1,
        1947, 22-55.

3616    ROMEYER, Blaise.  "La Liberté humaine d'après Bergson."
        Revue Néo-scolastique de Philosophie, 35, No. 2, mai 1933,
        190-219.  The author argues that the Essai is "seulement
        une analyse expérimentale suggestive et pénétrante."  It
        is not a metaphysics of liberty and hence cannot be op-
        posed to "la vraie métaphysique spiritualiste."

3617    ROMEYER, Blaise.  "Morale et religion chez Bergson."  Archi-
        ves de Philosophie, 9, No. 3, 1932, 283-317.  The author
        holds that Bergson "...manque à chercher la raison suffi-
        sante de cette valeur qui ne peut être que l'absolu subsis-
        tant, Dieu."

3618    ROMEYER, Blaise. "Review of La Pensée et le mouvant by Hen-
        ri Bergson." Archives de Philosophie, 10, No. 1, 1934,
        36-38.

3619    ROMEYER, Blaise. Le Problème moral et religieux. Paris:
        Bloud et Gay, 1945.

3620    ROMEYER, Blaise. "Le Problème moral et religieux: Maurice
        Blondel en regard d'Ollé-Laprune et de Bergson." Hommage
        à Maurice Blondel. Paris: Bloud et Gay, 1946, 49-80.

3621    ROMEYER, Blaise. "Spiritualité et survie d'après Bergson."
        Revue de Philosophie, 33, No. 2, mars-avril 1933, 117-156.

3622    ROOSEVELT, Theodore. "The Search for Truth in a Reverent
        Spirit." Outlook, 99, 2 December 1911, 819-826. This is
        a general account of Bergson's thought by a former Ameri-
        can president.

3623    ROSE, Mary C. "Three Hierarchies of Value: A Study in the
        Philosophies of Value of Henri Bergson, Alfred North White-
        head, and Søren Kierkegaard." Diss., Johns Hopkins, 1949.

3624    ROSENBERG, Maxmilian. "Die Erinnerungstäuschungen der 're-
        duplizierenden Paramnesie' und des 'déjà vu': Ihre klini-
        sche Differenzierung und ihre psychologische Beziehung
        zueinander." Zeitschrift für Pathopsychologie, 1, Mai
        1912, 561-602.

3625    ROSENBLOOM, Joseph. "The Internal Structure of Bergson's
        Philosophy." Diss., Chicago, 1949.

3626    ROSS, G. R. T. "The Satisfaction of Thinking." Proceedings
        of the Aristotelian Society, N.S. 9, 1908-1909, 119-140.
        Mathematical and intuitive accounts of motion are compared
        on pages 127-132; Bergson's biology is discussed on pages
        134-135. The author is generally critical.

3627    ROSS, G. T. "The Philosophy of Vitalism." Nation (London),
        4, 13 March 1909, 902-903.

3628    ROSS, Stephen D. Literature and Philosophy: An Analysis of
        the Philosophical Novel. New York: Appleton-Century-
        Crofts, 1969, 221.

3629    ROSTREVOR, Georges. Bergson and Future Philosophy: An Essay
        on the Scope of Intelligence. London: Macmillan and Co.,
        Ltd., 1921, 152.

3630    ROTENSTREICH, Nathan.  "Bergson and the Transformations of
        the Notion of Intuition."  Journal of the History of Phi-
        losophy, 10, No. 3, July 1972, 335-346.

3631    ROTENSTREICH, Nathan.  "The Changing Concept of Intuition
        and Bergson."  Iyyun, 20, January-October 1969, 1-13.
        This article is in Hebrew.

3632    ROUGEMONT, E. de.  "Portraits graphologiques: M. Henri Berg-
        son."  Mercure de France, 101, 16 février 1913, 736-756.
        This article contains an analysis of Bergson's handwriting.

3633    ROUGES, Alberto.  "La duración de Bergson, el tiempo físico
        y el acontecer físico."  Sustancia, 2, Nos. 7-8, septiem-
        bre 1941, 317-326.

3634    ROUGES, Alberto.  "La vida espiritual y la vida de la filo-
        sofía."  Sustancia, Año 1, No. 1, 1939.

3635    ROUGUE, Alberto.  "Le 4e Congrès international de philoso-
        phie."  Voprosy filosofii i psikhologii, 22, 1911.

3636    ROURE, Lucien.  "Review of Bergson by V. Jankélévitch."  Etu-
        des par des Pères de la Compagnie de Jésus, 210, 5 mars
        1932, 617-618.

3637    ROURE, Lucien.  "Un Livre danois sur M. H. Bergson."  Etudes
        par des Pères de la Compagnie de Jésus, 149, 5 novembre
        1916, 398-403.

3638    ROURE, Lucien.  Notes sur la psychologie de M. Bergson:
        L'Energie spirituelle."  Etudes par des Pères de la Com-
        pagnie de Jésus, 161, 5 novembre 1919, 295-303.

3639    ROUSSEAUX, André.  "De Bergson à Louis de Broglie."  Henri
        Bergson.  Ed. Béguin and Thévenaz, 271-280.  Bergson's
        philosophy, the author asserts, finds confirmation in the
        discoveries of twentieth-century physics.  The author com-
        pares Bergson's philosophy of science to that of the
        physicist Max Planck.

3640    ROUSSEAUX, André.  "Etudes Bergsoniennes."  Le Figaro Litté-
        raire, 4 juin 1949.

3641    ROUSSEAUX, André.  "Péguy, Bergson et Proust."  Fontaine, 4,
        No. 22, juin 1942, 123-127.

3642     ROUSTAN, Désiré. La Raison et la vie. Paris: Presses Uni-
         versitaires de France, 1946, 200. The introduction is by
         Armand Cuvillier.

3643     ROUTH, Harold Victor. Towards the Twentieth Century: Essays
         in the Spiritual History of the Nineteenth. Cambridge,
         England: Cambridge University Press; New York: Macmillan,
         1937, 329. Bergson is discussed on pages 346-366.

3644     ROW, T. V. Seshagiri. New Light on Fundamental Problems, in-
         cluding Nature and Function of Art: A Critical and Con-
         structive Study of the Problems of Philosophy from the New
         Point of View of Henri Bergson. Madras, India: University
         of Madras, 1932, 273.

3645     ROYCE, Josiah. "The Reality of the Temporal." Internation-
         al Journal of Ethics, 20, No. 3, 1910, 257-271. This is a
         criticism of Bergson's concept of duration by a prominent
         American philosopher.

3646     ROYERE, Jean. "Le Rire et l'art." Renaissance Politique et
         Littéraire, 27 novembre 1920.

3647     ROZ, Firmin. "Review of La Pensée contemporaine by Paul
         Gaultier." Correspondant, N.S. 213, No. 4, 25 novembre
         1912, 793-798.

3648     RUBI, Basili di. "Dues deus de la moral i de la religio se-
         gons Bergson." Criterion, 9, No. 34, ottobre-decembre
         1933. This is a critical appreciation of Les Deux Sources.

3649     RUGGIERO, Guido de. Filosofia contemporanea. Bari, Italy:
         Laterza e Figli, 1912, 485. The articles "Bergson," which
         appears on pages 203-214, and "I bergsoniani," on pages
         214-218, appeared originally in La Cultura, 1912.

3650     RUGGIERO, Guido de. Filosofia del novocento. Bari, Italy:
         Laterza, 1934, 296. Chapter X, entitled "L'ultimo Berg-
         son," is found on pages 148-172.

3651     RUGGIERO, Guido de. Filosofías del siglo XX. Buenos Aires:
         Abril, 1946, 289.

3652     RUGGIERO, Guido de. Lo svolgimento della filosofia di Berg-
         son. Trani, Italy: Ditta Vecchi, 1912, 12.

3653     RUGGIERO, Guido de. "Lo svolgimento della filosofia di En-
         rico Bergson." La Cultura, No. 4, 1912.

3654    RUGGIERO, Guido de. "L'ultimo." Critica, 27, No. 4, luglio
        1929, 264-277. The author proposes an idealistic, ration-
        alistic interpretation of Bergson.

3655    RUHE, Algot Henrik Leonard. Henri Bergson: Tänkesattet Berg-
        son i dess. grunddrag. Stockholm: Wahlstrom and Widstrand,
        1914, 174.

3656    RUMAYOR AGUIRRE, Alicia. La conciencia: Psicofenómeno e
        intencionalidad: Revision del tema a traves de Henri Berg-
        son. Monterrey, México, 1966, 87.

3657    RUSSELL, Bertrand. A History of Western Philosophy. New
        York: Simon and Schuster, 1945, 895. "Bergson" occurs on
        pages 791-810. This article is reprinted from the Monist,
        1912.

3658    RUSSELL, Bertrand. "Mysticism and Logic." Hibbert Journal,
        12, No. 48, July 1914, 780-803.

3659    RUSSELL, Bertrand. Mysticism and Logic. London: George
        Allen; New York: Norton, 1929, 234.

3660    RUSSELL, Bertrand. "On the Notion of Cause." Proceedings
        of the Aristotelian Society, 13, 1912-1913, 1-26. The au-
        thor argues that Bergson misconstrues the notion of causal-
        ity which scientists actually use. Hence his "attack on
        science" fails.

3661    RUSSELL, Bertrand. "The Philosophy of Bergson." Monist, 22,
        No. 3, July, 1912, 321-347.

3662    RUSSELL, Bertrand. The Philosophy of Bergson. Chicago:
        Open Court, 1912, 27.

3663    RUSSELL, Bertrand. The Philosophy of Bergson: With a Reply
        by Mr. H. Wildon Carr, and a Rejoinder by Mr. Russell.
        Cambridge, England: Bowes and Bowes; London: Macmillan;
        Glasgow: MacLehose, 1914, 36. This article is reprinted
        from the Monist, 1912.

3664    RUSSELL, Bertrand. Proposed Roads to Freedom: Socialism,
        Anarchism, and Syndicalism. London: George Allen, 1918;
        New York: Henry Holt and Company, 1919, 218. Bergson and
        syndicalism are mentioned on page 68.

3665    RUSSELL, John E. "Bergson's Anti-intellectualism." Journal
        of Philosophy, 9, No. 3, 1 February 1912, 128-131. The au-

thor replies to Ralph Barton Perry's earlier criticisms of Bergson in the Journal of Philosophy.

3666    RUTH-ADELAIDE.  "Charles Du Bos: Fils de Bergson."  Revue de L'Université d'Ottawa, 5, 1951, 857-863.

3667    RUTKEIWICS, Bodhan.  "L'Antimécanisme biologique."  Rivista di filosofia neoscolastica, 22, No. 3-4, 1930.  This is a translation of chapter III of a book published in Poland entitled L'Antimécanisme biologique et les bases du finalisme, Lublin, 1929.  The author defends finalism and intellectualism in biology against Bergson's criticisms.

3668    RUTTEN, Christian.  "La Méthode philosophique chez Bergson et chez Plotin."  Revue Philosophique de Louvain, 58, No. 3, août 1960, 430-452.

3669    RUYER, Ramond.  "Bergson et le sphex ammophile."  Revue de Métaphysique et de Morale, 64, No. 2, 1959, 165-179.  The author concludes that: "La conception bergsonienne de l'instinct est donc juste dans l'ensemble.  Ses faiblesses tiennent plutôt à ses contacts avec d'autres théories voisines, moins heureuses."  (176).

3670    RUYSSEN, Théodore.  "M. Bergson."  Eveil des Peuples, 1er janvier 1933.  This is a review of Les Deux Sources.

3671    RUYSSEN, Théodore.  "Table ronde: Liberté."  Actes du Xe Congrès des Sociétés de Philosophie de Langue Française (Congrès Bergson).  Paris: Armand Colin, 1, 1959, 167-189.

3672    RUYSSEN, Théodore.  "Table ronde: Néant et existentialisme."  Actes du Xe Congrès des Sociétés de Philosophie de Langue Française (Congrès Bergson).  Paris: Armand Colin, 2, 1959, 145-164.

3673    RYAN, Arthur H.  "Henri Bergson."  Studies, 31, No. 3, June 1942, 193-201.

3674    RYAN, John K.  "Aristotle's Concept of Place."  Ancients and Moderns.  Ed. John K. Ryan.  Washington: Catholic University of America Press, 1960, 12-72.  This is a translation of Bergson's Latin thesis, Quid Aristoteles de Loco Senserit.

3675    RYAN, John K.  "Henri Bergson: Heraclitus Redivivus."  Twentieth-Century Thinkers.  Ed. John K. Ryan.  New York: Alba House, 1964, 13-36.

3676     RYDER, H. Osborne. "The Philosophy of Change." Personalist,
         8, No. 4, October 1927, 246-254. This is an analysis of
         Bergson's two lectures on "The Perception of Change."

3677     SABATIER, Paul. L'Orientation religieuse de la France actu-
         elle. Paris: Armand Colin, 1911, 320.

3678     SAGERET, Jules. La Révolution philosophique et la science:
         Bergson, Le Dantec, J.-H. Rosny aîné. Paris: Félix Alcan,
         1924, 252.

3679     SAGERET, Jules. La Vague mystique: Henri Poincaré, Energé-
         tisme (W. Ostwald), Néo-thomisme (P. Duhem), Bergsonisme,
         Pragmatisme, Emile Boutroux. Paris: Flammarion, 1920, 180.

3680     SAENS, Hayes A. "Homenaje de Francia." La Prensa, 24 no-
         viembre 1939.

3681     SAINATI, V. "Review of Bergson by Lorenzo Giusso and Berg-
         son: L'Evoluzione creatrice by Félicien Challaye." Gior-
         nale di metafisica, 5, No. 2, 1950, 229-234.

3682     SAISSET, Frédéric. Qu'est-ce que la métaphysique? D'après
         Richet, Bergson et Osty. Paris: Editions Nicolaus, 1950,
         112.

3683     SAIT, Una Mirrieless (Bernard). The Ethical Implications
         of Bergson's Philosophy. New York: The Science Press,
         1914, 183.

3684     SALINAS QUIROGA, Genaro. "Bergson y la moral." Armas y
         Letras, 6, No. 8, agosto 1949, 1, 6.

3685     SALVAN, Jacques L. "Des Conceptions bergsonienne et sartri-
         enne de la liberté." French Review, 22, No. 2, 1948, 113-
         127. This essay contains interesting comparisons of Berg-
         son and Sartre, particularly as concerns temporality.

3686     SALVAN, Jacques L. To Be and Not To Be: An Analysis of Jean-
         Paul Sartre's Ontology. Detroit: Wayne State University
         Press, 1962, 155. Bergson's influence on existentialism
         is considered on pages xx, xxi, xxix, xxxiv, and xxxv.

3687     SAMARA, Adolfo Menéndez. Dos ensayos sobre Heidegger.
         México: Letras de México, 1939, 61. This study contains
         an essay entitled "La nada en Bergson y Heidegger."

3688     SANBORN, Alvan F. "Bergson: Creator of a New Philosophy."
         Outlook, 1913, 103, No. 7, 353-358.

3689    SANBORN, Alvan F.  "Henri Bergson: Pronounced 'The Foremost
        Thinker of France': His Personality, His Philosophy, and
        His Influence."  Century, 85, No. 2, December 1912, 172-
        176.  The author suggests insights into Bergson's charac-
        ter and personal life.

3690    SANBORN, Alvan F.  "The New Nationalism in France."  Forum,
        51, No. 2, January 1914, 9-26.  Bergson's opinions of
        French youth are mentioned on pages 21 of this article.

3691    SANCHES, Louis Alberto.  "Proyecciones de la intuición:
        Nuevos estudios sobre la filosofía bergsoniana por Enrique
        Molina."  Atenea, Año 24, No. 376.

3692    SANCHEZ-REULET, Aníbal.  "A Philosophy and its Consequences."
        Américas, 5, No. 7, July 1953, 36-37.

3693    SANCIPRIANO, Mario.  "Henri Bergson e Edmund Husserl."  Hu-
        manitas, 14, No. 11, 1959, 792-799.

3694    SANCIPRIANO, Mario.  "La 'metafisica induttiva' del Bergson."
        Giornale di metafisica, 14, No. 6, 1959, 818-825.  The au-
        thor holds that Bergson's thought involves the attempt to
        apply the inductive method to construct a metaphysics
        which can be presented as a science.  This attempt is dis-
        covered in the theory of psychological time, in the study
        of liberty, the substantiality of the soul, and the "élan
        vital."  Bergson's merit was to have brought again essen-
        tially empirical problems into the purview of philosophy.

3695    SANCTIS, Nicola de.  "Bergson l'esistenzialismo e il pro-
        blema della libertà come 'souci de soi'."  Studi urbinati
        di storia, Anno 28, N.S.(B) No. 1-2, 1964, 164-197.

3696    SANCTIS, Nicola de.  "Note su Bergson e l'esistenzialismo
        dal non-essere al nulla."  Studi urbinati di storia, Anno
        37, N.S.(B) No. 1, 1963, 135-142.

3697    SANCTIS, Sante De.  "Intuitions in Children."  Journal of
        Genetic Psychology, 25, No. 1, 1938, pp. 18-25.  The au-
        thor is at great pains to distinguish his concept of in-
        tuition as "immediate cognition" from the Bergsonian con-
        ception.

3698    SANDOZ, Ellis.  "Myth and Society in the Philosophy of Berg-
        son."  Social Research, 30, No. 2, Summer 1963, 171-202.
        This study deals largely with The Two Sources, the part
        played by myth in Bergson's thought, and Bergson's imma-
        netism and tendency towards pantheism.

3699 SANMARTIN GRAU, Juan. "Bergson." Annales de la Universidad de Cuenca, 24, Nos. 1-2, 1968, 204-211.

3700 SANMARTIN GRAU, Juan. "Bergson: La liberación del espíritu." Annales de la Universidad de Cuenca, 22, Nos. 3-4, 1966, 589-595.

3701 SANTAYANA, George. Winds of Doctrine: Studies in Contemporary Opinion. London: Dent and Sons; New York: Scribner's, 1913, 215. Chapter three, "The Philosophy of M. Henri Bergson," is found on pages 58-109. This is one of the most celebrated critiques of Bergson's philosophy by an English-speaking philosopher.

3702 SANTONASTASO, Giuseppe. "Sorel e Bergson." Mondo, 4, No. 44, 1952, 6.

3703 SANTOS, Delfim. "Una visita a Henry Bergsón." Luminar, 2, No. 4, Otoño 1938, 3-8.

3704 SANTOS, Jessy. "A influencia de Bergson no Brasil." Revista Brasileira de Filosofia, 15, No. 58, 1965, 237-244.

3705 SARLO, François de. "Le correnti filosofiche del Secolo XIX." Flegrea, 3, No. 6, 10 settèmbre 1901, 531-554.

3706 SAROLEA, Charles. The French Renascence. London: Allen and Unwin, 1916, 302. Bergson is discussed on pages 271-284.

3707 SARTRE, Jean-Paul. The Words. Greenwich, Connecticut: Fawcett Publications, Inc., 1964, 18. The author remarks in passing: "My grandfather had crossed Lake Geneva with Henri Bergson. 'I was wild with enthusiasm,' he would say. 'I hadn't eyes enough to contemplate the sparkling crests, to follow the shimmering of the water. But Bergson sat on his valise and never once looked up.' He would conclude from this incident that poetic meditation was preferable to philosophy."

3708 SARUILIEV, Ivan V. Quelques points obscurs dans la philosophie de Bergson. Sofia: Imprimerie de la Cour, 1934, 10. The text of this study is in Bulgarian.

3709 SASSEN, Ferdinand. "De ethiek van Bergson." Studia Catholica, 8, 1931-1932, 321-334.

3710 SASSEN, Ferdinand. Van Kant tot Bergson. Antwerp: Standaard-boekhandel, 1952, 232.

3711    SAULNIER, Claude. "Pour Une Compréhension intuitive du rire: Intériorité bergsonienne et intentionnalité axiologique." Actes du Xe Congrès des Sociétés de Philosophie de Langue Française (Congrès Bergson). Paris: Armand, Colin, 1, 1959, 285-288. In order to study the phenomen author adopts a reformulated introspective method, taking from Bergson the intuitive comprehension of the act in a state of becoming and from phenomenology the sense of true interiority. Laughter, an aesthetic play ("jeu"), pertains to felt life and verifies the laws of action which Parodi terms axiological laws.

3712    SAULNIER, Claude. "Table ronde: Matière, causalité, discontinu." Actes du Xe Congrès des Sociétés de Philosophie de Langue Française (Congrès Bergson). Paris: Armand Colin, 2, 121-142.

3713    SAULNIER, Claude. "Table ronde: Psychologie, phénoménologie, intuition." Actes du Xe Congrès des Sociétés de Philosophie de Langue Française (Congrès Bergson). Paris: Armand Colin, 2, 1959, 15-37.

3714    SAUSSURE, René de. "Le Temps en général et le temps bergsonien en particulier." Archives de Psychologie, 14, août 1914, 277-296. The author concedes the importance of time and agrees that philosophers, prior to Bergson, had neglected it. He argues, however, that time is both homogeneous and given-all-at-once like space. Time, thus, does not move: we move through time. The author concludes that there are three sorts of existence: (1) space, (2) time, and (3) events, conceived as the operation of forces.

3715    SAUVAGE, George M. "The New Philosophy in France." Catholic University Bulletin, 12, No. 4, April 1906, 147-159; 14, No. 3, March 1908, 268-286.

3716    SAVELLI, Rodolfo. Il pensiero di Henri Bergson. Città di Castello: Il Solco, 1921.

3717    SAVIOZ, Raymond. "Intellectualisme et intuition bergsonienne." Revue Philosophique de la France et de l'Etranger, 142, Nos. 4-6, 1952, 187-195.

3718    SAZBON, José. "Sobre algunas premisas comunes a Saussure y sus contemporáneos." Cuadernos de filosofía, 12, No. 2, julio-diciembre 1972, 279-286.

3719   SCHAEFKE, Friedrich.  "Bergsons 'L'Evolution créatrice' in
       den Hauptpunkten dargestellt und beurteilt."  Diss., Göt-
       tingen, 1914, 79.

3720   SCHARFSTEIN, Ben-Ami.  "Bergson and Merleau-Ponty: A Prelim-
       inary Comparison."  Journal of Philosophy, 52, No. 14,
       1955, 380-386.

3721   SCHARFSTEIN, Ben-Ami.  "Review of Bergsonian Philosophy and
       Thomism by Jacques Maritain."  Journal of Philosophy, 54,
       No. 3, 1957, 76-78.

3722   SCHARFSTEIN, Ben-Ami.  "Review of The Creative Mind by Henri
       Bergson."  Journal of Philosophy, 43, No. 10, 9 May 1946,
       278.  This is a brief, condescending review of the English
       translation of La Pensée et le mouvant.

3723   SCHARFSTEIN, Ben-Ami.  "Roots of Bergson's Philosphy."  Diss.,
       Columbia, 1943, 156.

3724   SCHARFSTEIN, Ben-Ami.  Roots of Bergson's Philosophy.  New
       York: Columbia University Press, 1943, 156.  The author
       holds that Bergson's ideas were largely borrowed from oth-
       er thinkers and that Bergson exhibited intellectual origi-
       nality in only a few instances.

3725   SCHEPERS, Eugène.  "Table ronde: Liberté."  Actes du Xe Con-
       grès des Sociétés de Philosophie de Langue Française (Con-
       grès Bergson).  Paris: Armand Colin, 2, 1959, 167-189.

3726   SCHEPERS, Eugène.  "Table ronde: Morale."  Actes du Xe Con-
       grès des Sociétés de Philosophie de Langue Française (Con-
       grès Bergson).  Paris: Armand Colin, 2, 1959, 237-257.

3727   SCHERER, René.  "Table ronde: Morale."  Actes du Xe Congrès
       des Sociétés de Philosophie de Langue Française (Congrès
       Bergson).  Paris: Armand Colin, 2, 1959, 237-257.

3728   SCHILLER, Ferdinand Channing Scott.  "Review of L'Energie
       spirituelle by Henri Bergson."  Mind, 29, N.S. No. 115,
       July 1920, 350-354.  This is a careful, generally lauda-
       tory review.

3729   SCHILPP, Paul Arthur.  Commemorative Essays in Celebration
       of the First Publication of Darwin's "Origin of the Spe-
       cies" and of the Seventieth Birthday of Henri Bergson,
       Edmond Husserl, John Dewey.  Stockton, California: Cali-
       fornia Private Publications, 1930, 47.

3730    SCHLAGEL, Richard H.    "Review of Bergson and the Evolution of Physics, Ed. and Trans. with Intro. P. A. Y. Gunter." Isis, 61, No. 4, 1970, 548-549.

3731    SCHLUMBERGER, Jean.    "Bergson."  Rencontres.  Paris: Gallimard, 1968, 133-135.

3732    SCHLUMBERGER, Jean.    "Trois Grands Hommes et une soeur abusive."  Revue de Paris, 74e Année, Nos. 7-8, juillet-août 1967, 93-96.  Bergson and Valéry are discussed in this article.

3733    SCHLUTER-HERMKES, Maria.    "Bergsons Verhältnis zum Chistentum."  Hochland, 42, No. 2, 1948-1950, 105-118.

3734    SCHNEEWEISS, A. J.    "Time and Speculative Philosophy."  Monist, 28, No. 3, October 1919, 601-610.

3735    SCHNEIDER.    "Les Cours de Bergson au Collège de France."  Le Temps, 9 février 1941.

3736    SCHNIPPENKÖTTER, J.    "Henri Bergson und seine Philosophie." Akademische Monatsblätter, 23, 1911, 170.

3737    SCHOEN, H.    "Heinrich Bergsons philosophischen Anschauungen." Zeitschrift für Philosophie und philosophische Kritik, 145, No. 2, Februar 1912, 40-129.

3738    SCHOEN, H.    "Review of L'Evolution créatrice by Henri Bergson."  Zeitschrift für Philosophie und Pädogogik, 15, No. 1, 1908, 39-41.

3739    SCHOLL, Klaus.    "Henri Bergson auf dem Wege zur Kirche." Begegnung, 13, 1958, 229.

3740    SCHOTTLAENDER, Felix.    "Henry Bergsons Gedächtnistheorie im Lichte der Psychoanalyse."  Psychoanalytische Bewegung, 3, 1931, 250-273.  The lack of mutual interest shown by philosophy and psychoanalysis is unfortunate.  The author attempts to show that each has value for the other.  There are similar points of interest in Bergson's thought-system and Freud's psychoanalysis.  Bergson recognizes two of the Freudian fundamentals, the unconscious and repression, but fails to recognize the place of sexuality.  Psychoanalysis begins where Bergson's philosophical construction ends. The author discusses the place of the theory of freedom of the will and the relationship between conscience and consciousness.

3741   SCHOUBOURG, Gary.  "Bergson's Intuitional Approach to Free
       Will."  Modern Schoolman, 45, No. 1, January 1968, 123-
       144.

3742   SCHRECKER, Paul.  Henri Bergsons Philosophie der Persönlich-
       keit.  München: Reinhardt, 1912, 61 (Schriften des Vereins
       für freie psychoanalytische Forschung, 3).  Written by a
       disciple of Freud, this study suggests close parallels be-
       tween Bergson and Freud, particularly in the matter of
       anti-intellectualism.

3743   SCHUHL, Pierre-Maxime.  "Carnet de notes."  Revue Philosophi-
       que de la France et de l'Etranger, 84, No. 3, 1959, 371-
       377.  This article contains an account of a visit with
       Bergson on 30 December 1938, as well as reminiscenses of
       other French philosophers.

3744   SCHUHL, Pierre-Maxime.  "Une Heure avec Bergson."  Revue Phi-
       losophique de la France et de l'Etranger, 149, No. 3, 1959,
       371.  Bergson and aesthetics are discussed in this account
       of an interview with Bergson.

3745   SCHUHL, Pierre-Maxime.  L'Imagination et le merveilleux:  La
       Pensée et l'action.  Paris: Flammarion, 1962, 242.  Aymé,
       Lévy-Bruhl, Bergson, Valéry, and others are discussed in
       this book.

3746   SCHUHL, Pierre-Maxime, ed.  "Lettres à Félix Ravaisson: 1846-
       1892."  Revue de Métaphysique et de Morale, 45, No. 2,
       1960, 173-202.  This article contains a letter by Bergson.

3747   SCHULTZE, Martin.  Das Problem der Wahrheitserkenntnis bei
       William James und Henri Bergson.  Erlangen, Germany: Junge
       und Sohn, 1913, 81.

3748   SCHUTZ, Alfred.  "Language, Language Disturbances, and the
       Texture of Consciousness: Philosophical Interpretatations
       of Language Disturbances: Henri Bergson."  Social Research,
       17, No. 3, September 1950, 374-378.

3749   SCHWIESSELMAN, Martin.  "Henri Bergson."  Neuphilologische
       Zeitschrift, 1, No. 3, 1949, 1-8.

3750   SCIACCA, Michele Federico.  La filosofia oggi.  Vol. 2, 2nd
       ed.  Milano e Roma: Fratelli Boca, 1952, 485.  "Il contin-
       gentismo di E. Boutroux e l'intuitionismo d. E. Bergson"
       appears on pages 48-58.

3751   SCIACCA, Michele Federico.  "Review of L'Intellectualisme de Bergson by Léon Husson."  Giornale di metafisica, 2, No. 3, 1948, 25-28.

3752   SCIACCA, Michele Federico (M. F. S.).  "Ommagio a Henry Bergson."  Humanitas, 14, No. 11, 1959, 769-770.

3753   SCIACCA, Michele Federico.  Philosophical Trends in the Contemporary World.  Trans. A. Salerno.  South Bend, Indiana: Notre Dame Press, 1964, 656.  A section entitled "Contingentism of E. Boutroux and Intuitionism of H. Bergson" may be found on pages 29-36.

3754   SCIACCA, Michele Federico.  "Review of La Philosophie religieuse de Bergson by Lydie Adolphe."  Giornale di metafisica, 2, No. 3, 1948, 258.

3755   SCIACCA, Michele Federico.  Il problema di Dio e della religione nella filosofia attuale.  Brescia, Italy: Morcelliana 1944, 379.  Bergson is discussed on pages 29-47.

3756   SCIACCA, Michele Federico.  Il secolo XX: Parte I: Dal pragmatismo allo spiritualismo cristiano: Parte II: Storici ed eruditi.  Milano: Bocca, 1942, 768, 263.

3757   "Science et humanisme."  La Nef, 3, No. 15, février 1946, 57-77.

3758   SCOTT, J. W.  "Bergsonism in England."  Monist, 27, No. 2, April 1917, 179-204.  The author concludes that Bergson's philosophy " . . . differs from other idealism in an essentially philosophical way only when it has something to say which is indefensible . . . ."  (204).

3759   SCOTT, J. W.  "Ethical Pessimism in Bergson."  International Journal of Ethics, 24, No. 2, January 1914, 147-167.  The author discusses Bergson's concept of laughter and its negative implications.

3760   SCOTT, J. W.  "The Pessimism of Bergson."  Hibbert Journal, 11, No. 1, October 1912, 99-116.

3761   SCOTT, J. W.  "The Pessimism of Creative Evolution."  Mind, 22, No. 87, July 1913, 344-360.

3762   SCOTT, J. W.  Syndicalism and Philosophical Realism: A Study in the Correlation of Contemporary Social Tendencies.  London: A. and C. Black, Ltd., 1919.  Bergson and syndicalism are discussed on pages 88-160.

3763    SCOTT, Nathan A.  The Broken Center: Studies in the Theolo-
        gical Horizon of Modern Literature.  New Haven, Connecti-
        cut, and London: Yale University Press, 1966, 237.

3764    SEBESTYEN, K.  "Die Gerüchte um Bergson."  Pester Lloyd, 29,
        No. 6, 1935.

3765    "Se convirtío Bergson?"  Revista Javeriana, 20, No. 99, 1943,
        176-177.

3766    "Secret of Henri Bergson."  Newsweek, 22, No. 4, 27 January
        1941, 59.  This is a brief mention of Bergson's relations
        with Catholicism.

3767    SEGOND, Joseph.  "Les Antithèses du bergsonisme."  Annales
        de Philosophie Chrétienne, 165, août 1912, 449-474.

3768    SEGOND, Joseph.  "Bergson."  Chronique, 22 février 1914.
        Possibly this journal is Chronique, published in London,
        1899-1924.

3769    SEGOND, Joseph.  La Guerre mondiale et la vie spirituelle.
        Paris: Félix Alcan, 1918, 167.  This study is an attempt-
        ed explanation of war based in part on L'Evolution créa-
        trice.

3770    SEGOND, Joseph.  "L'Intellectualisme et la philosophie berg-
        sonienne."  Revue Philosophique de la France et de l'Etran-
        ger, 84, No. 2, juillet-décembre 1917, 77-95.  The author
        reviews Höffding, Philosophie de Bergson and Grandjean,
        Une Révolution dans la philosophie.  In general, he de-
        fends Bergson against criticisms.

3771    SEGOND, Joseph.  L'Intuition bergsonienne.  1-2 ed.  Paris:
        Félix Alcan, 1913, 1930, 158.

3772    SEGOND, Joseph.  Intuition et amitié.  Paris: Félix Alcan,
        1918, 180 (Bibliothèque de Philosophie Contemporaine).

3773    SEGOND, Joseph.  "La Méthodologie bergsonienne."  Etudes
        Philosophiques, 9, No. 4, décembre 1935, 116-134.

3774    SEGOND, Joseph.  La Prière: Essai de psychologie religieuse.
        Paris: Félix Alcan, 1911, 364.

3775    SEGOND, Joseph.  "Le Rationalisme de Bergson."  Revue Poli-
        tique et Littéraire, Revue Bleue, 62e Année, No. 8, 19
        avril 1924, 263-266.

3776    SEGOND, Joseph. "Schématisme bergsonien et schématisme kantien." Henri Bergson. Ed. Béguin and Thévenaz, 241-247. The author considers Bergson's and Kant's conceptions of schematism and attempts to unify them.

3777    SEGUR, Nicolas. "Bergson et bergsonisme." La Revue, 23e Année, 1er octobre 1912, 297-315. This essay also appears in Wetenschap Bladen, 1913, 82-108.

3778    SEGUR, Nicolas. "La Philosophie à la mode: Le Bergsonisme." Le Matin, 25 juillet 1912.

3779    SEIDEMANN, Alfred. Bergsons Stellung zu Kant. Endigen-Kaiser-stahl, Germany: Wild, 1937, 98.

3780    SEILLIERE, Ernest. "L'Allemagne et la philosophie bergsonienne." L'Opinion, 11, No. 27, 3 juillet 1909, 13-14.

3781    SEILLIERE, Ernest. "L'Avenir de la philosophie bergsonienne." Revue Politique et Littéraire, Revue Bleue, 55, 1er semestre, No. 8, 1917, 235-239; No. 9, 1917, 261-266; No. 10, 1917, 299-304.

3782    SEILLIERE, Ernest. L'Avenir de la philosophie bergsonienne. Paris: Félix Alcan, 1917, 52.

3783    SEILLIERE, Ernest. "Review of La Pensée et le mouvant by Henri Bergson." Journal des Débats, 41, Pt. 1, 27 juillet 1934, 1198-1200.

3784    SEILLIERE, Ernest. "Schätzung und Wirkung d. Philosophie i. heut. Frankreich." Internationale Monatsschrift für Wissenschaft, 7, No. 1, 1913, 42-58.

3785    SELBIE, W. R. "Review of The Two Sources of Morality and Religion by Henri Bergson." Congregational Quarterly, 13, 1935,·367-368.

3786    SELIBER, G. "Der Pragmatismus und seine Gegner: Auf dem III. internationalen Kongress für Philosophie." Archiv für systematische Philosophie, N.S. 15, No. 3, 1909, 287-298.

3787    SELIGMANN, Raphael. "Die Entwicklungstheorie Bergsons." Sozialistisches Monatsheft, 1919, 462-472.

3788    SELIGMANN, Raphael. "Individuum und Ethos: Kurze Betrachtung über Bergson." Probleme d. Judentums. Wien: Löwit, 1919, 25-38.

3789    "Semaine Bergson au Maroc: 20-26 avril 1959." Etudes Philo-
        sophiques, N.S. 14e Année, No. 3, juillet-septembre 1959,
        347-350. The agenda and opening speech of a conference on
        Bergson are reported in this article.

3790    SEMERIA, Giuseppe. "Natura e genesi della metafisica di Hen-
        ri Bergson." Revista de filosofia neoscolastica, 9, No. 1,
        1917, 97-102. The author argues that Bergson raised cer-
        tain of Claude Bernard's ideas into a metaphysical schema.

3791    SERINI, Paulo. "Bergson e lo spiritualismo francese des
        secolo XIX." Logos, 5, No., 2-3, luglio-decembre 1922,
        315-357; 6, No. 1, gennaio-marzo 1923, 78-104. This mono-
        graph relates Bergson's thought to the philosophies of Vic-
        tor Cousin, Maine de Biran, Félix Ravaisson, Hyppolite
        Taine, Renan, and Jules Lachelier.

3792    SERINI, Paulo. Bergson e lo spiritualismo francese del seco-
        lo XIX. Genova: Perella, 1923, 68. 3793

3793    SEROUYA, Henri. "Bergson et la Kabbale." Revue Philosophi-
        que de la France et de l'Etranger, 149, No. 3, juillet-
        septembre 1959, 321-324. The author states: "Au cours
        d'une longue conversation, d'avant guerre, relative au mys-
        ticisme, Bergson nous a déclaré que, dans sa jeunesse, il
        avait appris l'hébreu, mais qu'il ignorait la Kabbale."
        (321). But the basis for his thought, according to the
        author, already existed in the Kabbala.

3794    SEROUYA, Henri. "Le Génie de Bergson." Actes du Xe Congrès
        des Sociétés de Philosophie de Langue Française (Congrès
        Bergson). Paris: Armand Colin, 1, 1959, 289-291. Kant
        attributed genius only to poets and artists. It is found
        nonetheless in certain great philosophers whose thought,
        like Bergsons's, has an intuitive character. Bergson pos-
        sesses to a considerable degree that subjectivity which is
        the attribute of the artist or poet.

3795    SEROUYA, Henri. Initiation à la philosophie contemporaine.
        Paris: Renaissance du Livre, 1933, 312. Chapter III, en-
        titled "Le Bergsonisme," is on pages 35-81.

3796    SEROUYA, Henri. "Table ronde: Sources et histoire du berg-
        sonisme." Actes du Xe Congrès des Sociétés de Philosophie
        de Langue Française (Congrès Bergson). Paris: Armand Co-
        lin, 2, 1959, 213-233.

3797    SEROUYA, Henri. "Table ronde: Unité, unicité, dialogue."
        Actes du Xe Congrès des Sociétés de Philosophie de Langue

Française (Congrès Bergson). Paris: Armand Colin, 2, 1959, 281-302 .

3798    SERRUS, Charles. "La Pensée symbolisée et la pensée pure." Revue de Metaphysique et de Morale, 48, No. 4, 1941, 268-282. The author concludes: "L'oeuvre de Bergson nous a présenté ainsi une théorie profonde et complète du symbolisme, dont la séméiologie tient aujourd'hui le plus grand compte et dont elle tire en même temps le plus grand profit." (282).

3799    SERTILLANGES, Antonin Gilbert. Avec Henri Bergson. Paris: Gallimard, 1941, 50 (Collection Catholique).

3800    SERTILLANGES, Antonin Gilbert. "Bergson apologiste." Henri Bergson. Ed. Béguin and Thévenaz, 57-72. The author views Bergson as an apologist for Christianity, but an apologist "from without." Bergson's philosophy, he holds, is not Christian but comes close to Christianity in many respects.

3801    SERTILLANGES, Antonin Gilbert. "Bergson devant le catholicisme." Nouvelles Littéraires, No. 322, 15 décembre 1928, 1.

3802    SERTILLANGES, Antonin Gilbert. Henri Bergson et le catholicisme. Paris: Flammarion, 1941, 151.

3803    SERTILLANGES, Antonin Gilbert. Le Christianisme et les philosophes. Vol. 2. Les Temps modernes. Paris: Aubier, 591. An essay entitled "Le Réalisme d'Henri Bergson" appears on pages 375-402.

3804    SERTILLANGES, Antonin Gilbert. "La Critica bergsoniana e la creazione 'ex nihilo'." Quaderni di Roma, Anno 1, No. 2, 1947.

3805    SERTILLANGES, Antonin Gilbert. Dieu ou rien. Paris: Flammarion, 1933, 19.

3806    SERTILLANGES, Antonin Gilbert. L'Idée de création et ses retentissements en philosophie. Paris: Aubier, 1945, 229.

3807    SERTILLANGES, Antonin Gilbert. "Le Libre Arbitre chez Saint-Thomas et chez Bergson." La Vie Intellectuelle, N.S. 39, No. 1, 10 avril 1937, 252-267. Bergson's reply to Sertillanges may be found on pages 268-269.

3808    SERTILLANGES, Antonin Gilbert. Lumière et périls du bergso-
        nisme. Paris: Flammarion, 1943, 64.

3809    SERTILLANGES, Antonin Gilbert. "Morale et religion d'après
        M. Bergson." La Vie Intellectuelle, 15, No. 2, 10 mai
        1932, 224-245. This is a review article concerning Les
        Deux Sources.

3810    SERTILLANGES, Antonin Gilbert. "La Politica bergsoniana e
        la creazione 'ex nihilo'." Quaderni di Roma, 1, No. 2,
        marzo 1947, 101-110.

3811    SERTILLANGES, Antonin Gilbert. "Questions à M. Bergson."
        La Vie Intellectuelle, 15, No. 3, 10 juin 1932, 356-385.

3812    SETA, Ugo della. L'intuizione nella filosofia di Enrico
        Bergson. Roma: Voghera, 1912, 26.

3813    SETZER, Ambrosio. "Conceito do homem no sistema metafisico
        de Bergson." Vozes de Petrôpolis, 2, No. 3, 1908.

3814    SEVERAC, J.-B. "Enquêtes: Influence de la philosophie de
        M. Bergson." Mouvement Socialiste, 29, No. 229, mars
        1911, 183-183.

3815    SEVER DE MONTSONIS, "Entorn de la filosofia bergsoniana."
        Criterion, 10, 1934, 241-246.

3816    SEWALL, Frank. Is the Universe Self-centered or God-cen-
        tered? An Examination of the Systems of Eucken and Berg-
        son: Presidential Address Delivered to the Swedenborg Sci-
        entific Association. Philadelphia, Pennsylvania: Sweden-
        borg Scientific Association, 1913, 13.

3817    SEYDL, E. "Henri Bergson." Allgemeine Literaturbericht, 25,
        1916, 65-70.

3818    SEYDL, E. "Henri Bergsons intuitive Philosophie." Neue Oes-
        terreich, 1, No. 4, April 1916, 49-54.

3819    SEYPPEL, Joachim H. "A Criticism of Heidegger's Time Con-
        cept with Reference to Bergson's 'durée'." Revue Interna-
        tionale de Philosophie, 10, No. 4, 1956, 503-508.

3820    SHASTRI, Prablu Datta. The Conception of Freedom in Hegel,
        Bergson and Indian Philosophy. Calcutta: Albion Press,
        1913, 26.

3821    SHELDON, Wilmon Henry. Strife of Systems and Productive Du-
        ality. London: Humphrey Milford, 1918, 528. Bergson is
        discussed on pages 287-316.

3822    SHEPHERD, Queen L. "Review of 'Le Souvenir du présent et la
        fausse reconnaissance' by Henri Bergson." Psychological
        Bulletin, 7, No. 9, 15 September 1910, 307.

3823    SHIMER, Hervey W. "Bergson's View of Organic Evolution."
        Popular Science Monthly, 82, No. 2, February 1913, 163-
        167.

3824    SHKLAR, Judith. "Bergson and the Politics of Intuition."
        Review of Politics, 20, No. 3, October 1958, 634-656.
        Faith in "creativity" and the "life force" is not a suf-
        ficient basis for a political theory, according to the
        author.

3825    SHOTWELL, James T. "Bergson's Philosophy." Political Sci-
        ence Quarterly, 28, No. 1, March 1913, 130-135. Bergson
        has difficulties with intuition, value, and anti-intellec-
        tualism, according to the author.

3826    SICE, Stanislas. "Hommage à Bergson." Revue des Deux Mon-
        des, N.S. 2, No. 10, 15 mai 1949, 364-367.

3827    SIEGFRIED, André. "Orateurs que j'ai connus: Silhouettes."
        Revue Générale Belge, No. 52, février 1950, 505-524. Berg-
        son, Brunetière, and Sorel are discussed in this article.

3828    SILBERMANN, Alphons. "Notizen zu Bergsons hunderstem Ge-
        burtstag." Theater und Zeit, 7, 1959-1960, 107-111.

3829    SILBERSTEIN. "Review of L'Evolution créatrice by Henri Berg-
        son." Przeglad filozoficzny, 1, 1908.

3830    SILVA GARCIA, Mario A. Plenitude y degradación a propósito
        del Bergsonismo. Montevideo, 1944.

3831    SIMMEL, Georg. "Bergson und d. deutsche 'Zynismus'." Inter-
        nationale Monatsschrift, 9, 1915, 197ff.

3832    SIMMEL, Georg. "La Philosophie d'Henri Bergson." Die Gül-
        denkammer, 4, No. 6, Juni 1914.

3833    SIMON, P. "Wissenschaftsideal und Philosophie mit bes.
        Berücks. von Bergson." Philosophia perennis. Vol. 2.
        Regensburg, Germany: Habbel, 1930, 351-376.

3834   SIMON, Paul.  Der Pragmatismus in der modernen französischen
       Philosophie.  Paderborn, Germany: Schoningh, 1920, 158.

3835   SIMON, W. M.  European Positivism in the Nineteenth Century.
       Ithaca, New York: Cornell University Press, 1963, 384.
       This study deals with many thinkers of whom Bergson is
       only one.  Bergson is discussed on pages 108-110.

3836   SIMON, Yves René.  "La Philosophie bergsonienne: Etude cri-
       tique."  Revue de Philosophie, 31, No. 7, juillet 1931,
       281-290.

3837   SINCLAIR, May.  A Defense of Idealism.  London: Macmillan,
       1917, 396.  Chapter II, entitled "Vitalism," appears on
       pages 51-74.  It is a discussion of Bergson's philosophy.

3838   SINGER, Edgar A. Jr.  "Review of Les Deux Sources de la mo-
       rale et de la religion by Henri Bergson."  Journal of Phi-
       losophy, 30, No. 1, 1933, 14-23.

3839   SINGERMAN, Ora.  "The Relation Between Philosophy and Sci-
       ence: A Comparison of the Positions of Bergson and White-
       head."  Iyyun, 9, No. 2, April 1968, 65-91.  This article
       is in Hebrew.  The sociologies of Whitehead and Bergson
       are discussed in this article.

3840   SIPFLE, David A.  "Abstract of 'Bergson's Theory of Matter
       and Modern Physics' by Milič Čapek."  Process Studies, 2,
       No. 2, Summer 1972, 169-170.  This is an abstract of a
       translation of Čapek's article in Bergson and the Evolu-
       tion of Physics, Ed. and Trans. with Intro. P. A. Y. Gun-
       ter.

3841   SIPFLE, David A.  "Henri Bergson and the Epochal Theory of
       Time."  Bergson and the Evolution of Physics.  Ed. and
       Trans. with Intro. P. A. Y. Gunter, 275-294.  Contrary to
       general opinion, the author holds, Bergson held the view
       that time (i.e., "durée") is epochal and occurs in quasi-
       discontinuous rhythms or pulsations.

3842   SIRVEN, Joseph.  "Review of La Pensée et le mouvant by Henri
       Bergson."  Polybiblion, N.S. 188 (Partie littéraire, 3),
       1934, 163-164.

3843   SKARD, Bjarne.  "Henri Bergson: 1859-1941."  Syn og segn,
       47, No. 1, 1941, 49-60.

3844   SLATER, Mary White.  "Vision of Bergson."  Forum, 52, No. 6,
       December 1913, 916-932.

3845    SLATER, Mary White. The Vision of Bergson: An Essay. New
         York: Exposition Press, 1954, 45.

3846    SLOSSON, Edwin Henry. Major Prophets of Today. Freeport,
         New York: Books for Libraries Press, 1968, 299.

3847    SLOSSON, Edwin Emery. "Recent Developments of Bergson's
         Philosophy." Independent, 74, No. 3368, 19 June 1913,
         1383-1385.

3848    SLOSSON, Edwin Emery. Twelve Major Prophets of Today. Bos-
         ton: Little, Brown and Company, 1914, 229.

3849    SLOSSON, Edwin Emery. "Twelve Major Prophets of Today: Hen-
         ri Bergson." Independent, 7o, No. 3262, 8 June 1911,
         1246-1261. This is a general account of Bergson's philoso-
         phy, containing many photographs.

3850    SMITH, Colin. Contemporary French Philosophy. New York:
         Barnes and Noble, 1964, 266. The content and influence of
         Les Deux Sources are discussed on pages 143-161.

3851    SMITH, Colin. "Philosophical Survey: Philosophy in France."
         Philosophy, 25, No. 134, July 1960, 265-271. Bergson and
         Jankélévitch are discussed in this article.

3852    SMITH, Colin. "The Philosophy of Vladimir Jankélévitch."
         Philosophy, 32, No. 123, 1957, 315-324.

3853    SMITH, Michael. "Considering a Poetic." Lace Curtain, No.
         3, Summer 1970, 45-50.

3854    SMITH, Norman Kemp. Commentary to Kant's Critique of Pure
         Reason. London: Macmillan, 1918, 651. Bergson is dis-
         cuesed on pages 86, 142, 359-360n, and 587n.

3855    SMITH, Norman Kemp. "Subjectivism and Realism in Modern
         Philosophy." Philosophical Review, 17, No. 2, March 1908,
         138-148. The author concludes that: "The two most coura-
         geous and thoroughgoing attempts to establish realism have
         been those of Avenarius and Bergson." (139).

3856    SMITH, Richard. "Review of Critical Exposition of Bergson's
         Philosophy by J. M. Stewart." International Journal of
         Ethics, 23, No. 1, January 1913, 211-216.

3857    SMITH, Richard. "Review of Laughter: An Essay on the Mean-
         ing of the Comic by Henri Bergson." International Journal

_of_ Ethics, 22, No. 2, January 1913, 216-218.  This is a
critical but appreciative review.  The author denies the
incompatibility of feeling and laughter.

3858    SMITH, Vincent Edward.  "Jurevičs: Eine Einführung in seine
        Philosophie."  Renascence, 3, No. 1, 1950, 66-67.

3859    SNELL, Laird Wingate.  "'Creative Evolution' and the Chris-
        tian Faith."  Anglican Theological Review, 2, No. 2, March
        1920, 255-289.

3860    SNEYERS, Germain.  Les Romanciers d'entre les deux guerres.
        Paris: Desclée de Brouwer, 1941, 326.  See pages 22-30 for
        a discussion of Bergson's intuitive method.

3861    SOBIESKI, Michal.  "H. Bergson."  Kurier Warsawski, 20 Jan-
        uary 1910.

3862    SODERBLOM, Mgr.  (Archevêque d'Upsal).  "Hommage."  Nouvel-
        les Littéraires, No. 322, 15 décembre 1928, 3.

3863    SOKOLOW, Nahum.  Ishim.  Tel-Aviv, 1935, III, 170-179.  De-
        tails of Bergson's ancestry are given in this article,
        which is in Hebrew.

3864    SOLOMON, Joseph.  Bergson.  London: Constable and Co., 1911,
        128.

3865    SOLOMON, Joseph.  Bergson.  1911 rpt.  Port Washington, New
        York, and London: Kennikat Press, 1970, 128.

3866    SOLOMON, Joseph.  "Review of Creative Evolution by Henri
        Bergson."  Mind, 20, No. 79, July 1911, 432-433.  This re-
        view includes a negative assessment of Mitchell's transla-
        tion.

3867    SOLOMON, Joseph.  "Philosophy of Bergson."  Mind, 20, No. 1,
        1911, 15-40.

3868    SOLOMON, Joseph.  "The Philosophy of Bergson."  Fortnightly
        Review, N.S. 90, No. 539, 1 November 1911, 1014-1031.
        This is a general review of Bergson's thought.

3869    SOLONITSI, Tatiana.  "A personalidade de Bergson."  Alio,
        No. 17, 1945-1946, 5.

3870    SOMMER, Erika.  Bergsons Einfluss auf die französische
        Schriftsprache: Inaugural-Dissertation.  München: "Poly-
        graph," 1935, 295.

3871    SOMMER, P.  "H. Bergson."  Warte, 15, No. 2, 15 Januar, 1920,
        93-97.

3872    SOREL, Georges.  "L'Ancienne et la Nouvelle Métaphysique."
        L'Ere nouvelle, 2, 1894.

3873    SOREL, Georges.  "Bergson et Pascal: Lettre inédite du 8
        avril 1913."  La Nef, 4, No. 32, juillet 1947, 59-60.

3874    SOREL, Georges.  "Review of L'Evolution créatrice by Henri
        Bergson."  Mouvement Socialiste, 12, No. 191, 15 octobre
        1907, 257-282; No. 193, 15 décembre 1907, 478-494; 13, No.
        194, 15 janvier 1908, 34-52; No. 196, 15 mars 1908, 184-
        194; No. 197, 15 avril 1908, 276-294.

3875    SOREL, Georges.  Reflections on Violence.  Trans. T. E.
        Hulme.  London: Allen and Unwin, 1916, 299.

3876    SOREL, Georges.  Reflections on Violence.  Trans. J. Roth.
        Glencoe, Illinois: Free Press, 1950, 311.

3877    SOREL, Georges.  Réflexions sur la violence.  Paris: "Pages
        libres," 1908, 257.  Numerous references to Bergson may be
        found throughout this study.

3878    SOREL, Georges.  "Sur L'Evolution créatrice."  L'Indépendant,
        1, mai 1911.  The author defends Bergson against the at-
        tacks of the right-wing Action française.

3879    SOREL, Georges.  "La Trilogie de l'esprit."  Etudes Bergso-
        niennes, 2, 1949, 226-227.  This is a previously unpub-
        lished passage by Sorel concerning the religious import
        of Bergson's thought.

3880    SOREL, Georges.  "Vues sur les problèmes de la philosophie."
        Revue de Métaphysique et de Morale, 17, No. 5, septembre
        1910, 581-613.

3881    SORLEY, W. R.  Moral Values and the Idea of God.  Cam-
        bridge, England: Cambridge University Press, 1918.  In-
        tuition and the vital impulse are discussed in this study.

3882    SOUCY, Claude.  "Technique et philosophie."  Recherches et
        Débats, No. 31, juin 1960, 109-123.  Various references to
        Bergson are included in this article.

3883    SOUDAY, Paul.  "Le Prix Nobel."  Annales Politiques et Litté-
        raires, No. 2323, 1er décembre 1928, 501.

3884    SOUDAY, Paul. "Le Prix Nobel à M. Bergson." Le Temps, No.
         24564, 19 novembre 1928, 1.

3885    SOUDAY, Paul. "Réception de M. Henri Bergson." Le Temps,
         No. 20657, 26 janvier 1918, 3.

3886    SOUDAY, Paul. "La Retraite de M. Bergson." Le Temps, No.
         21875, 24 juin 1921, 1.

3887    SOUDAY, Paul. "Taine, Bergson et M. Thibaudet." Le Temps,
         No. 24452, 30 juillet 1928, 1.

3888    SOUSA, Eudoro de. "Leonardo e Bergson, trecho do prefácio a
         una antologia de Leonardo." Acçao, 3, 4 aprile 1946.

3889    SOUSA, Filho J. B. "Bergson y la inteligencia." Sustancia,
         2, Nos. 7-8, septiembre 1941, 359-362.

3890    SOUZA, Sybil de. La Philosophie de Marcel Proust. Paris:
         Rieder, 1939, 176. The influence of Bergson on Proust is
         discussed on pages 49-61.

3891    SPEER, Catherine Ellis. "Bergson's Theory of Individuality
         and the Self." Diss., Texas, 1939, 97.

3892    SPENGLER, Boris de. "Table ronde: Physique." Actes du Xe
         Congrès des Sociétés de Philosophie de Langue Française
         (Congrès Bergson). Paris: Armand Colin, 2, 1959, 65-87.

3893    SPIRITO, Ugo. L'idealismo italiano e i suoi critici: Durata
         reale e intuizione. Firenze: Le Monnier, 1930, 266.

3894    SPIRITO, Ugo. Il pragmatismo nella filosofia contemporanea.
         Firenze: Vallecchi, 1921, 222. Bergson is discussed on
         pages 167-179.

3895    "Spiritual Philosopher." Review of Reviews, 47, No. 3,
         March 1913, 299.

3896    SPITZER, Leo. "Patterns of Thought in the Style of Albert
         Thibaudet." Modern Language Quarterly, 9, No. 3, 1948,
         259-272; No. 4, 1948, 478-491. The author denies that Thi-
         baudet was a follower of Bergson.

3897    SPURGEON, Caroline Frances Eleanor. Mysticism in English
         Literature. New York: Putman's Sons; Cambridge, England:
         University Press, 1913, 168. This is an account of mys-
         ticism based on Bergson's conceptions.

3898    STAHL, Roland. "Bergson's Influence on Whitehead." Person-
        alist, 36, No. 3, 1955, 250-257. Whitehead was deeply in-
        debted to Bergson, according to the author.

3899    STAHL, Roland. "The Influence of Bergson on Whitehead."
        Diss., Boston, 1950.

3900    STALLKNECHT, Newton Phelps. Bergson's Idea of Creation.
        Princeton, New Jersey, 1934, 113.

3901    STALLKNECHT, Newton Phelps. "Intuition and the Traditional
        Problems of Philosophy." Philosophical Review, 50, No. 4,
        July 1941, 396-409.

3902    STALLKNECHT, Newton Phelps. Studies in the Philosophy of
        Creation: With Special Reference to Bergson and Whitehead.
        Princeton, New Jersey: Princeton University Press, 1934,
        170. The author argues that Bergson has two theories of
        creation, one tenable, one not.

3903    STARK, Werner. "Henri Bergson: A Guide for Sociologists."
        Revue Internationale de Philosophie, 3, No. 10, 15 octobre
        1949, 407-443.

3904    STARK, Werner. "Diminishing Utility Reconsidered." Kyklos,
        1, No. 2, 1947, 321-344.

3905    STARK, Werner. "Stable Equilibrium Re-examined." Kyklos,
        4, No. 1, 1950, 218-232.

3906    STARKIE, Enid. "Bergson and Literature." The Bergsonian
        Heritage. Ed. Thomas Hanna. New York and London: Colum-
        bia University Press, 1962, 74-99. The author studies the
        influence of Bergson on his literary contemporaries: Gide,
        Proust, etc.

3907    STAUDENMAIER, John Michael. "Bergson's Latin Thesis: A Tex-
        tual Study." Diss., St. Louis, 1964.

3908    STEBBING, Lizzie Susan. "Henri Bergson." World Review, 10,
        Pt. 1, March 1941, 35-38.

3909    STEBBING, Lizzie Susan. "The Notion of Truth in Bergson's
        Theory of Knowledge." Proceedings of the Aristotelian So-
        ciety, 13, 1912-1913, 224-256. The author argues against
        Bergson that philosophy is not "life" but "the interpreta-
        tion of life by means of reason."

3910    STEBBING, Lizzie Susan.  Pragmatism and French Voluntarism.
        Cambridge, England: University Press, 1914, 168.

3911    STEEG, T.  "Henri Bergson: Notice biographique avec portrait."
        Revue Universelle, 12, No. 1, janvier 1902, 15-16.

3912    STEENBERGEN, Albert.  Henri Bergsons intuitive Philosophie.
        Iena: Diederichs, 1909, 110.

3913    STEFANO, R.  "Metafisica e scienza positiva in Bergson."
        Richerche filosofiche, 5, No. 1, 1951, 16-30.

3914    STEINSILBER, E.  Essai critique sur les idées philosophiques
        contemporaines.  Paris: Gauthier, 1912, 391.

3915    STEPELEVICH, Lawrence S.  "Benda's Attack on Bergson."  New
        Scholasticism, 34, No. 4, October 1960, 488-498.

3916    STEPELEVICH, Lawrence S.  Henri Bergson's Concept of Man: An
        Exposition and Critique.  Washington, D.C.: Catholic Uni-
        versity of America Press, 1963 (Microfilm).

3917    STEPHEN, Karin.  "The Misuse of Mind."  Psyche, 2, No. 4, Oc-
        tober 1921, 127-137.  This is an extract from the author's
        book, The Misuse of Mind.

3918    STEPHEN, Karin.  The Misuse of Mind: A Study of Bergson's At-
        tack on Intellectualism.  London: Kegan Paul, Trench, Trub-
        ner and Co., Ltd,; New York: Harcourt, Brace, and Company,
        1922, 107.  This careful study of Bergson's criticism of
        the intellect contains a prefatory letter by Bergson.

3919    STEPHEN, Karin.  "Thought and Intuition."  Proceedings of
        the Aristotelian Society, N.S. 18, 1917-1918, 38-74.

3920    STEPHENSON, Ralph.  "Space, Time and Montage."  British Jour-
        nal of Aesthetics, 2, No. 3, July 1962, 249-258.  Marcel
        Martin, Jean Epstein, Bergson, and Resnais are discussed
        in this article.

3921    STERN, Axel.  "Morale ouverte = morale rationelle."  Actes
        du Xe Congrès des Sociétés de Philosophie de Langue Fran-
        çaise (Congrès Bergson).  Paris: Armand Colin, 1, 1959,
        283-296.  We owe to Bergson the distinction between closed
        and open morality and the revival of the distinction be-
        tween intelligence and intuition.  Rejecting this latter
        distinction, the author shows that rational morality is
        open and that morality, in order to be open, must be ra-
        tional.

3922    STERN, Axel. "Table ronde: Morale." Actes du Xe Congrès des Sociétés de Philosophie de Langue Française (Congrès Bergson). Paris: Armand Colin, 2, 1959, 237-257.

3923    STERN, Axel. "Table ronde: Physique." Actes du Xe Congrès des Sociétés de Philosophie de Langue Française (Congrès Bergson). Paris: Armand Colin, 2, 1959, 65-87.

3924    STEWART, Allegra. "The Quality of Gertrude Stein's Creativity." American Literature, 28, No. 4, January 1957, 488-506. This essay deals with Stein in relation to Marcel and Bergson.

3925    STEWART, Herbert Leslie. Questions of the Day in Philosophy and Psychology. London: Edward Arnold, 1912, 284. Bergson's critique of psychophysics is discussed on pages 24-25 and Bergson's attack on intellectualism on pages 150-158.

3926    STEWART, J. McKellar. Critical Exposition of Bergson's Philosophy. New York: Macmillan, 1911, 304.

3927    STEWART, J. McKellar. "The Notion of the Unconscious in the New Psychology." Australasian Journal of Psychology and Philosophy, 1, No. 3, 1923, 191-196. The author reproaches psychoanalysts for constructing notions of the unconscious on the analogy of conscious processes. He counters with the concept of the "pre-conscious" inspired by Bergson's dynamism.

3928    STICKERS, Joe. "Bergson und sein Intuitionismus." Die monistiche Jahrhundert, 4, 1913, 635-641, 653-663.

3929    STODIECK, Henrique. Bergson e outros temas. Florianópolis, Brazil: Rotiero, 1966, 117. This study contains a chapter on Bergson and sociology.

3930    STOLPE, Sven. "Henri Bergson och kyrkan." Credo (Sweden), 32, No. 3, 1951, 138-141.

3931    STOLPE, Sven. "Henri Bergson und die katholische Kirche." Stimmen der Zeit, 149, No. 3, 1951-1952, 143-145.

3932    STORCK, Karl. "An Romain Rolland, Maeterlinck, Bergson, Shaw und Genossen! An die neutral. Protestler." Der Türmer, 17, No. 3, November 1914, 162-172.

3933    STORK, T. B. "Bergson and his Philosophy." Lutheran Quarterly, 47, 1913, 248-258.

3934     STOUT, George Frederick. "Free Will and Determinism."
         Speaker, 1, 10 May 1890, 520. This is a review of Berg-
         son's Essai sur les données immédiates de la conscience.

3935     STRANGE, E. "Bergson's Theory of Intuition." Monist, 25,
         No. 3, July 1915, 466-470.

3936     "Ein Streit um Bergson." Abendland, 2, No. 3, 1947, 89-90.

3937     STROMBERG, Roland N. An Intellectual History of Modern Eu-
         rope. New York: Appleton-Century-Crofts, 1966, 487. Berg-
         son is discussed on pages 340-343.

3938     STROWSKI, Fortunat. "Le Bergsonisme en littérature." Re-
         naissance Politique, Littéraire, et Artistique, 13, 9 juin
         1925, 14-15.

3939     STROWSKI, Fortunat. Tableau de la littérature française au
         XIXe siècle et au XXe siècle. Paris: Mellottée, 1925, 722.
         Maurras and Bergson are discussed on pages 670-676.

3940     STROZEWSKI, Władysław. "History of the Problems of Negation:
         Part 2: Ontological Problems of Negation in John Scotus
         Erigena and Henri Bergson." Studia mediewistyczne. Eds.
         Jan Legowicz and Stefan Swiezawski. Wroctaw-Warzawa: Os-
         solineum, 1968, 306.

3941     STUR, Svätopluk. "Henri Bergson." Tvorba, 1, Nos. 1-2,
         1947, 30-31. The author criticizes Bergson's dualism of
         intelligence and intuition.

3942     STURT, Mary. The Psychology of Time. London: Kegan Paul,
         Trench, Trubner and Co., Ltd., 1925, 152.

3943     STYX, Pierre-Maurice de. "Où J. Benda rencontrerait Henri
         Bergson." Nouvelle Revue, 110 (3e Livraison), No. 440
         (Quatrième série), 1930, 184-197.

3944     SUARES, André. "Bergson vu par André Suares." Nouvelles
         Littéraires, No. 1677, 22 octobre 1959, 2.

3945     SUBRAHMANYA, Iyer V. "The Last Interview with Bergson."
         Philosophy, 17, No. 68, 1942, 382-383.

3946     "Successo di Enrico Bergson." Rivista di filosofia neosco-
         lastica, 3, No. 6, dicembre 1911, 614-630.

3947 SUJOL, A. "Le Dieu calviniste et le dieu bergsonien." Christianisme Social, 45e Année, No. 3, mai 1932, 333-346. This is a review of Les Deux Sources.

3948 SUJOL, A. "Le Nouveau Spiritualisme de M. Henri Bergson." Le Protestant, 27e Année, No. 45, 9 novembre 1912, 353-355.

3949 SULZBERGER, Cyrus L. "Entretiens avec le général de Gaulle: II. De Bergson à Staline." Le Monde, No. 8003, 7 octobre 1970, 10.

3950 SUNDEN, Hjalmar. "Bergson en Suède." Revue Internationale de Philosophie, 3, No. 10, 1949, 445-458.

3951 SUNDEN, Hjalmar. La Théorie bergsonienne de la religion. Uppsala: Almquist et Wiksells Boktryckeri; Paris: Presses Universitaires de France, 1940, 319. This study contains an exchange of letters between Bergson and Soderblom. It is written from the vantage-point of a historian of religion.

3952 SUSMAN, Margarete. Gestalten und Kreise. Zürich: Diana Verlag, 1954, 365.

3953 SYMONS, Norman J. "Bergson's Theory of Intellect and Reality." Queen's Quarterly, 24, No. 2, 1915, 177-192.

3954 SYMONS, Norman J. "Bergson's Theory of Intellect and Reality." Scientific American Supplement, 82, No. 2936, 9 December 1916, 370-371; No. 2137, 16 December 1916, 390-391. This is a highly critical analysis of Bergson's biology.

3955 SYPKENS, D. "De Evolutieleer van Henri Bergson." Theologish Tijdschrift, 46, Nos. 1-2, 1912, 158-190.

3956 SZATHMARY, Arthur. The Aesthetic Theory of Bergson. Cambridge, Massachusetts: Harvard University Press, 1937, 74. This is a very clear and very suggestive account of Bergson's aesthetics.

3957 SZEMERE, S. "Henri Bergson: Zu seinem 75. Geburtstag." Pester Lloyd, 30, 1934.

3958 SZENDE, P. "Henri Bergson, d. Metaphysiker d. Gegenrevolution." Wirtschaftswissenschaftliche Gesellschaft, 7, No. 2, 1932, 542-568.

3959   T., C. "Le Testament de Bergson." Preuves, 4, No. 41, juillet 1954, 61-62.

3960   T., G. "De un buen estilo filosófico." Criterio, 5, No. 242, 20 octubre 1932, 58-59. This is a review of The Two Sources of Morality and Religion.

3961   TABORDA, Saúl. "El fenómeno político." Homenaje a Bergson. Córdoba, Argentina: Imprenta de la Universidad, 1936, 65-95.

3962   TACCONE GALLUCCI, Nicola. Introduzione all'etica del Bergson e dello Scheler. Lecce, Italy: Ediz. Milella, 1963, 70.

3963   TAKAYAMA, Takashi. Ide-forusu no Tetsugaku. Takyo, Japan: Yamamoto-shoter, 1959, 300. This is a study of Fouillée's philosophy of the "Idea-force." It deals with both Fouillée and Bergson.

3964   TAKEUCHI, Yoshirō. Jitsuzonteki Jiyū no Bōken. Tokyo: Gendai-shichōsha, 1963, 414. The English title of this book is The Adventure of Existential Freedom from Nietzsche to Marx. It contains articles on Nietzsche, Bergson, Sartre, and Marx.

3965   TALBOTT, E. Guy. "Eucken and Bergson: Two Modern Prophets." Methodist Review, 104, No. 6, November-December 1921, 940-943.

3966   TALVART, Hector and PLACE, Joseph. "Henri Bergson." Bibliographie des auteurs modernes de langue française. Paris: Chronique des Lettres Françaises, 1928, i, 432. Bibliographic materials concerning Bergson may be found on pages 379-389.

3967   TAMINIAUX, Jacques. "Le Congrès Bergson." Revue Philosophique de Louvain, 57, No. 3, août 1959, 438-442.

3968   TAMINIAUX, Jacques. "De Bergson à la phénoménologie existentielle." Revue Philosophique de Louvain, 54, No. 1, février 1956, 26-85.

3969   TANSEY, Anne. "Henri Bergson: Abridged." Catholic Digest, 10, No. 9, September 1946, 27-29.

3970   TANSEY, Anne. "The Triumph of a Soul." Context, 2, No. 2, October 1946, 13-15. This article is a condensation of an article which appeared originally in The Lamp.

3971     TARDE, G. de.   "Une Nouvelle Métaphysique de M. Bergson."
         Vie Contemporaine, 1, novembre 1907.

3972     TAROZZI, Giuseppe.   "Enrico Bergson."   Cultura moderna, Anno
         28, No. 1, 1929.

3973     TAROZZI, Giuseppe.   Della necessità del fatto naturale ed
         umano.   2 vols.   Torino: Ermanno Loescher, 1896-1897.

3974     TATARKIEWICZ, Ladislas.   "L'Esthétique de Bergson et l'art
         de son temps."   Actes du Xe Congrès des Sociétés de Philo-
         sophie de Langue Française (Congrès Bergson).   Paris: Ar-
         mand Colin, 1, 1959, 297-302.   The author explains that
         although Bergson had a great deal to say about art and the
         beautiful in his metaphysical writings, it is difficult to
         say what actual form of art corresponds to his opinions.
         The problem is to know what artistic currents influenced
         his way of viewing art and what artistic developments were
         influenced by him.

3975     TATARKIEWICZ, Ladislas.   "Table ronde: Esthétique."   Actes
         du Xe Congrès des Sociétés de Philosophie de Langue Fran-
         çaise (Congrès Bergson).   Paris: Armand Colin, 2, 1959,
         193-210.

3976     TATARKIEWICZ, Wlayslaw.   "Abstract Art and Philosophy."
         British Journal of Aesthetics, 2, No. 3, July 1962, 227-
         238.

3977     TAUTAIN, Gustave-Louis and PICARD, Gaston.   "Enquête sur M.
         Henri Bergson et l'influence de sa pensée sur la sensibi-
         lité contemporaine."   Grande Revue, 83, No. 3, 10 février
         1914, 544-560; No. 4, 25 février 1914, 744-760; 84, No. 5,
         10 mars 1914, 111-128; No. 6, 25 mars 1914, 309-328; No. 7,
         10 avril 1914, 513-528.

3978     TAUZIN, Sebastian.   Bergson e São Tomás: Conflicto entre a
         intuição e a inteligencia.   Rio de Janeiro: Desclée de
         Brouwer, 1946.   "Prefacio de Tritão de Athayde."

3979     TAVARES, Lima Rossine de.   "Libre arbitro e determinismo na
         filosofia Bergsoniana."   Sustancia, 2, Nos. 7-8, septiem-
         bre 1941, 347-350.

3980     TAYLOR, Alastair MacDonald.   "Vitalistic Philosophy of His-
         tory: What Can Bergsonism Contribute to Historiography?"
         Journal of Social Philosophy, 6, No. 1, January 1941, 137-
         150.

3981    TAYLOR, Alfred Edward.  A Commentary on Plato's Timaeus.
        Oxford: Clarendon Press, 1928, 700.  Bergson's concept of
        measurement is criticized on pages 689-691.

3982    TAYLOR, Alfred Edward.  "Creative Evolution by Henri Berg-
        son."  International Journal of Ethics, 22, No. 4, July
        1912, 467-469.  This is a largely appreciative review of
        Arthur Mitchell's translation with, however, certain criti-
        cisms.

3983    TAYLOR, Alfred Edward.  The Faith of a Moralist: Vol. 2.
        Natural Theology and the Positive Religions.  London: Mac-
        millan, 1937, 437.  The author offers various criticisms
        of Bergson's concepts of intuition, measurement, time, and
        space on pages 338-354.

3984    TAYLOR, Alfred Edward.  "Review of Matter and Memory by Hen-
        ri Bergson."  International Journal of Ethics, 22, No. 1,
        October 1911, 101-107.  The author criticizes Bergson's
        "lack of thorough grounding in epistemological criticism."

3985    TAYLOR, Alfred Edward.  "Review of Time and Free Will by
        Henri Bergson."  International Journal of Ethics, 21, No.
        3, April 1911, 350-352.  The author denies Bergson's the-
        sis that the spatial and measurable are equivalent.

3986    TAYLOR, E.  "Henri Bergson: A French Impression of the Phi-
        losopher."  Quest, 4, No. 1, 1912, 328-334.

3987    TAYLOR, Harold.  "A Philosophy for Modern Man."  Texas Quar-
        terly, 5, No. 1, Spring 1962, 150-161.

3988    TAYMANS, Adrien C.  "Tarde and Schumpeter: A Similar Vision."
        Quarterly Journal of Economics, 64, No. 4, August 1950,
        611-622.  The author explains: "I venture to say that the
        idea of dynamic development, so fully expressed by Bergson,
        the philosopher, and by Schumpeter, the economist, had
        first been crystallized by Gabriel Tarde (1834-1904), the
        French sociologist . . . ."  (611).

3989    "Tearing the Mask from Bergson."  Living Age, 320, No. 4157,
        8 March 1924, 479.  This is a brief mention of Enrico
        Leone's Anti-Bergson.

3990    TEIXEIRA, Lívio.  "Bergson e a história da filosofia."  Kri-
        terion, 13, Nos. 51-52, 1960, 9-20.

3991    TERAN, Sisto.  Aproximaciones a la doctrina tradicional.
        Buenos Aires: Juan Roldán y Cía., 1935, 402.  Bergson and

metaphor are discussed on pages 124-129; becoming, relativism, and novelty are discussed on pages 193-213.

3992   TERAN, Sisto. "Filosofía y metáfora." _Nosotros_, 22, No. 224, enero 1928, 5-32.

3993   TERAN, Sisto. "Sobre la difusión de la filosofía." _Criterio_, 2, No. 83, octubre 1929, 150, 212.

3994   TERZI, Carlo. "Henri Gouhier: _Bergson e il Cristo del Vangeli_." _Filosofia_, Anno 21, No. 4, ottobre 1970, 573-576. This is a review.

3995   THARAUD, Jérôme and Jean. "Encore le Panthéon." _Le Figaro_, 119, No. 134, 21-22 janvier 1945, 1-2.

3996   THAYER, V. T. "Comparison of Bergson and Spinoza." _Monist_, 29, No. 1, January 1919, 96-105.

3997   THAYER, V. T. "God, and the Knowledge of God, According to Bergson and Spinoza." _Journal of Philosophy_, 14, No. 14, 5 July 1917. This is an abstract of a talk. Close similarities between Bergson and Spinoza are stressed by the author.

3998   THEAU, Jean. _La Critique bergsonienne du concept_. Paris: Presses Universitaires de France; Toulouse, Privat, 1967, 621.

3999   THEODORESCU, Constantin A. _Die Erkenntnislehre Bergsons_. Jena: Frommansche, 1914, 56. This is an inaugural dissertation presented at the University of Jena. It is translated by the author from Rumanian.

4000   THERIVE, E. "Review of _Bergson: Mon Maître_ by G. Maire." _Europe Nouvelle_, 18, 26 octobre 1935, 1045-1046.

4001   THEVENAZ, Pierre. "Refus du réel et spiritualité." _Henri Bergson_. Ed. Béguin and Thévenaz, 97-104. The author considers Bergson's puzzling call to freedom for people who are, on his terms, already free. Difficulties in Bergson's concept of mystical intuition are also stressed.

4002   THIBAUD, Marguerite. "L'Effort chez Maine de Biran et Bergson." Diss., Grenoble, 1939, 199.

4003   THIBAUDET, Albert. "Bergson et le bergsonisme." _Candide_, 4, No. 4, 20 janvier 1927.

4004   THIBAUDET, Albert.  "Bergson et Proust."  Journal de Genève,
       15 février 1929.

4005   THIBAUDET, Albert.  "Bergson vu par Albert Thibaudet."  Nou-
       velles Littéraires, No. 1677, 22 octobre 1959, 2.

4006   THIBAUDET, Albert.  "Bergson, Henri."  Encyclopedia Britan-
       nica.  Chicago: Benton, 1962, Vol 3, 505-506.

4007   THIBAUDET, Albert.  "Henri Bergson écrivain."  Candide, 5,
       15 novembre 1928.

4008   THIBAUDET, Albert.  "Henri Bergson écrivain."  Messidor, 15,
       No. 11-12, novembre-décembre 1928.

4009   THIBAUDET, Albert.  "Conclusions sur le bergsonisme."  Nou-
       velle Revue Française, 21, No. 9, septembre 1923, 257-271.
       This article is quoted from the concluding pages of Thi-
       baudet's Bergson.

4010   THIBAUDET, Albert.  "Les Figures bergsoniennes de l'histoire."
       Revue de Genève, 7, No. 38, août 1923, 129-150.

4011   THIBAUDET, Albert.  Paul Valéry.  Paris: Grasset, 1923, 189.
       This is a rather Bergsonian interpretation of Valéry.

4012   THIBAUDET, Albert.  "Péguy et Bergson."  Nouvelle Revue Fran-
       çaise, 19, No. 211, avril 1931, 580-592.

4013   THIBAUDET, Albert.  "Le Style intérieur d'une philosophie."
       Nouvelles Littéraires, No. 322, 15 décembre 1928, 1-2.

4014   THIBAUDET, Albert.  "Taine, Bergson et M. Souday."  Nouvel-
       les Littéraires, No. 302, 28 juillet 1928, 1.

4015   THIBAUDET, Albert.  Trente ans de vie française: Vol. 3.  Le
       Bergsonisme.  Paris: Nouvelle Revue Française, 1913, 2
       vols., 256 et 253.

4016   THIBON, Gustave.  "La Notion de conscience d'après Bergson."
       Revue Thomiste, N.S. 16, No. 77, mai-juin 1933, 399-423.

4017   THIELMANS, H.  "Bergson."  Streven, 3, 1936, 246-270.

4018   THOMAS, James Bishop.  A Guide to Bergson.  Girard, Kansas:
       Handelman-Julius Company, 1924, 64 (Little Blue Book No.
       508).  This is a brief popular essay.

4019    THOMPSON, J. Arthur.  "Biological Philosophy."  Nature, 86,
        No. 2189, 12 octobre 1911, 475-477.  This is a review of
        Creative Evolution.

4020    THOMPSON, J. Arthur.  "Professor Henri Bergson's Biology."
        Royal Physical Society for the Promotion of Zoology and
        other Branches of Natural History (Proceedings).  Edin-
        burgh, 19, 1916, 79-92.

4021    THONNARD, F.-J.  Précis d'histoire de la philosophie.  Paris:
        Tournai, 1937, 810.  Bergson is viewed from a Thomist view-
        point on pages 707-740.

4022    THOROLD, Algar.  "Review of La Pensée et le mouvant by Henri
        Bergson."  Criterion, 14, No. 57, 1935, 690-694.

4023    "Threatened Collapse of the Bergson Boom in France."  Cur-
        rent Opinion, 56, No. 5, May 1914, 371-372.

4024    THYRION, Jacques.  "Bergson devant le désordre contemporain."
        Revue Générale Belge, No. 17, mars 1947, 703-709.

4025    THYRION, Jacques.  "Henri Bergson."  Revue Générale Belge, 2,
        1946, 74-79.

4026    THYSSEN, Johannes.  "Henri Bergson und die Deutsche-Philoso-
        phie der Gegenwart."  Kölnische Zeitung, 1925.

4027    TILGHER, Adriano.  "L'estetica di Enrico Bergson."  Nuova
        antologia, 6e Ser., 219, No. 6, 16 novembre 1920, 163-
        168.

4028    TILGHER, Adriano.  Filosofi e moralisti del novecento.  Roma:
        Bardi, 1932, 234.  This study contains a chapter on Berg-
        son.

4029    TILGHER, Adriano.  Homo faber: Storia del concetto del lavo-
        ra nella civilità occidentale.  Roma: Bardi, 1929, 200.
        Bergson's influence is found throughout this study of the
        part which work has played in the evolution of the human
        race.

4030    TILGHER, Adriano.  "Io, libertà, e moralità nella filosofia
        di Enrico Bergson."  La Cultura, 31, Nos. 22 and 23, 1912.

4031    TILGHER, Adriano.  Io, libertà, e moralità nella filosofia
        di Enrico Bergson.  Trani, Italy: Ditta Vecchi, 1912, 16.

4032    TILGHER, Adriano. "Il tempo." _Logos_, 16, No. 4, 1933. The author argues that time is one with consciousness and is nothing outside of consciousness.

4033    TILGHER, Adriano. _Voci del tempo_. Roma: Libr. di Sc. e Lettere, 1923, 224. Bergson is discussed on pages 190-203.

4034    TILGHER, Adriano. _Work: What it has Meant Through the Ages_. Trans. Dorothy Canfield Fisher. New York: Harcourt, Brace and Co., 1930, 225. Bergson's influence is found throughout this study of the part which work has played in the evolution of the human race.

4035    TILLEY, Ethel. "The Problem of Identity in Henri Bergson's Philosophy." Diss., Boston, 1936.

4036    TILLICH, Paul. "Existential Philosophy." _Journal of the History of Ideas_, 5, No. 1, January 1944, 44-70.

4037    "Review of _Time and Free Will_ by Henri Bergson." _Athenaeum_, No. 4330, 13 October 1910, 483-484.

4038    "Review of _Time and Free Will: An Essay on the Immediate Data of Consciousness_ by Henri Bergson." _Nation_, 91, No. 2369, 24 November 1910, 499-500. This is a general summary of Bergson's position in _Time and Free Will_.

4039    "Review of _Time and Free Will: An Essay on the Immediate Data of Consciousness_, by Henri Bergson." _Saturday Review_ (London), 90, No. 2866, 1 October 1910, 430.

4040    TISON-BRAUN, Micheline. _La Crise de l'humanisme: Le Conflit de l'individu et de la société dans la littérature française moderne_. Paris: Nizet, 1967, 468.

4041    TITCHENER, Edward Bradford. "Review of _Laughter: An Essay on the Meaning of the Comic_ by Henri Bergson." _American Journal of Psychology_, 23, No. 1, January 1912, 146-147. This is a review of the English translation of _Le Rire_ with critical comments.

4042    TOMEUCCI, Luigi. _La critica attualista del Bergson_. Messina, Italy, 1936.

4043    TOMEUCCI, Luigi. _La dottrina della durée e la critica italiana_. Messina, Italy, 1939.

4044    "Tomisme de Bergson al realismo de Santo Tomás." _Criterion_, 12, 1936. Articles on Bergson by R. Esquerra, J. Sanfelin,

Sever de Montsonis, and Augusti de Montclar are included in an issue of this journal in 1936.

4045    TONQUEDEC, Joseph de. "Bergson et la scolastique." Revue Critique des Idées et des Livres, 23, No. 137, 25 décembre 1913, 651-670.

4046    TONQUEDEC, Joseph de. "M. Bergson: Est-il moniste?" Etudes par des Pères de la Compagnie de Jésus, 130, No. 1, 10 février 1912, 506-516. This article is summarized in the Revue de Philosophie, avril 1912.

4047    TONQUEDEC Joseph de. "La Clef des Deux Sources." Etudes par des Pères de la Compagnie de Jésus, 208, 5 décembre 1932, 516-534; 20 décembre 1932, 667-683.

4048    TONQUEDEC, Joseph de. "Comment interpréter l'ordre du monde?" Etudes par des Pères de la Compagnie de Jésus, 114, 5 mars 1908, 577-597.

4049    TONQUEDEC, Joseph de. Comment interpréter l'ordre du monde à propos du dernier ouvrage de M. Bergson. Paris: Beauchesne, 1908.

4050    TONQUEDEC, Joseph de. "La Conception bergsonienne de Dieu." Actes du Xe Congrès des Sociétés de Philosophie de Langue Française (Congrès Bergson). Paris: Armand Colin, 1, 1959, 303-306. The author, who has written Bergson many letters concerning religion, expresses certain reservations concerning Bergson's concept of God. In spite of Bergson's rejection of a static monism, the evolutionary thesis of Creative Evolution, which plunges everything into becoming, has a certain monistic tinge. Further, Bergson's conception of mysticism differs from the Christian conception, according to the author.

4051    TONQUEDEC, Joseph de. "Le Contenu des Deux Sources." Etudes par des Pères de la Compagnie de Jésus, 214, 20 mars 1933, 641-668; 215, 5 avril 1933, 26-54.

4052    TONQUEDEC, Joseph de. "Discussion avec J. Maritain et R. Johannet sur Bergson." Les Lettres, 8, No. 2, 1er février 1920, 24-32.

4053    TONQUEDEC, Joseph de. "Les Lettres de Bergson sur Dieu." Revue des Deux Mondes, N.S. Année 5, No. 14, 15 juillet 1952, 252-263.

4054    TONQUEDEC, Joseph de.  "La Notion de vérité dans la philo-
        sophie nouvelle."  Etudes par des Pères de la Compagnie de
        Jésus, 110, 20 mars 1907, 721-749; 5 juillet 1907, 68-82;
        5 août 1907, 335-361.

4055    TONQUEDEC, Joseph de.  La Notion de la vérité dans la philo-
        sophie nouvelle.  Paris: Beauchesne, 1908, 150.  The au-
        thor offers numerous criticisms of Bergson and Le Roy.

4056    TONQUEDEC, Joseph de.  Sur La Philosophie bergsonienne.
        Paris: Beauchesne, 1936, 241.  This study consists of five
        articles published earlier in Etudes par des Pères de la
        Compagnie de Jésus (1905, 1908, 1932, and 1933) and the
        Revue Critique des Idées et des Livres (1913).

4057    TONQUEDEC, Joseph de.  "Table ronde: Religion."  Actes du Xe
        Congrès des Sociétés de Philosophie de Langue Française
        (Congrès Bergson).  Paris: Armand Colin, 2, 1959, 261-278.

4058    TOPCU, Nurettin.  Bergson.  Istanbul: Hareket Yayinlari,
        1968, 116.

4059    TORCHIA ESTRADA, J.  La filosofía del siglo XX.  Buenos
        Aires: Atlantida, 1955, 346.

4060    TORRES, Francisco W.  Dos filósofos de la vida: Bergson y
        Schopenhauer.  Córdoba, Argentina: Imprenta de la Univer-
        sidad, 1938, 155.  The author examines Bergson's basic
        ideas in metaphysics, ethics, and sociology.

4061    TORRES, J. V.  "El primado de la temporalidad."  Actas del
        Primero Congreso Nacional de Filosofía de Argentina, 2,
        1949, 858-864.

4062    TORREVEJANO, Mercedes.  "Bergson: En busca de una experien-
        cia de Dios."  Revista de la Institución Teresiana, agosto-
        septiembre 1963, 4-5.

4063    TORYHO, Jacinto.  "Bergson en anécdotas."  Argentina Libre,
        2, 1941.

4064    TOUCHARD, Pierre-Aimé.  Le Théâtre et l'angoisse des hommes.
        Paris: Edit. du Seuil, 1968, 221.  Beckett, Bergson, Clau-
        del, Cocteau, and others are discussed in this study.

4065    TOUPIN, Paul.  "Bergson et Proust."  L'Action Universitaire,
        13, novembre 1946, 18-30.

4066    TOUPIN, Paul. "Bergson et Proust." Amérique Française, 5, No. 8, novembre 1946, 18-30.

4067    TOWNSEND, James G. "Bergson and Religion." Monist, 22, No. 3, July 1912, 392-397.

4068    TREDICI, Giacinto. "New Tendencies in Contemporary Philosophy." Scuola cattolica, 49, No. 1, 1921. Blondel, Boutroux, Bergson, Varisco, Gentile, and Croce are discussed in this article.

4069    TREMBLAY, Jacques. "La Notion de philosophie chez Bergson." Laval Théologique et Philosophique, 14, No. 1, 1958, 30-76.

4070    TRESMONTANT, Claude. "Deux Métaphysiques bergsoniennes?" Revue de Métaphysique et de Morale, 64, No. 2, 1959, 180-193. The author examines contrary tendencies in Bergson's thought: his "metaphysics of creation" and his "neoplatonism."

4071    TRETHOWAN, Dom Illtyd. "Bergson and the Zeitgeist: With Excerpts from The Two Sources of Morality and Religion." Downside Review, 85, No. 2, April 1967, 138-147; No. 3, July 1967, 262-273.

4072    TREVISAN, Armindo. "Essai sur le problème de la création chez Bergson." Diss., Fribourg, Germany, 1963, 194.

4073    TROILO, Erminio. La conflagrazione: Indagini sulla storia dello spirito contemporaneo. Roma: Formiggini, 1918, 353.

4074    TROILO, Erminio. Figure e studi di storia della filosofia. Roma: Impr. Polyglotte l'Universelle, 1918, 324. This is a highly critical study of Bergson, James, Vailati, Bergi, and others.

4075    TROTIGNON, Pierre. L'Idée de vie chez Bergson et la critique de la métaphysique. Paris: Presses Universitaires de de France, 1968, 336.

4076    TROUCHE, H. "Review of L'Evolution créatrice by Henri Bergson." Revue de Philosophie, No. 11, novembre 1908, 520-534.

4077    TROUDE, R. "Review of La Pensée et le mouvant by Henri Bergson." Revue Scientifique, 73, No. 2, 1935, 772.

4078    TROUILLARD, Jean. "Sagesse bergsonienne, sagesse plotinienne." Actes du Xe Congrès des Sociétés de Philosophie de

Langue Française (Congrès Bergson).  Paris: Armand Colin,
1, 1959, 307-310.  Nothing could seem farther from a philosophy of spiritual creation than the common conception
of the Platonic Idea.  Nonetheless, there is in Bergson a
search for a simplicity at once original and creative,
whose anteriority, the author holds, can be an excellent
way of reinventing the Platonic Idea.

4079    TROUILLARD, Jean.  "Table ronde: Sources et histoire du bergsonisme."  Actes du Xe Congrès des Sociétés de Philosophie
de Langue Française (Congrès Bergson).  Paris: Armand Colin, 2, 1959, 213-233.

4080    TRUC, Gonzague.  "Belphégor ou le monde bergsonien."  L'Opinion, 12e Année, No. 17, 26 avril 1919, 373-374.

4081    TRUC, Gonzague.  "M. Benda et le bergsonisme."  Revue Critique des Idées et des Livres, 24, No. 138, 10 janvier 1914,
33-41.

4082    TRUC, Gonzague.  "Bergsonisme et catholicisme."  L'Opinion,
20e Année, No. 21, 21 mai 1927, 16-17.

4083    TRUC, Gonzague.  "Le Bergsonisme et le mouvement."  Revue
Hebdomadaire des Cours et des Conférences, 32e Année, No.
1, 3 mars 1923, 61-68.  This is purportedly a review of
Durée et simultanéité.  In it the author attacks insidi-
ous Bergsonism.

4084    TRUC, Gonzague.  "La Guerre et le bergsonisme."  L'Opinion,
11e Année, No. 36, 7 septembre 1918, 180-181.

4085    TRUC, Gonzague.  La Pensée: Tableau du XXe siècle 1900-1933.
Paris: Denoël et Steele, 1934, 300.

4086    TRUC, Gonzague.  "Le Spiritualisme bergsonien et la raison
moderne."  Revue de la Semaine Illustrée, 9, No. 38, 23
septembre 1921, 425-441.

4087    TRUC, Gonzague.  "Troisième Lettre à une institutrice sur la
culture de l'esprit: Bergson."  L'Ecole et la Vie, 3, No.
10, 20 décembre 1919.

4088    TSANOFF, Radoslav A.  "Evolution, Teleology and History."
Rice Institute Pamphlet, 46, No. 1, April 1959, 32-51.

4089    TUCHMAN, Barbara Wertheim.  The Guns of August.  New York:
Macmillan, 1962, 511.  Bergson and French militarism are
discussed on pages 21 and 436.

4090    TUCHMAN, Barbara Wertheim. The Proud Tower: A Portrait of the World Before the War, 1890-1914. New York: Macmillan, 1966, 528. Bergson and social psychology are discussed on pages 383-384.

4091    TUFTS, J. H. "Humor." Psychological Review, 8, No. 1, January 1901, 98-99. This is a brief review of Laughter.

4092    TUMMERS, F. "Bergson en de vrije wil." Tijdschrift voor Wijsbegeerte, 11, 1917, 488-504.

4093    TURNER, J. "The Future of Bergsonism." Monist, 33, No. 2, April 1923, 219-239.

4094    TURQUET-MILNES, Gladys Rosaleen. "Bergson and Tragedy." Contemporary Review, 136, August 1929, 205-212. Bergson construes the tragic emotion as an affirmation of life, according to the author.

4095    TURQUET-MILNES, Gladys Rosaleen. From Pascal to Proust: Studies in the Genealogy of a Philosophy. London: Cape Ltd., 1926, 192.

4096    TURQUET-MILNES, Gladys Rosaleen. Some Modern French Writers: A Study in Bergsonism. New York: McBride and Company, 1921, 302.

4097    TURQUET-MILNES, Gladys Rosaleen. Some Modern French Writers: A Study in Bergsonism. 1921 rpt. Freeport, New York: Books for Libraries Press, 1968, 302.

4098    TUTTLE, J. R. "Review of 'Creative Evolution and Philosophic Doubt' by A. J. Balfour in Hibbert Journal, 11, 1-23." Philosophical Review, 22, No. 1, January 1912, 122-123.

4099    TUTTLE, J. R. "Review of 'Life and Consciousness' by Henri Bergson in Hibbert Journal, 11, 24-44." Philosophical Review, 21, No. 1, January 1912, 125-126.

4100    "Review of The Two Sources of Morality and Religion by Henri Bergson." Catholic World, 142, No. 847, 1935, 112-113.

4101    "Review of The Two Sources of Morality and Religion by Henri Bergson." Journal of Nervous and Mental Disease, 84, 1936 221-223. This is a review of the English translation of Les Deux Sources, including an exposition of Bergson's basic position.

4102    "Review of The Two Sources of Morality and Religion by Henri
        Bergson." Modern Languages, 16, 1934-1935, 162.

4103    "Review of The Two Sources of Morality and Religion by Henri
        Bergson." Nature, 137, No. 3457, 1 February 1937, 171.

4104    "Review of The Two Sources of Religion and Morality by Henri
        Bergson." Thought, 11, No. 4, September 1936, 333-336.

4105    TYMIENIECKA, Anna Teresa. Why is There Something Rather
        Than Nothing? Prolegomena to the Phenomenology of Cosmic
        Creation. Assens, Denmark: Van Gorcum and Co., 1966, 168.

4106    TYRRELL, George. "Review of L'Evolution créatrice by Henri
        Bergson." Hibbert Journal, 6, No. 1, January 1908, 435-
        442. This is a lengthy, mainly expository review.

4107    TYRRELL, Henry. "Bergson." Art World, 2, No. 6, September
        1917, 520-521. This is a poem dedicated to Bergson.

4108    "Über die gegenwärtige Aufgabe der Philosophie." Logos, 2,
        No. 1, 1911-1912, 126-127. This is a review of Bergson's
        address at the 4th International Philosophical Congress.

4109    UGARTE DE ERCILLA, E. "Bergson: Idolo de la filosofía fran-
        cesa contemporánea." Razón y Fe, 39, No. 2, 1914, 298-311.

4110    UGARTE DE ERCILLA, E. "Boletín de filosofía contemporánea:
        Movimiento bergsoniano." Razón y Fe, 38, No. 4, 1914, 486-
        491.

4111    UNDERHILL, Evelyn. "Bergson and the Mystics." English Re-
        view, 10, No. 2, February 1912, 511-522. This study is re-
        published in Living Age, 272, No. 3532, 16 March 1912, 668-
        675. This is a suggestive account of the relevance of
        Bergson's thought to mysticism.

4112    UNDERHILL, Evelyn. Mysticism. New York: Dutton, 1912, 600.
        Bergson is discussed on pages 31-36.

4113    UNSOELD, William Francis. "Mysticism, Morality, and Freedom:
        The Role of the Vital Impulse in Bergson's Theory of Eth-
        ics." Diss., Washington (Seattle), 1959.

4114    UNSOELD, William Francis. Mysticism, Morality, and Freedom:
        The Role of the Vital Impulse in Bergson's Theory of Eth-
        ics. Ann Arbor, Michigan: University Microfilms, 1959
        (Microfilm AC-1 no. 59-3350).

4115    URMENETA, Fermín de.  "Henri Bergson et l'esthétique de la
        'jovialité'."  Actes du Xe Congrès des Sociétés de Philo-
        sophie de Langue Française (Congrès Bergson).  Paris: Ar-
        mand Colin, 1, 1959, 311-314.  In Laughter one discovers,
        the author holds, a faith in joviality which is at once
        conciliatory, objective, and exalting, and which makes
        Bergson's work such a stimulating incentive for its read-
        ers.  The author examines the aesthetic categories of the
        caricature and their closely allied categories.

4116    URMENETA, Fermín de.  "La estética en el 'Congreso Bergson'."
        Revista de Ideas Estéticas, 19, No. 74, 1961, 135-138.

4117    URMENETA, Fermín de.  "Louis Vives: Peldaño ideológico en-
        tre San Agustin y Enrique Bergson."  Revista de Filosifía,
        24, 1965, 373-383.

4118    URTIN, Henri.  "Le Fondement de l'intuition."  Actes du Xe
        Congrès des Sociétés de Philosophie de Langue Française
        (Congrès Bergson).  Paris: Armand Colin, 1, 1959, 315-318.
        It is possible to find within ourselves, the author holds,
        the essentials of intuition, which is basically the origi-
        nal character of our personal law ("statute").  It is nec-
        essary to search for this personal formula which consti-
        tutes our originality.  Also intuition intervenes neces-
        sarily in other domains.

4119    USCATESCU, George.  Profetas de Europa.  Madrid: Editoria
        Nacional, 1962, 172.

4120    USHENKO, Andrew.  The Logic of Events: An Introduction to a
        Philosophy of Time.  Berkeley, California: University of
        California Press, 1929, 180.  This study considers the
        views of Russell, Alexander, Bergson, Croce, Gentile, and
        Whitehead.

4121    USHENKO, Andrew.  "Zeno's Paradoxes."  Mind, 55, No. 218,
        April 1946, 151-165.  This article examines various at-
        tempted refutations of Zeno, including Bergson's, which
        is likened to Wisdom's.

4122    UZNADZE, D.  "Bergsons Monismus."  Archiv für Geschichte der
        Philosophie, 37, No. 1, 1925, 26-40.

4123    VALDEZ ALZAMORA, Mario.  "La filosofía de Bergson."  Revista
        de la Universidad Católica del Perú, 9, 1941, 144-161.

4124    VALENSIN, Auguste.  Profili: Platone, Cartesio, Pascal, Berg-
        son, Blondel.  Milano: IPL, 1968, 343.

4125    VALENSIN, Auguste. Regards sur Platon, Descartes, Pascal,
        Bergson, Blondel. Paris: Aubier, 1955, 327. The introduc-
        tion is by André Blauchet.

4126    VALERIU, Martin. "Das Verhältnis der Religion zur Gesell-
        schaft in der neuesten französischen Philosophie." Diss.,
        Jena, 1941.

4127    VALERY, Paul. "Allocution à l'occasion du décès de M. H.
        Bergson." Etudes Bergsoniennes. Paris: Presses Universi-
        taires de France, 1942, 1-4.

4128    VALERY, Paul. "Allocution à l'occasion du décès de M. Henri
        Bergson prononcée à la séance tenue par l'Académie fran-
        çaise, le 9 janvier 1941." Revue Philosophique de la
        France et de l'Etranger, 131, Nos. 3-8, mars-août 1941,
        121-124.

4129    VALERY, Paul. "Bergson: Extracts from the Notebooks." Mas-
        ters and Friends (Coll. works, IX). London: Routledge and
        Kegan Paul, 1968, 342-349.

4130    VALERY, Paul. "Henri Bergson: Allocution prononcée à l'Aca-
        démie française le 9 janvier 1941." Suisse Contemporaine,
        juin 1941.

4131    VALERY, Paul. "Henri Bergson: Allocution prononcée à l'Aca-
        démie française le 9 janvier 1941." Henri Bergson. Ed.
        Béguin and Thévenaz, 19-23.

4132    VALERY, Paul. Henri Bergson: Allocution prononcée à la sé-
        ance de l'Académie du jeudi 9 janvier 1941. Paris: Domat-
        Montchrestien, 1945, 11 (Collection "Au Voilier").

4133    VALERY, Paul. "Deux Lettres à Henri Bergson." Etudes Berg-
        soniennes, 5, 1960, 3-7.

4134    VALERY, Paul. "Discours sur la mort de Bergson." Lettres
        Françaises (Buenos Aires), 1re Année, No. 2, 1er octobre
        1941, 5-8.

4135    VALERY, Paul. "Funeral Address on Bergson." Masters and
        Friends. London: Routledge and Kegan Paul, 1968, 302-306.
        This is volume nine of the English translation of Valéry's
        collected works.

4136    VALERY, Paul. "In Memory of Henri Bergson." Partisan Re-
        view, 11, No. 1, Winter 1944, 18-21.

4137    VALERY, Paul. Lettres à quelques-uns. Paris: Gallimard, 1952, 256, 162-166. This book contains a letter by Valéry denying Bergson's influence on him. It was published previously in the prefac  to Martin Gillet, Paul Valéry et la métaphysique. Paris: La Tour d'Ivoire, 1927, 187.

4138    VALERY, Paul. "Sobre la muerte de Bergson." Abside, 6, No. 1, enero 1942, 3-8.

4139    VALLEJOS, M. A. Raúl. "El mundo especulativo de Henri Bergson." Universidad de San Carlos, 62, No. 1, 1964, 113-119.

4140    VANDEL, Albert. "Fils de Bergson." Nouvelles Littéraires, No. 1677, 22 octobre 1959, 6.

4141    VANDEL, Albert. "L'Importance de L'Evolution créatrice dans la genèse de la pensée moderne." Revue de Théologie et de Philosophie, 9, No. 2, 1960, 85-108. The author deals with the philosophy of evolution since Lamarck and Bergson's contribution to the philosophy of evolution. He also deals with Bergson's influence on F. Leenhardt, G. Mercier, and Teilhard de Chardin.

4142    VANDEL, Albert. "Table ronde: Vie et évolution." Actes du Xe Congrès des Sociétés de Philosophie de Langue Française (Congrès Bergson). Paris: Armand Colin, 2, 1959, 91-117.

4143    VAN DER BRUGH, Emmanuel Johannes. "Loisy contre Bergson." Nieuw Theologisch Tijdschrift, 24, 1935, 302-330.

4144    VAN DER BRUGH, Emmanuel Johannes. "De Philosophie van Bergson." Vragen van den Dag, 30, 1915.

4145    VANDEREM, Fernand. "Le Bergsonisme." Revue de France, 4, No. 7, 1er avril 1924, 621-626. This is a review of A. Thibaudet's Le Bergsonisme.

4146    VANDEREM, Fernand. "Review of L'Energie spirituelle by Henri Bergson." Revue de Paris, 26e Année, No. 16, 15 août 1919, 867-872.

4147    VANDEREM, Fernand. Le Miroir des Lettres: L'Energie spirituelle. Paris: Flammarion, 1921, 251.

4148    VAN DER KOOIJ, J. "Het Godsbegrip volgens het Bergsonisme." Kultuurleven, 4, 1935, 166-167.

4149    VAN DER KOOIJ, J. "De Methode van H. Bergson." Kultuurleven, 6, 1935.

4150   VAN DER MEERSCH, Joseph.  "Bergsonisme et catholicisme."
       Collationes Brugenses, 39, No. 1, 1949, 60-82; No. 2, 1939,
       154-162.

4151   VAN GINNEKEN, T.  "Nova et vetera."  Studiën, 86, 1916, 582-
       584.

4152   VAN HOLK, L. J.  "Van William James naar Henri Bergson."
       Wijsgerig Perspectief of Maatschappij en Wetenschap, 5,
       No. 2, 1964-1965, 101-110.

4153   VAN KLINKEN, L.  "De Profeet der intuitie."  Paedag. Tijd-
       schrift voor het Christelijk Onderwis, 29, 1937.

4154   VAN PEURSEN, C. A.  "Henri Bergson: Phénoménologie de la
       perception."  Revue de Métaphysique et de Morale, 65, No.
       3, 1960, 317-326.

4155   VAN SUCHTELEN, N.  "Over Bergson's Scheppende Evolutie."
       Wil en Weg, 4, 1925.

4156   VAN TIEGHEM, Paul.  "Review of Bergson und Proust by Kurt
       Jäckel."  Revue d'Histoire Littéraire de la France, 44,
       No. 3, 1937, 444.

4157   VARISCO, Bernardino.  "La creázióne."  Rivista filosofica,
       11, No. 2, marzo-aprile 1908, 149-180.  This is a review
       of L'Evolution créatrice.

4158   VARISCO, Bernardino.  "La filosofia della contingenza."
       Rivista filosofica, 8, No. 1, 1905, 3-37.  This is a cri-
       ticism of recent defenders of indeterminism, chiefly Berg-
       son.

4159   VARTIOVAARA, Klaus V.  "Nykyaikaisen filosofian johtana
       aateita."  Valvoja, No. 3, 1946, 53-58.

4160   VASCONCELOS, José.  "Bergson en México."  Homenaje a Bergson.
       Imprenta Universitaria México, 1941, 135-158.  This ar-
       ticle also appears in Filosofía y Letras, Universidad Na-
       cional Autónoma de México, No. 2, abril-junio 1941, 239-
       253.

4161   VASCONCELOS, José.  Historia del pensamiento filosófico.
       México: Universidad Nacional Autónoma de Mexico, 1937, 578.
       This is a history of philosophy containing a chapter on
       Bergson.

4162    VASSALLO, Angel. Bergson. Buenos Aires: Centro Editor de
America Latina, 1967, 116.

4163    VASSALLO, Angel. "Bergson y nosotros." Ciencia y Fe, 8,
Nos. 21-32, 1952, 41-55.

4164    VASSALLO, Angel. "Bergson y el problema de la metafísica."
Homenaje a Bergson. Córdoba, Argentina: Imprenta de la
Universidad, 1936, 13-31.

4165    VASSALLO, Angel. "Henri Bergson: Especialmente ética y filosofía de la religión." Cursos y Conferencias, 4, No. 7,
noviembre 1934, 707-718.

4166    VASSALLO, Angel. "Las dos fuentes de la moral." Cursos y
Conferencias, 5, No. 6, septiembre 1936, 603-654.

4167    VASSALLO, Angel. "En la muerte de Henri Bergson." Sur,
10, No. 76, enero 1941, 7-13.

4168    VASSALLO, Angel. "Inteligencia y instint: La intuición:
Mecanismo creador y devenir creador." Cursos y Conferencias, 4, No. 11, marzo 1935, 1175-1191.

4169    VASSALLO, Angel. "Para una visión y juicio del tiempo pre-
sente." Sur, 10, No. 65, febrero 1940, 77-86.

4170    VASSALLO, Angel. Retablo de la filosofía moderna: Figuras y
fervores. Buenos Aires: Universidad Nacional de la Pista,
1968, 140. This history of philosophy includes sections
on Leonardo, Spinoza, Blondel, and Bergson.

4171    VAX, Louis. "Du Bergsonisme à la philosophie première."
Critique, 11, No. 92, 1955, 36-52. This is a study of
Jankélévitch's Bergson.

4172    VAZ FERREIRA, Carlos. Lógica viva. Montevideo: Talleres
gráficos, 1920, 304. This work shows Bergson's and James'
influence.

4173    VEDALDI, Armando. Cinque profili di filosofi francesi: Montaigne, Pascal, Comte, Bergson, Blondel. Torino: Taylor,
1958, 267. The author gives a pantheistic interpretation
of Bergson on pages 127-253.

4174    VELEZ, Pedro. M. Dos lecturas filosóficos-teológicos: Bergson y el Indice, Pio X, el modernismo y Santo Tomás. "Con
las licencias necesarias." Lima: Impr. de "La Union,"
1915, 30.

4175    VELOSO, A.   "Bergson e la libertação do pensamiento."   Bro-
        teria, 75, 1962, 505-515.

4176    VERDENE, Georges.   Bergson le révolté ou l'ascension d'une
        âme.   Genève: P.-F. Perret-Gentil, 1942, 224.

4177    VERMOREL, L. J.   "Henri Bergson y su filosofía."   Universi-
        dad de Panamá, 1, No. 3, 1936, 8-16.

4178    VERNEAUX, Roger.   "Review of La Pensée et le mouvant by Hen-
        ri Bergson."   Revue de Philosophie, N.S. 4, No. 3, 1934,
        316-319.

4179    VERNEDE, Louis.   "Le Bergsonisme ou une philosophie de la
        mobilité."   Phalange, 7, No. 72, 1912, 485-507.

4180    VERSIANI VELLOSO, Arthur.   "Centenarios de 1959: Husserl,
        Bergson . . . ."   Kriterion, 12, No. 49-50, 1959, 499-516.

4181    VERTESI, Frigyes.   Bergson: Rendelmélete.   Pécs, Hungary:
        1927, 40.

4182    VESTDIJK, J.   "De beeldende philosoof."   Groot-Nederland, 1,
        No. 4, 1941, 269-280.   This is an obituary article.

4183    VETTARD, Camille.   "Review of Le Bergsonisme ou une philoso-
        phie de la mobilité by Julien Benda."   Nouvelle Revue Fran-
        çaise, 8, 1er novembre 1912, 940-944.

4184    VETTER, Johannes.   "Das Ästhetische in der Wirklichkeits-
        lehre Bergsons."   Diss., Erlangen, 1923, 69.

4185    VIAL, Fernand.   "Bergson et Proust: L'Idée de Temps."   Pub-
        lications of the Modern Language Association of America,
        55, No. 4, 1940, 1191-1212.

4186    VIAL, Fernand.   "Review of The Bergsonian Heritage.   Ed.
        Thomas Hanna."   French Review, 37, No. 5, April 1964, 594-
        596.

4187    VIAL, Fernand.   "Le Bergsonisme de Paul Claudel."   Publica-
        tions of the Modern Language Association of America, 60,
        No. 2, June 1945, 437-462.   Claudel's is an integral Berg-
        sonism.

4188    VIAL, Fernand.   "Henri Bergson: Spiritual and Literary In-
        fluence."   Thought, 16, No. 61, June 1941, 241-258.

4189    VIAL, Fernand. "Méconnaissance du temps." Revue des Sciences Philosophiques et Théologiques, 20, No. 3, août 1931. Uchenko, Bergson, and Russell are all wrong, according to the author. Time is not a movement, but its measure.

4190    VIAL, Fernand. "Le Symbolisme bergsonien du temps dans l'oeuvre de Proust." Publications of the Modern Language Association of America, 55, No. 4, December 1940, 1191-1212. The author argues that the novelist Marcel Proust transposed Bergsonism into literature.

4191    VIALATOUX, Joseph. De Durkheim à Bergson. Paris: Bloud et Gay, 1939, 200.

4192    "Review of La Vie Personnelle by Albert Bazaillas." Revue de Métaphysique et de Morale, 13, No. 2 (Supplément), mars 1912, 62-64.

4193    VIETROFF, J. "L'Influence de la philosophie de M. Bergson. VI." Mouvement Socialiste, 31, No. 237, janvier 1912, 62-64.

4194    VIGNON, Paul. "Review of L'Energie spirituelle by Henri Bergson." Revue de Philosophie, 27, No. 4, 1920, 361-376.

4195    VIGONE, Lucette. "Quelques Etudes bergsoniennes en Italie." Actes du Xe Congrès des Sociétés de Philosophie de Langue Française (Congrès Bergson). Paris: Armand Colin, 1, 1959, 319-326. This is a bibliography of writing concerning Bergson in Italy from 1900-1958. It deals with the more important works.

4196    VIGONE, Lucette. "Table ronde: Sources et histoire du bergsonisme." Actes du Xe Congrès des Sociétés de Philosophie de Langue Française (Congrès Bergson). Paris: Armand Colin, 1959, 2, 213-233.

4197    VIGONE, Luciana. "Bibliografia bergsoniana in Italia (1940-1959)." Giornale di metafisica, 14, No. 6, 1959, 853-856.

4198    VIGONE, Luciana. "Congresso Bergson (Parigi, 17-19 maggio 1959)." Rivista di filosofia neoscolastica, 51, No. 4, 1959, 372-376.

4199    VILLASSERE, H. "Review of L'Evolution créatrice by Henri Bergson." Bulletin Critique, 3e Sér., 2, septembre 1908, 392-411. This is an exposition of the major arguments developed by Bergson in L'Evolution créatrice.

4200    VILLEGAS, Angel Camilo.  Bergson y la filosofía clásica.
        Bogotá: Tip. Mogollón, 1929, 69.  The introduction is by
        Fernando de la Vega.

4201    VINCENT, A.  "Les Religions statiques et dynamiques de M.
        Bergson et l'histoire des religions."  Revue des Sciences
        Religieuses, 15, 1935, 44-58.  This is a series of reflec-
        tions on Les Deux Sources.

4203    VIOLETTE, René.  "Review of Henri Bergson by Vladimir Janké-
        lévitch."  Revue Philosophique de la France et de l'Etran-
        ger, 85, No. 4, octobre-décembre 1960, 501-504.

4203    VIOLETTE, René.  La Spiritualité de Bergson: Essai sur l'é-
        laboration d'une philosophie spirituelle dans l'oeuvre
        d'Henri Bergson.  Toulouse: Privat, 1968, 575.

4204    VIRIEUX-REYMOND, Antoinette.  "A Propos du problème du dis-
        continu dans la philosophie bergsonienne."  Actes du Xe
        Congrès des Sociétés de Philosophie de Langue Française
        (Congrès Bergson).  Paris: Armand Colin, 1, 1959, 327-331.
        In Bergson's thought discontinuities are, the author holds,
        always displayed against a background of contintuity.
        What are these discontinuities and how can they be inte-
        grated into Bergson's continuist hypotheses?  Are they due
        to the conceptual fragmentation which our intelligence pro-
        jects onto reality, or do they pertain to reality itself?

4205    VIRIEUX-REYMOND, Antoinette.  "Review of Les Etudes Bergso-
        niennes, vol. III."  Revue de Théologie et de Philosophie,
        3e Série, 3, No. 1, 1953, 75-76.

4206    VIRIEUX-REYMOND, Antoinette.  "Réflexions sur la nature du
        temps: Bergson."  Giornale di metafisica, 14, No. 6, 1959,
        826-834.  This is an explanation of Bergson's conception
        of the nature of time.  It deals with time as conceived
        in Greek philosophy and Zeno's paradoxes.  Bergson's dura-
        tion is seized from within through an act of intuition,
        the author explains.  Heterogeneous in its flow, it is cre-
        ative and embodies liberty.

4207    VIRIEUX-REYMOND, Antoinette.  "Table ronde: Esthétique."
        Actes du Xe Congrès des Sociétés de Philosophie de Langue
        Française (Congrès Bergson).  Paris: Armand Colin, 2, 1959,
        193-210.

4208    VIRIEUX-REYMOND. Antoinette.  "Table ronde: Matière, causa-
        lité, discontinu."  Actes du Xe Congrès des Sociétés de

Philosophie de Langue Française (Congrès Bergson). Paris: Armand Colin, 2, 1959, 121-142.

4209    VISAN, Tancrède de. L'Attitude du lyrisme contemporain. Paris: Mercure de France, 1911, 476. The last chapter of this study concerns Bergson and symbolism and appears on pages 125-140.

4210    VISAN, Tancrède de. "Ce que nous devons à Bergson." Temps Présent, 1, 2 février 1914, 153-163.

4211    VISAN, Tancrède de. "L'Idéal symboliste: Essai sur la mentalité lyrique contemporaine." Mercure de France, 69, No. 241, 15 juillet 1907, 193-208. The author stresses a basic agreement of Bergson and symbolism on pages 206-208.

4212    VISAN, Tancrède de. "Review of Kant: Choix de textes by René Gillouin and H. Bergson: Choix de textes by René Gillouin." Revue de Philosophie, 18, No. 1, janvier 1911, 101-102.

4213    VISAN, Tancrède de. Paysages introspectifs: Poésies: Avec un essai sur le symbolisme. Paris: Jouve, 1904, 152.

4214    VISAN, Tancrède de. "La Philosophie de M. Henri Bergson et l'esthétique contemporaine." Vie et Lettres, 1, No. 21, avril 1913, 124-137.

4215    VISAN, Tancrède de. "La Philosophie de M. Bergson et le lyrisme contemporain." Vers et Prose, 6, No. 21, avril 1910, 125-140.

4216    VISENOT. "Review of 'La Signification de la guerre' by Henri Bergson." Polybiblion, 2e Série, 81 (Partie littéraire), 1915, 317-318.

4217    VISENTIN, Giovanni. "Testimonianza." Idea, 6, No. 35, 1954, 3.

4218    "Visiting French Philosopher." Literary Digest, 46, No. 1193, 1 March 1913, 460-461. This is a report on Bergson's lectures at Columbia University.

4219    VITA, Luís Washington. "O bergsonismo na filosofia latino-americana." Revista Brasiliense, 25, set.-out. 1959, 137-145.

4220   VITA, Luís Washington.  "O bergsonismo na filosofia latino-
       americana."  Revista Brasileira de Filosofia, 10, No. 4,
       1960, 536-542.

4221   VITA, Luís Washington.  Momentos decisivos do pensamento
       filosófico.  São Paulo: Melhoramentos, 1964, 518.  Bergson
       is discussed on pages 355-366.

4222   VIVANTE, Leone.  Il concetto della indeterminazione.  Firen-
       ze:  Vallecchi, 1938, 231.

4223   VIVANTE, Leone.  Della intelligenza nell'espressione.  Roma:
       Maglione e Strini, 1922, 229.  Bergson's concept of the
       function of the brain is discussed on pages 48-61; his con-
       cept of concrete duration on pages 166-167.

4224   VIVANTE, Leone.  Notes on the Originality of Thought.  Trans.
       Brodrick-Bullock.  London: John Lane, 1927, 227.  Bergson
       is discussed on pages 92 and 208n.

4225   VIVIANI, René.  La Mission française en Amérique, 24 avril-
       13 mai 1917.  Paris: Flammarion, 1917, 264.  The preface
       is by Henri Bergson, i-ii.

4226   VLOEMANS, Antoon.  Bergson.  Den Haag: Kruseman, 1967, 144.

4227   VLOEMANS, Antoon.  "Review of Les Deux Sources de la morale
       et de la religion by Henri Bergson."  Gids, 2, 1932.

4228   VLOEMANS, Antoon.  "De philosophie van Bergson."  Erasmus,
       2, 1934.

4229   VLOEMANS, Antoon.  "De philosophie van H. Bergson."  De
       Ploeg, 12, 1930.

4230   VLOEMANS, Antoon.  "Terugblik op Bergson."  Nieuw Vlaams
       Tijdschrift, 19, No. 6, 1966, 603-610.

4231   VOEGELIN, Eric.  New Science of Politics.  Chicago: Univer-
       sity of Chicago Press, 1952, 193.  Bergson is discussed on
       pages 26, 60, and 61; Bergson's philosophy of history, on
       pages 79-80.

4232   VOELKE, A.  "Les Thèmes fondamentaux de la métaphysique de
       Raymond Ruyer."  Revue de Théologie et de Philosophie, 6,
       No. 1, 1956, 11-28.  The author explains: "Partant de tra-
       vaux scientifiques, Ruyer a formulé une philosophie que
       l'on peut rapprocher de celle de Bergson."

4233    VOGT, Fritz J.   "Review of Henri Bergson: Eine Einführung
        in seine Philosophie by Paulis Jurevičs."   Philosophischer
        Literaturanzeiger, 3, No. 1, 1951, 17-22.

4234    VOISINE, G.   "La Durée des choses et la relativité: A Propos
        d'un livre récent de M. Bergson."   Revue de Philosophie,
        22, No. 5, septembre 1922, 498-522.   This is a review of
        Durée et simultanéité.

4235    VOISINE, F.   "Obligation morale et pression sociale."   Revue
        de Philosophie, 33, No. 4, 1933, 384-390.   This is a cri-
        tique of Les Deux Sources.

4236    VOORTHUISEN, Th.   "H. Bergson."   De Opbouw, 2, 1919.

4237    VORST, B. van.   "M. Bergson et les Américains."   Le Gaulois,
        ler février 1914.

4238    "Le Voyage espagnol d'Henri Bergson (avril-mai 1916): Docu-
        ments rassemblés par Juan-Miguel Palacios: Traduction Mi-
        chel Gauthier."   Etudes Bergsoniennes, 9, 1970, 7-122.

4239    VUARNET, Jean-Noël.   "Bergson vu par Madeleine Barthélemy-
        madaule."   Lettres Françaises, No. 1258, 20-26 novembre
        1968, 17.

4240    VUILLEMIN, J.   "Review of Henri Bergson: Quellen und Kon-
        sequenzen einer induktiven Metaphysik by G. Pflüg."   Ar-
        chiv für Geschichte der Philosophie, 43, No. 3, 1961, 323-
        324.

4241    W., B. C. A.   "Review of Laughter by Henri Bergson."   Dublin
        Review, 151, No. 302, July 1912, 181-184.

4242    WAELHENS, Alphonse de.   "Notes on Some Trends of Contempo-
        rary Philosophy."   Diogenes, No. 5, Winter 1954, 39-56.
        Similarities between Bergson and Hegel, Marx, Kierkegaard,
        and Nietzsche are pointed out by the author.

4243    WAELHENS, Alphonse de.   "Over Bergson en het Bergsonisme."
        Tijdschrift voor Philosophie, 3, No. 1, 1941, 185-195.

4244    WAGNER, Geoffrey.   "Wyndham Lewis and Bergson."   Romantic
        Review, 46, No. 2, 1955, 112-124.   Lewis owed an inadver-
        tent debt to Bergson, according to the author.

4245    WAHL, Jean.   "Au Sujet des relations de Bergson avec l'Egli-
        se catholique."   Nouvelle Relève, 4, No. 1, avril 1945, 1-
        11.

4246    WAHL, Jean.  Bergson.  Paris: Centre de documentation uni-
        versitaire, 1965, 161.  These are the lecture notes from a
        course on Bergson at the Sorbonne.

4247    WAHL, Jean.  "Henri Bergson."  From the N.R.F.  Ed. Justin
        O'Brien.  New York: Farrar, Straus and Cudahy, 1958, 282-
        284, 383.

4248    WAHL, Jean.  "Concerning Bergson's Relation to the Catholic
        Church."  Review of Religion, 9, No. 1, November 1944, 45-
        50.

4249    WAHL, Jean.  "Deux Ouvrages récents sur la philosophie de M.
        Bergson."  Revue du Mois, 7, No. 4, août 1912, 153-180.
        This is a critical discussion of Le Bergsonisme by Julien
        Benda and Une Philosophie nouvelle by Le Roy.

4250    WAHL, Jean.  "Discours sur Bergson."  Bulletin de la Société
        Française de Philosophie, 54, No. 1, janvier-mars 1960,
        49-52.

4251    WAHL, Jean.  "L'Espèce à part."  Etudes Bergsoniennes, 8,
        1968, 173-175.

4252    WAHL, Jean.  "L'Espèce à part."  Nouvelles Littéraires, No.
        2071, 11 mai 1967, 13.  This is an address delivered at
        the dedication of a Bergson plaque at the Panthéon.

4253    WAHL, Jean.  "Les Hommages à Henri Bergson (11 mai 1967)."
        Annales de l'Université de Paris, 37, 1967, 571-573.

4254    WAHL, Jean.  "M. Jean Wahl apporte du nouveau sur Bergson."
        Le Figaro Littéraire, 22 mai 1954, 9.  This concerns hith-
        erto unpublished portions of Bergson's will.

4255    WAHL, Jean.  "Présence de Bergson."  Henri Bergson.  Ed.
        Béguin and Thévenaz, 25-28.  The author discusses Berg-
        son's thought in the context of the history of Western phi-
        losophy and mentions a brief visit with Bergson in Novem-
        ber 1940.

4256    WAHL, Jean.  "Présence de Bergson."  Poésie, pensée, percep-
        tion.  Paris: Calmann-Lévy, 1948, 116-118.

4257    WAHL, Jean.  "The Present Situation and the Present Future
        of French Philosophy."  Philosophic Thought in France and
        the United States.  Ed. Marvin Farber.  Albany, New York:
        State University of New York Press, 1968, 35-49.  The in-
        fluence of Bergson is discussed on pages 35-36.

4258    WAHL, Jean. Tableau de la philosophie française. Paris:
        Fontaine, 1946, 235. Descartes, Comte, and Bergson are
        discussed at length in this study.

4259    WAHL, Jean. "Table ronde: Matière, causalité, discontinu."
        Actes du Xe Congrès des Sociétés de Philosophie de Langue
        Française (Congrès Bergson). Paris: Armand Colin, 2, 1959,
        121-142.

4260    WAHL, Jean. "Table ronde: Néant et existentialisme." Actes
        du Xe Congrès des Sociétés de Philosophie de Langue Fran-
        çaise (Congrès Bergson). Paris: Armand Colin, 2, 1959,
        145-164.

4261    WAHL, Jean. "Table ronde: Sources et histoire du bergsonis-
        me." Actes du Xe Congrès des Sociétés de Philosophie de
        Langue Française (Congrès Bergson). Paris: Armand Colin,
        2, 1959, 213-233.

4262    WAHL, Jean. "Témoignages." Nouvelles Littéraires, No. 322,
        15 décembre 1928, 4.

4263    WAHL, Jean. "A Tribute to Bergson on the Occasion of the
        Bergson Centennial in Paris, 1959." The Bergsonian Heri-
        tage. Ed. Thomas Hanna. New York and London: Columbia
        University Press, 1962, 150-154. Bergson, for all his op-
        timism, retains "a profound disquiet about this life," ac-
        cording to the author.

4264    WAHL, Jean; JANKELEVITCH, Vladimir; TROTIGNON, Pierre; and
        MAZARS, Pierre. "Cet invisible Bergson que nous portons."
        Le Figaro Littéraire, No. 1048, 19 mai 1966, 10, 11. This
        "table ronde" contains discussions of Bergson's philosophi-
        cal system, his influence on literature and music, and of
        his disciples.

4265    WALKER, Charles. "M. Bergson's Creative Evolution." Lancet,
        182, 17 February 1912, 456. In this letter to the editor,
        Walker criticizes R. F. Licorish's neo-Lamarckian inter-
        pretation of Bergson and criticizes Bergson for his fail-
        ure to understand Darwinism.

4266    WALKER, Leslie J. "L'Evolutionisme dans la théorie de la
        connaissance et de la vérité." Revue de Philosophie, 19,
        Nos. 9-10, septembre-octobre 1911, 417-466.

4267    WALL, Bernard. Headlong into Change: An Autobiography and a
        Memoir of Ideas Since the Thirties. London: Harvill Press,

1969, 288.  Claudel, Gide, Desjardins, Du Bos, Maritain,
Valéry, and Bergson are discussed in this book.

4268    WALLIS, Robert.  Le Temps, quatrième dimension de l'esprit:
        Etude de la fonction temporelle de l'homme du point de vue
        physique, biologique et métaphysique.  Paris: Flammarion,
        1966, 288.  "Préface d'O. Costa de Beauregard."  The au-
        thor notes: "Avec Henri Bergson, nous pouvons nous deman-
        der s'il est vrai que 'le temps est création ou il n'est
        rien du tout'."  (29).  References to Bergson may be found
        on pages 29, 51-53, 173n, 177n, 186-187, 189-190, 192-193,
        235, 242, 246, 246, and 257.

4269    WALLON, Henri.  "Le Problème biologique de la conscience."
        Nouveau Traité de psychologie.  Vol. 1.  Ed. Georges Dumas.
        Paris: Félix Alcan, 1930, 293-331.  Bergson is discussed
        on pages 303-305.

4270    WARD, Anne.  "Speculations on Eliot's Time-World: An Analy-
        sis of The Family Reunion in Relation to Hulme and Bergson."
        American Literature, 21, No. 1, March 1949, 18-34.  The au-
        thor explores the extent to which the poet T. S. Eliot was
        influenced by Bergson through the thought of T. E. Hulme.

4271    WARD, Mary.  "James Ward on Sense and Thought."  Mind, 35,
        N.S. No. 140, October 1926, 452-456.  Bergson and Ward
        agree on the nature of experienced duration, according to
        the author.

4272    WARD, James.  The Realm of Ends.  Cambridge, England: Univer-
        sity Press, 1911, 490.  Bergson is mentioned on pages 306-
        307.

4273    "Was Bergson a Catholic?"  Tablet, 177, 15 February 1941,
        128.

4274    WASSERBERG, J.  "Irracjonalizm Bergsona."  Przeglad Filo-
        zoficzny, 16, No. 2, 1912, 145-160.

4275    WATANABE, Satosi.  "Le Concept du temps en physique moderne
        et la durée de Bergson."  Revue de Métaphysique et de Mo-
        rale, 56, No. 2, 1951, 128-142.  Translated, with an in-
        troduction, in Bergson and the Evolution of Physics, Ed.
        P. A. Y. Gunter, 62-77.

4276    WATERHOUSE, E. S.  "Henri Bergson."  Religions, April, 1941.

4277    WATERHOUSE, E. S.  "Obituary."  London Quarterly Review, 166,
        No. 2, April 1941, 127-137.

4278    WATERLOW, Sydney.  "Review of An Introduction to Metaphysics by Henri Bergson."  International Journal of Ethics, 24, No. 1, 1913-1914, 100-102.

4279    WATERLOW, Sydney.  "The Philosophy of Bergson."  London Quarterly Review, 76, No. 3292, 4 January 1912, 152-176.

4280    WATKIN, E.  "Philosophy of Henri Bergson: With a Summary of his Two Sources of Morality and Religion."  Dublin Review, 209, No. 3, July 1941, 7-22.

4281    WATSON, B.  "The Bergsonism of Marcel Proust."  Diss., Chicago, 1938.

4282    WAUTIER D'AYGALLIERS, A.  "El Dios de Bergson."  Luminar, 2, No. 4, Otoño 1938, 63-85.

4283    WAVRE, Rolin.  La Figure du monde: Essai sur le problème de l'espace des Grecs à nos jours.  Neuchâtel, Switzerland: La Baconnière, 1950, 170.  This study contains sections on Bergson's and Sartre's concepts of space.

4284    WAVRE, Rolin.  "Les Possibles de Diodora à Bergson."  Alma Mater, 3, 1946, 223-227.

4285    WEBER, Alois.  Der Begriff Intuition bei Descartes, Pascal und Bergson.  Luzern, Switzerland, 1948, 67 (Jahresber. d. Kanton höheren Lehranstalten 1947/1948).

4286    WEBER, Eugen.  Action Française: Royalism and Reaction in Twentieth-Century France.  Stanford, California: Stanford University Press, 1962, 594.  Bergson and Claudel are discussed as disruptive issues withing the Action française on page 82.

4287    WEBER, Louis.  "Review of L'Evolution créatrice by Henri Bergson."  Revue de Métaphysique et de Morale, 15, No. 5, septembre 1907, 620-670.  This is a lengthy exposition of Bergson's views in L'Evolution créatrice.

4288    WEBER, Louis.  "Review of Matière et mémoire by Henri Bergson."  Mercure de France, 23, No. 7, juillet 1897, 150-152.

4289    WEBER, Louis.  "Review of La Pensée et le mouvant by Henri Bergson."  Revue de Métaphysique et de Morale, 42, No. 1, 1935, 53-75.  This is an exposition of Bergson's position as expressed on La Pensée et le mouvant, with critical comments.

4290    WEBER, Louis. "Review of Le Rire by H. Bergson." Mercure
        de France, 35, No. 7, juillet 1900, 225-227.

4291    WEILER, Maurice and JACOB, Jean. Ecrivains français du
        vingtième siècle: Textes choisis. Paris: Belin, 1966, 375.

4292    WEISS, Konrad. Die Reine Wahrnehmung im psychophysischen
        Problem Bergsons. Diss., Berlin, Humboldt-Universität,
        1930, 75; Ilsenburg-Harz, Germany: Ruland, 1930, 75.

4293    WENGER, Marguerite. "Bibliographie der Schriften von und
        über Bergson." Das Buch, 3, No. 2, 1951, 64-70.

4294    WERNER, A. "Henri Bergsons Philosophie." Internationale
        Monatsschrift für Wissenschaft, 9, 1915, 1431.

4295    WERNER, Charles. La Philosophie moderne. Paris: Payot,
        1954, 326. A section on the reaction against rationalism
        in this study contains discussions of Nietzsche, Bergson,
        and existentialism.

4296    WERNER, Charles. "Table ronde: Durée et mémoire." Actes du
        Xe Congrès des Sociétés de Philosophie de Langue Française
        (Congrès Bergson). Paris: Armand Colin, 2, 1959, 41-61.

4297    WERNER, Charles. "Table ronde: Liberté." Actes du Xe Con-
        grès des Sociétés de Philosophie de Langue Française (Con-
        grès Bergson). Paris: Armand Colin, 2, 1959, 167-189.

4298    WESTCOTT, Malcom R. Toward a Contemporary Psychology of In-
        tuition. New York: Holt, Rinehart and Winston, Inc.,
        1968, 228. Bergson is discussed on pages 6-11, 19-21, 75-
        77, and elsewhere.

4299    WEYEMBERGH, Maurice. "La Personnalité charismatique chez M.
        Weber et le héros chez Bergson." Morale et Enseignement,
        Bulletin de l'Institut de Philosophie, 16, 1967, 121-175.

4300    WHEELER, Leonard Richmond. Vitalism: Its History and Valid-
        ity. London: J. F. and G. Witherby, 1939, 275. This
        study contains references to Bergson throughout. The au-
        thor deals with Matter and Memory on pages 182-185.

4301    WHEELER, Olive Annie. Bergson and Education. New York:
        Longmans, Green and Co., 1922, 130.

4302    WHITE, E. M. "Bergson and Education." Educational Review,
        47, No. 5, May 1914, 433-443. This article is reprinted

from the London Journal of Education. It is a general and speculative attempt to describe a Bergsonian pedagogy.

4303    WHITE, Morton. "Time, Instinct, and Freedom." The Great Ages of Western Philosophy: The Age of Analysis--20th Century Philosophers. New York: New American Library, 1955, 253. An introduction and readings from Bergson are on pages 65-81.

4304    WHITEHEAD, Alfred North. "The Problem of Simultaneity." Proceedings of the Aristotelian Society, Supplementary Volume, 3, 1923, 34-41. Here Whitehead presents his alternative to Bergson's criticism of relativity theory.

4305    WHITTAKER, Albert L. "Bergson: First Aid to Common Sense." Forum, 51, No. 3, March 1914, 410-414.

4306    WHITTAKER, Thomas. "Review of Essai sur les données immédiates de la conscience by Henri Bergson." Mind, 51, No. 58, April 1890, 292-293. This review is largely an exposition of Bergson's position in the Essai.

4307    WHYTE, Lancelot Law. "Review of Bergson and the Evolution of Physics, Ed. and Trans. with Intro. P. A. Y. Gunter." British Journal for the Philosophy of Science, 22, No. 1, February 1971, 75-76.

4308    WICKHAM, Harvey. The Unrealists: James, Bergson, Santayana, Russell, Dewey, Alexander, and Whitehead. New York: Dial, 1930, 314. A thoroughly critical, equally superficial account of Bergson's philosophy is given on pages 68-93.

4309    WIDART, H. "A Propos de la philosophie bergsonienne." Collectanea Mechliniensia, N.S. 15, No. 1, février 1945, 15-60; No. 5-6, novembre 1945, 503-529.

4310    WILBOIS, Joseph. "L'Esprit positif." Revue de Métaphysique et de Morale, 9, 1901, 154-209, 597-645; 10, 1902, 69-105, 334-370, 565-612.

4311    WILD, John. "The New Empiricism and Human Time." Review of Metaphysics, 7, No. 4, June 1954, 537-557. The author discusses Bergson's opposition between lived time and spatial extension on pages 541-542.

4312    WILD, K. W. Intuition. Cambridge, England: University Press; New York: Macmillan, 1938, 240. An analysis of Bergson's concept of intuition begins this study.

4313    WILLCOX, Louise Collier. "Implications of Bergson's Philos-
         ophy." North American Review, 199, No. 700, March 1914,
         448-451.

4314    WILLCOX, Louise Collier. "Impressions of M. Bergson." Har-
         per's Weekly, No. 2933, 8 March 1913, 6. This is a brief
         discussion of Bergson's lectures at Columbia University.

4315    WILLIAMS, D. C. "The Myth of Passage." Journal of Philoso-
         phy, 58, No. 15, 1951, 457-472. The author criticizes var-
         ious modern concepts of "passage."

4316    WILLIAMS, Ernest. "Religious Bearing of Bergson's Philoso-
         phy." Hibbert Journal, 24, No. 2, January 1926, 264-269.

4317    WILLIAMS, T. Rhonnda. "Syndicalism in France and its Rela-
         tion to the Philosophy of Bergson." Hibbert Journal, 12,
         No. 46, February 1914, 389-403. The author criticizes syn-
         dicalists for misinterpreting Bergson's concept of the in-
         tellect.

4318    WILLOCH, Helga Aubert. "Bergson." Edda, 40, bind 53, No. 1,
         1953, 110-130.

4319    WILM, Emil Carl. "Bergson and Philosophy of Religion." Bib-
         lical World, N.S. 42, No. 5, November 1913, 279-283.

4320    WILM, Emil Carl. Henri Bergson: A Study in Radical Evolu-
         tion. New York: Sturgis and Walton Company, 1914, 193.

4321    WILM, Emil Carl. Theories of Instinct. New Haven, Connec-
         ticut: Yale University Press, 1925, 188. Bergson's evolu-
         tionary theory is discussed on pages 177-179.

4322    WILSON, Alexander P. "The Concept of Human Freedom in Berg-
         son and James." Diss., Washington at Seattle, 1950.

4323    WINDELBAND, Wilhelm. "Preface." Materie und Gedächtnis.
         Jena: Diederichs, 1908, 264, I-XV.

4324    WIRIATH, Marcel. Notes du soir. Paris: Plon, 1968, 201.
         Surrealism, Bergson, Donnay, Gide, Green, and Sartre are
         discussed in this book.

4325    WITHOF, A. "Een nieuwe wijsbegeerte: H. Bergson." Het
         Nieuwe Levens, 1, 1915.

4326    WIZE, K. F. "Der vierte Kongress für die Philosophie in
         Bologna." Vierteljahrschrift für wissenschaftliche Philo-

sophie, 35, No. 4, 1911, 459-483.  Bergson is discussed on pages 464-466.

4327    WODEHOUSE, Helen.  "Bergson and World-Loyalty; Based on The Two Sources of Morality and Religion."  Hibbert Journal, 38, No. 4, July 1940, 457-468.  This essay also appears in Menorah Journal, 29, April 1941, 125-137.

4328    WOLF, A.  "Mr. Balfour on Teleology and Creative Evolution." Hibbert Journal, 10, Part 1, January 1912, 469-472.  The author concludes that: "Not teleology, but only an externally imposed and completely determined teleology, is incompatible with creative evolution."  (472).

4329    WOLF, A.  "The Philosophy of Probability."  Proceedings of the Aristotelian Society, 13, 1912-1913, 328-361.  Bergson is discussed on pages 328, 336-337, and 360-361.

4330    WOLFF, Edgar.  "D'Un Progrès dialectique dans la pensée de Bergson: Changement, mémoire, durée."  Archives de Philosophie, 12, No. 1, octobre-décembre 1959, 521-528.  The author argues that Bergson was driven to assert the paradoxical doctrine of the integral conservation of the past because, having defined the inner life as radical change, he needed a stable vantage-point from which to appreciate change.  He found this vantage-point in the extra-temporality of memory, which he could have demanded of the characterological unity of the profound self.

4331    WOLFF, Edgar.  "Mémoire et durée."  Actes du Xe Congrès des Sociétés de Philosophie de Langue Française (Congrès Bergson).  Paris: Armand Colin, 1, 1959, 333-337.  According to the author, in Matter and Memory Bergson asserts that pure memory constitutes, in the strongest sense of the term, a representation of the past, i.e., an intuitive vision of once-experienced events.  This pure memory is the essence of real memory.  This interior contemplation of the past permits us, in an instantaneous apprehension, to recover all its elements.  The author examines the objections to this thesis.

4332    WOLFF, Edgar.  "Table ronde: Durée et mémoire."  Actes du Xe Congrès des Sociétés de Philosophie de Langue Française (Congrès Bergson).  Paris: Armand Colin, 2, 1959, 41-61.

4333    WOLFF, Edgar.  "Table ronde: Matière, causalite, discontinu." Actes du Xe Congrès des Sociétés de Philosophie de Langue Française (Congrès Bergson).  Paris: Armand Colin, 2, 1959, 121-142.

4334    WOLFF, Edgar.  "Table ronde: Morale."  Actes du Xe Congrès
        des Sociétés de Philosophie de Langue Française (Congrès
        Bergson).  Paris: Armand Colin, 2, 1959, 237-257.

4335    WOLFF, Edgar.  "La Théorie de la mémoire chez Bergson."  Ar-
        chives de Philosophie, 20, No. 1, 1957, 42-77.  The author
        holds that: "Il faut repenser Matière et mémoire à travers
        L'Effort intellectuel et L'Evolution créatrice."

4336    WOODBRIDGE, Frederick James Eugene.  The Purpose of History:
        Reflections on Bergson, Dewey and Santayana.  New York:
        Columbia University Press, 1916, 89.

4337    WREDE, Otto.  Pädagogische Probleme bei Henri Bergson.
        Forchheim, Germany: Mauser, 1935, 79.

4338    WRIGHT, William Kelley.  A History of Modern Philosophy.
        New York: Macmillan, 1941, 633.  Bergson is discussed on
        pages 560-577.

4339    WYANT, G. G.  "Bergson and his Philosophy."  Bookman, 41, No.
        1, March 1915, 22-27.

4340    WYLIE, Laurence and BEGUE, Armand, in collaboration with
        BEGUE, Louise.  Les Français.  Englewood Cliffs, New Jer-
        sey: Prentice-Hall, Inc., 1970, 444.  The authors discuss
        Bergson's concept of laughter and the comedies of Molière
        on pages 392-394, 397, and 402.

4341    WYRICK, Green D.  "Hemingway and Bergson: The Elan Vital."
        Modern Fiction Studies, 1, No. 3, August 1955, 17-19.
        Parallels between Bergson and Hemingway are sought after
        in this brief article.

4342    XIRAU, Joaquín.  "Crisis: Husserl and Bergson."  Personalist,
        27, No. 3, July 1946, 269-284.

4343    XIRAU, Joaquín.  "La plenitude orgánica."  Homenaje a Berg-
        son.  Imprenta Universitaria México, 1941, 159-189.

4344    XIRAU, Joaquín.  Vida, pensamiento y obra de Bergson.  Méxi-
        co: Edit. Leyenda, 1944, 157 (Col. Atalaya, 4).

4345    XIRAU, José R.  "Filosofía y política."  Revista Interameri-
        cana de Bibliografía, 2, No. 2, mayo-agosto 1953, 141-145.
        This is a review of Bergsonismo y política by Quintanilla.

4346    XIRAU, Ramon. El péndulo y el espiral. Xalapa, México
        Universidad Veracurzana, 1959, 146. This is a study of
        modern philosophy of history based on Les Deux Sources.

4347    YAMAGUCHI, Minoro. The Intuition of Zen and Bergson: Compar-
        ativ intellectual approach to Zen: Reason of divergences
        between East and West. Tokyo: Enderle Bookstore, 1970,
        235.

4348    YEPEZ, Gumersindo. "Henri Bergson, su vida y su obra."
        Revista del Colegio Nacional Vicente Rocafuerte, 17, No.
        52, 1940.

4349    YOUNOSZAI, Barbara. "El tiempo de Bergson en la obra de
        Jorge Luis Borges." Dissertation Abstracts International,
        32, 1971, 2715A. The author explores similarities between
        Bergson's and Borges' concepts of time.

4350    YUSHKEVICH, P. S. "Бергсон и его философия интуи-
        ции." Русское богатство, 11, № 2, 1914, 33-59;
        № 3, 1914, 47-67.

4351    YUSHKEVICH, P. S. Мировоззрение и мировоззрения.
        Петербург: 1912, 194. This study contains a section
        on Bergson.

4352    ZAC, Sylvain. "Review of Bergson et le Christ des Evangiles
        by Henri Gouhier." Revue de Synthèse, 84, No. 32, 1963,
        502-509.

4353    ZAC, Sylvain. "Les Thèmes spinozistes dans la philosophie
        de Bergson." Etudes Bergsoniennes, 8, 1968, 123-158.
        This is a thoughtful comparison of Bergson and Spinoza.
        It suggests interesting similarities between the two phi-
        losophers.

4354    ZACKS, Hanna. "Perception and Action in Henri Bergson and
        Allied Philosophers." Dissertation Abstracts, 27, No. 3,
        September 1966, 803A.

4355    ZAMBELLONI, Franco. "Bergson e la filosofia italiana (1900-
        1915)." Filosofia, Anno 21, No. 3, luglio 1970, 331-360.
        The author discusses the reception of Bergson's thought in
        Italy during the first years of this century. In general
        Bergson's thought was not understood correctly and as a
        whole. Papini and Prezzolini described Bergson's thought
        as a "magical pragmatism." Croce used Bergson against the
        positivists.

4356    ZANER, Richard M.  "The Subjectivity of the Human Body."
        Main Currents, 29, No. 1, January-February 1973, 117-120.

4357    ZANTA, Léontine.  "La posizione del Bergson di frontragli
        studi psichici."  Luce e ombra, 11, No. 2, febbrao 1911.

4358    ZANTA, Léontine.  "Le Rayonnement de la philosophie fran-
        çaise."  Journal des Débats, 35, Pt. 2, 15 novembre 1928,
        863-864.

4359    ZARAGUETA, Juan.  "Henri Bergson (1859-1941)."  Revista de
        Filosofía, 1, No. 1, 1942, 167-174.

4360    ZARAGUETA, Juan.  La intuición en la filosofía de Henri Berg-
        son.  Madrid: Espasa-Calpe, 1941, 320.

4361    ZARAGUETA, Juan.  "La intuición y la inteligencia en la filo-
        sofía de Henri Bergson."  Estudios filosóficos.  Madrid:
        Instituto "Luis Vives" de Filosofía, C.S.I.C., 1963, 375-
        383.

4362    ZARAGUETA, Juan.  "La libertad en la filosofía de Henri Berg-
        son."  El Escorial, 4, 1941, 91-116.

4363    ZARAGUETA, Juan.  "La Liberté dans la philosophie d'Henri
        Bergson."  Actes du Xe Congrès des Sociétés de Philosophie
        de Langue Française (Congrès Bergson).  Paris: Armand Co-
        lin, 1, 1959, 339-342.

4364    ZARAGUETA, Juan.  "Table ronde: Liberté."  Actes du Xe Con-
        grès des Sociétés de Philosophie de Langue Française (Con-
        grès Bergson).  Paris: Armand Colin, 2, 1959, 167-189.

4365    ZARAGUETA, Juan.  "Table ronde: Psychologie, phénoménologie,
        intuition."  Actes du Xe Congrès des Sociétés de Philoso-
        phie de Langue Française (Congrès Bergson).  Paris: Armand
        Colin, 2, 1959, 15-37.

4366    ZASLAWSKY, Denis.  "Bergson, le finalisme et la philosophie
        analytique."  Revue de Théologie et de Philosophie, 3e
        Série, 14, No. 6, 1964, 335-347.

4367    ZAWIRSKI, Zygmunt.  L'Evolution et la notion du temps.  Kra-
        ków: Gebethner and Wolff, 1936, 357.

4368    ZDANOWICZ, C.  "Molière and Bergson's Theory of Laughter."
        University of Wisconsin Studies in Literature, 20, No. 1,
        1924, 99-125.

4369    ZEIFEL, Eugène. "Jules Romains und H. Bergson." Das lit-
        erarische Echo, 20, No. 2, 1917-1918, 84-87.

4370    ZIEHEN, Theodor. "Review of Matière et mémoire by Henri
        Bergson." Zeitschrift für Philosophie und philosophische
        Kritik, N.S. 113, No. 12, Dezember 1898, 295-299.

4371    ZIEHEN, Theodor. "Review of Le Rire by Henri Bergson."
        Zeitschrift für Philosophie und philosophische Kritik,
        N.S. 123, No. 2, 1904, 215-216.

4372    Zoological Studies. Aberdeen: Printed for the University of
        Aberdeen, 1914, 138. Articles by J. Arthur Thomson, J. J.
        Simpson, J. Alexander Innes, and A. Landsborough Thomson
        are contained in this volume.

4373    ZUBIRI, Xavier. "Bergson." Cinco lecciones di filosofía.
        Madrid: Sociedad de Estudios y Publicaciones, 1963, 163-
        211.

4374    ZULEN, Pedro Salvino. La filosofía de lo inexpresable: Bos-
        quejo de una interpretación y una crítica de la filosofía
        de Bergson. Lima: Impreso en los talleres tipocráficos
        de Sanmarti y Cía., 1920, 62.

4375    ZUNINI, G. "Henri Bergson." Revue de Synthèse, 5, Nos. 5-6,
        1946.

4376    ZWIEBEL, Daniel. "Durée de Dieu et imprévisibilité des
        actes libres chez Bergson." Actes du Xe Congrès des Soci-
        étés de Philosophie de Langue Française (Congrès Bergson).
        Paris: Armand Colin, 1, 1959, 343-346. The author claims
        that the free act is for Bergson creative and unforseeable.
        God is for Bergson creative and free, but Bergson's God en-
        dures and must be distinguished from the un-temporal Deity
        of classical theology. But God's duration is not man's,
        and the descent of God into the soul of the mystic in-
        volves the elevation of the human duration to the divine
        tension.

4377    ZWIEBEL, Daniel. "Table ronde: Liberté." Actes du Xe Con-
        grès des Sociétés de Philosophie de Langue Française (Con-
        grès Bergson). Paris: Armand Colin, 2, 1959, 167-189.

# PART IV

# SOURCES USED IN COMPILING THIS BIBLIOGRAPHY

## 1. BERGSON BIBLIOGRAPHIES

"Bibliografia bergsoniana." Giornale di metafisica, 14, No. 6, 1959, 835-872. 1945-1959, France, Italy, Spain, Latin America.

Centre nationale de bibliographie. Les Bibliographies (Bruxelles), 6. Henri Bergson, 1966, 24 pp.

A Contribution to a Bibliography of Henri Bergson. New York: Columbia University Press, 1913, 56.

Coviello, Alfredo. "Bibliografía bergsoniana." Sustancia, 11, No. 7-8, septiembre 1941, 394-440.

Coviello, Alfredo. El processo filosófico de Bergson y su bibliografía. Tucumán, Argentina: Revista Sustancia, 1941, 117.

Dossier Henri Bergson. Salle des imprimés. Bibliothèque nationale. (Several review articles and expositions of Bergson's philosophy.)

Gonzalo Casas, Manuel. "Bibliografia bergsoniana in Spagna e nell'America Latina." Giornale di metafisica, 14, No. 6, 1959, 866-872.

Gonzalo Casas, Manuel. "Bibliografía hispanoamericana de Bergson." Humanitas, 7, No. 12, 1959, 103-108.

Lameere, J. "Bibliographie de Bergson." Revue Internationale de Philosophie, 3, No. 10, 15 octobre 1949, 459-478.

Mathieu, Vittorio. "Bibliografia bergsoniana in Francia (1945-1959)." Giornale di metafisica, 14, No. 6, 1959, 835-852.

Mathieu, Vittorio. "Bibliografia bergsoniana in Germania (1945-1959)." Giornale di metafisica, 14, No. 6, 1959, 853-856.

Meckauer, Walter. "Literaturverzeichnis." Der Intuitionismus und seine Elemente bei Henri Bergson. Leipsic: Meiner, 1917, 160, ix-xiv.

Mossé-Bastide, Rose-Marie. "Bibliographie de Bergson." Bergson éducateur. Paris: Presses Universitaires de France, 1955, 465, 359-379.

Mossé-Bastide, Rose-Marie. "Bibliographie générale des études sur le bergsonisme." Bergson éducateur. Paris: Presses Universitaires de France, 1955, 465, 381-448.

Mourélos, Georges. Bergson et les niveaux de la réalité. Paris: Presses Universitaires de France, 1964, 256.

References on Henri Bergson. Washington, D.C.: Library of Congress, 1913, 3.

"Séminaire Bergson de Louvain, bibliographie de Bergson." Revue Internationale de Philosophie, 4, No. 13, 15 juin 1950, 341-350.

Vigone, Luciana. "Bibliografia bergsoniana in Italia." Giornale di metafisica, 14, No. 6, 1959, 857-865.

Wenger, Marguerite. "Bibliographie der Schriften von und über Bergson." Das Buch, 3, No. 2, 1961, 64-70.

## 2. ISSUES OF JOURNALS, REVIEWS, ETC. DEDICATED TO BERGSON

Actes du Xe Congrès des Sociétés de Philosophie de Langue Française (Congrès Bergson). Paris: Armand Colin, 1959, 355 (Bulletin de la Société Française de Philosophie, 53e Année, 1959. Numéro spécial).

Archives de Philosophie, 17, No. 1, 1947, 1-172 (Bergson et bergsonisme).

Béguin, Albert and Thévenaz, Pierre, Eds. Henri Bergson: Essais et témoignages. Neuchâtel, Switzerland: La Baconnière, 1943, 373 (Les Cahiers du Rhône, hors série, août 1943). An earlier edition of this collection of articles appeared in 1941 at Neuchâtel.

Bulletin de la Société Française de Philosophie, 10, No. 1, 1960, 2-108. This issue contains talks given in September 1959 at the Congrès Bergson of the Société romande de philosophie.

Criterion, 11, 1936 (Tomismo de Bergson al realismo de Santo Tomàs).

Etudes Bergsoniennes. Paris: Presses Universitaires de France, 1942, 222 (Tiré à part de la Revue Philosophique).

Giornale di metafisica, 14, No. 6, novembre-dicembre 1959, 753-872.

Homenaje a Bergson.   Córdoba, Argentina: Imprenta de la Universidad, 1936, 191.

Homenaje a Bergson.   México: Imprenta Universitaria, 1941.

Humanitas, 14, No. 11, 1959, 769-852 (Ommagio a Henry Bergson).

Kriterion, 13, No. 1, 1960, 1-20.

Luminar, 2, No. 4, 1938, 1-99 (Homenaje a Bergson).

La Nef, 4, No. 32, juillet 1947 (Bergson et la justice).

Nouvelles Littéraires, No. 322, 15 décembre 1928.   This issue was dedicated to Bergson on the occasion of his receiving the Nobel Prize for literature.

Nouvelles Littéraires, No. 1677, 22 octobre 1959.   This issue is dedicated to Bergson on the centennial of his birth.

The Personalist, 14, No. 2, April 1933.

Revista brasileira de filosofia, 11, 1961, 106-113 (Centenário de Bergson.  Depoimentos).

Revue de Métaphysique et de Morale, 48, No. 4, 1941 (Controverses bergsoniennes).

Revue de Métaphysique et de Morale, 64, No. 2, 1959, 129-256 (Pour le centenaire de Bergson).

Revue de Théologie et de Philosophie, 54, No. 1, janvier-mars 1960, 1-63 (Hommage solonnel à Bergson).

Revue Internationale de Philosophie, 13, No. 2, 1959, 171-290.

Revue Philosophique de la France et de l'Etranger, 131, No. 3-8, mars-août 1941, 121-342 (Hommage à Henri Bergson).

Revue Philosophique de la France et de l'Etranger, 149, No. 3, juillet-septembre 1959 (Autour de Bergson).

Revue Thomiste, N.S. 16, No. 77, mai-juin 1933, 347-502.   This issue is devoted to Bergson's philosophy of religion.

Richerche filosofiche, 5, No. 1, 1951.

Sustancia.  Revista de Cultura Superior, Año 2, No. 7-8, septiembre 1941, 317-439.

## 3. GENERAL BIBLIOGRAPHIC SOURCES

Archiv für Begriffsgeschichte: Band 5. Eine Begriffsgeschichte deutscher Hochschulschriften von 1900-1955. Bonn: Bouvier und Ges., Verlag, 1960, 718. Henri Bergson: 127f, 1094, 1267f, 3850ff, 4089, 4099, 4422ff, 4584, 4604f, 6477, 8828, 8900, 9176, 9400.

A.T.L.A. Index to Religious Periodical Literature. 1949-1971 (Jan.-June).

"Biblio." 1-37, 1934-1970.

Bibliografía Argentina de Filosofía. La Plata, Argentina: Ministerio de Educación. 2-4, 1960-1962.

Bibliografia filosofica italiana. Dal 1900 al 1950. Roma: Edizioni Delfino, 1950, 298. Vol. 1, 116-118.

Bibliographie de la philosophie. Paris: Vrin. 1937-1971.

Bibliographie der deutschen Zeitschriften-Literatur. Ergänzungsband. 1899-1917.

Bibliographie der deutschen Zeitschriften-Literatur. New York: Kraus Reprint, 1961. Orig. Osnabrück: Verlag Dietrich, 1896-1944 (1); 1944-1946 (2); 1947-1949; 1950 (Abt. A)-1963 (1).

Biblioteca Nazionale Centrale Firenze: Catologo Cumulativo: 1886-1957. New York: Kraus Reprint. Vol. 5, 103-104.

Bibliothèque nationale. Catalogue matières, ouvrages entrés de 1894-1959, et depuis 1960.

Books Abroad. 2-24, 1928-1950.

Brie, G. A. de. Bibliographica Philosophica. Bruxelles: Editiones Spectrum, 1950, 1954. 2 vols. (Esp. Vol. 1, 546-551.)

British Museum, General Catalogue of Printed Books. London: Trustees of the British Museum, 1965. Vol. 15, 509-518.

Bulletin Analytique de Philosophie. 1-14, 1947-1960. This publication is continued as Bulletin Signalétique: Sciences Humaines: Philosophie.

Bulletin Signalétique: Sciences Humaines: Philosophie.  15-24, 1961-
1970.

Catalogue of the Latin American Collection: University of Texas Library: Austin.  Vol. 4.  Bergson: 144-145.

Catholic Periodical Index.  1930-1936; 1939-1971.

Dreher, S. and Rolli, M.  Bibliographie de la littérature française:
1930-1939.  Genève: Droz, 1948, 438.  Successor to H. P.
Thieme's bibliography.

Drevet, Marguerite L.  Bibliographie de la littérature française:
1940-1949.  Genève: Droz, 1954, 644.  Successor to H. P.
Thieme's bibliography.

French 7 Bibliography.  1-22, 1949-1968.

French 20 Bibliography.  21-23, 1969-1971.

Handbook of Latin American Studies.  Nos. 5-26, 28, 30, 32, 1939-
1970.

Index to Latin American Periodical Literature: 1929-1950.  Boston:
Hall and Co., 1962.  Vol. 1.

Index to Latin American Periodicals: Humanities and Social Sciences.
1-10, 1961-1970, Nos. 1 and 2.

Index to Little Magazines, 1920-1939; 1943-1947.

International Index to Periodicals.  1907-1965.  This publication
is continued, as concerns philosophy, in the Social Sciences
and Humanities Index.

Koehler und Volckmar Fachbibliographien Philosophie und Grenzgebie-
te.  1945-1964.  Bergson: 29, 70, 305, 327.

Library of Congress Catalogue.  Books: Subjects.  1950-1971.

Manuel de la recherche documentaire en France: Tome II, 1re Partie,
7e Section.  Philosophie (Sous la direction de Raymond Bayer).
Paris: Vrin, 1950, 417.  Bergson: 27, 60, 65, 70, 96, 121, 147,
158, 190, 225.

New York Public Library Slavonic Collection Catalogue.  Boston:
Hall and Co., 1959.  Vol. 2.

Palau y Dulcet, Antonio. Manuel del Librero Hispanoamericano. Barcelona: Librería Palau, 1949, 494. Bergson: 180.

Philosophen-Lexikon. Berlin: Walter de Gruyter und Ges., 1949, I, 700. Brief article on Bergson with bibliography.

Philosophers Index. Bowling Green, Ohio: Philosophy Documentation Center. 2-6, 1968-1973.

Die Philosophie des Ausländers vom Beginn des 19. Jahrhunderts bis auf die Gegenwart. Berlin: Mittler, 1928, 431. Bergson: 21, 35, 53, 56ff, 78, 195, 240, 396, 418.

Philosphische Dokumentation aus dem Philosophischen Institut der Universität Düsseldorf. Gesamtregister zur Zeitschrift für philosophische Forschung 1-21 (1946-1967). Meisenheim am Glan: Verlag Anton Hain, 1968, 618. Bergson: 130.

Reader's Guide to Periodical Literature. 1900-1971.

Répertoire bibliographique de la philosophie. 1949-1971.

Social Sciences and Humanities Index. 1965-1972.

Subject Index to Periodicals (American and English). 1915-1961.

Thieme, Hugo Paul. Bibliographie de la littérature française de 1800 à 1930. Paris: Droz, 1933, I, 1061. Bergson: 185-189.

Thils, Gustave. Theologica e Miscellaneis. Louvain: Warny, 1960, 434 (Festschriften and memorial volumes since World War I). Bergson: 1630, 2244, 2340, 2700, 3107, 3614.

Tijdschrift voor Philosophie. Bibliographisch Repertorium. 1939-1956; 1964-1967.

Turner, Mary C. Libros en Venta en Hispanoamérica y España. New York: Bowker, 1964, 1891. Bergsonismo: 1276.

Varet, Gilbert. Manuel de bibliographie philosophique. Paris: Presses Universitaires de France, 1956, 2 vols., 1058. Bergson: 153n, 260, 448, 605, 674, 744, 869, 894-895.

# PART  V

# INDICES

INDEX: WORKS BY BERGSON

INDEX: WORKS CONCERNING BERGSON

Note: References in this index to an author do not include works by this author.  Works by the various authors listed below may, however, often be found listed alphabetically under his name in Section II of the bibliography.

Barrès, Maurice: 630, 776, 878, 3411.

Bazaillas, Albert: 1261, 4192.

Behaviorism: 509, 1575, 3277, 3278.

Benda, Julien: 906, 1339, 1698, 2159, 2574, 3915, 3943, 4048, 4080, 4081, 4179, 4183.

Berkeley, George: 565, 817, 1953, 2573, 3202.

Bernard, Claude: 1476, 3790.

Binet, Alfred: 575, 817, 1597.

Biology (See also Creative Evolution, Instinct): 626, 689, 795, 987, 1030, 1031, 1157, 1158, 1272, 1281, 1314, 1518, 1519, 1520, 1535, 1566, 1750, 1815, 1980, 1982, 1984, 2019, 2086, 2115, 2160, 2196, 2242, 2278, 2279, 2336, 2394, 2397, 2444, 2468, 2521, 2535, 2580, 2584, 2635, 2665, 2666, 2667, 2722, 2735, 2748, 2749, 2795, 2796, 2916, 2957, 3032, 3058, 3065, 3092, 3095, 3096, 3097, 3098, 3173, 3185, 3235, 3402, 3453, 3524, 3557, 3558, 3626, 3627, 3667, 3669, 3701, 3787, 3823, 3953, 3954, 3955, 4020, 4075, 4141, 4266, 4268, 4269, 4300, 4320, 4321, 4372.

Biran, Maine de: 921, 1062, 1427, 1612, 1676, 1898, 1901, 2388, 2473, 2581, 2951, 3523, 3792, 4002.

Blondel, Charles: 2233.

Blondel, Maurice: 882, 890, 1061, 1193, 1477, 2422, 2981, 3620,

4068, 4124, 4125, 4170, 4173.

Borges, Jorge Luis: 4349.

Bosanquet, Bernard: 3499.

Boutroux, Emile: 706, 857, 1012, 1708, 1796, 3679, 3750, 3753, 4068.

Bradley, Francis Herbert: 471, 947, 1827, 2225, 2655, 2696, 3067.

Brain (See Aphasia, Memory, Mind-Body Problem).

Bréhier, Emile: 486, 644, 1965, 2110, 2165.

Bruno, Giordano: 3137.

Brunschvicg, Léon: 706, 738, 924, 1055, 1437, 1484, 1751, 1950, 1965.

Butler, Samuel: 1389, 1583, 1714.

Camus, Albert: 811, 1398, 1512, 2276, 2889, 2890, 2892, 2895.

Carteron, Henri: 1522.

Casona, Alejandro: 3046.

Cassirer, Ernst: 1978.

Catholicism, Roman (See also Aquinas, Augustine, Péguy, Teilhard de Chardin): 503, 595, 619, 747, 751, 755, 756, 798, 813, 814, 895, 935, 946, 1162, 1171, 1176, 1186, 1340, 1369, 1489, 1700, 1728, 1854, 1855, 1872, 1957, 2105, 2300, 2315, 2525, 2533, 2534, 2692, 2721, 2746, 2809, 2810, 2811, 2812, 2813, 2814, 2815, 2816, 2815,

2873, 3780, 3831, 4026.

Gide, André: 577, 1703, 2433, 2891, 3486, 4324.

God (See also Aquinas, Augustine, Catholicism, Christianity, Judaism, Metaphysics, Mysticism, Plotinus): 487, 521, 569, 597, 610, 691, 771, 914, 1050, 1070, 1187, 1188, 1189, 1190, 1200, 1264, 1267, 1268, 1306, 1330, 1334, 1336, 1456, 1490, 1491, 1511, 1702, 1713, 1818, 1873, 1928, 2030, 2035, 2045, 2046, 2047, 2048, 2268, 2623, 2577, 2834, 2978, 2979, 2995, 3022, 3040, 3048, 3153, 3182, 3300, 3342, 3463, 3466, 3549, 3570, 3591, 3592, 3599, 3755, 3805, 3816, 3881, 3947, 3997, 4050, 4062, 4067, 4053, 4282, 4316, 4376.

Gouhier, Henri: 746, 1409, 1707.

Great Britain: 1348, 1387, 1388, 1389, 1613, 2342, 2769, 3153, 3317, 3582, 3759.

Gunter, P. A. Y.: 489, 742, 829, 1038, 1350, 1748, 2021, 2220, 3422, 3730, 4307.

Guyau, Georges: 1978, 2244, 3027.

Hamelin, Octave: 1484, 1521, 2235, 2605, 3233, 3442.

Harrison, Frederic: 3540.

Hegel, Georg Wilhelm: 609, 792, 1198, 1199, 1309, 2400, 3067, 3820, 4242.

Heidegger, Martin: 539, 1703, 1778, 2699, 3139, 3181, 3612, 3687, 3819.

Hemmingway, Ernest: 4341.

Heraclitus: 515, 1040, 1494, 3675.

History: 1579, 1615, 1897, 2171, 2179, 2467, 2625, 2801, 3123, 3156, 3352, 3353, 3381, 3980, 4088, 4231, 4336, 4346.

Hörbinger, Hans: 1604.

Hulme, Thomas Ernest: 2044, 3584, 4270.

Humanism: 909, 1056, 1057, 1838, 2152, 2359, 3043, 3163, 3213, 3757, 4040.

Husserl, Edmund: 734, 1315, 1703, 1778, 1886, 2123, 2181, 2182, 2826, 3693, 3729, 4180, 4342.

Huxley, Julian: 3163.

Hypnotism: 1597.

Images (See also Matter, Matter and Memory, Perception): 485, 587, 644, 709, 920, 925, 1656, 1751, 2044, 2071, 2165, 2350, 2864, 2871, 3129, 3577.

Immortality (See Death).

Impressionism: 1025, 1332, 3293.

Ingarden, Roman: 1652.

Instinct (See Biology, Creative Evolution, The Creative Mind, Intuition).

Intellect: 1039, 1571, 1572, 1582, 1720, 1755, 1848, 1916, 1925, 1979, 1980, 1981, 1982, 1984, 1984a, 2023, 2050, 2051, 2078, 2089, 2093, 2144, 2149,